125

D0904314

Everyman, I will go with thee, and be thy guide,
In thy most need to go by thy side.

EVERYMAN'S LIBRARY

Founded 1906 by J. M. Dent (d. 1926)
Edited by Ernest Rhys (d. 1946)

No. 983

THEOLOGY

ST. AUGUSTINE: THE CITY OF GOD
JOHN HEALEY'S TRANSLATION, WITH A
SELECTION FROM VIVES' COMMENTARIES
EDITED BY R. V. G. TASKER, M.A., B.D.
INTRODUCTION BY SIR ERNEST BARKER
IN TWO VOLS.   VOL. II

AUGUSTINE, born in 354 in Tagaste in Numidia. Went to the university of Carthage and embraced Manichaeism. While living in Milan the oratory of Ambrose led to his conversion to the Christian Church in 386. Died at Hippo in 430.

THE CITY OF GOD
(DE CIVITATE DEI)
VOLUME TWO

SAINT AUGUSTINE

LONDON: J. M. DENT & SONS LTD.
NEW YORK: E. P. DUTTON & CO. INC.

All rights reserved
Made in Great Britain
at The Temple Press Letchworth
for
J. M. Dent & Sons Ltd.
Aldine House Bedford St. London
First published in this edition 1945
Last reprinted 1947

THE THIRTEENTH BOOK OF
THE CITY OF GOD

CHAPTER I

Of the first man's fall, and the procurement of mortality

HAVING got through the intricate questions of the world's origin, and mankind's, our method now calls us to discourse of the first man's fall, nay the first fall of both in that kind, and consequently of the origin and propagation of our mortality. For God made not men as He did angels, that although they sinned yet they could not die; but so that having performed their course of obedience, no intervention of death could prevent them from partaking for ever of blessed and angelical immortality: but having left this course, death should take them into just condemnation, as we said in the last book.

CHAPTER II

Of the death that may befall the immortal soul, and of the body's death

BUT I see I must unfold this kind of death a little plainer. For man's soul (though it be immortal) dies a kind of death. It is called immortal, because it can never cease to be living and sensitive: and the body is mortal, because it may be destitute of life, and cannot live by itself. But the death of the soul is when God leaves it; and the death of the body is when the soul leaves it; so that the death of both is when the soul, being left of God, leaves the body. And this death of the whole man is followed by that which the scripture calls the second death. This our Saviour signified, when He said: 'Fear Him which is able to destroy both body and soul in hell':[1] which coming not to pass before the body is joined to the soul never to be separated, it is strange that the body can be said to die by that death, which severs not the soul from it, but torments them both together. For that eternal pain (of which we will speak hereafter) is fitly called the soul's death, because it lives not with God: but how is it the body's which lives by the soul? For if it did not so live it could not feel the corporal pains that await it after the resurrection. Is it because all life whatsoever is good, and all pain evil, that the body is said to die, wherein the soul is cause of sorrow rather than life? Therefore the

[1] Matt. x. 28.

soul lives by God, when it lives well (for it cannot live without God
working good in it): and the body lives by the soul, when the soul
lives in the body, whether it live by God or no. For the wicked
have life of body, but none of soul: their souls being dead (that is,
forsaken of God) having power through such little of their immortal life as they may retain to afford them this. But in the last
damnation, though man be not insensitive, yet this sense of his
being neither pleasing nor peaceful, but sore and painful, is justly
termed death rather than life; and therefore is it called the second
death, because it follows the first breach of nature, either between
God and the soul, or the soul and the body. Of the first death
therefore we may say that it is good to the good, and bad to the
bad. But the second, as it happens to none of the good, so is good
to none.

CHAPTER III

*Whether death, propagated unto all men from the first, be punishment
of sin to the saints*

But here is a question not to be omitted: whether the first death
be good to the good. If it be so, how can it be the punishment of
sin? For had not our first parents sinned, they had never tasted
it. How then can that be good to the upright that can happen
only to offenders? And if it happen only to offenders, it should
not be good, for it should not be at all unto the upright: for why
should they have punishment that have no guilt? We must confess, then, that had not our first parents sinned, they had not died;
but sinning, the punishment of death was inflicted upon them and
all their posterity: for they should not produce anything but what
themselves were, and the greatness of their crime depraved their
nature, so that that which was penal in the first man's offending,
was made natural in the birth of all the rest; for they came not of
man, as man came of the dust. The dust was man's material; but
man is man's parent. That which is earth is not flesh, though
flesh be made of earth: but that which man the father is, man the
son is also. For all mankind was in the first man, to be derived
from him by the woman, when this couple received their sentence
of condemnation. And that which man was made, not in his
creation, but in his fall and condemnation, that he begot, in
respect (I mean) of sin and death. For the first man was not
reduced by his sin to that state of weakness and mental dullness,
which we see in infants. Those God would have as the origin of
the infants, whose parents he had cast down to bestial mortality,
as it is written: 'Man was in honour, and understood not, but
became like to the beasts that perish'[1] (unless we are to say that

[1] Ps. xlix. 12.

infants are weaker in motion and appetite than all the other creatures, to show man's mounting excellence above them all, comparable to a shaft that flies the stronger when it is drawn farthest
back in the bow). Therefore the first man's presumption and
just sentence condemned him not to those imbecilities of nature:
but his nature was depraved unto the admission of concupiscential
disobedience in his members against his will: and thereby was
bound to death by necessity, and to produce his offspring under
the same conditions that his crime deserved. From which bond
of sin if infants by the mediator's grace be freed, they shall only
suffer the first death, that of body; but from the eternal, penal
second death, their freedom from sin shall free them absolutely.

CHAPTER IV

*Why the first death is not withheld from those regenerated from sin
by grace*

IF any man think they should not suffer this death, which is the
punishment of guilt, whose guilt is cleared by grace, his problem is
solved in our book called *De Baptismo Parvulorum*. There we say
that the separation of soul and body is not done away with though
its connection with sin be dissolved, because if the sacrament of regeneration should be immediately followed by immortality of body,
our faith were disannulled, faith being an expectation of a thing
unseen. But by the strength and vigour of faith was this fear of
death to be in time past conquered, especially by the martyrs:
whose conflicts had had no victory, nor any glory, nay, had been no
conflicts, if they had been deified and freed from corporal death
immediately upon their regeneration. For if it were so, who would
not run unto Christ along with the children to be baptized, lest
he should die? Would his faith be approved by this visible reward? No, it would be no faith, because he received his reward
immediately. But now the wonderful grace of our Saviour has
turned the punishment of sin unto the greater good of righteousness. Then it was said to man: 'Thou shalt die if thou sin'; now
it is said to the martyr: 'Die to avoid sin.' Then: 'If you break
My laws, you shall die'; now: 'If you refuse to die, you break My
laws.' That which we feared then if we offended, we must now
choose, not to offend. Thus by God's ineffable mercy the punishment of sin is become the instrument of virtue, and the pain due
to the sinner's guilt is the just man's merit. Then did sin purchase
death, and now death purchases righteousness—I mean, in the
martyrs, whom their persecutors bade either renounce their faith
or their life; and those just men chose rather to suffer that for
believing which the first sinners suffered for not believing: for

unless they had sinned they had not died, and martyrs had sinned
if they had not died. They died for sin, these sin not because
they die. The others' crime brought death to them as a punishment; the punishment of these by death prevented them from
committing crime. It is not that death, which before was an evil,
has now become good, but God has given such grace to faith, that
death, which is life's contrary, is here made the ladder whereby
to ascend to life.

CHAPTER V

*As the wicked use the good law ill, so the good use death,
which is evil, well*

FOR the apostle, desiring to show the hurt of sin when it is un-
prevented by grace, did not hesitate to say that the law which
forbids sin is the strength of sin. 'The sting of death,' says he, 'is
sin, and the strength of sin is the law.' [1] Most true: for the forbidding of unlawful desires increases them, where righteousness is
not of power to suppress all such desires to sin. And righteousness can never be loved without the aid of God's grace. But yet
to show that the law is not evil, though he calls it the strength of
sin, he says in another place, when treating the same question:
'The law is holy, and the commandment holy and just and good.'
'Was that then which is good,' says he, 'made death to me? God
forbid: but sin, that it might appear sin, wrought death in me by
that which is good, that sin might be out of measure sinful by the
commandment.' [2] 'Out of measure,' says he, because transgression
is added; the law being also contemned through the lust of sin.
Why do we recite this? Because as the law is not evil when it
excites concupiscence in the bad, so death is not good when it increases the glory of the good; neither the law, when it is forsaken
by sinners, and makes them transgressors: nor death, when it is
undertaken for truth, and makes them martyrs. Consequently
the law forbidding sin is good, and death being the reward of sin
is evil. But as the wicked use all things, good and evil, badly, so
the just use all things, evil and good, well. Therefore the wicked
use the law, that is good, badly, and the just use death, that is
bad, well.

CHAPTER VI

The general evil of that death that severs soul and body

WHEREFORE, as for the death that divides soul and body, when they
suffer it who we say are a-dying, it is good unto none. For it
is a sharp unnatural experience, by which nature is wrung this

[1] 1 Cor. xv. 56.   [2] Rom. vii. 12, 13.

way and that in the composition of the living creature, until it be dead, and until all the feeling be gone wherein the soul and body were combined. Which great trouble, one stroke of the body or one rapture of the soul oftentimes prevents, and outruns feeling in swiftness. But whatsoever it is in death, that takes away our sensation with so grievous a sensation, being faithfully endured, it augments the merit of patience, but takes not away the name of punishment. It is certainly the death of the first man, duly propagated, though if it be endured for faith and justice, it becomes the glory of the regenerate. Thus death, though the award of sin, sometimes frees sin from all award.

CHAPTER VII

Of the death that such as are not regenerate do suffer for Christ

FOR whosoever he is that being not yet regenerate dies for confessing Christ, it frees him of his sin as well as if he had received the sacrament of baptism. For He that said: 'Unless a man be born again of water, and of the Holy Spirit, he shall not enter into the kingdom of God,' [1] excepts these elsewhere, in as general a saying: 'Whosoever confesses Me before men, him will I confess before My Father which is in heaven': [2] and again: 'He that loseth his soul for Me, shall find it.' [3] Hereupon it is that 'Precious in the sight of the Lord is the death of the saints.' [4] For what is more dear, than that death wherein all a man's badness is abolished, and his good augmented? Those that die baptized, because they could live no longer, have not equal merit with those that die willingly when they might have lived longer; because these had rather die in confessing Christ, than deny Him and so come to baptism. Which if they had done, this sacrament would have forgiven it, because they denied Him for fear of death. For in it even their villainy was forgiven that murdered Christ. But how could they love Christ so dearly, as to contemn life for Him, but by abounding in the grace of that Spirit that inspires where it pleases? Precious, therefore, is the death of those saints, who took such gracious hold of the death of Christ, that they did not flinch from facing death themselves in their quest of Him, and whose death showed that they made use of that which before was the punishment of sin to the producing of a greater harvest of glory. But death ought not to seem good, because it is God's help and not a man's own power that has made it of such good use, that being once propounded as a penalty laid upon sin, it is now elected as a deliverance from sin, and an expiation of sin, to the crowning of righteousness with glorious victory.

[1] John iii. 5.   [2] Matt. x. 32   [3] Matt. xvi. 25.   [4] Ps. cxvi. 15.
II—* A 9⁸3

CHAPTER VIII

That the saints in suffering the first death for the truth are free from the second

For if we mark the matter well, we see that in dying well and laudably for the truth is a worse death avoided, and therefore we take a part of it, lest the whole should fall upon us, even a second that should never have end. We submit to the separation of the body from the soul, lest we should come to have the soul severed from God, and then from the body: and so man's first death being past, the second, that endless one, should fall presently upon him. Wherefore the death as I say that we suffer when we die, and that causes us to die, is good unto no man, but it is well tolerated for attaining of good. But when men once are in death, and called dead, then we may say that it is good to the good, and bad to the bad. For the good souls, being severed from their body, are in rest, and the evil in torment, until the bodies of the first rise to life eternal, and the latter unto the eternal or second death.

CHAPTER IX

Whether a man at the hour of his death may be said to be amongst the dead, or the dying

But now for the time of the soul's separation from the body (be it good or bad), may we say it is in death, or after it? If it be after death, it is not death then being past and gone, which is good or bad, but rather the present life of the soul. For the death was evil to them whilst it was death, that is, whilst they dying suffered it, because it was a grievous suffering (though the good make good use of this evil). How then can death being past be either good or bad? Again, if we mark well, we shall find that that grievous suffering in man is not death. For as long as we feel, we live; and as long as we live, we are before death, and not in it: for when death comes, it takes away all sense, yea, even that which is grieved by death's approach. And therefore how we may call those that are not dead, but in the pangs of deadly affliction, dying, is hard to explain, though they may be called ordinarily so: for when death is come, they are no more in dying, but in death, or dead. Therefore is none dying but the living: because when one is in the greatest extremity, or giving up the ghost, as we say, if his soul be not gone, he is yet alive then. Thus is he both living and dying, going to death and from life, yet living as long as the soul is in the body, and not yet in death, because the soul is undeparted. And when it is departed, then is he not in death, but rather after death. Who then can say who is in death? No man dying is, if no man can be both living and dying at once; for as long as the soul is in the body we cannot deny that he lives. But if it be said that he is dying who is drawing towards death, and yet that the dying and the living cannot be both in one at once, then I do not know who is living.

CHAPTER X

Whether this mortal life be rather to be called death than life

FOR as soon as ever man enters this mortal body, he begins a perpetual journey unto death. For that this changeable life enjoins him to, if I may call the course unto death a life. For there is none but is nearer death at the year's end than he was at the beginning, to-morrow than to-day, to-day than yesterday, by and by than just now, and now than a little before. Each part of time that we pass, cuts off so much from our life, and the remainder still decreases; so that our whole life is nothing but a course unto death, wherein one can neither stay nor slack his pace; but all run in one manner, and with one speed. For the short liver ran his course no faster than the long; both had a like passage of time, but the first had not so far to run as the latter, both making speed alike. It is one thing to live longer, and another to run faster. He that lives longer, runs farther, but not a moment faster. And if each one begin to be in death as soon as his life begins to shorten (because when it is ended he is not then in death but after it), then is every man in death as soon as ever he is conceived. For what else do all his days, hours, and minutes declare, but that they being done, the death, wherein he lived, is come to an end; and that his time is now no more in death (he being dead), but after death? Therefore if man cannot be in life and death both at once, he is never in life as long as he is in that dying rather than living body. Or is he in both? In life that is still being diminished, and in death because he dies, whose life diminishes? For if he be not in life, what is it that is diminished, until it be ended; and if he be not in death, what is it that diminishes the life? For life being taken finally from the body could not be said now to be after death, unless death ended it and unless it was death whilst it was being diminished. And if man be not in death, but after it, when his life is ended, where is he but in death whilst it is diminishing?

CHAPTER XI

Whether one may be living and dead both together

BUT if it be absurd to say a man is in death before he come to it (for what is it that his course runs unto, if he be there already?) chiefly because it is too strange to say one is both living and dying, since we cannot say one is both sleeping and waking, we must find when a man is dying. Dying before death come, he is not, for then he is living: dying when death is come, he is not, for then he is dead. The one is after death, and the other is before it. When is he in death then? For he is in death when dying, to equate three things, *living*, *dying*, and *dead*, with three times, *before death*, *in death*, and *after*. Therefore when he is in death, that is, neither living, or before death, nor dead, or after death, is hard to be defined. For whilst the soul is in the body (especially with feeling) man assuredly lives, as yet being soul and body, and therefore is before death, and not in it. But when the soul and feeling are gone, then is he dead, and after death. These two then take away his means of being in death, or dying, for if he live he is before death, and if he cease to live he is after death. Therefore he is never dying nor in death. So in the passing of time the present cannot be found, since it occupies no space but is the transition from the past to the future. Do we not see then that by this reason the death of the body does not exist? If it does, how is it anything, being in nothing, and nothing being in it? For if we live, death is not anything yet, because we are before it, not in it; if we live not, death is nothing still, for now we are after it and not in it. But now, if death be nothing before nor after, what sense is there in saying 'before,' or 'after, death'? I would to God we had lived well in paradise that death might have been nothing indeed. But now, there is not only such a thing, but it is so grievous unto us, as neither tongue can tell nor reason avoid. Let us therefore speak according to custom (for so we should) and call the time ere death come 'before death': as it is written: 'Judge none blessed before his death.' [1] Let us call the time when it has already come 'after death' (this or that was 'after his death') and let us speak of the present time, as we can: 'he dying gave such a legacy,' 'he dying left this much, or that much,' though no man could do this but the living, and rather before his death, than at or in his death. And let us speak as the holy scripture speaks of the dead, saying they were not after death but in death, 'For in death there is no remembrance of thee': [2] for until they rise again they are justly said to be in death as one is in sleep until he awake. Though such as are in sleep we say are sleeping, yet may we not say that such as are dead are dying. For they that are once separate wholly from their

<hr>

[1] Ecclus. xi. 28.   [2] Ps. vi. 5.

bodies are past dying the bodily death (whereof we speak) any more. But this that I say, one cannot declare, namely how the dying man may be said to live, or how the dead man can be said to be in death: for how can he be after death, if he be in death, since we cannot call him dying, as we may call him that is in sleep, sleeping, or him that is in languor, languishing, or him that is in sorrow, sorrowing, or in life, living? But the dead until they arise are said to be in death, yet we cannot say they are dying. And therefore I think it was not for no cause (perhaps God decreed it) that *morior*, the Latin word for 'to die,' could not by any means be brought by grammarians unto the form of other verbs. *Orior*, 'to arise,' hath *ortus* in the perfect tense, and so have other verbs that are declined by the participle of the perfect tense. But *morior* must have *mortuus* for the perfect tense, doubling the letter *u*, for *mortuus* ends like *fatuus*, *arduus*, *conspicuus*, and suchlike that are no perfect tenses, but adjectives, declined without signification of time: and this, as if it were a declinable adjective that cannot be declined, is put for the participle of the past tense. So that it is convenient, that as the thing which the word signifies cannot be defined, so the word itself cannot be declined. Yet by the grace of our Redeemer, we may decline (that is, avoid) the second death. For this is the sore one, and the worst of evils, being no separation but rather a combination of body and soul unto eternal torture. Therein shall none be before death nor after death, but eternally in death: never living, never dead, but ever dying. For man can never be in worse death, than when the death he is in is endless.

CHAPTER XII

Of the death that God threatened to promise the first man with if he transgressed

IF therefore it be asked what death God threatened man with upon his transgression and breach of obedience, whether it were bodily or spiritual, or that second death, we answer: It was all. The first consists of two, and the second is a complete death. For as the whole earth consists of many lands, and the whole Church of many churches, so doth the universal death consist of all, the first consisting of two, the body's and the soul's, being the death wherein the soul, being forsaken of God, forsakes the body, and endures pains for the time: but the second being that wherein the soul, being forsaken of God, endures pains for ever. Therefore when God said to the first man that He placed in paradise, as concerning the forbidden fruit: 'Whensoever thou eatest thereof, thou shalt die the death,' [1] He comprehends therein, not only the first

[1] Gen. ii. 17.

part of the first death, wheresoever the soul loses God, nor the
latter only, wherein the soul leaves the body, and is punished after
that separation, but also that last part, or the second which is the
last of deaths, eternal, and following after all. All this is compre-
hended in that commination.

CHAPTER XIII

What punishment was first laid on man's transgression

FOR after man had broken the precept, he was first forsaken of
God's grace and confounded with his own nakedness: and so
with the fig leaves (the first perhaps that came to hand), he
covered his nakedness and shame. His members were before
as they were then, but they were not shameful before, whereas
now he felt a new impulse of his disobedient flesh, as the
reciprocal punishment of his disobedience. For the soul, being
now delighted with perverse liberty and scorning to serve God,
could not have the body as formerly at its command: and having
willingly forsaken God its superior, it could not have its inferior so
serviceable as it desired, nor could it have the flesh subject as it
might have had always, had it remained itself God's subject. For
then the flesh began to covet, and contend against the spirit; and
with this contention are we all born, drawing death from our
origin, and bearing nature's corruption, and contention or victory
of the first transgression in our members.

CHAPTER XIV

In what state God made man, and into what state he fell by his voluntary choice

FOR God (the Creator of nature, and not of vice) made man upright:
who being willingly depraved and justly condemned, begot all his
offspring under the same depravation and condemnation. For in
him were we all, since we all were that one man, who, through the
woman who was made of himself before sin, fell into sin. We
had not our particular forms yet, but there was the seed of our
natural propagation, which being corrupted by sin must needs
produce man of that same nature, the slave to death, and the object
of just condemnation. And therefore this came from the bad
using of free will. Thence arose all this train of calamity, drawing
all men on into misery (excepting those that by God's free grace
are delivered) from their corrupt origin, even to the beginning of
the second death which has no end.

CHAPTER XV

That Adam forsook God ere God forsook him, and that the soul's first death was the departure from God

WHEREFORE in that it was said: 'Ye shall die the death,' because it was not said the 'deaths,' if we understand that death, wherein the soul leaves the life, that is God (for it was not forsaken ere it forsook Him, but contrariwise, the one will being their first leader to evil, and the Creator's will being the first leader to good, both in the creation of it, before it had being, and the restoring of it when it had fallen)—wherefore if we do understand that God meant but this death, where He says: 'Whensoever thou eatest thereof thou shalt die the death': as if He had said, Whensoever you forsake Me in disobedience, I will forsake you in justice: yet verily do all the other deaths follow the denunciation of this death. For in that the soul felt a disobedient impulse of the flesh, and thereupon covered the body's secret parts, in this was the first death felt, that is, the departure of the soul from God. Which was signified in this, that when the man in mad fear had gone and hid himself, God said to him: 'Adam, where art thou?' [1] not ignorantly seeking him, but watchfully warning him to look well where he was, seeing God was not with him. But when the soul forsakes the body decayed with age, then is the other death felt, whereof God said in imposing man's future punishment: 'Earth [2] thou art, and unto earth shalt thou return': [3] that by these two the first death, which is of the whole man, might be accomplished, which the second should follow, if God's grace procure not man's freedom from it: for the body, which is earth, returns not to earth but by the one death, that is, the departure of the soul from it. Wherefore all Christians holding the Catholic faith believe that the bodily death lies upon mankind by no law of nature, as if God had made man mortal, but as a due punishment for sin: because God in scourging this sin, said unto that man, from whom we are all descended: 'Earth thou art, and unto earth shalt thou return.'

CHAPTER XVI

Of the philosophers that held corporal death not to be penal, though Plato brings in the Creator promising the lesser gods that they should never leave their bodies

BUT the philosophers (against whose calumnies we defend this city of God, that is, His Church) think they give us a witty scoff for saying that the soul's separation from the body is to be held as part of the punishment; whereas they affirm that then is the soul

---

[1] Gen. iii. 9.   [2] St. Augustine follows the Septuagint.—ED.
[3] Gen. iii. 19.

perfectly blessed when it leaves the body, and goes up pure and
naked unto God. If I should find no battery against this opinion
out of their own books, I should have a great ado to prove that it is
not the body but the corruptibility of the body which is the soul's
burden: in accordance with that which we cited in our last book:
'A corruptible body is heavy unto the soul.'[1] In adding 'corruptible' he shows that this being inflicted as sin's punishment
upon the body, and not the body itself, is heavy to the soul: and if
he had not added it, yet must we have understood it so. But Plato
affirming plainly that the gods that the Creator made have incorruptible bodies, and bringing in their Maker as Himself promising them (as a great benefit) to remain therein eternally, and never
to be separated from them, why then do those men dissemble
their own knowledge, to procure Christianity trouble, and contradict themselves in seeking to argue against us? Plato's words[2]
Tully translates thus, bringing in the great God speaking thus to
the gods He had made: 'You that are of divine origin, whom I
have created, attend: these your bodies by My will, are indissoluble, although every compound may be dissolved. But it is
evil to desire to dissolve a thing compounded by reason; but seeing
that you are created, you are neither immortal nor indissoluble;
yet shall you never be dissolved, nor die: these shall not prevail
against My will, which is a greater assurance of your eternity than
all your forms and compositions are.' Behold, Plato says that
their gods by their creation and combination of body and soul are
mortal, and yet immortal by the decree and will of Him that made
them. If therefore it be pain to the soul to be bound in any body,
why should God seem to take away their fear of death, by promising
them eternal immortality, not because of their nature, which is
compounded and not simple, but because of His holy will, which
can render creatures eternal, and preserve compounds immortally
from dissolution? Whether Plato holds this true of the stars is
another question. For we may not consequently grant him that
those luminous globes or bodies, shining night and day upon earth,
have each one a particular soul whereby it lives, being blessed and
intellectual, as he affirms directly of the world also. But this,
as I said, is no question for this place. This I held fit to recite
against those that affecting the name of Platonists are proudly
ashamed of the name of Christians, lest the association of this name
with the vulgar should debase the proud (because small) number
of the *palliati*.[3] These, seeking holes in the coat of Christianity,
bark at the eternity of the body, as if the desire of the soul's eternity
and the continuance of it in the frail body were contraries; whereas
their master Plato holds it as a gift given by the great God to the
lesser ones, that they should not die, that is, be severed from the
bodies He gave them.

[1]Wisd. of Sol. ix. 15.   [2] *Tim.*, p. 41 A and B.   [3] See Commentary, p. 430.

CHAPTER XVII

Against the opinion that earthly bodies cannot be made incorruptible nor eternal

THEY agree in this also, that earthly bodies cannot be eternal, and yet they hold the whole earth, which they regard as a central part of their great god (though not of their highest) the world, to be eternal. Seeing then their greatest God made another god greater than all the rest beneath him, that is, the world, and seeing they hold that this is a creature having an intellectual soul included in it by which it lives, having the parts consisting of four elements, whose connection that great God (lest this other should ever perish) made indissoluble and eternal: why should the earth then, being but a central member of a greater Creature, be eternal, and yet the bodies of earthly creatures (God willing the one as well as the other) may not be eternal? Aye, but, say they, earth must be returned unto earth, whence the bodies of earthly creatures are shapen, and therefore (say they) these must necessarily be dissolved, and die, to be restored to the eternal earth from whence they were taken. Well, if one should affirm the same of the fire, and say that all the bodies taken thence should be restored unto it again, such as the heavenly bodies thereof consisting—were not that promise of immortality, that Plato said God made unto those gods, utterly broken by this argument? Or can it not be so, because it pleases not God, whose will, as Plato says, is beyond all other assurance? Why may not God then have so resolved of the earthly bodies, that being brought forth they should perish no more; that once composed, they should be dissolved no more; nor should that which is once taken from the elements ever be restored; and that the souls being once placed in them the bodies should never forsake them, but enjoy eternal happiness in this combination? Why does not Plato confess that God can do this? Why cannot He preserve earthly things from corruption? Is His power as the Platonists, but not as the Christians avouch? How very likely that the philosophers know God's counsels, but not the prophets! Rather it was thus: the Spirit of truth revealed what God permitted unto the prophets, but the weakness of human conjecture in these questions wholly deluded the philosophers. But they should not have been so far besotted in obstinate ignorance as to contradict themselves in public assertions, saying first that the soul cannot be blessed unless it abandons all body whatsoever, and by and by after that asserting that the gods have blessed souls, and yet are continually tied unto celestial and fiery bodies; and with regard to Jupiter's (the world's) soul, that it is eternally inherent in the four elements composing this universe.

For Plato holds it to be diffused from the midst of earth, geometri-
cally called the centre, unto the extremest parts of heaven through
all the parts of the world by musical numbers: making the world a
blessed creature, whose soul enjoys full happiness of wisdom and
yet leaves not the body, and whose body lives eternally by it; and
although the body consist of so many different parts, yet can it
neither dull nor hinder the soul. Seeing then that they give
their conjectures this scope, why will they not believe that God
has power to make eternal mortal bodies, wherein the souls without
being parted from them by death, or being burdened by them at all
in life, may live in most blessed eternity, as they say their gods do
in fiery bodies, and their Jupiter in all the four elements? If the
souls cannot be blessed without their bodies being quite forsaken,
why then let their gods get them out of the stars, let Jupiter be
free from the elements: or if they cannot go, then are they wretched.
But they will allow neither of these. They dare not aver that the
gods may leave their bodies, lest they should seem to worship
mortals: neither dare they deny them bliss, lest they should confess
them wretches. Wherefore all bodies are not impediments to
beatitude, but only the corruptible, transitory, and mortal ones;
not such as God made man at first, but such as his sin procured him
afterwards.

CHAPTER XVIII

*Of the earthly bodies which the philosophers hold cannot be in heaven,
but must fall to earth by their natural weight*

OH, but, they say, an earthly body is either kept on earth, or carried
to earth by its natural weight, and therefore cannot be in heaven.
The first men indeed were in a woody and fruitful land, which was
called paradise. But because we must resolve this doubt, seeing
that both Christ's body is already ascended, and that the saints at
the resurrection shall do so also, let us ponder these earthly weights
a little. If man's art out of a metal, that being put into the water
sinks, can frame a vessel that shall swim, how much more
credible is it for God's secret power, whose omnipotent will, as
Plato says, can both keep things produced from perishing, and
parts combined from dissolving (whereas the combination of
corporal and incorporeal is a stranger and harder operation than
that of corporals with corporals), to take all weight from earthly
things, whereby they are carried downwards, and to qualify the
bodies of the blessed souls, so that, though they be terrene, yet
they may be incorruptible, and fit to ascend, descend, or use what
motion they will with all celerity. Or if the angels can transport
bodily weights whither they please, must we think they do it with

toil and feeling the burden? Why then may we not believe that
the perfect spirits of the blessed can carry their bodies whither
they please, and place them where they please? For whereas in
our bodily carriage of earthly things, we feel that the larger it is,
the heavier it is, and the heavier, the more toilsome to bear, it is
not so with the soul. The soul carries the bodily members better
when they are big and strong than when they are small and meagre;
and whereas a big sound man is heavier to others' shoulders than a
lean sick man, yet will he move his healthy heaviness with far
more agility than the other can do his infirm lightness, or than he
can himself if famine or sickness have shaken off his flesh. Thus the
state of the constitution is of more importance than great weight
in considering our mortal, earthly, and corruptible bodies. And
who can describe the infinite difference between our present
health and our future immortality? Let not the philosophers
therefore oppose us with any corporal weight or earthly ponderosity. I will not ask them why an earthly body may not be in
heaven as well as the whole earth may hang alone without any
support: for perhaps they will withdraw their disputation to the
centre of the world unto which all heavy things do tend. But this
I say, that if the lesser gods (whose creatures Plato makes man and
all other living things with him to be) could take away the quality
of burning from the fire, and leave it the light, which transfuses the
eye; shall we then doubt that that God, unto whose will he ascribes
their immortality, the eternal coherence and indissolubility of those
strange and diverse combinations of corporals and incorporeals,
can give a man a nature that shall make him live incorruptible and
immortal, keeping the form of him, and avoiding the weight? But
of the faith of the resurrection, and the quality of the immortal
bodies, I will speak more exactly (God willing) in the end of the
work.[1]

CHAPTER XIX

*Against those that hold that man would not have been immortal if he
had not sinned*

BUT now let us proceed with the bodies of the first men, who if they
had not sinned, had never tasted of that death which we say is good
only to the good, being, as all men know, a separation of soul and
body, wherein the body of the creature, that had evident life, has
evident end. For although we may not doubt that the souls of
the faithful that are dead are in rest; yet it were so much better
for them to live with their bodies in good state, that they, that hold
it most blessed to be without a body, may see themselves convinced

---

[1] XXII. xii sqq.

herein directly. For no man dare compare those wise men, that have either left their bodies, or are to leave them, unto the *immortal gods* to whom the great God promised perpetuity of bliss, and inherence in their bodies. And Plato thought [1] it the greatest blessing man could have, to be taken out of the body (after a course virtuously run) and placed in the bosoms of those gods, that are never to leave their bodies.

> Scilicet immemores supra ut convexa revisant
> Rursus, et incipiant in corpora velle reverti. [2]

> The thought of heaven is quite out of their brain,
> Now can they wish to live on earth again.

Which Virgil is commended for speaking after the fashion of Plato. So that he holds that the souls of men can neither be always in their bodies, but must needs be loosed from them: nor can they be always without their bodies, but must be forced successively, now to live, and now to die; making this difference, that wise men when they die are carried up to the stars, and every one stays a while in a star fit for him, thence to return again to misery, in time; and to follow the desire of being embodied again, and so to live again in earthly calamity: but your fools are bestowed after their deaths in other bodies, of men or beasts, according to their merits. In this hard and wretched case places he the wisest souls, who have no other bodies given them to be happy in, but such as they can neither be eternally within, nor eternally abandon. Of this Platonism, Porphyry (as I said elsewhere) was ashamed because of the Christian dispensation, excluding the souls not only from the bodies of beasts, and from that revolution, but affirming them (if they lived wisely) to be set free from their bodies, so that they should nevermore be incorporate, but live in eternal bliss with the Father. Wherefore lest he should seem in this point to be outbid by the Christians that promised the saints eternal life, the same does he give to the purified souls: and yet, to contradict Christ, he denies the resurrection of their bodies in incorruptibility, and places the soul in bliss without any body at all. Yet did he never teach that these souls should be not subject in matters of religion unto the gods who dwelt in bodies. Why so? Because he did not think them better than the gods, though they had no bodies. Wherefore if they dare not (as I think they dare not) prefer human souls before their most blessed though corporal gods, why do they think it absurd for Christianity to teach that our first parents, had they not sinned, had been immortal, this being the reward of their true obedience; and that the saints at the resurrection shall have the same bodies that they laboured in here, but so that they shall be as light and incorruptible as their bliss shall be perfect and unchangeable.

---

[1] *Phaedr.*, pp. 107C–108C; 246D–249D.   [2] Virg. *Aen.* vi. 750–1.

CHAPTER XX

That the bodies of the saints now resting in hope shall become better than our first father's was

THE death that severs the souls of the saints from their bodies is not troublesome unto them, because their bodies do rest in hope, and therefore they seemed insensible to all reproach here upon earth. For they do not (as Plato will have men to do) desire to forget their bodies, but rather, remembering what the Truth that deceives no one said unto them that they should not lose a hair of their head,[1] they desire and wait for the resurrection of their bodies wherein they suffered such pains and are never to suffer more. For if they hated not their flesh when they were fain to bind it by the law of the Spirit from rebelling, how much shall they love it, when it is itself spiritual? For if we may justly call the spirit serving the flesh carnal, then so may we call the flesh serving the spirit spiritual, not because it shall be turned into the spirit (as some think, because it is written: 'It is sown a natural body, but it is raised a spiritual body'[2]): but because it shall serve the spirit in all wonderful and ready obeisance, to the fulfilling of the most secure will of indissoluble immortality, all sense of trouble, heaviness, and corruptibility being quite taken from it. For it shall not be so bad as it is now in our best health; nor as it was in our first parents before sin; for they (though they had not died except they sinned) were fain to eat bodily food as men do now, having earthly, and not spiritual, bodies: and though they would never have grown old and so have died (the tree of life that stood in the midst of paradise along with that which it was unlawful for them to taste of, affording them this estate by God's wonderful grace), yet they ate of more trees than that one, which was forbidden them, not because it was bad, but for their instruction in pure and simple obedience, which is a great virtue in a reasonable creature placed under God the Creator; for though a man touched no evil, yet in touching that which was forbidden him, the very act was the sin of disobedience. They lived therefore on other fruits, and ate, lest their carnal bodies should have been troubled by hunger, or thirst: but the taste of the tree of life was given them, to confirm them against death, and weakness by age; the rest serving them for nutriment, and this one for a sacrament, the tree of life in the earthly paradise being as the wisdom of God is in the heavenly, whereof it is written: 'It is a tree of life to them that embrace it.'[3]

---

[1] Luke xxi. 18.   [2] 1 Cor. xv. 44.   [3] Prov. iii. 18.

CHAPTER XXI

Of the paradise wherein our first parents were placed, that it may be taken spiritually also without any wrong to the truth of the history as touching the real place

WHEREUPON some referred that paradise wherein the first man was placed, as the scripture records, all unto a spiritual meaning, taking the trees to be virtues, as if there were no such visible things, but only that they were writ to signify things allegorical. As if there were not a real paradise, because we may understand a spiritual one: as if there were not two such women as Hagar and Sarah, and two sons of Abraham by them, the one being a bondwoman and the other free, because the apostle says that they signified the two covenants: or as if the rock gushed not forth with water, when Moses smote it, because that rock may prefigure Christ, the same apostle saying, 'the rock was Christ'![1] No man denies that the paradise may be understood as the bliss of the saints; the four floods, four virtues, prudence, fortitude, temperance, and justice; the trees, all good learning; the tree of life, wisdom the mother of the rest; the tree of the knowledge of good and evil, the experience of transgression, for God decreed a punishment for sin, justly and well, if man could have made use of it to his own good. These things may also be understood of the Church, and that in a better manner, as prophetic tokens of things to come. Paradise may be taken for the Church, as we read in the Canticles thereof. The four floods are the four gospels; the fruitful trees, the saints; their fruits, their works; the tree of life, the holy of holies, Christ; the tree of the knowledge of good and evil, free election of will, so that if a man once forsake God's will, he can only use himself to his own destruction; and therefore he learns either to adhere unto the good of all goods, or to love his own only. For loving himself he is given to himself, that being in troubles, sorrows, and fears (and feeling them withal) he may sing with the psalmist: 'My soul is cast down within me':[2] and being reformed: 'I will wait upon thee, O God, my defence.'[3] These and suchlike may be lawfully understood by paradise, taken in a spiritual sense, provided that the history of the true and local one be as firmly believed.

CHAPTER XXII

That the saints' bodies after resurrection shall be spiritual, and yet not changed into spirits

THE bodies of the saints in the resurrection shall need none of the tree of life to preserve them in life, health, or strength, nor any meat to keep away hunger and thirst. They shall have in every

[1] 1 Cor. x. 4.   [2] Ps. xlii. 6.   [3] Ps. lix. 9.

way such absolute immortality, that they shall never need to eat. Power they shall have to do it if they will, but no necessity. For so the angels did appearing visibly and sensibly, not of necessity, but from power and will, to afford their ministry unto man more conveniently. For we may not think that when they lodged in men's houses, they did but eat seemingly: though to those who knew not that they were angels they may have seemed to be under the same necessity to eat as ordinary men. And therefore the angel says in Tobias: 'You saw me eat, but you saw it but in vision': [1] that is, you thought I had eaten as you did, to refresh my body. But if another view may be probably held of the angels, yet verily we doubt it not to be true of Christ, that He in His spiritual flesh after His resurrection (yet was it His true flesh) ate and drank with His disciples. The need only, not the power, is taken from those glorified bodies, which are spiritual not because they cease to be bodies, but because they subsist by the quickening of the Spirit.

CHAPTER XXIII

*Of bodies animate and spiritual, these dying in Adam, and those being
quickened in Christ*

FOR as the bodies that have a living soul (though as yet unquickened by the Spirit) are called animate, yet are not souls but bodies, so are the other called spiritual, yet God forbid we should believe them to be spirit, or other than substantial fleshly bodies, yet incorruptible and without weight by the quickening of the Spirit. For man shall not then be earthly but celestial, not that he shall leave his earthly body, but because he shall be so endowed from heaven, that he may inhabit it without loss of his nature, but by attaining a celestial quality. The first man was made earth of earth into a living creature, but not into a quickening spirit, as he would have been had he persevered in obedience. Doubtless therefore his body needing meat and drink against hunger and thirst, and being not kept in youth and from death by indissoluble immortality, but only by the 'tree of life,' was not spiritual, but only animate: yet would it not have died, unless it had incurred God's heavy sentence by offending. And though he might take of other meats outside of paradise, yet being forbidden to touch the 'tree of life,' he became liable to time and corruption, in regard to that life, which, had he continued in spiritual obedience, though it were merely animate life yet might it have been eternal in paradise. Wherefore though by these words of God: 'Whensoever you eat thereof you shall die the death,' we understand by death the separation of soul and body, yet ought it not to seem absurd, in that they died not the very day that they took this deadly

[1] Tobit xii. 19.

meat; for that very day their nature was depraved, and by their just exclusion from the tree of life, the necessity of death entered upon them, wherein we all are brought forth. And therefore the apostle says not: 'The body shall die for sin,' but: 'The body is dead because of sin, and the spirit is life for righteousness' sake.' And then he adds: 'But if the Spirit of Him that raised up Jesus from the dead dwell in you, He that raised up Christ from the dead, shall also quicken your mortal bodies by His Spirit dwelling in you.'[1] Then therefore, as the apostle says, the body shall become a quickening spirit, which is now a living soul, and yet dead, because it must necessarily die. But in the first man, it was made a living soul, and not a quickening spirit, yet could it not be called dead, because had not he broken the commandment, he had not been bound to death. But whereas God signified the death of the soul in leaving Him, by saying: 'Adam, where art thou?' and whereas in saying: 'Earth thou art, and unto earth shalt thou return,' He signified the death of the body in leaving of the soul, therefore we must think He spoke not of the second death, reserving that secret for His New Testament, where it is plainly discovered: that the first, which is common to all, might be shown to proceed from that sin, which one man's act made common to all; but that the second death is not common to all, because of those holy ones whom He has foreknown and predestinated (as the apostle says) 'to be made like the image of His Son, that He might be the First-born of many brethren,'[2] whom the grace of God by this mediator had saved from the second death.

Therefore the first man's body was but animate, as the apostle witnesses, who, desiring to distinguish our animate bodies now from those spiritual ones that they shall become in the resurrection, says: 'It is sown in corruption, but is raised in incorruption: it is sown in reproach, it is raised in glory: it is sown in weakness, it is raised in power: it is sown an animated body, but shall arise a spiritual body.'[3] And then to prove this, he proceeds: 'For if there be a natural (or animated) body, there is also a spiritual body.' And to show what a natural body is, he says: 'The first man, Adam, was made a living soul.' Thus then showed he what a natural body is, though the scripture does not say of the first man, Adam, when God breathed in his face the breath of life, that man became a living body, but man became a living soul. 'The first man was made a living soul,' says the apostle, meaning he was made a natural body. But how the spiritual body is to be taken, he shows also, adding, 'but the last man, a quickening spirit': meaning Christ assuredly, who rose from death to die no more. Then he continues, saying: 'That was not first made which is spiritual, but that which is natural, and afterward that which is spiritual.' Here he shows most plainly that he did mean by the 'living soul' the

---

[1] Rom. viii. 10, 11.   [2] Rom. viii. 28, 29.   [3] 1 Cor. xv. 42–9.

natural body, and by the 'quickening spirit' the spiritual. For the natural body that Adam had, was first (though it had not died unless he had sinned), and such have we now, our nature drawing corruption and necessity of death from him and from his sin. Such also did Christ take upon Him for us, not needfully, but in His power. But the spiritual body is afterwards; and such had Christ our Head in His resurrection; such also shall we, His members, have in ours. Then does the apostle describe the difference of the two thus: 'The first man is of the earth, earthy; the second is heavenly, from heaven; as the earthy one was, so are all the earthy: and as the Heavenly One is, such shall all the heavenly ones be. As we have borne the image of the earthy, so shall we bear the image of the heavenly.' This the apostle infers from the sacrament of regeneration, as he says elsewhere: 'All ye that are baptized into Christ have put on Christ': [1] which shall then be really performed, when that which is natural in our birth shall become spiritual in our resurrection, for, to use his own words, 'we are saved by hope.' [2] We put on the image of the earthy man, by the propagation of sin and corruption, adherent unto our first birth: but we put on that of the Heavenly Man by grace, pardon, and promise of life eternal; which regeneration is efficacious for us only by the mercy of the mediator between 'God and man, the Man Christ Jesus,' whom the apostle calls the Heavenly Man because He came from heaven to take upon Him the shape of earthly mortality, and to shape it into heavenly immortality. He calls the rest heavenly also, because they are made members of Christ by grace, they and Christ being one, as the members and the head are one body. This he avers plainly in the chapter aforesaid: 'By man came death, and by man came also the resurrection from the dead: for as in Adam all die, even so in Christ shall all be made alive': [3] that is, in a quickening spirit, that is a spiritual body. Not that all that die in Adam shall become members of Christ; for many more of them shall fall into the eternal second death: but it is said, 'all,' and 'all,' because as none die naturally except in Adam, so none shall rise spiritually except in Christ. We may not then think that our bodies at the resurrection shall be such as Adam's was at the creation, nor that this text: 'As the earthy one was, so are all the earthy,' is meant of that which was effected by the transgression; for we may not think that Adam had a spiritual body ere he fell, and in his fall was made a natural one. He that conceives it so, gives but little regard to that great teacher, who says: 'If there be a natural body, then is there also a spiritual'; as it is also written: 'The first man Adam was made a living soul.' Surely this was not done after sin, since it was the first estate of man, whence the blessed apostle took this testimony of the law, to show what a natural body was?

[1] Gal. iii. 27.   [2] Rom. viii. 24.   [3] 1 Cor. xv. 21, 22.

CHAPTER XXIV

*How God's breathing life into Adam, and Christ's breathing upon
His apostles when He said: 'Receive the Holy Spirit,' are to be
understood*

SOME therefore do unadvisedly think that God, when He breathed
into his face the breath of life and man became a living soul, did
not then give him a soul but by the Holy Spirit only quickened a
soul that was in him before.   They ground this view upon Christ's
breathing upon His apostles after His resurrection and saying,
'Receive the Holy Spirit:' [1] thinking that this was such another
breathing, so that the evangelist might have said, 'they became
living souls'; which if he had done, it would have caused us to
imagine all reasonable souls dead that are not quickened by God's
Spirit, though their bodies seem to be alive.   But it was not so
when man was made, as the scripture shows plainly in these words:
'And God formed [2] man being dust of the earth': [3] which some
thinking to explain, translate: 'And God framed [4] man of the loam
of the earth,' because it was said before, 'a mist went up from the
earth and watered all the earth': that loam should seem to be produced by this mixture of earth and water, for immediately follows:
'And God framed man being dust of the earth,' as the Greek
translations whence our Latin is, do read it.   But whether the
Greek ἔπλασεν be 'formed,' or 'framed,' makes no difference.
'Framed' is the more proper word, but they that used 'formed'
thought they avoided ambiguity, because *fingo* in the Latin is used
commonly for 'to feign' by lying or delusion.   This man therefore
being framed of dust, or loam (for loam is moistened dust), that
this dust of the earth (to speak with the scripture more expressly)
when it received a soul was made an animate body, the apostle
affirms, saying: 'The man was made a living soul': that is, this dust
being formed was made a living soul.   Aye, say they, but he had
a soul now already, otherwise he could not have been man, being
neither soul only, nor body only, but consisting of both.   It is true,
the soul is not the whole man but the better part only; nor the body
the whole man but the worse part only, and both conjoined make
man; yet when we speak of them disjoined, they lose not that name.
For who may not follow custom, and say, 'Such a man is dead';
'Such a man is now in joy, or in pain,' and speak but of the soul
only: or 'Such a man is in his grave,' and mean but the body only?
Will they say the scripture uses no such phrase?   Yes, it both
calls the body and soul conjoined by the name of man, and also
dividing them, calls the soul the inward man, and the body the
outward, as if they were two men, and not both composing one.
    And mark in what respect man is called God's image, and man

---

[1] John xx. 22.   [2] Latin *formavit*.   [3] Gen. ii. 7.   [4] Latin *finxit*.

of earth returning to earth.   The first is in respect of the reasonable
soul which God breathed or inspired into man, that is, into man's
body; and the latter is in respect of the body which God made of
the dust, and gave it a soul, whereby it became a living body;
that is, man became a living soul.   And therefore when Christ
breathing upon His apostles said: 'Receive the Holy Spirit,' this
was to show that the Spirit was His, as well as the Father's, for the
Spirit is the Father's and the Son's, making up the Trinity of
Father, Son, and Holy Spirit, being no creature but a Creator.
That breath which was carnally breathed was not the substantial
nature of the Holy Spirit, but rather a signification (as I said) of
the Son's communication of the Spirit with His Father, it being
not particular to either, but common to both.   The scriptures in
Greek call it always πνεῦμα, as the Lord called it here, when by
signifying it with His breath, He gave it to His disciples: and I
never read it otherwise called in any place of God's book.   But
here, whereas it is said that 'God formed man being dust of the
earth, and breathed into his nostrils the Spirit (or breath) of life':
the Greek is not πνεῦμα, but πνοή; which word is read oftener for
the creature than the Creator, and therefore some Latinists (for the
sake of variety) do not interpret this word πνοή, spirit, but breath,
for so it is in Isaiah, where God saith: 'I have made all breath': [1]
meaning doubtless, 'every soul.'   Therefore that which the Greeks
call πνοή we do sometimes call breath, sometimes spirit, sometimes inspiration, sometimes aspiration, and sometimes soul: but
πνεῦμα, never but spirit, either of man, as the apostle says: 'What
man knoweth the things of a man but the spirit of a man which is
in him?' [2] or of a beast, as we read in the Preacher: 'Who knoweth
whether the spirit of man ascendeth upwards, and the spirit of
the beast downwards to the earth?' [3] or that bodily spirit which we
call 'wind,' as the psalm says, 'fire, hail, snow, ice, and the spirit
of tempests': [4] or of no creature, but the Creator Himself: whereof
our Saviour said in the gospel: 'Receive the Holy Spirit': [5]
signifying it in His bodily breath: and there also where He says:
'Go and baptize all nations in the name of the Father, the Son,
and the Holy Spirit,' plainly and excellently intimating the full
Trinity unto us: and there also where we read: 'God is a Spirit,' [6]
and in many other places of scripture.   In all those places of
scripture, the Greek, we see, hath πνεῦμα, and not πνοή, and the
Latin not flatus, but spiritus.   And therefore if in that place 'He
breathed into his face the breath of life,' the Greek had not πνοή
(as it hath), but πνεῦμα: yet it would not follow that we should
take it for the Holy Spirit, the third person in the Trinity, because
πνεῦμα is used for a creature, as well as the Creator, and as

---

[1] Isa. lvii. 16.   [2] 1 Cor. ii. 11.   [3] Eccles. iii. 21.   [4] Ps. cxlviii. 8.
              [5] Matt. xxviii. 19.   [6] John iv. 24.

ordinarily. Oh, but (say they) He would not have added *vitae*, 'of
life,' unless He had meant that Holy Spirit. And whereas He
said: 'Man became a soul,' He would not have added 'living,' but
that He meant that soul's life, which is given from above by the
Spirit of God: for the soul having a proper life by itself, why
should He add 'living,' but to intimate the life given by the Holy
Spirit? But what is this but to contend foolishly for conjecture,
and wholly to neglect scripture? For why need we go further
than one chapter, and behold: 'Let the earth bring forth the living
soul': speaking of the creation of all earthly creatures. And
besides, only five or six chapters after, why might they not observe this: 'Everything in whose nostrils the spirit of life did
breathe, whatsoever was in the dry land, died';[1] relating the
destruction of every living thing upon the earth by the deluge?
If then we find a living soul and a spirit of life in beasts, as the
scripture says plainly, using πνοή and not πνεῦμα in this very last
place: why may we not as well say: Why added He 'living' there,
seeing that a soul cannot be unless it live? And why added He
'of life' here, having named 'spirit'? But we understand the scripture's ordinary usage of the 'living soul,' and the 'spirit of life,'
for animated bodies, natural and sensitive; and yet forget this
usual phrase of scripture when it comes to be used concerning the
state of man: whereas it implies that man received a reasonable
soul of God, created by His breath, not as the others were, produced out of water and earth, and yet so that it was made in that
body to live therein and make it an animate body and a living soul,
as the other creatures were, whereof the scripture said: 'Let the
earth bring forth a living soul': and that 'in whose nostrils was the
spirit of life,' which the Greek text calleth not πνεῦμα, but πνοή,
meaning not the Holy Spirit, but their life. But we (say they) do
conceive God's breath to come from the mouth of God; now if
that be a soul, we must hold it equal and consubstantial with that
Wisdom or Word of God, which says: 'I come out of the mouth
of the Most High.'[2] Well, it says not that it was breathed from
His mouth, but came out of it. And as we men, not out of our
own nature, but of the air about us, can take an influx into ourselves, and give it out again in a breath, so Almighty God, not
only out of His own nature, or of any inferior creature, but even
of nothing, can make a breath, which He may be most fitly said to
breathe or inspire into man, it being as He is, incorporeal, but
not as He is, immutable, because it is created, as He is not. But
to let those men see that will talk of scriptures, and yet mark not
what they do intend, that something may be said to come forth of
God's mouth besides that which is equal and consubstantial with
Him, let them read or hear God's own words: 'Because thou art

---

[1] Gen. vii. 22, 23.   [2] Ecclus. xxiv. 3.

lukewarm, and neither cold nor hot, it will come to pass that I shall spew thee out of My mouth.' [1]   Therefore we have no cause to contradict the apostle's plainness in distinguishing the natural body wherein we now are, from the spiritual wherein we shall be: where he says: 'It is sown a natural body, it is raised a spiritual body.'   As it is also written: 'The first man Adam was made a living soul, and the last Adam a quickening spirit. The first was of the earth, earthy, the second of heaven, heavenly: as is the earthy, such are all the earthy, and as the heavenly is, such are the heavenly. And as we have borne the image of the earthy, so shall we bear the image of the heavenly.' Of all which words we spake before.   Therefore the natural body wherein man was first made was not made immortal: but yet was made so that it would not have died, unless man had offended.   But the body that shall be spiritual and immortal shall never have power to die, as the soul is created immortal, which though it do in a manner lose its life by losing the Spirit of God, which should advance it unto beatitude, yet it retains its own life, even though it lives in misery for ever, for it cannot die wholly.   The apostate angels, after a sort, are dead by sinning, because they forsook God, the fountain of life, whereat they might have drunk eternal felicity: yet could they not die in such a way that their proper life and sense should leave them, because they were made immortal; and at the last judgment they shall be thrown headlong into the second death, yet shall they live therein for ever, in perpetual sense of torture.   But the saints (the angels' fellow citizens), belonging to the grace of God, shall be so clothed with spiritual bodies, that from thenceforth they shall neither sin nor die; becoming so immortal (as the angels are) that sin can never subvert their eternity.   The nature of flesh shall still be theirs, but quite extracted from all corruption, unwieldiness, and ponderosity.   Now followeth another question, which (by the true God's help) we mean to decide.   And that is this.   If the motion of concupiscence arose in the rebelling members of our first parents immediately upon their transgression, whereupon they saw, that is, they did more curiously observe, their own nakedness, and, because the unclean impulse resisted their wills, covered their privy parts—how should they have begotten children, had they remained as they were created, before they sinned?   But this book being fit for an end, and this question not fit for a too succinct discussion, it is better to leave it to the next book.

[1] Rev. iii. 16.

THE FOURTEENTH BOOK OF
THE CITY OF GOD

CHAPTER I

*That the disobedience of the first man had drawn all mankind into
the perpetuity of the second death, but that God's grace hath freed
many from it*

WE said in our precedent books that it was God's pleasure to
propagate all men from one, both for the keeping of human nature
in one sociable similitude, and also to make their unity of origin
the means of their concord in heart. Nor would any of this kind
have died had not the first two (the one whereof was made from
the other, and the other from nothing) incurred this punishment
by their disobedience. In committing so great a sin their whole
nature, being hereby depraved, was so transfused through all their
offspring in the same degree of corruption and necessity of death;
whose kingdom hereupon became so great in man, that all would
have been cast headlong into the second death, that has no end,
by this due punishment, had not the undue grace of God acquitted
some from it. Whereby it comes to pass that, whereas mankind
is divided into so many nations, distinct in language, discipline,
habit, and fashion: yet are there but two sorts of men that do
properly make the two cities we speak of; the one is of men that
live according to the flesh, and the other of those that live according
to the spirit, each wishing, when they have attained their desire,
to enjoy their own particular peace.

CHAPTER II

*Of the carnal life, apparent in the soul's viciousness as well as the
body's*

WE must first then see what it is to live according to the flesh, and
what according to the spirit. The rash and inconsiderate con-
siderer hereof, not attending well to the scriptures, may think
that the Epicureans were those that lived according to the flesh,
because they made bodily pleasure that *summum bonum*, and all
such as in any way held corporal delight to be man's chiefest good,

together with the vulgar, which not out of philosophy, but out of their own proneness to lust, can delight in no pleasures but such as are bodily and sensible; but that the Stoics that placed this *summum bonum* in the mind, live according to the spirit (for what is man's mind but his spirit?). But the scriptures prove them both to follow the courses of the flesh, calling the flesh not only an earthly animate body, as it doth saying: 'All flesh is not the same flesh; for there is one flesh of men, and another flesh of beasts, and another of fishes, and another of birds': [1] but it uses the word in far other significations, amongst which one is, that it calls the whole man, that is, his entire nature, flesh, using the part for the whole: as: 'By the works of the law shall no flesh living be justified.' [2] What means he by 'no flesh,' but no man? He explains himself immediately: 'A man is justified by faith without the works of the law.' And in another place: 'No man is justified by the law.' 'The Word was made flesh.' What is that but man? Some, misconceiving this passage, held that Christ had no human soul. For as the part is taken for the whole in these words of Mary Magdalene: 'They have taken away my Lord and I know not where they have laid Him': [3] meaning only the flesh of Christ, which she thought they had taken out of the sepulchre: so is the part taken for the whole, when we say 'flesh,' for man, as in the quotations before. Seeing therefore that the scripture uses flesh in so many significations (too tedious here to recollect) to find what it is to live according to the flesh (such living being evil though the flesh is not evil), let us look a little diligently into that text of the Apostle Paul to the Galatians, where he says: 'The works of the flesh are manifest, which are adultery, fornication, uncleanness, wantonness, idolatry, witchcraft, hatred, debate, emulation, wrath, contentions, seditions, heresies, envy, drunkenness, gluttony, and suchlike; whereof I tell you now, as I told you before, that they which do those things shall not inherit the kingdom of God.' [4]

The due consideration of this text of the apostle will presently give us sufficient demonstration (as far as here needs) of what it is 'to live according to the flesh,' for in the works of the flesh which he says are manifest, rehearsing and condemning them, we find not only such as appertain to bodily and luxurious delight, as fornications, uncleanness, luxury, and drunkenness, but such also as discover the viciousness of the mind, truly distinct from fleshly pleasures. For who does not think that idolatry, witchcraft, enmity, contention, emulation, wrath, envy, sedition, and heresy, are rather mental vices than corporal? A man may for very reverence to some idolatrous or heretical error abstain from the lusts of the body, and yet though he do so, by the apostle's words, 'He lives according to the flesh': and in avoiding fleshly lusts commits most damnable works 'of the flesh.' Who has not enmity

[1] 1 Cor. xv. 39.   [2] Rom. iii. 20.   [3] John xx. 13.   [4] Gal. v. 19–21.

in his heart? Or who says to his enemy, or him that he thinks his
enemy: 'You have an evil flesh against me'? Nobody. They
say: 'You have an evil mind against me.' Lastly, as all men, that
heard those carnal vices recited, would affirm they were meant of
the flesh, so none that hears those mental crimes, but refers them
to the mind. Why then doth this true and faithful teacher of the
Gentiles call them 'the works of the flesh,' except he takes flesh
for man, as the part for the whole?

CHAPTER III

*That sin came from the soul, and not the flesh: and that the corruption
which sin has procured is not sin, but the punishment of sin*

IF any man say that the flesh is cause of the viciousness of the soul,
he is ignorant of man's nature, for the corruptible body does
but burden the soul. Therefore the apostle, speaking of this corruptible body whereof he had said before: 'Although our outward
man be corrupted,' [1] adds: 'That if our earthly house of habitation
be destroyed, we have a building given of God, an house not made
with hands, eternal in the heavens; therefore we sigh, desiring to
be clothed with that habitation which we have in heaven; if so be
that being clothed we shall not be found naked. For we that are
in this habitation, sigh, and are burdened, because we would not
be unclothed, but clothed upon, that mortality might be swallowed
up of life.' [2] We are therefore burdened with this corruptible
body, and yet knowing that it is not the body's nature, but corruption, that causes this burden, we would not be despoiled of it,
but be clothed upon it with the immortality thereof. It shall then
be a body still, but burdensome to us no more, because it is become
incorruptible. So then, as yet, the corruptible body is heavy unto
the soul and the earthly mansion keeps down the comprehensive
mind. But such as think that the evils of the mind arise from
the body do err. For though Virgil seems to express a plain
Platonism in these verses:

> Igneus est illis vigor et caelestis origo
> Seminibus, quantum non noxia corpora tardant,
> Terrenique hebetant artus, moribundaque membra,[3]

> Those seeds have fiery vigour, heavenly spring,
> So far as bodies hinder not with fullness,
> Or earthly dying members clog with dullness,

seeming to derive the four known passions of the mind, desire,

---

[1] 2 Cor. iv. 16.   [2] 2 Cor. v. 1–4.   [3] *Aen.* vi. 730–2.

fear, joy, and sorrow, as the origins of all guilt, wholly from the body, by these verses following:

> Hinc metuunt cupiuntque, dolent gaudentque, nec auras
> Suspiciunt, clausae tenebris et carcere caeco,[1]

> Here hence they fear, desire, displeased, content,
> Nor look to heaven, in dark blind prison pent,

yet our faith teaches us otherwise. For this corruption, that is so burdensome to the soul, is the punishment of the first sin, not the cause. The corruptible flesh made not the soul to sin, but the sinning soul made the flesh corruptible. From which corruption although there arise some incitements unto sin, and some vicious desires, yet are not all the sins of an evil life to be laid upon the flesh; otherwise we shall make the devil, that has no flesh, sinless: for though we cannot call him a fornicator, a drunkard, or by any one of those carnally vicious names (though he be a secret provoker of man unto all those), yet is he truly styled most proud and envious, which vices have possessed him so far, that on account of them he is destined unto eternal torment in the prisons of this obscure air. Now those vices that domineer in him the apostle calls the works of the flesh, though certain it is that he has no flesh. For he says that enmity, contention, emulation, wrath, and envy are the works of the flesh; to all which pride gives being, yet rules pride in the fleshless devil. For who hates the saints more than he? Who is more envious, contentious, emulating, and wrathful against them than he? Doing all this without the flesh, how are these the works of the flesh, but because they are the works of man, whom as I said before, the apostle means by flesh? For man became like the devil not in being in the flesh (for so was not the devil) but in living according to his own lust, that is, according to the fleshly man: for so chose the devil to do, when he left the truth, to become a liar, not through God, but through himself, who is both a liar and the father of lying. For he lied first, and from him sinning and lying had their beginning.

CHAPTER IV

What it is to live according to man, and to live according to God

THEREFORE a man living according to man, and not according to God, is like the devil: because an angel indeed should not live according to an angel, but according to God—to remain in the truth, and speak truth from Him, and not lies from himself. For the apostle speaks thus of man: 'If the truth of God hath abounded

[1] *Aen.* vi. 733–4.

through my lying': [1] calling lying his, and the truth, of God.
Therefore he that lives according to the truth lives according unto
God, not according to himself. For God said: 'I am the truth.' [2]
But he that lives not so, but according to himself, lives according
to lying: not that man (whom God, that never created a lie, did
create) is the author of lying, but because man was created upright,
to live according to his Creator and not himself, that is, to do His
will rather than his own. But not to live as he was made to live,
this is a lie. For he would be blessed, and yet will not live in a
course possible to attain it. What can there be more lying than
such a will? And therefore it is not unfitly said that every sin is a
lie. For we never sin except with a desire to do ourselves good,
or not to do ourselves hurt.

Therefore is it a lie when that which we think shall do us good
turns unto our hurt; or that which we think to better ourselves
by makes us worse. Whence is this, but because man can only
have his good from God, whom he forsakes in sinning, and none
from himself, in living according to whom he sins? Whereas
therefore we said that the contrariety of the two cities arose hereupon, because some lived according to the flesh, and others according to the Spirit, we may likewise say it is because some live
according unto man, and others unto God. For Paul says plainly
to the Corinthians: 'Seeing there is emulation and contention
amongst you, are ye not carnal, and walk according to man?' [3]
To walk therefore according to man is carnal, man being understood in his inferior part, flesh. For those whom he calls carnal
here, he calls natural before, saying: 'What man knoweth the
things of a man but the spirit of a man which is in him? Even so,
no man knoweth the things of God but the Spirit of God. Now we
have not received the spirit of the world, but the Spirit which is of
God, that we might know the things that God hath given us,
which things also we speak, not in the words which man's wisdom
teacheth, but being taught by the Spirit, comparing spiritual things
with spiritual things. But the natural man perceiveth not the
things of the Spirit of God, for they are foolishness unto him.' [4]
Unto those natural men he spake this a little afterwards: 'I could
not speak unto you brethren as unto spiritual men, but as unto
carnal.' [5] And here is that figure of speech that uses the part
for the whole to be understood; for the whole man may either be
meant by the soul or by the flesh, both which are his parts; and so
a natural man and a carnal man are not several, but all one, namely
one that lives according to man; as those texts afore-cited do
intend: 'By the works of the law shall no flesh be justified'; [6]
and that where it is said that 'Seventy-five souls went down with
Jacob into Egypt.' [7] In the former, by 'flesh' is meant 'man';

[1] Rom. iii. 7.   [2] John xiv. 6.   [3] 1 Cor. iii. 3.   [4] 1 Cor. ii. 11–14.
[5] 1 Cor. iii. 1.   [6] Rom. iii. 20   [7] Gen. xlvi. 27

and in the latter, by 'seventy-five souls,' are meant 'seventy-five persons.' And in this: 'Not in the words which man's wisdom teaches,' he might have said: 'which carnal wisdom teaches': as also, 'according to the flesh,' for 'according unto man,' if he had pleased. And it was more apparent in what follows: for 'when one says, I am of Paul, and another, I am of Apollos, are ye not men?' [1] That which he had called natural and carnal before, he now more expressly calls man: meaning, you live according to man, and not according to God, whom if you followed in your lives, you should be made gods.

CHAPTER V

That the Platonists teach the natures of soul and body better than the Manichees, yet they err in ascribing sin unto the nature of the flesh

WE should not therefore injure our Creator in imputing our vices to our flesh. The flesh is good, but to leave the Creator and live according to this created good is the mischief; whether a man chooses to live according to the body or the soul or both, which make a full man, who therefore may be called by either of them. For he that makes the soul's nature the greatest good, and the body's the greatest evil, does both carnally desire the soul, and carnally avoid the flesh: conceiving of both as human vanity, not as divine verity teaches. Indeed the Platonists are not so mad as the Manichees, that hate the carnal body as the natural cause of all mischief, since they make God the Creator of all the elements, parts, and qualities that this visible world is composed of. But the Platonists hold that these, our mortal members, produce the feelings of fear, desire, joy, and sorrow in our bodies; from which four perturbations (as Tully calls them [2]) or passions (as other translators give them) the whole inundation of man's enormities has its source and spring. If this be so, why does Aeneas in Virgil, hearing by his father that the souls were to return back into the bodies, wonder at this opinion, and cry out:

> O pater, anne aliquas ad caelum hinc ire putandum est,
> Sublimes animas, iterumque ad tarda reverti
> Corpora? quae lucis miseris tam dira cupido? [3]

> What, father, do you think the souls are ta'en
> To heaven, and thence, to this dull flesh return?
> What dread desire should urge them to their pain?

Is this same dread desire still remaining in the soul, being now free from the carnal burden in such a commended purity? Does he

[1] 1 Cor. iii. 4.   [2] *Tusc. Disp.* iv. 6, 11.   [3] *Aen.* vi. 719–21.

not say they are purged from all bodily infection, when they
desire to return into the body again? If it were the case (as it is
most vain to hold so) that there were an eternal revolution of the
pollution and the purgation of souls going from and returning to
the body, yet could it not be truly said that all vicious desires are
the effects of the flesh: for as this noble speaker says, 'that dread
desire which doth compel the soul being purged from all earthly
contagion to desire the body again,' is not of the body. And therefore they confess that all the soul's evil affections arise not from
the flesh, as desire, fear, joy, and sorrow, but that it may have
those passions of itself.

CHAPTER VI

*Of the quality of man's will, unto which all affections, good and bad,
are subject*

BUT the quality of man's will is of some moment; for if it be bad
so are all those motions of the soul; if good, they are both blameless and praiseworthy. For there is a will in them all. Nay,
they are all direct wills. What is desire, and joy, but a will consenting to that which we affect? And what is fear, and sorrow,
but a will contrary unto what we like? But when we consent to
the desire of anything, that is desire: and when we consent in
enjoying anything, this is delight. So, when we dislike a thing,
and would not have it come to pass, this will is fear: when we
dislike it after it has come to pass, this is grief or sorrow. And
according to the variety of the things desired and avoided, as the
will consents or dislikes, so are our diversity of passions. Whereof
a man that makes God and not man the steersman of his life, ought
to love good, and consequently to hate evil. And because none is
evil by nature, but all by vice, he that lives after God's love owes
his full hate unto the evil; not to hate the man for his vice, nor to
love the vice for the man, but hate the vice and love the man: for
the vice being cured, he shall find no object of his hate, but all
for his love.

CHAPTER VII

*That 'amor' and 'dilectio' are of indifferent use in the scriptures both
for good and evil*

FOR he, that is resolved to love God and his neighbour according
unto God and not man, is for this love called a man of a good
will; and this is called more commonly charity in the scriptures,

though sometimes it be called love therein also. For the apostle will have his magistrate to be a lover of good. And our Lord asking Peter thus: 'Simon, son of Jonas, lovest thou Me more than these,' [1] he answered: 'Lord, thou knowest that I love Thee.' He asked him so again, and he answered so again; then He asked him the third time, by φιλῶ, amo, whereas he had used ἀγαπάω, diligo, in the other two; only to show that diligere and amare were both one, to love, as Peter had used the one word in reply to all the three questions. This I thought worth recital, but some say dilectio, charity, is one thing, and amor, love, another: and that the first is used in the good, and the latter in the bad sense. But sure it is that the profane authors never used them so. But let the philosophers look to their distinctions. For their books use amor, love, in good senses, and in reference to God most frequently. But we wished to show that our scriptures, which we place far above their authorities, do not use amor and dilectio with any such distinct difference: for we have shown that they use amor in a good sense. If any one think it is used both in a good sense and bad, and dilectio only in the good, let him look into that verse of the psalm: 'He that loveth [diligit] iniquity hateth his own soul.' [2] Here is diligo upon a bad object. And here the apostle John: 'If any man love [dilexerit] the world, the love [dilectio] of the Father is not in him.' [3] Behold here dilectio used in one verse with both a good and a bad object. But if any one seek to know whether amor be used in an evil sense (we have shown it in good), let him read this: 'Men shall be lovers of themselves,' [4] etc.; lovers of pleasures more than lovers of God. For an upright will is good love, and a perverse will is bad love. Love then desiring to enjoy what it loves is desire: and enjoying it, is joy: flying what it hates, it is fear; feeling it, it is sorrow.

These are evils if the love be evil, and good if it be good. What we say let us prove by scripture. The apostle 'desires to be dissolved, and to be with Christ'; [5] and: 'My heart breaketh for the continual desire I have unto Thy judgments'; [6] or if this be better: 'My soul hath coveted to desire Thy judgments'; and: 'Desire of wisdom leadeth to the kingdom.' [7] Yet custom has made it a law, that where concupiscentia or cupiditas is used without addition of the object, it is ever taken in a bad sense. But joy, or gladness, the psalm uses in a good sense: 'Be glad in the Lord, and rejoice, ye righteous,' [8] and: 'Thou hast given gladness to mine heart,' [9] and: 'In Thy presence is the fullness of joy.' [10] Fear is also used by the apostle in a good sense: 'Work out your salvation with fear and trembling'; [11] and: 'Be not high-minded, but fear'; [12]

---

[1] John xxi. 15–17.   [2] Ps. xi. 5.   [3] 1 John ii. 15.   [4] 2 Tim. iii. 2.
[5] Phil. i. 23.   [6] Ps. cxix. 20.   [7] Wisd. of Sol. vi. 21.
[8] Ps. xxxii. 11.   [9] Ps. iv. 7.   [10] Ps. xvi. 11.
[11] Phil. ii. 12.   [12] Rom. xi. 20.

and: 'But I fear lest as the serpent beguiled Eve through his subtlety, so your minds should be corrupted from the simplicity that is in Christ.' [1]   But as for that sorrow (which Tully had rather call *aegritudo*, sickness, and Virgil, *dolor*, pain; where he says, *dolent gaudentque*, yet I had rather call it *tristitia*, sadness, because *aegritudo* and *dolor* are more often used for bodily desires) —the question whether it be used in a good sense or no, is fit to be more curiously examined.

CHAPTER VIII

Of the three passions that the Stoics allow a wise man, excluding sadness as a foe to a virtuous mind

THOSE emotions which the Greeks call εὐπάθειαι, and Tully *constantiae*, the Stoics make to be three; and instead of speaking of three perturbations in a wise man's mind, they substitute will for desire, joy for exultation, and wariness for fear: but as for that *aegritudo* or *dolor* which we, to avoid ambiguity, call sadness, they deny that a wise mind can entertain anything of it; for the will (say they) desires the good, which a wise man effects; joy concerns the good he has attained, and wariness avoids what he is to avoid. But seeing that sadness arises from an evil cause already fallen out (and no evil happens to a wise man), therefore wisdom admits no place thereof in the mind.   Therefore (say they) none but wise men can will, rejoice, and beware; and none but fools can covet, exult, fear, and be sad.   The first are the three constancies (says Tully), and the latter the four perturbations. The Greeks, as I said, call the first three εὐπάθειαι, and these four πάθη. In seeking the correspondency of this with the language of holy writ, I found this of the prophet: 'There is no joy (saith the Lord) unto the wicked,' [2] as if the wicked might rather exult, than have joy in their mischiefs, for joy is properly peculiar to the good and godly.   That saying also in the gospel: 'Whatsoever ye would that men should do unto you, even so do ye to them,' [3] seems to intimate that a man cannot will any evil thing but only covet it: by reason of which custom of interpretation some translators added 'good': 'What good soever,' etc., for they thought it not fit for man to desire that men should do them any dishonesty, and therefore put in this, lest some should think that in their luxurious banquets (to be silent on more obscene matters) they should fulfil this precept, in doing to others as others did unto them.   But 'good' is not in the original Greek, but only, as we read before: 'Whatsoever ye would,'

[1] 2 Cor. xi. 3.   [2] Isa. lvii. 21.   [3] Matt. vii. 12.

etc.; for in saying 'ye would,' he means 'good.' He said not, 'whatsoever you covet.' Yet must we not always tie our phrases to this strictness, but take leave to do so on needful occasions; and when we read those writers that we may not resist, we must conceive their phrases in this way when their true sense can be discovered in no other way, as, for example sake, in the said verses of the prophet and the apostle. Who knows not that the wicked exult in pleasure? And yet 'there is no joy (says the Lord) to the wicked.' Why? Because joy is properly and strictly used in this place. So may some say that precept, 'Whatsoever you would' etc., is not well delivered; and they may pollute one another with uncleanness or suchlike in consequence of it. Notwithstanding, the command is well given, and is a most true and healthful one. Why? Because will, which properly cannot be used of evil, is put in the most proper signification in this place. But as for ordinary usage of speech, we would not say: 'Have no will to tell any lie'— but that there is a bad will also, distinct from that which the angels praised saying: 'Peace on earth to men of good will.' [1] Good were here superfluous, if there was no will but good. And how coldly had the apostle praised charity by saying that it rejoiceth not in iniquity,[2] but that envy rejoiceth therein. For the pagan authors do use these differences. 'I desire,' says Tully, 'conscript fathers, I desire to be merciful.' [3] Here he uses *cupio* in a good sense, and who is so perverse as to say he should have used *volo* rather? And Terence's lascivious youth: 'I would have none but Philumena,' says he. That this will was lust, his ancient servant's answer declares, saying to his master: 'How much better were it for you, to cast this love out of your heart, rather than seek to inflame it more therein!' [4] That they used joy in an evil sense, Virgil's verse of the four perturbations records:

> Hinc metuunt cupiuntque, dolent gaudentque.[5]
> Here hence they fear, desire, displeased, content.

And the same author in another place says:

> Mala mentis gaudia.[6]
> The mind's bad joys.

So then both good and evil do will, desire, beware, and rejoice; and to rehearse them in other terms, the good and bad do desire, fear, and are joyful: but the one does it well, and the other badly, according as their wills are. And that sadness, for which the Stoics can find no place in a wise man, is apparent in good men, especially of our profession. For the apostle praises the Corinthians for that they sorrowed after a godly manner. Aye, but (some may say) the apostle congratulates their sorrow in repentance, and that is proper to none but sinners: for his words run thus:

¹ Luke ii. 14.   ² 1 Cor. xiii. 6.   ³ 1 *Cat.* ii. 4.
⁴*Andr.* ii. 1, 6–8.   ⁵ *Aen.* vi. 733.   ⁶ *Aen.* vi. 278–9.

'For I perceive that the same epistle hath made you sorry
though it were but for a season. Now I rejoice not that ye were
made sorry but that ye sorrowed to repentance: for ye were made
sorry after a godly manner, so that in nothing you were hurt by
us. For godly sorrow causeth repentance unto salvation, not to
be repented of: but the worldly sorrow causeth death; for behold
this godly sorrow, what carefulness it hath wrought in you.' [1]
Verily the Stoics may answer for themselves, that this sorrow
seemed useful unto their repentance, but it cannot be in a wise
man because he cannot do a sinful act worthy of repentance, nor
can admit anything that should produce sadness in him. For
they say that Alcibiades (if I have not forgotten the man's name)
thinking himself happy, and Socrates disputing against it and
proving him miserable, because he was not wise, fell a-weeping.
So here was his want of wisdom cause of this good sorrow, whereby
he grieved that he was not as he should be; but a wise man (say
the Stoics) can never have this sorrow.

CHAPTER IX

*Of the perturbations of mind which the righteous moderate and rule
aright*

BUT concerning these questions of perturbations, the philosophers
are already answered in the ninth book, in which we show that
their contention is rather verbal than real. But according to our
religion and the scriptures, the citizens of God, as long as they are
pilgrims, and in the way of God, do fear, desire, rejoice, and
sorrow. But their love, being right, straightens all those emotions.
They fear eternal pain, and desire eternal joy. They sorrow for
the present, because as yet they sigh in themselves, waiting for
their adoption, even the redemption of their bodies. They rejoice
in hope, because that shall be fulfilled which is written: 'Death is
swallowed up in victory.' [2] They fear to offend, and desire to
persevere. They sorrow for sin, and rejoice in doing good. They
fear to sin, because, 'for that iniquity shall be increased, the love
of many shall wax cold.' [3] They desire to persevere, because, 'He
that endureth to the end shall be saved.' [4] They sorrow for sin,
because, 'If we say that we have no sin, we deceive ourselves and
the truth is not in us.' [5] They rejoice in good works, for 'God
loveth a cheerful giver.' [6] And as they are strong or weak, so do
they desire or fear to be tempted: rejoicing, or sorrowing in temptations. They fear to be tempted, for, 'If any man fall into a fault

[1] 2 Cor. vii. 8–11.   [2] 1 Cor. xv. 54.   [3] Matt. xxiv. 12.
[4] Matt. x. 22.   [5] 1 John i. 8.   [6] 2 Cor. ix. 7.

by any occasion, ye which are spiritual, restore such an one in the spirit of meekness, considering thyself, lest thou also be tempted.'[1] They desire to be tempted, for, 'Prove me, O Lord, and try me, examine my reins and mine heart,'[2] said David.   They sorrow in temptations, for they hear how Peter wept.   They rejoice in them, for, 'Brethren, count it exceeding joy when ye fall into divers temptations,'[3] says James.

And they do not feel emotions for themselves only, but for others also, whom they desire should be freed, and fear lest they perish, sorrowing at their fall and rejoicing at their deliverance. For if we that are come from paganism to Christianity may give an especial instance in that worthy and dauntless man that boasted of his infirmities, that teacher of faith and truth to the nations, that toiler above all his fellow apostles, that edifier of God's people by sermons being present, and by more epistles than they all being absent, that blessed man Paul (I mean), Christ's champion, taught by Him, anointed from Him, crucified with Him, glorified in Him, in the theatre of this world where he was made a spectacle to God, angels, and men, fighting a lawful and great fight, and 'following hard towards the mark for the prize of the high calling':[4] how gladly do we with the eyes of faith behold him 'weep with them that weep, and rejoice with them that rejoice';[5] 'fightings without, and fears within';[6] 'longing to depart and to be with Christ,'[7] desiring to see the Romans, and to receive fruit from them as well as the others;[8] being jealous over the Corinthians, and fearing lest their minds should be corrupted 'from the chastity which is in Christ';[9] having great sadness and continual sorrow of heart for Israel, that being ignorant of God's righteousness would erect one of their own, and not be subject unto God: and bitterly grieving that divers had not repented them of their fornication and uncleanness!   If these emotions, arising from the love of good, be vicious, then let true vices be called virtues: but seeing their use is levelled by the rule of reason, who dare call them frail or imperfect passions of the mind?   Our Lord Himself, living in the form of a servant (yet without sin), used them when He thought it requisite; for we may not think that having man's essential body and soul, He had but seeming affections.

And therefore His sorrow for Jerusalem's hardness of heart, His joy for the believers, His tears for Lazarus, His desire to eat the passover with His disciples, and His deadly heaviness of soul upon the approach of His passion, these are no feigned narrations.

But these emotions of man He felt when it pleased Him, as He was made man when it pleased Him.   Wherefore we confess that those emotions, in their best kind, are but pertinent to this present life, not unto that which we hope for hereafter; and that we are

---

[1] Gal. vi. 1.   [2] Ps. xxvi. 2.   [3] Jas. i. 2.   [4] Phil. iii. 14.   [5] Rom. xii. 15.
[6] 2. Cor. vii. 5.   [7] Phil. i. 23.   [8] Rom. i. 11, 13.   [9] 2 Cor. xi. 3.

often overpressed by them. A laudable desire or charity may
move us: yet shall we weep whether we will or no. For we have
them by our human infirmity, but so had not Christ; for He had
His very infirmity itself from His own power. But as long as we
live in this infirmity, we shall live worse if we lack those emotions.
For the apostle dispraises and detests such as want natural affection. And so does the psalmist, saying: 'I looked for some to
pity me, and there was none.' [1] For to lack the sense of sorrow in
this mortal life (as a great scholar held) never befalls a man without
great stupidity of body and barbarism of mind. Therefore the
Greek ἀπάθεια, or impassibility, being meant of the mind, and
not the body, if it be understood as a lack of those perturbations
only which disturb the mind and resist reason, is to be defended
and desired. For the godly wise and holy men (not ordinary
wranglers) say all directly: 'If we say that we have no sin, we deceive
ourselves, and the truth is not in us.' [2] But if a man had this same
ἀπάθεια (meant as before), he had no sin indeed in him. In truth it
is well if we can live here without crime: but he that thinks he
lives without sin does not avoid sin but rather excludes all pardon.
But now if ἀπάθεια be an utter abandoning of all mental affections
whatsoever, who will not say that such a stupidity is worse than
sin? We may fitly say indeed that true happiness shall be utterly
void of fear and sorrow: but who can say it shall be void of love
and joy, but he that professes to oppose the truth? But if this
ἀπάθεια be a freedom from fear and sorrow, we must not aim at
it in this life, if we mean to live after the law of God. But in the
other promised life of eternity all fear shall be excluded from us.
For that fear whereof the apostle John says: 'There is no fear in
love, but perfect love casteth out fear, and he that feareth is not
perfect in love,' [3] is not that kind of fear wherewith the apostle Paul
feared the fall of the Corinthians, for love has this fear in it, and
nothing has it but love: but the other fear is not in love, whereof
the same apostle Paul says: 'For ye have not received the spirit of
bondage to fear again.' [4] But that chaste fear, remaining world
without end, if it be in the world to come (and how else can it
remain world without end?), shall be no fear terrifying us from
evil, but a fear keeping us in an inseparable good. For where the
good attained is unchangeably loved, there is the fear to lose it
inseparably chained. For by this chaste fear is meant the will that
we must necessarily have to avoid sin: not with an ungrounded
carefulness lest we should sin, but being founded in the peace of
love, to beware of sin. But if that firm and eternal security be
free from all fear, and conceive only the fullness of joy, then the
saying that 'the fear of the Lord is clean, and endureth for ever,' [5]

---

[1] Ps. lxix. 20.   [2] 1 John i. 8.   [3] 1 John iv. 18.
                  [4] Rom. viii. 15.   [5] Ps. xix. 9

is meant as that other passage is: 'The patience of the afflicted shall not perish for ever.'[1]

Their patience shall not be eternal, which is necessary only where miseries are to be eternally endured. But that which their patience shall attain, shall be eternal. So it may be that this pure fear is said to remain for ever, because the scope whereat it aims is everlasting: which being so, and a good course alone leading to beatitude, then has a bad life bad affections, and a good life good ones. And everlasting blessedness shall have both joy and love, not only right, but firm and unmoving: but shall be utterly free from fear and sorrow. Hence is it apparent what courses God's citizens ought to run in this earthly pilgrimage, making the spirit not the flesh, God and not humanity the lantern to their paths: and here also we see their estate in their eternal future. But the city of the impious that steer by the compass of carnality, and in their most divine matters reject the truth of God, and rely upon the instructions of men, is shaken with these affections, as with earthquakes, and infected with them as with pestilent contagions. And if any of the citizens seem to curb themselves from these courses, they grow so impiously proud and vainglorious, that the less their trouble is by these passions, the greater their disease. And if any of them be so wonderfully vain and barbarous as to embrace downright callousness, becoming insensible of all affection, they do rather abjure true manhood than attain true peace. Roughness does not prove a thing right; nor can dullness produce solid soundness.

CHAPTER X

Whether man had those perturbations in paradise before his fall

BUT it is a fair question whether our first parent, or parents (for they were two in marriage), had those natural affections ere they sinned, which we shall be free from when we are perfectly purified. If they had them, how had they that memorable bliss of paradise? Who can be directly happy that either fears or sorrows? And how could they either fear or grieve in that copious affluence of bliss, where they were out of the danger of death and sickness, having all things that a good will desired, and lacking all things that might give their happiness just cause of offence? Their love to God was unmoved, their union sincere, and thereupon exceeding delightful, having power to enjoy in full what they loved. They were in a peaceable avoidance of sin, which tranquillity kept out all external annoyance. Did they desire (do you

[1] Ps. ix. 18.

think?) to taste the forbidden fruit, and yet feared to die? God
forbid we should think this to be where there was no sin, for it
were a sin to desire to break God's command, and to forbear it
rather for fear of punishment than love of righteousness. God
forbid, I say, that ere that sin was, that should be proved true in
relation to the forbidden fruit which Christ saith in relation to
woman: 'Whosoever looketh upon a woman to lust after her hath
already committed adultery with her in his heart.' [1]   How happy
were our first parents, being troubled with no perturbations of
mind nor any sickness of body! Even so happy should all mankind have been if they had not transfused that misery, which their
sin incurred, into their posterity: nor would any of their seed have
committed an act worthy of condemnation.   And this bliss remaining, until, by the words 'Increase and multiply,' [2] the number of the
predestinate were fulfilled, then should a better have been given
us, namely, that which the angels have, wherein there is an eternal
security from sin and death: and so should the saints have lived
then without tasting of labour, sorrow, and death, as they shall do
now in the resurrection, after they have endured them all.

CHAPTER XI

*The fall of the first man, in whom nature was made good, but can only
be repaired by the Maker*

BUT God, foreknowing all things, could not but know that man
would fall.   Therefore we must ground our city upon His prescience and ordinance, not upon that which we know not, and
God has not revealed.   For man's sin could not disturb God's
decree, nor force Him to change His purpose.   God foreknew
and anticipated both, that is, how bad man (whom He had made)
should become, and what good He meant to derive from him, for
all his badness.   For though God be said to change His resolution
(as the scriptures figuratively say that He repented, etc.), yet this is
in respect of man's hope, or nature's order, not according to His
own prescience.   So then God made man upright, and consequently well-willed: otherwise he could not have been upright.
And so this good will was God's work, man being therewith
created.   But the evil will, which was in man before his evil work,
was rather a falling from the work of God to its own works than
any positive work.   And therefore were the works evil, because they
were according to themselves, and not according to God, this evil
will or man himself in respect of his evil will being as a tree bearing
such bad fruit.   Now this evil will, though it does not follow, but

[1] Matt. v. 28.   [2] Gen. i. 28.

oppose nature, being a fault; yet is it of the same nature that vice is, which cannot but be in some nature: but it must be in that nature which God made of nothing, not in that which He has begotten of Himself, as He begot the Word by whom all things were made. For although God made man of dust, yet He made dust out of nothing; and He made the soul out of nothing, which He joined with the body, making a complete man. But evils are so far under that which is good, that though they be permitted to exist to show what good use God's provident justice can make of them, yet may that which is good exist without them, as that true and glorious God Himself, and all the visible resplendent heavens do, above this darkened and misty air of ours: but evils cannot exist apart from that which is good, for all the natures wherein they abide, being considered merely as natures, are good. And evil is removed from nature, not by abscission of any other nature contrary to this or any part of this, but by purifying of that nature only, which was thus depraved. Then therefore is the will truly free, when it serves neither vice nor sin. Such God gave us, such we lost, and can only recover by Him that gave it: as the Truth says: 'If the Son shall make you free, ye shall be free indeed.'[1] It is as if He should say: 'If the Son save you, you shall be truly saved,' for He is the Liberator, that is the Saviour. Wherefore in a paradise both local and spiritual man made God his rule to live by; for it was a paradise local for the body's good, and not spiritual for the spirit's; nor was it a paradise spiritual for the spirit's good, and not local for the body's: no, it was both for both. But after that proud and therefore envious angel fell through that pride from God unto himself, and chose to rule in a tyrannical vainglory rather than be ruled, fell from the spiritual paradise (of whose fall, and his fellows, that thereupon from being good angels became his, I disputed in my eleventh book, as God gave grace and means), desiring to creep into man's mind by his ill-persuading subtlety, and envying man's constancy in his own fall, he chose the serpent, one of the creatures that then lived harmlessly with the man and woman in the earthly paradise, a creature slippery and pliable, wreathed in knots, and fit for his work. This he chose to speak through, abusing it, as subject unto the greater excellency of his angelical nature; and, making it the instrument of his spiritual wickedness, through it he began to speak deceitfully unto the woman; beginning at the meaner part of mankind, to invade the whole by degrees, thinking the man was not so credulous nor so soon deluded as he would be seeing another so served before him. For as Aaron consented not by persuasion, but yielded by compulsion unto the Hebrews' idolatry, to make them an idol, and as Solomon (as it is thought) yielded no worship to idols of his own erroneous belief, but was brought unto that sacrilege by his

[1] John viii. 36.

wives' persuasions; so is it to be thought that the first man did not yield to his wife in this transgression of God's precept, as if he thought she spoke the truth; but only being compelled to it by his social love to her, being but one with one, and both of one nature and kind. For it is not in vain that the apostle says: 'Adam was not deceived: but the woman was deceived': [1] but it shows that the woman did think the serpent's words were true, but Adam would not break company with his partner, though it were in sin, and so sinned wittingly. Wherefore the apostle says not, 'He sinned not': but, 'He was not seduced,' for he shows that he sinned, saying: 'By one man sin entered into the world': and a little after more plainly: 'after the manner of the transgression of Adam.' [2] And those he means are seduced, that think the first to be no sin, which he knew to be a sin. Otherwise why should he say: 'Adam was not seduced'? But he that is not acquainted with the divine severity might therein be deceived to conceive that his sin was but venial. And therefore while the woman was seduced, he was not; but this it was that deceived him, that he was to be judged for his false excuse: 'The woman that Thou gavest me to be with me, she gave me of the tree, and I did eat.' [3] What need we any more then? Though they were not both seduced, they were both taken in sin and made the devil's captives.

CHAPTER XII

Of the quality of man's first offence

BUT if the difference of the effects of others' sins from that of the first man do trouble any one, in that other sins do not alter man's nature, as that first transgression did; making him liable to that death, torture of the affections, and corruption which we all feel now, and which originally he felt not at all, nor would have felt, if he had not sinned: if this (I say) move any one, he must not therefore think that it was a light fault that he committed in eating of that fruit which was not hurtful at all, but only as it was forbidden. For God would not have planted any hurtful thing in that delicious paradise. But upon this precept was grounded obedience, the mother and guardian of all the other virtues of the soul. And it is good for the soul to be subject, and pernicious for it to leave the Creator's will and to follow its own. This command then of forbearing one fruit when there were so many besides it, being so easy to observe and so short to remember, especially since no lust then opposed the will (for this was a penalty that came after the transgression), was the more unjustly broken, by how much it was the easier to keep.

[1] 1 Tim. ii. 14.   [2] Rom. v. 12, 14.   [3] Gen. iii. 12.

CHAPTER XIII

That in Adam's offence his evil will was before his evil work

BUT evil began within them secretly at first, to draw them into open disobedience afterwards. For there would have been no evil work, but there was an evil will before it: and what could begin this evil will but pride, that is 'the beginning of all sin'?[1] And what is pride but a perverse desire of height, in forsaking Him to whom the soul ought solely to cleave, as the beginning thereof, to make itself seem its own beginning. This is when it likes itself too well, or when it so loves itself that it will abandon that unchangeable Good which ought to be more delightful to it than itself. This defect now is voluntary. For if the will remained firm in the love of that higher and stronger Good which gave it light to see it, and zeal to love it, it would not have turned from that, to take delight in itself, and thereupon have become so blind of sight and so cold of zeal that either Eve should have believed the serpent's words as true, or Adam should have dared to prefer his wife's will before God's command, and to think that he offended but venially, if he bare the partner of his life company in her offence. The evil therefore, that is, this transgression, was not done but by such as were evil before. Such ate the forbidden fruit. There could be no evil fruit, but from an evil tree. The tree was made evil against nature, for it had not become evil but by the unnatural viciousness of the will: and no nature can be depraved by vice, but such as is created of nothing. And therefore in that it is nature it has it from God: but in that it falls from God, it was made of nothing. Yet man was not made nothing upon his fall, but he was lessened in excellence by inclining to himself, after having been most excelling in his adherence to God. But leaving Him to adhere to and delight in himself, he grew not to be nothing, but towards nothing. Therefore the scripture calls proud men otherwise pleasers of themselves. It is good to lift up the heart, but not unto one's self, for that is pride, but unto God, for that is obedience inherent only in the humble.

In humility therefore there is this to be wondered at, that it elevates the heart; and in pride this, that it dejects it. This seems strangely contrary, that elevation should be below, and dejection aloft. But godly humility subjects one to his superior: and God is above all; therefore humility exalts one, in making him God's subject. But pride the vice refusing this subjection falls from Him that is above all, and so becomes more base by far, fulfilling this verse of the psalm: 'Thou hast cast them down in their own exaltation.'[2] He says not 'when they were exalted,' as if they were degraded afterwards: but, in their very exaltation were they cast down. Their elevation was their ruin. And therefore in

---

[1] Ecclus. x. 13.   [2] Ps. lxxiii. 18.

that humility is so approved of, and commended to the city of God that is yet a pilgrim upon earth, and so highly extolled by Christ the King thereof; and pride, the just contrary, shown by holy scripture to be so predominant in His adversaries the devil and his angels—in this very thing the great difference of the two cities, the godly and the ungodly, with both their angels accordingly, lies most apparent; God's love prevailing in the one, and self-love in the other. So that the devil could not have seduced mankind to such a palpable transgression of God's express charge, had not evil will and self-love got place in them before, for he delighted in that which was said: 'Ye shall be as gods': [1] which they might sooner have been by obedience and coherence with their Creator than by proud opinion that they were their own beginners; for the created gods are not gods of themselves but by participation of the God that made them; but man desiring more became less, and choosing to be sufficient in himself fell from that all-sufficient God.

This then is the mischief: man liking himself as if he were his own light turned away from the true light, which if he had pleased himself with, he might have been like. This mischief, I say, was first in his soul, and thence was drawn on to the subsequent mischievous act, for the scripture is true that says: 'Pride goeth before destruction, and a haughty mind before the fall.' [2] The fall which was in secret foreruns the fall which was in public, the first being taken for no fall at all: for who takes exaltation to be ruin, though there is already a fall in the forsaking of the Highest?

But who fails not to see that ruin lies in the express breach of God's precepts? For therefore did God forbid an action, that if it were done, all excuse and pretence of justice might be excluded. And therefore I dare say it is good that the proud should fall into some broad and disgraceful sin, thereby to take a dislike of themselves, who fell by liking themselves too much: for Peter's sorrowful dislike of himself when he wept was more healthful to his soul than the unsound pleasure that he took in himself when he presumed. Therefore says the psalmist: 'Fill their faces with shame, that they may seek Thy name, O Lord': [3] that is, that they may delight in Thee and seek Thy name, who before delighted in themselves, and sought their own.

CHAPTER XIV

Of the pride of the transgression, which was worse than the transgression itself

But pride, that makes man seek to colour his guilt, is far more damnable than the guilt itself is. Such pride was in the first of

[1] Gen. iii. 5.   [2] Prov. xvi. 18.   [3] Ps. lxxxiii. 16.

mankind. She could say: 'The serpent beguiled me, and I did eat.' He could say: 'The woman Thou gavest me, she gave me of the tree, and I did eat.' Here is no word of asking mercy, no breath of desiring help: for though they do not deny their guilt, as Cain did, yet their pride seeks to lay their own evil upon another, the man's upon the woman, and hers upon the serpent. But this indeed does rather accuse them of worse than acquit them of so plain and palpable a transgression of God's command. For the woman's persuading of the man, and the serpent's seducing of the woman to this, in no way acquits them of the guilt: as if there were anything to be believed, or obeyed, before God, or rather than the Most High.

CHAPTER XV

Of the just reward that our first parents received for their sin

THEREFORE because God (that had made man according to His image, placed him in paradise above all creatures, given him plenty of all things, and laid no hard nor long laws upon him, but only that one brief command of obedience, to show that Himself was Lord of that creature whom free service best befitted) was thus contemned; thereupon followed that just condemnation, being such, that man, who might have kept the command and been spiritual in body, became now carnal in mind; and because he had before delighted in his own pride, now he tasted of God's justice; becoming not as he desired his own master, but falling even from himself, he became his slave that taught him sin, changing his sweet liberty into wretched bondage, being willingly dead in spirit, and unwilling to die in the flesh, forsaking eternal life, and condemned to eternal death, had not God's good grace delivered him. He that holds this sentence too severe, cannot truly apportion the guilt incurring it, and the easiness of avoiding it: for as Abraham's obedience is highly extolled, because the killing of his son (a hard matter) was commanded him, so was their disobedience in paradise so much the more extreme, as the precept was easy to perform. And as the obedience of the second was the more rarely excellent, in that he kept it unto the death: so was that disobedience of the first man the more truly detestable, because he brake his obedience to incur death. For where the punishment of the breach of obedience is so great, and the precept so easily kept, who can fully relate the guilt of that sin that breaks it, standing neither in awe of the commander's majesty, nor in fear of the terrible affliction following the breach?

And in one word, what reward, what punishment, is laid upon

disobedience but disobedience? What is man's misery other than his own disobedience to himself: that seeing he would not what he might, now he cannot what he would? For although in paradise all was not in his power during his obedience, yet then he desired nothing but what was in his power, and so did what he would.

But now, as the scripture says, and we see by experience, 'Man is like to vanity.' [1] For who can recount his innumerable desires of impossibilities, the flesh and the mind (that is himself) disobeying the will (that is himself also), for his mind is troubled, his flesh pained, age and death approach, and a thousand other emotions seize on us against our wills, which they could not do if our nature were wholly obedient unto our will? And the flesh suffers something that hinders the service of the soul. But what does it matter, as long as it is God's almighty justice, to whom we would not be subject, that our flesh should not be subject to the soul, but trouble it, whereas it was subject wholly unto it before, though we in not serving God do trouble ourselves and not Him? For He needs not our service, as we need our bodies: and therefore it is our pain to have a body, not any hurt to Him that we have made it such a body. Besides, those that we call fleshly pains are the soul's pains, in and from the flesh; for what can the flesh either feel or desire without the soul? But when we say 'the flesh' does either, we mean either the man (as I said before) or some part of the soul than the fleshly passion affects, either by sharpness procuring pain and grief, or by sweetness producing pleasure. But fleshly pain is only an offence given to the soul by the flesh, and a dislike of that passion that the flesh produces: as that which we call sadness is a distaste of things befalling us against our wills. But fear commonly foreruns sadness, and that is wholly in the soul, and not in the flesh. But whereas the pain of the flesh is not forerun by any fleshly fear, felt in the flesh before that pain; pleasure indeed is ushered in by certain appetites felt in the flesh, as the desires thereof, such as hunger and thirst and the carnal appetite usually called lust. Lust, however, is a general name to all desires: for wrath is nothing but a lust of revenge, as the ancient writers defined it; although a man sometimes without sense of revenge will be angry at senseless things, as when he breaks his pen in anger when it writes badly; but even this is a certain desire of revenge, and though it be reasonless, it is a certain shadow of rendering evil to them that do evil. So then wrath is a lust of revenge; avarice, a lust of having money; obstinacy, a lust of getting victory; boasting, a lust of vainglory. And many such lusts there are; some specifically named, and some nameless: for who can give a fit name to the lust of sovereignty, which notwithstanding the tyrants show by their intestine wars that they stand well affected unto?

[1] Ps. cxliv. 4.

CHAPTER XVI

Of the evil of lust: how the name is general to many vices, but proper unto sexual concupiscence

ALTHOUGH therefore there be many lusts, yet when we read the word 'lust' alone, without mention of the object, we commonly take it for the unclean motion of the generative parts. For this holds sway in the whole body, moving the whole man, without and within, with such a mixture of mental emotion and carnal appetite that hence is the highest bodily pleasure of all produced: so that in the very moment of consummation, it overwhelms almost all the light and power of cogitation. And what wise and godly man is there, who being married, and knowing, as the apostle says, 'how to possess his vessel in holiness and honour, and not in the lust of concupiscence, as the Gentiles do, which know not God,' [1] had not rather (if he could) beget his children without this lust, that his members might obey his mind in this act of propagation, as his other members in fulfilling their particular functions, and be ruled by his will, not compelled by concupiscence? But the lovers of these carnal delights themselves cannot have this emotion at their will, either in nuptial conjunctions, or wicked impurities. The motion will be sometimes importunate against the will, and sometimes immovable when it is desired, and being fervent in the mind, yet will be frozen in the body. Thus wondrously does this lust fail man, both in honest desire of generation, and in lascivious concupiscence; sometimes resisting the restraint of the whole mind, and sometimes opposing itself by being wholly in the mind and in no way in the body at the same time.

CHAPTER XVII

Of the nakedness that our first parents discovered in themselves after their sin

JUSTLY is man ashamed of this lust, and justly are those members (which lust moves or suppresses against our wills, as it lusts) called shameful. Before man sinned, they were not so; for it is written, 'They were both naked, and were not ashamed,' [2] not that they saw not the nakedness, but because their nakedness was not yet shameful: for lust did not as yet move these parts against their wills; nor was the disobedience of the flesh as yet made a testimony of the disobedience of man. They were not made blind, as the

[1] 1 Thess. iv. 4, 5.   [2] Gen. ii. 25.

unenlightened crowd imagine, for the man saw the creatures whom
he named, and the woman saw 'that the tree was good for food,
and pleasing to the eyes.' [1]   Their eyes therefore were open, but
they were not yet opened, that is they were not occupied in beholding what good the garment of grace bestowed upon them, in
keeping from them the knowledge of the members' rebellion
against the will; which grace being gone, that disobedience might
be punished by disobedience, there entered a new shame upon
those bodily motions that made their nakedness seem indecent.
This they observed, and this they were ashamed of.   Thence it is,
that after they had broken the command, it was written of them:
'And the eyes of them both were opened, and they knew that they
were naked, and they sewed fig-tree leaves together and made
themselves breeches.' [2]   Their eyes were opened, not to see, for
they saw before, but to discern between the good that they had
lost and the evil that they had incurred.   And therefore the tree
was called 'the tree of the knowledge of good and evil,' because if
it were tasted of against the commandment by them, they must
perforce see this difference, for the pain of the disease being known,
the pleasure of health is the sweeter.   So they knew that they were
naked, naked of that grace that made their bodily nakedness innocent, and unresisting the will of their minds.   This knowledge
they got.   Happy they, if they had kept God's precepts, and
believed Him, and never come to know the hurt of faithless disobedience.   But then being ashamed of this fleshly disobedience
that was both a punishment for and a witness to their disobedience
unto God, they sewed fig-tree leaves together, and made them
breeches, or covers for their privities.   The Latin word is *cam-
pestria*, taken from the vestures wherewith the youths that wrestled
or exercised themselves naked in the field (*in campo*) did cover their
genitals withal, being therefore called by the vulgar *campestrati*.
Thus their shamefastness wisely covered that which lust dis-
obediently incited as a memory of their disobedient wills justly
herein punished: and from hence all mankind, springing from one
origin, have it naturally in them to keep their members covered;
that even some of the barbarians will not bathe with them bare,
but wash them with their coverings.   And whereas there are some
philosophers called Gymnosophists, because they live naked in the
dark parts of India, yet do they cover their genitals, whereas all
the rest of their bodies are bare.

---

[1] Gen. iii. 6.   [2] Gen. iii. 7.

CHAPTER XVIII

Of the shame that accompanies copulation, as well in harlotry as in marriage

BUT the act of lust, not only in punishable adulteries, but even in the use of harlots which the earthly city allows, is ashamed of the public view, although the deed be liable unto no pain of law: and houses of ill fame themselves have their secret provisions for it, even because of natural shame.   Thus was it easier for unchasteness to obtain permission, than for impudence to give it public practice.   Yet such as are filthy themselves, will call this filthiness, and though they love it, yet dare not display it.   But now for copulation in marriage, which according to the laws of matrimony must be used for propagation's sake: does it not seek a corner for performance, though it be honest and lawful?   Does not the bridegroom turn all the feast-masters, the attendants, the music, and all others out of his chamber, before he begins to embrace his bride?   And whereas, as 'that great author of Roman eloquence' [1] said, all honest deeds desire the light, that is, love to be known; [2] this honest deed alone if it desires to be known yet blushes to be seen. For who knows not what the man must do to the woman to have a child begotten, seeing the wife is solemnly married for this end? But when this is done, the children themselves, if they have had any before, shall not know.   For this act does desire the sight of the mind, yet so as it flies the view of the eye.   Why, unless this lawful act of nature is (from our first parents) accompanied with our penal shame?

CHAPTER XIX

That the motions of wrath and lust are so violent that they do necessarily require to be suppressed by wisdom: and that they were not in our nature before our fall depraved it

HEREUPON the most acute and judicious philosophers held wrath and lust to be two vicious parts of the mind; because they moved man without all order and measure to acts condemned by wisdom, and therefore needed to be overswayed by judgment and reason: which third part of the soul they placed as in a tower to be sovereign over the rest, that this commanding, and they obeying, the harmony of justice might be fully kept in man.   These parts which they confess to be vicious in the most wise and temperate

---

[1] Lucan, *Phars.* vii. 62, 63   [2] Cicero, *Tusc. Disp.* ii. 26, 64.

man, so that the mind had need still to tie them from exorbitance to order, and allow them that liberty only which wisdom prescribes, as wrath in a just repulse of wrong, and lust in the propagation of one's offspring: these I say were not vicious at all in man whilst he lived sinless in paradise. For they never aimed at anything besides rectitude, reason directing them without reins. But now whensoever they move the just and temperate man, they must be moderated by restraint, which some do easily, and others with great difficulty. They are now no parts of a sound, but pains of a sick, nature. And whereas shamefacedness does not hide wrath, nor other emotions, in their immoderate acts, as it does lusts: what is the reason except it is not the emotion but the consenting will that moves the other members, performing those acts of the emotions, because it rules as chief in their use? For he that being angry rails or strikes, could not do it unless the tongue and the hand are appointed to do so by the will, which moves them also when anger is absent; but in the members of generation, lust has so peculiarly made them its own property, that they cannot move, if it be away, nor stir unless it (being either voluntary, or forcibly excited) do move them. This is the cause of shame and avoidance of beholders in this act: and the reason why a man being in unlawful anger with his neighbour, had rather have a thousand look upon him, than one when he is in carnal copulation with his wife.

CHAPTER XX

Of the vain obscenity of the Cynics

THIS the canine philosophers, that is, the Cynics, observed not, averring that truly canine, impure, and shameless sentence against man's shamefacedness, that the matrimonial act being lawful is not shame, but ought, if one lust, to be done in the street. Even very natural shame subverted this foul error. For though Diogenes is said to have done thus once, glorying that his impudence would make his sect the more famous: yet afterwards the Cynics left it, and shame prevailed more with them, as they were men, than that absurd error to become like dogs. And therefore I think that he, or those that did so, did rather show the motions of persons in copulation unto the beholders that saw not what was done under the cloak, than that they performed the sexual act in their view indeed. For the philosophers were not ashamed to make show of their desire for copulation there, where lust was ashamed to provoke them. We see there are Cynics to this day, wearing cloaks and bearing clubs, yet none of them dare do this. If they should, they would have all the street upon their backs either with stones or spittle. Without a doubt therefore man's nature is justly ashamed of this act: for that disobedience, whereby the genital members are taken from the will's rule and given to lust's, is a plain demonstration of the reward that our first father had for his sin, and that ought to be most apparent in those parts, because thence is our nature derived which was so depraved by that his first offence. From this bond none is freed, unless that, which was committed for the ruin of us all (we being then all in one) and is now punished by God's justice, be expiated in every one by the same grace of God.

CHAPTER XXI

Of the blessing of fecundity before sin, which the transgression did not abolish but only linked to lust

GOD forbid then that we should believe that our first parents in paradise should have fulfilled that blessing, 'Increase and multiply, and replenish the earth,' in that lust that made them blush and hide their privities. This lust was not in them until after sin; and then, their shamefaced nature, having the power and rule of the body, perceived it, blushed at it, and concealed it. But that blessing of marriage, for increase, multiplication, and peopling of the earth, though it remained in them after sin, yet was it given them before sin that they might know that procreation of children belonged to the glory of marriage, and not to the punishment of sin. But the men that are now on earth, knowing not that happiness of paradise, think that children cannot be begotten, but by this lust which they have tried. This it is that makes honest marriage ashamed to act it.

Others reject and impiously deride the holy scriptures that say they were ashamed of their nakedness after they had sinned, and covered their privities; and others though they receive the scriptures, yet hold that this blessing, 'Increase and multiply,' is meant of a spiritual, and not a corporal fecundity: because the psalm says: 'Thou shalt multiply me with strength in my soul,'[1] and so they interpret the following words of Genesis, 'And replenish the earth and subdue it,' thus: Earth, they say, is the flesh, which the soul fills with the presence, and rules over it when it is multiplied in virtue. But they hold that the carnal propagation could not be performed without that lust which arose in man, was discovered by him, shamed him, and made him conceal it, after sin:

[1] Ps. cxxxviii. 3.

and that his progeny could not have lived in paradise, but outside it, as they did: for they begot no children until they were put forth from paradise and did first conjoin and beget them.

CHAPTER XXII

That God first instituted and blessed the bond of marriage

BUT we doubt not at all that his increase, multiplying, and filling of the earth was by God's goodness bestowed upon the marriage which He ordained in the beginning, ere man sinned, when He made them male and female, sexes evident in the flesh. This work was no sooner done, but it was blessed: for the scripture having said: 'He created them male and female,' adds at once: 'And God blessed them, saying, Increase and multiply,' etc. All which though they may not unfitly be applied spiritually, yet male and female can in no wise be appropriate even in a figure of speech to two things in one man, as though there were one thing in him which rules and another which is ruled: but as it is evident in the real distinction of sex, they were made male and female, to bring forth fruit by generation, to multiply and fill the earth. This plain truth none but fools will oppose. It cannot be meant of the spirit ruling, and the flesh obeying; of the reason governing and the emotion serving; of the contemplative part excelling, and the active serving; nor of the mind's understanding and the body's sense; but directly, of the bond of marriage, combining both the sexes in one. Christ being asked whether one might put away his wife for any cause, because Moses by reason of the hardness of their hearts suffered them to give her a bill of divorce, answered saying: 'Have ye not read, that He which made them at the beginning, made them male and female?' and said: 'For this cause shall a man leave his father and mother and cleave unto his wife, and they twain shall be one flesh. So that now they are no more two but one. Let no man therefore sunder what God has coupled together.' [1]   Sure it is therefore that male and female were ordained at the beginning in the same form and difference that mankind is now in. And they are called one, either because of their conjunction, or the woman's origin, who came out of the side of man: for the apostle warns all married men by this example to love their wives.

[1] Matt. xix. 4–6.

CHAPTER XXIII

Whether if man had not sinned, he would have begotten children in paradise, and whether there should there have been any contention between chastity and lust

BUT he that says that there should have been neither copulation nor propagation but for sin, what does he else but make sin the origin of the holy number of saints? For if they two should have lived alone, not sinning, seeing sin (as these say) was their only means of generation, then verily was sin necessary to make the number of saints more than two. But if it be absurd to hold this, it is fit to hold that the number of God's citizens should have been as great then, if no man had sinned, as now shall be gathered by God's grace out of the multitude of sinners, as long as this worldly multiplication of the sons of the world shall endure; and therefore that marriage, that was held fit to be made in paradise, should have had increase, but no lust, had not sin been. How this might be, here is no fit place to discuss: but it need not seem incredible that one member might serve the will without lust then, so many serving it now. Do we now move our hands and feet so easily when we will unto their offices without resistance, as we see in ourselves and others, chiefly handicraftsmen, where industry has made dull nature nimble; and may we not believe that those members might have served our first father unto procreation, without their having been seized with lust, the reward of his disobedience, as well as all his others served him to other acts? Does not Tully, disputing of the difference of governments (in his treatise *Of the Commonwealth* [1]), and drawing a simile from man's nature, say, that we command our bodily members as sons, they are so obedient, and that we must keep a harder form of rule over our mind's vicious parts, as our slaves? In order of nature the soul is above the body, yet is it harder to rule than the body. But this lust whereof we speak is the more shameful in this, that the soul does neither rule itself therein, so that it may not lust, nor the body either, so that the will rather than lust might move these parts, which, if it were so, would be nothing to be ashamed of. But now the soul is ashamed that the body its inferior should resist it. It feels less shame in other rebellious emotions, because the resistance in this case comes from itself; and when it is conquered of itself, it conquers itself (although it be inordinately and viciously); for although these parts be reasonless that conquer it, yet are they parts of itself, and so, as I say, it is conquered of itself. For when it conquers itself in an orderly manner, and brings all the parts under reason, this is a laudable and virtuous conquest, if the soul be God's subject. But it is less ashamed when it is resisted

[1] *De Re Publ.* iii. 25.

by the vicious parts of itself, than when the body disobeys it, because the body is under it, depends on it, and cannot live without it. But so long as the other members are all under the will, without which members nothing can be performed against the chastity by those members which are incited by lust so to do, the chastity is kept unviolated, and the delight in sin is not permitted. This contention, fight, and altercation of lust and will, this need of lust to the sufficiency of the will, had not been laid upon wedlock in paradise, unless disobedience had become the punishment for the sin of disobedience. Otherwise these members had obeyed their wills as well as the rest. The seed of generation should have been sown in the vessel, as corn is now in the field. What I would say more in this kind, modesty bids me forbear a little, and first ask pardon of chaste ears. I need not do it, but might proceed in any discourse pertinent to this theme freely, and without any fear to be obscene, or imputation of impurity to the words, being as honestly spoken of these as others are of any other bodily members. Therefore he that reads this with unchaste suggestions, let him accuse his own guilt, not the nature of the question: and let him brand the effect of turpitude in himself, not the words necessity compels us to use, which the chaste and religious reader will easily allow us to use in confuting our experienced (not our credulous) adversary, who draws his arguments from proof not from belief. For he that abhors not the apostle's reprehension of the horrible beastliness of women, 'who perverted natural use and acted against nature,' [1] will read this without offence, especially seeing we neither rehearse nor reprehend that damnable bestiality that he condemns, but are investigating the emotions of human generation, yet with avoidance of obscene terms, as much as he avoids them.

CHAPTER XXIV

That our first parents, had they lived without sin, should have had their members of generation as subject unto their wills as any of the rest

MAN therefore would have sown the seed, and woman have received it, as need required, without any lust, and as their wills desired. For as we now are, not only do our articulate members obey our will—our hands, or feet, or fingers—but even those also that we move only by small sinews and tendons we contract and turn as we list; as you see in the voluntary motions of the mouth and face. And the lungs, the softest of all the organs except

[1] Rom. i. 26.

the brain, and therefore placed in the hollow of the breast for more
safety in taking in and giving out the breath, and in modulating
the voice, do serve a man's will entirely, like a pair of smith's or
organist's bellows, to breathe, to speak, to cry, or to sing.   I omit
that it is natural in some creatures if they feel anything bite them,
to move the skin there where it bites, and nowhere else; shaking off
not only flies, but even darts or shafts by this motion of the skin.
Man cannot do this.   What then?   Could not God give it unto
what creatures He listed?   Even so might man have had the
obedience of his lower parts, which his own disobedience debarred.
For God could easily have made him with all his members subjected to his will, even that which now is not moved but by lust:
for we see some men's natures far different from others; acting
those things strangely in their bodies, which others can neither do
nor hardly will believe.   There are those who can move their
ears, one or both, as they please: there are those that can move all
their hair towards their forehead, and back again, and never move
their heads.   There are those that can swallow twenty things
whole, and pressing their stomach lightly, give you every thing up
as whole as if they had but put into a bag.   There are those that
can mimic the voices of birds and other men so cunningly, that
unless you see them, you cannot distinguish them at all.   There are
those that can break wind backward so artificially, that you would
think they sung.   I have seen one sweat whenever he pleased, and
it is sure that some can weep when they list, and shed tears plenti-
fully.   But even more wonderful was the case lately seen by some
of the brethren in a priest called Restitutus, of the village of
Calama, who when he pleased (and they requested him to show
them this rare experiment), at the imitation of funeral wailing
drew himself into such an ecstasy, that he lay as if dead, senseless
of all pinching, pricking, nay even of burning, but that he felt it
sore after his awaking.   And this rapture was found to be true,
and not counterfeit in him, in that he lay still without any breathing: yet he said afterward, that if one spake aloud, he thought he
heard him, as if he were afar off.   Seeing therefore that in this
frail state of ours, the body serves the will in such extraordinary
emotions; why should we not believe that before his disobedience
the first man might have had his means and members of generation
without lust?   But he taking delight in himself was left by God
unto himself, and therefore could not obey himself, because he
would not obey God.   And this proves his misery the plainer, in
that he cannot live as he would.   For if he would do so, he might
think himself happy; yet living, in obscenity, he would not be
so indeed.

CHAPTER XXV

Of the true beatitude—that it is unattainable in this life

BUT if we observe aright, none lives as he wishes but he is happy, and
no one is happy without being righteous; yet the just man lives not
as he pleases, until he attain that sure, eternal, hurtless, undeceiving
state. This he naturally desires, nor can he be perfect until he
have his desire. But what man here upon earth can say he lives
as he pleases, when his life is not in his own hand? He would fain
live, and he must die. How then lives he as he pleases, that lives
not as long as he pleases? But if he desires to die, how can he
live as he desires when he does not wish to live at all? And if he
desires to die, not to forgo all life, but to change it for a better, then
lives he not as he likes, but attains that by dying. But admit this,
he lives as he likes, because he has forced himself and brought
himself to this, to desire nothing but what is in his power, as
Terence says: 'Since you cannot have what you would have, desire
that which you may have': [1] yet is he not blessed, because he is
patiently wretched. For beatitude is not attained unless it be
loved. And if it be both attained and loved, then must this love
needs surmount all other, because all other things are loved for
this. And if this be loved as it ought to be (for he that loves not
beatitude as it ought to be loved cannot be happy) then he cannot
help desiring it to be eternal. So that the blessed life must needs
be joined with eternity.

CHAPTER XXVI

*That our first parents in paradise might have produced mankind
without any shameful appetite*

THEREFORE man lived in paradise as he desired, whilst he only
desired what God commanded. He enjoyed God, from whence
was his good. He lived without need, and had life eternal in his
power. He had meat for hunger, drink for thirst, the tree of life
to keep off age. He was free from all bodily corruption and
feeling of molestation. He feared neither disease within nor
violence without. Height of health was in his flesh, and fullness
of peace in his soul; and as paradise was neither fiery nor frosty,
no more was the inhabitants' good will offended either with desire,
or fear. There was no true sorrow, nor vain joy. Their joy
continued by God's mercy, whom they loved with a pure good

[1] *Andr.* ii. 1, 5.

conscience and an unfeigned faith.   Their wedlock love was holy and honest; their vigilance and custody of the precept without any toil or trouble.   They were neither weary of leisure, nor unwillingly sleepy.   And can we not suppose that in all this happiness they might beget their children without lust, and move those members without concupiscential desire, the man being laid in his wife's lap without corruption of integrity?   Lack of experience need not drive us from believing that their generative parts might be moved by will only, without exorbitance of hotter desire; and that the sperm of man might be conveyed into the place of conception without corruption of the instrument receiving, just as now it doth give forth the menstruous flux without breach of virginity.   The one might be cast in as the other is cast forth. For as their childbirth would not have been forerun by pain but by maturity, which should open a way for the child without torment; so would their copulation have been performed without lustful appetite, only by voluntary use.   This theme is immodest, and therefore let us conjecture as we can, how the first parents of man were, ere they were ashamed.   Needs must our discourse hereupon rather yield to shamefacedness than trust to eloquence. The one restrains us much, and the other helps us little.   For seeing they that might have tried, did not try this that I have said, desiring by sin to be expelled from paradise, before they had used their means of propagating man, how can man now conceive it should be done, except by the means of that headlong lust, not by any quiet will?   This is that which stops my mouth, though I behold the reason in mine heart.   But however, Almighty God, the Creator of all nature, the helper and rewarder of all good wills, the just condemner of the bad, and the ordainer of both, lacked no prescience how to fulfil the number of those whom He had destined to be of His city, even out of the condemned progeny of man, distinguishing them not by their merits (for the whole fruit was condemned in the corrupted stock) but by His own grace, freeing them both from themselves and the slavish world, and showing them what He bestowed on them; for each one now acknowledges that it is not his own deserts, but God's goodness that has freed him from evil, and from their society with whom he would have shared a just condemnation.   Why then might not God create such as He knew would sin, thereby to show in them and their progeny both what sin deserved, and what His mercy bestowed; and that the perverse inordinate offence of them, under Him, could not pervert the right order which He had resolved?

CHAPTER XXVII

That the sinners, angels and men, cannot with their perverseness disturb God's providence

AND therefore the offending angels and men in no way hindered the great works of God, who is absolute in all that He wills. His omnipotence distributes all unto all, and knows how to make use both of good and bad. And therefore why might not God, using the evil angel (whom He had deservedly condemned for his evil will, and cast from all good) unto a good end, permit him to tempt the first man in whom He had placed an upright will, and who was in such a state, that if he would build upon God's help, a good man would conquer an evil angel, but if he fell proudly from God, to delight in himself, he would be conquered, having a reward laid up for his uprightness of will assisted by God, and a punishment for his perverseness of will in forsaking God. Trust upon God's help he could not, unless God helped him: yet follows it not, that he had no power of himself, to leave this divine help in relying wholly upon himself. For as we cannot live in the flesh without nourishment, yet may we leave the flesh when we please, as do suicides; even so, man being in paradise could not live well without God's help, but yet it was in his power to live badly, and to select a false beautitude, and a sure misery. Why then might not God that knew this beforehand permit him to be tempted by the malicious wicked spirit, not being ignorant that he would fall, but knowing withal, how doubly the devil would be overthrown by those that His grace should select out of man's posterity. Thus God neither was ignorant of the future event, neither compelled He any one to offend: but showed by succeeding experience both to men and angels, what difference there was between presuming of one's self, and trusting unto Him. For who dare say or think that God could not have kept both men and angels from falling? But He would not take it out of their powers, but showed thereby the wickedness of their pride, and the goodness of His own grace.

CHAPTER XXVIII

The state of the two cities, the heavenly and the earthly

TWO loves therefore have given origin to these two cities, self-love in contempt of God unto the earthly, love of God in contempt of one's self to the heavenly. The first seeks the glory of men, and the latter desires God only as the testimony of the conscience, the

greatest glory. That glories in itself, and this in God. That
exalts itself in self-glory: this says to God: 'My glory and the lifter
up of my head.'[1]   That boasts of the ambitious conquerors led by
the lust of sovereignty: in this all serve each other in charity,
both the rulers in counselling and the subjects in obeying. That
loves worldly virtue in the potentates: this says unto God: 'I will
love Thee, O Lord, my strength.'[2]   And the wise men of that
follow either the good things of the body, or mind, or both: living
according to the flesh; and such as might know God, 'honoured
Him not as God, nor were thankful, but became vain in their own
imaginations, and their foolish heart was darkened; for professing
themselves to be wise, that is, extolling themselves proudly in their
wisdom, they became fools; changing the glory of the incorruptible
God to the likeness of the image of a corruptible man, and of birds
and four-footed beasts and serpents':[3] for they were the people's
guides or followers unto all those idolatries, and served the creature
more than the Creator who is blessed for ever. But in this other,
this heavenly city, there is no wisdom of man, but only the piety
that serves the true God and expects a reward in the society of the
holy angels, and men, 'that God may be all in all.'[4]

[1] Ps. iii. 3.   [2] Ps. xviii. 1.   [3] Rom. i. 21-3.   [4] 1 Cor. xv. 28.

THE FIFTEENTH BOOK OF
THE CITY OF GOD

CHAPTER I

Of the two contrary courses taken by the human race from the beginning

OF the place and felicity of the local paradise, together with man's life and fall therein, there are many opinions, many assertions, and many books, as several men thought, spoke, and wrote. What we held hereof, or could gather out of holy scriptures, correspondent unto their truth and authority, we related in some of the foregoing books. If they be farther looked into, they will give birth to more questions and longer disputations than we have now room for. Our time is not so large as to permit us to argue scrupulously upon every question that may be asked by busy heads that are more curious of inquiry than capable of understanding. I think we have sufficiently discussed the doubts concerning the beginning of the world, the soul, and mankind; which last is divided into two sorts, such as live according to man, and such as live according to God. These we mystically call two cities or societies, the one predestined to reign eternally with God, the other condemned to perpetual torment with the devil. This is their end, of which hereafter. Now seeing we have said sufficient concerning their origin, both in the angels whose number we know not, and in the two first parents of mankind, I think it fit to pass on to their progression from man's first offspring until he cease to beget any more. All the time included between these two points, wherein the livers ever succeed the diers, is the progression of these two cities. Cain therefore was the first begotten of those two that were mankind's parents, and he belongs to the city of man; Abel was the later, and he belongs to the city of God. For as we see that in an individual man (as the apostle says) that which is spiritual is not first, but that which is natural first, and then the spiritual (whereupon all that comes from Adam's corrupted nature must needs be evil and carnal at first, and then if a man be regenerate by Christ, becomes good and spiritual afterward): so in the first propagation of man, and progression of the two cities of which we dispute, the carnal citizen was born first, and the pilgrim on earth or heavenly citizen afterwards, being by grace predestined, and by grace elected, by grace a pilgrim upon earth, and by grace a citizen in heaven. For as for his birth, it was out of the same corrupted mass that was condemned from the beginning; but God

60

like a potter (for this simile the apostle himself uses) out of the same lump, made 'one vessel to honour and another to reproach.' [1] The vessel of reproach was made first, and the vessel of honour afterwards. For in each individual, as I said, there is first reprobation, whence we must needs begin (and wherein we need not remain), and afterwards goodness, to which we come by profiting, and coming thither therein make our abode. Whereupon it follows that no one can be good that has not first been evil, though all that be evil become not good; but the sooner a man betters himself the quicker does this name follow him, abolishing the memory of the other. Therefore it is recorded of Cain that he built a city, but Abel was a pilgrim, and built none. For the city of the saints is above, though it have citizens here upon earth, wherein it lives as a pilgrim until the time of the kingdom come; and then it gathers all the citizens together in the resurrection of the body, and gives them a kingdom to reign in with their King for ever and ever.

CHAPTER II

Of the sons of the flesh and the sons of promise

THE shadow and prophetical image of this city (not making it present but signifying it) served here upon earth, at the time when such a foreshadowing was needed; and was called the holy city, because it was a symbol of the city that was to be, though not the reality. Of this city serving as an image, and the free city herein prefigured, the apostle speaks thus unto the Galatians: 'Tell me, ye that desire to be under the law, do ye not hear the law? For it is written that Abraham had two sons, one by a bondwoman, and the other by a free: but the son of the bondwoman was born of the flesh, and the son of the freewoman by promise. Which things are an allegory: for these are the two Testaments, the one given from Mount Sinai, begetting man in servitude, which is Hagar; for Sinai is a mountain in Arabia, joined to the Jerusalem on earth, for it serves with her children. But our mother the celestial Jerusalem is free, for it is written: "Rejoice, thou barren that bearest not: break forth into joy, and cry out, thou that travailest not with child, for the desolate hath many more children than the married wife." But we, brethren, are the sons of promise according to Isaac. But as then he that was born of the flesh persecuted him that was born after the spirit, even so it is now. But what says the scripture? "Cast out the bondwoman and her son, for the bondwoman's son shall not be heir with the freewoman's."

[1] Rom. ix. 21.

Then, brethren, we are not children of the bondwoman, but of the free.'[1]   Thus the apostle authorizes us to conceive of the Old and New Testaments.   For a part of the earthly city was made an image of the heavenly, not signifying itself but another, and therefore serving: for it was not ordained to signify itself but another, and itself was signified by another precedent type; for Hagar, Sarah's servant, and her son, were an image hereof.   And because, when the light comes, the shadows must flee away, Sarah the freewoman signifying the free city (which that shadow of the earthly Jerusalem signified in another manner) said: 'Cast out the bondwoman and her son: for the bondwoman's son shall not be heir with my son Isaac': whom the apostle calls the freewoman's son. Thus then we find this earthly city in two forms; the one presenting itself, and the other prefiguring the celestial city, and serving it.'[2] Our nature corrupted by sin produces citizens of earth; and grace freeing us from the sin of nature makes us citizens of heaven: the first are called the vessels of wrath, the last of mercy.   And this was signified in the two sons of Abraham, the one of whom being born of the bondwoman was called Ishmael, being the son of the flesh: the other, the freewoman's, Isaac, the son of promise.   Both were Abraham's sons; but natural custom begot the first, and gracious promise the latter.   In the first was a demonstration of man's use, in the second was a revelation of God's goodness.

CHAPTER III

Of Sarah's barrenness, which God turned into fruitfulness

FOR Sarah was barren and despaired of having any child; and desiring to have a child, though it were from her slave, she gave her to Abraham to bring him children, seeing she could bring him none herself.   Thus exacted she her due of her husband, although it were by the womb of another.   So was Ishmael born, being begotten by the usual commixture of both sexes in the law of nature and thereupon was he said to be born after the flesh—not because such births are not God's benefits or works (for 'His working wisdom,' as the scripture says, 'reaches from end to end, mightily and sweetly orders all things'[3]); but because in order that there might be a signification of that free grace that God meant to give unto man, such a son should be born as the laws and order of nature did not require.   For nature denies children unto all such

[1] Gal. iv. 21–31.
[2] i.e. (a) Jerusalem in itself; (b) Jerusalem as a type of the heavenly Jerusalem.—ED.
[3] Wisd. of Sol. viii. 1.

copulations as Abraham's and Sarah's were, age and barrenness both ruling in her then: whereas she could have no child in her younger days, when her age seemed not to lack fruitfulness, though fruitfulness was lacking in that youthful age.   Therefore in that her nature being thus affected could not expect the birth of a son, is signified this, that man's nature, being corrupted and consequently condemned for sin, had no claim afterward unto any part of felicity.   But Isaac being born by promise is a true type of the sons of grace, of those free citizens, of those dwellers in eternal peace, where no private or self-love shall be predominant, but all shall joy in that universal good, and many hearts shall meet in one, forming a perfect model of charity and obedience.

CHAPTER IV

Of the conflict and peace of the earthly city

BUT the temporal, earthly city (temporal, for when it is condemned to perpetual pains it shall be no more a city) has all its good here upon earth, and therein takes that joy that such an object can afford. But because it is not a good that acquits the possessors of all troubles, therefore this city is divided in itself into wars, alter- cations, and appetites of short-lived or destructive victories. For any part of it that wars against another desires to be the world's conqueror, whereas indeed it is vice's slave.   And if it conquer, it extols itself and so becomes its own destruction.   But if it con- siders the condition of worldly affairs, and grieves at man's open- ness to adversity, rather than delights in the events of prosperity, thus is the victory short-lived; for it cannot keep a sovereignty for ever over those whom it has subjugated by conquest.   Nor can we rightly call the objects of this city's desires good, since it is only better itself in its own human fashion.   It desires an earthly peace for very low ambitions, and seeks it by war, where if it subdue all resistance, it attains peace: which notwithstanding the other side, that fought so unfortunately for the same reasons, lack. This peace they seek by laborious war, and obtain (they think) by a glorious victory.   Yet when they conquer that had the juster cause, who will not congratulate their victory, and be glad of their peace?   Doubtless those results are good, and God's good gifts. But if the things appertaining to that celestial and supernal city where the victory shall be everlasting, be neglected for those goods, and those goods desired as the only goods, or loved as if they were better than the others, misery must needs follow and increase that which is inherent before.

CHAPTER V

*Of that murderer of his brother, that was the first founder of the
earthly city, whose act the builder of Rome paralleled in murdering
his brother also*

THEREFORE this earthly city's foundation was laid by a murderer
of his own brother, whom he slew through envy, and who was a
pilgrim upon earth of the heavenly city. Whereupon it is no
wonder if the founder of that city which was to become the world's
chief, and the queen of the nations, followed this his first example
or archetype in the same fashion. One of their poets records the
fact in these words:

> Fraterno primi maduerunt sanguine muri.[1]
> The first walls stained with a brother's blood.

Such was Rome's foundation, and such was Romulus' murder
of his brother Remus, as their histories relate. This difference
only there is. These brethren were both citizens of the earthly
city and propagators of the glory of Rome, for whose institution
they contended. But they both could not have that glory, that if
they had been but one, they might have had. For he that glories
in dominion must needs see his glory diminished when he has a
partner to share with him. Therefore the one, in order to have all,
killed his partner, and by villainy grew into bad greatness, whereas
innocence would have rendered him less great but better. But
those two brethren, Cain and Abel, stood not both alike desirous
of earthly matters. Nor did this produce envy in them, that, if
they both should reign, he that could kill the other should arise to a
greater pitch of glory; for Abel sought no dominion in that city
which his brother built, but that devil envy did all the mischief,
which the bad bear unto the good, only because they are good.
For the possession of goodness is not lessened by being shared:
nay, it is increased when it has many possessing it in one link and
league of charity. Nor shall he ever have it, that will not have it
in common; and he that loves a partner in it, shall have it more
abundantly. The strife therefore of Romulus and Remus shows
the division of the earthly city in itself; and that of Cain and Abel
shows the opposition of the city of men and the city of God. The
wicked oppose the good; but the good, being perfect, cannot contend amongst themselves: but whilst they are imperfect they may
contend one against another in that manner that each contends
against himself, for in every man the flesh is against the spirit and
the spirit against the flesh. So then the spiritual desire in one
may fight against the carnal in another, or contrariwise the carnal
against the spiritual, as the evil do against the good; or the two

[1] Lucan, *Phars.* i. 95.

carnal desires of two good men that are imperfect may contend
as the bad do against the bad, until their diseases be cured, and
themselves brought to everlasting health of victory.

CHAPTER VI

*Of the weaknesses God's citizens endure in earth as the punishments
of sin during their pilgrimage, and of the grace of God curing them*

BUT the weakness or disobedience (spoken of in the last book) is
the punishment of the first disobedience, and therefore it is no
nature, but a corruption; for which it is said unto those earthly
pilgrims and those growing in grace: 'Bear ye one another's
burdens, and so ye shall fulfil the law of Christ': [1] and again:
'Admonish the unruly, comfort the feeble, be patient towards all,
overcome evil with good, see that none render evil for evil': [2]
and again: 'If a man be fallen by occasion into any sin, ye that are
spiritual restore such an one in the spirit of meekness, considering
thyself, lest thou also be tempted': [3] and besides: 'Let not the sun
go down upon your wrath': [4] and in the gospel: 'If thy brother
trespass against thee, take him and tell him his fault between thee
and him alone.' [5]

And concerning the scandalous offenders, the apostle says:
'Them that sin, rebuke openly that the rest may fear': [6] and in
this respect many things are taught concerning pardoning. And
a great charge is laid upon us to keep that peace in the passage
dealing with the great fear of the servant being commanded to pay
the ten thousand talents he owed, because he forcibly exacted his
fellow's debt of a hundred pence. Unto which simile the Lord
Jesus added this clause: 'So shall My heavenly Father do unto you,
except ye forgive each one his brother's trespasses from your
hearts.' [7] Thus are God's citizens upon earth cured of their
diseases, whilst they are longing for the celestial habitation. But
the Holy Spirit works within to make the salve work that is outwardly applied. Otherwise, though God should speak to mankind out of any creature, either sensibly or in dreams, and not
dispose our hearts with His inward grace, the preaching of the
truth would not further man's conversion a whit. But this does
God in His secret and just providence, dividing the vessels of
wrath and mercy. And it is His admirable and secret work, that
sin being in us rather the punishment of sin, as the apostle says,

[1] Gal. vi. 2. St. Augustine follows the Vulgate. The Greek has the imperative 'fulfil.'—ED.
[2] 1 Thess. v. 14, 15.   [3] Gal. vi. 1.   [4] Eph. iv. 26.
[5] Matt. xviii. 15.   [6] 1 Tim. v. 20.   [7] Matt. xviii. 34, 35.

and dwelling in our members, when it does not reign in our mortal body obeying the desires of it, and when we do not give up our members as instruments of iniquity to serve it, the soul is converted into a mind consenting not unto it in any evil, by God's government; and man that possesses it somewhat quietly here, shall have it afterwards most perfectly settled, sinless, and in eternal peace.

CHAPTER VII

Of the cause and obstinacy of Cain's wickedness, which was not repressed by God's own words

BUT the fact that God spake unto Cain in the same way that (as we have showed) He was wont to do to the first men by assuming the form of a subject creature, what good did it do him? Did he not fulfil his wicked intent to murder his brother, after God had warned him? For after God had distinguished both their sacrifices, rejecting the one and receiving the other (no doubt by some visible sign), and that because the one wrought evil and the other good, Cain grew exceeding wroth, and his look was dejected. And God said unto him: 'Why is thy look dejected? If thou offer well, and dividest not well, hast thou not sinned? Be quiet, unto thee shall his desire be subject, and thou shalt rule over him.'[1] In this admonition of God unto Cain, because the first words: 'If thou offer well and dividest not well, hast thou not sinned?' are of doubtful understanding, the translators have drawn it unto divers senses, each one seeking to interpret it in an orthodox manner. A sacrifice that is offered to the true God, to whom only such are due, is well offered. But the division may be ill made upon a bad distinction of the times, place, offering, offerers, or of him to whom it is offered, or of them to whom the offering is distributed: meaning here by division a discerning between offering at due times, in due places, due offerings, due distributions, and the contraries of all these: as if we offer, where, when, and what we should not: or reserve better to ourselves than we offer to God: or distribute the offering to the unsanctified, herein profaning the sacrifice. In which of these Cain offended God we cannot easily find. But as the apostle John said of these two brethren: 'Not as Cain who was of that wicked one, and slew his brother. And wherefore slew he him? Because his own works were evil and his brother's good.'[2] This proves that God respected not his gifts, because he divided evil, giving God only some of his cattle, and giving himself to himself; as all do that leave God's will to follow their own, and

<hr>

[1] Gen. iv. 6, 7.   [2] 1 John iii. 12.

living in perverseness of heart, offer gifts unto God as it were to buy Him, not to cure their vicious desires but to fulfil them. This is the property of the earthly city to worship one or many gods, for victory and terrestrial peace, never for charitable instruction, but all for lust of sovereignty. The good use this world to the enjoying of God, but the wicked, just contrariwise, would use God to enjoy the world—such I mean as hold there is a God and that He is interested in mankind: for there are those that are far worse and believe not this. So then Cain knowing that God respected his brother's sacrifice and not his ought to have changed himself and fallen to imitation of his good brother; not to have swollen up in envy against him. But because he was sad, and his looks cast down, this grief at another's good, chiefly his brother's, God finds great fault with, for thereupon He asked him, saying: 'Why art thou sad, and why is thy countenance cast down?' His envy of his brother God saw and reprehended. Man, that knows not the heart, might well have doubted whether he was sad for his own badness that displeased God, or for his brother's goodness, for which God accepted his sacrifice. But God giving a reason why He would not accept his, that he might have juster cause to dislike himself than his brother, having not 'divided,' that is, not lived well, and being not worthy to have his sacrifice accepted, shows that he was far more wicked, in this, that he hated his just brother for no cause: yet He sends him not away without a good and holy command: 'Be quiet,' quoth He, 'for unto thee shall his desire be subject and thou shalt rule over him.' What, over his brother? God forbid. No, but over sin; for He had said before: 'Hast thou not sinned?' and now He adds: 'Be quiet, for unto thee,' etc. Some may take it thus, that sin shall be turned upon man, so that he that sins shall have none to blame for it but himself; for this is the wholesome medicine of repentance, and the fit plea for pardon, that these words of God be understood as a precept, and not as a prophecy: for then shall every man rule over sin, when he does not support it by excuse, but subdues it by repentance: otherwise he that becomes the protector of it, shall surely become prisoner to it. But if we understand this sin to be that carnal concupiscence whereof the apostle says: 'The flesh lusteth against the spirit,' [1] amongst whose works, envy is reckoned for one, which incited Cain to his brother's murder, then we may well take these words thus: 'It shall be turned unto thee, and thou shalt rule over it'; for the carnal part being moved (which the apostle calls sin, saying: 'I do not this, but the sin which dwelleth in me' [2]), which part the philosophers call the vicious part of the soul, that ought not to rule but to serve the mind, and be thereby curbed from unreasonable acts—when this moves us to any mischief, if we follow the apostle's counsel, saying: 'Yield not your members as weapons of

[1] Gal. v. 17.   [2] Rom. vii. 17.

unrighteousness unto sin,' [1] then is this part conquered and brought under the mind and reason. This rule God gave him that was in malice with his brother, and desired to kill him whom he ought to follow. 'Be quiet,' quoth He—that is, keep thine hands out of mischief, let not sin get predominance in thy body, to effect what it desires, nor give thou thy members up as weapons of unrighteousness thereunto, for unto thee shall the desires thereof become subject, if thou restrain it by suppression and increase it not by giving it scope. And 'thou shalt rule over it.' Permit it not to perform any external act, and thy goodness of will shall exclude it from all internal motion. Such a saying there is also of the woman, when God had examined and condemned our first parents after their sin, the devil in the serpent, and man and woman in themselves: 'I will greatly increase thy sorrows and thy conceptions,' says He, 'in sorrow shalt thou bring forth children'; and then He adds: 'And thy desire shall be subject to thine husband and he shall rule over thee.' [2] Thus what was said to Cain concerning sin or concupiscence, the same was said here to the offending woman: where we must learn, that the man must govern the woman, as the soul should govern the body. Whereupon the apostle said: 'He that loveth his wife loveth himself, for no man ever hated his own flesh.' [3] These we must cure, as our own, not cast away, as strangers. But Cain conceived of God's command like a wicked reprobate, and yielding to his height of envy, lay in wait for his brother and slew him. This was the founder of the fleshly city. How he furthermore was a type of the Jews, that killed Christ the true Shepherd prefigured in the shepherd Abel, I spare to relate, because it is a prophetical allegory, and I remember that I said somewhat hereof in my work against Faustus the Manichee.

CHAPTER VIII

The reason why Cain was the first of mankind that ever built a city

BUT now must I defend the authority of the divine history that says that this one man built a city, when there were but three or four men upon earth. After he had killed his brother, there were but Adam, the first father, Cain himself, and his son Enoch, whose name was given to the city. But they that find this a difficulty consider not that the scriptures need not name all the men that were upon earth at that time: but only those that were pertinent to their purpose. The purpose of the Holy Ghost in Moses was to draw a pedigree and genealogy from Adam through certain men unto

[1] Rom. vi. 13.   [2] Gen. iii. 16.   [3] Eph. v. 28, 29.

Abraham, and so by his seed unto the people of God: which being distinct from all other nations might contain all the types and pre-figurations of the eternal city of Heaven and Christ the King and Founder (all of which were spiritual and to come): yet are these so recorded, that the men of the earthly city have mention made of them also, as far as was necessary to show them as the adver-saries of the said glorious city of God. Therefore when the scriptures reckon up a man's time, and conclude he lived thus long, and had sons or daughters, must we imagine that because he names not those sons and daughters, there might not have been in so many years as one man lived in those times as many children gotten and born as would serve to people divers cities? But it belonged to God, who inspired the Spirit by which the scriptures were penned, to distinguish these two states by their several generations from the first, that the several genealogies of the carnal citizens and of the spiritual might be collected by themselves up to the deluge, at which point their difference and their association are made clear: their difference, in that the one is recited down from the murderer Cain, and the other from the righteous Seth, whom Adam had given for him whom Cain had murdered, and their association, in that all men grew from bad to worse, so that they deserved to be all overwhelmed with the flood, excepting one just man called Noah, his wife, his three sons, and their wives. Only these eight persons did God vouchsafe to deliver in the ark, of all the whole generation of mankind. Whereas therefore it is written: 'And Cain knew his wife which conceived and bare Enoch, and he built a city and called it by his son's name, Enoch': [1] this proves not that he was his first son, for we may not think that because it is said here, that he knew his wife, that he had not known her before, for this is said of Adam also, not only when Cain was begotten, who was his first son, but when Seth, his younger son, was born also. 'Adam knew his wife and she con-ceived and bare a son and called his name Seth.' Plain it is then, that the scripture uses this phrase in all copulations, and not only in those wherein the first begotten are born. Nor is it necessary that Enoch should be Cain's first son, because the city bore his name; there might be some other reason why his father loved him above the rest. For Judah, of whom the name of Judah and Jews came, was not Israel's first-born: but admit Enoch was this builder's first son, it does not follow that his father named the city after him as soon as he was born, for then could not he have founded a city, which is nothing else but a multitude of men combined in one band of society. Therefore when this man's children and family grew populous, then he might sort them into a city, and call it after his first son, for the men lived so long in those days, that of all that are recorded together with their years, he that lived the

[1] Gen. iv. 17.

least time lived seven hundred and fifty-three years. And some
exceeded nine hundred, yet all were short of a thousand. Who
makes any doubt now that in one man's time, mankind might increase to a number able to replenish many cities more than one?
It is a good proof hereof, that of Abraham's seed only, the Hebrew
people in less than five hundred years grew to such a number that
there went six hundred thousand persons of them out of Egypt,
and those all warlike youths; to omit the progeny of the Idumaeans,
that Esau begot, and the nations that came of Abraham's other son
not by Sarah; for these belong not to Israel.

CHAPTER IX

Of the length of life and bigness of body that men had before the deluge

THEREFORE no wise man need doubt that Cain might built a city,
and that a large one, men living so long in those days; unless some
faithless people will take occasion of incredulity from the number
of years which our authors recite men to have lived, and say it is
impossible. So also they may deny that the bigness of men's
bodies in those days far exceeded ours; whereof their famous poet
Virgil gives a testimony of a boulder stone, that a valiant man caught
up in fight, and running upon his foe threw this at him:

> Vix illud lecti bis sex cervice subirent,
> Qualia nunc hominum producit corpora tellus,[1]
>
> It passed the power of twelve strong men to raise
> That stone from ground, as men go nowadays,

intimating that men of elder times were of far larger bodies. How
much more then before that famous deluge in the world's infancy!
This difference of growth is proved out of old sepulchres which
either ruins, or ruiners, or some chance have opened, and wherein
have been found bones of an incredible bigness. Upon the shore
of Utica, I myself and many with me saw a man's molar tooth of
such bigness, that if it had been cut into pieces, it would have made
a hundred of ours. But I think it was some giant's tooth; for
though the ancients' bodies exceeded ours, the giants exceeded all
others: and our times have seen some (though very few) that have
overgrown the ordinary stature exceedingly. The elder Pliny,
that great scholar, affirms [2] that the longer the world lasts, the
lesser bodies shall nature produce, as Homer (he says) does often
complain, not deriding it as a fiction, but recording it as a writer
of the miracles of nature. But, as I said, the bones of the en-
tombed ancients have left great proofs of this unto posterity: but

[1] *Aen.* xii. 899, 900.   [2] *Nat. Hist.* vii. 16, 73–5.

as for the continuance of their times, that cannot be proved by any of those testimonies; yet may we not derogate from the credit of the holy scriptures, nor be so impudent as to be incredulous of what they relate, seeing we see that those things have so certainly come to pass, that they foretell. Pliny says [1] that there is as yet a country wherein men live two hundred years. If then we believe that this length of life which we have not known is yet extant in some unknown countries, why may we not believe that it has been general in ancient times? Is it possible that that which is not here may be in another place, and is it impossible that that which is not now, might have come at some other time?

CHAPTER X

Of the difference that seems to be between the Hebrews' computation and ours

WHEREFORE though there seem to be some difference between the Hebrews' computation and ours, I know not upon what cause, yet it does not disprove that those men lived as long as we say they did. For Adam, ere he begot Seth, is said by our books to have lived two hundred and thirty years, by the Hebrews' but one hundred and thirty. But after he had begotten Seth, he lived seven hundred years by our account, and eight hundred by the Hebrews'. Thus both agree in the main sum. And so in the following generations, the Hebrews are still at such or such a one's birth, a hundred years behind us in the father's age, but in his years after his son's birth, they still come up unto our general sum, and both agree in one. But in the sixth generation they differ not a letter. In the seventh generation wherein Enoch was (not he that died, but he that pleased God and was translated) there is the same difference of the one hundred years before he begot his son: but all come to one end still, both the books making him live three hundred and sixty-five years ere his translation.

The eighth generation has some difference, but of less moment, and not like to this. For Methuselah having begotten Enoch before he had his next whom the scriptures name is said by the Hebrews to have lived twenty years longer than we say he lived; but in the account of his years after this son, we added the twenty, and both agree in one just sum. Only in the ninth generation, that is, in the years of Lamech the son of Methuselah and the father of Noah, we differ in the whole sum, but it is a difference of but four and twenty years, which they have more than

[1] *Nat. Hist.* vii. 48, 154

we. For his age, ere he begot Noah, in the Hebrew is six years less than in ours; and their sum of his years afterwards is thirty more than ours, which six taken from thirty leaves four-and-twenty, as I said before.

CHAPTER XI

Of Methuselah's years, who seems to have lived fourteen years after the deluge

BUT here is a notable question arising upon this difference between us and the Hebrews, where Methuselah is reckoned to have lived fourteen years after the deluge, whereas the scripture reckons but eight persons that were saved therein of all mankind, and of these Methuselah was not one. For in our books, Methuselah lived ere he begot Lamech one hundred and sixty-seven years, and Lamech until he begot Noah one hundred fourscore and eight years, which joined make three hundred and fifty-five years; unto which add Noah's six hundred years (for then began the deluge), and so the time between Methuselah's birth and the deluge is nine hundred and fifty-five years. Now Methuselah's days are reckoned to be nine hundred and sixty-nine years: for being one hundred and sixty-seven years of age ere he begot Lamech, he lived eight hundred and two years after, which make in all nine hundred and sixty-nine; from whence take nine hundred and fifty-five (the time from his birth to the deluge) and there remains fourteen, which he is thought to live after the deluge. Whereupon some think that he lived this time not upon earth, for there was not a soul of those escaped, but in the place to which his son was translated with him until the deluge were come and gone; because they will not call the authority of these truths into question, seeing the Church has allowed them, nor believe that the Jews have the truth rather than we; nor allow that this should rather be an error in us than in those out of whom we have it by the Greek. But, say they, it is incredible that the seventy interpreters, who translated all at one time, and in one sense, could err, or would falsify in a matter indifferent to them: but that the Jews, envying our translations of their law and their prophets, altered divers things in their books, to subvert the authority of ours. This suspicion, a matter of opinion, every one may take as he please: but this at least is certain; Methuselah lived not after the deluge, but died in the same year, if the Hebrews' account be true. Concerning the Septuagint's translation, I will speak my mind hereafter, when I come (by God's help) to the times themselves, as the method of the work shall exact. Suffice it for this present question to have shown by both books, that the patriarchs of old lived so long, that one man might see a number of his own propagation sufficient to build a city.

CHAPTER XII

Of those who do not believe that men of old time lived so long as recorded

NOR is any ear to be given unto those that think that one of our ordinary years would make ten of the years of those times, they were so short: and therefore, say they, nine hundred years of theirs, that is to say, ninety of ours: their ten is our one, and their hundred our ten. Thus they think that Adam was but twenty and three years old when he begat Seth, and Seth but twenty and a half when he begat Enos, which the scriptures call two hundred and five years. For as these men hold, the scripture divided one year into ten parts, calling each part a year: and each part has a sixfold quadrate, because in six days God made the world, resting upon the seventh (on which I have already argued in the eleventh book). Now six times six (for six makes the sixfold quadrate) is thirty-six: and ten times thirty-six is three hundred and sixty, that is twelve months of the moon. The five days remaining and that quarter of a day, which causes another day to be added to the leap year, were added by the ancients afterwards to make up the number of other years, and the Romans called them *dies intercalares*— days intercalated. So Enos was nineteen years of age when he begat Cainan, the scriptures saying he was one hundred fourscore and ten years. And so down through all generations to the deluge, there is not one in all our books that begat any son at a hundred, or a hundred and twenty years, or thereabouts, but he that was the youngest father was one hundred and threescore years of age: because (say they) none can beget a child at ten years of age, which that number of a hundred makes: but at sixteen years they are competent to have children, and that is as the scriptures say, when they are one hundred and threescore years old. And to prove this diversity of years likely, they allude to the Egyptian years of four months, the Acarnanian of six months, and the Lavinian of thirteen months. Pliny having recorded that some lived one hundred and fifty years, some ten more, some two hundred years, some three hundred, some five hundred, some six hundred, nay, some eight hundred, held that all this grew upon ignorance in computation. For some (says he) made two years of summer and winter; some made four years of the four quarters, as the Arcadians did with their year of three months. And the

Egyptians (says he) besides their little years of four months (as
we said before) made the course of the moon to conclude a year
every month. Thus amongst them (says he) are some recorded to
have lived a thousand years. These probabilities have some
brought, not to overthrow the authority of holy scriptures, but
to prove it credible that the patriarchs might live so long, and have
persuaded themselves (thinking it no folly either to persuade others
so in like manner) that their years in those days were so little, that
ten of them made but one of ours, and a hundred of theirs ten of
ours. But I will lay open the evident falseness of this immediately. Yet ere I do it, I must first mention a more credible
suspicion. We might overthrow this assertion out of the Hebrew
books, which say that Adam was not two hundred and thirty, but
a hundred and thirty years old when he begat his third son, which
if they make but thirteen years, then he begat his first son at the
eleventh or twelfth year of his age. And who can in nature's
ordinary course now beget a child so young? But let us except
Adam, perhaps he might have begotten one as soon as he was
created: for we may not think that he was created a little one, as
our children are born. But now his son Seth was not two hundred
years old (as we read) but a hundred and fifty, when he begat
Enos, and by their account but eleven years of age. What shall I
say of Cainan who according to us begat Mahalaleel at seventy,
not at a hundred and seventy years of age, as say the Hebrews?
If those were but seven years, what man can beget a child then?

CHAPTER XIII

*Whether we ought to follow the Hebrew computation, or that of the
Septuagint*

BUT if I say thus or thus, I shall immediately be told it is one of the
Jews' lies. I have already said sufficient about this, for it is incredible that such laudable and honourable fathers as the translators of the Septuagint were would record an untruth. Now if I
should ask them whether it be likely that a nation so large and so
far dispersed as the Jews should all lay their heads together to
forge this lie, and through envy that others should have the
authority over them should subvert their own truths; or that the
Seventy being Jews also and all shut up in one place (for Ptolemy
had them assembled for that purpose), should be envious that the
Gentiles should enjoy their scriptures, and put in those errors by a
common consent; who does not see which is easier to believe?
But God forbid that any wise man should think that the Jews

(however perverse) could have such power, or so many and so widely scattered books, or that the Seventy had any such common intent to conceal the truth of their history from the Gentiles. One might more easily believe that the error was committed in the transcription of the copy from Ptolemy's library, and that so it had a successive propagation through all the copies dispersed. This may well be suspected indeed in Methuselah's life, and in that other, where there is four-and-twenty years' difference in the whole sum. But in those where the fault is continued, so that a hundred years in the one are still in excess before the generation, and wanting after it; and in the other, still wanting before, and in excess after, still agreeing in the main; and where this continued through the first, second, third, fourth, fifth, and seventh generation—this shows a constancy in error, and intimates rather industrious endeavour to make it so than any negligent omission to let it pass so. So that this disparity in the Greek and Latin from the Hebrew, where these years are first lacking and then added to procure the agreement of the two, is neither to be ascribed to the Jews' malice nor the diligence of the translators of the Septuagint, but to the transcriber's error that copied it first from Ptolemy's library. For unto this very day, numbers, where they are either hard to be understood or seem to denote a thing not very needful, are negligently transcribed and more negligently corrected. For who thinks that he need learn how many thousands there were in every tribe of Israel? It is held useless. How few are those that can discern what use to make of such knowledge? But, where in all these generations here a hundred years are lacking and here are a hundred too many (lacking afterward when they exceeded before the birth of such or such a son, and exceeding afterward when they were lacking before), he that did this, desiring to persuade us that the patriarchs were able to live so long just because the years were so short, and desiring to point out their maturity, when they were fit to generate, hereby thought to persuade the incredulous that a hundred of those years were but ten of ours. This made him, where he found an age which his account would prove incapable of generation, add a hundred years, and, after the generation was past, to take it from the main sum of his days of life. For thus he sought to show these ages convenient for generation (by his account) and yet not to diminish from the true computation of their whole years. And the fact that he did it not in the sixth generation persuades us the rather to think that he did it where it was needed, because where it is not necessary he adds not nor alters anything. For there in the Hebrew he found that Jared lived a hundred and sixty-two years before he begat Enoch, which time comes to sixteen years, two months, and some odd days by his account. That age is fit for generation, and therefore he would not add a hundred here, to make them up twenty-six of our years by his reckoning; nor would

he detract anything from the time of Jared after Enoch's birth.
This is what made the totals of both books agree. Another persuasion is that in the eighth generation before Methuselah had
begotten Lamech, the Hebrews reading one hundred and eighty-
two, our books have twenty years less, when we generally find a
hundred more: and after Lamech's birth, they are added again to
make up the total, which is the same in both the books. For if he
would take a hundred and seventy years to be seventeen, because
of the ability to get children, he should neither have added nor
subtracted anything from thence; for he found a time full enough
here, for want of which he was fain to add a hundred years elsewhere. Wherefore we should verily think that this error of the
twenty years was occasioned by some fault in transcription, but
that the sum of twenty is added to the grand total again, to make
both books agree. Shall we think it was cunning in him to cover
his addition and subtraction of those years when need was, by
practising it also (not with hundreds, but with less sums) where he
needed not? Whether we think it was thus or no, or that the
right is this or that, I do not question that the best course of all in
all those controversies concerning computations, if the two books
differ (seeing both cannot be true) is to believe the original rather
than the translation. For some of the Greek copies, besides a
Latin one and a Syriac one, affirm that Methuselah died six years
before the deluge.

CHAPTER XIV

Of the equal length of years as formerly measured and now

Now let us see how plainly we can show that ten of their years is
not one of ours, but that one of their years is as long as one of ours;
both determined by the course of the sun, and all their ancestors'
long lives measured by that reckoning. It is written that the flood
happened in the sixth hundredth year of Noah's age. But why do
the scriptures say: 'In the six hundredth year of Noah's life, in the
second month, and the twenty-seventh day of the month,'[1] if the
year were but thirty-six days? For so little a year must either
have no months, or it must have but three days in a month, to make
twelve months in a year. How then can it be said, 'the six hundredth year, the second month, and the twenty-seventh day of the
month,' unless their years and months were as ours are? How
can it be otherwise said that the deluge happened the twenty-
seventh of the month? Again, at the end of the deluge it is
written: 'In the seventh month and the twenty-seventh day of the

[1] Gen. vii. 10, 11.

month, the ark rested upon Mount Ararat: and the waters decreased until the eleventh month: and in the eleventh month, on the first day, were the tops of the mountains seen.' [1] So then if they had such months, their years were like ours; for a three-dayed month cannot have twenty-seven days. Or if they diminish all proportionably, and make the thirteenth part of three days stand for one day, why then that great deluge, that continued increasing forty days and forty nights, lasted not full four of our days! Who can endure this absurdity? Cast aside this error then which seeks to procure the scriptures credit in one thing by falsifying it in many. The day without any question was as great then as it is now, begun and ended in the compass of four-and-twenty hours; the month as it is now, concluded in one performance of the moon's course; and the year as it is now, completed in twelve lunary revolutions eastward, five days and a quarter more being added for the proportioning of it to the course of the sun. Six hundred of such years had Noah lived, two such months and seven-and-twenty such days, when the flood began, wherein the rain fell forty days continually, not days of two hours and a piece, but of four-and-twenty hours with the night; and therefore those patriarchs lived some of them nine hundred of such years, as Abraham lived but one hundred and eighty of, and his son Isaac near a hundred and fifty, and such as Moses passed over to the number of a hundred and twenty, and such as our ordinary men nowadays do live seventy or eighty of, or some few more, of which it is said, 'their overplus is but labour and sorrow.' [2] For the difference of reckoning between us and the Hebrews does not concern the length of the patriarchs' lives; and where there is a difference between them both that truth cannot reconcile, we must trust to the tongue whence we have our translation. And though every man has power to do so, yet it is not for naught that no man dares adventure to correct that which the Seventy have made different in their translation from the Hebrew. For this diversity is no error. Let no man think so. I do not. But if there be no fault of the transcriber, it is to be thought that the Holy Spirit meant to alter some things concerning the truth of the sense, and that alteration was made by them, not according to the custom of interpreters, but the liberty of prophets. And therefore the apostles are found not only to follow the Hebrews, but the translators also, in citing the holy scriptures. But hereof (if God will) hereafter: now to our purpose. We may not therefore doubt, that the first child of Adam living so long might have issue enough to people a city—an earthly one I mean, not that of God's, which is the principal subject of which this whole work treats.

---

[1] Gen. viii. 4, 5.   [2] Ps. xc. 10.

CHAPTER XV

*Whether the men of old abstained from women until the scriptures
say they begat children*

BUT some will say: Is it credible that a man should live eighty or
ninety, nay, more than a hundred years without a woman, and
without purpose of continency, and then commence begetting
children as the Hebrews record of them? Or if they had pleased,
could they not get children before? This question has two answers,
for either they lived longer immature than we do, according to the
length of time exceeding ours; or else (which is more likely) their
first-born are not reckoned, but only such as are requisite for the
drawing of a pedigree down from Adam unto Noah, from whom
we see a derivation to Abraham; and so until a certain period, as
far as those pedigrees were held fit to prefigure the course of God's
glorious pilgrim city, until it ascend to eternity. It cannot be
denied that Cain was the first that ever was born of man and
woman. For Adam would not have said: 'I have gotten a man
from the Lord,' [1] at his birth, but that he was the first man born
before the other two. Him Abel followed, whom the first or elder
killed; and herein was prefigured what persecutions God's glorious
city should endure at the hands of the wicked members of the
terrestrial society, those sons of earth as I may call them. But how
old Adam was at the begetting of these two, it is not evident. From
thence is a passage made to the generations of Cain, and to his whom
God gave Adam in murdered Abel's stead, called Seth: of whom
it is written: 'God hath appointed me another seed for Abel
whom Cain slew.' [2] Seeing therefore that these two generations,
Cain's, and Seth's, do perfectly represent the two cities; the one
celestial, and labouring upon earth; the other earthly, and following
our terrestrial affections; there is not one of all Cain's progeny,
from Adam to the eighth generation, whose age is set down when
he begat his next son; yet is his whole generation rehearsed: for
the Spirit of God would not record the times of the wicked before
the deluge, but of the righteous only, as only worthy. But when
Seth was born, his father's years were not forgotten, though he had
begotten others before, as Cain and Abel. And who dare say
whether he had more besides them? For it does not follow that
they were all the sons he had, because they were only named for
the fit distinction of the two generations: for we read that he had
sons and daughters, all of whom are unnamed. Who dare affirm
how many they were, and be free from a charge of rashness? Adam
might by God's instinct say at Seth's birth: 'God hath raised me
up another seed for Abel,' in that Seth was to fulfil Abel's sanctity,
not that he was born after him by course of time. And whereas

[1] Gen. iv. 1.   [2] Gen. iv. 25.

it is written, Seth lived one hundred and five or two hundred and five years, and begat Enos, would any but the heedless gather from hence that Enos was Seth's first son, to give us reason for wondering that Seth could live so long continent without purpose of continency, or without use of the marriage bed unto generation? For it is written of him: 'He begat sons and daughters, and the days of Seth were nine hundred and twelve years, and he died.' [1] And thus, the rest also that are named are all recorded to have had sons and daughters. But here is no proof that he that is named to be son to any of them should be their first son: nor is it credible that their fathers lived all this while either immature, or unmarried, or without offspring, nor that they were their father's firstborn. But the scripture intending to descend by a genealogical scale from Adam unto Noah to the deluge recounted not the firstborn of every father, but only such as fell within the compass of these two generations. Take this example, to clear all further or future doubt. St. Matthew the evangelist, intending to record the generation of the Man Christ, beginning at Abraham, and descending down to David, 'Abraham,' says he, 'begat Isaac': [2] Why not Ishmael? He was his first son. 'Isaac begat Jacob': Why not Esau? He was his first son too. The reason is, he could not descend by them unto David. It follows: 'Jacob begat Judah and his brethren.' Why? Was Judah his first-born? 'Judah begat Phares and Zara.' Why? Neither of these were Judah's first sons. He had three before either of them. So the evangelist kept only the genealogy that descended directly down to David, and so to his purpose. Hence may we therefore see plain that the men's first-born before the deluge were not considered on this account, but those only through whose loins the propagation passed from Adam to Noah the patriarch. And thus the fruitless and obscure question of their late maturity is discussed as far as is necessary. We will not tire ourselves therein.

CHAPTER XVI

Of the differing laws of marriage, which the first women might have, from after ages

THEREFORE while mankind (after the forming of the first man out of clay, and the first woman out of his side) needed the conjunction of male and female for propagation's sake, it being impossible for man to be increased but by such means, the brethren married the sisters. This was lawful then, through the compulsion of necessity:

[1] Gen. v. 6–8.   [2] Matt. i. 2, 3.

but now it is equally as worthy of condemnation, through the prohibition of it in religion: for there was a just care had of charity,
that they to whom concord was most useful might be joined
together in divers bonds of kindred and affinity; not that one
should in his sole person occupy many relationships, but that every
special relationship should be bestowed among many, and so many,
by as many, should be joined together in honourable marriage.
As father and father-in-law are names for two different relationships, and two different people discharge them, there is a larger extent of charity. Adam is compelled to be both unto his sons and his
daughters, who were matched together being brothers and sisters.
So was Eve both mother and stepmother to them both. But if
there had been two women for these two names, the love of charity
had extended further. The sister also here, that was made a wife,
comprised two alliances in herself, which, had they been divided,
the sister to one, and wife to another, the combination had taken
in more persons than then it could, there being no mankind
upon earth but brothers and sisters, the progeny of the first
created. But it was necessarily right to end this as soon as possible,
and that then wives and sisters should be no more one: it being no
need, but great abomination to practise it any more. For if the
first men's grandsons, that married their cousins-german, had
married their sisters, there had been three alliances (not two) included in one: which three ought for the extension of love and
charity to have been communicated unto three several persons.
For one man would in that case be father, stepfather, and uncle
unto his own children, brother and sister, should they two marry
together; and his wife would be mother, stepmother, and aunt
unto them; and they themselves would be not only brother and
sister, but brother's and sister's children also. Now those alliances
that combine three men unto one, would conjoin nine persons
together in kindred and amity if they were severed. One may
have one his sister, another his wife, another his cousin, another
his father, another his uncle, another his stepfather, another his
mother, another his aunt, and another his stepmother. Thus
were the social amity scattered, and not gathered together all into
two or three. And this upon the world's increase we may observe
even in heathen and infidels, that although some of their bestial
laws allowed the brethren to marry their sister, yet better custom
abhorred this bad liberty; and although in the world's beginning it
was lawful, yet they avoid it now as if it had never been lawful;
for custom has great power to make a man hate or feel a desire for
anything; and custom herein suppressing the immoderate im-
modesty of concupiscence has justly set a brand of ignominy upon
it as an irreligious and inhuman act. For if it be a wrong to
plough beyond your boundary, for greediness of more ground, how
far does this exceed it, for lust of carnality to transgress all bound,

nay, subvert all ground of good manners? And we have observed that the marriage of first cousins, because of the degree it holds next unto brother and sister, has been very rare in these later times of ours: and this because of good custom to the contrary, though the laws allowed it, for the law of God has not forbidden it, nor as yet had the law of man. But this, although it were lawful, is avoided, because it is so near to that which is unlawful; and that which one does with his cousin, he almost thinks that he does with his sister: for these, because of their near consanguinity, are called brothers and sisters, and are indeed very near it. But the patriarchs had a religious care to keep the kindred within such limits, lest it should spread unto nothing: binding of it back again into itself, when it was a little diffused, and calling it still to a new combination in itself. And hereupon when the earth was well replenished with men, they desired no more to marry brother unto sister, yet notwithstanding each one desired a wife in his own kindred. But without any question the prohibition of the marriages of first cousins is very proper, partly for the aforesaid reasons, because one person therein shall have two alliances, which two persons ought rather to have, for the increase of affinity, and partly because there is a certain laudable natural instinct in a man's shamefacedness, to abstain from using that lust (though it tend unto propagation) upon such as propinquity has bound him chastely to respect, seeing that blameless wedlock is ashamed of this very act. In respect of mankind, therefore, the coupling of man and woman is the seed-bed of a city: and the earthly city needs only this generation, but the heavenly city needs a further matter called regeneration, to avoid the corruption of the first generation. But whether there were any sign, or at least any corporal or visible sign of regeneration before the deluge, or until circumcision was commended unto Abraham, the scripture does not manifest. That these first men sacrificed unto God, Holy Writ declares, as in the two first brethren, and Noah after the deluge, when he came out of the ark, is said to offer unto God. But of this we have spoken already, to show that the devils desire to be accounted gods, and offered unto, only for this end, because they know that true sacrifice is due to none but the true God.

CHAPTER XVII

Of the two heads and princes of the two cities, born both of one father

ADAM therefore being the father of both the races belonging to the earthly and heavenly city, and Abel being slain, and in his death a wonderful mystery commended unto us, Cain and Seth became the heads of the two parties; in whose sons such as are named, the two cities began to show themselves upon earth, in mankind: for Cain begat Enoch, and built an earthly city after his name, no such city as should be a pilgrim in this earthly world, but an enjoyer of the terrestrial peace. Cain is interpreted 'possession,' whereupon either his father or his mother at his birth said: 'I have gotten a man by God.'[1] Enoch is interpreted 'dedication': for the earthly city is dedicated here below where it is built: for here is the scope and end that it aspires to and aims at. Now Seth is called 'resurrection,' and Enos his son is called 'man,' not as Adam was; for Adam is man, but in the Hebrew it is common to male and female: for it is written: 'Male and female made He them, and called their name Adam':[2] so that Eve doubtless was so properly called Eve, but that Adam was a name common to them both. But Enos is so properly a man, that it excludes all womankind (as the Hebrew linguists affirm), as importing the son of the resurrection where they shall not marry nor take a wife. For regeneration shall exclude generation from thence. Therefore I hold this no idle note, that in the whole generation drawn from Seth there is not one woman named as begotten in this generation. For thus we read it: 'Mathusael begat Lamech, and Lamech took unto him two wives, Adah and Zillah; and Adah bare Jabal, the father of such as lived in tents and were keepers of cattle: and his brother's name was Jubal, who was the father of musicians. And Zillah also bare Tubal, who wrought in brass and iron: and the sister of Tubal was Naamah.'[3] Thus far are Cain's generations recited, being eight from Adam inclusive, seven to Lamech that had these two wives, and the eighth in his sons, whose sisters are also reckoned. This is eminently worthy of remark, that the earthly city shall have carnal generations until it end: such I mean as proceed from the copulation of male and female. And therefore the wives of him that is the last father here are named by their proper names, and so are none besides them before the deluge, except Eve. But even as Cain being interpreted 'possession,' of the earthly city's founder, and Enoch his son, interpreted 'dedication,' who gave the city his name, show that it is to have both an earthly beginning and ending, in which there is no hope but of things of this world: so likewise Seth is interpreted the 'resurrection,' and being the father of the other generations, we must see what Holy Writ delivers concerning his son.

[1] Gen. iv. 1.   [2] Gen. v. 2.   [3] Gen. iv. 18–22.

CHAPTER XVIII

That the signification of Abel, Seth, and Enos are all pertinent unto Christ and His body, the Church

AND Seth (says the scripture) [1] had a son, and he called his name Enos. This man hoped to call upon the name of the Lord, for, says the truth, it is true that the son of the resurrection lives in hope, all the while that he continues in his pilgrimage here below, together with the city of God, which arises out of the faith of Christ's resurrection: for by these two men, Abel, interpreted 'sorrow,' and Seth, 'resurrection,' is the death and rising again of Christ prefigured, from which faith the city of God has its rising, namely in these men that hoped to call upon the Lord God. 'For we are saved by hope,' says the apostle. 'But hope which is seen is no hope; for how hopeth he for that he seeth? But if we hope for that which we see not, then do we with patience wait for it.' [2] Who can say that this does not concern the depth of this mystery? Did not Abel hope to call upon the name of the Lord God when his sacrifice was so acceptable unto Him? And did not Seth so also, of whom it is said: 'God hath appointed me another seed for Abel'? [3] Why then is this peculiarly bound unto Seth's time, which applies to the time of all the godly, but that it was fitting that in him, the first begotten of the father of the generations which were to form part of the heavenly city, there should be prefigured that society of men who live in the hope of blessed eternity not according to man but God? It is not said, 'he hoped in God': nor 'he called upon God': but 'he hoped to call upon God.' Why 'hoped to call' but that it is a prophecy that from him should arise a people who by the election of grace should call upon the name of the Lord God? This is that which the apostle has from another prophet, and shows it to pertain unto the grace of God, saying: 'Whosoever shall call upon the name of the Lord, shall be saved.' [4] This is that which is said: 'He called his name Enos' (which is 'man'), and then is added: 'This man hoped to call upon the name of the Lord': wherein is plainly shown that man ought not to put his trust in himself. For 'Cursed is the man that trusteth in man,' [5] as we read elsewhere, and consequently in himself: which if he do not, he may become a citizen of that city which is founded above in the eternity of bliss, not of that which Cain built and named after his son, being of this world, wavering and transitory.

---

[1] Gen. iv. 26.   [2] Rom. viii. 24, 25.   [3] Gen. iv. 25, 26.
[4] Rom. x. 13; Joel ii. 32.   [5] Jer. xvii. 5.

CHAPTER XIX

What the translation of Enoch signified

FOR Seth's progeny has that name of dedication also for one of the
sons, the seventh from Adam, who was called Enoch, and was the
seventh of that generation: but he was translated, or taken up
because he pleased God, and lived in that famous number of the
generation whereupon the sabbath was sanctified, namely, the
seventh from Adam; and from the first distinctions of the generations in Cain and Seth, the sixth: in which number man was made,
and all God's works perfected.   The translation of this Enoch is
the prefiguration of our dedication which is already performed in
Christ, who rose from death to die no more, and was taken up also.
The other dedication of the whole house remains yet, whereof
Christ is the foundation, and this is deferred until the end, and final
resurrection of all flesh to die no more.   We may call it the house
of God, the Church of God, or the city of God: the phrase matters
not.   Virgil called Rome the house of Assaracus,[1] because the
Romans were descended from Troy and the Trojans from Assaracus: and he calls it the house of Aeneas,[2] because he led the Trojans
into Italy, and they built Rome.   Thus the poet imitated the
scriptures, that calls the populous nations of the Hebrews the
house of Jacob.

CHAPTER XX

Concerning Cain's succession, being but eight from Adam, whereas Noah is the tenth

AYE, but (say some), if the scripture meant only to descend down
from Adam to Noah in the deluge, and from him to Abraham,
where Matthew the Evangelist began the generation of the King
of the Heavenly city, Christ, what meant it to meddle with Cain's
succession?   I answer, It meant to descend down to the deluge by
Cain's progeny, and then was the earthly city utterly consumed,
though it was afterwards repaired by Noah's sons.   For the society
of these worldlings shall never be wanting until the world's end:
of whom the scripture saith: 'The children of this world marry and
are married.'   But it is regeneration that takes the city of God
from the pilgrimage of this world, and places it in the other, where
the sons neither marry nor are married.   Thus, then, generation
is common to both the cities here on earth; though the city of

[1] *Aen.* i. 284.   [2] *Aen.* iii. 97.

God hath many thousands that abstain from generation, and the other hath some citizens that do imitate these, and yet go astray: for unto this city do the authors of all heresies belong, as livers according to the world, not after God's prescription. The Gymnosophists of India, living naked in the deserts, are of this society also; and yet abstain from generation. For this abstinence is not good, unless it be in the faith of God, that great good. Yet we do not find any that professed it before the deluge. Even Enoch himself the seventh from Adam, whom God took up, and suffered not to die, had sons and daughters, of whom Methuselah was the man through whom the generation passed downwards. But why then are so few of Cain's generations named, if they were to be counted down to the flood, and their length of years hindered not their maturity, which continued a hundred or more years without children? For if the author intended not to draw down this progeny unto one man, as he does to Noah in Seth's, and so to proceed, why omitted he the first-born to come unto Lamech, in whose sons that line reaches its completion, in the eighth generation from Adam, and the seventh from Cain, as if there were somewhat more to be added, for the descent down, either unto the Israelites (whose terrestrial city Jerusalem was a type of the city of God), or down unto Christ's birth in the flesh (who is that eternal God and blessed Founder and Ruler), whereas all Cain's posterity were abolished in the flood? Whereby we may see that the first-born were reckoned in this recital of the offspring. Why are they so few then? So few there could not be, unless the length of their fathers' ages stayed them from maturity a hundred years at the least. For to admit that they began all alike to beget children at thirty years of age: eight times thirty (for there are eight generations from Adam to Lamech's children inclusively) is two hundred and forty: did they beget no children then, all the residue of the time before the deluge? What was the cause then that this author does not mention the rest: for our books account from Adam to the deluge two thousand two hundred and sixty-two years, and the Hebrews one thousand six hundred and fifty-six. To allow the lesser number for the truer, take two hundred and forty from one thousand six hundred and fifty-six, and there remains one thousand four hundred and sixteen years. Is it likely that Cain's offspring had no children all this time? But let him whom this troubles observe what I said before, when the question was put, how it were credible that the first men could forbear generation so long. It was answered two ways; either because of their late maturity, proportioned to their length of life: or because that they which were reckoned in the descents were not necessarily the first-born, but such only as conveyed the generation of Seth through themselves down unto Noah.

And therefore if in Cain's posterity no one occurs whom there

would be special reason for mentioning (omitting the first-born,
and including only such as were needful), we must impute it to the
lateness of maturity, whereby they were not capable of generation
until they were above one hundred years old, that so the generation
might still pass through the first-born, and so descending through
these multitudes of years, meet with the flood. I cannot tell
whether there may be some more secret cause why the earthly
city's generation should be rejected until Lamech and his sons,
and then the rest unto the deluge wholly suppressed by the author.
And (to avoid this late maturity) the reason why the pedigree
descends not by the first-born may be that Cain might reign long
in his city of Enoch, and beget many kings who might each beget a
son to reign in his own stead.   Of these Cain, I say, might be the
first, Enoch his son the next (for whom the city was built that he
might reign there), Irad the son of Enoch the third, Mehujael
the son of Irad the fourth, Methusael the son of Mehujael the fifth,
Lamech the son of Methusael the sixth, and this man is the seventh
from Adam by Cain.   Now it follows not that each of these should
be their father's first begotten.   Their merits, virtue, policy,
chance, or indeed their father's love might easily enthrone them.
And the deluge might befall in Lamech's reign, and drown both
him and all on earth but for those in the ark; for the diversity of
their ages might make it no wonder that there should be but seven
generations from Adam by Cain to the deluge, and ten by Seth;
Lamech as I said being the seventh from Adam, and Noah the
tenth: and therefore, Lamech is not said to have one son but many,
because it is uncertain who should have succeeded him, had he died
before the deluge.   But howsoever Cain's race be recorded, by
kings or by eldest sons, this I may not omit, that Lamech, the
seventh from Adam, had as many children as made up eleven, the
number of prevarication.   For he had three sons and one daughter
(his wives have a reference to another thing not here to be dwelt
upon: for here we speak of descents; but theirs is unknown).
Wherefore seeing that the law has a symbol in the number ten,
as the ten commandments testify, eleven, exceeding ten by one,
signifies the transgression of the law or sin.   Hence it is that there
were eleven haircloth veils made for the tabernacle, or movable
temple of God,[1] during the Israelites' travels.   For in haircloth is
the remembrance of sin included, because of the goats that shall be
set on the left hand: for in repentance we prostrate ourselves in
haircloth, saying as it is in the psalm, 'My sin is ever in my sight.'[2]
So then the line of Adam by wicked Cain ends in the eleventh, the
number of sin: and the last that consummates the number is a
woman, in whom that sin began, for which we are all death's slaves;
and which was committed, that disobedience unto the spirit and
carnal desires might take place in us.   For Naamah, Lamech's

---

[1] Exod. xxvi. 7.   [2] Ps. li. 3.

daughter, is interpreted 'beautiful pleasure.' But from Adam to Noah by Seth, ten, the number of the law, is completed: unto which Noah's three sons are added. Two their father blessed, and the third fell off, so that the reprobate being rejected, and the elect added to the whole, twelve, the number of the patriarchs and apostles, might herein be intimated; which is glorious because of the multiplication of the parts of seven producing it, for four times three or three times four is twelve. This being so, it remains to discuss how these two progenies distinctly intimating the two cities, of the reprobate and the regenerate, came to be so commixed and confused, that all mankind except eight persons deserved to perish in the deluge.

CHAPTER XXI

Why the generation of Cain is continued without a break from the naming of his son Enoch, whereas the scripture having named Enos, Seth's son, goes back again to being Seth's generation at Adam

BUT first we must see the reason why Cain's generation is described continuously to the deluge, from the naming of his son Enoch, who was named before all his other posterity, and yet, when Seth's son Enos is born, the author does not proceed downward to the flood, but goes back to Adam in this manner: 'This is the book of the generation of Adam. In the day that God created Adam, in the likeness of God made He him, male and female created He them and blessed them, and called their name Adam that day that they were created.' [1] This I hold is interposed, to go back to Adam, from him to reckon the times: which the author would not do in his description of the earthly city; as if God remembered that without taking account of its duration. But why returns he to this re-capitulation after he has named the righteous son of Seth, who hoped to call upon the name of the Lord, but that he will present the two cities in this manner—one by a homicide until he come to a homicide (for Lamech confesses unto his two wives that he had been a homicide) and the other by him that hoped to call upon the name of the Lord? For the principal business that God's city has in this pilgrimage upon earth is that which was commended in that one man who was appointed a seed for him that was slain. For in him only was the unity of the supernal city, not really complete, mystically comprised. Wherefore the son of Cain, the son of 'possession,' what shall he have but the name of the earthly city on earth, which was built in his name?

[1] Gen. v. 1, 2.

Hereof sings the psalmist: 'They have called their lands after their own names':[1] whereupon that follows which he says elsewhere: 'Thou, O Lord, in Thy city shalt bring their image to nothing.'[2] But let the son of the resurrection, Seth's son, hope to call upon the Lord's name, for he is a type of that society that says: 'I am like a green olive in the house of God, for I trusted in His mercy';[3] and let him not seek vainglory upon earth, for 'Blessed is the man that maketh the Lord his trust, and regardeth not vanity, and false folly.'[4]

Thus the two cities are described to be seated, the one in worldly possession, the other in heavenly hope, both coming out at the common gate of mortality, which was opened in Adam, out of whose condemned race, as out of a putrefied lump, God elected some vessels of mercy and some of wrath; giving due pains unto the one, and undue grace unto the other, that the citizens of God upon earth may take this lesson from those vessels of wrath, never to rely on their own freedom of will, and may hope to call upon the name of the Lord, because the natural will which God made (yet the Unchangeable made it not changeless) may both decline from Him that is good, and from all good to do evil, and that by freedom of will, and from evil also to do good, but that not without God's assistance.

CHAPTER XXII

Of the fall of the sons of God by loving strange women, whereby all (but eight) perished

THIS freedom of will, increasing and partaking with iniquity, produced a confused mixture of both cities. And this mischief arose from woman also, but not as the first did; for the women now did not seduce men to sin, but the daughters that had been of the earthly city from the beginning, and of evil conditions, were beloved of the citizens of God for their bodily beauty, which is indeed a gift of God, but given to the evil also, lest the good should imagine it of any such great worth. Thus was the greatest good pertaining only to the good left, and a declination made unto the least good, that is common to the bad also; and thus the sons of God were taken with the love of the daughters of men, and for their sakes fell into the society of the earthly, leaving the piety that the holy society practised. And thus was carnal beauty (a gift of God indeed, but yet a temporal, base, and transitory one) sinfully elected and loved before God, that eternal, inward, and sempiternal

[1] Ps. xlix. 11.   [2] Ps. lxxiii. 20.   [3] Ps. lii. 8.   [4] Ps. xl. 4.

good. Just as the covetous man forsakes justice and loves gold, the gold being not in fault but the man, even so is it in all other created things. They are all good, and may be loved well, or badly; well, when our love is moderate; badly, when it is inordinate: as one wrote in praise of the Creator:

> Haec tua sunt, bona sunt, quia tu bonus ista creasti,
> Nil nostrum est in eis, nisi quod peccamus amantes
> Ordine neglecto pro te quod conditur abs te.

> These are Thy goods, for Thou (Chief Good) didst make them,
> Not ours, yet seek we them instead of Thee:
> Perverse desire the motive to misuse them.

But we love the Creator truly if He be beloved for Himself, and nothing that is not of His essence be loved, for of Him we cannot love anything amiss. For that very love, whereby we love what is to be loved, is itself to be moderately loved in ourselves, as being a virtue directing us in honest courses. And therefore I think that the best and briefest definition of virtue is this. It is an order of love: for which Christ's spouse the city of God says in the holy Canticles: 'He hath ordered his love in me.' [1] This order of love did the sons of God break, neglecting Him, and running after the daughters of men, in which two names both the cities are fully distinguished; for they were the sons of men by nature, but grace had given them a new style. For in the same scripture, where it is said that 'The sons of God loved the daughters of men,' they are also called the angels of God. [2] Whereupon some thought them to be angels and not men that did thus.

CHAPTER XXIII

Whether it be credible that the angels being of an incorporeal nature, should lust after the women of earth, and marrying them, beget giants of them

THIS question we touched at in our third book, but left it undiscussed, whether the angels, being spirits, could have carnal knowledge of women: for it is written: 'He maketh His angels spirits': [3] that is, those that are spirits He makes His angels, by sending them on messages as he please: for the Greek word ἄγγελος, which the Latins call *angelus*, is interpreted 'a messenger.' But whether he meant of their bodies, when he added: 'And his ministers a flaming fire,' or whether he intimated that God's ministers should

---

[1] Cant. ii. 4.
[2] Genesis vi. 4. (The Septuagint has 'the angels of God.' The Hebrew and the Vulgate 'the sons of God.')
[3] Ps. civ. 4.

burn with fiery zeal and charity, is doubtful: yet do the scriptures
plainly aver that the angels have appeared both in visible and
palpable figures.   And seeing it is so general a report, and so many
aver it either from their own experience or from others, that are of
indubitable honesty and credit, that the silvans and fauns, commonly called incubi, have often injured women, desiring and acting
carnally with them, and that certain devils whom the Gauls call
dusii do continually practise this uncleanness, and tempt others
to it, which is affirmed by such persons, and with such confidence
that it were impudence to deny it, I dare not venture to determine
anything here as to whether the devils being embodied in air (for
this air being violently moved is felt) can suffer this lust, or
move it so as the women, with whom they commix, may feel it;
yet do I firmly believe that God's angels could never fall so at that
time, nor that the apostle Peter did allude to them when he said:
'If God spared not the angels that had sinned, but cast them down
into hell, and delivered them into chains of darkness to be kept
unto damnation': [1] but rather to those that turned apostates with
the devil their prince at first, him I mean that deceived mankind
in the serpent.   That men were also called the angels of God, the
scripture testifies also, saying of John: 'Behold, I send mine angel
before Thy face which shall prepare the way before Thee.' [2]   And
Malachi the prophet by a peculiar grace given him was called
an angel.

But some stick at this, that in this mingling of them that were
called God's angels with the women of earth there were giants
begotten and born: as though we have no such extraordinary huge-
statured creatures even in these our times.   Was there not a
woman of late at Rome, with her father and mother, a little before
it was sacked by the Goths, that was of a giant-like height in respect
of all others?   It was wonderful to see the concourse of those that
came to see her, and she was the more admired, in that her parents
exceeded not our tallest ordinary stature.   Therefore there might
be giants born before the sons of God (called also His angels) had
any carnal confederacy with the daughters of men—men living I
mean as men naturally do: that is, ere the sons of Seth meddled
with the daughters of Cain, for the scripture in Genesis says thus:
'So when men were multiplied upon earth, and there were daughters
born unto them, the sons of God saw the daughters of men that
they were fair, and they took them wives of all that they liked.
Therefore the Lord said, My spirit shall not alway strive with man
because he is but flesh; and his days shall be a hundred and twenty
years.   There were giants in the earth in those days, yea and after
that the sons of God came unto the daughters of men, and they
had borne them children; these were giants, and in old time were
men of renown.' [3]   These words of Holy Writ show plainly that

[1] 2 Pet. ii. 4.   [2] Mark i. 2; Mal. iii. 1.   [3] Gen. vi. 1–4.

there were giants upon earth when the sons of God took the fair daughters of men to be their wives, for the scripture is wont to call that which is fair, good. But there were giants born after this: for it says: 'There were giants upon earth in those days, and after that the sons of God came in unto the daughters of men': so that there were giants both then and before. And whereas it says, 'They begat unto themselves,' this shows that they had begotten children unto God before, and not unto themselves, that is, not for lust, but for their duty of propagation, nor to make themselves up any flaunting family, but to increase the citizens of God, whom they (like God's angels) instructed to ground their hope on Him, as the Son of the resurrection, Seth's son did, who hoped to call upon the name of the Lord: in which hope, he and all his sons might be sons and heirs of life everlasting. But we may not take them to be such angels as were no men. Men they were without doubt, and so says the scripture, which having first said, 'The angels of God saw the daughters of men that they were good, and they took them wives of all whom they liked,' adds at once, 'And the Lord said, My Spirit shall not always strive with man, because he is but flesh.' For His Spirit made them His angels and sons, but they declined downwards, and therefore He called them men, by nature, not by grace, and flesh, being the forsaken forsakers of the Spirit. The Septuagint calls them the angels and sons of God. Some copies call them only the sons of God, leaving out angels. But Aquila, whom the Jews prefer before all, calls them neither, but the sons of gods. Both are true, for they were both the sons of God, and by having Him as their father, the brethren of their earthly fathers; and they were the sons of the gods as born of the gods, and their equals, according to the words of the psalm: 'I have said, Ye are gods, and ye are all the sons of the Most High.' [1] For we do worthily believe that the Seventy had the spirit of prophecy, and that whatsoever they altered is set down according to the truth of divinity, not after the pleasure of translators, yet the Hebrew, they say, is doubtful, and may be interpreted either the 'sons of God,' or 'of gods.' Therefore let us omit the scriptures that are called Apocrypha, because the old fathers, of whom we had the scriptures, knew not the authors of those works, wherein, though there be some truths, yet their multitude of falsehoods makes them of no canonical authority. Some scriptures questionless were written by Enoch the seventh from Adam, as the canonical Epistle of Jude records; [2] but it is not for nothing that they were left out of the Hebrew canon which the priests kept in the temple. The reason was, their antiquity incurred a suspicion that they were not truly divine, and an uncertainty whether Enoch were the author or no; seeing that such as should have given them their credit unto posterity never named them. And therefore those books that are under his name and contain those stories of the giants saying that their fathers were no men, are by good judgments held to be none of his; but counterfeit, as the heretics have produced many under the names of the apostles and prophets, which were all afterward examined, and thrust from canonical authority. But according to the Hebrew canonical scriptures, there is no doubt that there were giants upon the earth before the deluge, and that they were the sons of the men of earth, and citizens of the carnal city, unto which the sons of God, being Seth's in the flesh, forsaking righteousness, adjoined themselves. Nor is it strange if they begat giants. They were not all giants, but there were far more before the deluge than have been since; whom it pleased the Creator to make, that we might learn that a wise man should neither respect hugeness of body nor fairness of face, but find his blessedness in the undecaying spiritual and eternal goods that are peculiar to the good, and not shared with the bad: which another commends to us, saying: 'There were the giants famous from the beginning that were of so great stature and so expert in war. These did not the Lord choose, neither gave He the way of knowledge unto them: but they were destroyed because they had no wisdom, and perished through their own foolishness.' [1]

CHAPTER XXIV

How the words that God spake of those that were to perish in the deluge: 'and their days shall be a hundred and twenty years,' are to be understood

BUT whereas God said: 'Their days shall be a hundred and twenty years,' [2] we must not take it as though it were a forewarning, that none after that should live above that time, for many after the deluge lived five hundred years. But it is to be understood that God spake this about the end of Noah's five hundred years, that is, when he was four hundred and fourscore years old, which the scripture ordinarily calls five hundred, taking the greater part for the whole: for in the six hundredth year of Noah, and the second month, the flood began, and so the hundred and twenty years were passed, at the end of which mankind was to be universally destroyed by the deluge. Nor is it fruitless to believe that the deluge came thus, when there were none left on earth, that were not worthy of such a death—not that a good man dying such a death would be a jot the worse for it after it is past. But of all those of Seth's line whom the scripture names there was not one

---

[1] Baruch iii. 26–8.   [2] Gen. vi .3.

that died by the deluge.   This flood the scripture says came about thus: 'The Lord saw that the wickedness of man was great in the earth, and all the imaginations of his heart were only and continually evil: and He revolved in His heart how He had made man in the earth, and said: I will destroy from the face of the earth the man whom I have made, from man to beast, and from the creeping things to the fowls of the air, for I am angry that I have made them.' [1]

CHAPTER XXV

Of God's anger without passion or change

GOD's anger is no disturbance of mind in Him, but His judgment assigning sin the deserved punishment; and His revolving of thought is an unchanged ordering of changeable things.   For God repents not of anything He does, as man does: but His knowledge of a thing ere it be done, and His thought of it when it is done, are both alike firm and fixed.   But the scripture without these phrases cannot instil into our understandings the meaning of God's works, nor terrify the proud, nor stir up the idle, nor exercise the inquirers, nor delight the understanders.   This it cannot do without declining to our low capacities.   And whereas it relates the future destruction of beasts and birds, it shows us the greatness of the dissolution, but does not threaten it unto the irrational creation as if they had sinned.

CHAPTER XXVI

That Noah's ark signifies Christ and His Church in all things

Now whereas Noah being (as the truth says) a just man in his time, and perfect in his generation (yet not as the citizens of God shall be perfect in that immortality wherein they shall be as the angels, but perfect as a mortal pilgrim of God may be upon earth), was commanded by God to build an ark, wherein he, his family, and the creatures which God commanded to come into the ark unto him, might be saved from the waters: this verily is a figure of God's city here upon earth, that is, His Church which is saved by wood, that is, by that whereupon Christ the mediator between God and man was crucified.   For the dimensions of the length, depth, and

[1] Gen. vi. 5–7.

83

breadth of the ark do signify man's body, in which the Saviour
was prophesied to come, and did so: for the length of man's body
from head to foot, is six times his breadth from side to side, and
ten times his thickness measuring perpendicularly from back to
front.   Lay a man prone and measure him, and you shall find his
length from head to foot to contain his breadth from side to side
six times, and his height from the earth whereon he lies, ten times;
whereupon the ark was made 300 cubits long, 50 broad, and 30
deep.   And the door in the side was the wound that the soldier's
spear made in our Saviour, for by this do all men go in unto Him:
for thence came the sacraments of the faithful.   And the ark being
made all of square wood, signifies the unmoved constancy of the
saints; for cast a cube or square body which way you will, it will
ever stand firm.   So all the rest that concerned the building of this
ark were types of ecclesiastical matters.   But here we have no
time to spend on them.   We have done so already, against Faustus
the Manichee, who denied that the Old Testament had any prophetical thing concerning Christ.   It may be one may take this one
way, and another another way, so that all be referred to the holy
city whereupon we discourse, which as I say often laboured here
in this terrestial pilgrimage.   Otherwise he shall go far from his
meaning that wrote it.   As for example, if any one will not expound this text, 'Make it with the lowest, second, and third
rooms,' [1] as I do in that work against Faustus, namely, that because
the Church is gathered out of all nations, it had two rooms, for the
two sorts of men circumcised and uncircumcised, whom the apostle
otherwise calls Jews and Greeks: and it had three rooms, because
all the world descended from Noah's three sons after the flood—
if any one like not this exposition, let him follow his own pleasure,
so he keeps in harmony with the true rule of faith in it.   For the
ark had rooms below and rooms above, and therefore was called
double-roomed: and it had rooms above those upper rooms, and
so was called triple-roomed, being three storeys high.   In these
may be meant the three things that the apostle praises so: faith,
hope, and charity; or (and that far more fitly) the three evangelical
increases: thirtyfold, sixtyfold, and a hundredfold—chaste marriage dwelling in the first, chaste widowhood in the second, and
chaste virginity in the highest of all.   Thus or otherwise may
this be understood, ever respecting the reference it has to this holy
city.   And so I might say of the other things here to be expounded,
which, although they have more than one exposition, yet all they
have must be liable to one rule of concordance with the Catholic
faith.

[1] Gen. vi. 16.

CHAPTER XXVII

Of the ark, and the deluge, that the meaning thereof is neither merely historical, nor merely allegorical

BUT let none think that these things were written only to relate a historical truth without any typical reference to anything else; or contrariwise, that there were no such things really acted, but that it is all allegorical; or that whatsoever it is, it is of no use, nor includes any prophetical meaning concerning the Church. For who but an atheist will say that these books are of no use, which have been so religiously kept, and so carefully delivered from one age to another, so many thousand years together; or that they are only historical, when (to let all the rest pass) the bringing in of the unclean creatures by pairs, and the clean by sevens, must needs have some other meaning, for they might have been preserved had they been but pairs, as well as the others. Could not God, that taught this means of restoration, re-pair them as He had created them? And now for those that say that all this was but mystical only. First they imagine it impossible that any flood should become so huge as to exceed the height of any mountain fifteen cubits, because of the top of Mount Olympus which, they say, reaches above the clouds, and is as high as heaven, so that the thicker air that engenders winds and rain cannot mount so high: never observing that the grossest element of all, the earth, can lie so high. Or will they say that the top of this mountain is not earth? No. Why then do those bad measurers allow the earth to lie so high, and yet deny the water to mount higher, averring notwithstanding that the water is higher and has more ability to ascend than the earth? What reason can they show why earth should hold so high a place in air for so many thousand years, and yet that water may not arise to the same height for a little space? They say also that the ark was too little to hold such a number of creatures, seven of every clean one, and two of every unclean one. It seems they make account only of three hundred cubits in length, fifty in breadth, and thirty in depth; never marking that every room therein was of this size, making the whole ark to be nine hundred cubits in length, one hundred and fifty in breadth, and ninety in depth or height. And if that be true that Origen elegantly proves, that Moses, being learned, as it is written, in all the wisdom of the Egyptians, who were great geometricians, meant a geometrical cubit in this case, one of which make six of ours, who sees not what a huge room-space lies within this measure? For when they say that an ark of such greatness could in no way be built, they talk idly, for huger cities than this ark have been built; and they never consider the hundred years that it took to build it throughout; unless they will say that one stone may be bound

fast unto another by lime only, and walls in this manner be carried
out many miles in compass, and yet timber cannot be fastened
unto timber by mortices, bolts, nails, and pitch, whereby an ark
might be made, not with curved ribs, but in a straight lineal form,
not to be launched into the sea by the strength of men, but lifted
from earth by the natural force of the waters themselves, having
God's providence, rather than man's practice, both for steersman
and pilot.   And for their scrupulous question concerning the
vermin, mice, lizards, locusts, hornets, flies, and fleas, whether
there were any more of them in the ark than there should be by
God's command, they that are concerned with this question ought
first to consider this, that such things as might live in the waters,
needed not to be brought into the ark, whether they be the fishes
that swam in the water, or divers birds also that swam above it.

And whereas it is said, 'They shall be male and female,' that
concerns the renewal of kind; and therefore such creatures as do
not generate, but are produced themselves out of mere putrefaction,
needed not be there.   If they were, it was as they are now in our
houses, without any known number.   If the greatness of this holy
mystery included in this true and real act could not be perfected
without there were the same order of number kept in all those
creatures, which nature would not permit to live within the waters,
that care belonged not unto man but unto God.   For Noah did
not take the creatures and turn them into the ark, but God sent
them in all.   Noah only suffered them to enter.   For so says the
book: 'Two of every sort shall come unto thee': not by his fetching,
but by God's bidding.   Yet may we well hold that none of the
creatures without sex were there: for it is precisely said: 'They
shall be male and female.' [1]   There are creatures that arising out
of corruption, do afterwards engender, as flies; and some also
without sex, as bees: some also that have sex and yet engender not,
as he-mules and she-mules.   It is probable they were not in the
ark, but that their parents, the horse and the ass, served to produce
them afterwards: and so likewise of all other creatures begotten
between divers kinds.   But if this concerned the mystery, there
they were, for they also were male and female.

Some also scruple at the diversity of meats that they had, and
what they ate, that could eat nothing but flesh; and whether there
were any more creatures there than was in the command, that the
rest might feed upon them; or rather (which is more likely) that
there were some other meats besides flesh, that contented them.
For we see many creatures that eat flesh eat fruits such as apples, and
especially figs and chestnuts.   What wonder then if God had taught
this just man to prepare a meat for every creature's eating, and yet
not flesh?   What will not hunger make one eat?   And what
cannot God make wholesome, and delightsome to the taste, who

[1] Gen. vii. 16.

might make them (if He pleased) to live without any meat at all?
It was, however, befitting to the perfection of this mystery that they
should be fed.   And thus all men but those that are obstinate
are bound to believe that each of these manifold circumstances
prefigured in some way the Church: for the Gentiles have now
so filled the Church with clean and unclean, and shall do so until
the end; and now are all so enclosed in those ribs, that it is unlawful to see no mystical references in those more difficult and
obscurer ceremonies.   Which being so, if no man may either think
these things are written to no end, nor as bare and insignificant
actions, nor as unhistorical allegories, nor as discourses not concerning the Church; but if each ought rather to believe that
they are written in wisdom, and are both true histories and mystical
allegories, all concerning the prefiguration of the Church; then
this book is brought unto an end; and from hence we are to proceed with the progress of both our cities, the one celestial, and that
is God's, and the other terrestrial, and that is man's, touching
both of which we must now observe what fell out after the deluge.

THE SIXTEENTH BOOK OF
THE CITY OF GOD

CHAPTER I

Whether there be any families of God's citizens named between Noah and Abraham

To find in the evidences of Holy Writ whether the glorious city of God continued on in a good course after the deluge, or whether through further inundations of impiety it was so interrupted that God's religion lay wholly unrespected, is a very difficult matter: because in all the canonical scriptures, after Noah and his three sons with his and their wives were saved by the ark from their deluge, we cannot find any one person until Abraham's time evidently commended for his piety: only from Noah's prophetical blessing of his two sons, Shem and Japheth, do we see and know that he knew what was to follow a long time after. Whereupon he cursed his middlemost son who had offended him not in himself, for he laid not, I say, the curse upon himself, but upon his grand-child, saying: 'Cursed be Canaan, a servant of servants shall he be unto his brethren.'[1] This Canaan was Ham's son, his that did not cover, but rather uncovered his father's nakedness. And then did he follow this with a blessing upon his eldest sons, saying: 'Blessed be the Lord God of Shem, and let Canaan be his servant. The Lord make Japheth rejoice that he may dwell in the tents of Shem';[2] all of which, together with Noah's planting a vineyard, being drunken with the wine, and uncovered in his sleep, are circumstances which have their prophetical interpretations and mystical references.

CHAPTER II

What prophetic mysteries were in the sons of Noah

BUT their true event has now cleared their former obscurity; for what diligent observer sees them not all in Christ? Shem, of whose seed Christ's humanity came, is interpreted 'named.' And who is more named than Christ, whose name is now so fragrant that the prophetical Canticle compares it to 'an ointment poured

[1] Gen. ix. 25.   [2] Gen. ix. 26–7

forth': [1] in whose houses, that is, in whose churches, the diffused nations shall inhabit. For Japeth is 'diffused.' But Ham, who is interpreted 'hot,' Noah's middle son being distinct from both, and remaining between both, being neither of the first fruits of Israel, nor of the fullness of the nations—what is he but a type of our hot heretics, not hot in the spirit of wisdom, but of turncoat subtlety, that burns in their hearts to the disturbance of the saints' quiet? But this is useful to the good proficients in the Church, as the apostle says: 'There must be heresies amongst you that they which are approved might be known.' [2] Whereupon also it is written: 'The learned son will be wise, and use the fools as his minister.' [3] For there are many things pertaining to the Catholic faith, which the heretics turbulently tossing and turning cause them that are to defend them against them both to observe them the more fully, understand them the more clearly, and avow them the more confidently. Thus the enemy's question adds the perfection of understanding. However, not only the professed infidels, but even the cloaked heretics also lurking under the name of Christians, and yet living wickedly, may be justly comprised in Noah's middle son: for in word they declare and in deed they dishonour the passion of Christ prefigured in Noah's nakedness. Of these it is said: 'By their fruits ye shall know them': [4] and therefore was Ham cursed in his son, as in his fruit, that is, his work: whereupon Canaan is fitly interpreted 'their motion,' and what is that but 'their work'? But Shem and Japheth, prefiguring circumcision and uncircumcision, or as the apostle says, the Jews and the Greeks (those I mean that are called and justified), hearing of their father's nakedness (the Redeemer's typical passion) took a garment, and putting it upon their shoulders, went backward, and so covered their father's nakedness, not seeing what they covered. [5] In like manner, we, in Christ's passion, do reverence that which was done for us, yet abhor we the Jews' villainy herein. The garment is the sacrament; their backs, the remembrance of things past, because the Church now celebrates the passion of Christ, Japheth dwelling in the tents of Shem, and Ham between them both. It looks now no more for a passion to come, but the evil brother is servant to his good brethren in his son, that is, his work; because the good can make use of the evil to their increase of wisdom: 'for there be some' (says the apostle) 'that preach not Christ purely, but howsoever Christ be preached, whether sincerely, or in pretence, I do joy, and will joy therein.' [6] For He had planted the vineyard whereof the prophet says: 'The vineyard of the Lord of hosts is the house of Israel,' [7] etc., and he drinks of the wine thereof; whether it be of that cup whereof it is said: 'Are ye able to drink of the cup that I shall drink of?' [8] and, 'O My Father, if it be

---

[1] Cant. i. 3.   [2] 1 Cor. xi. 19.   [3] Prov. x. 5 (LXX).   [4] Matt. vii. 20.
[5] Gen. ix. 23.   [6] Phil. i. 18.   [7] Isa. v. 7.   [8] Matt. xx. 22.

possible, let this cup pass from Me': [1] wherein doubtless He meant
His passion: or whether it were signified (seeing that wine is the
fruit of the vineyard) that He took our flesh and blood out of the
vineyard, that is, the house of Israel, and was drunk, and uncovered, that is, suffered the passion.   For there was His nakedness discovered, that is, His infirmity, whereof the apostle says:
'He was crucified concerning His infirmity': [2] whereof also he
says elsewhere: 'The weakness of God is stronger than men, and
the foolishness of God is wiser than men.' [3]   But the scripture
having said, 'He was uncovered,' and adding, 'in the midst of His
own house,' makes us an excellent demonstration that He was to
suffer death by the hands of His own countrymen, fellows and
kinsmen in the flesh.   This passion of Christ the reprobate preach
verbally only; for they know not what they preach.   But the elect
lay up this great mystery within, and there they honour it in their
hearts, being God's infirmity and foolishness, but far stronger and
wiser than man in his best strength and wisdom.   The type of this
is Ham's going out and telling his brethren what he had seen of his
father, and Shem's and Japheth's going in, that is, disposing themselves inwardly, for to cover and reverence that which he had seen
and told them of.   Thus as we can we search the sense of scripture,
finding it more congruent to some applications than to others, yet
doubting not but that every part of it has a further meaning than
merely historical, and that, to be referred to none but Christ and
His Church the city of God, which was preached from man's first
creation, as we see the events do confirm.   So then from these
two blessed sons of Noah, and that cursed one betwixt them, down
unto the days of Abraham, is no mention made of any righteous
man, which time continued more than one thousand years.   I do
not imagine there were no just men in this time, but that it would
have been too tedious to have rehearsed them all, and rather to
have concerned the diligence of a history than the substance of a
prophecy.   The writer of these divine books (or rather the Spirit
of God in him) goes only about such things as both declare the
things past and prefigure the things to come, pertinent only to the
city of God: for whatsoever is herein spoken concerning her
opposites, it is all to make her glory the more illustrious by entering
comparison with their iniquity, or to procure her augmentation by
teaching her to observe their ruin, and be warned thereby.   Nor
are all the historical relations of these books mystical, but such as
are not are added for the more illustration of such as are.   It is the
ploughshare only that turns up the earth, yet may not the plough
lack the other instruments.   The strings only do cause the sound in
harps and other such instruments, yet must the harp have pins, and
the others frets, to make up the music, and the organs have other
devices linked to the keys, which the organist touches not, but only

---

[1] Matt. xxvi. 39.   [2] 2 Cor. xiii. 4.   [3] 1 Cor. i. 25.

their keys, to make the sound proportionate and harmonious. Even so in those prophetic stories, some things are merely relations, yet are they adherent unto those that are significant, and in a manner linked to them.

CHAPTER III

Of the generations of the three sons of Noah

Now must we see what we can find concerning the generations of these sons, and lay that down as we go on, to show the procession of both the cities in their courses, heavenly and earthly. The generation of Japheth, the youngest, is the first that is recorded, who had eight sons, two of which had seven sons further, three the one and four the other: so that Japheth had in all fifteen descendants. Now Ham, the middle brother, had four sons, one of which had five more, and one of these had two, which in all make eleven. These being reckoned, the scripture returns as to the head, saying: 'And Cush begat Nimrod, who was a giant upon the earth. He was a mighty hunter against the Lord, wherefore it is said: As Nimrod the mighty hunter against the Lord. And the beginning of his kingdom was Babylon, Erech, Accad, and Calneh in the land of Shinar. Out of that land came Asshur and builded Nineveh, and the city Rehoboth, and Calah, and Resen, between Chalah and Nineveh: this was a great city.' [1] Now this Cush, the giant Nimrod's father, is the first of Ham's generation that is named, five of whose sons and two of his grandchildren were reckoned before. But he either begot this giant after them all, or else (and that I rather hold) the scripture names him for the sake of his fame, because his kingdom is named also (whereof Babylon was the chief city), and so are the other cities and regions that he possessed. But where it is said that Asshur came out of the land of Shinar, which belonged unto Nimrod, and builded Nineveh and the other three cities, this was long after, but it is named here, because of the greatness of the Assyrian kingdom, which Ninus, Belus' son, enlarged wonderfully—he that was the founder of the great city Nineveh, which was called after his name, Nineveh from Ninus. But Asshur, the father of the Assyrians, was none of Ham's sons, but of the race of Shem, Noah's eldest son. So that it is evident that some of Shem's sons afterward attained the kingdom of this great giant, and went further than it, and builded other cities, the first of which was called Nineveh from Ninus. From this the scripture returns to another son of Ham's, Mizraim, and his generation is reckoned up, not by particular men, but by seven

[1] Gen. x. 8–12.

nations: out of the sixth whereof, as from a sixth son, came the
Philistim which make up eight.   Thence it returns back again to
Canaan in whom Ham was cursed, and his generation is comprised
in eleven; and all their boundaries are related, together with some
cities.   Thus casting all into one sum, of Ham's progeny are one-
and-thirty descended.   Now it remains to recount the stock of
Shem, Noah's eldest son: for the generations began to be counted
from the youngest, and so upwards gradually unto him.   But it is
somewhat hard to find where his race begins to be recounted;
yet must we explain it some way, for it is very relevant to our
purpose.

Thus we read it: 'Unto Shem also, the father of all the sons of
Heber, and elder brother of Japheth, were children born.'   The
order of the words is this: 'And Heber was born unto Shem, and
all his children, even unto Shem, who was Japheth's elder brother.'
Thus it makes Shem the patriarch unto all that were born of his
stock, whether they were his sons, or his grandsons, or their sons,
or their grandsons, and so of the rest: for Shem begat not Heber,
Heber is the fifth from him in lineal descent.   For Shem (besides
others) begat Arphaxad, he Canaan, Canaan Salah, and Salah was
Heber's father.   It is not for nothing then that Heber is named the
first of Shem's line, and before all Shem's sons, being but grandchild to his grandchild, for in truth the Hebrews had their name
from him: though it may be held that they were called Hebrews
from Abraham.   But true it is, they were called Hebrews from
Heber; and Israel alone attained that language, and was the
people wherein God's city was both prefigured and made a pilgrim.   So then Shem first has his six sons reckoned, and four
other sons by one of them: and then another of Shem's sons
begat a son, and this son of this last son was father unto Heber.
And Heber had two sons, one called Peleg, that is, 'division.'
The scripture adds this reason of his name: 'For in his time
the earth was divided': which shall be manifested hereafter.
Heber's other son had twelve sons, and so the lineage of Seth
were in all seven-and-twenty.   Thus then the grand sum of all
the generations of Noah's three sons is threescore and thirteen,
fifteen from Japheth, thirty and one from Ham, and seven-and-
twenty from Shem.   Then the scripture proceeds, saying: 'These
are the sons of Shem according to their families and their tongues,
in their countries and nations.'[1]   And then of them all: 'These
are the families of the sons of Noah after their generations
amongst their people'; and out of these were the nations of
the earth divided after the flood.   Whence we gather that they
were threescore and thirteen, or rather (as we will show hereafter)
threescore and twelve nations; not seventy-two single persons; for
when the sons of Japheth were reckoned, it concluded thus: 'Of

[1] Gen. x. 31.

these were the islands of the Gentiles divided in their hands, each one according to his tongue and families in their nations.' And the sons of Ham are plainly made the founders and storers of nations, as I showed before. Mizraim begat all those that were called the Ludiim, and so of the other six. And having reckoned Ham's sons, it concludes in like manner: 'These are the sons of Ham according to their tongues and families in their countries and their nations.' Wherefore the scripture could not reckon many of their sons, because they grew up, and went to dwell in other countries; and so could not people whole lands themselves. For why are but two of Japheth's eight sons' progenies named, three of Ham's four, and two of Shem's six? Had the others no children? Oh, we may not imagine that; but they did not grow up into nations worth recording, as the others did, but joined themselves with other people.

CHAPTER IV

Of the confusion of tongues and the building of Babylon

WHEREAS therefore the scripture reckons those nations each according to its proper tongue, yet it returns back to the time when they had all but one tongue, and then shows the cause of the diversity. 'Then the whole earth,' it saith, 'was of one language and one speech. And as they went from the east, they found a plain in the land of Shinar, and there they abode. And they said one to another, Come, let us make brick and burn it in the fire: so they had brick for stone, and pitch for lime. They said also, Come, let us build us a city and a tower whose top may reach to the heaven, that we may get us a name, lest we be scattered upon the whole earth. And the Lord came down to see the city and tower which the sons of men builded. And the Lord said, Behold the people is all one, and have all one language, and this they begin to do, neither can they now be stopped from whatsoever they have imagined to effect. Come on, let us go down and confound their language there, that each one of them understand not his fellow's speech. So the Lord scattered them from thence over the whole earth and they left off to build the city and the tower. Therefore the name of it was called "confusion," because there the Lord confounded the language of the whole earth: and from thence did the Lord scatter them upon all the earth.'[1] This city now which was called 'confusion' is that Babylon, whose wonderful building is admired even in profane histories: for Babylon is interpreted 'confusion.' Whence we gather that Nimrod the giant was (as we said before) the builder of it; the scripture saying: 'The

[1] Gen. xi. 1–9.

beginning of his kingdom was Babylon.' This was the metro-
politan city of the realm, the king's residence, and the chief of all the
rest, though it were never brought to that strange perfection that the
wicked and the proud would have it to be, for it was built too high,
being, it was said, 'up to heaven,' whether this were the fault of
some one tower which they wrought more upon than all the rest,
or whether all were named under one (as we will say, 'the soldier,'
or 'enemy,' when we mean many thousands, and as the multitude of
frogs and locusts that plagued Egypt were called only in the singular
number, 'the frog and locust'). But what intended man's vain
presumption herein? Even if they could have exceeded all the
mountains with their building's height, could they ever have gotten
above the element of air? And what hurt can elevation either of
body or spirit do unto God? Humility is the true pathway unto
heaven, lifting up the spirit unto God, but not against God, as that
giant was said 'to be an hunter against the Lord': which some not
understanding, were deceived by the ambiguity of the Greek and
translated, 'before the Lord,' ἐναντίον being both 'before,' and
'against': for the psalm uses it so: 'And kneel before the Lord our
maker.' And it is also in Job: 'He hath stretched out his hand
against God.' [1] Thus then is that hunter against the Lord to be
understood. But what is the word hunter but an entrapper,
persecutor, and murderer of earthly creatures. So rose this hunter
and his people, and raised this tower against God, which was a type
of the impiety of pride; and an evil intent, though never effected,
deserves to be punished. But how was it punished? Because
all sovereignty lies in command, and all command in the tongue,
thus pride was plagued, that the commander of men should not be
understood, because he himself would not understand the Lord
his commander. Thus was this conspiracy dissolved, each one
departing from him whom he understood not; nor could he adapt
himself to any but those that he understood; and thus these languages divided them into nations and dispersed them over the
whole earth, as God, who wrought those strange effects, had
resolved.

CHAPTER V

Of God's coming down to confound the language of those tower-builders

FOR whereas it is written: 'The Lord came down to see the city
and tower which the sons of men builded' (that is, not the sons of
God, but that earthly-minded crew which we call the terrestrial
city): we must think that God removed from no place, for He is
always all in all, but He is said to 'come down,' when He does

[1] Job xv. 13.

anything in earth beyond the order of nature, wherein His omnipotency is as it were presented. Nor gets He temporary knowledge by seeing, who can never be ignorant in anything; but He is said to see and know that which He lays open to the sense and knowledge of others. So then He did not so much see that city, but rather He made it be seen, when He showed how far He was displeased with it. We may say God came down to it, because His angels came down, wherein He dwells, as that also which follows makes clear. The Lord said: 'Behold, the people are one, and they have all one language,' etc.: and then, 'Come, let us go down, and there confound their language.'[1] This is a recapitulation, showing how the Lord came down; for if He were come down already, why should He say, 'Let us go down,' etc.? He spoke to the angels in whom He came down. And He says not, 'Come, and go you down, and there confound their language,' but 'Come, let us go,' etc., showing that they are His ministers, and yet He co-operates with them and they with Him, as the apostle says, 'For we are fellow-labourers with God.'[2]

CHAPTER VI

The manner in which God speaks to His angels

THAT passage also where God says, 'Let us make man in our image,' might have been understood as spoken to the angels, because He says not, 'I will make.' But as He adds, 'in our image': it is wicked to think that God made man in the angels' image, or that God's and the angels' image is all one. This therefore is an intimation of the Trinity: which Trinity being, nevertheless, but one God, when He had said, 'Let us make,' He continues, 'Thus God created the man in His image.' He does not say, 'The Gods created,' nor 'in the image of the Gods.' And so here may the Trinity be understood, as if the Father had said to the Son and the Holy Spirit: 'Come now, let us go down, and there confound their language': if there be any reason for excluding the angels at this point, as those whom it rather befitted to come unto God in holy motions and godly cogitations, having recourse unto the unchangeable Truth, the eternal law of that upper court. For they themselves are not the truth, but partakers of the Truth that created them, and approach to that, as the fountain of their life, taking out of it what is wanting in themselves; and this motion of theirs is steady, by which they approach to that from which they never depart. Nor does God speak to His angels as we do one to another, or unto God; or as His angels to us, or we to them, or God by them to us; but in an ineffable manner, shown to us after our manner: and His high speech to them before the effect is the unaltered cause of the effect, not admitting sound, or reverberation of air, but having an eternal power in itself, working upon a temporal object. Thus does God speak to His angels; but unto us, being far from Him, He speaks in a far other manner: and when we conceive anything by the first manner, we come near the angels. But I am not here to discourse of God's ways of opening His will to others. The unchangeable Truth does speak either ineffably from Himself unto reasonable creatures, or by reasonable creatures, mutable or spiritual, either unto our imagination and spirit, or to our bodily sense.

And whereas it is said: 'Not all their many schemes shall fail, which they imagine,'[1] this is no confirmation, but rather a question, such as we use in threatening, as in this verse Virgil declares:

Non arma expedient, totaque ex urbe sequentur?[2]

And shall not all my powers take arms, and run?

We must therefore take it as a question, Shall not all their many schemes fail, which they imagine? Otherwise it shows not as a threatening. We must needs therefore add the interrogative point. Thus then the issue of Noah's three sons were seventy-three, or rather (as we have said) threescore and twelve nations, who filled the earth and the islands thereof; and the number of nations was far above the number of languages; for now in Africa we have many barbarous countries that speak all one language; and who doubts that, mankind increasing, divers took ships and went to inhabit the islands abroad?

CHAPTER VII

Whether the remote isles were supplied with the beasts of all sorts that were saved in the ark

BUT now there is a question concerning those beasts, which man cares not for, and yet are not produced by putrefaction, as frogs are, but only by the copulation of male and female (as wolves, etc.) —the question how they after the deluge, wherein all perished but those in the ark, could come into those islands. Unless they were propagated from them that were preserved in the ark, we may think that they might swim to the nearest isles: but there are some far from the main lands, to which no beast could swim. If men desired to catch them and transport them thither, questionless they might do it by hunting; though we cannot deny that the angels by God's command might carry them thither. But if they were produced from the earth, as at first, because God said: 'Let

[1] Gen. xi. 6.   [2] Virg. *Aen.* iv. 592.

the earth bring forth the living soul': then is it most apparent that the diversity of beasts were preserved in the ark rather for a figure of the divers nations, than for restoration, if the earth brought them forth in those isles to which they could not otherwise come.

CHAPTER VIII

Whether Adam's or Noah's sons begat any monstrous kinds of men

IT is further demanded whether Noah's sons, or rather Adam's (of whom all mankind came) begat any of those monstrous men that are mentioned in profane histories: as some that have but one eye in their mid forehead; some with their heels where their toes should be; some with both sexes in one, and their right breast a man's, and the left a woman's, and both begetting and bearing children in one body; some without mouths, living only by air and smelling; some but a cubit high, called pygmies by the Greeks; in some places the women bear children at the fifth year of their age, dying at the eighth; some that have but one leg, and bend it not, and yet are of wonderful swiftness, being called Sciopodes, because they sleep under the shade of this their foot; some neckless, with the face of a man in their breasts; and such others as are wrought in chequer-work in Sea Street at Carthage, being taken out of their most curious and exact histories. What shall I say of the Cynocephali, that had dogs' heads, and barked like dogs? Indeed we need not believe all the monstrous reports that run concerning this point. But whatsoever he be, that is man, that is, a mortal reasonable creature, be his form, voice, or whatever, ever so different from an ordinary man's, none of the faithful ought to doubt that he is of Adam's race: yet is the power of nature shown and strangely shown in such; but the same reasons that we can give for this or that extraordinary birth amongst us, the same may be given for those monstrous nations; for God made all, and when or how He would form this or that, He knows best, having the perfect skill to beautify this universe by opposition and diversity of parts. But he that cannot contemplate the beauty of the whole stumbles at the deformity of the part, not knowing the harmony that it has with the whole. We see many that have above five fingers, or toes, and this is only a small difference: yet God forbid that any one should be so besotted as to think the Maker erred in the creation of this, though we know not why He made it thus. Be the diversity never so great, He knows what He does; and none must reprehend Him. At Hippo we had one born with feet like half moons, and hands likewise; with two fingers only, and two toes. If there were such a nation now, curious history would ring with it as of a wonder. But must we therefore say that this creature came not from Adam? An age can seldom be without a hermaphrodite, though they be not ordinary—persons I mean that are so perfect in both sexes that we know not what to term them, man, or woman: though custom has given the pre-eminence to the chief, and calls them still, men. For none speak of them in the female sense. In our time (some few years ago) was one born that was two from the middle upwards, and but one downward. This was in the east. He had two heads, two breasts, four hands, one belly, and two feet: and lived so long that a multitude of men were eye-witness of this shape of his.

But who can reckon all the extraordinary births? Wherefore as we may not deny that these are really descended from the first man, so what nations soever have shapes different from that which is in most men, and seem to be different from the common form, if they be definable to be reasonable creatures, and mortal, they must be acknowledged for Adam's issue (if it be true that there be such diversity of shapes in whole nations, varying so far from ours). For if we knew not that apes, monkeys, and baboons were not men but beasts, those brave and curious historiographers would allege them confidently to be nations and generations of men. But if they be men of whom they write these wonders, what if God's pleasure was to show us in the creating of whole nations from such monsters, that His wisdom did not, like an imperfect carver, fail in the framing of such shapes, but purposely formed them in this fashion? It is no absurdity therefore to believe that there may be such nations of monstrous men, just as we see our times are often witnesses of monstrous births here amongst ourselves. Wherefore to close this question up with a sure lock—either the stories of such monsters are plain lies; or if there be such, they are either no men, or if they be men, they are descended from Adam.

CHAPTER IX

Whether there be any inhabitants of the earth called the Antipodes

BUT whereas they fable of a people that inhabit that land where the sun rises when it sets with us, and go with their feet towards ours, it is incredible. They have no authority for it, but only conjecture that such a thing may be, because the earth hangs within the orbits of heaven, and each part of the world is above and below alike, and thence they gather that the other hemisphere cannot lack inhabitants. Now they consider not that although it be globous as ours is, yet it may be all covered with sea: and if it be bare, yet it follows not that it is inhabited, seeing that the scripture (that

proves all that it says to be true, by the true events that it foretells)
never makes mention of any such thing. And it were too absurd
to say that men might sail over that huge ocean, and go and dwell
there, and that the race of the first man might people that part also.
But let us go and seek among those seventy-two nations and their
languages, whether we can find that city of God which remained
a continual pilgrim on earth until the deluge, and is shown to
have continued amongst the sons of Noah after their blessing,
chiefly in Shem, Noah's eldest son; for Japheth's blessing was to
dwell in the tents of his brother.

CHAPTER X

*Of the generation of Shem, in which the city of God lies down unto
Abraham*

SHEM'S generation it is then that we must follow to find the city of
God after the deluge, as it was derived from Seth long before.
Therefore the scripture, having shown the earthly city to be in
Babylon, that is, in confusion, returns to the patriarch Shem, and
carries his generation down unto Abraham, counting every man's
years, when he had his son, and how long he lived. And here by
the way I think of my promise of explaining why one of Heber's
sons was called Peleg, because in his days the earth was divided.
How was it divided? By the confusion of tongues.
So then the sons of Shem that concern not this purpose being
let pass, the scripture recites those that convey his seed down unto
Abraham; as it did with those that conveyed Seth's seed before the
deluge, down unto Noah. It begins therefore thus: 'These are
the generations of Shem: Shem was a hundred years old, and begat
Arphaxad, two years after the flood. And Shem lived after he
begat Arphaxad five hundred years, and begat sons and daughters,
and died.' [1] And thus of the rest, showing when every one begat
his son that belonged to this generation that descended to Abraham, and how long every one lived after he had begotten his son,
and begat more sons and daughters, to show us what a great
multitude might come of one, lest we should make any childish
doubt because of the few that it names; Shem's seed being sufficient
to replenish so many kingdoms, chiefly for the Assyrian monarchy,
where Ninus, the subduer of all the east, reigned in majesty, and
left a mighty empire to be possessed many years after by his
posterity. But let us not stay upon trifles longer than needs
must. We will not reckon the number of every man's years till
he died, but only until he begat the son who is enranked in

[1] Gen. xi. 10, 11.

this genealogical roll. And gathering these from the deluge to Abraham, we will briefly touch on other events as occasion shall necessarily import. In the second year therefore after the deluge, Shem, being two hundred years old, begat Arphaxad: Arphaxad, being a hundred and thirty-five years old, begat Canaan: he, being a hundred and thirty years old, begat Salah, and so old was Salah when he begat Heber: Heber was a hundred and thirty and four years old when he begat Peleg: Peleg a hundred and thirty and begat Reu: he one hundred and thirty and two and begat Serug: Serug one hundred and thirty and begat Nahor: Nahor seventy and nine and begat Terah: Terah seventy and begat Abram, whom God afterward called Abraham. So then from the deluge to Abraham are one thousand and seventy and two years, according to the vulgar translation, that is, the Septuagint's. But in the Hebrew the years are far fewer, whereof we can hear little or no reason shown.

Now therefore in this quest of the city of God, we cannot say in this time wherein those men were all of one language (those seventy and two nations, I mean, wherein we seek it), that all mankind was fallen from God's true service, but that it remained only in Shem's generation, descending to Abraham by Arphaxad. But the earthly city was visible enough in that presumption of building the tower up to heaven (the true type of devilish exaltation); therein was it apparent, and ever after that. But whether this other were not before, or lay hid, or whether rather both remained in Noah's sons, the godly in the two blessed ones, and the wicked in that one accursed, from whom that great giant hunter against the Lord descended, it is hard to discern, for it may be (and that most likely) that before the building of Babylon, God might have servants of some of Ham's children, and the devil of some of Shem's and Japheth's. For we may not believe that the earth lacked either sort. For after that saying, 'They are all gone out of the way, they are all corrupt, there is not one that doeth good, no, not one,' in both the psalms that record it, this follows: 'Do not all that work iniquity know that they eat up My people as it were bread?' [1] so that God had His people then. And therefore that same, 'No, not one,' is meant restrictively of the sons of men, and not the sons of God, for He said before: 'The Lord looked down from heaven upon the sons of men, to see if there were any that would understand and seek after God': [2] and then the following words show that it was those that lived after the law of the flesh, and not of the spirit, of whom the psalmist speaks.

[1] Ps. xiv. 3, 4; liii. 3, 4.   [2] Ps. liii. 2.

CHAPTER XI

That the Hebrew tongue (so called afterward of Heber) was the first language upon the earth, and remained in his family when that great confusion was

WHEREFORE even as sin lacked not sons when they had all but one language (for so it was before the deluge, and yet all deserved to perish therein but Noah and his family), so when man's presumption was punished with his language's confusion, whence the city Babylon their proud work had its name, Heber's house failed not, but kept the old language still. Whereupon as I said, Heber was reckoned the first of all the sons of Shem, who begat each of them a whole nation; yet was he the fifth from Seth in descent. So then because this language remained in his house, that was confounded in all the rest (being credibly held the only language upon earth before this), hence it had the name of the Hebrew tongue, for then it was to be nominally distinct from the other tongues, as other tongues had their proper names. But when it was the tongue of all, it had no name, but it was the tongue or language of mankind, wherein all men spake. Some may say: If the earth was divided by the languages in Peleg's time, Heber's son, it should rather have been called by his name than Heber's. Oh, but we must understand that Heber did give his son Peleg such a name, that is, 'division,' because he was born unto him just at the time when the earth was divided; so means the scripture when it says: 'In his days the earth was divided.' [1] For if Heber were not living when the confusion befell, the tongue that was to remain in his family would not have had the name from him. And therefore we must think that it was first universal, because the confusion of tongues was a punishment, which God's people were not to taste of. Nor was it for nothing that Abraham could not communicate this his language unto all his generation, but only to those that were descended from Jacob and, becoming eminently the people of God, were to receive his testament and the Saviour in the flesh. Nor did all the children of Heber bear away this language, but only that branch from whence Abraham descended. Wherefore though there be no godly men definitely named, that lived at the time when the wicked built Babylon; yet this concealment ought not to dull, but rather to incite one to inquire further. For whereas we read that at first men had all one language, and that Heber is first reckoned of all the sons of Shem, being but the fifth of his house downward, and that language which the patriarchs and prophets used in all their words and writings was the Hebrew: verily when we seek where that tongue was preserved in the confusion (being kept amongst them to whom the confusion could be

[1] Gen. x. 25.

no punishment), what can we say but that it was preserved unto this man's family of whom it had the name, and that this is a great sign of righteousness in him, that whereas the rest were afflicted with the confusion of their tongues, he only and his family were free from that affliction?

But there is yet another doubt. How could Heber and his son Peleg become two several nations, having both but one language? And truly the Hebrew tongue descended to Abraham from Heber, and so down from him until Israel became a great people. How then could every son of Noah's son's line become a particular nation whereas Heber and Peleg had both but one language? The greatest probability is that Nimrod became a nation also, and yet was reckoned separately for the eminence of his dignity and corporal strength, to keep the number of seventy-two nations inviolate; but Peleg was named not for growing into a nation, but because that strange accident of the earth's division fell out in his days: for of the nation and language of Heber was Peleg also. We need not stumble at this, how Nimrod might live up to that time when Babylon was built, and the confusion of tongues befell. For there is no reason, because Heber was the sixth from Noah, and he but the fourth, but that they might both live unto one time and in one time; for this fell out so before, where they that had the least progeny lived the longest, and they that had the more died sooner; or they that had few sons had them later than those that had many; for we must conceive this, that when the earth was divided Noah's sons had not only all their issue (who were called the fathers of those nations) but that these also had great and numerous families, worthy the name of nations. Nor may we think then that they were born as they are reckoned. Otherwise, how could Joktan's twelve sons (another son of Heber's) become authors of those nations, if he were born after Peleg as he is reckoned, for in Peleg's days was the earth divided?

We must take it thus then: Peleg is first named, but was born long after his brother Joktan, whose twelve sons had all their families so great that each might be sufficient to share one tongue in the confusion; for so might he that was last born be first reckoned, as Noah's youngest son is first named, namely Japheth; Ham, the second, the next; and Shem, the eldest, the last. Now some of these nations' names continued, so that we may know to this day whence they are derived, as the Assyrians of Assur; the Hebrews of Heber; and some continuance of time has abolished, in so much that the most learned men can scarcely find any memory of them in antiquity. For some say that the Egyptians were they that came of Mizraim, Ham's son. Here is no similitude of names at all; nor in the Aethiopians, who they say came of Cush, another son of Ham's. And if we consider all, we shall find far more names lost than remaining.

CHAPTER XII

Of that point of time wherein the city of God began a new order of succession in Abraham

Now let us see how the city of God proceeded from that minute wherein it began to be more eminent and evident in promises unto Abraham, which now we see fulfilled in Christ. Thus the holy scripture teaches us, that Abraham was born in a part of Chaldaea which belonged unto the empire of the Assyrians. And now had superstition got great head in Chaldaea, as it had everywhere else: so there was only the house of Terah, Abraham's father, that served God truly, and (by all likelihood) kept the Hebrew tongue pure, though (as Joshua tells the Hebrews) just as they did in Egypt when they had become a more distinct people, so in Mesopotamia they fell to idolatry, all Heber's other sons becoming other nations, or being commixed with others. Therefore even as in the deluge of waters, Noah's house remained alone to repair mankind, so in this deluge of sin and superstition, Terah's house alone remained as the place wherein God's city was planted and kept. And even as before the deluge, the generations of all from Adam, the number of years, and the reason of the deluge being all reckoned up, before God began to speak of building the ark, the scripture says of Noah: 'These are the generations of Noah': [1] even so here, having reckoned all from Shem, the son of Noah, down unto Abraham, he puts this to the conclusion, as a point of much moment: 'These are the generations of Terah. Terah begat Abraham, Nahor, and Haran: and Haran died before his father Terah in the land wherein he was born, being a part of Chaldaea. And Abraham and Nahor took them wives: the name of Abraham's wife was Sarah, and the name of Nahor's wife was Milcah, the daughter of Haran': [2] who was father both to Milcah and Iscah, whom some hold also to be Sarah, Abraham's wife.

CHAPTER XIII

Why there is no mention of Nahor, Terah's son, in his departure from Chaldaea to Mesopotamia

THEN the scripture proceeds, and declares how Terah and his family left Chaldaea, and came into Mesopotamia, and dwelt in Haran. But of his son Nahor there is no mention, as if he had not gone with him. Thus says the scripture: 'Thus Terah took Abraham his son, and his grandson Lot, the son of Haran, and Sarah his daugher-in-law, his son Abraham's wife, and he led them out of the country of Chaldaea, into the land of Canaan, and

[1] Gen. vi. 9.   [2] Gen. xi. 27-9.

he came to Haran and dwelt there.'[1]   Here is no word of Nahor, nor his wife Milcah.   But afterward, when Abraham sent his servant to seek a wife for his son Isaac, we find it written thus: 'So the servant took ten of his master's camels, and of his master's goods with him, and departed and went into Mesopotamia, into the city of Nahor.'[2]   This place, and others beside, do prove, that Nahor went out of Chaldaea also, and settled himself in Mesopotamia where Abraham and his father had dwelt.   Why did not the scriptures then remember him, when Terah went thence to dwell elsewhere, when it makes mention both of Abraham and Lot, that was but his grandchild, and Sarah his daughter-in-law, in this transmigration?   What should we think but that he had forsaken his father's and brother's religion, and received the Chaldees' superstition; and afterward, either repenting of his deed, or being persecuted by the country, suspecting him to be hollow-hearted, departed thence himself also?   For Holofernes, Israel's enemy, in the book of Judith, inquiring what nation they were, and whether he ought to fight against them, was thus answered by Achior, captain of the Ammonites: 'Let my lord hear the word of the mouth of his servant, and I will show thee the truth concerning this people that inhabit these mountains, and there shall no lie come out of thy servant's mouth.   This people came out of the stock of the Chaldaeans, and they dwelt before in Mesopotamia, because they would not follow the gods of their fathers, that were glorious in the land of Chaldaea: but they left the way of their ancestors and worshipped the God of heaven, whom they knew: so that they cast them out from the face of their gods, and they fled into Mesopotamia, and dwelt there many days. Then their God commanded them to depart from the place where they dwelt, and to go into the land of Canaan where they dwelt,'[3] and so forth, as Achior the Ammonite relates.   Hence it is plain that Terah's family were persecuted by the Chaldaeans for their religion, because they worshipped the true and only God.

CHAPTER XIV

Of the age of Terah, who lived in Haran until his dying day

TERAH died in Mesopotamia, where it is said he lived two hundred and five years; and after his death the promises that God made to Abraham began to be manifested.   Of Terah, it is thus recorded: 'The days of Terah were two hundred and five years, and he died in Haran.'   He lived not there all this time, you must think, but because he ended his time (which amounted unto two hundred and five years) in that place, it is said so.   Otherwise we could not tell

[1] Gen. xi. 31.   [2] Gen. xxiv. 10.   [3] Judith v. 5–9.

how many years he lived, because we have not the time recorded
when he came to Haran: and it were foolish to imagine that in that
catalogue where all their ages are recorded, his only should be left
out; for whereas the scripture names some, and yet names not
their years, it is to be understood that they belong not to that
generation that is so lineally drawn down from man to man.   For
the stem that is derived from Adam unto Noah, and from him unto
Abraham, names no man without recording the number of his
years also.

CHAPTER XV

*Of the time wherein Abraham received the promise from God, and
departed from Haran*

WHEN, therefore, we read, that after Terah's death the Lord said
unto Abraham, 'Get thee out of thy country, and from thy kindred,
and from thy father's house,'¹ etc., we must not think that this
followed immediately in order of time, though it follows immediately
in the scriptures, for so we shall fall into an inextricable doubt: for
after these words unto Abraham, the scripture continues thus: 'So
Abraham departed, as the Lord spake unto him, and Lot went
with him: and Abraham was seventy-five years old when he went
out of Haran.'   How can this be true now, if Abraham went not
out of Haran until after the death of his father; for Terah begat
him, as we said before, in the seventieth year of his age; unto
which add seventy-five years (the age of Abraham at this his departure from Haran) and it makes a hundred and forty-five years.
So old therefore was Terah when Abraham departed from Haran,
that city of Mesopotamia: for Abraham was then but seventy-five
years of age, and his father begetting him when he was seventy
years old, must needs be a hundred and forty-five years old (and
no more) at his departure.   Therefore he went not after his
father's death, who lived two hundred and five years, but before,
in the seventy-fifth year of his own age, and consequently the
hundred and forty-fifth of his father's.   And thus the scripture
(in a usual course) returns to the time which the former relation
had gone beyond; as it did before, saying that the sons of Noah's
sons were divided into nations and languages, etc., and yet afterwards continues: 'Then the whole earth was of one language,' etc.,
as though this had really followed.

How then had every man his nation and his tongue, but that
the scriptures return back again unto the times now past?   Even
so here, where it is said: 'The days of Terah were two hundred and five years, and he died in Haran': and then the scripture,
returning to that which it passed over in order to finish the discourse

¹ Gen. xii. 1.

of Terah first, proceeds: 'The Lord said unto Abraham, Get thee
out of thy country,' etc., after which is added: 'So Abraham
departed as the Lord spake unto him, and Lot went with him:
and Abraham was seventy-five years old when he went from
Haran.' This therefore was when his father was a hundred and
forty-five years of age, for then was Abraham seventy-five. This
doubt is also otherwise dissolved by counting Abraham's seventy-
five years when he went to Haran, from the time when he was
freed from the fire of the Chaldaeans, and not from his birth, as if
he had rather been born then. But St. Stephen in the Acts discoursing hereof, says thus: 'The God of glory appeared to our
father Abraham in Mesopotamia, before he dwelt in Charran, and
said unto him, Get thee out of thy country from thy kindred and
come into the land which I will give thee.' [1] According to these
words of Stephen it was not after Terah's death that God spake
to Abraham (for Terah died in Haran), but it was before he dwelt
in Haran, yet was in Mesopotamia. But he was gone out of
Chaldaea first. And whereas Stephen says, 'Then came he out
of the land of the Chaldaeans and dwelt in Charran': this is a record
of a thing done after those words of God; for he went out of
Chaldaea after God had spoken to him (for says he, 'God spake to
him in Mesopotamia') but that word, 'then,' comprises all the
time from Abraham's departure until the Lord spoke to him.
And as to what follows: 'After that his father was dead, God
placed him in this land wherein he now dwelleth'; [2] the meaning of
the passage is: 'And God brought him from thence, where his father
died afterwards, and placed him here.' So then we must understand that God spoke unto Abraham, being in Mesopotamia, yet
not as yet dwelling in Haran: but that he came into Haran with his
father, holding God's commandment fast, and in the seventy-fifth
year of his age departed thence, which was in his father's one
hundred and forty-fifth year. Now he says that he was placed in
Canaan (not he came out of Haran) after his father's death, for
when he was dead, he began to buy land there, and became rich in
possessions. But whereas God spoke thus to him after he came
from Chaldaea and was in Mesopotamia, 'Get thee out of thy
country, from thy kindred and from thy father's house': this concerned not his bodily removal (for that he had done before) but
the separation of his soul from them, for his mind was not departed from them if he ever had any hope to return, or desired it.
This hope and desire by God's command was to be cut off. It is
not incredible that afterwards when Nahor followed his father,
Abraham then fulfilled the command of God, and took Sarah his
wife and Lot his brother's son, and so went out of Haran.

[1] Acts vii. 2, 3.   [2] Acts vii. 4.

CHAPTER XVI

The order and quality of God's promises made unto Abraham

Now must we examine the promises made unto Abraham; for in them the oracles of the true God, prophesying of our Lord Jesus Christ, began to appear, who was to come of that godly people, whom the prophecies foretold. The first of them is this: 'The Lord said unto Abraham: Get thee out of thy country, and from thy kindred, and from thy father's house unto the land that I will show thee. And I will make of thee a great nation, and will bless thee, and make thy name great, and thou shalt be blessed: I will also bless them that bless thee, and curse them that curse thee, and in thee shall all the families of the earth be blessed.'[1] Here we must observe a double promise made unto Abraham: the first, that his seed should possess the land of Canaan, in these words: 'Go unto the land that I will show thee, and I will make thee a great nation'; the second, of far more worth and moment, concerning his spiritual seed, whereby he is not only the father of Israel, but of all the nations that follow his faith: and that is in these words: 'And in thee shall all the families of the earth be blessed.' This promise was made in Abraham's seventy-fifth year, as Eusebius thinks; as if Abraham did soon afterwards depart out of Haran, because the scripture may not be contradicted, that gives him these many years at the time of his departure. But if it were made then, then was Abraham with his father in Haran; for he could not depart from thence, unless he had first dwelt there. Does not this then contradict Stephen's saying, that God appeared unto him in Mesopotamia, before he dwelt in Charran? But we must conceive that this took place in one year, God's promise to Abraham first; Abraham's dwelling in Haran next; and lastly his departure; not only because Eusebius' computation is thus, accounting four hundred and thirty years from this year unto the Israelites' freedom out of Egypt, but also because the Apostle Paul mentions it likewise.[2]

CHAPTER XVII

Of the three most eminent kingdoms of the world, the chief of which in Abraham's time was most excellent of all

At this time there were divers famous kingdoms upon earth, that is, the society of men living carnally, and in the service of the fallen angels, three of which were most illustrious, the Sicyonians, the Egyptians, and the Assyrians, which was the greatest of all. For Ninus, the son of Belus, conquered all Asia, excepting India only. I do not mean by Asia what is now but one province of the greater

[1] Gen. xii. 1–3.   [2] Gal. iii. 17.

Asia, but that which contained it all, which some make the third part of the world, dividing the whole earth into Asia, Europe, and Africa; and some make it the half, dividing the whole into two only. Others divide all into three equal parts. Asia in the east, from the north to the south; Europe from the north to the west; and Africa from the west unto the south; so that Europe and Africa are but the half of the world, and Asia the other half: but the two first were made two parts, because all the water that comes from the ocean, runs in between them two, making our great sea. So that dividing the world into two, Asia will be one half, and Europe and Africa the other. Therefore Sicyonia, one of the three eminent kingdoms, was not under the Assyrian monarchy, for it lay in Europe. But Egypt must needs be inferior unto Assyria, seeing that the Assyrians were lords of all Asia, excepting India. So then the city of the wicked kept the chief court in Assyria, whose chief city was Babylon, most fitly called so, that is, 'confusion'; and there Ninus succeeded his father Belus, who had held that sovereignty threescore and five years; and his son Ninus lived fifty-two years, and had reigned forty and five years when Abraham was born, which was about one thousand two hundred years before Rome was built, that other Babylon of the west.

CHAPTER XVIII

Of God's second promise to Abraham, that he and his seed should possess the land of Canaan

So Abraham in the seventy-fifth year of his own age and the hundred and forty-fifth of his father's, left Haran, and took Lot his brother's son with him, and Sarah his wife, and came into the land of Canaan, even unto Sichem, where he received his second promise: 'The Lord appeared unto Abraham and said, Unto thy seed will I give this land.'[1] This promise concerned not that seed of his, whereby he was to become the father of all the nations, but the issue of his body only, by Isaac and Israel, for their seed possessed this land.

CHAPTER XIX

How God preserved Sarah's chastity in Egypt, when Abraham would have it known that she was not his wife but his sister

THERE Abraham built an altar, and then departed and dwelt in a wilderness, and from thence was driven by famine to go into Egypt, where he called his wife his sister, and yet he lied not.

[1] Gen. xii. 7.

For she was his cousin-german, and Lot being his brother's son
was called his brother.   So that he did only conceal and not deny
that she was his wife, commending the custody of her chastity unto
God, and avoiding man's deceits, as man: for if he would not have
endeavoured to eschew danger as much as in him lay, he would
rather have become a tempter of God, than a truster in Him,
whereof we have disputed against Faustus the Manichee's calumnies.   And as Abraham trusted upon God, so came it to pass: for
Pharaoh the king of Egypt, seeking to have her to wife, was sore
afflicted, and forced to restore her to her husband.   In this God
forbid that we should think her defiled by him in any way; for it is
much more credible that the great plagues that he suffered would
in no way permit him to commit any such outrage.

CHAPTER XX

*Of the separation of Lot and Abraham without breach of charity or
love between them*

So Abraham departing out of Egypt to the place whence he came,
Lot (without any breach of love between them) departed to dwell
in Sodom.   For being both very rich, their shepherds and herdsmen could not agree, and so to avoid that inconvenience they
parted.   For amongst such (as all men are imperfect) there might
no doubt be some contentions now and then arising; to avoid which
evil, Abraham said thus unto Lot: 'Let there be no strife I pray
thee between thee and me, nor between my herdsmen and thine,
for we be brethren.   Is not the whole land before thee?   I pray
thee depart from me: if thou wilt take the left hand, I will go to
the right, or if thou wilt go to the right hand, then I will take the
left.' [1]   And hence, it may be, there arose amongst men an honest
quiet custom, that the elder should evermore divide the land, and
the younger should choose.

CHAPTER XXI

*Of God's third promise, of the land of Canaan to Abraham and his
seed for ever*

But when Abraham and Lot were parted, and dwelt apart (for
necessity's sake and not for discord), Abraham in Canaan, Lot in
Sodom, God spake the third time to Abraham, saying: 'Lift up
thine eyes now, and look from the place where thou art; northward
and southward, and eastward, and to the sea, for all the land thou

                         [1] Gen. xiii. 8, 9.

seest will I give to thee and thy seed for ever: and I will make thy seed as the sands of the earth, so that if a man may number the sands of the earth, then shall thy seed be numbered also. Arise, walk through the land in the length and breadth thereof, for I will give it unto thee.'[1] Whether these promises concern his being the father of all the nations, it is not evidently apparent. These words, 'I will make thy seed as the sands of the sea,' may have some reference to that, being a figure of speech which the Greeks call hyperbole. But how the scripture uses this and the rest, none that has read them but understands. This figure then is when the words do far exceed the meaning. For who sees not that the number of the sands is more than all Adam's seed can make from the beginning to the end of the world? How much more then than Abraham's, though it include both the Israelites and the believers of all other nations? Compare this latter with the number of the wicked, and it is but a handful; though this handful be such a multitude as Holy Writ thought to signify hyperbolically by the sands of the earth. And indeed the seed promised Abraham is innumerable unto men, but not unto God, nor the sands either. And therefore because not only the Israelites, but all Abraham's seed besides, which he shall propagate in the spirit, are fitly compared with the sands; therefore this promise includes both. But this, we say, is not apparent, because his bodily issue alone in time amounted to such a number that it filled almost all the world, and so might (by a hyperbole) be comparable to the sands of the earth, because this multitude is only innumerable unto man. But that the land He spoke of was Canaan alone, no man makes question. But some may stumble at this: 'I will give it to thee and thy seed for ever': whether He mean eternally here or no. But if we understand this 'ever,' to be meant until the world's end, as we do firmly believe it is, then the doubt is cleared. For though the Israelites be chased out of Jerusalem, yet do they possess other cities in Canaan, and shall do until the end; and were all the land inhabited with Christians, there were Abraham's seed in them.

CHAPTER XXII

How Abraham overthrew the enemies of the Sodomites, freed Lot from captivity, and was blessed by Melchizedek the priest

ABRAHAM having received this promise departed and remained in another place, by the wood of Mamre, which was in Hebron. And then Sodom being spoiled, and Lot taken prisoner by five kings that came against them, Abraham went to fetch him back

[1] Gen. xiii. 14–17.

with three hundred and eighteen of those that were born and bred in his house, and overthrew those kings, and set Lot at liberty, and yet would take nothing of the spoil though the king for whom he warred proffered it him.   But then was he blessed of Melchizedek, who was priest of the high God, of whom there is written in the Epistle to the Hebrews (which the most affirm to be Paul's, though some deny it) many and great things.   For there the sacrifice that the whole Church offers now unto God was first apparent, and that was prefigured which was long after fulfilled in Christ, of whom the prophet said, before He came in the flesh: 'Thou art a priest for ever, after the order of Melchizedek':[1] not after the order of Aaron, for that was to be removed, when the true things came to pass, whereof those were figures.

CHAPTER XXIII

Of God's promise to Abraham that He would make his seed as the stars of heaven, and that he was justified by faith, before the circumcision

THEN the word of the Lord came unto Abraham in a vision, who having many great promises made to him, and yet doubting of posterity, said that Eliezer his steward should be his heir; but presently he had an heir promised him, not Eliezer, but one of his own body: and in addition he was promised that his seed should be innumerable, not as the sands of earth now, but as the stars of heaven;[2] wherein the celestial glory of his posterity seems to be plainly intimated.   But as for their number, who sees not that the sands do far exceed the stars?   Herein you may say they are comparable in that they are both innumerable.   For we cannot think that one can see all the stars, but the more earnestly he beholds them, the more he sees: so that we may well suppose that there are some that deceive the sharpest eye, besides those that arise in other horizons out of our sight.   Lastly, such as understand and record one certain and definite number of the stars, as Aratus, or Eudoxus, or others, this book overthrows them wholly.   And here is that recorded that the apostle recites in commendation of God's grace, 'Abraham believed the Lord, and that was counted unto him for righteousness,'[3] lest circumcision should exalt itself, and deny the uncircumcised nations access unto Christ: for Abraham was uncircumcised as yet, when he believed thus, and it was imputed unto him for righteousness.

[1] Ps. cx. 4; Heb. vii. 17.   [2] Gen. xv. 1–5.
[3] Gen. xv. 6; Rom. iv. 3; Gal. iii. 6.

CHAPTER XXIV

*Of the signification of the sacrifice which Abraham was commanded
to offer when he desired to be confirmed in the things he believed*

GOD said also unto him in the same vision: 'I am the Lord that
brought thee out of the country of the Chaldees, to give thee this
land to inherit it.' Then said Abraham: 'Lord, how shall I know
that I shall inherit it?' And God said unto him: 'Take me an
heifer of three years old, a she goat of three years old, a ram of three
years old, a turtle-dove, and a pigeon.' So he did, and divided
them in the midst, and laid one piece against another, but the birds
he did not divide. Then came fowls, as the book says, and fell on
the carcasses, and sat thereupon, and Abraham sat by them: and
about sunset there fell a heavy sleep upon Abraham, and lo a
horror of great darkness fell upon him. And God said unto
Abraham: 'Know this assuredly that thy seed shall be a stranger
in a land that is not theirs, four hundred years, and they shall serve
there, and shall be evil entreated. But the nation whom they
shall serve will I judge, and afterwards they shall come out with
great substance. But thou shalt go unto thy fathers in peace, and
shalt die in a good age: and in the fourth generation they shall come
hither again, for the wickedness of the Amorites is not yet full.
And when the sun went down there was a darkness, and behold a
smoking furnace, and a fire-brand went between those pieces. In
that same day the Lord made a covenant with Abraham, saying,
Unto thy seed have I given this land from the river of Egypt unto
the great river of Euphrates, the Kenites, and the Kenizzites, and
the Kadmonites, the Hittites, the Perizzites, the Rephaims, the
Amorites, the Canaanites, the Girgashites, and the Jebusites.'[1]
All this did Abraham hear and see in his vision. To deal with
each particular were tedious, and alien to our purpose. Suffice it
that we must know that whereas Abraham believed before, and
that was counted unto him for righteousness, he fell not from his
faith now, in saying: 'Lord, how shall I know that I shall inherit
it?'—namely, that land which God had promised him. He says
not, From whence shall I know, but How or whereby shall I know,
by what similitude shall I be further instructed in my belief?
Nor did the Virgin Mary distrust, saying: 'How shall this be,
seeing I know no man?'[2] She knew it would be, but she inquired
of the manner and was answered thus: 'The Holy Ghost shall
descend upon thee, and the power of the Highest shall over-
shadow thee.'

And in this manner had Abraham his simile in his three beasts,
his heifer, his goat, and ram, and the two birds, the turtle-dove, and
the pigeon: to learn that that was to come to pass thus which he

[1] Gen. xv. 7–21.   [2] Luke i. 34.

was firmly persuaded should come to pass some way. Either therefore the heifer signified the people's yoke under the law, the goat their offending, and the ram their dominion (which three creatures were all three years old, because of the three spaces of time being so famous which lay from Adam to Noah, from Noah to Abraham, and from Abraham to David, who was the first elected King of Israel, Saul being a reprobate, of these three, this third, from Abraham to David, contained Israel's full growth to glory: or else they may signify some other thing more conveniently; but without any doubt the turtle-dove and the pigeon are types of his spiritual seed, and therefore it is said: 'Them he divided not': for the carnal are divided between themselves, but the spiritual never; whether they retire themselves from conversing with the affairs of man, like the turtle-dove, or live amongst them, like the pigeon.

Both these birds are simple and harmless, signifying that even in Israel who should possess that land, there should be individual sons of promise, and heirs of the kingdom of eternity. The birds that fell upon the sacrifice signified nothing but the airy powers, that feed upon the contentions and divisions of carnal men. But whereas Abraham sat by them, that signified that there should be some faithful amongst these contentions, even unto the end of the world: and the heaviness that fell upon Abraham towards sunsetting, and that fearful darkness signifies the sore trouble that the faithful shall endure towards the end of this world, whereof Christ said in the gospel: 'Then shall be a great tribulation, such as was not from the beginning,' [1] etc. And whereas it was said to Abraham, 'Know assuredly that thy seed shall be a stranger,' etc., this was a plain prophecy of Israel's servitude in Egypt, not that they were to serve four hundred years in this slavish affliction, but that within four hundred years this was to befall them. For as there where it is written of Terah, the father of Abraham, that 'he lived in Haran two hundred and five years,' we must note that he lived not there all this while, but that there he ended these his days; so it is here said, 'They shall be strangers in a land that is not theirs, four hundred years,' not that their bondage lasted all this time, but that it was ended at this time. And it is said four hundred years for the roundness of the number, although there were some more years in the account, whether you reckon from Abraham's first receiving of the promise, or from the birth of his son Isaac, the first of the seed unto whom this was promised; for from Abraham's seventy-fifth year, wherein, as I said before, he first received the promise, unto the departure of Israel out of Egypt, are reckoned four hundred and thirty years, which the apostle mentions in these words: 'This I say, that the law which was four hundred and thirty years after, cannot disannul the covenant which was confirmed of God

[1] Matt. xxiv. 21.

before, or make the promise of none effect.' [1] Now these four hundred and thirty years might have been called four hundred, because they are not much more, especially as some of them were past when Abraham had this vision, or when Isaac was born unto his father, being then one hundred years old, it being five-and-twenty years after the promise, so that there remained four hundred and five years of the four hundred and thirty that were to come; and those it pleased God to call four hundred. So likewise in the other words of God, there is no man who doubts but that they belong unto the people of Israel. But that which follows: 'When the sun went down there was a darkness, and behold, a smoking furnace and a firebrand went between the pieces': this signifies that in the end the carnal are to be judged by fire; for as the great and exceeding affliction of the city of God was signified by the heaviness that fell upon Abraham towards sunset, that is, towards this world's end: even so, at sunset, that is, at this world's end, does this fire signify that fire that shall purge the righteous and devour the wicked. And then the promise made unto Abraham is a plain mention of the land of Canaan, naming the eleven nations thereof from the river of Egypt unto the great river Euphrates—not from the Nile, the great river of Egypt, but from that little one which divides Egypt and Palestine, on whose bank the city Rhinocorura stands.

CHAPTER XXV

Of Hagar, Sarah's bondwoman, whom she gave as concubine unto Abraham

Now follow the times of Abraham's sons, one of Hagar the bondwoman, the other of Sarah the freewoman, of whom we spoke also in the last book. But with regard to this act, Abraham offended not in using this woman Hagar as a concubine; for he did it for the sake of offspring, and not for lust, nor as insulting but obeying his wife, who held that it would be a comfort unto her barrenness if she got children from her bondwoman by will, seeing she could get none of herself by nature, using that law that the apostle speaks of: 'The husband hath not power over his own body, but the wife.' [2] The woman may procure herself children from the womb of another if she can bear none herself. There is neither lust nor uncleanness in such an act. The maid was therefore given by the wife to the husband for issue's sake, and for that end he took her. Neither of them desires the effects of lust, but the fruits of nature; and when the bondwoman being now with child began to despise her barren mistress, and Sarah suspected her husband for bearing

[1] Gal. iii. 17.   [2] 1 Cor. vii. 4.

with her in her pride, Abraham showed that he was not a captive lover, but a free father in this; that it was not his pleasure, but her will that he had fulfilled, and that by her own seeking; that he meddled with Hagar, yet was in no way entangled in desire unto her: and that he sowed the seed of future fruit in her, yet without yielding to any exorbitant affection for her: for he told his wife: 'Thy maid is in thine hand: use her as it pleaseth thee.' O worthy man, that could use his wife with temperance and his servant with obedience, and both without any touch of uncleanness!

CHAPTER XXVI

Of God's promise unto Abraham, that Sarah (though she were old) should have a son that should be the father of the nations, and how this promise was sealed in the mystery of circumcision

AFTER this Ishmael was born of Hagar, in whom it might be thought God's promise to Abraham was fulfilled, for, when he talked of making his steward his heir, God said: 'Nay, but thou shalt have an heir of thine own body.' [1] But lest he should build upon this, in the fourscore and nineteenth year of his age, God appeared unto him, saying: 'I am the all-sufficient God, walk before Me, and be thou upright: and I will make My covenant between Me and thee, and will multiply thee exceedingly.' Then Abraham fell on his face, and God talked with him, saying: 'Behold, I make My covenant with thee. Thou shalt be a father of many nations. Nor shall thy name be called Abram any more, but Abraham: for a father of many nations have I made thee. I will make thee exceeding fruitful, and many nations, yea even kings shall proceed of thee: and I will establish My covenant between Me and thee, and thy seed after thee in their generations, for an everlasting covenant to be God to thee and thy seed after thee. And I will give thee and thy seed after thee a land wherein thou art a stranger, even all the land of Canaan for an everlasting possession, and I will be their God': and God said further unto Abraham: 'Thou shalt keep My covenant, thou and thy seed after thee in their generations. This is My covenant which thou shalt keep between thee and Me, and thy seed after thee. Let every man-child of you be circumcised; that is, you shall circumcise the foreskin of your flesh, and it shall be a sign of the covenant between Me and you. Every man-child of eight days old amongst you shall be circumcised in your generations, as well he that is born in thine house, as he that is bought of any stranger which is not of thy seed: both must be circumcised; so My covenant shall be eternally in you. But the uncircumcised man-child, and he in whose flesh the foreskin is

[1] Gen. xvi. 6.

not circumcised, shall be cut off from his people, because he hath
broken My covenant.' And God said moreover unto Abraham:
'Sarai thy wife shall be no more called Sarai, but Sarah, and I will
bless her, and will give thee a son of her, and I will bless her, and
she shall be the mother of nations, yea even of kings.' Then
Abraham fell upon his face and laughed in his heart, saying: 'Shall
he that is a hundred years old have a child? And shall Sarah that
is ninety years old, bear?' And Abraham said unto God: 'Oh, let
Ishmael live in Thy sight': and God said unto Abraham: 'Sarah thy
wife shall bear a son indeed, and thou shalt call his name Isaac.
I will establish My covenant with him as an everlasting covenant,
and I will be his God, and the God of his seed after him. As
concerning Ishmael, I have heard thee; for I have blessed him,
and will multiply and increase him exceedingly. Twelve princes
shall he beget, and I will make him a great nation. But My
covenant will I establish with Isaac, whom Sarah shall bear unto
thee next year by this time.' [1] Here now is the calling of the nations
plainly promised in Isaac, that is, in the son of promise, signifying
grace, and not nature; for a son is promised unto an old man, by
a barren old woman; and although God works according to the
course of nature, yet where that nature is withered and wasted,
there such an effect as this is God's evident work, more evidently
manifesting grace. And because this was not to come by generation, but regeneration afterwards, therefore was circumcision
commanded now, when this son was promised unto Sarah And
whereas not only all children, but servants home-born and bought
and strangers, are commanded to be circumcised, this shows that
grace belongs unto all the world: for what does circumcision signify
but the putting off corruption, and the renewal of nature? And what
does the eighth day signify but Christ that rose again in the end
of the week, the sabbath being fulfilled? The very names of these
parents being changed, all signifies that newness, which is shadowed
in the types of the Old Testament, in which the New Testament
lies prefigured. For why is it called the Old Testament, except
that it shadows the New? And what is the New Testament but
the revelation of the Old? Now Abraham is said to laugh, but
this was the extremity of his joy, not any sign of his deriding this
promise upon distrust: and his thoughts being these: 'Shall he
that is a hundred years old,' etc., are not doubts of the events,
but marvellings caused by so strange an event. Now if some stop
at that where God says, 'He will give him all the land of Canaan
for an eternal possession,' how this may be fulfilled, seeing that no
man's issue can inherit the earth everlastingly; he must know that
eternal is here taken as the Greeks take αἰώνιον, which is derived
of αἰών, that is *saeculum*, an age: but the Latin translation durst not
say *saeculare* here, lest it should have been taken in another sense:

[1] Gen. xvii. 1–21.

for *saeculare* and *transitorium* are both alike used for things that last but for a little space: but αἰώνιον is that which is either endless or ends not until the world's end: and in this latter sense is *eternal* used here.

CHAPTER XXVII

Of the man-child, that if it were not circumcised the eighth day, it perished for breaking of God's covenant

SOME also may scruple at the understanding of these words: 'The man-child in whose flesh the foreskin is not circumcised, that person shall be cut off from his people, because he has broken My covenant.' Here is no fault of the child's who is here exposed to destruction. He broke no covenant of God's, but his parents, that looked not to his circumcision; unless you say that the youngest child has broken God's command and covenant as well as the rest, in the first man, in whom all mankind sinned. For there are many testaments or covenants of God, besides the Old and New, those two so great ones, that every one may read and know. The first covenant was this, unto Adam: 'Whensoever thou eatest thereof, thou shalt die the death.' Whereupon it is written in Ecclesiasti-cus: 'All flesh waxeth old as a garment, and it is a covenant from the beginning that all sinners shall die the death.' [1] For whereas the law was afterwards given, and that brought the more light to man's judgment in sin, as the apostle says: 'Where no law is there is no transgression': [2] how is that true that the psalmist said: 'I accounted all the sinners of the earth transgressors,' [3] unless every man is guilty in his own conscience of somewhat that he has done against some law? And therefore seeing that little children (as the true faith teaches) be guilty of original sin, though not of actual, whereupon we confess that they must necessarily have the grace of the remission of their sins: then verily in this they are breakers of God's covenant made with Adam in paradise: so that both the psalmist's saying and the apostle's are true; and conse-quently, seeing that circumcision was a type of regeneration, justly shall the child's original sin (breaking the first covenant that ever was made between God and man) cut him off from his people, unless that regeneration engraft him into the body of the true religion. This then we must conceive that God spake: 'He that is not regenerate, shall perish from amongst his people, because he has broken My covenant, in offending Me in Adam.' For if He had said, 'he has broken this My covenant,' it could have been meant of nothing but the circumcision only: but seeing He says not what covenant the child breaks, we must needs understand Him to mean a covenant applicable to the transgression of the

[1] Ecclus. xiv. 17.   [2] Rom. iv. 15.   [3] Ps .cxix. 119 (LXX)

child.   But if any one will refer it unto circumcision, and say that
that is the covenant which the uncircumcised child has broken, let
him beware of absurdity in saying that he breaks their covenant
which is not broken by him, but in him only.   Yet even so we
shall find the child's condemnation to come only from his original
sin, and not from any negligence of his own incurring this breach
of the covenant.

CHAPTER XXVIII

Of the changing of Abram's and Sarai's names, who being, the one too
barren, and both too old to have children, yet by God's bounty were
both made fruitful

THUS this great and evident promise being made unto Abraham in
these words: 'A father of many nations have I made thee, and I
will make thee exceeding fruitful: and nations, yea even kings shall
proceed from thee' [1] (which promise we see most evidently fulfilled in Christ), from that time the man and wife are called no more
Abram and Sarai, but, as we called them before, and all the world
calls them, Abraham and Sarah.   But why was Abram's name
changed?   The reason follows immediately upon the change, 'for
a father of many nations have I made thee.'   This is signified by
Abraham.   Now Abram (his former name) is interpreted a high
father.   But for the change of Sarah's name, there is no reason
given: but as they say that have interpreted those Hebrew names,
Sarai is 'my princess'; and Sarah, 'strength': whereupon it is
written in the Epistle to the Hebrews: 'By faith Sarah received
strength to conceive seed,' [2] etc.   Now they were both old, as the
scripture says, but she was barren also.   It had ceased to be with
Sarah after the manner of women, so that she could no longer have
borne children even if she had not been barren.   And if a woman
be well on in years, and yet retains the custom of women, she may
conceive by a young man, but never by an old: as the old man may
beget children, but it must be upon a young woman, as Abraham
after Sarah's death did upon Keturah, because she was of a youthful
age as yet.

This therefore is that which the apostle so highly wonders at,
and hereupon he says that Abraham's body was dead, because he
was not able to beget a child upon any woman who only retained
something of the natural vigour for child-bearing, but only upon
those that were in the prime and flower thereof.   For his body
was dead to some purposes though not to all; otherwise it should
have been a corpse fit for a grave, not an ancient father upon earth.
Besides, the gift of begetting children that God gave him lasted

[1] Gen. xvii. 5, 6, 16.   [2] Heb. xi. 11.

after Sarah's death, and he begat divers upon Keturah; and this
clears the doubt that his body was dead only unto generation.
But I like the other answer better, that a man in those days was
not in his weakest age at a hundred years, although the men of our
times be so and cannot beget a child of any woman.   They might,
for they lived far longer, and had abler bodies than we have.

CHAPTER XXIX

*Of the three men, or angels, in whom God appeared to Abraham in
the plain of Mamre*

GOD appeared unto Abraham in the plain of Mamre in three men,
who doubtless were angels, though some think that one of them
was Christ, and that He was visible before His incarnation.   It is
indeed in the power of the unchangeable, incorporeal, and invisible Deity to appear unto man visible whensoever He pleases,
without any alteration of Himself: not in His own form but in some
creature subject unto Him; and what is it that He rules not over?
But if they ground their affirmation that one of these three was
Christ upon this, that Abraham when he saw three men, saluted
the Lord separately, bowing to the ground at the door of his tent,
and saying: 'Lord, if I have found favour in Thy sight,' etc., why
do they not observe that when two came to destroy Sodom, Abraham spoke yet but unto one of them that remained (calling him
Lord, and entreating him not to destroy the righteous with the
wicked), and those two were entertained by Lot, who notwithstanding called each of them by the name of Lord?   For speaking
to them both, 'My Lords,' said he, 'I pray you turn in unto your
servant's house,' etc., and yet afterwards we read: 'And the angels
took him, and his wife, and his two daughters by the hands, the
Lord being merciful unto him: and they brought him forth, and
set him without the city,' and when they had so done, the angels
said: 'Escape for thy life, look not behind thee, neither tarry in all
the plain, but escape to the mountains lest thou be destroyed,' and
he said: 'Not so, I pray Thee, my Lord,' etc., and afterward, the
Lord being in these two angels answered him as in one, saying:
'Behold, I have received thy request,' etc.   Therefore it is far
more likely that Abraham knew the Lord to be in them all three,
and Lot in the two, unto whom they continually spoke in the
singular number, even then when they thought them to be men,
than otherwise.   For they entertained them at first only to give
them meat and lodging in charity, as unto poor men; but yet there
was some excellent mark in them whereby their hosts might be
assured that the Lord was in them, as He used to be in the prophets:
and therefore they sometimes called them Lords in the plural

number, as speaking to themselves, and sometimes Lord, in the
singular, as speaking to God in them.   But the scriptures themselves testify that they were angels, not only in this place of Genesis,
but in the Epistle to the Hebrews where the apostle commending
hospitality, 'Thereby some,' says he, 'have entertained angels
unawares.'[1]   These three men therefore confirmed the promise of
Isaac the second time, and said of Abraham: 'He shall be a great
and mighty nation, and in him shall the nations of the earth be
blessed.'[2]   Here is a plain prophecy both of the bodily nation of
the Israelites, and the spiritual nations of the righteous.

CHAPTER XXX

*Lot's deliverance; Sodom's destruction; Abimelech's lust; Sarah's
chastity*

AFTER this promise was Lot delivered out of Sodom, and the
whole territory of that wicked city consumed by a shower of fire
from heaven, and all those parts where masculine bestiality was as
allowable by custom as any other act is by the laws.   Besides, this
punishment of theirs was a type of the day of judgment.   And
what does the angels' forbidding them to look back signify, but
that the regenerate must never return to his old courses, if he mean
to escape the terror of the last judgment?   Lot's wife, where she
looked back, there was she fixed; and being turned into a pillar of
salt serves to season the hearts of the faithful, to take heed by such
example.[3]   After this, Abraham did with his wife Sarah at Gerar,
in King Abimelech's court, as he had done before in Egypt; and
her chastity was in like manner preserved, and she returned to her
husband.   And there Abraham, when the king chided him for
concealing that she was his wife, revealed his fear, and withal told
him, saying: 'She is my sister indeed, for she is my father's daughter
but not my mother's, and she is my wife':[4] and so she was indeed
both these, and withal of such beauty, that she was lovable even at
that great age.

CHAPTER XXXI

*Of Isaac, born at the time promised, and named so because of his
parents' laughter*

AFTER this Abraham, according to God's promise, had a son by
Sarah, and called him Isaac, that is, 'laughter': for his father
laughed for joy and wonder when he was first promised: and his
mother, when the three men confirmed this promise again, laughed

---

[1] Heb. xiii. 2.   [2] Gen. xviii. 18.   [3] Gen. xix. 16, 24–8.   [4] Gen. xx. 12.

also, between joy and doubt, the angel showing her that her laughter was not full of faith, though it were joyful. Hence had the child his name; for this laughter belonged not to the recording of reproach, but to the celebration of gladness, as Sarah showed when Isaac was born and called by this name; for she said: 'God has made me to laugh, and all that hear me will rejoice with me.' [1] And soon after the bondwoman and her son are cast out of the house, signifying the old covenant, as Sarah does the new (as the apostle says), and that glorious city of God, Jerusalem which is above.

CHAPTER XXXII

Abraham's faith and obedience proved in his intent to offer his son: Sarah's death

To omit many events for brevity's sake, Abraham (for a trial) was commanded to go and sacrifice his dearest son Isaac, that his true obedience might show itself to all the world in that shape, which God knew already that it bore. This now was a temptation without blame in itself (and some such there be) and was to be taken thankfully, as one of God's trials of man. And generally man's mind can never know itself well, but by putting forth itself upon trials and experimental hazards; and by their events it learns its own state, wherein, if it acknowledge God's enabling it, it is godly, and confirmed in solidity of grace, against all the bladder-like humours of vainglory. Abraham would never believe that God could take delight in sacrifices of man's flesh, though God's thundering commands are to be obeyed, not questioned. Yet is Abraham commended for having a firm faith and belief that his son Isaac should rise again after he were sacrificed. For when he would not obey his wife in casting out the bondwoman and her son, God said unto him: 'In Isaac shall thy seed be called': and adds: 'Of the bondwoman's son will I make a great nation also, because he is thy seed.' [2] How then is Isaac only called Abraham's seed, when God calleth Ishmael so likewise? The apostle expounds it in these words: 'That is, They which are the children of the flesh, are not the children of God, but the children of the promise are accounted for the seed.' [3] And thus are the sons of promise called to be Abraham's seed in Isaac, that is, gathered into the Church by Christ's free grace and mercy. This promise the father holding fast, seeing that it must be fulfilled in him whom God commanded to kill, doubted not but that that God could restore him after sacrificing, who had given him at first beyond all hope. So the scripture takes his belief to have been, and explains it. 'By faith Abraham, when he was tried, offered

[1] Gen. xxi. 6.   [2] Gen. xxi. 12, 13.   [3] Rom. ix. 7, 8.

up Isaac: and he that had received the promises offered up his only-begotten son: to whom it was said, In Isaac shall thy seed be called: accounting that God was able to raise him even from the dead': and then follows, 'from whence also he received him in a figure.' [1] In what figure but as He received His son, of whom it is said: 'Who spared not His own Son, but gave Him to die for us all'? [2] And so did Isaac carry the wood of sacrifice to the place, even as Christ carried the cross.   Lastly, seeing that Isaac was not to be slain indeed, and that his father was commanded to hold his hand, who was that ram that was offered as a full and typical sacrifice, namely, that which Abraham first of all espied entangled in the bushes by the horns? What was this but a type of Jesus Christ, crowned with thorns ere He was crucified? But mark the angel's words: 'Abraham,' says the scripture, 'lifted up his hand and took the knife to kill his son': but the angel of the Lord called unto him from heaven saying, 'Abraham!' and he answered, 'Here, Lord'; then he said: 'Lay not thy hand upon the lad, neither do thou anything unto him, for now I know thou fearest God, seeing that for My sake thou hast not spared thine only son.' 'Now I know,' that is, 'now I have made known': for God knew it ere now. And then Abraham, having offered the ram for his son Isaac, called the place 'the Lord hath seen': as it is said unto this day: 'In the mount hath the Lord appeared.' And the angel of the Lord called unto Abraham again out of heaven, saying: 'By myself have I sworn,' says the Lord, 'because thou hast done this thing and hast not spared thine only son for Me: surely I will bless thee and multiply thy seed as the stars of heaven or the sands of the sea; and thy seed shall possess the gate of his enemies: and in thy seed shall all the nations of the earth be blessed, because thou hast obeyed My voice.' This is that promise sworn unto by God concerning the calling of the Gentiles after the offering of the ram, the type of Christ. God had often promised before, but never sworn. And what is God's oath but a confirmation of His promise and a reprehension of the faithless?

After this died Sarah, being one hundred and twenty-seven years old, in the hundred and thirty-seventh year of her husband's age, for he was ten years older than she: as he showed when Isaac was first promised, saying: 'Shall I that am a hundred years old have a child? And shall Sarah that is fourscore and ten years old, bear?' And then did Abraham buy a piece of ground and buried his wife in it. And then (as Stephen says) was he settled in that land: for then began he to be a possessor, namely, after the death of his father, who was dead some two years before.

---

[1] Heb. xi. 17-19.   [2] Rom. viii. 32.

CHAPTER XXXIII

Of Rebecca, Nahor's grand-daughter, whom Isaac married

THEN Isaac, being forty years old, married Rebecca, the grand-daughter to his uncle Nahor, three years after his mother's death, his father being one hundred and forty years old. And when Abraham sent his servant into Mesopotamia to fetch her, and said unto him: 'Put thine hand under my thigh, and I will make thee swear by the Lord God of heaven and the Lord of earth that thou shalt not take my son Isaac a wife of the daughters of Canaan'—what is meant by this, but the Lord God of heaven and the Lord of earth that was to proceed of those loins? Are these small prophecies and presages of that which we see now fulfilled in Christ?

CHAPTER XXXIV

Of Abraham marrying Keturah after Sarah's death, and the meaning therefore

BUT what is meant by Abraham's marrying Keturah after Sarah's death? God defend us from suspicion of incontinency in him, being so old, and so holy and faithful. Desired he more sons, God having promised 'to make the seed of Isaac as the stars of heaven and the sands of the earth'? But if Hagar and Ishmael did signify the carnal people of the Old Testament (as the apostle teaches), why may not Keturah and her sons signify the carnal people belonging to the New Testament? They both were called Abraham's wives, and his concubines. But Sarah was never called his concubine, but his wife only; for it is thus written of Sarah's giving Hagar unto Abraham: 'Then Sarah, Abraham's wife, took Hagar the Egyptian, her maid, after Abraham had dwelt ten years in the land of Canaan, and gave her to her husband Abraham for his wife.' And of Keturah we read thus of his taking her after Sarah's death: 'Now Abraham had taken him another wife called Keturah.' Here now you hear them both called his wives; but the scripture calls them both his concubines also, saying afterwards: 'Abraham gave all his goods unto Isaac, but unto the sons of his concubines he gave gifts, and sent them away from Isaac his son (while he yet lived) eastward, into the east country.' Thus the concubines' sons have some gifts, but none of them attain the promised kingdom, neither the carnal Jews, nor the heretics, for none are heirs but Isaac: 'For they which are the children of the flesh, these are not the children of God: but the children of the promise are counted for the seed, of whom it was said, In Isaac shall thy seed be called.' [1] For I cannot see how Keturah whom he married after Sarah's death should be called his concubine but in this respect. But he

[1] Rom. ix. 8.

that will not understand these things thus, let him not slander Abraham: for what if this were appointed by God, to show those future heretics that deny second marriage in this great father of so many nations, that it is no sin to marry after the first wife be dead? Now Abraham died, being a hundred and seventy-five years old, and Isaac (whom he begat when he was a hundred) was seventy-five years of age at his death.

CHAPTER XXXV

The appointment of God concerning the two twins in Rebecca's womb

Now let us see the proceedings of the city of God after Abraham's death. So then from Isaac's birth to the sixtieth year of his age (wherein he had children) there is this one thing to be noted, that when, after he had prayed for her fruitfulness (who was barren), God had heard him, and opened her womb, and she conceived, the two twins played in her womb: wherewith she being troubled asked the Lord's pleasure, and was answered thus: 'Two nations are in thy womb, and two manner of people shall be divided out of thy bowels, and the one shall be mightier than the other, and the elder shall serve the younger.' [1]   Wherein Paul the apostle understands the great mystery of grace; in that ere they were born, and either done evil or good, the one was elected and the other rejected: and doubtless as concerning original sin, both were alike, and guilty, and as concerning actual, both alike and clear.   But my intent in this work curbs me from further discourse of this point. We have handled it in other volumes.   But that saying 'The elder shall serve the younger' all men interpret of the Jews serving the Christians; and though it seem fulfilled in Idumaea, which came of the elder, Esau or Edom (for he had two names), because it was afterward subdued by the Israelites that came of the younger, yet, notwithstanding, that prophecy must needs have a greater implication: and what is that but to be fulfilled in the Jews and the Christians?

CHAPTER XXXVI

Of a promise and blessing received by Isaac, in the manner that Abraham had received his

Now Isaac received such an instruction from God, as his father had done divers times before.   It is recorded thus: 'There was a famine in the land besides the first famine that was in Abraham's time: and Isaac went to Abimelech, king of the Philistines in Gerar. And the Lord appeared unto him and said, Go not down into

[1] Gen. xxv. 23.

Egypt, but abide in the land which I shall show thee: dwell in this land, and I will be with thee and bless thee; for to thee and thy seed will I give this land, and I will establish mine oath which I sware to Abraham thy father; and will multiply thy seed as the stars of heaven, and give all this land unto thy seed; and in thy seed shall all the nations of the earth be blessed, because thy father Abraham obeyed My voice, and kept My ordinances, My commandments, My statutes, and My laws.' Now this patriarch had no wife nor concubine more than his first, but rested content with the two sons that God sent him at one birth. And he also feared his wife's beauty amongst those strangers, and did as his father had done before him, calling her sister only, and not wife. She was indeed his kinswoman both by father and mother: but when the strangers knew that she was his wife, they let her quietly alone with him. We do not prefer him before his father though, because he had only one wife. Without all doubt his father's obedience was of the greater merit, so that for his sake God says that He will do Isaac that good that He did him. 'In thy seed shall all the nations of the world be blessed,' says He, 'because thy father Abraham obeyed My voice,' etc. Again, says He, 'I am the God of Abraham thy father, fear not: for I am with thee, and have blessed thee, and will multiply thy seed for my servant Abraham's sake.' By this He shows all those carnally minded men that think it was lust that made Abraham do as it is recorded, that he did it with no lust at all, but a chaste intent; and He teaches us besides that we ought not to compare men's worth by their single deeds, but to take all their qualities together. For a man may excel another in this or that virtue, who excels him as far in another as good. And albeit it be true that continence is better than marriage, yet the faithful married man is better than the continent infidel: for such a one is not only not to be praised for his continency, since he believes not, but rather highly to be dispraised for not believing, seeing he is continent. But to grant them both good, a married man of great faith and obedience in Jesus Christ is better than a continent man with less: but if they be equal, who makes any question that the continent man is the more excellent?

CHAPTER XXXVII

Of Esau and Jacob, and the mysteries included in them both

So Isaac's two sons, Esau and Jacob, were brought up together. Now the younger got the birthright of the elder by a bargain made for lentils and pottage which Jacob had prepared, and Esau longed for exceedingly, and so sold him his birthright for some of them, and confirmed the bargain with an oath. Here now may we learn that it is not the kind of meat, but the gluttonous desire that hurts. To proceed. Isaac grew old, and his sight failed him. He would willingly bless his elder son, and not knowing, he blessed the younger, who had counterfeited his brother's roughness of body by putting goats' skins upon his neck and hands, and so let his father feel him. Now, lest some should think that this were fraudulent deceit in Jacob, the scripture says before: 'Esau was a cunning hunter, and lived in the fields, but Jacob was a simple plain man, and kept at home.' The word 'simple' is ἄπλαστος, 'deceitless,' one without counterfeiting. What was the deceit then of this plain-dealing man in getting of this blessing? What can the guile of a guiltless, true-hearted soul be in this case, but a deep mystery of the truth? What was the blessing? 'Behold,' says he, 'the smell of my son is as the smell of a field which the Lord hath blessed; God give thee therefore of the dew of heaven and the fatness of earth and plenty of corn and wine: let the nations be thy servants, and princes bow down unto thee; be lord over thy brethren, and let thy mother's children honour thee: cursed be he that curseth thee, and blessed be he that blesseth thee.' Thus this blessing of Jacob is the preaching of Christ unto all the nations. This is the whole scope, in Isaac is the law and the prophets, and by the mouths of the Jews is Christ blessed, unknown to them because He knows not them. The odour of His name fills the world like a field, the dew of heaven is His divine doctrine, the fertile earth is the faithful Church, the plenty of corn and wine is the multitude engrafted in Christ by the sacraments of His body and blood. Him do nations serve and princes adore. He is Lord over His brethren, for his people rule over the Jews. The sons of His father, that is, Abraham's sons in the faith, do honour Him, for He is Abraham's son in the flesh. 'Cursed be he that curseth him, and blessed he be that blesseth him'—Christ I mean, our Saviour, is blessed. That is truly taught by the prophets of the wandering Jews: and is still blessed by others of them that as yet erroneously expect His coming. And now comes the elder for the blessing promised. Then is Isaac afraid, and knows he had blessed the one for the other. He wonders, and asks who he was, yet complains he not of the deceit, but having the mystery thereof revealed in his heart, he forbears fretting, and confirms the blessing. 'Who was he then,' says he, 'that hunted and took venison for me, and I have eaten of it all before thou camest, and I have blessed him, yea, and he shall be blessed?' Who would not have here expected a curse rather, but that his mind was altered by a divine inspiration? O deeds truly done, but yet all prophetical; on earth, but all by heaven; by men, but all for God! Whole volumes would not hold all the mysteries that they contain: but we must restrain ourselves. The process of the work calls us on unto other matters.

CHAPTER XXXVIII

Of Jacob's journey into Mesopotamia for a wife: his vision in the night, as he went: his return with four women, whereas he went but for one

JACOB'S parents sent him into Mesopotamia, there to get a wife. His father dismissed him with these words: 'Thou shalt take thee no wife of the daughters of Canaan: arise, get thee to Mesopotamia, to the house of Bethuel, thy mother's father, and thence take thee a wife of the daughters of Laban, thy mother's brother. My God bless thee, and increase thee, and multiply thee, that thou mayest be a multitude of people: and give the blessing of Abraham to thee and to thy seed after thee, that thou mayest inherit the land (wherein thou art a stranger) which God gave Abraham.' Here we see Jacob, the one half of Isaac's seed, severed from Esau the other half. For when it was said: 'In Isaac shall thy seed be called,' that is, the seed pertaining to God's holy city, then was Abraham's one seed (the bondwoman's son) severed from this other, as Keturah's was also to be treated afterwards. But now there was this doubt risen about Isaac's two sons, whether the blessing belong but unto one, or unto both: if unto one only, unto which of them? This was resolved when Isaac said: 'That thou mayest be a multitude of people, and God give the blessing of Abraham unto thee': namely, to Jacob. Jacob going forward into Mesopotamia, had a vision in a dream, recorded thus: 'And Jacob departed from Beersheba, and came to Haran: and he came to a certain place and tarried there all the night, because the sun was down, and he took of the stones of the place, and laid them under his head, and slept. And he dreamed, and behold a ladder, and the top of it reached up to heaven, and lo the angels of God ascended and descended by it, and the Lord stood above it and said, I am the Lord God of Abraham thy father, and the God of Isaac, fear not. The land on which thou sleepest, will I give thee and thy seed; and thy seed shall be as the dust of the earth, and thou shalt spread over the sea, to the east, the north, and the south. And lo, I am with thee and will keep thee wheresoever thou goest, and will bring thee again into this land, for I will not forsake thee, until I have performed that which I promised unto thee. And Jacob arose from his sleep, and said, Surely the Lord is in this place, and I knew it not; and he was afraid, and said, How dreadful is this place! Surely this is none other but the house of God and the gate of heaven. And he arose up and took the stone that he had laid under his head and set it up for a memorial [1] and poured oil upon the top of it, and called the name

---

[1] J. H. translates 'like a Title'; St. Augustine, following the Vulgate, *titulum*. The Septuagint has 'pillar.'—ED.

of that place the house of God.' This now was prophetical. He did not idolatrize in pouring oil on the stone, nor make it a god, nor adore it, nor sacrifice unto it; but because the name of Christ was to come of *chrisma*, that is unction, of that was this a very significant mystery. Now for the ladder, our Saviour himself mentions it in the gospel; for having said of Nathanael, 'Behold an Israelite indeed, in whom is no guile' (because Israel, that is, Jacob, saw this sight), he adds: 'Verily, verily I say unto you, Hereafter ye shall see heaven open and the angels of God ascending and descending upon the Son of Man.'[1] But to proceed. Jacob went into Mesopotamia to seek a wife; where he happened to have four women given him, of whom he begat twelve sons and one daughter, without desiring any of them lustfully, as the scripture shows, for he came but for one. And being deceived by one for another, he would not turn her away whom he had unwittingly known, lest he should seem to make her a laughing-stock; and so because the law at that time did not prohibit plurality of wives for the sake of increase, he took the other also whom he had promised to marry before; who, being barren, gave him her maid to beget her children upon, as her sister had done, who was not barren, and yet did so to have the more children. But Jacob never desired but one: nor used any but to the augmentation of his posterity, and that by law of marriage; nor would he have done this, but that his wives urged it upon him, who had lawful power of his body because he was their husband.

CHAPTER XXXIX

Jacob now called Israel. The reason of this change

OF these four women Jacob begot twelve sons and one daughter. And then came the entrance into Egypt by his son Joseph, whom his brethren envied, and sold thither, who was preferred there unto great dignity.

Jacob was also called Israel (as I said before), which name his progeny bore after him. This name the angel that wrestled with him as he returned from Mesopotamia gave him, being an evident type of Christ. For whereas Jacob prevailed against him, by his own consent, to form this mystery, is signified the passion of Christ, wherein the Jews seemed to prevail against him. And yet Jacob got a blessing from him whom he had overcome; and the changing of his name was that blessing: for Israel means 'seeing God,' which shall come to pass in the end of the world. Now the angel touched him (prevailing) upon the breadth of his thigh, and so he became lame. So the blessed and the lame was all but one

[1] John i. 47, 51.

Jacob, blessed in his faithful descendants, and lame in the unfaithful. For the breadth of his thigh is the multitude of his issue: 'of which the greatest part,' as the prophet says, 'have halted in their ways.' [1]

CHAPTER XL

Jacob's departure into Egypt with seventy-five souls; how to be taken, seeing some of them were born afterwards

IT is said there went with Jacob into Egypt seventy-five souls, counting himself and his sons, his daughter, and his grand-daughter. But if you mark well, you shall find that he had not so numerous a progeny at his entrance into Egypt. For in this number are Joseph's great-grandchildren reckoned, who could not then be with him. For Jacob was then a hundred and forty years old, and Joseph thirty-nine, who marrying (as it is recorded) but at thirty years old, how could his sons in nine years have any sons to increase this number by? Seeing, then, that Ephraim and Manasseh, Joseph's sons, had no children, being but nine years of age at this removal of Jacob's stock, how can their sons' sons, or their sons, be accounted amongst the seventy-five that went in this company unto Egypt? for there is Machir reckoned, Manasseh's son, and Gilead, Machir's son, and there is Shuthelah, Ephraim's son, reckoned, and Shuthelah's son Ezer, the grandson of Ephraim and great-grandson of Joseph. Now these could not be there, Jacob finding at his coming that Joseph's children, the fathers and grandfathers of those four last named, were but children of nine years old at that time. But this departure of Jacob thither with seventy-five souls, contains not one day, nor a year, but all the time that Joseph lived afterwards, by whose means they were placed there: of whom the scripture says: 'Joseph dwelt in Egypt, and his brethren with him, a hundred years, and Joseph saw Ephraim's children even run to the third generation': that was, until he was born who was Ephraim's grandchild. Unto him was he great-grandfather. The scripture then proceeds: 'The sons of Machir (the son of Manasseh) were brought up on Joseph's knees.' This was Gilead, Manasseh's grandchild: but the scripture speaks in the plural, as it does of Jacob's one daughter, calling her daughters, as the Latins are wont to call a man's only child if he have no more, *liberi*, 'children.' Now Joseph's felicity being so great as to see the fourth from him in descent, we may not imagine that they were all born when he was but thirty-nine years old, at which time his father came into Egypt: and this is that that deceived the ignorant, because it is written: 'These are the names of the children of Israel

[1] Ps. xviii. 45 (LXX).

which came into Egypt with Jacob their father.'[1] For this is said
because the seventy-five are reckoned with him, not that they all
entered Egypt with him. But in this transmigration and settling
in Egypt, is included all the time of Joseph's life, who was the
means of his settling here.

CHAPTER XLI

Jacob's blessing unto his son Judah

So then if we seek the fleshly descent of Christ from Abraham
first (for the good of the city of God, that is still a pilgrim upon
earth) Isaac is the next: and from Isaac, Jacob or Israel, Esau or
Edom being rejected: and from Israel, Judah (all the rest being
debarred), for from his tribe came Christ. And therefore Israel
at his death blessing his sons in Egypt, gave Judah this prophetical
blessing: 'Judah, thy brethren shall praise thee: thine hand shall
be on the neck of thine enemies: thy father's sons shall adore thee.
As a lion's whelp (Judah) shalt thou come up from the spoil, my
son. He shall lie down and sleep as a lion, or a lion's whelp.
Who shall rouse him? The sceptre shall not depart from Judah,
nor a law-giver from between his feet, until Shiloh come, and the
people be gathered unto him. He shall bind his foal unto the
vine, and his ass's foal unto the choice vine.[2] He shall wash his
robe in wine, and his garment in the blood of the grape; his eyes
shall be red with wine, and his teeth white with milk.'[3] These I
have explained against Faustus the Manichee, as far, I think, as the
prophecy requires. Christ's death is presaged in the word sleep,
as denoting not His necessity, but His power to die, as the lion
had to lie down and sleep: which power He Himself avows in
the gospel: 'I have power to lay down My life, and power to
take it again: no man taketh it from Me, but I lay it down of Myself.'[4] So the lion roared, so fulfilled what was spoken: for that
same, 'Who shall rouse him?' belongs to the resurrection; for
none could raise Him again, but He Himself that said of His body:
'Destroy this temple and in three days I will raise it up again.'[5]
Now this manner of death upon the high cross is intimated in this:
'shalt thou come up': and these words, 'He shall lie down and
sleep,' are even these: 'He bowed down His head and give up the
ghost.'[6] Or it may mean the grave wherein He slept, and from
whence none could raise Him up, as the prophets and He Himself
had raised others, but Himself raised Himself as from a sleep.
Now His robe which He washed in wine, that is, cleansed from sin

---

[1] Gen. xlvi. 8.
[2] St. Augustine reads *cilicio*.   J. H. translates 'with a rope of hair.'   The
Vulgate has *ad vitem*, and the Septuagint τῇ ἕλικι.—ED.
[3] Gen. xlix. 8–12.   [4] John x. 17, 18.   [5] John ii. 19.   [6] John xix. 30.

in His blood (intimating the sacrament of baptism, as that addition, 'And His garment in the blood of the grape,' expresses), what is it but the Church? And 'eyes being red with wine' are His spiritual sons that are drunk with her cup, as the psalmist says: 'My cup runneth over'; [1] and 'His teeth whiter than the milk,' are His nourishing words wherewith He feeds His little weaklings as with milk. This is He in whom the promises to Judah were laid up, which until they came, there never lacked kings of Israel of the stock of Judah. And unto Him shall the people be gathered. This is plainer to the sight to conceive, than the tongue to utter.

CHAPTER XLII

Of Jacob's changing his hands over the heads of Joseph's sons when he blessed them

BUT as Esau and Jacob, Isaac's two sons, prefigured the two peoples of Jews and Christians (although in the flesh, the Idumaeans, and not the Jews, came of Esau, nor the Christians from Jacob, but rather the Jews), for thus must the words, 'The elder must serve the younger,' be understood; even so it was in Joseph's two sons, the elder prefiguring the Jews, and the younger the Christians. In blessing which two, Jacob laid his right hand upon the younger, who was on his left side, and his left upon the elder, who was on his right side. This displeased their father, who told his father of it, to get him to reform the supposed mistake, and showed him which was the elder. But Jacob would not change his hands, but said: 'I know, my son, I know very well: he shall be a great people also: but his younger brother shall be greater than he, and his seed shall fill the nations.' Here are two promises now, a people to the one, and a fullness of nations to the other. What greater proof need we than this, to establish that the Israelites, and all the world besides, are contained in Abraham's seed: the first in the flesh, and the latter in the spirit?

CHAPTER XLIII

Of the times of Moses, Joshua, the Judges, the Kings, Saul the first, David the chief, both in merit and in mystical reference

JACOB and Joseph being dead, the Israelites in the other hundred and forty-four years (at the end of which they left Egypt) increased wonderfully, though the Egyptians oppressed them sore, and once killed all their male children for fear of their marvellous increase. But Moses was saved from those butchers, and brought up in the

[1] Ps. xxiii. 5.

court by the daughter of Pharaoh (the name of the Egyptian kings),
God intending great things by him; and he grew up to that worth
that he was held fit to lead the nation out of this extreme slavery, or
rather God did it by him, according to His promise to Abraham.
First, he fled into Midian, for killing an Egyptian in defence of an
Israelite: and afterwards returning full of God's Spirit, he foiled
the enchanters of Pharaoh in all their opposition; and laid the ten
great plagues upon the Egyptians, because they would not let
Israel depart—namely, the changing of the water into blood, the
frogs and lice, the flies, the murrain of cattle, the botches and sores,
the hail, the locusts, the darkness, and the death of all the first-born.
And lastly the Israelites being permitted, after all the plagues that
Egypt had groaned under, to depart, and yet being pursued afterwards by them again, passed over the Red Sea dry-foot, and left
all the host of Egypt drowned in the middle. The sea opened
before the Israelites, and shut after them, returning upon the
pursuers and overwhelming them. And then forty years after was
Israel in the deserts with Moses, and there had they the tabernacle
of the testimony, where God was served with sacrifices that were
all figures of future events; the law being now given with terror
upon Mount Sinai, for the terrible voices and thunders were full
proofs that God was there. And this was presently after their
departure from Egypt in the wilderness, and there they celebrated
their passover fifty days after, by offering of a lamb, the true type
of Christ's passing unto His Father by His passion in this world.
For *pascha*, in Hebrew, is a passing over: and so the fiftieth day
after the revelation of the New Testament, and the offering of
Christ our Passover, the Holy Spirit descended from heaven (He
whom the scriptures call the Finger of God), to renew the memory
of the first miraculous prefiguration in our hearts, because the law
in the tables is said to be written by the finger of God. Moses
being dead, Joshua ruled the people, and led them into the land
of promise, dividing it amongst them. And by these two glorious
captains were strange battles won, and they were ended with happy
success; God Himself avouching that the losers' sins and not the
winners' merits were the causes of those conquests. After these
two, the land of promise was ruled by judges, that Abraham's
seed might see the first promise fulfilled, concerning the land of
Canaan, though not as yet concerning the nations of all the earth;
for that was to be fulfilled by the coming of Christ in the flesh, and
the faith of the gospel, not the precepts of the law, which was in-
sinuated in this, that it was not Moses, who received the law, but
Joshua, whose name God also changed, that led the people into
the promised land. But in the times of the judges, as the people
offended or obeyed God, so varied their fortunes in war. On unto
the Kings. Saul was the first king of Israel, who being a reprobate
and dead in the field, and all his race rejected from ability of

succession, David was enthroned, whose son our Saviour is especially called. In him is as it were a point, from whence the people of God do flow, whose origin (as David's time was the period of its advanced youth) is drawn from Abraham unto David. For it is not out of neglect that Matthew the evangelist reckoned the descents so, that he puts fourteen generations between Abraham and David. For a man may be able to beget in his early youth, and therefore he begins his genealogies from Abraham, who upon the changing of his name was made the father of many nations. So that before him, the Church of God was in the infancy, as it were, from Noah I mean unto him; and therefore the first language, the Hebrew, was then invented. For from the end of one's infancy, man begins to speak, being previously called an infant, *a non fando*, from not speaking, which age of himself every man forgets as fully as the first age of the human race was destroyed by the deluge. For who can remember his infancy? Wherefore in this progress of the city of God, as the previous book contains the first age thereof, so let this contain the second and the third, when the yoke of the law was laid on their necks, the abundance of sin appeared, and the earthly kingdom had beginning, etc., intimated by the heifer, the goat, and the ram of three years old: in which there were not lacking some faithful persons, as the turtle-dove and the pigeon portended.

THE SEVENTEENTH BOOK OF
THE CITY OF GOD

CHAPTER I

Of the times of the prophets

THUS have we attained the understanding of God's promises made unto Abraham, and due unto Israel, his seed in the flesh, and to all the nations of earth as his seed in the spirit. How they were fulfilled the progress of the city of God in those times did manifest. Now because our last book ended at the reign of David, let us in this book proceed with the same reign, as far as is requisite. All the time, therefore, between Samuel's first prophecy and the return of Israel from seventy years' captivity in Babylon, to repair the temple (as Jeremiah had prophesied), all this is called 'the time of the prophets.' For although the patriarch Noah, in whose time the universal deluge befell, and divers others living before there were kings in Israel, for some holy and heavenly predictions of theirs may not undeservedly be called prophets (especially as we see Abraham and Moses chiefly called by those names, and more expressly than the rest), yet the days wherein Samuel began to prophesy, were called peculiarly 'the times of the prophets.' Samuel anointed Saul first, and afterwards (he being rejected) he anointed David for king, by God's express command; and from David's loins was all the blood-royal to descend during that kingdom's continuance. But if I should rehearse all that the prophets (each in his time) successively foretold of Christ during all this time that the city of God continued as its members died and new members were born, I should never make an end. First, because the scriptures, though they seem but a bare relation of the successive deeds of each king in his time, yet being considered with the assistance of God's Spirit, will prove either more, or as fully, prophecies of things to come, as histories of things past. And how laborious it were to stand upon each particular hereof, and how huge a work it would amount unto, who knows not that has any insight herein? Secondly, because the prophecies concerning Christ and His kingdom (the city of God) are so many in multitude, that the disputations arising hereof would not be contained in a far bigger volume than is necessary for my intent. So that as I will restrain my pen as much as I can from all superfluous relations in this work, so will I not omit anything that shall be really pertinent unto our purpose.

CHAPTER II

At what time God's promise concerning the land of Canaan was fulfilled, and Israel received it to dwell in and possess

WE said in the last book that God promised two things unto Abraham. One was the possession of the land of Canaan for his seed, in these words: 'Go into the land that I will shew thee, and I will make thee a great nation,' [1] etc. The other was of far more excellence, not concerning the carnal, but the spiritual seed; nor Israel only, but all the believing nations of the world: in these words: 'In thee shall all nations of the earth be blessed,' [2] etc. This we confirmed by many testimonies. Now, therefore, was Abraham's carnal seed, that is, the Israelites, in the land of promise. Now had they towns, cities, yea, and kings therein, and God's promises were performed unto them in great measure, not only those that He made by signs, or by word of mouth unto Abraham, Isaac, and Jacob, but even those also that Moses who brought them out of the Egyptian bondage or any other after him unto this instant had promised them from God. But the promise concerning the land of Canaan, that Israel should reign over it from the river of Egypt unto the great Euphrates, was neither fulfilled by Joshua, that worthy leader of them into the land of promise, who divided the whole amongst the twelve tribes, nor by any other of the judges in all the time after him: nor were there any more prophecies that it was to come, but at this instant it was expected. And by David, and his son Solomon, it was fulfilled indeed, and their kingdom enlarged as far as was promised; for these two made all those nations their servants and tributaries. Thus then was Abraham's seed in the flesh so settled in this land of Canaan by these kings, that now no part of the earthly promise was left unfulfilled; except that the Hebrews, obeying God's commandments, might continue their dominion therein, without any disturbance, and in all security and happiness of estate. But God knowing they would not do it used some temporal afflictions to exercise the few faithful therein that He had left, and by them to give warning to all His servants that the nations were afterwards to contain, in whom He was to fulfil His other promise, in the revelation of the New Testament through the incarnation of Christ.

---

[1] Gen. xii. 1, 2.   [2] Gen. xii. 3.

CHAPTER III

The prophets' three meanings: of the earthly Jerusalem, of the heavenly Jerusalem, and of both

WHEREFORE, as those prophecies spoken to Abraham, Isaac, Jacob, or any other in the times before the kings, so likewise all that the prophets spoke afterwards, had their double reference, partly to Abraham's seed in the flesh, and partly to that wherein all the nations of the earth are blessed in him, being made co-heirs with Christ in the glory and kingdom of heaven, by this new covenant. So then they concern partly the bondwoman, bringing forth unto bondage, that is, the earthly Jerusalem, which serves with her sons, and partly to the free city of God, the true Jerusalem, eternal and heavenly, whose children are pilgrims upon earth walking in the way of God's word. And there are some that belong unto both, properly to the bondwoman, and figuratively unto the freewoman. For the prophets have a triple meaning in their prophecies; some concerning the earthly Jerusalem, some the heavenly, and some both. For example, the prophet Nathan was sent to tell David of his sin, and to foretell him the evils that should ensue thereof. Now who doubts that these words concerned the temporal city, whether they were spoken publicly for the people's general good, or privately for some man's knowledge, for some temporal use in the life present? But where we read, 'Behold the days come, saith the Lord, that I will make a new covenant with the house of Israel, and the house of Judah: not according to the covenant that I made with their fathers when I took them by the hand to bring them out of the land of Egypt, which covenant they brake, although I was an husband unto them, saith the Lord: but this is the covenant that I will make with the house of Israel; After those days, saith the Lord, I will put my law in their minds, and write it in their hearts, and I will be their God, and they shall be My people' [1]— this without all doubt is a prophecy of the celestial Jerusalem, to which God Himself stands as a reward, and unto which the enjoying of Him is the perfection of good. Yet belongs it unto them both in that the earthly Jerusalem was called God's city, and His house promised to be therein, which seemed to be fulfilled in Solomon's building of that magnificent temple. These things were both relations of things acted on earth, and figures of things concerning heaven; which kind of prophecy compounded of both is of great efficacy in the canonical scriptures of the Old Testament, and does exercise the readers of scripture very laudably in seeking how the things that are spoken of Abraham's carnal seed are allegorically fulfilled in his seed by faith; insomuch that some held that there was nothing in the scriptures foretold and effected, or

[1] Jer. xxxi. 31–3.

effected without being foretold, that intimated not something belonging unto the city of God, and that ought not to be referred unto the holy pilgrims thereof upon earth.   But if this be so, we shall tie the prophets' words unto two meanings only, and exclude the third; and not only the prophets, but even all the Old Testament.   For therein must be nothing peculiar to the earthly Jerusalem, if all that is spoken or fulfilled of that have a farther reference to the heavenly Jerusalem; so that the prophets must needs speak but in two ways, either in respect of the heavenly Jerusalem, or else of both.   But as I think it a great error in some, to hold no relation of things done, in the scriptures, to be more than merely historical: so do I hold it a great boldness in them that bind all the relations of scripture unto allegorical reference; and therefore I avouch the meanings in the scriptures to be triple and not twofold only.   This I hold, yet blame I not those that can pick a good spiritual sense out of anything they read, so they do not contradict the truth of the history.   But what true believer will not say that those are vain sayings that can belong neither to divinity nor humanity?   And who will not avow that these of which we did speak, are to have a spiritual interpretation also, or leave them unto those that can interpret them in that manner?

CHAPTER IV

The change of the kingdom and priesthood of Israel. Hannah, Samuel's mother, a prophetess, and a type of the Church: what she prophesied

THE progress therefore of the city of God in the kings' time, when Saul was reproved, and David chosen in his place to possess the kingdom of Jerusalem for him and his posterity successively, signifies and prefigures that which we may not omit, namely, the future change concerning the two covenants, the old and the new; where the old kingdom and priesthood was changed by that new and eternal King and Priest Christ Jesus; for Eli being rejected, Samuel was made both the priest and the judge of God; and Saul being rejected, David was chosen for the king; and these two being thus seated signified the change that I spake of.   And Samuel's mother, Hannah, being first barren, and afterwards by God's goodness made fruitful, seems to prophesy nothing but this in her song of rejoicing, when having brought up her son she dedicated him unto God as she had vowed, saying: 'My heart rejoiceth in the Lord, my horn is exalted in the Lord: my mouth is enlarged on mine enemies, because I rejoiced in Thy salvation.   There is none holy as the Lord: there is no God like our God, nor any holy besides Thee.   Speak no more presumptuously, let no arrogancy come out of your mouth, for the Lord is a God of knowledge, and by Him are enterprises established. The bow of the mighty men hath He broken, and girded the weak with strength. They that were full are hired forth for hunger; and the hungry have passed the land: for the barren hath borne seven, and she that had many children is enfeebled. The Lord killeth, and quickeneth: bringeth down to the grave, and raiseth up. The Lord impoverisheth, and enricheth: humbleth, and exalteth. He raiseth the poor out of the dust, and lifteth the beggar from the dunghill, to set them amongst princes, and make them inherit the seat of glory. He giveth vows unto those that vow unto Him, and blesseth the years of the just: for in his own might shall no man be strong. The Lord, the holy Lord shall weaken His adversaries. Let not the wise boast of his wisdom, nor the rich in his riches, nor the mighty in his might, but let their glory be to know the Lord, and to execute His judgment and justice upon the earth. The Lord from heaven hath thundered. He shall judge the ends of the world, and shall give the power unto our kings, and shall exalt the horn of His anointed.' [1] Are these the words of a woman giving thanks for her son? Are men's minds so benighted, that they cannot discern a greater spirit herein than merely human? And if any one be moved at the events that now began to fall out in this earthly process, does he not discern and acknowledge the very true religion and city of God whose King and Founder is Jesus Christ, in the words of His Hannah, who is fitly interpreted, 'His grace'; and that it was the spirit of grace (from which the proud decline and fall, and to which the humble cleave and are advanced as this hymn says) which spake those prophetical words? If any one will say that the woman did not prophesy, but only commended and extolled God's goodness for giving her prayers a son, why then what is the meaning of this: 'The bow of the mighty hath He broken, and girded the weak with strength. They that were full are hired forth for hunger, and the hungry have passed over the land: for the barren hath borne seven, and she that had many children is enfeebled'? Had she (being barren) borne seven? She had borne but one when she said thus, nor had she seven afterward, or six either (for Samuel to make up seven), but only three sons and two daughters. Again, there being no king in Israel at that time, to what end did she conclude thus 'He shall give the power unto our kings, and exalt the horn of His anointed'? Did she not prophesy in this?

Let the Church of God therefore, that fruitful mother, that gracious city of that great King, be bold to say that which this prophetical mother spoke in her person so long before: 'My heart rejoiceth in the Lord and my horn is exalted in the Lord.' True joy, and as true exaltation, because both were in the Lord, and not in herself! 'My mouth is enlarged over mine enemies,' because

[1] 1 Sam. ii. 1-10.

God's word is not pent up even in distressing straits, nor in preachers that are taught what to speak.[1] 'I have rejoiced,' says she, 'in Thy salvation'—that was, in Christ Jesus, whom old Simeon (in the gospel) had in his arms, and knew His greatness in His infancy, saying, 'Lord, now lettest Thou Thy servant depart in peace: for mine eyes have seen Thy salvation.'[2] Let the Church then say: 'I have rejoiced in Thy salvation. There is none holy, as the Lord is; no God like to our God, for He is holy, and maketh holy; just Himself, and justifying others. None is holy besides Thee, for none is holy but from Thee.' Finally she says: 'Talk no more so exceeding proudly; let not arrogancy come out of your mouth; for the Lord is a God of knowledge, and by Him are all enterprises established.' None knows what He knows; for he that thinks himself to be something, seduces himself, and is nothing at all. This now is against the presumptuous Babylonian enemies of God's city, glorying in themselves and not in God, as also against the carnal Israelites, who (as the apostle says [3]) 'being ignorant of the righteousness of God' (that is, that which He being alone righteous, and justifying, giveth man), 'and going about to establish their own righteousness' (that is, as if they had gotten such themselves, and had none of His bestowing), 'submitted not themselves unto the righteousness of God; but thinking proudly to please God by a righteousness of their own, and none of His' (who is the God of knowledge, and the arbiter of consciences, and the discerner of all man's thoughts, which being vain, derive not from Him), 'so they fell into reprobation.' And by Him (says the said hymn) 'are all enterprises established'—and what are they but the suppression of the proud, and the advancement of the humble? These are God's intents, stated in what follows: 'The bow of the mighty hath He broken, and girded the weak with strength.' 'Their bow' means their proud opinions that then could sanctify themselves without His inspirations: and they that are 'girded with strength' are they that say in their hearts: 'Have mercy on me, O Lord, for I am weak.'[4] 'They that were full are hired out for hunger,' means they are made lesser than they were; for in their very bread, that is, the divine words, which Israel as then had alone of all the world, they savour nothing but the taste of earth. But the hungry nations that had not the law, coming to those holy words by the New Testament, have passed over the earth, and found bread because they relished a heavenly taste in those holy doctrines, and not a savour of earth. And this follows as the reason: 'For the barren hath brought forth seven, and she that had many children is enfeebled.' Here is the whole prophecy revealed to such as know the number of the Jews for what it is, to wit, the number of the Church's

---

[1] St. Augustine, *nec in praeconibus alligatis*; which may be taken literally, 'nor in preachers that are bound.'—ED.

[2] Luke ii. 29, 30.   [3] Rom. x. 3.   [4] Ps. vi. 2.

perfection; and therefore John the apostle writes unto the seven
Churches, implying in that the fullness of one only.   And so it is
figuratively spoken in Solomon: 'Wisdom hath built her an house
and hewn out her seven pillars':[1] for the city of God was barren
in all the nations, until she obtained that fruit whereby we now see
her a fruitful mother; and the earthly Jerusalem that had so many
sons we now behold to be weak and enfeebled; because all the freewoman's sons were her virtues; but now seeing she has the letter
only without the spirit, she has lost her virtue and is become weak.
'The Lord killeth and the Lord quickeneth.'   He kills her that
had so many sons; He quickens her womb that was dead before,
and has made her bring forth seven; although properly His quickening fell upon those whom He has killed, for she does, as it were,
repeat it, saying: 'He bringeth down to the grave, and raiseth up.'
For they, unto whom the apostle says: 'If ye be dead with Christ,
seek the things that are above, where Christ sitteth at the right
hand of God,' are killed unto salvation by the Lord; unto which
purpose he adds: 'Set your affections upon things above, and not
on things that are on the earth.   For ye are dead,' quoth he.   Behold here how healthfully the Lord killeth: and then he adds: 'And
your life is hid with Christ in God.'[2]   Behold here how God
quickens.   Aye, but does He bring them to the grave and back
again?   Yes, without doubt, all we that are faithful see that fulfilled
in our Head, with whom our life is hid in God.   For He that
spared not His own Son but gave Him for us all, He killed Him in
this manner, and in raising Him from death, He quickened Him
again.   And because we hear Him say in the psalm: 'Thou shalt
not leave My soul in the grave,'[3] therefore He brought Him unto
the grave and back again.   By His poverty are we enriched: for 'the
Lord makes poor and enriches,' that is nothing else but the Lord
humbles and exalts, humbling the proud and exalting the humble.
For that same passage: 'God resisteth the proud and giveth
grace unto the humble,'[4] is the text whereupon all this prophetess'
words have dependence.   Now that which follows: 'He raiseth
the poor out of the dust and lifteth the beggar from the dunghill,'
is the fittest understood of Him who became poor for us, whereas
He was rich, by His poverty (as I said) to enrich us.   For He raised
Him from the earth so soon that His flesh saw no corruption.   Nor
is what follows, 'And lifteth the beggar from the dunghill,' meant
of any but Him, for the beggar and the poor is all one.   The dunghill whence he was lifted, is the persecuting multitude of Jews,
amongst whom the apostle had been one; but afterwards, as he
says, 'That which was advantage unto me I held loss for Christ's
sake: nay, not only loss, but I judge them all dung, that I might win
Christ.'[5]   Thus, then, was this poor man raised above all the rich

[1] Prov. ix. 1.   [2] Col. iii. 1–3.   [3] Ps. xvi. 10.
          [4] Jas. iv. 6; 1 Pet. v. 5.   [5] Phil. iii. 7, 8.

men of the earth, and this beggar was lifted up from the dunghill
to sit with the princes of the people, to whom He says: 'Ye shall
sit on twelve thrones,' [1] etc., 'and to make them inherit the seat of
glory': for those mighty ones had said: 'Behold we have left all,
and followed Thee.' This vow had those mighties vowed. But
whence had they this vow but from Him 'that gives vows unto
those that vow'? Otherwise, they should be of those mighties
whose bow He has broken. 'That gives vows' (says she) 'unto
them that vow.' For none can vow any set thing unto God but he
must have it from God. It follows, 'and blesses the years of the
just,' that is, that they shall be with Him eternally, unto whom it
is written: 'Thy years shall never fail: for that they are fixed': but
here they either pass or perish; for they are gone ere they come,
bringing still their end with them. But of these two, 'He gives
vows to those that vow' and 'blesses the years of the just': the one
we perform, and the other we receive; but this latter we only receive
by God's giving, when by His strength we have been enabled to
do the former, because in his own might shall no man be strong.
'The Lord shall weaken his adversaries,' namely, such as resist
and envy His servants in fulfilling their vows. The Greek may
also signify 'His own adversaries': for he that is our adversary
when we are God's children is His adversary also, and is overcome
by us, but not by our strength: for in his own might shall no man
be strong. 'The Lord, the holy Lord, shall weaken His adversaries,' and make them be conquered by those whom He, the most
Holy, has made holy also. And therefore 'let not the wise glory
in his wisdom, the mighty in his might, nor the rich in his riches,
but let their glory be to know God, and to execute His judgments
and justice upon earth.' He is a good proficient in the knowledge
of God, that knows that God must give him the means to know
God. 'For what hast thou,' says the apostle, 'which thou hast
not received?' [2] that is, what hast thou of thine own to boast of?
Now he that does right executes judgment and justice, even he that
lives in God's obedience. And the 'end of the commandment is
charity out of a pure heart, and a good conscience and faith unfeigned.' [3] But this charity (as the apostle John says) 'is of God.' [4]
Then, to do judgment and justice, is of God. But what is 'on the
earth'? Might it not have been left out, and it have only been
said, 'to do judgment and justice'? The precept would be more
common both to men of land and sea; but lest any should think
that after this life there were a time elsewhere to do justice and
judgment in, and so to avoid the great judgment for not doing
them in the flesh, therefore, 'in the earth' is added, to confine
those acts within this life: for each man bears his earth about with
him in this world, and when he dies, bequeaths it to the great earth,
that must return it to him at the resurrection. In this earth,

[1] Matt. xix. 27, 28.   [2] 1 Cor. iv. 7.   [3] 1 Tim. i. 5.   [4] 1 John iv. 7.

therefore, in this fleshly body must we do justice and judgment to
do ourselves good hereafter when every one shall receive according
to his works done in the body, good or bad: in the body, that is, in
the time that the body lived; for if a man blaspheme in heart
though he do no hurt with any bodily member, yet shall not he be
unguilty, because though he did it not in his body, yet he did it in
the time wherein he was in the body. And so may we understand
that verse of the psalm: 'The Lord, our King, hath wrought salvation in the midst of the earth before the beginning of the world': [1]
that is, the Lord Jesus our God before the beginning (for He made
the beginning) has wrought salvation in the midst of the earth,
namely, then, when the Word became flesh, and dwelt corporally
amongst us.

But to proceed. Hannah having shown how each man ought
to glory, viz. not in himself but in God, for the reward that follows
the great judgment, proceeds thus: 'The Lord went up into
heaven, and hath thundered. He shall judge the ends of the
worlds, and shall give the power unto our kings, and exalt the
horn of His anointed.' This is the plain faith of a Christian.
'He ascended into heaven, and thence He shall come to judge the
quick and the dead.' For who is ascended, saith the apostle, 'but
He who first descended into the lower parts of the earth?' [2] He
thundered in the clouds, which He filled with His Holy Spirit in
His ascension, from which clouds He threatened Jerusalem, that
ungrateful vine, to send no rain upon it. [3] Now it is said: 'He shall
judge the ends of the world,' that is, the ends of men: for He
shall judge no real part of the earth, but only all the men thereof;
nor judges He them that are changed into good or bad in the meantime, but as every man ends, so shall he be judged. Whereupon
the scripture says: 'He that endureth unto the end shall be saved.' [4]
He therefore that does justice in the midst of the earth shall not
be condemned, when the ends of the earth are judged. 'And shall
give power unto our kings,' that is, in not condemning them by
judgment. He gives them power because they rule over the flesh
like kings, and conquer the world in Him who shed His blood for
them. 'And shall exalt the horn of His anointed.' How shall
Christ the anointed exalt the horn of His anointed? It is of Christ
that those sayings, 'The Lord went up to heaven,' etc., are all
meant, and so is this same last, of exalting the horn of His anointed.
'Christ therefore shall exalt the horn of His anointed,' that is, of
every faithful servant of His, as she said at first: 'My horn is
exalted in the Lord'; for all that have received the unction of His
grace, may well be called His anointed, all which, with their Head,
make but one Anointed. This Hannah prophesied, holy Samuel's
mother, in whom the change of ancient priesthood was figured and
now fulfilled, when the woman with many sons was enfeebled, that

[1] Ps. lxxiv. 12.   [2] Eph. iv. 9, 10.   [3] Isa. v. 6.   [4] Matt. x. 22.

the barren which brought forth seven might receive the new priesthood in Christ.

CHAPTER V

The prophet's words unto Eli the priest, signifying the taking away of Aaron's priesthood

BUT this was more plainly spoken unto Eli the priest by a man of God, whose name we read not, but his ministry proved him a prophet. Thus it is written: 'There came a man of God unto Eli, and said unto him: Thus saith the Lord, Did not I plainly appear unto the house of thy father when they were in Egypt in Pharaoh's house, and I chose him out of all the tribes of Israel to be My priest, to offer at Mine altar, to burn incense, and to wear an ephod, and I gave thy father's house all the burnt-offerings of the house of Israel, for to eat. Why then have you looked in scorn upon My sacrifices, and offerings, and honoured thy children above me, to bless the first of all the offerings of Israel in My sight? Wherefore thus saith the Lord God of Israel: I said thy house and thy father's house should walk before Me for ever: but not so now, the Lord saith; for them that honour Me, will I honour, and them that despise Me, will I despise. Behold, the days come that I will cast out thy seed, and thy father's seed, that there shall not be an old man in thine house. I will destroy every one of thine from Mine altar, that thine eyes may fail and thine heart faint, and all the remainder of thy house shall fall by the sword; and this shall be a sign unto thee, that shall befall thy two sons, Hophni and Phineas. In one day shall they both die. And I will take myself up a faithful priest that shall do according to mine heart. I will build him a sure house, and he shall walk before my Christ for ever. And the remains of thy house shall come and bow down to him for an halfpenny of silver, saying, Put me, I pray thee, in some office about the priesthood, that I may eat a morsel of bread.' [1]

We cannot say that this prophecy, plainly announcing the change of their old priesthood, was fulfilled in Samuel; for though Samuel were of that tribe that served the altar, yet was he not of the sons of Aaron, to whose offspring God tied the priesthood: and therefore in this was that change shadowed that Christ was to perform; and so it belonged to the Old Testament properly, but figuratively unto the New: being now fulfilled both in the event foretold by the prophecy, and in the history that records these words of the prophet unto Eli. For afterwards there were priests of Aaron's race, as Abiathar and Zadok in David's reign, and many more, before the time came wherein the change was to be effected by Christ. But who sees not now (if he observe it with the eye of

[1] 1 Sam. ii. 27–36.

faith) that all is fulfilled? The Jews have now no tabernacle, no
temple, no altar, nor any priest of Aaron's pedigree, as God commanded them to have; just as this prophet said: 'Thou and thy
father's house shall walk before Me for ever. Nay, not so now; for
them that honour Me, will I honour,' etc. 'By his father's house'
he means not Eli's last fathers, but Aaron's, from whom they all
descended, as these words: 'Did I not appear to thy father's house
in Egypt,' etc., do plainly prove. Who was his father in the
Egyptian bondage, and was chosen priest after their freedom, but
Aaron? Of his stock then it was here said there should be no
more priests, as we see now come to pass. Let faith be but vigilant,
and it shall discern and apprehend the truth, even whether it will
or no. 'Behold,' says he, 'the days do come, that I will cast out
thy seed,' etc. It is true: the days are come. Aaron's seed has
now no priest; and his whole offspring behold with failing eyes
and fainting hearts the sacrifice of the Christians gloriously offered
all the world through. But that which follows: 'All the remainder
of thine house shall fall by the sword,' etc., belongs properly to
the house of Eli. And the death of his sons was a sign of the
change of the priesthood of Aaron's house: and signified the death
of the priesthood, rather than the men. But the next passage
belongs to the priest that Samuel, Eli's successor, prefigured, I
mean Christ, the priest of the New Testament. 'I will take Me
up a faithful priest, that shall do all according to Mine heart: I
will build him a sure house,' etc. This house is the heavenly
Jerusalem. 'And he shall walk before mine anointed for ever':
that is, he shall converse with them, as He said before of the house
of Aaron: 'I said, thou and thine house shall walk before Me for
ever.' 'Before Mine anointed,' that is, mine anointed flesh, not
mine anointed priest, for that is Christ Himself, the Saviour. So
that his house and stock it is that shall walk before Him. It may
be meant also of the passage of the faithful from death unto life at
the end of their mortality, and the last judgment. But whereas it
is said: 'He shall do all according to Mine heart,' we may not think
that God has any heart, being the heart's maker; but it is figuratively spoken of Him, as the scripture does of other members,
'the hand of the Lord,' 'the finger of God,' etc. And lest we
should think that in this respect man bears the image of God, the
scripture gives Him wings, which man doth lack: 'Hide me under
the shadow of Thy wings,'[1] to teach men indeed, that those things
are spoken with not a literal, but a figurative reference unto that
ineffable essence. Let us proceed. 'And the remains of thine
house shall come and bow down unto him,' etc. This is not meant
of the house of Eli, but of Aaron's, of which some were remaining
until the coming of Christ, yea, and are unto this day. For that
above, 'The remainder of thy house shall fall by the sword,' re-

[1] Ps. xvii. 8.

ferred to Eli's lineage.   How then can both these sayings be true, that some should come to bow down, and yet the sword should devour all, unless they be meant of two, the first of Aaron's lineage, and the second of Eli's?   If then they be of that predestinate remnant whereof another prophet says: 'The remnant shall be saved,' [1] and the apostle: 'At this present time is there a remnant through the election of grace' [2] (which may well be understood of that remnant that the man of God speaks of here), then doubtless they believed in Christ, as many of their nation (Jews) did in the apostle's time, and some (though very few) do now, fulfilling the words of the prophet, which follow: 'And bow down to him for an halfpenny of silver.'   To whom but unto the great Priest, who is God eternal?   For in the time of Aaron's priesthood the people came not to the temple to adore or bow down to the priest.   But what is that, 'for an halfpenny of silver'?   Only the brevity of the word of faith, as the apostle says, 'The Lord will make a short account in the earth.' [3]   That silver is put for the word, the psalmist proves, saying: 'The words of the Lord are pure words, as silver, tried in the fire.' [4]   What are his words now, that bows to this God's priest, this priest who is God?   'Place me in some office about the priesthood, that I may eat a morsel of bread.   I will not have my father's honours, they are nothing; but place me anywhere in thy priesthood.   I would fain be a doorkeeper, or anything in thy service and amongst thy people,' for priesthood is put here for the people, to whom Christ the mediator is the High Priest: which people the apostle called 'an holy nation and a royal priesthood.' [5]   Some read 'sacrifice' in the former place for 'priest-hood.'   All is one.   Both signify the Christian flock.   Whereof St. Paul says: 'We are one bread, being many, and one body'; [6] and again: 'Give up your bodies a living sacrifice.' [7]   So then the addition, 'That I may eat a morsel of bread,' is a direct expression of the sacrifice, whereof the Priest Himself says: 'The bread which will give is My flesh,' [8] etc.   This is the sacrifice not after the order of Aaron, but of Melchizedek: he that reads let him under-stand.   So then these words, 'Place me in some office about thy priesthood that I may eat a morsel of bread,' are a direct and succinct confession of the faith.   This is the 'halfpenny of silver,' because it is brief, and it is God's word, that dwells in the house of the believer: for having said before that He had given Aaron's house meat of the offering of the house of Israel which were the sacrifices of the Jews in the Old Testament, therefore adds he the eating of bread in this conclusion, which is the sacrifice of the New Testament.

[1] Isa. x. 22.   [2] Rom. xi. 5.   [3] Rom. ix. 28.   [4] Ps. xii. 6.
[5] 1 Pet. ii. 9.   [6] 1 Cor. x. 17.   [7] Rom. xii. 1.   [8] John vi. 51.

CHAPTER VI

The promise of the priesthood of the Jews, and their kingdom, to stand eternally, not fulfilled in the way that other promises of that unbounded nature are

ALTHOUGH these things were then as deeply prophesied, as they now are plainly fulfilled, yet some may put this doubt. How shall we expect all the event therein presaged, when this that the Lord said, 'Thine house, and thy father's house, shall walk before Me for ever,' [1] can be in no way now effected, the priesthood being now quite abolished; nor in any way expected, because eternity is promised to the priesthood that succeeded? He that objects this conceives not that Aaron's priesthood was but a type and shadow of the other's future priesthood, and therefore that the eternity promised to the shadow was due but unto the substance only; and that the change was prophesied to avoid this supposition of the shadow's eternity. For so the kingdom of Saul, the reprobate, was a shadow of the kingdom of eternity to come, the oil wherewith he was anointed being a great and reverend mystery: which David so honoured, that when he was hid in the dark cave into which Saul came to ease himself of the burden of nature, he was afraid, and only cut off a piece of his skirt, to have a token whereby to show him how causelessly he suspected him and persecuted him. He feared, I say, in doing this much, lest he had wronged the mystery of Saul's being anointed. 'He was touched in heart,' says the scripture, 'for cutting off the skirt of his raiment.' His men that were with him persuaded him to seize the opportunity, Saul being now in his hands, and to kill him. 'The Lord keep me,' says he, 'from doing so unto my master the Lord's anointed; to lay mine hands on him, for he is the anointed of the Lord.' [2] Thus honoured he this figure, not for itself, but for the thing it shadowed. And therefore these words of Samuel unto Saul: 'The Lord had prepared thee a kingdom for ever in Israel, but now it shall not remain unto thee, because thou hast not obeyed His voice: therefore will He seek Him a man according to His heart,' [3] etc., are not to be taken as if Saul himself should have reigned for evermore, and then that his sin made God break His promise afterwards (for He knew that he would sin, when He did prepare him this kingdom), but this He prepared for a figure of that kingdom that shall remain for evermore; and therefore He adds: 'It shall not remain unto thee': it remains and ever shall, in the signification, but not unto him, for neither he nor his progeny were to reign there everlastingly.

'The Lord will seek him a man,' says He, meaning either David or the mediator, prefigured in the unction of David and his posterity. He does not say, 'He will seek,' as if He knew not where to find, but He speaks as one that seeks our understanding; for we were all known both to God the Father and His Son, the seeker of the lost sheep, and elected in Him also, before the beginning of the world. 'He will seek,' means 'He will have as His own.' He will show the world that which He Himself knows already. And so have we *acquiro* in the Latin, *quaero* with a preposition, 'to attain': and may use *quaero*, in that sense also: as *quaestus*, the substantive, for 'gains.'

CHAPTER VII

The kingdom of Israel rent: prefiguring the perpetual division between the spiritual and carnal Israel

SAUL fell again by disobedience, and Samuel told him again from God: 'Thou hast cast off the Lord and the Lord has cast off thee, that thou shalt be no more king over Israel.'[1] Now when Saul confessed this sin, and prayed for pardon, and that Samuel would go with him to entreat the Lord, 'Not I,' says Samuel, 'thou hast cast off the Lord,' etc. And Samuel turned himself to depart, and Saul held him by the lap of his coat, and it rent. Then quoth Samuel: 'The Lord hath rent the kingdom of Israel from thee this day, and hath given it unto thy neighbour who is better than thee: and Israel shall be parted into two, and shall no more be united, for He is not a man that He should repent,' etc.[2] Now he unto whom these words were said ruled Israel forty years, even as long as David, and yet was told this in the beginning of his kingdom, to show us that none of his race should reign after him, and to turn our eyes upon the line of David, whence Christ our mediator took His humanity. Now the original does not read in this place as the Latin copies do: 'The Lord shall rend the kingdom of Israel from thee this day,' but, 'The Lord hath rent the kingdom from Israel out of thine hand,' from thee, that is, from Israel, so that this man was a type of Israel, that was to lose the kingdom as soon as Christ came with the New Testament, to rule spiritually, not carnally. And these words, 'and hath given it unto thy neighbour,' show His consanguinity with Israel in the flesh, and so with Saul: and that following, 'who is better than thee,' implies not any good in Saul or Israel, but that which the psalmist says: 'Until I make thine enemies thy footstool,' whereof Israel the persecutor (whence Christ rent the kingdom) was one. Howbeit there was Israel the wheat amongst Israel the chaff also: for the apostles were thence, and Stephen, with many martyrs besides; and from their seed grew up so many churches as Saint Paul reckons, all glorifying God in his conversion. And that which follows, 'Israel shall be parted into two,' refers to the division into

[1] 1 Sam. xv. 23.   [2] 1 Sam. xv. 26–9.

Israel, Christ's friend, and Israel, Christ's foe: into Israel the freewoman and Israel the slave. For these two were first united,
Abraham accompanying with his maid until his wife's barrenness
being fruitful she cried out: 'Cast out the bondwoman and her son.'
Indeed because of Solomon's sin, we know that in his son Rehoboam's time Israel divided itself into two parts; and each had a
king, until the Chaldaeans came and subdued and overthrew all.
But what was this unto Saul? Such an event was rather to be
threatened unto David, Solomon's father. And now in these
times, the Hebrews are not divided, but dispersed all over the
world, continuing still in their error. But that division that God
threatened unto Saul, who was a type of this people, was a foreshadowing of the eternal irrevocable separation, because forthwith
there follows: 'And shall no more be united, and He will not be
changed, neither will He repent: for He is not as a man that He
should repent; a man who threatens and does not persist.' But
what God once resolves is irremovable. For where we read that
'God repented,' it portends an alteration of things out of His eternal
prescience. And likewise where we read 'He did not repent' it
portends a fixing of things as they are. So here we see the division
of Israel, perpetual and irrevocable, grounded upon this prophecy.
For they that come from thence to Christ were to do so by God's
providence, though human conceit cannot apprehend it: and their
separation is in the spirit and not according to the flesh. And
those Israelites that shall stand in Christ unto the end, shall never
partake with those that stayed with His enemies unto the end,
'but be,' as it is here said, 'eternally separate.' For the Old
Testament of Sinai, begetting in bondage, serves no other purpose
than to bear witness to the New. Otherwise, as long as Moses is
read, the veil is drawn over their hearts: and when they come to
Christ, then is it removed. For the thoughts of those that pass
from them to Him, are changed and bettered in their pass: and
thence, the felicity they seek is spiritual, no more carnal. Wherefore the great prophet Samuel before he had anointed Saul, when
he cried to the Lord for Israel, and He heard him; and when he
offered the burnt-offering (the Philistines coming against Israel,
and the Lord thundered upon them and scattered them, so that
they fell before Israel), took a stone, and placed it between the two
Mizpehs, the Old and the New, and named the place Ebenezer,
that is, 'the stone of help': saying: 'Hitherto the Lord hath
helped us.' [1] That stone is the mediation of our Saviour, by
which we come from the Old Mizpeh to the New, from the
thought of a carnal kingdom in all felicity, unto the expectation of
a crown of spiritual glory (as the New Testament teaches us), and
seeing that this is the sum and scope of all, that hitherto hath
God helped us.

[1] 1 Sam. vii. 12.

CHAPTER VIII

Promises made unto David, concerning his son, not fulfilled in
Solomon but in Christ

Now must I relate God's promises unto David, Saul's successor
(which change prefigured the spiritual and great one, which all the
scriptures have relation unto), because it concerns our purpose.
David having had continual good fortune, intended to build God
a house, namely that famous and memorable temple that Solomon
built after him. While this was in his thought, Nathan came to
him from God, to tell him what was His pleasure: wherein, when
God had said that David should not build Him a house, and
that He had not commanded Israel in all this time to build Him
any house of cedar, then He proceeds thus: 'Tell My servant
David, that thus saith the Lord: I took thee from the sheepcote, to
make thee a ruler over My people Israel: and I was with thee wheresoever thou didst walk, and have destroyed all thine enemies out of
thy sight, and given thee the glory of a mighty man upon earth.
I will appoint a place for My people Israel, and will plant him. He
shall dwell by himself, and move no more, nor shall wicked people
trouble him any more, as they have done, since I appointed judges
over Israel. And I will give thee rest from all thine enemies, and
the Lord telleth thee also that thou shalt make Him an house. It
shall be when thy days be fulfilled, and thou sleepest with thy fathers,
then will I set up thy seed after thee, even him that shall proceed
from thy body, and will prepare his kingdom. He shall build an
house for My name, and I will direct his throne for ever. I will be
his Father, and he shall be My son. If he sin I will chasten him
with the rod of men, and with the plagues of the children of men.
But My mercy will I not remove from him, as I removed it from
Saul, whom I have rejected. His house shall be faithful, and his
kingdom eternal before Me: his throne shall be established for
ever.' [1] He that holds this mighty promise fulfilled in Solomon,
is far out. For mark how it lies: 'He shall build Me an house.'
Solomon did so: and this he marks. But, 'His house shall be
faithful, and his kingdom eternal before Me': this he marks not.
Well, let him go to Solomon's house, and see the flocks of strange
idolatrous women, drawing this so wise a king into the same depth
of condemnation with them. Does he see it? Then let him
neither think God's promises false, nor His prescience ignorant of
Solomon's future perversion by idolatry. We need never doubt
here, nor idly run with the harebrained Jews to seek for some
other here in whom these may be fulfilled. We should never have
seen them fulfilled but in our Christ, the son of David in the flesh.
For they know well enough that this son of whom these promises

[1] 2 Sam. vii. 8–16.

spoke was not Solomon: but (oh, wondrous blindness of heart!) stand still expecting another to come, who is already come, in most clean and manifest appearance. There was some shadow of the thing to come in Solomon, it is true, in his erection of the temple, and that laudable peace which he had in the beginning of his reign, and in his name (for Solomon is 'a peacemaker'), but he was only in his person a shadow, but no presentation of Christ our Saviour, and therefore some things are written of him that concern our Saviour; the scripture including the prophecy of the one in the history of the other. For besides the books of the Kings and Chronicles that speak of his reign, the seventy-second psalm is entitled with his name. Wherein there are so many things impossible to be true in him, and most apparent in Christ, that it is evident that he was but the figure, not the truth itself. The bounds of Solomon's kingdom were known, yet (to omit the rest) that psalm says: 'He shall reign from sea to sea, and from the river to the land's end.' [1] This is most true of Christ. For He began His reign at the river, when John baptized and declared Him, and His disciples acknowledged Him, calling Him Lord and Master. Nor did Solomon begin his reign in his father's time (as no other of their kings did) save only to show that he was not the aim of the prophecy that said: 'It shall be when thy days are fulfilled, and thou sleepest with thy fathers, then will I set up thy seed after thee, and prepare His kingdom.' Why then shall we lay all this upon Solomon, because it is said: 'He shall build Me an house'; and not the rather understand that it is the other peacemaker that is spoken of, who is not promised to be set up before David's death (as Solomon was) but after, according to the precedent text? And though Christ was ever so long ere He came, yet clearly He came after David's death. He came at length as He was promised, and built God the Father a house, not of timber and stones, but of living souls, wherein we all rejoice. For to this house of God, that is, His faithful people, St. Paul says: 'The temple of God is holy, which temple are ye.' [2]

CHAPTER IX

A prophecy of Christ in the eighty-ninth psalm, like unto this of Nathan in the book of Kings

THE eighty-ninth psalm also, entitled, 'An instruction for himself by Ethan the Israelite,' reckons up the promises of God unto David, and there are some like those of Nathan, as this: 'I have sworn to David My servant, Thy seed will I establish for ever': and this: 'Then spakest Thou in a vision unto Thy sons, and said, I have

[1] Ps. lxxii. 8.   [2] 1 Cor. iii. 17.

laid help upon the mighty one. I have exalted one chosen out of My people. I have found David My servant; with My holy oil have I anointed him. For Mine hand shall help him, and Mine arm shall strengthen him. The enemy shall not oppress him, nor shall the wicked hurt him. But I will destroy his foes before his face, and plague them that hate him. My truth and mercy shall be with him, and in My name shall his horn be exalted. I will put his hand in the sea, and his right hand in the floods. He shall call upon Me, Thou art my Father, my God, and the rock of my salvation. I will make him My first-born, higher than the kings of the earth. My mercy will I keep unto him for ever, and My covenant shall stand fast with him. His seed shall endure for ever, and his throne as the days of heaven.'[1] All this is meant of Christ under the type of David, because from a virgin of his seed Christ took man upon Him. Then is there mention of David's sons, as in the case of Nathan's words meant properly of Solomon. He said there: 'If they sin, I will chasten them with the rod of men, and with the plagues of the sons of men' (that is, corrective afflictions), 'but My mercy will I not remove from him.' Whereupon it is said, 'Touch not Mine anointed, hurt them not.'[2] And now here in this psalm (speaking of the mystical David) he says the like: 'But if his children forsake My law, and walk not in My righteousness, etc., their transgressions will I visit with rods and their sins with scourges: yet My mercy will I not take from him.'[3] He says not 'from them,' though He speak of His sons, but 'from him,' which being well marked, is as much: for there could no sins be found in Christ, the Church's Head, worthy to be corrected of God with or without reservation of mercy, but in His members, that is, His people. Wherefore in the Kings it is called 'His sin,' and in this psalm, 'His children's,' that we might see that all things spoken of His body have some reference unto Himself. So it is when Saul persecuted His members, His faithful, He said from heaven: 'Saul, Saul, why persecutest thou Me?'[4] There follows in the said psalm: 'My covenant will I not break, nor alter the thing I have spoken. I have sworn only by My holiness that if I fail David,' that is, 'I will not fail David' (it is the scriptures' usual phrase, that He will not fail). He then adds: 'His seed shall remain for ever, and his throne shall be as the sun before Me, perfect as the moon, and as a faithful witness in heaven.'[5]

[1] Ps. lxxxix. 3, 4, 19–29.   [2] Ps. cv. 15.   [3] Ps. lxxxix. 30–3.
[4] Acts ix. 4.   [5] Ps. lxxxix. 34–7.

CHAPTER X

Of divers actions done in the earthly Jerusalem, and the kingdom, differing from God's promises, to show that the truth of His words concerned the glory of another kingdom, and another king

Now after the confirmation of all these promises, lest it should be thought that they were to be fulfilled in Solomon (as they were not), the psalm adds: 'Thou hast cast him off, and brought him to nothing.' [1] So did He indeed with Solomon's kingdom in his posterity, even unto the destruction of the earthly Jerusalem, the seat of that royalty, and unto the burning of that temple that Solomon built. But yet lest God should be thought to fail in His promise, he adds: 'Thou hast delayed Thine anointed.' This was not Solomon, nor David, if the Lord's anointed were delayed; for though all the kings that were consecrated with that mystical chrism were called anointed, from Saul their first king (for so David calls him), yet was there but one True Anointed whom all these did prefigure, who (as they thought that looked for him in David, or Solomon) was long delayed, but yet was prepared to come in the time that God had appointed. What became of the earthly Jerusalem in the meantime where He was expected to reign, the psalmist shows, saying: 'Thou hast overthrown Thy servant's covenant, profaned his crown, and cast it on the ground. Thou hast pulled down his walls, and laid his fortresses in ruin. All that pass by do spoil him. He is the scorn of his neighbours. Thou hast set up the right hand of his foes, and made his enemies glad. Thou hast turned the edge of his sword, and given him no help in battle. Thou hast dispersed his dignity, and cast his throne to the ground. Thou hast shortened the days of his reign, and covered him with shame.' [2] All this befell Jerusalem the bondwoman, wherein nevertheless some sons of the freewoman reigned in the time appointed, hoping for the heavenly Jerusalem in a true faith, being the true sons thereof in Christ. But how those things befell that kingdom, the history shows unto those that will read it.

CHAPTER XI

The substance of the people of God who were in Christ through His assumption of flesh, who alone had power to redeem the soul of man from hell

After this, the prophet begins to pray. Yet is this prayer a prophecy also: 'Lord, how long wilt Thou turn away for ever?' [3]—as

[1] Ps. lxxxix. 38.   [2] Ps. lxxxix. 39–45.   [3] Ps. lxxxix. 46.

is said elsewhere: 'How long wilt Thou turn thy face from me?'[1]
Some books read it in the passive, but it may be understood of
God's mercy also in the active. 'For ever,' that is, 'unto the end';
which end is the last times, when that nation shall believe in Christ,
before which time it is to suffer all those mysteries that he bewails.
Wherefore it follows: 'Shall Thy wrath burn like fire? O remember of what I am, my substance.'[2] Here is nothing fitter
to be understood than Jesus the substance of this people, for hence
He had His flesh.

Didst Thou create the children of men in vain? Unless there
were one son of man, of the substance of Israel, by whom a multitude should be saved, they were all created in vain indeed. For
now all the seed of man is fallen by the first man from truth to
vanity: 'Man is like to vanity (says the psalm): his days vanish like
a shadow.'[3] Yet did not God create all men in vain, for He frees
many from vanity by Christ the mediator His Son; and such as
He knows will not be freed He makes use of, to the good of the
free, and the greater eminence of the two cities. Thus is there
good reason for the creation of all reasonable creatures.

It follows: 'What man liveth that shall not see death; or shall
free his soul from the hand of hell?'[4] Why none but Christ Jesus
the substance of Israel, and the son of David; of whom the apostle
says: 'Who being raised from death, dieth no more: death hath no
more dominion over Him.'[5] For He lives and shall not see death,
'but freed His soul from the hand of hell,' because He descended
into the lower parts to loose some from the bonds of sin by that
power that the Evangelist records of His: 'I have power to lay down
My life and I have power to take it up again.'[6]

CHAPTER XII

Another verse of the former psalm, and the persons to whom it refers

THE rest of this psalm, in these words: 'Lord, where are Thy old
loving-kindnesses which Thou swarest unto David in Thy truth?
Lord, remember the rebuke of Thy servants (by many nations
that have scorned them), because they have reproached the footsteps[7] of Thine Anointed'[8]—whether it have reference to the
Israelites that expected this promise made unto David, or to the
spiritual Israelites the Christians, is a question worth deciding.

[1] Ps. xiii. 1.   [2] Ps. lxxxix. 46, 47.   [3] Ps. cxliv. 4.   [4] Ps. lxxxix. 48.
[5] Rom. vi. 9.   [6] John x. 18.
[7] J. H.'s translation here follows the Hebrew. St. Augustine follows the
Vulgate and Septuagint, which have the mistranslation 'change': on which
St. Augustine here bases his exegesis.—ED.
[8] Ps. lxxxix. 49–51.

This was written or spoken in the time of Ethan, whose name the title of the psalm bears; which was also in David's reign, so that these words: 'Lord, where are Thine old mercies which Thou swarest unto David in Thy truth?' could not then be spoken, unless the prophet is speaking in the name of those who would come a long time after, to wit, at such time as the time of David wherein those mercies were promised might seem ancient. It may further be thus understood, because many nations, that persecuted the Christians, cast in their teeth the passion of Christ, which scripture calls His 'change,' to wit, being made immortal by death.

Christ's 'change' may also in this respect be a reproach unto the Israelites, because they expected Him, and the nations alone received Him, and for this the believers of the New Testament reproach them, seeing that they continue in the Old: so that the prophet may say: 'Lord, remember the reproach of Thy servants,' because hereafter (God not forgetting to pity them) they shall believe also. But I like the former meaning better: for the words, 'Lord, remember the reproach of Thy servants,' etc., cannot be said of the enemies of Christ, to whom it is a reproach that Christ left them and came to the nations (for such Jews are no 'servants of God'): but of them only, who having endured great persecutions for the name of Christ, can remember that high kingdom promised unto David's seed, and say in desire thereof, knocking, seeking, and asking, 'Where are Thine old loving-kindnesses, Lord, which Thou swaredst unto Thy servant David? Lord, remember,' etc., 'because Thine enemies have held Thy "change" a destruction, and upbraided it in Thine anointed.'

And what is 'Lord, remember,' but 'Lord, have mercy, and for my patience give me that height which Thou swarest unto David in Thy truth'? If we make the Jews speak this, it must be those servants of God, that suffered the captivity in Babylon before Christ's coming, and knew what the 'change' of Christ was, and that there was no earthly nor transitory felicity to be expected by it, such as Solomon had for a few years, but that eternal and spiritual kingdom, which the infidel nations not then apprehending exulted over, and insulted the people of God for being captives. Thus they in their ignorance reproached those who knew the real meaning of the 'change.' And therefore that last verse of the psalm, 'Blessed be the Lord for evermore, amen, amen,' agrees fitly enough with the people of the celestial Jerusalem; place them as you please, hidden in the Old Testament before the revelation of the New, or manifested in the New when it was fully revealed. For God's blessing upon the seed of David is not to be expected only for a while, as Solomon had it, but for ever, and therefore follows 'Amen, amen.' The hope confirmed, the word is doubled.

David understanding this in the second book of Kings (whence we digressed in this psalm) says: 'Thou hast spoken of Thy servant's house for a great while to come.' [1]   And then a little after: 'Now therefore begin and bless the house of Thy servant for ever,' etc., because then he was to beget a son, by whom his posterity should descend unto Christ, in whom his house and the house of God should be one, and that eternal.   It is David's house, because of David's seed, and the same is God's house, because of His temple, built of souls and not of stones, wherein God's people may dwell for ever, in and with Him, and He for ever in and with them, He filling them, and they being full of Him; God being all in all, their reward in peace and their fortitude in war.   And whereas Nathan had said before, 'Thus saith the Lord, Shalt thou build me an house?' now David says after that, 'Thou, O Lord of hosts, the God of Israel, hast revealed unto Thy servant, saying, I will build thee an house.'   This house do we build, by living well, and the Lord by giving us power to live well, for, 'except the Lord build the house, their labour is but lost that build it.'   And at the last dedication of this house, shall the word of the Lord be fulfilled that Nathan spoke, saying: 'I will appoint a place for My people Israel, and will plant him, and he shall dwell by himself, and be no more moved, nor shall the son of iniquity trouble him any more, as from the beginning when I appointed judges over My people Israel.'

CHAPTER XIII

Whether the truth of the promised peace may be ascribed unto Solomon's time

HE that looks for this great good in this world is far wrong.   Can any one bind the fulfilling of it unto Solomon's time?   No, no, the scriptures commend it excellently as the figure of a future good.   But this one passage, 'the son of iniquity shall not trouble him any more,' dissolves this suspicion fully: adding this further, 'as from the beginning when I appointed judges over My people Israel.'   For the judges began to rule Israel before the kings, as soon as ever they had attained the land of promise: and the wicked, that is, the enemy, troubled them sore, and always was there the chance of war, yet had they longer peace in those times than ever they had in Solomon's, who reigned but forty years; for under judge Ehud they had eighty years' peace.   Solomon's time, therefore, cannot be held the fulfilling of those promises; and much less any king's besides his; for no king had that peace that he had; nor has any nation ever had a kingdom wholly free from fear of foe, because the mutability of human estate can never grant any realm an absolute security from all incursions of hostility.   The place, therefore,

[1] 2 Sam. vii. 19.

where this promised peace will dwell and abide, is eternal. It is that heavenly Jerusalem, that freewoman where the true Israel shall have their blessed abode: as the name imports, Jerusalem, that is, 'beholding God': in the desire of which reward we must live our life in godliness, through all this sorrowful pilgrimage.

CHAPTER XIV

Of David's endeavours in composing of the Psalms

GOD'S city having this progress, David reigned first in the type thereof, the terrestrial Jerusalem. Now David had great skill in songs, and loved music, not out of his private pleasure, but in his zealous faith: whereby, in the service of his (and the true) God, in diversity of harmonious and proportionate sounds, he mystically describes the concord and unity of the celestial city of God, composed of divers particulars. Almost all his prophecies are in his psalms. A hundred and fifty whereof, that which we call the book of Psalms, or the Psalter, contains. Of which, some will have them only to be David's, that bear his name over their title. Some think that only they that are entitled, each peculiarly 'a psalm of David,' are his. The rest, that are entitled 'to David,' were made by others, and fitted unto his person. But this our Saviour confutes His own self, saying, 'that David called Christ in the Spirit his Lord': citing the hundred and tenth psalm that begins thus: 'The Lord said unto my Lord, Sit thou on my right hand until I make thine enemies thy footstool.' Now this psalm is not entitled, 'of David,' but 'for David,' as many more are. But I like their opinion best that say he made all the hundred and fifty, entitling them sometimes with other names, which prefigured something relevant to the subject-matter, and leaving some others untitled at all, as God was pleased to inspire these dark mysteries and hidden varieties (all useful howsoever) into his mind. Nor is it anything against this that we read the names of some great prophets that lived after him, upon some of his psalms, as if they were made by them; for the spirit of prophecy might as well foretell him their names, as other matters that appertained to their persons, as the reign of King Josiah was revealed unto a prophet,[1] who foretold his doings and his very name above three hundred years before they came to pass.

[1] 1 Kings xiii. 2.

CHAPTER XV

Whether all things concerning Christ and His Church in the Psalms ought to be rehearsed in this work

I SEE my reader expects now, that I should deliver all the prophecies concerning Christ and His Church contained in the Psalms. But the abundance thereof, rather than the want, hinders me from explaining all the rest as I have done one, and as the cause seems to require. I should be too tedious, in reciting all, and fear to choose any part lest some should think I had omitted any that were more necessary. Again, another reason is, because the testimony we brought is to be confirmed by the whole body of the Psalter, so that though all do not affirm it yet nothing may be against it: lest we should otherwise seem to snatch out verses for our purpose, like fragments of some cento, whose intent concerns a theme far different. Now to show this testimony in every psalm of the book, we must expound the whole psalm: a stupendous task as both others and our volumes wherein we have done it expressly declare. Let him that can and will read those; and there he shall see how abundant the prophecies of David concerning Christ and of His Church were, namely concerning that celestial King, and the city which He builded.

CHAPTER XVI

Of the forty-fifth psalm: what is said openly or figuratively concerning Christ and the Church

FOR although there be some manifest prophecies, yet are they mixed with figures, putting the learned unto a great deal of labour, in making the ignorant understand them; yet some show Christ and His Church at first sight though we must at leisure expound the difficulties that we find therein. As for example Psalm xlv, 'Mine heart hath given out a good word: I dedicate my works to the King. My tongue is the pen of a ready writer: Thou art fairer than the children of men, grace is poured in Thy lips, for God hath blessed Thee for ever. Gird Thy sword upon Thy thigh, O Thou most Mighty: proceed in Thy beauty and glory: and reign prosperously because of Thy truth, Thy justice, and Thy gentleness. Thy right hand shall guide Thee wondrously. Thine arrows are sharp, Most Mighty, against the hearts of the King's enemies: the people shall fall under Thee. Thy throne, O God, is everlasting, and the sceptre of Thy kingdom a sceptre of direction. Thou lovest justice, and hatest iniquity: therefore God, even Thy God, hath anointed Thee with the oil of gladness above Thy fellows.

All Thy garments smell of myrrh, aloes, and cassia, from the ivory palaces, wherein the King's daughters had made Thee glad, in their honour.' Who is so dull that he discerns not Christ our God, in whom we believe, in this passage? Hearing Him called God, whose throne is for ever, and anointed by God, not with visible but with spiritual chrism, who is so barbarously ignorant in this immortal and universal religion, that he hears not that Christ's name comes of *chrisma*, 'unction'? Here we know Christ. Let us examine then the types. How is He fairer than the sons of men? In a beauty far more amiable than that of the body. What is His sword, His shafts, etc.? All these are figurative of His power. And how they are all so, let him that is subject to this true, just, and gentle King, inquire into at his leisure. And then behold His Church, that spiritual spouse of His, and that divine wedlock of theirs. Here it is: 'The queen stood on Thy right hand; her clothing was of gold embroidered with divers colours. Hear, O daughter, and mark, attend, and forget thy people and thy father's house. For the King taketh pleasure in thy beauty: and He is the Lord thy God. The sons of Tyre shall adore Him with gifts, the rich men of the people shall woo Him with presents. The King's daughter is all glorious within, her clothing is of wrought gold. The virgins shall be brought after her unto the King, and her kinsfolk and companions shall follow her; with joy and gladness shall they be brought, and shall enter into the King's chamber. Instead of thy fathers thou shalt have children, that thou mayest make them princes in all lands. They shall remember Thy name, O Lord, from generation to generation; therefore shall the people give thanks unto Thee, world without end.' I do not think any one so stupid as to think this to be meant of any personal woman. No, no, she is His spouse to whom it is said: 'Thy throne, O God, is everlasting; and the sceptre of Thy kingdom a sceptre of direction. Thou hast loved justice and hated iniquity, therefore the Lord thy God hath anointed Thee with the oil of gladness before Thy fellows': namely, Christ before the Christians. For they are His fellows, of whose concord out of all nations is formed this queen, as another psalm says: 'the city of the great King,' meaning the spiritual Zion. Zion is *speculatio* (discovery): for so she descries the future good that she is to receive, and thither directs she all her intentions. This is the spiritual Jerusalem, whereof we have all this while spoken. This is the foe of that devilish Babylon, high confusion; and that the foe of this. Yet is this city, by regeneration, freed from the Babylonian bondage, and passes over the worst king for the best that ever was, turning from the devil and coming home to Christ: for which it is said: 'Forget thy people and thy father's house,' etc. The Israelites were a part of this city in the flesh, but not in the faith, being foes both to this great King and to His queen.

Christ was killed by them, and came from them to those that He never saw in the flesh. And therefore our King says by the mouth of the psalmist in another place: 'Thou hast delivered Me from the contentions of the people, and made Me the head of the heathen: a people whom I have not known hath served Me: and as soon as they heard Me obeyed Me.'[1] This was the Gentiles who never saw Christ in the flesh, nor He them: yet hearing Him preached they believed so steadfastly, that He might well say: 'As soon as they heard Me, they obeyed Me': for faith comes by hearing. This people, conjoined with the true Israel, both in flesh and spirit, is that city of God, which when it was only in Israel, brought forth Christ in the flesh: for thence was the Virgin Mary, from whom Christ took our manhood upon Him. Of this city, thus says another psalm: 'Men shall call it our Mother Zion: He became man therein, the Most High hath founded her.'[2] Who was this Most High but God? So did Christ found her in His patriarchs and prophets before He took flesh in her from the Virgin Mary. Seeing, therefore, that the prophet so long ago said that of this city which now we behold come to effect: 'Instead of fathers thou shalt have children, whom thou mayest make princes over all the earth' (for so has she when whole nations and their rulers come freely to confess and profess Christ's truth for ever and ever), then without all doubt there is no figure herein, however understood, but it has direct reference unto these manifestations.

CHAPTER XVII

Of the references of the hundred and tenth psalm unto Christ's priesthood: and the twenty-second unto His passion

FOR in that psalm that styles Him a Priest (as this calls Christ a King), beginning: 'The Lord said unto my Lord, Sit Thou at My right hand until I make Thine enemies Thy footstool': we believe that Christ sits at God's right hand, but we see it not: nor that His enemies are all under His feet (which must appear in the end, and is now believed, as it shall hereafter be beheld). But with regard to the rest: 'The Lord shall send the rod of Thy power out of Sion, and be Thou ruler amidst Thine enemies'—this is so plain that naught but impudence itself can contradict it. The enemies themselves confess that the law of Christ came out of Sion, that which we call the gospel, and avouch to be the rod of His power. And that He rules in the midst of His enemies, they themselves His slaves with grudging and fruitless gnashing of teeth do really acknowledge. Furthermore: 'The Lord sware and will not repent' (which proves that what follows is eternally established),

[1] Ps. xviii. 43, 44.   [2] Ps. lxxxvii. 5.

'Thou art a priest for ever after the order of Melchizedek.' The
reason is, Aaron's priesthood and sacrifice are abolished; and now
in all the world under Christ the Priest we offer that which Melchizedek brought forth when he blessed Abraham. Who doubts
now of whom this is spoken? And unto this manifestation are the
other figures of the psalm referred, as we have declared them
peculiarly in our sermons, and in that psalm also wherein Christ
prophesies of His passion by David's mouth, saying: 'They
pierced My hands and My feet: they counted all My bones, and
stood gazing upon me.' These words are a plain description of
His posture on the cross, the nailing of His hands and feet, His
whole body stretched at length, and made a rueful gazing-stock to
the beholders. Nay, more: 'They parted My garments among
them, they cast lots upon My vesture.'[1] How this was fulfilled,
let the gospel tell you. And so in this, there are divers obscuri-
ties, which notwithstanding are all congruent with the purpose
and scope of the psalm, and are manifested in the passion; especially seeing that those things which the psalm presaged so long
before, we survey as present, being now opened unto the eyes of
the whole world. For it says a little after: 'All the ends of the
world shall remember themselves, and turn unto the Lord: all
the kindreds of the earth shall worship before Him; for the kingdom
is the Lord's, and He shall rule among the nations.'

CHAPTER XVIII

*Christ's death and resurrection prophesied in the third, sixteenth,
forty-first, and sixty-eighth psalms*

NEITHER were the psalms silent of His resurrection. For what is
that of the third psalm: 'I laid me down, and slept, and rose again,
for the Lord sustained me'?[2] Will any one say that the prophet
would record it as such a great thing, to sleep, and to rise, but that
he means by sleep, death, and by rising again, the resurrection—
things that were fit to be prophesied of Christ? This in the forty-
first psalm is most plain: for David in the person of the mediator,
discoursing (as he usually does) of things to come as if they were
already past (because they are already past in God's predestination
and prescience), says thus: 'Mine enemies speak evil of me, saying,
When shall he die, and his name perish? And if he come to see
me, he speaketh lies, and his heart heapeth up iniquity within
him; and he goeth forth and telleth it. Mine enemies whisper
together against me, and imagine how to hurt me. They have
spoken an unjust thing upon me. Shall not He that sleepeth,
arise again?'[3] This is even as much as if he had said, 'Shall not

[1] Ps. xxii. 16–18.   [2] Ps. iii. 5.   [3] Ps. xli. 5–8.

He that is dead revive again?' The previous words show how they conspired His death, and how he that came in to see Him, went out to betray Him to them. And why is not this that traitor Judas, His disciple? Now because he knew they would effect their wicked purpose, to kill Him, He, to show the futility of their malice in murdering Him that should rise again, says these words: 'Shall not He that sleepeth, arise again?' as if he had said: 'O fools, your wickedness procureth but My sleep.' But lest they should do such a villainy unpunished, He meant to repay them in full: saying: 'My friend and familiar, whom I trusted, and who ate of My bread, even he hath kicked at Me: but Thou, Lord, have mercy upon Me, raise Me up and I shall requite them.' [1] Who is he now that beholds the Jews beaten out of their land, and made vagabonds all the world over since the passion of Christ, that conceives not the scope of this prophecy? For He rose again after they had killed Him, and repaid them with temporal plagues, besides those that He reserves for the rest until the great judgment. For Christ Himself showing His betrayer to the apostles by reaching him a piece of bread remembered this verse of the psalm, and showed it fulfilled in Himself, 'he that did eat of My bread, even he hath kicked at Me.' The words, 'in whom I trusted,' agree not with the head but with the members properly; for our Saviour knew him well beforehand, when He said: 'One of you is a devil'; but Christ used to transfer the special qualities of His members unto Himself, as being their Head, body and head being all one Christ. And therefore those words of the gospel, 'I was hungry, and you gave Me to eat,' He expounded afterward thus: 'In that ye did it to one of these, ye did it unto Me.' [2] He says therefore, that He trusted in him, as the apostles trusted in Judas, when he was made an apostle. Now the Jews hope that their Christ that they hope for shall never die: and therefore they hold that the law and the prophets prefigured not ours, but one that shall be free from all touch of death, whom they do look for, and may do, long enough. And this miserable blindness makes them take that sleep and rising again (of which we now speak) in the literal sense, not for death and resurrection.

But the sixteenth psalm confounds them, thus: 'My heart is glad, and my tongue rejoiceth, my flesh also resteth in hope, for Thou wilt not leave my soul in hell, neither wilt Thou suffer Thine Holy One to see corruption.' [3] What man could say that his flesh rested in that hope that his soul should not be left in hell, but return presently to the flesh to save it from the corruption of a carcass, excepting Him only that rose again the third day? It cannot be said of David. The sixty-eighth psalm says also: 'Our God is the God that saveth us, and the issues from death are the Lord's.' [4] What can be more plain? Jesus Christ is the God

[1] Ps. xli. 9, 10.   [2] Matt. xxv. 35, 40.   [3] Ps. xvi. 9, 10.   [4] Ps. lxviii. 20.

that saves us: for Jesus is a Saviour, this being the reason why His name was given in the gospel: 'He shall save His people from their sins.' [1] And seeing that His blood was shed for the remission of sins, the issues from death ought to belong unto none but unto Him; nor could He have passage out of this life, but by death. And therefore it is said: 'Unto Him belong the issues from death'; to show that He by death should redeem the world. And this last is spoken in wonder, as if the prophet should have said: 'Such is the life of man, that the Lord Himself leaveth it not, but by death!'

CHAPTER XIX

The obstinate infidelity of the Jews declared in the sixty-ninth psalm

BUT all those testimonies and prefigurations being so miraculously come to effect could not move the Jews. Wherefore that of the sixty-ninth psalm was fulfilled in them; which speaking in the person of Christ of the events of His passion, says this also among the rest: 'They gave Me gall to eat, and when I was thirsty they gave Me vinegar to drink' [2] And this banquet which they afforded Him, He thanks them thus for: 'Let their table be a snare for them, and their prosperity their ruin; let their eyes be blinded that they see not, and bend their backs for ever,' [3] etc., which are not wishes, but prophecies of the plagues that should befall them. What wonder then if they whose eyes are blinded, discern not this; and if they whose backs are eternally bended, do keep their eyes fixed upon earth? For these words, being drawn from the literal reference to the body, do import the vices of the mind. So much for the psalms of David, to keep our intended limits. Those that read these and known them already, must needs pardon me for being so copious; and if they know that I have omitted aught that is more concerning mine object, I pray them to forbear complaints of me for it.

CHAPTER XX

David's kingdom and merit. His son Solomon. Prophecies of Christ in Solomon's books, and in books that are annexed unto them

DAVID, the son of the celestial Jerusalem, reigned in the earthly one, and was much commended in the scriptures. His piety and true humility so conquered his imperfections, that he was one of whom we might say, with him: 'Blessed are those whose iniquity is forgiven and whose sins are covered.' [4] After him, his son Solomon reigned in all his kingdom, beginning to reign (as we

---

[1] Matt. i. 21.   [2] Ps. lxix. 21; Matt. xxvii. 34.   [3] Ps. lxix. 22, 23.
[4] Ps. xxxii. 1.

said) in his father's time. He began well, but he ended badly. Prosperity, the moth of wisdom, did him more hurt than his famous and memorable wisdom itself profited him. He was a prophet, as his works, namely the Proverbs, the Canticles, and Ecclesiastes, do prove: all which are canonical. But Ecclesiasticus and the book of Wisdom were only called his, for some similitude between his style and theirs. But all the learned affirm them none of his, yet the Churches of the west hold them of great authority, and have done long. And in the book of Wisdom is a plain prophecy of Christ's passion, for his wicked murderers are brought in, saying: 'Let us circumvent the just, for He displeases us, and is contrary unto our doings, checking us for offending the law, and shaming us for our breach of discipline. He boasts Himself of the knowledge of God, and calls Himself the Son of the Lord. He is made to reprove our thoughts. It grieves us to look upon Him, for His life is not like other men's. His ways are of another fashion. He counts us triflers, and avoids our ways, as uncleanness. He commends the ends of the just, and boasts that God is His Father. Let us see then if He say true. Let us prove what end He shall have. If this just man be God's Son, He will help Him and deliver Him from the hands of His enemies. Let us examine Him with rebukes and torments, to know His meekness, and to prove His patience. Let us condemn Him unto a shameful death, for He says He shall be preserved.' Thus they imagine, all astray, for their malice has blinded them.'[1] In Ecclesiasticus also is the future faith of the Gentiles prophesied, in these words: 'Have mercy upon us, O Lord God of all, and send Thy fear amongst the nations. Lift up Thine hand upon the nations that they may see Thy power: and as Thou art sanctified in us before them, so be Thou magnified in them before us: that they may know Thee as we know Thee, that there is no god but only Thou, O Lord.'[2] This prophetical prayer we see fulfilled in Jesus Christ. But the Scriptures that are not in the Jewish canon are no good proofs against our adversaries.

But it would be a tedious dispute, and carry us far beyond our aim, if I should here stand to refer all the prophecies of Solomon's three true books that are in the Hebrew canon, unto the truth of Christ and His Church. Although what is said in the Proverbs, in the persons of the wicked: 'Let us lay wait for the just without a cause, and swallow them up alive, as they that go down into the pit; let us raze His memory from earth, and take away His rich possession'[3]—this may easily and in few words be reduced unto Christ and His Church: for such a saying has the wicked husbandman in His evangelical parable: 'This is the Heir, come let us kill Him, and take His inheritance.'[4] In the same book likewise, that

---

[1] Wisd. of Sol. ii. 12–21.   [2] Ecclus. xxxvi. 1–6.   [3] Prov. i. 11–13.
[4] Matt. xxi. 38.

which we touched at before (speaking of the barren that brought forth seven) cannot be meant except of the Church of Christ, and Himself, as those do easily apprehend that know Christ to be called the 'Wisdom of His Father.' The words are: 'Wisdom hath built her an house, and hath hewn out her seven pillars: she hath sacrificed her victims, mingled her wine in the cup, and prepared her table. She hath sent forth her maidens to cry from the heights, saying, He that is simple come hither to me; and to the weak-witted she saith, Come and eat of my bread, and drink of the wine that I have mingled.'[1] Here we see that God's Wisdom, the Co-eternal Word, built Him a house of humanity in a virgin's womb, and unto this head has annexed the Church as the members: 'hath sacrificed her victims,' that is, sacrificed the martyrs, 'and prepared the table with bread and wine' (there is the sacrifice of Melchizedek), 'hath called the simple and the weak-witted,' for 'God,' says the apostle, 'hath chosen the weakness of the world to confound the strength by.'[2] To whom notwithstanding is said as follows: 'Forsake your foolishness, that ye may live; and seek wisdom, that ye may have life.' The participation of that table is the beginning of life: for in Ecclesiastes, where it says: 'It is good for man to eat and drink,'[3] we cannot understand it better than of the participation of that table which our Melchizedekian priests instituted for us in the New Testament. For that sacrifice succeeded all the Old Testament sacrifices, that were but shadows of the future good: as we hear our Saviour speaks prophetically in the fortieth psalm, saying: 'Sacrifice and offering Thou didst not desire, but a body hast Thou perfected for me.'[4] For His body is offered and sacrificed now instead of all other offerings and sacrifices. For Ecclesiastes refers not to carnal eating and drinking in those words that he repeats so often, as that one passage shows sufficiently: 'It is better to go into the house of mourning than of feasting': and a little after: 'The heart of the wise is in the house of mourning: but the heart of fools is in the house of feasting.'[5] But there is one passage in this book, of chief note, concerning the two cities, and their two kings, Christ and the devil: 'Woe to the land whose king is a child, and whose princes eat in the morning. Blessed art thou, O land, when thy King is the Son of nobles, and thy princes eat in due time for strength and not for drunkenness.'[6] Here he calls the devil a child, for his foolishness, pride, rashness, petulance, and other vices incident to the age of boyish youths. But Christ he calls the Son of nobles, to wit, of the patriarchs of that holy and free city: for from them came His humanity. The princes of the former eat in the morning, before their hour, expecting not the true time of felicity, but hurrying unto the world's delights headlong: but they of the city of Christ await their future

---

[1] Prov. ix. 1–5.   [2] 1 Cor. i. 27.   [3] Eccles. viii. 15.   [4] Ps. xl. 6.
[5] Eccles. vii. 2, 4.   [6] Eccles. x. 16, 17.

beatitude with patience.   This is for strength: for their hopes never fail them.   'Hope,' says Saint Paul, 'maketh not ashamed.'[1]   'All they that hope in Thee,' says the psalm, 'shall not be ashamed.'[2] As for the Canticles, it is a certain spiritual and holy delight in the marriage of the King and Queen of this city, that is, Christ and the Church.   But this is all in mystical figures, to inflame us the more to search the truth and to delight the more in finding the appearance of that Bridegroom to whom it is said there: 'Truth hath loved Thee'; and of that Bride that receives this word: 'Love is in thy delights.'   I omit many things with silence, to draw the work towards an end.

CHAPTER XXI

Of the kings of Israel and Judah, after Solomon

WE find few prophecies of any of the Hebrew kings after Solomon, either of Judah or Israel, pertinent unto Christ or the Church. For so were the two parts termed into which the kingdom after Solomon's death was divided, for his sins, and in his son Rehoboam's time.   The ten tribes that Jeroboam, Solomon's servant, retained, being under Samaria, were called properly Israel (although the whole nation went under that name), and the two others, Judah and Benjamin, which remained under Jerusalem, lest David's stock should have utterly failed, were called Judah: of which tribe David was.   But Benjamin stuck unto it, because Saul (who was of that tribe) had reigned there the next before David. These two (as I say) were called Judah, and so distinguished from Israel, under which the other ten tribes remained subject: for the tribe of Levi, being the seminary of God's priests, was freed from both, and made the thirteenth tribe.   Joseph's tribe was divided into two tribes, Ephraim and Manasseh; whereas all the other tribes make but single ones apiece.   But yet the tribe of Levi was most properly under Jerusalem because of the temple wherein they served.   Upon this division, Rehoboam, King of Judah, Solomon's son, reigned in Jerusalem, and Jeroboam, King of Israel, formerly servant to Solomon, in Samaria.   And whereas Rehoboam would have made wars upon them for falling from him, the prophet forbade him from the Lord, saying that it was the Lord's doing. So then that it was no sin either in the king or people of Israel but the Lord's will, that was herein fulfilled: which being known, both parties pacified themselves, and rested; for they were only divided in rule, not in religion.

[1] Rom. v. 5.   [2] Ps. xxv. 3.

CHAPTER XXII

How Jeroboam infected his subjects with idolatry : yet did God never
fail them in prophets, nor in keeping many from that infection

BUT Jeroboam, the King of Israel, fell perversely from God (who
had truly enthroned him as He had promised), and fearing that the
huge resort of all Israel to Jerusalem (for they came to worship and
sacrifice in the temple, according to the law) might be a means to
withdraw them from him unto the line of David (their old king),
began to set up idols in his own realm, and to seduce God's people
by this damnable and impious subtlety, yet God never ceased to
reprove him for it by His prophets, and not only him but the
people also that obeyed him and his successors in it. For in
that time were the two great men of God, Elijah and his disciple
Elisha. And when Elijah said unto God: 'Lord, they have slain
Thy prophets, and digged down Thine altars, and I only am left,
and now they seek my life': he was answered, that God had yet
seven thousand in Israel that had not bowed down the knee to
Baal.[1]

CHAPTER XXIII

The state of Israel and Judah until both their captivities, which
happened in different times and circumstances. Judah united to
Israel : and lastly, both unto Rome

NOR were there lacking prophets in Judah (that lay under Jerusalem)
in all these successions of kings. God's pleasure was still to have
them ready, to send out either for prediction of events, or reformation of manners. For the kings of Judah did offend God also
(though in far less measure than Israel) and deserved punishment,
both they and their people. All their good kings have their due
commendations. But Israel had not one good king from thence, but
all were wicked, more or less. So that both these kingdoms (as it
pleased God) had their revolutions of fortune, now prosperous, now
adverse, through foreign and civil wars, as God's wrath, or mercy,
was moved: until at length, their sins provoking Him, He gave
them all into the hands of the Chaldaeans, who led most part of them
captives into Assyria, first the ten tribes of Israel, and then Judah
also, destroying Jerusalem, and that goodly temple: and that
captivity lasted seventy years. And then being freed, they repaired the ruined temple, and then (although many of them lived
in other nations) yet was the land no more divided, but one prince
only reigned in Jerusalem, and thither came all the whole land to

[1] 1 Kings xix. 10, 14,18.

sacrifice and to celebrate their feasts at the time appointed. But they were not yet secure from all the nations; for then came the Romans, and under their subjection must Christ come and find His Israel.

CHAPTER XXIV

Of the last prophets of the Jews, about the time that Christ was born

AFTER their return from Babylon (at which time they had the prophets, Haggai, Zechariah, and Malachi, and Ezra) they had no more prophets until our Saviour's birth, except another Zechariah, and Elizabeth his wife: and hard before His birth, old Simeon and Anna, a widow, and John the last of all, who was about Christ's years, and did not prophesy His coming, but announced His presence, it being before unknown. Therefore said Christ: 'The prophets and the law prophesied unto John.'[1] The prophecies of these five last we find in the gospel, where the Virgin, our Lord's mother, prophesied also before John. But these prophecies the wicked Jews reject, yet an innumerable company of them did believe, and received them. For then was Israel truly divided, as was prophesied of old by Samuel unto Saul: and foretold as never to be altered. But the reprobate Jews also have Malachi, Haggai, Zechariah, and Ezra in their canon, and they are the last books thereof: for their books are as the others full of great prophecies: otherwise they were but few that wrote worthy of canonical authority. Of these aforesaid I see I must make some abstracts to insert into this work, as far as shall concern Christ and His Church: but that I may do better in the next book.

[1] Matt. xi. 13.

THE EIGHTEENTH BOOK OF
THE CITY OF GOD

CHAPTER I

A recapitulation of the seventeen books past, concerning the two cities, continuing unto the time of Christ's birth, the Saviour of the world

IN my confutations of the perverse contemners of Christ in respect of their idols, and of the envious enemies of Christianity (which was all that I did in my first ten books), I promised to continue my discourse through the origin, progress, and limits of the two cities, God's and the world's, as far as should concern the generation of mankind. Of this my triple promise, one part, the origin of the cities, have I declared in the next four books: part of the second, the progress from Adam to the deluge, in the fifteenth book: and so from thence unto Abraham I followed the story of both cities together. But from Abraham's father's time until the kingdom of the Israelites (where I ended the sixteenth book), and from thence unto our Saviour's birth (where I ended the seventeenth) I have only carried the city of God along with my pen, whereas both the cities ran on together in the generations of mankind. This was my reason. I desired first to manifest the descent of those great and manifold promises of God, from the beginning, until He, in whom they all were bounded and were to be fulfilled, was come to be born of the Virgin, without any interposition of aught done in the worldly city during the meantime; so as to make the city of God more apparent, although all this while, until the revelation of the New Testament, it did but lie involved in figures. Now, therefore, must I begin where I left off, and bring along the earthly city, from Abraham's time unto this point where I must now leave the heavenly: that, having brought both their times to one extent, their comparison may show them both with greater clearness.

CHAPTER II

Of the kings and times of the earthly city, correspondent unto those of Abraham

MANKIND, therefore, being dispersed through all the world far and wide (differing in place, yet one in nature), and each one following his own affections, and the thing they desired being either

178

insufficient for one, or all (being not the true good), began to be divided in itself. The weaker were oppressed by the stronger: for men preferred any sort of peace and safety even to freedom, so that they were wondered at, that had rather perish than serve; for nature cries with one voice almost all the world through: 'It is better to serve the conqueror, than to be destroyed by war.' Hence it is that some are kings and some are subjects (not without God's providence, for prince and subject are unto Him alike, and both in His power). But in all those earthly dominions, wherein divided mankind followed each his temporal profit and interest, we find two more eminent than all the others, first Assyria, and then Rome. Each arose in different times and places, the one in the east long before the other, that was in the west; while the end of the first was the beginning of the latter. The other kingdoms were but as appendages unto these two. In Assyria, Ninus ruled, the second king thereof after his father Belus the first, in whose time Abraham was born.

Then was Sicyonia but a small thing, whence the great scholar Varro begins his discourse, writing of the Roman nation, and coming from the Sicyonians to the Athenians, from them to the Latins, and so to the Romans. But those were trifles in respect of the Assyrians, before Rome was built. Though the Roman Sallust says that Athens was very famous in Greece, I think indeed it was more famous than fameworthy, for he, speaking of them, says thus: 'The Athenians' exploits I think were worthy indeed but short of their report, as being enhanced by their eloquence in narrating, and so came the world to ring of Athens and the Athenians' virtues, held to be as powerful in their acts, as their wits were able to represent them in their reports.' [1] Besides, the philosophers continually abode thereabouts, and the nourishment of such studies there added much unto the fame of Athens. But as for dominion, there was none in those times so famous nor so spacious as the Assyrians; for Ninus, Belus' son, ruled there with all Asia, the world's third part in population, and half part in extent, under his dominion, out as far as the furthest limits of Libya. Only the Indians (of all the east) he had not subdued; but his wife, Semiramis, warred upon them after his death. Thus were all the viceroys of those lands at the command of the princes of Assyria. And in this Ninus' time was Abraham born in Chaldaea. But because we know the state of Greece better than that of Assyria, and the ancient writers on Rome's origin have traced it from the Greeks to the Latins, and so unto the Romans (who are indeed Latins), therefore must we here reckon the Assyrian kings only as far as need is, to show the progress of Babylon (the first Rome) together with that heavenly pilgrim on earth, the holy city of God: but for the things themselves that shall concern this work, and the

[1] *Catil.* 8.

comparison of both cities, them we must rather fetch from the
Greeks and Latins, where Rome (the second Babylon) is seated.

At Abraham's birth, therefore, Ninus was the second king of
Assyria, and Europs of Sicyonia, for Belus was the first of the one,
and Aegialeus of the other: but when Abraham left Chaldaea upon
God's promise of that universal blessing to the nations in his seed,
the fourth king ruled in Assyria, and the fifth in Sicyonia; for
Ninus, the son of Ninus, reigned there after his mother Semiramis,
whom they say he slew because she bore an incestuous lust towards
him. Some think she built Babylon. Indeed she might have
repaired it; but when and by whom it was built our sixteenth book
declares. Now this son of Ninus and Semiramis, that succeeded
his mother, some call Ninus and some Ninius by a derivative from
his father's name. And now was Sicyonia governed by Telexion,
who had so happy a reign that when he was dead, they adored him
as a god with sacrifices and plays, whereof it is said they were the
first inventors.

CHAPTER III

*What kings reigned in Assyria and Sicyonia in the hundredth year of
Abraham's age, when Isaac was born according to the promise: or
at the birth of Jacob and Esau*

IN his time also did Sarah, being old, barren, and past hope of
children, bring forth Isaac unto Abraham, according to the promise
of God. And then reigned Aralius, the fifth king of Assyria. And
Isaac, being threescore years of age, had Esau and Jacob both at one
birth of Rebecca, Abraham his father being yet living and of the
age of one hundred and sixty years, who lived fifteen years longer
and then died; Xerxes the elder, called also Balaeus, reigning the
seventh king of Assyria, and Thuriachus (called by some Thurimachus) the seventh of Sicyon. Now the kingdom of the Argives
began with the time of these sons of Isaac; and Inachus was the
first king there. But this we may not forget out of Varro, that the
Sicyonians used to offer sacrifices at the tomb of the seventh king
Thurimachus. But Armamitres being the eighth king of Assyria,
and Leucippus of Sicyonia, and Inachus the first king of Argos,
God promised the land of Canaan unto Isaac for his seed, as he
had done unto Abraham before, and the universal blessing of the
nations therein also. And this promise was thirdly made unto
Jacob, afterwards called Israel, Abraham's grandchild, in the time
of Belocus the ninth Assyrian monarch, and Phoroneus, Inachus'
son, the second king of the Argives, Leucippus still reigning in
Sicyon. In this Phoroneus' time, Greece grew famous for divers
good laws and ordinances: but yet his brother Phegous after his

death built a temple over his tomb, and made him to be worshipped
as a god, and caused oxen to be sacrificed unto him, holding him
worthy of this honour, I think, because in that part of the kingdom
which he held (for their father divided the whole between them) he
set up oratories to worship the gods in, and taught the true course
and observation of months and years: which the rude people ad-
miring in him, thought that at his death he was become a god, or
else would have it to be thought so.   For so they say that Io was
the daughter of Inachus, she that afterwards was called Isis, and
honoured for a great goddess in Egypt; though some write that she
came out of Ethiopia to be queen of Egypt, and because she was
mighty and gracious in her reign, and taught her subjects many
good arts, they gave her this honour after her death, and that with
such diligent respect, that it was death to say she had ever been
mortal.

CHAPTER IV

Of the times of Jacob and his son Joseph

BALEUS being the tenth king of Assyria, and Mesappus otherwise
called Cephisus (if both these names were by several authors used
for one man) being the ninth of Sicyonia, and Apis the third of
Argos, Isaac died, being a hundred and eighty years old, leaving
his twin sons at the age of a hundred and twenty years: the younger,
Jacob, belonging to God's city, and the elder to the world's.   The
younger had twelve sons, one of whom called Joseph his brothers
sold unto merchants going into Egypt, in their grandfather Isaac's
time.   Joseph lived (by his humility) in great favour and advancement with Pharaoh, being now thirty years old.   For he interpreted the king's dreams, foretelling the seven plenteous years, and
the seven dear ones, which would consume the plenty of the other:
and for this the king set him at liberty (being before imprisoned
for his true chastity, in not consenting to his lustful mistress, but
rather fleeing and leaving his raiment with her, who hereupon
falsely complained to her husband of him), and afterwards he made
him viceroy of all Egypt.   And in the second year of scarcity
Jacob came into Egypt with his son, being one hundred and thirty
years old, as he told the king.   Joseph was thirty-nine when the
king advanced him thus, the seven plentiful years and the two
dear ones being added to his age.

CHAPTER V

Of Apis, the Argive king, called Serapis in Egypt, and there adored as a deity

AT this time did Apis, king of Argos, sail into Egypt, and dying there, was called Serapis, the greatest god of Egypt. The reason for changing his name, says Varro, is this. A dead man's coffin (which all do now call σαρκοφάγος), is σορός also in Greek. So at first they worshipped at his coffin and tomb, ere his temple was built, calling him at first Sorosapis or Sorapis: and afterwards (by change of a letter, as is ordinary) Serapis. And they made a law, that whosoever should say he had been a man should die the death. And because in all the temples of Isis and Serapis there was an image with the finger laid upon the mouth, as commanding silence, this was (says Varro) to show them that they must not say that those two were ever mortal. And the ox which Egypt (being wondrously and stupidly seduced) nourished in all pleasures and fatness unto the honour of Serapis, because they did not worship him in a coffin, was not called Serapis but Apis: which ox being dead, and they seeking him and finding another flecked of colour just as he was, here they thought was something miraculous and divinely provided. It was not such a hard matter indeed for the devils to imprint the imagination of such a shape in any cow's phantasy at her time of conception, so as to subvert the souls of men; and the cow's imagination would surely model the conception into such a form, as Jacob's ewes did and his she-goats, by seeing the particoloured sticks; for that which man can do with true colours, the devil can do with apparitions, and so very easily frame such shapes.

CHAPTER VI

The kings of Argos and Assyria, at the time of Jacob's death

APIS the king of Argos (not of Egypt) died in Egypt. Argus his son succeeded him in his kingdom, and from him came the name of the Argives. For neither the city nor the country bare any such name before his time. He reigning in Argos, and Eratus in Sicyonia, Balaeus ruling still in Assyria, Jacob died in Egypt, being one hundred and forty-seven years in age, having blessed his sons and grandsons at his death, and prophesied clearly of Christ, saying in the blessing of Judah: 'The sceptre shall not depart from Judah, nor the law-giver from between his feet, until that come which is promised him: and He shall be the nations' expectation.'[1]

[1] Gen. xlix. 10.

Now in Argus' time Greece began to know husbandry and tillage, fetching seeds from other countries. For Argus after his death was counted a god, and honoured with temples and sacrifices. Which honour a private man, one Homogyrus, who was slain by lightning, had before him, because he was the first that ever yoked oxen to the plough.

CHAPTER VII

In what king's time Joseph died in Egypt

In Mamitus' time, the twelfth Assyrian king, and Plemnaeus', the eleventh king of Sicyonia (Argus being still alive in Argos), Joseph died in Egypt, being a hundred and ten years old. After the death of him, God's people remaining in Egypt increased wonderfully for a hundred and forty-five years together, until all that knew Joseph were dead. And then because their great increase was so envied, and their freedom suspected, a great and heavy bondage was laid upon them, in the which nevertheless they grew up still, for all that they were so persecuted and kept under. And at this time the same princes ruled in Assyria and Greece, whom we named before.

CHAPTER VIII

What kings lived when Moses was born: and what gods the pagans had as then

In Saphrus' time, the fourteenth Assyrian king, Orthopolus being then the twelfth of Sicyon, and Criasus the fifth of Argos, Moses was born in Egypt, who led the people of God out of their slavery, wherein God had exercised their patience during His pleasure. In the aforesaid king's time Prometheus (as some hold) lived, who was said to make men of earth, because he taught them wisdom so excellently well, yet are there no wise men recorded to have lived in his time. His brother Atlas indeed is said to have been a great astronomer, whence the fable arose of his supporting heaven upon his shoulders; yet there is a huge mountain of that name, whose height may seem to an ignorant eye to hold up the heavens. And now began Greece to fill the stories with fables, but from the first unto Cecrops' time (the king of Athens) in whose reign Athens got that name, and Moses led Israel out of Egypt, some of the dead kings were recorded for gods by the folly and customary superstition of the Greeks. Such were Melantonice, Crias' wife; Phorbas their son, the sixth king of Argos; and Jasus the son of

Triopas the seventh king; and Sthelenas or Stheleneus, or Sthenelus (for he is diversely written), the ninth. And in these times also lived Mercury, Atlas' grandchild, born of Maia his daughter. His story is familiar. He was a perfect artist in many good inventions, and therefore was believed (at least men desired he should be believed) to be a deity. Hercules lived after this, yet was he about those times of the Argives. Some think he lived before Mercury, but I think they are deceived. But howsoever, the gravest historians that have written of them both to be men, and that for the good that they did mankind in matters pertaining to the more convenient conduct of human life, they were rewarded with those divine honours. But Minerva was long before this, for she (they say) appeared in Ogyges' time, at Lake Triton, in a virgin's shape, whereupon she was called Tritonia, a woman indeed of many good inventions, and the likelier to be held a goddess, because her origin was unknown, for the story that she sprang from Jove's brain is absolutely poetic, and in no way real history. There was indeed a great deluge in Ogyges' time, not so great as that wherein all perished save those in the ark (for that neither Greek authors nor Latin do mention), but greater than that which befell in Deucalion's days. But of this Ogyges' time the writers have no certainty, for where Varro begins his book, I showed before: and indeed he traces the Romans' origin no further than the deluge that befell in Ogyges' time. But our chroniclers, Eusebius first, and then Jerome, following other more ancient authors herein, record Ogyges' deluge to have fallen in the time of Phoroneus, the second king of Argos, three hundred years after the time aforesaid. But however, this at least is certain, that in Cecrops' time (who was either the builder or restorer of Athens) Minerva was there adored with divine honours.

CHAPTER IX

The time when Athens was built, and the reason that Varro gives for the name

OF the name of Athens (coming from 'Aθήνη, which is Minerva) Varro gives this reason. An olive-tree grew suddenly up in one place, and a fountain burst out as suddenly in another. These prodigies drew the king to Delphos, to know the oracle's mind, which answered him that the olive-tree signified Minerva, and the fountain Neptune, and that the citizens might after which of these they pleased name their city. Hereupon Cecrops gathered all the people of both sexes together (for then it was a custom in that place to call the women unto consultations also) to give their voices in this election, the men being for Neptune, and the women for

Minerva; and the women being more, won the day for Minerva.
At this Neptune, being angry, overflowed all the Athenians' lands
(for the devils may draw the waters which way they will); and to
appease him the Athenian women had a triple penalty set on their
heads. First, they must never hereafter have a vote in council.
Second, that they should never hereafter be called Athenians; and
third, that they should never leave their name unto their children.
Thus this ancient and goodly city, the only mother of arts and
learned inventions, the glory and lustre of Greece, by a scoff of
the devil's, in a contention of their gods a male and female, and
by a feminine victory obtained by women, was styled Athens
after the female's name that was victor, Minerva: and yet being
plagued by him that was conquered was compelled to punish the
means of the victor's victory, and showed that it feared Neptune's
waters worse than Minerva's arms. For Minerva herself was
punished in those her women champions; nor did she assist those
that advanced her, so much as to the bare reservation of her name
unto themselves, besides the loss of their votes in elections, and
the leaving of their names unto their sons. Thus they lost the
name of this goddess, whom they had made victorious over a male
god: whereof you see what I might say, but that mine intent carries
my pen on unto another purpose.

CHAPTER X

*Varro's relation of the original of the word Areopagus: and of
Deucalion's deluge*

BUT Varro will believe no fables that make against their gods, lest
he should disparage their majesty: and therefore he will not derive
that Areopagus (the place where St. Paul disputed with the
Athenians, and whence the judges of the city had their names)
from the fact that Mars (in Greek, "Άρης) being accused of homicide
was tried by twelve gods in that court, and acquitted by six
(for the number being equal on both sides the absolution was wont
to overpoise the condemnation). But this, though it be the
common opinion, he rejects, and endeavours to defend another
cause of this name, that the Athenians should not offer to derive
Areopagus from "Άρης and πάγος, 'field'; for this were to injure the
gods by imputing broils and contentions unto them; and therefore
he affirms this, and the goddesses' contention about the golden
apple, to be both alike false, though the stage may present them to
the gods as true, and the gods take pleasure in them, be they true or
false. This Varro will not believe, for fear of disgracing the gods
in it. And yet he tells a tale concerning the name of Athens about
the contention between Neptune and Minerva as frivolous as this,
and makes that the likeliest origin of the city's name. When they

two were contending by prodigies, Apollo durst not be judge between them, but as Paris was called to decide the strife between the three goddesses, so he was made an umpire in this wrangling of these two, where Minerva conquered by her supporters and yet was conquered in the punishment of her supporters, and getting the name of Athens to herself could not leave the name of Athenians unto them. In these times, as Varro says, Cranaus, Cecrops' successor, reigned at Athens, or Cecrops himself, as our Eusebius and Jerome do affirm: and then befell that great inundation called the flood of Deucalion, because it was most extreme in his kingdom. But it came not near Egypt nor the confines thereof.

CHAPTER XI

About whose times Moses brought Israel out of Egypt. Of Joshua: in whose times he died

IN the latter end of Cecrops' reign at Athens came Moses with Israel out of Egypt, Ascatades, Marathus, and Triopas being kings of Assyria, Sicyon, and Argos. To Sinai did Moses lead them, and there received the law from above called the Old Testament, containing all terrestrial promises; the New one, containing the spiritual, being about to come with Christ our Saviour. For this order was fittest, as it is in every man, as St. Paul says, that the natural should be first, and the spiritual afterwards, because (as he said truly) 'the first man is of earth, earthy, and the second man is of heaven, heavenly.'[1] Forty years did Moses rule this people in the desert, dying a hundred and twenty years old, having prophesied Christ by innumerable types of carnal observances in the tabernacle, the priesthood, the sacrifices, and other mystical commands. Unto Moses was Joshua the successor, and he led the people into the land of promise, and by God's conduct expelled all the pagans that swarmed in it; and having ruled seven-and-twenty years, he died in the time that Amintas ruled as eighteenth king of Assyria; Corax, the sixteenth of Sicyonia; Danaus, the tenth of Argos; and Ericthonius, the fourth of Athens.

CHAPTER XII

The false gods adored by those Greek princes which lived between Israel's freedom and Joshua's death

BETWIXT the departure of Israel out of Egypt and the death of Joshua, who led them into the land of promise, the Greek princes ordained many sorts of sacrifices to their false gods, as solemn

[1] 1 Cor. xv. 46, 47.

memorials of the deluge and the freedom of mankind from it, and the miserable time that they had in it, and upon it, now being driven up to the hills, and soon after coming down again into the plains. For this they say the Luperci running up and down the holy street portray, namely, how the men ran up to the mountains in that great inundation, and when it ceased, came all down again into the plains. And at this time they say that Dionysus (otherwise called Father Liber, and made a god after his decease) did first show the planting of the vine in Attica. And then were there musical plays dedicated to Apollo of Delphos, to appease him whom they thought had afflicted all Greece with barrenness, because they defended not his temple which Danaus, in his invasion, burned: and the oracle itself charged them to ordain those plays. Ericthonius was the first that presented them in Attica, both unto him and Minerva, where he that conquered had a reward of oil, which Minerva they say discovered, as Liber had found out the wine. And in these times did Xanthus, King of Crete, carry off Europa, and begat Rhadamanthus, Sarpedon, and Minos, who are commonly reported to be the sons of Jove and Europa. But the pagans regard as the truth of history what we have said of the king of Crete: and this story about Jove that falls from every poet's pen, and is on every player's lips, they do account as a fable, to prove their deities wholly delighted in beastly untruths. And now was Hercules famous at Tyre; not he that we spoke of before (for the more secret histories say there were many Hercules, and many Father Libers). And this Hercules they make famous for twelve sundry rare exploits (not counting the death of the African Antaeus amongst them, for that belongs to the other Hercules). And this same Hercules do they make to burn himself upon Mount Oeta, his virtue whereby he had subdued so many monsters failing him now in the patient endurance of his own pains. And at this time Busiris the son of Neptune and Libya, daughter to Epaphus, and king, or rather tyrant, of Egypt, used to murder strangers and offer them to his gods. Oh, but we must never think Neptune could have committed this adultery or the gods will be incriminated; but let the poets have this scope to fill the stage and please the gods withal! It is said that Vulcan and Minerva were parents to this Ericthonius, in the end of whose reign Joshua died. But because they hold Minerva a virgin, therefore (say they) in their striving together, Vulcan projected his seed upon the earth, and thence came this king as his name shows: for ἔρις is 'strife,' and χθών is 'earth': which joined do make Ericthonius. But indeed the best learned of them do reject this filthiness from their gods, and say that the fable arose hereupon, that in the temple of Vulcan and Minerva, which both shared at Athens, there was a little child found with a dragon wound about him, which was a sign that he should prove a famous man; and because of this temple's knowing

no other parents that he had, they called him the son of Vulcan
and Minerva. Yet that fable does manifest his name better than
this history. But what is that to us, seeing that this is written in
true books to instruct religious men, and that is presented on
public stages to delight the unclean devils, whom notwithstanding
their truest writers honour as gods, with those religious men? And
though they may deny this of their gods, yet can they not acquit
them of all crime, in desiring the presenting of those filthinesses,
and in taking pleasure to behold those things filthily acted, which
wisdom seems to say might better be denied. For even if the
fables belie them, yet if they do delight to hear those lies of themselves, this makes their guilt most true.

CHAPTER XIII

*What fictions got footing in the nations when the judges began
first to rule Israel*

JOSHUA being dead, Israel came to be ruled by judges: and in those
times they prospered, or suffered, according to the goodness of
God's mercies, or the defeat of their sins. And now the fiction
of Triptolemus was invented, who by Ceres' appointment flew all
over the world with a yoke of dragons, and taught the use of corn;
and another fiction of the Minotaur, shut in the labyrinth, a place
which none that entered could ever get out of: of the Centaurs
also, half men and half horses: of Cerberus, the three-headed dog
of hell: of Phryxus and Helle, who flew away on the back of a ram:
of the Gorgon, whose hairs were snakes, and who turned all that
beheld her into stones: of Bellerophon, and his winged horse
Pegasus: of Amphion, and his stone-moving music on the harp:
of Oedipus, and his answer to the monster Sphinx's riddle, making
her break her own neck by casting herself headlong: of Antaeus,
earth's son, killed by Hercules in the air, for that he never smote
him to the ground but he arose up as strong again as he was when
he fell: and others more than I perhaps have omitted. Those
fables, unto the Trojan war, where Varro ended his second book
De Gente Romanorum, were by men's inventions so skilfully
drawn from the truth of history that their gods were in no way by
them disgraced. But as for those that feigned that Jupiter stole
Ganymede, that goodly boy, for his lustful use (a villainy done by
Tantalus and ascribed unto Jove), or that he came down to lie with
Danae in a shower of gold (the woman being tempted by gold
unto dishonesty); and all this being either done or devised in those
times, or done by others, and feigned to be Jove's; it cannot be
said how mischievous those fable-forgers presumed the hearts of
all mankind to be, that they would bear with such ungodly slanders

of their gods: which they did notwithstanding, and gave them gracious acceptance, whereas had they truly honoured Jupiter, they would severely have punished his slanderers. But now they are so far from checking them, that they fear their gods' anger if they do not nourish them, and present their fictions unto a numerous audience. About this time Latona bore Apollo, not that god of the oracles aforesaid, but him that kept the herds of King Admetus with Hercules: yet was he afterwards held a god, and counted one and the same with the other. And then did Father Liber make war in India, leading a crew of women about with him in his army, called Bacchae, being more famous for their madness than their virtue. Some write that this Liber was conquered and imprisoned: some, that Perseus slew him in the field, mentioning his place of burial also: and yet were those wicked sacrilegious sacrifices called the Bacchanals appointed by the unclean devils unto him, as unto a god. But the senate of Rome at length (after long use of them) saw the barbarous filthiness of these sacrifices, and expelled them from the city. And in this time Perseus and his wife Andromeda being dead were verily believed to be taken up into heaven, and thereupon the world was neither ashamed nor afraid to give their names unto two goodly constellations, and to form their images therein.

CHAPTER XIV

Of the theological poets

ABOUT that time lived poets, who were called theologians, versifying of their men-made gods, or of the world's elements (the true God's handiwork) or the principalities and powers (whom God's will, and not their merit, had so advanced). Of these as of gods did they make their poems. If their fables contained anything that concerned the true God, it was so intermingled with the rest, that He was neither to be discerned from their false gods thereby, nor could they give Him that complete service that was His only due, but must needs worship the creatures as gods, with God the Creator, and could not abstain from disgracing these same gods with obscene fables. Such poets were Orpheus, Musaeus, and Linus. But those were only the gods' servants, not made gods themselves; though Orpheus, I know not by what means, has been placed over the infernal sacrifices or rather sacrileges in the city of the devil. The wife of Athamas also, Ino, cast herself headlong into the sea with her child Melicertes, and yet both were reputed gods; as others of those times were also, as Castor and Pollux. Ino was called by the Greeks Leucothea, and by the Latins Matuta, and held a goddess by both.

CHAPTER XV

The ruin of the Argive kingdom: Picus, Saturn's son, succeeding him in Laurentum

THEN was the Argive kingdom translated to Mycenae, where Agamemnon ruled: and then arose the kingdom of the Laurentines, in which Picus, Saturn's son, was the first successor, Deborah, a woman, being judge of the Jews. God's Spirit indeed judged in her, for she was a prophetess (her prophecy is too obscure to refer unto Christ without a long discourse). And now had the Laurentines a kingdom in Italy, from whence (after their descent from Greece) the Romans' pedigree is drawn. Still the Assyrian monarchy kept up: Lampares, the twentieth king, ruling there now, when Picus began his kingdom in Laurentum. His father Saturn (the pagans say) was no man. Let the pagans look to that. Some of them have written that he was, and that he was king here before his son Picus. Ask these verses of Virgil, and they will tell you:

> Is genus indocile ac dispersum montibus altis
> Composuit, legesque dedit, Latiumque vocari
> Maluit, his quoniam latuisset tutus in oris.
> Aurea, quae perhibent, illo sub rege fuere
> Saecula.[1]

> The undocile sort on mountains high dispersed
> He did compose, and gave them laws, and first
> Would call it Latium, when he latent lay,
> In whose reign was the golden age, men say.

But these they say are poetical fictions. Sterces was Saturn's father, he that invented manuring of the ground with dung, which from him was called *stercus*. Some say they called him Stercutius. Well, howsoever he got the name of Saturn, he was the same Sterces or Stercutius whom they deified for his husbandry. And Picus, his son, was deified after him also, a cunning soothsayer, and a great soldier as they report him to be. He begat Faunus, the second king of Laurentum, and he too was made a god. All these men were deified before the Trojan war.

CHAPTER XVI

How Diomedes was deified after the destruction of Troy, and his companions said to be turned into birds

TROY (whose destruction the excellent wits of elder times have left recorded unto all memory, as well as its greatness) being now destroyed in the reign of Latinus, son to Faunus (and from

---

[1] *Aen.* viii. 321–5.

him came the Latin name, instead of the Laurentine): the Grecian victors, returning each one to his home, were sore afflicted on all sides, and destroyed in great numbers; yet some of them became gods. For Diomedes was made one, who never returned home, and his companions they say became birds. This now they have history for, not poetry only, yet neither could his new godhead nor his entreaty of Jove prevail so much as to turn his fellows unto men again. It is said also that he has a temple in the island of Diomedea, not far from Mount Garganus in Apulia, where these birds continually fly about the temple, and dwell there with such wonderful obedience, that they will wash the temple with water which they bring in their beaks; and when any Grecian comes thither, or any of a Greek race, they are quiet, and will be gentle with them; but if any one else come they will fly at his face with great fury, and hurt some even to death, for their beaks are very big, sharp, and strong, as it is said.

CHAPTER XVII

Of the incredible changes of men that Varro believed

VARRO, to get credit for this, reports many strange tales of that famous witch Circe, who turned Ulysses' companions into beasts; and of the Arcadians, who swimming over a certain lake became wolves, and lived with the wolves of the woods, and if they ate no man's flesh, at nine years' end, swimming over the said lake they became men again. Nay, he names one Daemaenetus, who tasting of the sacrifices, which the Arcadians (killing a child) offered to their god Lycaeus, was turned into a wolf, and becoming a man again at ten years' end, he grew to be a champion, and was victor in the Olympic games. Nor does he think that Pan and Jupiter were called Lycaei in the Arcadian history for any other reason than for their transforming of men into wolves; for this they held impossible to any but a divine power. A wolf is called λυκός in Greek, and thence came their name Lycaeus: and the Roman Luperci (says he) had their origin from their mysteries.

CHAPTER XVIII

Of the devils' power in transforming man's shape. What a Christian may believe herein

SOME perhaps will look for our opinion here, touching this deceit of the devils, as to what a Christian should do, upon this report of miracles amongst the infidels. What shall we say but 'Get you out of the midst of Babylon'? This prophetical command wills

us to ply our faith's feet as fast as we can, and be quit of this
worldly city compact of a confused crew of sinners and evil angels,
and hie us unto the living God. For the greater power we behold
in the deceiver, the firmer hold must we lay upon our mediator, by
whom we leave the dregs and ascend unto the height of purity.
So then if we should say all those tales are lies, yet are there some
that will avow they have either heard them for truth from persons
of credit, or have experienced them themselves. For when I was in
Italy, I heard such a report there, how certain women of one place
there would but give one a little drug in cheese, and presently he
became an ass, and so they made him carry their necessaries whither
they would; and having done, they restored him to his proper
shape; yet had he his human reason still, as Apuleius had while
he was an ass, as himself writes in his book of *The Golden Ass*;
be it a lie or a truth that he writes.

Well either these things are false, or incredible, because so un-
usual. But we must firmly hold God's power to be omnipotent
in all things; but the devils can do nothing beyond the power of
their nature (which is angelical, although malevolent) unless He
whose judgments are ever secret, but never unjust, permit them.
Nor can the devils create anything (whatever appearances of theirs
produce these doubts) but only cast a changed shape over that
which God has made, altering it only in show. Nor do I think
the devils can form any soul or body into bestial or brutal members
and essences: but they can in an indescribable way transport
man's phantasm in a bodily shape unto the senses of others (this
passes ordinarily in our dreams through a thousand several things,
and though it be not corporal, yet it seems to carry itself in corporal forms through all these things) while the bodies of the men
thus affected lie in another place, being alive, but yet in a trance
far more deep than any sleep. Now this phantasm may appear
unto the senses of others in a bodily shape, and a man may seem
to himself to be such a one as he often thinks himself to be in his
dream, and to bear burdens, which if they be true burdens indeed,
the devils bear them, to delude men's eyes with the appearance of
true burdens, and false shapes. For one Praestantius told me that
his father took that drug in cheese at his own house, whereupon
he lay in such a sleep that no man could awake him: and after a few
days he awoke of himself and told all he had suffered in his dreams
in the meanwhile; how he had been turned into a horse and carried
the soldiers' victuals about in a sack. This had truly happened as
he recorded it, yet seemed it but a dream unto him. Another
told how one night before he slept, an old acquaintance of his, a
philosopher, came to him and expounded certain Platonisms unto
him, which he would not expound to him before. So afterwards he
asked him why he did there what he would not do in his own house
when he was entreated? 'I did it not,' quoth the other, 'but I

dreamed that I did it.' And so that which the one dreamed while
asleep, the other in a phantasmal appearance beheld while awake.
These now were related by such as I think would not lie, for had
any one told them, they would not have to be believed. So then
those Arcadians, whom the gods (nay the devils rather) turned
into wolves, and those companions of Ulysses being charmed by
Circe into bestial shapes, had only their phantasm occupied in such
forms, if there were any such matter. But as for Diomedes' birds,
seeing they reproduce their kind, 'I hold them not to be transformed men, but that the men were taken away, and they brought
in their places, as the hind was in place of Iphigenia, Agamemnon's
daughter. The devils can play such juggling tricks with ease, by
God's permission; but the virgin being found alive afterwards,
this was a plain deceit of theirs to take her away, and set the hind
there. But Diomedes' companions, because they were never seen
(the evil angels destroying them), were believed to be turned into
those birds that were brought out of their unknown habitations
into these places. As for their washing of his temple, their love
for the Greeks, and their fury against others, they may have all this
by the devils' instigation: because it was their endeavour to persuade that Diomedes was become a god, thereby to make them
injure the true God, by adoring feigned ones, and dead persons
(with temples, altars, priests, and sacrifices) who when they lived
had no life: all which honours being rightly bestowed are peculiar
to that one true and only God.

CHAPTER XIX

That Aeneas came into Italy when Abdon was judge of Israel

TROY being now taken and razed, Aeneas with ten ships filled
with the remains of Troy came into Italy, Latinus being king there,
Mnestheus at Athens, Polyphides in Sicyon, Tautanes in Assyria,
and Abdon judging Israel. Latinus dying, Aeneas reigned three
years in the same time of the same kings, excepting that Pelasgus
was king of Sicyon, and Samson judge of the Hebrews, who
was counted Hercules for his wonderful strength. Aeneas being not
to be found after his death, was canonized for a god by the Latins.
So was Sangus or Sanctus by the Sabines. And at this time
Codrus, the king of Athens, went in disguise to be slain of the
Peloponnesians, the Athenians' enemies; and so he was, hereby
delivering his country from ruin. For the Peloponnesians had
an oracle which told them that they should conquer if they killed
not the Athenian king. So he deceived them by his disguise, and
giving them evil words, provoked them to kill him; whereof Virgil

says: 'Or the quarrels of Codrus.'[1] And him the Athenians
sacrificed unto as a god.   Now in the reign of Silvius, the fourth
Latin king (Aeneas' son by Lavinia, not by Creusa, nor brother to
Ascanius), Oneus, the nine-and-twentieth of Assyria, Melanthus,
the sixteenth of Athens, and Eli the priest judging Israel, the
Sicyonian kingdom fell to ruin, which endured (as it is recorded)
959 years.

CHAPTER XX

Of the succession of the kingdom in Israel after the judges

SOON after (in those kings' times) the judges ceased, and Saul was
anointed the first king of Israel, in Samuel the prophet's time.
And now began the Latin kings to be called Silvii, after Silvius,
Aeneas' son.   All after him had their proper names different, and
this surname in common, as the emperors that succeeded Caesar
were called Caesars long after.   But Saul and his issue being
rejected, and he dead, David was crowned forty years after Saul
began his reign.   Then had the Athenians no more kings after
Codrus, but began an aristocracy.   David reigned forty years, and
Solomon his son succeeded him, he that built that goodly temple
of God at Jerusalem.   In his time the Latins built Alba, and their
kings were thenceforth called Alban kings, though ruling in
Latium.   Rehoboam succeeded Solomon, and in his time Israel
was divided into two kingdoms, and each had a king by itself.

CHAPTER XXI

Of the Latian kings: Aeneas (the first) and Aventinus (the twelfth)
are made gods

LATIUM, after Aeneas, their first deified king, had eleven more, and
none of them deified.   But Aventinus, the twelfth, being slain in
war, and buried on that hill that bears his name, was put into the
calendar of their men-gods.   Some say he was not killed, but
vanished away, and that Mount Aventine had not the name from
him but from another.   After him were no more gods made in
Latium but Romulus, the builder of Rome, betwixt whom and
Aventinus were two kings.   One Virgil names, saying,

> Proximus ille Procas Troianae gloria gentis.[2]

In whose time, because Rome was now nearly born, the great
monarchy of Assyria came to an end.   For now after one thousand
three hundred and five years (counting Belus' reign also in that little

---

[1] *Eclog.* v. 11.   [2] *Aen.* vi. 767.

kingdom at first) it was transferred to the Medes. Procas reigned before Amulius. Now Amulius had made Rhea (or Ilia) his brother Numitor's daughter, a vestal virgin; and Mars they say lay with her (thus they honour and excuse her whoredom) and begat two twins on her; who (for a proof of their aforesaid excuse for her) they say were cast out, and a she-wolf, the beast of Mars, came and fed them with her teats, thus acknowledging the sons of her lord and master. Now some do say that there was a whore who found them when they were first cast out, and that she nurtured them. (Now they called whores *lupae*, she-wolves, and the bawdy-houses unto this day are called *lupanaria*). Afterwards Faustulus, a shepherd, had them (they say), and his wife Acca brought them up. Well, what if God, to reprove the bloody mind of the king that commanded to drown them, preserved them from the water and sent this beast to give them nourishment? Is this any wonder? Numitor, Romulus' grandsire, succeeded his brother Amulius in the kingdom of Latium, and in the first year of his reign was Rome built, so that from thenceforward he and Romulus reigned together in Italy.

CHAPTER XXII

Rome founded at the time of the Assyrian monarchy's fall, Hezekiah being king of Judah

BRIEFLY, Rome, the second Babylon, daughter of the first by which it pleased God to quell the whole world, and fetch it all under one sovereignty, was now founded. The world was now full of hardy men, painful and well practised in war. They were stubborn, and not to be subdued but with infinite labour and danger. In the conquests of the Assyrians over all Asia, the wars were of far lighter account; the people were weak in their defences, nor was the world so populous. For it was not above a thousand years after that universal deluge, wherein all died but Noah and his family, that Ninus conquered all Asia excepting India. But the Romans came not to their monarchy with that ease that he did. They spread by little and little, and found sturdy hindrances in all their proceedings. Rome, then, was built when Israel had dwelt in the land of promise 718 years, 27 under Joshua, 329 under the Judges, and 362 under the Kings, until Ahaz, or as others count, until his successor Hezekiah, was king of Judah, Hezekiah that good and godly king, who reigned (assuredly) in Romulus' time, Hosea in the meantime being king of Israel.

CHAPTER XXIII

Of the evident prophecy of the Erythraean Sibyl concerning Christ

IN those days a proconsul (some say) prophesied. There were many sibyls (says Varro), and not merely one. But this sibyl of Erythraea wrote some apparent prophecies of Christ, which we have read in rough Latin verses, not correspondent to the Greek, the interpreter, as we learned afterwards, being none of the best poets. For Flaccianus, a learned and eloquent man (one that had been a proconsul), being in a conference with us concerning Christ, showed us a Greek book, saying it contained this sibyl's verses, wherein in one place he showed us a sort of verses so composed, that the first letter of every line being taken, they all made these words, Ἰησοῦς Χριστὸς Θεοῦ Υἱός, Σωτήρ, *Jesus Christus, Dei Filius, Salvator,* 'Jesus Christ, Son of God the Saviour.' Now these verses, as some have translated into Latin, are thus:

> J udicii signum tellus sudore madescet.
> E caelo rex adveniet per saecla futurus,
> S cilicet in carne praesens ut judicet orbem.
> U nde Deum cernent incredulus atque fidelis
> C elsum cum sanctis aevi jam termino in ipso.
> S it animae cum carne aderunt, quas judicat ipse,
> C um jacet incultus densis in vepribus orbis.
> R ejicient simulacra viri, cunctam quoque gazam.
> E xuret terras ignis pontumque polumque
> I nquirens taetri portas effringet Averni.
> S anctorum sed enim cunctae lux libera carni
> T radetur, sontes aeterna flamma cremabit.
> O ccultos actus retegens, tunc quisque loquetur
> S ecreta, atque Deus reserabit pectora luci.
> T unc erit et luctus, stridebunt dentibus omnes:
> E ripitur solis jubar et chorus interit astris
> V olvetur coelum, lunaris splendor obibit;
> D eiciet colles, valles extollet ab imo.
> N on erit in rebus hominum sublime vel altum.
> J am aequantur campis montes et caerula ponti.
> O mnia cessabunt, tellus confracta peribit:
> S ic pariter fontes torrentur fluminaque igni.
> S ed tuba tum sonitum tristem demittet ab alto
> O rbe, gemens facinus miserum variosque labores,
> T artareumque chaos monstrabit terra dehiscens.
> E t coram hic Domino reges sistentur ad unum.
> R eccidet e caelo ignisque et sulphurus amnis.[1]

Now this translator could not make the initial letters of each line the same as those in the Greek. For example, the Greek letter υ is at the head of some lines, but the Latins have no word begin-

---

[1] An English version of the Greek of these lines in acrostic form is given in the selections from Vives' commentary at the end of the volume.—ED.

ning with *u* that could fit the sense. And this is in three lines, the
fifth, the eighteenth, and the nineteenth. And so if we link together
the initial letters of all the lines, substituting *u* for those in the
fifth, the eighteenth, and the nineteenth, we find expressed the
Greek equivalents of *Jesus Christus Dei Filius, Salvator*. The
verses are in all twenty-seven, which number is the cube of three.
For three times three is nine, and three times nine is twenty-seven.
Now take the five first letters from the five first words of the Greek
sentence included in the verse's heads, and they make ἰχθύς, 'a
fish,' a mystical name of Christ, who could be in this mortal world
as in a deep sea, without any sin. Now this Erythraean Sibyl, or
(as some rather think) Cumaean, has not one word in all her verses
(whereof these are a portion) tending to idolatry, but all are against
the false gods and their worshippers, so that she seems to me to
have been a citizen of the city of God. Lactantius [1] also has
prophecies of Christ out of some sibyl, but he says not from which.
But that which he scatters in short fragments I think it is good to
lay together, and make one large prophecy of his many little ones.
This it is: 'Afterwards He shall be taken by the ungodly, and they
shall strike God with wicked hands, and spit their venomous spirits
in His face. He shall yield His holy back to their strokes, and take
their blows with silence, lest they should know that He is the
Word, or whence He came to speak to mortals.[2] They shall crown
Him with thorn. They gave Him gall, instead of vinegar to eat.
This table of hospitality they shall afford Him! Thou foolish
nation, that knewest not thy God, but crownedst Him with thorn,
and didst feast Him with bitterness. The veil of the temple shall
rend in two, and it shall be dark for three hours at noonday. Then
shall He die and sleep three days, and then shall He arise again
from death and shew the first fruits of the resurrection to them that
are called.' All this has Lactantius used in several places, as he
needed, from the sibyl. We have laid it together, distinguishing
it only by the heads of the chapters, if the transcriber have the care
to observe and follow us. Some say the Erythraean Sibyl lived in
the Trojan war, long before Romulus.

CHAPTER XXIV

*The seven sages in Romulus' time. Israel led into captivity.
Romulus dies, and is deified*

IN Romulus' time lived Thales, one of those who (after the theological poets, in which Orpheus was chief) were called the wise men
or sages. And now did the Chaldaeans subdue the ten tribes of
Israel (fallen before from Judah), and lead them into Chaldaea

---

[1] *Inst.* iv. 18.   [2] Latin *inferis*—which may mean 'the departed.'—ED.
II—* G 9⁸3

captive, leaving only the tribes of Judah and Benjamin free, who
had their king's seat at Jerusalem. Romulus dying, and not able
to be found, was hereupon deified, which use was now almost given
up, until it was revived in the Caesar's times when they did it
rather for flattery than in error, and Tully [1] commends Romulus
highly in that he could deserve those honours in so wise and
learned an age, though philosophy was not yet at her height of
subtle and acute disputations. But although in the later days
they made no new gods of men, yet kept they their old ones still,
and gave not over the worship of them, increasing superstition by
their swarms of images, whereof antiquity had none; and the
devils working so powerfully with them, that they got them to make
public presentations of the gods' shames, though they were now
ashamed to invent them. After Romulus reigned Numa, who
stuffed all the city with false religion; yet could he not find a godhead for himself as a result of all this chaos of his consecrations.
It seems he stowed heaven so full of gods that he left no room for
himself. He reigning at Rome, and Manasseh over the Hebrews
(that wicked king that killed the prophet Isaiah), the Samian Sibyl
lived, as it is reported.

CHAPTER XXV

*Philosophers living in Tarquinius Priscus' time, and in Zedekiah's,
when Jerusalem was taken, and the temple destroyed*

ZEDEKIAH ruling over the Hebrews, and Tarquinius Priscus (successor to Ancus Martius) over the Romans, the Jews were carried
captive to Babylon, Jerusalem was destroyed, and Solomon's
temple razed. The prophets had told them long before that their
wickedness would be the cause of this, chiefly Jeremiah, who told
them the very time that it would last. About this time lived
Pittacus of Mitylene, another of the sages. And the other five
also (which with Thales and this Pittacus make seven) lived all
(as Eusebius says) within the time of the Israelites' captivity in
Babylon. Their names were Solon of Athens, Chilo of Lacedaemon, Periander of Corinth, Cleobulus of Lindus, and Bias of
Priene. These were all after the theological poets, and were
more famous than others for their better discipline of life, and because they gave sundry good instructions touching the reformation
of manners. But they left no records of their learning to posterity,
excepting only Solon, that left the Athenians some laws of his
making. Thales was a naturalist, and left books of his opinions:
and in this time also lived Anaximander, Anaximenes, and Xeno-
phanes, all natural philosophers, and Pythagoras also, in whose
time men began to be called philosophers.

[1] *De Re Publ.* ii. 10.

CHAPTER XXVI

*The Romans were freed from their kings, and Israel from captivity
both at one time*

AT the same time Cyrus, king of Persia, Chaldaea, and Assyria,
gave the Jews a kind of release, for he sent fifty thousand of them
to rebuild the temple.   But these only built the altar, and laid the
foundations; for their foes troubled them with so frequent incursions that the building was left off until Darius' time.   The
story of Judith fell out also in the same times; which they say the
Jews receive not into their canon.   The seventy years therefore
being expired in Darius' reign (the time that Jeremiah had foretold), the Jews had their full freedom; Tarquin the Proud being
the seventh king of Rome, whom the Romans expelled, and never
would be subject to any more kings.   Until this time had Israel
prophets in great numbers, but indeed we have but few of their
prophecies canonically recorded.   Of these I said in ending my
last book, that I would make some mention in this, and here is a
suitable place.

CHAPTER XXVII

*Of the times of the prophets whose books we have : how they prophesied
(some of them) of the calling of the nations in the declining of the
Assyrian monarchy, and the erecting of the Romans*

To know the times well, let us go back a little.   The prophecy of
Hosea, the first of the twelve, begins thus: 'The word of the Lord
that came to Hosea, in the days of Uzziah, Jotham, Ahaz, Hezekiah, kings of Judah.'   Amos writes also that he prophesied in
Uzziah's days, adding that Jeroboam lived in those times also, as
he did indeed.   Isaiah, also the son of Amos (either the prophet or
some other, and this latter is more generally held), names the same
four in the beginning of his prophecy, that Hosea named.   So does
Micah also.   All these their prophecies prove to have lived in one
time; together with Jonah and Joel, the first under Uzziah, and the
latter under his son Jotham.   But we find not the times of the two
latter in their books, but in the Chronicles.   Now these times
reach from Procas or Aventinus' predecessor, king of the Latins,
unto Romulus, now king of Rome, nay even unto Numa Pompilius,
his successor; for so long reigned Hezekiah in Judah.   And therefore in the fall of the Assyrian empire and the rising of the Roman
did these fountains of prophecy break forth; that even as Abraham
had received the promise of all the world's being blessed in his
seed, at the first origin of the Assyrian State, so likewise might the

testimonies of Him in whom the former was to be fulfilled, be as
frequent both in word and writing in the origin of the western
Babylon. For those prophets that were continually in Israel,
from the first of their kings, were all for their peculiar good, and
in no way pertaining to the nations. But for the more manifest
prophecies, which tended also to the nation's good, it was fit they
should begin, when that city began that was the mistress of the
nations.

CHAPTER XXVIII

Prophecies concerning the gospel in Hosea and Amos

HOSEA is a prophet as divine as he is deep. Let us perform our
promise, and see what he says: 'In the place where it was said unto
them, Ye are not My people, it shall be said, Ye are the sons of the
living God.' This testimony the apostles themselves interpreted of
the calling of the Gentiles; who, because they are the spiritual sons of
Abraham and therefore rightly called Israel, it follows of them thus:
'Then the children of Judah and the children of Israel shall be
gathered together and appoint themselves one head, and they shall
come up out of the land.'[1]   If we seek for farther exposition of this,
we shall mar the sweet taste of the prophet's eloquence. Remember but the corner stone, and the two walls, the Jews and the
Gentiles, either of them under those several names, being founded
upon that one head, and acknowledged to ascend from the earth.
And that those carnal Israelites that believe not now shall one day
believe (or rather their sons succeeding them in their places) the
same prophet avouches, saying: 'The children of Israel shall sit
many days without a king, without a prince, without an offering,
without an altar, without a priesthood, and without manifestations.'[2]   Who does not see that these are the Jews? Now mark
the sequel. 'Afterwards shall the children of Israel return, and
seek the Lord their God, and David their king, and shall fear the
Lord and His goodness in these latter days.' Nothing can be
plainer spoken. Here is Christ meant by David, as He was the
Son of David in the flesh (says the apostle). Nay, this prophet
foretold the third day of His resurrection also. Hear himself:
'After two days will He revive us, and in the third day He will raise
us up.'[3]   Just in this key spake St. Paul, saying: 'If ye then be
risen with Christ, seek those things which are above.'[4]   Such a
prophecy has Amos also: 'Prepare to meet thy God, O Israel, for
lo, I form the thunder and the winds, and declare mine anointed
in men.'[5]   And in another place: 'In that day will I raise up the
tabernacle of David that is fallen down, and close up the breaches

---

[1] Hos. i. 10, 11.   [2] Hos. iii. 4, 5.   [3] Hos. vi. 2.   [4] Col. iii. 1.
[5] Amos iv. 12, 13.

thereof, and will raise up his ruins, and build it as in the days of old; that the residue of mankind and all the heathen may seek Me, because My name is called upon them, said the Lord that doeth this.'[1]

CHAPTER XXIX

Isaiah's prophecies concerning Christ

ISAIAH is not one of the twelve prophets. They are called the minor prophets, because their prophecies are brief in comparison with others that wrote large volumes, of whom Isaiah was one, whom I add here, because he lived in the times of the two aforenamed. In his precepts against sin, and unto goodness, and his prophecies of tribulation for offending, he forgets not also to proclaim Christ and His Church more amply than any other, insomuch that some call him an evangelist rather than a prophet. One of his prophecies hear in brief, because I cannot spend time now upon many. In the person of God the Father, thus he says: 'Behold, My Son shall understand. He shall be exalted and be very high. As many were astonied at Thee (Thy form was so despised by men, and Thy beauty by the sons of men), so shall many nations admire Him, and the kings shall be put to silence at His sight: for that which they have not heard of Him shall they see, and that which hath not been told them, they shall understand. Lord, who will believe our report? To whom is the Lord's arm revealed? We will declare Him as an infant, and as a root out of a dry ground. He hath neither form nor beauty. When we shall see Him He shall have neither goodliness nor glory; but His look shall be despised and rejected before all men. He is a man full of sorrows, and hath experience of infirmities. For His face is turned away. He was despised and we esteemed Him not. He hath borne our sins and sorrows for us; yet did we judge Him as plagued of God, and smitten and humbled. But He was wounded for our transgressions, and broken for our iniquities. Our peace we learned by Him, and with His stripes we are healed. We have all strayed like sheep. Man had lost his way, and upon Him hath God laid all our guilt. He was afflicted, yet never opened He His mouth. He was led as a sheep to the slaughter, and as a lamb before the shearer is dumb, so was He, and opened not His mouth. He was brought from prison unto judgment. O who shall declare His generation? For He shall be taken out of life. For the transgression of My people was He plagued; and I will give the wicked for His grave, and the rich for His death; because He hath done no wickedness, nor was there any deceit found in His mouth! The Lord will purge Him from His affliction. If ye give your soul for

[1] Amos ix. 11, 12.

sin, ye shall see the seed continue long, and the Lord shall take His soul from sorrow, to show Him light, to confirm His understanding, to justify the righteous, serving many, for He bare their iniquities. Therefore I will give Him a portion with the great. He shall divide the spoils of the strong, because He hath poured out His soul unto death. He was reckoned with the transgressors, and hath borne the sins of many, and was betrayed for their trespasses.' [1]   Thus much of Christ. Now what says He of His Church? 'Rejoice, O barren, that bearest not. Break forth and cry out for joy, thou that bringest not forth: for the desolate hath more children than the married wife. Enlarge the place of thy tents, and fasten the curtains of thy tabernacles. Spare not, stretch out thy cords, and make fast thy stakes. Spread it yet further to the right hand and the left, and thy seed shall possess the Gentiles, and dwell in the desolate cities. Fear not, because thou art ashamed. Be not afraid, because thou art upbraided, for thou shalt forget thine everlasting shame, and shalt not remember the reproach of thy widowhood any more, for the Lord that made thee is called the Lord of Hosts, and the Redeemer, the Holy One of Israel, shall be called the God of all the world,' etc.[2] Here is enough, needing but little explanation, for the places are so plain that our enemies themselves are forced (despite their hearts) to acknowledge the truth. These then suffice.

CHAPTER XXX

Prophecies of Micah, Jonah, and Joel, correspondent unto the New Testament

THE prophet Micah, prefiguring Christ by a great mountain, says thus: 'In the last days shall the mountain of the Lord be prepared upon the tops of the hills, and shall be exalted above the hills: and the nations shall haste them to it, saying: Come, let us go up into the mountain of the Lord, into the house of the God of Jacob; and He will teach us His ways, and we will walk in His paths, for the law shall go forth of Zion, and the word of the Lord from Jerusalem. He shall judge amongst many people, and rebuke mighty nations afar off.' [3]   The same prophet foretells Christ's birth-place also, saying: 'And thou, Bethlehem, of Ephratah, art little to be amongst the thousands of Judah, yet out of thee shall a captain come forth unto me that shall be the Prince of Israel, whose goings forth have been from everlasting. Therefore will He give them up until the time that the child-bearing woman doth travail, and the remnant of her brethren shall return unto the children of Israel. And He shall stand and look, and feed His flock in the strength of the Lord. In the honour of God's name shall they continue; for

[1] Isa. lii. 13–liii. 12.   [2] Isa. liv. 1–5.   [3] Mic. iv. 1–3.

now shall He be magnified unto the world's end.'[1]   Now Jonah prophesied Christ rather in suffering than in speaking, and that most manifestly considering the passion and resurrection.   For why was he three days in the whale's belly and then let out, but to signify Christ's resurrection from the depth of hell upon the third day?   Joel's prophecies of Christ and the Church require great explanation, yet one of his (and that was remembered by the apostles, at the descent of the Holy Ghost upon the faithful, as Christ had promised) I will not omit: 'Afterwards,' says he, 'I will pour out My Spirit upon all flesh.   Your sons and daughters shall prophesy, and your old men shall dream dreams, and your young men see visions.   Even upon the servants and the handmaids in those days will I pour My Spirit.'[2]

CHAPTER XXXI

Prophecies of Obadiah, Nahum, and Habakkuk, concerning the world's salvation in Christ

THREE of the lesser prophets, Obadiah, Nahum, and Habakkuk, never mention the times they lived in: nor does Eusebius or Jerome supply that defect.   They place Obadiah and Micah both together, but not there where they record the time of Micah's prophesying, of which the negligence of the transcribers was, I think, the only cause.   The two others we cannot once find named in our copies; yet since they are canonical, we may not omit them.   Obadiah in his writing is the briefest of them all.   He speaks against Idumaea, the reprobate progeny of Esau, the elder son of Isaac, and grand-child of Abraham.   Now if we take Idumaea, by a *synecdoche partis*,[3] for all the nations, we may take this prophecy of his to be meant of Christ: 'Upon Mount Zion shall be salvation, and it shall be holy.'[4]   And a little after: 'They shall be saved, shall come out of Zion' (that is, the believers in Christ, the apostles, shall come out of Judah) 'to defend Mount Esau.'   How to defend it, but by preaching the gospel, to save the believers, and translate them into the kingdom of God out of the power of darkness as the sequel shows: 'And the kingdom shall be the Lord's'?[5]   For Mount Zion signifies Judaea, the storehouse of salvation, and the holy mother of Christ in the flesh: and Mount Esau is Idumaea, prefiguring the church of the Gentiles, whom they that were saved came out of Zion to defend, that the kingdom might be the Lord's. This was unknown ere it were done, but being come to pass, who did not discern it?

----

[1] Mic. v. 2–4.   [2] Joel ii. 28, 29.
[3] A form of speech in which a part is put for the whole.—ED.
[4] Obad. 17.   [5] Obad. 21.

Now the prophet Nahum (nay, God in him) said: 'I will abolish the graven and molten image, and make them their grave. Behold upon the hills the feet of him that declareth and publisheth peace. O Judah, keep thy solemn feasts, perform thy vows; for the wicked shall no more pass through thee; he is utterly cut off. He that breatheth in thy face, and freeth thee from tribulation, ascendeth.' [1] Who is this that does thus? Remember the Holy Ghost, remember the gospel. For this belongs to the New Testament whose feasts are renewed, never more to cease. The gospel we see has abolished all those graven and molten images, those false idols, and has laid them in oblivion, as in a grave. Herein we see this prophecy fulfilled. Now for Habakkuk, what does he mean but the coming of Christ, when he said: 'The Lord answered, saying, Write the vision, and make it plain on tables that he may run that readeth it. For the vision is yet for an appointed time, but at the last it shall speak and not lie; though it tarry wait for it, for it shall surely come, and shall not tarry.' [2]

CHAPTER XXXII

The prophecy contained in the song and prayer of Habakkuk

AND in his prayer and song [3] whom does he speak unto but Christ, saying: 'O Lord, I heard Thy voice, and was afraid. Lord, I considered Thy works, and was terrified.' What is this but an ineffable admiration of that sudden and unknown salvation of man? 'In the midst of two shalt Thou be known.' What are those two, the two Testaments, the two thieves, or the two prophets Moses and Elias? 'In the approach of years shalt Thou be known.' This is plain, and needs no exposition. But that which follows, 'My soul being troubled therewith, in Thy wrath remember mercy,' is meant of the Jews, of whose nation He was. When they were mad in their wrath and crucifying Christ, He remembering His mercy, said: 'Father, forgive them, for they know not what they do.' 'God shall come from Teman, and the Holy One from the thick and dark mountain.' From Teman (say some), that is from the south, signifying the heat of charity and the light of truth. 'The thick dark mountain' may be taken diversely; but I rather choose to hold it referred to the depth of the holy scriptures prophesying Christ: for therein are many depths for the industrious to exercise themselves in, and which they find out when they find Him whom they concern. 'His glory covers the heavens, and the earth is full of His praise.' That is just as the psalm says: 'Exalt Thyself O God above the heavens, and let Thy glory be above all the earth.' 'His brightness was as the light' means His glory shall

---

[1] Nahum i. 14–ii. 1.   [2] Hab. ii. 2, 3.   [3] Hab. iii. 2–19.

enlighten the nations. 'He had horns coming out of His hands.'
That was His trophy on the cross. 'There was the hiding of His
power.' This is plain. 'Before Him went the word, and followed
Him into the field.' He was prophesied ere He came, and preached
after His departure. 'He stood, and the earth moved.' He stood
to save, and the earth was moved with believing in Him. 'He
beheld the nations, and they were dissolved.' That is, He pitied,
and they repented. 'He broke the mountains with violence.' His
miracles amazed the proud. 'The eternal hills did bow.' The
people were temporarily humbled, to be eternally glorified. 'For
my pains I saw His goings in.' That is, I had the reward of
eternity for my labours in charity. 'The tents of Ethiopia
trembled, and so did they of Midian.' Even those nations that
were never under Rome, by the terror of Thy name and power
preached, shall become subject to Christ. 'Was the Lord angry
against the rivers, or was Thine anger against the sea?' This
implies that He came not to judge the world, but to save it. 'Thou
rodest upon horses, and Thy chariot brought salvation.' The
evangelists are His horses, for He rules them, and the gospel His
chariot, salvation to all believers. 'Thou shalt bend Thy bow
above sceptres. Thy judgment shall restrain even the kings of
the earth. Thou shalt cleave the earth with rivers.' Thine
abundant doctrine shall open the hearts of men to believe them:
unto such it is said: 'Rend your hearts, and not your garments.'
'The people shall see Thee, and tremble. Thou shalt spread the
waters as Thou goest.' Thy preachers shall pour out the streams
of Thy doctrine on all sides. 'The deep made a noise.' The
depth of man's heart expressed what it saw. 'The height of his
fantasy.' That is, the deep gave out the voice, expressing (as I said)
what it saw. This fantasy was a vision, which he concealed not,
but proclaimed in full. 'The sun was extolled, and the moon kept
her place.' Christ was taken up into heaven, and by Him is the
Church ruled. 'Thine arrows flew in the light.' Thy word was
openly taught, and by the brightness of Thy shining arms Thine
arrows flew: for Christ Himself had said: 'What I tell you in darkness, that speak ye in the light.' [1] 'Thou shalt tread down the land
in anger.' Thou shalt humble high spirits by afflicting them.
'Thou shalt thresh the heathen in displeasure.' Thou shalt quell
the ambitious by Thy judgments. 'Thou wentest forth to save
Thy people and Thine anointed, Thou laidest death upon the
heads of the wicked.' All this is plain. 'Thou hast cut them off
with amazement.' Thou hast cut down bad, and set up good, in
wonderful manner. 'The mighty shall crown their heads, which
marvel at this. They shall gape after Thee as a poor man eating
secretly.' For so divers great men of the Jews being hungry after
the bread of life came to eat secretly, fearing the Jews, as the

[1] Matt. x. 27.

gospel shows. 'Thou puttest Thine horses into the sea, which troubled the waters'—that is, the people; for unless all were troubled, some would not become fearful converts, and others furious persecutors. 'I marked it, and my body trembled at the sound of the prayer of my lips: fear came into my bones, and I was altogether troubled in myself.' See, the height of his prayer and his prescience of those great events amazed even himself; and he is troubled with those seas, to see the imminent persecutions of the Church, whereof he lastly avouches himself a member, saying, 'I will rest in the day of trouble,' as if he were one of the hopeful sufferers and patient rejoicers; 'that I may go up to the people of my pilgrimage,' leaving his carnal kindred that wander after nothing but worldly matters, never caring for their supernal country. 'For the fig tree shall not fructify, nor shall fruit be in the vines: the olive shall fail, and the fields shall be fruitless. The sheep have left their meat, and the oxen are not in their stalls.' Here he sees the nation that crucified Christ, deprived of all spiritual goods, prefigured in those corporal fertilities; and because the country's ignorance of God had caused these plagues, forsaking God's righteousness through their own pride, he adds this: 'I will rejoice in the Lord, and joy in God my Saviour. The Lord my God is my strength, He will establish my feet. He will set me upon high places, that I may be victorious in His song.' What song? Even such as the psalmist speaks of: 'He has set my feet upon the rock, and ordered my goings; and has put into my mouth a new song of praise unto God.' [1] In such a song (and not in one of his own praise) does Habakkuk conquer, glorying in the Lord his God. Some books read this passage better, 'I will joy in my Lord Jesus.' But the translators had not the name itself in Latin, otherwise we like the word a great deal better.

CHAPTER XXXIII

Prophecies of Jeremiah and Zephaniah concerning the former themes

JEREMIAH is one of the greater prophets. So is Isaiah not of the lesser, of some of whom I now spoke. He prophesied under Josiah, king of Judah, Ancus Martius being king of Rome, just before Israel's captivity unto the fifth month of the captivity, as his own book proves. Zephaniah, a lesser prophet, was also in his time, and prophesied in Josiah's time also (as himself says), but how long he says not. Jeremiah's time lasted all Ancus Martius' and part of Tarquinius Priscus' reign, the fifth Roman king. For in the beginning of his reign the Jews were carried captive. This prophecy of Christ we read in Jeremiah: 'The breath of our

[1] Ps. xl. 2, 3.

mouth, the Anointed of our Lord was taken in our sins.'[1]   Here
he shows briefly both Christ's deity and His sufferance for us.
Again: 'This is my God, nor is there any besides Him.   He hath
found all the ways of wisdom, and taught them to His servant
Jacob, and to Israel His beloved.   Afterwards was He seen upon
earth, and He conversed with men.'[2]   This, some say, is not
Jeremiah's but Baruch's, his transcriber's.   But the most hold it to
be Jeremiah's.   He says further: 'Behold, the days come (saith
the Lord) that I will raise unto David a just branch, which shall
reign as king, and be wise; and shall execute justice and judgment
upon the earth.   In His days shall Judah be saved, and Israel
shall dwell safely, and this is the name that they shall call Him—
The Lord our Righteousness.'[3]   Of the calling of the Gentiles
(which we see now fulfilled) he says thus: 'O Lord my God and
refuge in the day of evil, unto Thee shall the Gentiles come from
the ends of the world, and shall say, Our fathers have adored false
images wherein there was no profit.'[4]   And because the Jews
would not acknowledge Christ, but should kill Him, the prophet
says: 'The heart is heavy in all things.   He is a man and who shall
know Him?'[5]   His was the testimony also of the New Testament
and Christ the mediator, which I recited in my tenth book: for he
says: 'Behold the days come that I will make a new covenant with
the house of Israel,' etc.[6]   Now Zephaniah, that was of this time
also, has this of Christ: 'Wait upon Me (saith the Lord) in the day
of My resurrection, wherein My judgment shall gather the nations.'[7]
And again: 'The Lord will be terrible unto them.   He will consume
all the gods of the earth.   Every man shall adore Him from his
place, even all the isles of the heathen.'[8]   And a little after: 'Then
will I turn to the people a pure language, that they may all call
upon the Lord, and serve Him with one consent, and from beyond
the rivers of Ethiopia shall they bring Me offerings.   In that day
shalt thou not be ashamed for all the works wherein thou hast
offended Me, for then will I cleanse thee of the wicked that have
wronged thee: and thou shalt no more be proud of Mine holy
mountain, and I will leave a meek and lowly people in the midst of
thee, and the remnant of Israel shall reverence the name of the
Lord.'[9]   This is the remnant that is prophesied of elsewhere, and
that the apostle mentions, saying: 'There is a remnant at this
present time through the election of grace.'[10]   For a remnant of
that nation believed in Christ.

[1] Lam. iv. 20.   [2] Baruch iii. 35–7.   [3] Jer. xxiii. 5, 6.
[4] Jer. xvi. 19.   [5] Jer. xvii. 9.   [6] Jer. xxxi. 31.
[7] Zeph. iii. 8.   [8] Zeph. ii. 11.   [9] Zeph. iii. 9–13.
                            [10] Rom. ix. 27.

CHAPTER XXXIV

Daniel's and Ezekiel's prophecies concerning Christ and His Church

Now in the captivity itself, Daniel and Ezekiel, two of the greater prophets, prophesied first. Daniel foretold the very number of years until the coming of Christ, and His passion. It is too tedious to particularize, and others have done it before us. But of His power and glory, thus he said: 'I beheld a vision by night, and behold, the Son of Man came in the clouds of heaven, and approached unto the Ancient of days; and they brought Him before Him, and He gave Him dominion and honour, and a kingdom, that all people, nations, and languages should serve Him. His dominion is an everlasting dominion, and shall never be taken away. His kingdom shall never be destroyed.'[1] Ezekiel also prefiguring Christ as David (as the prophets are wont), because Christ took his flesh, and the form of a servant from David's seed, in the person of God the Father, does thus prophesy of Him: 'I will set up a Shepherd over My sheep, and He shall feed them, even My servant David; He shall feed them and be their Shepherd. I, the Lord, will be their God, and My servant David shall be Prince amongst them. I the Lord have spoken it.'[2] And again: 'One King shall be King to them all. They shall be no more two peoples, nor be divided from thenceforth into two kingdoms; nor shall they be any more polluted with their idols, nor with their abominations, nor with all their transgressions: but I will save them out of all their dwelling-places, wherein they have sinned, and will cleanse them. They shall be My people, and I will be their God. And David My servant shall be King over them, and they all shall have one Shepherd.'[3]

CHAPTER XXXV

Of the three prophecies of Haggai, Zechariah, and Malachi

THREE of the minor prophets, Haggai, Zechariah, and Malachi, all prophesying in the end of this captivity, still remain. Haggai prophesies of Christ and His Church thus, briefly and plainly: 'Yet a little while and I will shake the heavens, and the earth, and the sea, and the dry land: and I will move all nations, and the Desire of all nations shall come, saith the Lord of Hosts.'[4] This prophecy is partly come to effect, and partly to be effected at the final consummation. The angels and the stars are witness of heaven's moving at Christ's birth. The miracle of a virgin's child-birth moved the earth. The preaching of Christ in the islands

[1] Dan. vii. 13–14.   [2] Ezek. xxxiv. 23–4.   [3] Ezek. xxxvii. 22–4.
[4] Hag. ii. 6, 7.

and the continent moved both sea and dry land. The nations
we see are moved to the faith. The coming of the Desire of all
nations, that we do expect at this day of judgment: for first He
must be loved of the believers and then be desired of the expecters.
The words of Zechariah, 'Rejoice greatly, O daughter of Zion,' he
speaks of Christ and His Church; 'shout for joy, O daughter of
Jerusalem. Behold, thy King cometh to thee. He is just, and thy
Saviour; poor, and riding upon an ass, and upon a colt the foal of
an ass. His dominion is from sea to sea, and from the river to the
land's end.' [1] Of Christ's riding in this manner, the gospel speaks;
where this prophecy (as much as needs) is recited. In another
place, speaking prophetically of the remission of sins by Christ, he
says thus to Him: 'Thou in the blood of Thy testament hast loosed
Thy prisoners out of the lake wherein is no water.' [2] This lake
may be diversely interpreted without injuring our faith. But I
think he means that barren, boundless depth of human miseries,
wherein there is no stream of righteousness, but all is full of the
mud of iniquity: for of this is that saying of the psalm meant: 'He
hath brought me out of the lake of misery, and out of the miry
clay.' [3]

   Now Malachi, prophesying of the Church (which we see so
happily propagated by our Saviour Christ), has these plain words
to the Jews in the person of God: 'I have no pleasure in you,
neither will I accept an offering at your hand: for from the rising
of the sun unto the going down thereof My name shall be great
amongst the Gentiles, and in every place shall be incense offered
unto Me, and a pure offering unto My name: for My name is great
among the heathen, saith the Lord.' [4] This we see offered in every
place by Christ's priesthood after the order of Melchizedek: but
the sacrifice of the Jews, wherein God took no pleasure but refused,
that they cannot deny is ceased. Why do they expect another
Christ, and yet see that this prophecy is fulfilled already, which
could not be except by the true Christ? For He says soon
after in the person of God: 'My covenant was with Him of life
and peace. I gave Him fear, and He feared Me, and was afraid
before My name. The law of truth was in His mouth. He
walked with Me in peace and equity, and turned many away from
iniquity. For the priest's lips should preserve knowledge, and they
should seek the law at His mouth; for He is the messenger of the
Lord of hosts.' [5] No wonder if Christ be called so, for as He is a
servant because of the servant's form He took, when He came to
men, so is He a messenger, because of the glad tidings which He
brought unto men. For *evangelium* in Greek, is in our tongue,
'glad tidings.' And He says again of Him: 'Behold I will send
My messenger and He shall prepare the way before Me. The

---
[1] Zech. ix. 9, 10.   [2] Zech. ix. 11.   [3] Ps. xl. 2.   [4] Mal. i. 10, 11.
[5] Mal. ii. 5–7.

Lord, whom ye seek, shall come suddenly into His temple, and the Messenger of the covenant whom you desire. Behold, He shall come, saith the Lord of Hosts: but who may abide the day of His coming? Who shall endure when He appeareth?'[1] This passage is a direct prophecy of both the comings of Christ. Of the first: 'He shall come suddenly into His temple His flesh,' as He said Himself: 'Destroy this temple, and in three days I will raise it again.'[2] Of the second: 'Behold, He shall come, saith the Lord of Hosts, but who may abide the day of His coming?' etc. But those words, 'the Lord whom ye seek, and the Messenger of the covenant whom ye desire,' imply that the Jews, in that manner that they conceive the scriptures, desire and seek the coming of Christ. But many of them acknowledged Him not, when He came, for whose coming they so longed, their evil deserts having blinded their hearts.

The covenant, named both here, and there where He said, 'My covenant was with Him,' is to be understood of the New Testament, whose promises are eternal, not of the Old, which is full of temporal promises, such as weak men esteeming too highly do serve God wholly for, and stumble when they see the sinful enjoying them. Wherefore the prophet, to put a clear difference between the bliss of the New Testament, peculiar to the good, and the abundance of the Old Testament, shared with the bad also, adjoins this: 'Your words have been stout against Me (saith the Lord) and yet ye said, Wherein have we spoken against Thee? Ye have said it is in vain to serve God: and what profit have we in keeping His commandments, and in walking humbly before the Lord God of hosts? And now we regard aliens as blessed. They that work wickedness are set up, and they that oppose God, they are delivered. Thus spake they that feared the Lord, each to his neighbour. The Lord hearkened, and heard it, and wrote a book of remembrance in His sight for such as fear the Lord and reverence His name.'[3] That book refers to the New Testament. Hear the sequel: 'They shall be to Me, saith the Lord of Hosts, in that day wherein I do this, for a flock: and I will spare them as a man spareth his own son that serveth him. Then shall ye return, and discern between the righteous and the wicked, and between him that serveth God and him that serveth Him not. For behold the day cometh that shall burn as an oven: and all the proud and the wicked shall be as stubble; and the day that cometh shall burn them up, saith the Lord of Hosts, and shall leave them neither root nor branch. But unto you that fear My name shall the Sun of Righteousness arise, and health shall be under His wings, and ye shall go forth and grow up as fat calves. Ye shall tread down the wicked. They shall be as dust under the soles of your feet in the day that I shall do this, saith the Lord of Hosts.'[4] This is that day that is called

[1] Mal. iii. 1–2.   [2] John ii. 19.   [3] Mal. iii. 13–16.   [4] Mal. iii. 17–iv. 3.

the day of judgment, whereof, if it please God, we mean to say somewhat in a place convenient.

CHAPTER XXXVI

Of the books of Esdras, and the Maccabees

AFTER Haggai, Zechariah, and Malachi, the three last prophets, in the time of the said captivity, Esdras wrote. But he is rather held an historiographer than a prophet: as the book of Esther is also, containing events happening about those times, all tending to the glory of God. It may be said that Esdras prophesied in this, that when the question arose amongst the young men what thing was most powerful, and the first answered kings, the next wine, and the third women for they often command kings, yet did the third add more, and said that truth conquered all things. Now Christ in the gospel is found to be the truth. From this time, after the temple was rebuilt, the Jews had no more kings but princes unto Aristobulus' time. The account of which times we have not in the canonical scriptures, but in the others, amongst which the books of the Maccabees are also, which the Church indeed holds for canonical because of the vehement and wonderful sufferings of some martyrs for the law of God before the coming of Christ. Such there were that endured intolerable torments, yet these books are but apocryphal to the Jews.

CHAPTER XXXVII

The prophets more ancient than any of the Gentile philosophers

IN our prophets' time (whose works are now so far divulged) there were no philosophers stirring as yet; for the first of them arose with Pythagoras of Samos, who began to be famous at the end of the captivity. So that all other philosophers must needs be much later; for Socrates of Athens, the chief moralist of his time, lived after Esdras, as the chronicles record. And soon after was Plato born, the most excellent of all his scholars. To whom if we add also the former seven, who were called sages, not philosophers; and the naturalists that followed Thales' study, to wit, Anaximander, Anaximenes, Anaxagoras, and others, before Pythagoras professed philosophy, not one of these was before the prophets; for Thales, the most ancient of them all, lived in Romulus' time, when this prophetical doctrine flowed from the fountain of Israel, to be derived unto all the world. Only, therefore, the theological poets, Orpheus, Linus, Musaeus, and the others (if there were any more) were before our canonical prophets. But they were not more ancient than our true divine Moses, who taught them one true God, and whose books are in the front of our canon. And therefore though the learning of Greece warms the world at this day, yet need they not boast of their wisdom, being neither so ancient nor so excellent as our divine religion, and the true wisdom. We confess, not that Greece, but that the barbarians, as Egypt for example, had their peculiar doctrines before Moses' time, which they called their wisdom. Otherwise our scripture would not have said that Moses was learned in all the wisdom of the Egyptians; for there was he born, adopted, and brought up worthily by the daughter of Pharaoh. But their wisdom could not be before our prophets, for Abraham himself was a prophet. And what wisdom could there be in Egypt, before Isis, their supposed goddess, taught them letters? This Isis was daughter to Inachus, king of Argos, who reigned in the times of Abraham's grandchildren.

CHAPTER XXXVIII

Of some scriptures too ancient for the Church to allow, because that might cause a suspicion that they are rather counterfeit than true

Now if I should go any further back, there is the patriarch Noah, before the great deluge. We may very well call him a prophet, for his very ark, and his escape in that flood, were prophetical references unto these our times. What was Enoch, the seventh from Adam? Does not the canonical epistle of Jude say that he prophesied? The reason that we have not their writings, nor the Jews either, is their too great antiquity, which may cause a suspicion that they are rather feigned to be theirs, than theirs indeed. For many that believe as they like, and speak as they will, defend themselves with quotations from books. But the canon neither permits that such holy men's authority should be rejected, nor that it should be abused by counterfeit pamphlets. Nor is it any marvel that such antiquity is to be suspected when, as we read in the histories of the kings of Judah and Israel (which we hold canonical) of many things touched at there which are not there explained, but are said to be found in other books of the prophets, who are sometimes named, and yet whose works we have not in our canon, nor the Jews in theirs. I know not the reason of this; only I think that those prophets whom it pleased the Holy Spirit to inspire, wrote some things historically as men, and other things prophetically as from the mouth of God, and that these works were really distinct; some being held their own, as they were men, and some the Lord's, as speaking out of their bosoms, so that the first might belong to the bettering of knowledge, and the latter to the confirming of religion, to which the canon only has respect. Outside this canon, if there be any works going under prophets' names, they are not of authority even to better knowledge, because it is doubtful whether they are the works of those prophets or no. Therefore we may not trust them, especially when they speak against the canonical truth, wherein they prove themselves directly false births.

CHAPTER XXXIX

That the Hebrew letters have been ever continued in that language

WE may not therefore think as some do, that Hebrew as a spoken language only was derived from Heber and passed on to Abraham, and that Moses first gave the Hebrew letters with the law. No, that tongue was derived from man to man successively by letters as well as language. For Moses appointed men to teach them before the law was given. These the scriptures call *grammaton eisagogeis*, that is, introducers of letters, because they did as it were bring them into the hearts of men, or rather their hearts into them. So then no nation can vaunt itself over our prophets and patriarchs in antiquity of wisdom, for they had divine inspirations. And the Egyptians themselves, that usually give out such extreme and palpable lies about their learnings, are proved behindhand in comparison with our patriarchs. For none of them dare say that they had any excellence of understanding before they had letters, that is, before Isis came and taught them. And what was their goodly wisdom, think you? Truly nothing but astronomy, and such other sciences as rather seemed to exercise the wit than to elevate the knowledge. For as for morality, it stirred not in Egypt until Trismegistus' time, who was indeed long before the sages and philosophers of Greece, but after Abraham, Isaac, Jacob, Joseph, yea, and Moses also: for at the time when Moses was born, was Atlas, Prometheus' brother, a great astronomer, living; and he was grandfather by the mother's side to the elder Mercury, who begat the father of this Trismegistus.

CHAPTER XL

The Egyptians' abominable lyings, to claim their wisdom the age of 100,000 years

IT is therefore a monstrous absurdity to say, as some do, that it is above 100,000 years since astronomy began in Egypt. What records have they for this, seeing that they had their letters but two thousand years ago (or little more), from Isis? Varro's authority is of worth here, agreeing herein with the holy scriptures. For seeing it is not yet six thousand years from the first man

Adam, how ridiculous are they that overrun the truth such a multitude of years! Whom shall we believe in this so soon as him that
foretold what now we see accordingly effected? The disagreement
of historians gives us leave to lean to such as do accord with our
divine writings. The citizens of Babylon, indeed, being diffused
all over the earth, when they read two authors of like (and acceptable) authority, differing in relating matters of a bygone age,
know not which to believe. But we have a divine history to sustain us, and we know that whatsoever secular author he be, famous
or obscure, if he contradict that, he goes far astray from truth;
but be his words true or false, they are of no value to the attainment
of true felicity.

CHAPTER XLI

*The dissension of philosophers, and the concord of the canonical
scriptures*

But to leave history, and come to the philosophers whom we left
long ago. Their studies seemed wholly to aim at the attainment
of beatitude. Why did the scholars then contradict their masters,
but that both were whirled away with human affections? And
although there might be some spice of vainglory, each thinking
himself wiser and quicker witted than the other, and affecting
to be an arch-dogmatist himself, and not a follower of others;
notwithstanding, let us grant that it was the love of truth that
carried some (or the most of them) from their teachers' opinions,
to contend for truth, whether it were truth or the reverse. But
what course, what act can mortal misery perform to the obtaining
of true blessedness, unless it have a divine instruction? As for
our canonical authors, God forbid that they should differ. No,
they do not. And therefore worthily did so many nations believe
that God spoke either in them or by them. This the multitude
in other places, learned and unlearned, do avow, though your
petty company of janglers in the schools deny it. Our prophets
were but few, lest being more, their esteem should have been less,
which religion ought highly to reverence; yet are they not so few
but that their concord is justly to be admired. Let one look
amongst all the multitude of philosophers' writings, and if he find
two that tell both one tale in all respects, it may be registered for a
rarity. It were too much for me to try to set out their diver-
sities in this work. But what dogmatist in all this demon-honour-
ing city has any such privilege that he may not be reproved, and
opposed by others, who likewise enjoy some favourable approval?
Were not the Epicureans in great account at Athens, who held that
God had naught to do with man? And were not the Stoics, their
opponents, that held the gods to be the directors of all things, ever

as acceptable as they? Wherefore I marvel that Anaxagoras was accused for saying that the sun was a fiery stone, denying the godhead thereof; Epicurus being allowed and honoured in that city, who denied deity to sun, stars, yea, and to Jove himself and all the rest, as being present in the world and able to receive men's supplications. Was not Aristippus there with his bodily *summum bonum*, and Antisthenes with his mental? Both were famous Socratists, and yet both were far contrary to each other in their subjects of beatitude. The one bade a wise man escape from ruling, the other bade him take it; and both had full and frequent audience. Did not all of them defend their opinions in public, in the famous porch, in schools, in gardens, and likewise in all private places? One held there was one world, another a thousand. Some hold that the world was created, some not created. Some hold it eternal, some not eternal. Some say it is ruled by the power of God, others by chance. Some say the souls are immortal, others mortal. Some transfuse them into beasts, others do not. Some of those that make them mortal say they die soon after the body; others say they live longer, yet not for ever. Some place the chiefest good in the body, some in the soul, some in both. Some add external goods to the soul and the body. Some say the senses are always true, some say but sometimes, some say never. These and millions more of dissensions do the philosophers bandy. And what people, state, kingdom, or city of all the diabolical society has ever brought them to the test, or rejected the one and received the other? Has it not rather given nourishment to all confusion in its very bosom, and upheld the rabble of curious janglers, not about lands, or cases in law, but upon main points of misery and bliss? Wherein if they spake true, they had as good leave to speak false, so fully and so fitly was their society suited to the name of Babylon, which (as we said) signifies confusion. Nor cares their king, the devil, how much they jangle, for it procures him the larger harvest of variable impiety. But the people, state, nation, and city of Israel, to whom God's holy laws were left, did not confound with that licentious confusion the false prophets with the true, but all in one consent held and acknowledged the latter for the true authors recording God's testimonies. These were their sages, their poets, their prophets, their teachers of truth and piety. He that lived after their rules, followed not man, but God, who spake in them. The sacrilege forbidden there, God forbids. The commandment of 'Honour thy father and mother,' God commands. 'Thou shalt not commit adultery, nor murder, nor shalt steal.' [1] God's wisdom pronounces this, not the wit of man. For what truth soever the philosophers attained and disputed of amidst their falsehood, as, namely, that God framed the world, and governed it most excellently; the honesty of virtue; the love of

[1] Exod. xx. 12–15.

our country; the faith of friendship; just dealing, and all the things belonging to good manners—they knew not to what end the whole was to be referred. The prophets taught these things from the mouth of God in the persons of men, not with inundations of arguments, but inculcating fear and reverence of the Lord in all that understood them.

CHAPTER XLII

Of the translations of the Old Testament out of Hebrew into Greek, by the ordinance of God for the benefit of the nations

THESE scriptures one Ptolemy, a king of Egypt, desired to understand; for after the strange and wonderful conquest of Alexander of Macedon, surnamed 'the Great,' wherein he brought all Asia and almost all the world under his subjection, partly by fair means and partly by force (who came also into Judaea), his nobles after his death making a turbulent division, or rather a dilaceration of his monarchy, Egypt came to be ruled by the Ptolemies. The first of which was the son of Lagus, who brought many Jews captive into Egypt; the next was Philadelphus, who freed all those captives, sent gifts to the temple, and desired Eleazar the priest to send him the Old Testament, whereof he had heard great commendations, and therefore he meant to put it into his famous library. Eleazar sent it in Hebrew, and then he desired interpreters of him, and he sent him seventy-two, six of every tribe, all most perfect in the Greek and Hebrew. Their translation do we now usually call the Septuagint. The report of their divine concord therein is admirable: for Ptolemy having (to try their faith) made each one translate by himself, there was not one word of difference between them, either in sense or order, but all was one, as if only one had done it all, because indeed there was but one spirit in them all. And God gave them that admirable gift, to give a divine commendation to so divine a work, wherein the nations might see that presaged, which we all see now effected.

CHAPTER XLIII

That the translation of the Seventy has most authority, next unto the Hebrew

THERE were other translators out of the Hebrew into the Greek, as Aquila, Symmachus, Theodotion, and that nameless interpreter whose translation is called the fifth edition. But the Church has received that of the Seventy, as if there were no other, as many of the Greek Christians, using this wholly, know not whether there be or no. Our Latin translation is from this also; although one Jerome, a learned priest, and a great linguist, has translated the same scriptures from the Hebrew into Latin. But although the Jews affirm his learned labour to be all truth, and avouch the Seventy to have oftentimes erred, yet the Churches of Christ hold no one man to be preferred before so many, especially being selected by the high priest for this work. For although their concord had not proceeded from their unity of spirit but from their collations, yet were no one man to be held more sufficient than they all. But seeing there was so divine a demonstration of it, truly whosoever translates from the Hebrew, or any other tongue, either must agree with the Seventy, or if he dissent, we must hold by their prophetical inspiration. For the same Spirit that spake in the prophets was in their translators. And that Spirit might say otherwise in the translation than in the prophet, and yet speak alike in both, the sense being one unto the true understander though the words be different unto the reader. The same Spirit might add also, or diminish, to show that it was not man's labour that performed this work, but the working Spirit that guided the labours. Some held it good to correct the Septuagint by the Hebrew, yet durst they not reject what was in it and not in the Hebrew, but only added what was in that and not in it, marking the places with asterisks at the heads of the verses; and noting what was in the Septuagint, and not in the Hebrew, with lines, as we mark ounces of weight with. And many Greek and Latin copies are interspersed with these marks. But as for the alterations, whether the difference be great or small, they are not to be discerned but by a collation of the books. If therefore we look for the spirit of God and nothing else, as is fittest, whatsoever is in the Septuagint, and not in the Hebrew, it pleased God to speak by those latter prophets, and not by these first. And so contrariwise of that which is in the Hebrew and not in the Septuagint, herein showing them both to be prophets; for so did He speak this by Isaiah, that by Jeremiah, and other things by others as His pleasure was. But what we find in both, that the Spirit spake by both; by the first as prophets, by the latter as prophetical translations: for as there was one Spirit of peace in the first who spake so many several things without discordance, so was there in these who translated so consistently without conference.

CHAPTER XLIV

Of the destruction of Nineveh, which the Hebrew prefixes forty days unto, and the Septuagint but three

AYE, but some will say, How shall I know whether Jonas said, 'Yet forty days and Nineveh shall be destroyed,'[1] or, 'Yet three days'? Who does not see that the prophet, presaging their destruction,

[1] Jonah iii. 4.

could not say both? If at three days' end they were to be destroyed, then it could not be at forty; if at forty, then not at three.
    If I be asked the question, I answer for the Hebrew. For the
Septuagint being long after, might say otherwise, and yet not saying
something against the sense, but as pertinent to the matter as the
other, though in another signification; advising the reader not to
leave out the signification of the history for the circumstance of a
word, nor to contemn either of the authorities. For those things
were truly done at Nineveh, and yet had a reference farther than
Nineveh. It was true that the prophet was three days in the
whale's belly, and yet it intimated the being of the Lord of all
the prophets three days in the womb of the grave. Wherefore if
the Church of the Gentiles were prophetically figured by Nineveh,
as being destroyed in repentance, to become quite different from
what it was; Christ doing this in the said Church, it is He that is
signified both by the forty days, and by the three: by forty, because
he was so long with His disciples after His resurrection, and then
ascended into heaven; by three, for on the third day He arose
again. It is as if the Septuagint intended to stir the reader to look
further into the matter than the mere history, and that the prophet
had intended to intimate the depth of the mystery; as if he had
said: 'Seek Him in forty days whom thou shalt find in three'—
this in His Resurrection, and the other in His Ascension. Wherefore both numbers have their fit signification. Both are spoken
by one Spirit, the first in Jonah, the latter in the translators. Were
it not for tediousness, I could reconcile the Septuagint and the
Hebrew in many places wherein they are held to differ. But I
study brevity, and according to my talent have followed the
apostles, who assumed what made for their purposes out of both
the copies, knowing the Holy Spirit to be one in both. But to
proceed with our purpose.

CHAPTER XLV

*The Jews had no prophets ever after the repairing of the temple, and
were afflicted even from thence until Christ came: to show that the
prophets spoke of the building of the other temple*

AFTER the Jews were left destitute of prophets, they grew daily
worse and worse; namely, from the end of their captivity, when
they hoped to grow into better state upon the repairing of the
temple. For so that carnal nation understood Haggai's prophecy,
saying: 'The glory of this last house shall be greater than the first.' [1]
And yet he shows that he meant this to refer to the New Testament
in the words before, where he promised Christ expressly saying:
'I will move all nations, and the Desire of all nations shall come.' [2]

[1] Hag. ii. 9.   [2] Hag. ii. 7.

In this passage the Septuagint used a sense rather applicable to the members than the Head, saying: 'And they that are God's elect shall come out of all nations,' to wit, the men of whom Christ said in the gospel, 'Many are called, but few are chosen.'[1] For those chosen are the house of God built by the New Testament of living stones, far more glorious than that which was built by Solomon, and repaired after the captivity.   Therefore from thence had this nation no more prophets, but were sore afflicted by aliens, even by the Romans themselves, to teach them that Haggai was not speaking of that house which they had repaired.   For Alexander came soon after that, and subdued them; who, although he made no massacre of them (for they durst do no other but yield at his first beck), yet there was the glory of that temple proved inferior to what it had been in the times of their own free kings.   For in the temple did Alexander sacrifice, not in any true worship unto God, but giving Him a place in the adoration of his false deities. Then came the forenamed Ptolemy, son of Lagus, after Alexander's death, and he led many of them captive into Egypt; yet his son Philadelphus did courteously free them afterwards, and caused the seventy to translate the Old Testament for him, as I said before, from whence it came into our hands.

After all this, the wars mentioned in the Maccabees fell upon them.   And in process of time, Ptolemy, king of Alexandria, subdued them (he that was called Epiphanes), and then were they extremely plagued, forced to offer to idols, and their temple filled with sacrilegious pollution by Antiochus, king of Syria; whose leaders nevertheless Judas Maccabeus utterly subverted, and restored the temple to the ancient dignity.

Within a while after, did Alcimus (a man born out of the priests' blood) by ambition aspire to the priesthood; and then about fifty years after, all which were passed under the variable chance of war, did Aristobulus assume a diadem, and became both king and priest. For all the time before, ever since the captivity, they had no kings, but captains and generals, or princes (though a king may be called a prince, because of his pre-eminence, but all that are captains and princes are not kings, as Aristobulus was).   To him did Alexander succeed both in the kingdom and the priesthood, and is recorded to have been a tyrant over his people.   He left the throne to his wife Alexandra, and from thence began the Jews' extremities of affliction.   For her two sons, Aristobulus and Hyrcanus, contending for the principality, called in the Roman forces to come against Israel, Hyrcanus demanding their aid against his brother. Then had the Romans conquered all Africa and Greece; and having command over a multitude of other nations, the state seemed too heavy for itself, and broke itself down with its own burden.   For now had sedition got strong hold amongst them,

[1] Matt. xxii. 14.

breaking out into confederacies and civil wars, wherewith it was so
maimed, that now all declined into a monarchic form of government. But Pompey, the great general of Rome's forces, brought
his powers into Judaea, took Jerusalem, opened the temple doors
(not to go in to pray unto God, but rather to prey upon God) and
not as a worshipper, but as a profaner, entered the *sanctum sanctorum,* a place only lawful for the high priest to be seen in. And
having seated Hyrcanus in the priesthood, and made Antipater
provost of the province, he departed, carrying Aristobulus away
with him prisoner. Here began the Jews to be the Romans'
tributaries. Afterwards came Cassius and spoiled the temple.
And within a few years after, Herod an alien was made their
governor, and in his time was our Saviour Christ born.

For now was the fullness of the time come which the patriarch
prophetically implied, saying: 'The sceptre shall not depart from
Judah, nor the lawgiver from between his feet, until Shiloh come,
and He shall gather the nations unto Him.'[1] For the Jews had
never been without a prince of their blood, until Herod's time,
who was their first alien king. Now then was the time of Shiloh
come, now was the New Testament to be promulgated, and the
nations to be reconciled to the truth. For it were impossible that
the nations should desire Him to come in His glorious power to
judge (as we see they do), unless they had first been united in their
true belief in Him, when He came in His humility to suffer.

CHAPTER XLVI

*Of the Word's becoming flesh, our Saviour's birth; and the dispersion
of Jews*

HEROD reigning in Judaea, Rome's government being changed,
and Augustus Caesar being emperor, the world being all at peace,
Christ (according to the precedent prophecy) was born in Bethlehem of Judah, being manifestly man of His virgin mother, and
secretly God of God His Father: for so the prophet had said:
'Behold, a virgin shall conceive, and bear a Son: and she shall call
His name Emmanuel, that is, God with us.'[2] Now He showed
His deity by many miracles, which, as far as concerns His glory
and our salvation, are recorded in the gospel. The first is His
miraculous birth, the last His as miraculous ascension. But the
Jews who rejected Him, and slew Him (according to the need-
fulness of His death and resurrection), after that were miserably
spoiled by the Romans, under the domination of strangers, and
dispersed over the face of the whole earth. For they are in all
places with their testament, to show that we have not forged

[1] Gen. xlix. 10.   [2] Isa. vii. 14.

those prophecies of Christ, which many of them considering, both before His passion and after His resurrection, believed in Him; and they are the remnant that are saved through grace. But the rest were blind, as the psalm says: 'Let their table be made a snare unto them, and their prosperity their ruin: let their eyes be blinded that they see not, and make their loins alway to tremble.'[1] For in refusing to believe our scriptures, their own (which they read with blindness) are fulfilled upon them.

Some may say that the sibyl's prophecies which concern the Jews are but fictions of the Christians. But that suffices us which we have from the books of our enemies, which we acknowledge in that they preserve it for us against their wills, themselves and their books being dispersed as far as God's Church is extended and spread, in every corner of the world, as that prophecy of the psalm, which they themselves do read, foretells them. 'My merciful God will prevent me. God will let me see my desire upon mine enemies. Slay them not, lest my people forget it, but scatter them abroad with Thy power.'[2] Here did God show mercy to His Church, even by the Jews His enemies, because, as the apostle says, 'through their fall cometh salvation to the Gentiles.'[3] And therefore He slew them not, that is, He left them their name of Jews still, although they be the Romans' slaves, lest their utter dissolution should make us forget the law of God concerning this testimony of theirs. So it were nothing to say, 'Slay them not,' but that He adds, 'Scatter them abroad': for if they were not dispersed throughout the whole world with their scriptures, the Church would lack their testimonies concerning those prophecies fulfilled in our Messiah.

CHAPTER XLVII

Whether any but Israelites, before Christ's time, belonged to the city of God

WHEREFORE any stranger, be he no Israelite born, nor his works regarded as canonical by them, if he have prophesied of Christ, and we can know or quote him, may be added unto the number of our testimonies. Not that we need his words, but because it is no error to believe that there were some of the Gentiles to whom this mystery was revealed, and who were inspired by the spirit of prophecy to declare it, whether they were elect, or reprobate and taught by the evil spirits, who we know confessed Christ being come, though the Jews denied Him. Nor do I think the Jews dare aver that no man was saved after the propagation of Israel, on the rejection of his elder brother, but Israelites. Indeed there was no other people properly called the people of God, but

they cannot deny that some particular men lived in this world and
in other nations that were belonging to the heavenly hierarchy.
If they deny this, the story of holy Job convinces them, who was
neither a native Israelite nor a proselyte, adopted by their law,
but born and buried in Idumaea; and yet is he so highly commended in the scriptures, that there was none of his time (it seems)
that equalled him in righteousness, whose date though the chronicles express it not, yet out of the canonical authority of his own
book we gather him to have lived in the third generation after
Israel. God's providence (no doubt) intended to give us an instance
in him, that there might be others in the nations that lived after the
law of God, and in His service, thereby attaining a place in the
celestial Jerusalem: which we must think none did but such as
foreknew the coming of the Messiah, mediator between God and
man, who was prophesied unto the saints of old that He should
come just as we have seen Him to have come in the flesh. Thus
did one faith unite all the predestinated into one city, one house,
and one temple for the living God. But what other prophecies
soever there pass abroad concerning Christ, the vicious may
suppose that we have forged. Therefore there is no way so sure
to batter down all contentions of this kind, as by citing the prophecies contained in the Jews' books; by whose dispersion from
their proper habitations all over the world the Church of Christ is
happily increased.

CHAPTER XLVIII

*Haggai's prophecy of the glory of God's house fulfilled in the Church,
not in the temple*

THIS is that House of God more glorious than the former for all
the precious material. For Haggai's prophecy was not fulfilled in
the repairing of the temple, which never had that glory after the
restoring that it had in Solomon's time, but rather lost it all, the
prophets ceasing, and destruction ensuing, which was performed
by the Romans as I formerly related. But the House of the New
Testament is of another lustre, the workmanship being more
glorious, and the stones being more precious. But it was figured
in the reparation of the old temple, because the whole New Testament was figured in the Old. God's prophecy, therefore, that
saith, 'In this place will I give peace,'[1] is to be meant of the
place signified, not of the place which signifies: that is, as the
restoring of that house prefigured the Church which Christ was
to build, so God said, 'In this place' (that is, in the place that this
prefigures) 'will I give peace.' For all things signifying seem to

[1] Hag. ii. 9.

carry with them the persons of the things signified, as St. Paul said: 'the Rock was Christ';[1] for it signified Christ. So then, far is the glory of the House of the New Testament above the glory of the Old, as shall appear in the final dedication. Then shall the Desire of all nations appear (as it is in the Hebrew): for His first coming was not desired of all the nations, for some knew not whom to desire, nor in whom to believe. And then also 'shall they that are God's elect out of all nations come' (as the Seventy read it), for none shall come truly at that day but the elect, of whom the apostle says: 'As He hath elected us in Him, before the beginning of the world.'[2] For the Architect Himself, that said: 'Many are called, but few are chosen,'[3] spake not of those that were called to the feast and then cast out; but meant to show that He had built a house of His elect, which time's worst spite could never ruin. But since the churches are now full of those who are to be hereafter sifted, the corn from the chaff, the glory of this House cannot be so great now as it shall be then, when every man shall be always there where he once comes.

CHAPTER XLIX

The Church's increase uncertain, because of the commingling of elect and reprobate in this world

THEREFORE in these mischievous days, wherein the Church works for her future glory in present humility, in fears, in sorrows, in labours, and in temptations, joying only in hope when she joys as she should, many reprobate live amongst the elect. Both come into the gospel's net, and both swim at random in the sea of mortality, until the fishers draw them to shore, and then the bad are thrown from the good, in whom as in His temple God is all in all. We acknowledge therefore His words in the psalm: 'I would declare and speak of them, but they are more than I am able to express, to be truly fulfilled.'[4] This multiplication began at that instant when first John His messenger, and then Himself in person, began to say: 'Amend your lives,[5] for the kingdom of God is at hand.'[6] He chose Him disciples, whom He named the apostles, poor, ignoble, unlearned men, that what great work soever was done He might be seen to do it in them. He had one, who abused His goodness, yet used He this wicked man to a good end, to the fulfilling of His passion, and presenting His Church an example of patience in tribulation. And having sown sufficiently the seed of salvation, He suffered, was buried, and rose again; showing by

[1] 1 Cor. x. 4.   [2] Eph. i. 4.   [3] Matt. xxii. 14.   [4] Ps. xl. 5.
[5] St. Augustine quotes the Vulgate, *paenitentiam agite.*—ED.
[6] Matt. iii. 2.

His suffering what we ought to endure for the truth, and by His resurrection what we ought to hope for from eternity, besides the ineffable sacrament of His blood, shed for the remission of sins. He was forty days on earth with His disciples afterwards, and in their sight ascended to heaven, ten days later sending down His promised Spirit upon them; who in His coming gave that manifest and necessary sign of the knowledge of the languages of all nations, to signify that there was but one Catholic Church, which in all those nations should use all those tongues.

CHAPTER L

The gospel preached, and gloriously confirmed by the blood of the preachers

AND then it happened as it was prophesied: 'The law shall go forth from Sion, and the word of the Lord from Jerusalem,' [1] and as Christ had foretold, when (His disciples being astonished at His resurrection) He opened their understandings in the scriptures, and told them that it was written thus: 'It behoved Christ to suffer, and to rise again the third day, and that repentance and remission of sins should be preached in His name amongst all nations, beginning at Jerusalem'; [2] and when they asked Him of His second coming, and He answered: 'It is not for you to know the times and seasons which the Father hath put in His own power: but ye shall receive power of the Holy Ghost when He shall come upon you, and ye shall be witnesses of Me in Jerusalem, and in all Judaea, and in Samaria, and unto the utmost part of the earth.' [3] First the Church spread itself from Jerusalem, and then through Judaea, and Samaria; and those lights of the world bare the gospel unto other nations. For Christ had armed them, saying: 'Fear not them that kill the body but are not able to kill the soul.' [4] They had the heat of love which kept out the cold of fear. Finally, by their persons who had seen Him alive, and dead, and alive again; and by the horrible persecutions endured by their successors after their death, and by the diverse tortures and deaths of the martyrs, the gospel was diffused through all the habitable world; God going with it in miracles, in virtues, and in gifts of the Holy Ghost, insomuch that the nations believing in Him who suffered for their redemption, in Christian love did hold the blood of those martyrs in reverence, which before they had shed in barbarousness; and the kings whose edicts afflicted the Church came humbly to be warriors under that banner which they cruelly before had sought utterly to abolish, beginning now to persecute the false gods, for whom before they had persecuted the servants of the true God.

[1] Isa. ii. 3.   [2] Luke xxiv. 45–7.   [3] Acts i. 7, 8.   [4] Matt. x. 28.

CHAPTER LI

That the Church is confirmed even by the schisms of heresies

Now the devil, seeing his temples empty and all running unto this Redeemer, set heretics on foot to subvert Christ, in a Christian mask, as if there were that room for them in the heavenly Jerusalem which there was for contrariety of philosophers in the devil's Babylon. Such therefore as in the Church of God are sickly and perverse, and being checked and advised to beware do obstinately oppose themselves against good instructions, and rather defend their abominations than discard them, those become heretics, and going forth out of God's house, are to be held as our most eager enemies. Yet they do the members of the Catholic Church this good, that their fall makes them take better hold upon God, who uses evil to a good end, and works all for the good of those that love Him. So then all the Church's enemies, even if they have the power to impose corporal affliction, yet do they exercise her patience. If they bait her with opposition only verbal, they practise her in her wisdom. And she in loving these enemies exercises her benevolence and bounty, whether she go about them with gentle persuasion or severe correction. And therefore though the devil her chief opponent move all his vessels against her virtues, still he cannot injure her an inch. Comfort she has in prosperity, to be confirmed and constant in adversity; and exercised is she in adversity, to be kept from corruption in prosperity; God's providence managing the whole, and so tempering the one with the other that the psalmist said fitly: 'In the multitude of the cares of mine heart Thy comforts have rejoiced my soul.'[1] And the apostle also: 'Rejoicing in hope and patient in tribulation.'[2] For the same apostle's words saying, 'All that will live godly in Christ shall suffer persecution,'[3] must be held to be in continual action. For though *ab externo*, abroad, all seem quiet, no gust of trouble appearing, and that is a great comfort, to the weak especially: yet at home, *ab intus*, there do we never lack those that offend and molest the godly pilgrim by their devilish demeanour, blaspheming the Christian and catholic name; which the dearer the godly esteem it, so much more grief do they feel to hear, it being less respected by their pernicious brethren than they desire it should be. And the heretics themselves, being thought to have the name of Christ, the sacraments, the scriptures, and the holy profession[4] amongst them, grieve the hearts of the righteous extremely, because many that have a good desire to Christianity stumble at their dissessions, and again many that oppose it take occasion hereby to burden it with greater calamities; the heretics bearing the name of Christians also. These persecutions befall God's true servants by the vanity of others' errors, although they be quiet in their bodily estate. This persecution

[1] Ps. xciv. 19.   [2] Rom. xii. 12.   [3] 2 Tim. iii. 12.   [4] = the Creed.'—ED.

touches the heart, and not the body: as the psalm says: 'In the multitude of the cares of mine heart'; not 'of my body.' But then again, when we revolve the immutability of God's promises, who, as the apostle says, 'knoweth them that are His,'[1] whom He has predestinated to be made like the image of His Son, there shall not one of these be lost. Therefore the psalm adds: 'Thy comforts have rejoiced my soul.' Now the sorrow that the godly feel for the perverseness of evil or false Christians is good for their own souls, if it proceed from charity, not desiring their destruction nor the hindrance of their salvation: and the reformation of such yields great comfort to the devout soul, redoubling the joy now for the grief that it felt before for their errors. So then in these malignant days, not only from Christ and His apostles' time, but even from holy Abel whom his wicked brother slew, so along unto the world's end, does the Church travel on her pilgrimage, now suffering worldly persecutions, and now receiving divine consolations.

CHAPTER LII

Whether the opinion of some be credible, that there shall be no more persecutions after the ten passed, but the eleventh, which is that of Antichrist

BUT I think that that is not to be rashly affirmed, which some do think, viz. that the Church will suffer no more persecutions until Antichrist's time than the ten already passed, and that his shall be the eleventh and last. The first was under Nero, the second by Domitian, the third by Trajan, the fourth by Antoninus, the fifth by Severus, the sixth by Maximin, the seventh by Decius, the eighth by Valerian, the ninth by Aurelian, the tenth by Diocletian and Maximian. For some hold the plagues of Egypt being ten in number before Israel's freedom to have reference unto these, Antichrist's eleventh persecution being like the Egyptians' pursuit of Israel in the Red Sea, in which they were all drowned. But I take not those events in Egypt to be in any way pertinent unto these, either as prophecies or figures, although they that hold otherwise have made a very ingenious adaptation of the one to the other, but not by the spirit of prophecy, but only by human conjecture, which sometimes may err, as well as not. For what will they that hold this affirm of the persecution wherein Christ was killed? What rank shall that have amongst the rest? If they except this, and hold that such only are to be reckoned as belong to the body and not to the Head, what do they say to those persecutions after the ascension, where Stephen was stoned, and James the brother of John beheaded, and Peter shut up for the slaughter, but that the angel freed him; where the brethren were chased from Jerusalem,

[1] 2 Tim. ii. 19.

and Saul (afterwards made an apostle and called Paul) played the
pursuer amongst them, haling them out to destruction; and where
he himself also being converted, and preaching the faith which he
had persecuted, suffered such afflictions as aforetimes he had laid
upon others, wheresoever he preached unto Jews or Gentiles?
Why do they begin at Nero, when the Church was never without
persecutions through all the time before, whereof it is too tedious
to recount the particulars? If they will not begin but at persecutions by a king, why, Herod was a king, who did the Church
extreme injury after Christ's ascension. Again, why are not
Julian's villainies reckoned amongst the ten? Was not he a persecutor that forbade the Christians to be taught the liberal arts?
Was not Valentinian the elder (who was third emperor after him)
deprived of his generalship for confessing Christ, to omit all the
massacres begun at Antioch by this wicked apostate, until one
faithful and constant young man lying in tortures a whole day,
continually singing psalms, and praying to God, did with his
patience so terrify the persecuting atheist, that he was both afraid
and ashamed to proceed? Now, lastly, Valens an Arian, brother
to the above-named Valentinian—hath not he afflicted the eastern
Church with great trouble even now before our eyes? What a
lame consideration is it to collect the persecutions endured by a
universal Church under one prince, and in one nation, and not in
another? Cannot a Church so far diffused suffer affliction in one
particular nation but it must suffer in all? Perhaps they will not
reckon the Christian persecution in Gothland, by their own king,
who martyred many true Catholics, as we heard of divers brethren
who had seen it, when living in those parts as children. And
what can they say about Persia? Have not the persecutions there
chased divers even unto the towns of the Romans? It may be
now quiet, but it is more than we can tell. Now all these con-
siderations laid together, and others like them, make me think
that the number of the Church's persecutions is not to be defined;
but to affirm that there may be many inflicted by other kings before
that great and assured one of Antichrist, were as rash an assertion
as the other. Let us therefore leave it in the midst, neither
affirming nor contradicting, but only controlling the rashness of
both in others.

CHAPTER LIII

Of the unknown time of the last persecution

THE last persecution under Antichrist, Christ's personal presence
shall extinguish: for, 'He shall consume him with the breath of
His mouth, and abolish him with the brightness of His presence,' [1]

[1] 2 Thess. ii. 8.

says the apostle. And here is a usual question: 'When shall this be?' It is a saucy [1] one. If the knowledge of it would have done us good, who would have revealed it sooner than Christ unto His disciples? For they were not silent when with Him, but asked Him, saying: 'Lord, wilt Thou at this time restore the kingdom to Israel'? But what said He? 'It is not for you to know the times or seasons which the Father hath put in His own power.' [2] They asked Him not of the day or hour, but of the time, when He answered them thus. In vain therefore do we try to reckon the remainder of the world's years, when we hear the plain truth telling us: 'It befits us not to know them.' Some say that it shall last four hundred, some five hundred, some a thousand years after the ascension. Every one has his view, it were in vain to try to show upon what grounds. In a word, their conjectures are all human, grounded upon no certainty of scripture. For He that said, 'It is not for you to know the times,' etc., stops all your accounts and bids you leave your calculations.

But this being an evangelical sentence, I wonder not that it was not powerful enough to repress the audacious fictions of some infidels touching the continuance of Christian religion. For those, observing that these greatest persecutions did rather increase than suppress the faith of Christ, invented a sort of Greek verses (as if they had been oracular), explaining that Christ was clear from this sacrilege, but that Peter had by magic founded the worship of the name of Christ for three hundred threescore and five years, and that at that date it should utterly cease. Oh, learned heads! Oh, rare inventions fit to believe those things of Christ, since you will not believe in Christ; to wit, that Peter learned magic of Christ, yet was He innocent; and that His disciple was a wizard, and yet would rather have his Master's name honoured than his own, working to that end with his magic, with toil, with perils, and lastly with the effusion of his blood! If Peter's witchcraft made the world love Christ so well, what had Christ's innocence done that Peter should love Him so well? Let them answer, and (if they can) conceive that it was that supernal grace that fixed Christ in the hearts of the nations for the attainment of eternal bliss; which grace also made Peter willing to endure a temporal death for Christ, by Him to be received into the said eternity. And what goodly gods are these, that can presage things and yet not prevent them; but are forced by one wizard and (as they affirm) by one child-slaughtering sacrifice, to suffer a sect so injurious to them to prevail against them for so long, and to bear down all persecutions by bearing them with patience, and to destroy their temples, images, and sacrifices! Which of their gods is it (none of ours it is) that is compelled to work these effects by so wicked an oblation? For the verses say that Peter dealt not with a devil, but with a god in his

---

[1] Latin *importune omnino*.—ED.   [2] Acts i. 6, 7.

magical operation. Such a god have they, that have not Christ
for their God.

CHAPTER LIV

*The pagans' foolishness in affirming that Christianity should last but
three hundred and sixty-five years*

I COULD gather many arguments such as this, if the year were not
past that those lies prefixed and those foolish men expected. But
seeing it is now above three hundred and sixty-five years since
Christ's coming in the flesh, and the apostles' preaching His name,
what need is there of any plainer confutation? For to omit
Christ's infancy and childhood wherein He had no disciples, yet
after His baptism in Jordan, by John, as soon as He called some
disciples to Him, His name assuredly began to be divulged, of
whom the prophet had said: 'He shall rule from sea to sea, and
from the river to the land's end.'[1] But because the faith was not
definitely decreed until after His passion, to wit, in His resurrection; for so says St. Paul to the Athenians: 'Now He admonisheth
all men everywhere to repent, because He hath appointed a day in
which He will judge the world in righteousness by that Man in
whom He hath appointed a faith unto all men, in that He hath
raised Him from the dead';[2] we shall do better for the solution of
this question to begin at that time, chiefly because then the Holy
Spirit descended upon that society wherein the second law, the
New Testament, was to be professed, according as Christ had
promised. For the first law, the Old Testament, was given in Sinai
by Moses, but the latter which Christ was to give was prophesied
in these words: 'The law shall go forth out of Sion, and the word
of the Lord from Jerusalem.'[3] Therefore He said Himself that it
was fit that repentance should be preached in His name throughout
all nations, yet beginning at Jerusalem. There then began the
belief in Christ crucified and risen again. There did this faith
heat the hearts of divers thousands already, who sold their goods
to give to the poor, and came cheerfully to Christ and to voluntary
poverty, withstanding the assaults of the bloodthirsty Jews with a
patience stronger than an armed power.

If this now were not done by magic, why might not the rest
that was done in all the world be as clearly due to the same divine
power? But if Peter's magic had made those men honour Christ,
who both crucified Him and derided Him being crucified, then
I ask them when their three hundred threescore and five years must
have an end? Christ died in the consulship of the two Gemini,
the eighth of the calends of April, and rose again the third day,
as the apostles saw with their eyes, and felt with their hands. Forty

<hr>

[1] Ps. lxxii. 8.   [2] Acts xvii. 30, 31.   [3] Isa. ii. 3.

days after ascended He into heaven, and ten days after (that is
fifty after the resurrection) came the Holy Ghost, and then three
thousand men believed in the apostles' preaching of Him.   And
so then His name began to spread, as we believe, and as it was truly
proved, by the operation of the Holy Ghost; but as the infidels
feign, by Peter's magic.   And soon after five thousand more
believed through the preaching of Peter and his miraculous curing
of one that had been born lame and lay begging at the porch of the
temple; Peter with one word, 'In the name of our Lord Jesus
Christ,' set him sound upon his feet.   Thus the Church got up by
degrees.   Now reckon the years by the consuls from the descent
of the Holy Spirit that was in the ides of May, unto the consulship
of Honorius and Eutychian, and you shall find full three hundred
threescore and five years expired.   Now in the next year, in the
consulship of Mallius Theodorus, when Christianity should have
been utterly gone (according to that oracle of devils, or fiction of
fools), what is done in other places we need not inquire; but as for
that famous city of Carthage we know that Junius and Gaudentius,
two of Honorius' officers, came thither on the tenth of the calends
of April, and broke down all the idols, and pulled down their
temples.

   It is now almost thirty years ago since then, and what increase
Christianity has had since is apparent enough, and especially
amongst many whom the expectation of the fulfilling of that oracle
kept from being reconciled to the truth, but who since are come
into the bosom of the Church, discovering the ridiculousness of
that former expectation.   But we that are Christians *re et ore*, in
deed and in name, do not believe in Peter, but in Him that Peter
believed in.   We are edified by Peter's sermons of Christ, but
not bewitched by his charms nor deceived by his magic, but
furthered by his religion.   Christ, that taught Peter the doctrine
of eternal life, teaches us also.   But now it is time to set an end
to this book, wherein as far as need was we have run along with
the courses of the two cities in their confused progress; the one of
which, the Babylon of the earth, has made her false gods of mortal
men, serving them and sacrificing to them as she thought good;
but the other, the heavenly Jerusalem, has stuck to the only and
true God, and is His true and pure sacrifice herself.   But both of
these do feel one touch of good and evil fortune, but not with one
faith, nor one hope, nor one law: and at length, at the last judgment,
they shall be severed for ever, and each shall receive the endless
reward of their works.   Of these two ends we are now to discourse.

THE NINETEENTH BOOK OF
THE CITY OF GOD

CHAPTER I

*That Varro observed two hundred and eighty-eight sects of the
philosophers in their question of the perfection of goodness*

WHEREAS I am now to draw my discourse from the progress unto
the consummation of the state of those two hierarchies, the celestial
and the terrestrial, I must therefore lay down their arguments
(as far as the limits of this volume may permit) who intend to
make for themselves a beatitude extant even in the continual misfortunes of man's temporal mortality. And herein my purpose is
to parallel their empty dreams with our assured hope, which God
has given us, and with the object of that assurance, namely, the
true blessedness which He will give us; that so confirming our
assertions both with holy scriptures, and with such reasons as are
fit to be produced against infidels, the difference of their grounds
and ours may be the more fully apparent. About that question
of the final good the philosophers have kept a wonderful coil
amongst themselves, seeking in every cranny and cavern thereof
for the true beatitude; for that is the final good, which is desired
only for itself, all other goods having in their attainments a reference unto that alone. We do not call that the final good, which
ends goodness, that is, which makes it nothing, but that which
perfects it, and gives it fullness of perfection. Nor do we call that
the end of all evil, whereby it ceases to be evil; but that point
which mischief arises unto, still preserving the mischievous nature,
that we call the end of mischief. So then the great good and the
greatest evil, are the ends of all good and evil, the final goodness
and the final badness. About which two there has been wonderful research, to avoid the final evil and attain the final good.
This was the daily endeavour of our worldly philosophers, who
though they were guilty of much exorbitance of error, yet the
bounds of nature were such limits to their aphorisms that they
sought no further than either the body, the mind, or both, wherein
to place this *summum bonum* of theirs. From this tripartite foundation has M. Varro, in his book *De Philosophia*, most subtly and
diligently observed two hundred and eighty-eight possible though
not actual sects, for so many different results may be drawn from
those three fountains.

And to make a brief demonstration of these I must begin with that which he rehearses in the book aforenamed, that there are four things which every one desires by nature, without help of master or industry or that habit of life which is called virtue, and is learned by degrees; namely, either sensible pleasure, or sensible rest, or both (which Epicurus calls by one name of pleasure), or the universal first objects of nature, wherein these and the rest are included, as in the body health and strength, and in the mind sharpness of wit and soundness of judgment. These four, therefore, pleasure, rest, both of these together, and nature's first objects, are in the fabric of man under these respects, that either virtue (the effect of doctrine) is to be desired for them, or for itself, or they for virtue or for themselves. And here are foundations for twelve sects, for by this means they are all tripled. I will show it in one, and that will make it apparent in all the rest. Bodily pleasure being either set under virtue, above it, or equal with it, gives life to three different opinions. It is under virtue when virtue rules it and uses it, for it is a virtue to live for our country's good, and for the same end to beget our children; neither of which can be excluded from corporal delight, for without that we neither eat to live, nor use the means of carnal generation. But when this pleasure is preferred before virtue, then is it affected in mere respect of itself, and virtue's attainment is wholly referred unto that; that is, all virtue's acts must tend to the production of corporal pleasure, or else to the preservation of it: which is a deformed kind of life, because therein virtue is slave to the commands of voluptuousness (though, indeed, that cannot properly be called virtue that is so). But even this deformity could not lack patronage, and that by many philosophers. Now, pleasure and virtue are joined in equality when they are both sought for themselves, no way respecting others. Wherefore, as the subjection, pre-eminence, or equality of virtue unto voluptuousness, make three sects, so do rest, delight and rest, and the first objects of nature make three more in this kind, for they have their three places under, above, or equal to virtue, as well as pleasure. Thus does the number become twelve. Now add but one difference, to wit, social life, and the whole number is doubled; because, whosoever follows any one of these twelve sects, does so either as respecting himself or his fellow, for whom he ought to wish what he wishes for himself. So there may be twelve men that hold those twelve opinions each one for their own respect, and another twelve that hold them in respect of others, whose good they desire as much as their own. Now, bring in but your new Academics, and these twenty-four sects become forty-eight, for every one of these positions may be either maintained Stoically to be certain (as in the case of virtue, which the Stoics regard as the sole good) or Academically, as uncertain, and not so much assuredly true, as likely to be true. Thus are there twenty-four affirming the certain truth of those positions, and twenty-four standing wholly for their uncertainty. Again, each of these positions may be defended either in the manners of any other philosopher or of a Cynic, and this instead of forty-eight makes the whole ninety-six. Again, these may either be disputed of by such as merely profess philosophy, in no way intermeddling with affairs of State; or by such as love argument and yet nevertheless keep a place in political affairs and employments of public life; or by such as profess both, and by a certain vicissitude, do now play the mere philosopher's part, and now the mere politician's: and thus is the number trebled, amounting to two hundred and eighty-eight.

Thus much as briefly as I could have I taken out of Varro, laying down his doctrine in mine own forms. But to show how he refutes all the rest but one, and chooses that, the one belonging to the old Academics of Plato's institution (continuing to defend certain aphorisms from him to Polemo, the fourth that succeeded him), who are quite different from the new Academics who lay down nothing positively, and who were instituted by Arcesilas, Polemo's successor—to show Varro's opinion in this, that the old Academics were free both of uncertainty and error, is too tedious for me to make a full relation of it, yet may we lawfully (nay, and must necessarily) take a view of it in some part. First therefore he removes all the differences producing this multitude of sects. His reason is that they aim not at the perfection of goodness. For he holds that to be alone worthy of the name of a sect in philosophy which differs from all others in the main ends of good and evil; the end of all philosophy being only beatitude, which is the main end and perfection of all goodness. This then is the aim of all philosophers; and such as do not aim at this are unworthy of that name. Wherefore in that question of the social life, whether a wise man should respect the perfection of goodness in his friend as much as in himself, or do all he does for his own beatitude's sake—this does in no way concern the good itself, but only the assuming or not assuming of a companion into the participation of it, not for one's own sake, but for his sake that is admitted, whose good the other desires as he does his own. And likewise when it is asked by these new Academics, whether all these assertions are to be held as uncertain, or with that assurance that other philosophers defended them, the question is not concerned with the nature of that which we are to attain as the end of all good, but it asks whether there be such a thing or no, averring a doubt hereof rather than an affirmation: that is, to be more plain, the controversy is, whether the follower of this perfection may affirm his final good to be certain, or only that it seems so, but may be uncertain; and yet both these pursue one good. And likewise again in the matter of the manners of the Cynics, the reality of the good is not called in question, but whether it is to be followed in such a fashion of life and conversation or no. Finally, there have been philosophers that have affirmed diversely of the final good, some placing it in virtue, and some in pleasure, and yet have they all observed the manners and form of carriage of the Cynics; so that the cause of their being styled so, had no manner of reference to the perfection that they studied to attain. For if it had, then should that end be peculiar to those manners, and not be associated with any other.

CHAPTER II

Varro's reduction of the final good out of all these differences unto three heads and three definitions, one only of which is the true one

MOREOVER in regard to these three sorts of life, the contemplative, the active, and the mixed, if our question be which of these we should observe, we are not concerned with the final good, but with the easy or hard attainment of that good, which accompanies those three several courses; for being attained, the final good does immediately make the attainer blessed. But it is neither contemplation, nor action, nor these two proportioned together, that make a man blessed; for one may live in any of these three fashions, and yet be far wide from the true course to beatitude. So then the questions touching the end of goodness, which distinguish all those sects, are far different from those of social life, Academical doubt, the manners of the Cynics, and that of the three courses of conversation, the philosophical, the political, and the mixed. For none of all these do once touch upon the natures of good and evil. Wherefore Varro having recited the last four, whereby the whole sum of opinions amounts to two hundred and eighty-eight—because they are not worthy of the name of sects, in that they make no mention of the good that is chiefly to be desired, he leaves them all, and returns to those first twelve, whose controversy is about the main point, man's chief good. Out of these will he gather one direct truth, and show all the rest to be false. For first he removes the three sorts of life, and they carry two parts of the number with them; so there remains but ninety-six. Then go the Cynics, and they carry forty-eight with them, so there remains but forty-eight. Then send away the new Academics with their parts, so there remains but thirty-six. And then the social conversation, with the multitude that it brought, so there remains only twelve, which no man can deny to be twelve several sects. For their only difference is about the supreme good and evil. For the ends of good being found, the evils lie directly opposite. So these twelve sects are produced by the triplication of these four, pleasure, rest, both of these together, and nature's primitive desires and habits, which Varro calls *primogenia*. For they are all made

either virtue's inferiors, and desired only in respect of her; or her
superiors, and she desired only for their sake; or equals, and both
are desired for their own sakes: thus do they amount to twelve
several sects. Now from these four heads Varro takes away
three, pleasure, rest, and both united; not that he disproves them,
but that they are already included in the fourth, namely the first
objects of nature, and so are many things more, and therefore
why need they keep a number in this rank? So then of the three
remaining that can be deduced from the fourth head, his discourse
must wholly be framed, to know which of them is the truth. There
can be but one true one by reason, be it in these three, or in some
other thing, as we shall see afterwards. Meantime let us briefly
see Varro's choice of the three: which are these: 'Whether nature's
primary desires ought to be desired for virtue's sake, or virtue
for theirs, or both for themselves.'

CHAPTER III

*Varro's choice amongst the three fore-named sects, following therein
the opinion of Antiochus, founder of the old Academical sect*

THUS he begins to show in which of them the truth is contained.
First, because the question concerns not the beatitude of gods, or
beasts, or trees, but of man, he holds it fit to examine what man is.
Two things he finds in his nature, body and soul, whereof the soul
he affirms to be the far more excellent part. But whether the soul
alone be man, and the body be unto it as the horse is to the horseman, that he makes another controversy of (for the horseman is the
man alone, not the horse and man both together; yet is it the man's
reference to the horse that gives him that name). Or whether the
body alone be the man, having that relation unto the soul that the
cup has to the drink (for it is not the cup and the drink both that
are called *poculum* in Latin, but the cup only; yet only in respect
that it contains the drink). Or whether it be both body and soul
conjoined, and not several, that is called man, and these two are
but his parts; as two oxen are called a yoke (which though it consist
of one on this side, and another on that, yet call we neither of them
separately a yoke, but both combined together). Now of those
three positions he chooses the last, calling the essence composed of
body and soul, man, and denying the appellation unto either of
them being severally considered. And therefore (says he) man's
beatitude must be included in the goods that belong jointly both to
body and soul; so that the prime gifts of nature are to be desired
for themselves, and that virtue which doctrine does gradually
engraft in a good mind is the most excellent good of all. And this
virtue or method of life, having received those first gifts of nature

(which notwithstanding had being before they had virtue), now desires all things for itself, and itself also for its own sake; using all things together with itself unto its own pleasure and delightful fruition, taking pleasure in them all, whether greater or smaller, and yet if necessity require, rather refusing the smaller goods, for the attainment or preservation of the greater, than otherwise. But it holds itself entirely in higher respect than any other good whatsoever, mental or corporal: for it knows both the use of itself and of all other good things that makes a man happy. But where it is wanting, be there never so many good things, they are none of his that has them, because he cannot give them their true natures by good application of them. That man, therefore, alone is truly blessed, that can use virtue, and the other bodily and mental goods which virtue cannot be without, all unto their true end. If he can make good use of those things also that virtue may easily do without, he is the happier in that. But if he can so use all things whatsoever, as to turn them either to the good of the body or of the mind, then is he the happiest man on earth: for life and virtue are not one and the same. The wise man's life alone is it, that deserves that name; for some kinds of life may be wholly void of virtue, but no virtue can be without life. And so likewise is it with memory, reason, and other qualities in man. All these are before learning, it cannot be without them any more than virtue can, which it does teach. But swiftness of foot, beauty of face, strength of body, and such, may be all without virtue; and all of them are good of themselves without virtue; yet is virtue desired for itself nevertheless, and uses these good things as befits. Now this blessed estate of life they hold to be sociable also, desiring the neighbours' good as much as its own, and wishing for them in their own respects what it wishes for itself; whether it be wives and children, or fellow citizen, or any mortal men whatsoever, or it may be even the gods whom they hold the friends of wise men, and whom we call by a more familiar name angels. But of the ends of the good and evil they make no doubt, wherein alone (they say) they differ from the new Academics; nor care they whether a man follow the Cynic's mode of life or some other, so long as he aver their ends. Now of the three lives, contemplative, active, and mixed, they choose the last. Thus (says Varro) the old Academy taught, Antiochus, master to him and Tully, being author hereof, though Tully makes him rather a Stoic than an old Academician in most of his opinions. But what is that to us? We are rather to look how to judge of the matter, than how others judge of the men.

CHAPTER IV

The Christian's opinion of the chiefest good and evil, which the philosophers held to be within themselves

IF you ask us now what the city of God says, first to this question of the supreme good and evil, it will answer you at once: Eternal life is the perfection of good, and eternal death the consummation of evil; and the aim of our life must be to avoid the one, and attain the other. Therefore it is written: 'The just shall live by faith.'[1] For we see not our greatest good, and therefore are to believe and hope for it; nor have we power to live accordingly, unless our belief and prayer obtain help of Him who has given us that belief and hope that He will help us. But such as found the perfection of felicity upon this life, placing it either in the body, or in the mind, or in both: or, to speak more plainly, either in pleasure or in virtue, or in pleasure and rest together, or in virtue, or in both; or in nature's first desires, or in virtue, or in both, fondly and vainly are these men persuaded to find true happiness here. The prophet laughs at them, saying: 'The Lord knoweth the thoughts of men' (or, as St. Paul has it, 'of the wise') 'that they are vain.'[2] For who can discourse exactly of the miseries of this life? Tully, upon his daughter's death, did what he could. But what could he do? In what person can the first objects of nature be found without alteration? What, have not sorrow and disquiet full power to disturb the pleasure and quiet of the wisest? Even so strength, beauty, health, vigour, and activity, are all subverted by their contraries, by loss of limbs, deformity, sickness, faintness, and unwieldiness. And what if a member suffers from some tumour or other disease? What if weakness of the back bend a man down to the ground, making him near to a four-footed beast? Is not all the grace of his posture quite gone? And then the first gifts of nature, whereof sense and reason are the two first, because of the apprehension of truth, how easily are they lost! How totally does deafness or blindness take away hearing and sight! And then for the reason, how soon is it subverted by a frenzied passion, or lethargy! Oh, it is able to wring tears from our eyes to see the actions of insane persons so wholly different, nay, so directly contrary unto reason's direction! Why need I speak of the demoniacs, whose understanding the devil wholly dulls, and uses all their powers of soul and body at his own pleasure? And what wise man can fully secure himself from these incursions? Again, how weak is our apprehension of truth in this life when, as we read in the book of true Wisdom, 'the corruptible body is heavy unto the soul, and the earthly mansion keepeth down the mind that is full of cares.'[3]

[1] Hab. ii. 4.   [2] Ps. xciv. 11; 1 Cor. iii. 20.   [3] Wisd. of Sol. ix. 15.

And that same ὁρμή, that violent impulse unto action, which they
reckon for one of nature's first benefits in good men, is it not that
that causes those strange and horrible acts of madness when the
reason and sense are both besotted and darkened? Besides,
virtue, which is not from nature, but comes afterwards from learning, when it has got the highest place in humanity, what other
work has it but a continual fight against the inbred vices that are
inherent in our own bosoms, not in others—especially the virtue
σωφροσύνη, that temperance which suppresses the lusts of the
flesh, and curbs them from carrying the mind away into mischief?
For it is a vice when, as the apostle says, 'the flesh lusteth against
the spirit'; and on the contrary it is a virtue, when 'the spirit
lusteth against the flesh': for they, says he, 'are contrary, so that
ye cannot do what you would.' [1]   And what would we?   What is
our desire in this perfection of good, but that the flesh should not
lust against the spirit, and that there were no vice in us against
which the spirit should lust?   Which since we cannot attain in
this life, however much we try, let us by God's grace endeavour
this, that we do not subject our spirit unto the concupiscence of
our flesh, and so set our seal unto the bond of sin with a free
consent.

So then far be it from us ever to think that we have attained the
true happiness whilst we live here.   Who is so wise but has now
and then divers fights against his own lusts?   What is the office
of prudence?   Is it not to discern between things to be chosen
and things to be refused, to the end that no error be incurred in
either?   This testifies that there is evil in us, and that we are in
evil.   It teaches us that it is evil to assent unto sin, and good to
avoid it.   But yet neither can prudence nor temperance rid our
lives of that evil which they forewarn us of and arm us against.
And what of justice, that gives every one his due?   And the just
order of nature is that the soul be under God, the flesh under the
soul, and both together under God.   Is it not plain that this is
rather continually laboured after than truly attained in this life?
For the less that the soul does meditate on God, the less it serves
Him, and the more that the flesh lusts against the soul, the less
command has the soul over it.   Wherefore as long as we are subjected unto this languor and corruption, how dare we say we are
safe, and if not safe, much less blessed by the perfection of attained
bliss?

Now there is also fortitude, another authentic testimony of
human miseries endured with patience.

I wonder with what face the Stoics deny these to be evils, of
which they confess that if a wise man cannot or ought not to
endure them, he may lawfully (nay, he must needs) kill himself,
and avoid this life.   To this height is their proud stupidity grown

[1] Gal. v. 17.

(building all their beatitude upon this life), that if their wise man were blind, deaf, lame, and made the very hospital of all agonies and anguish, which should lie so sore on him that they should force him to be his own death, yet this life that is environed with all those plagues are they not ashamed to call blessed. Oh, sweet and blessed life, which it is requisite that death do conclude! For if it be blessed why then not keep it still? But if those evils make it to be avoided, what is become of the bliss? Or what are these but evils, that have such power to subvert the good of fortitude, making it not only guilty of dejection, but of dotage in affirming that one and the same life is blessed, and yet must be avoided? Who is so blind that sees not that if it be the one, it cannot possibly be the other? Oh, but, say they, the avoidance is caused by the effect of the overpressing infirmity. Why may they not as well bid adieu to obstinacy, and confess that it is wretched? Was it patience that made Cato kill himself? No, he would not have done it but that he took Caesar's victory so impatiently. Where was his fortitude now? Gone; it yielded, and was so trodden down that it fled both light and life, blessed as it was! Or was not his life then blessed? Then it was wretched. Why then are not they true evils that can make one's life so wretched as to be avoided? And therefore the Peripatetics and old Academics (whose sect Varro stands wholly for) did better in calling these accidents plainly evil. But they have one foul error, to hold his life that endures these evils blessed, if he rid himself from them by his own voluntary destruction. The pains and torments of the body are evil, say they, and the greater the worse, which to avoid you must willingly betake yourself to death, and leave this life. What life? This, that is so encumbered with evils. What, is it then blessed among so many evils that must be avoided, or call you it blessed, because you may abandon these evils when you will by death? What if some divine power should hold you from dying, and keep you continually in those evils? then you would say this were a wretched life indeed! Well, the early leaving of it makes not against the misery of it; because if it were eternal, yourself would judge it miserable. It is not free from misery therefore because it is short, nor (much less) is it happiness in that the misery is short. It must needs be a forcible evil, that has power to make a man (nay, and a wise man) to be his own executioner, it being truly said by themselves, that it is as it were nature's first and most forcible precept, that a man should cherish a respect of himself, and therefore avoid the hand of death, by sheer natural instinct, and so befriend himself, that he should still desire to be a living creature, and enjoy the conjunction of his soul and body. Mighty are the evils that subdue this natural instinct, which is in all men to desire to avoid death, and subdue it so far, that what was before abhorred should now be desired, and (rather than being done without)

effected by a man's own hand.   Mighty is the mischief that makes
fortitude a homicide, if that can be called fortitude which yields
so to these evils, that it is fain to force him to kill himself to avoid
these inconveniences whom it has undertaken to defend against all
inconveniences.

A wise man is indeed to endure death with patience, but that
must come *ab externo*, from another man's hand and not from his
own.   But these men teaching that he may do it himself, must
needs confess that the evils are intolerable which force a man to
such an extreme impropriety.   The life therefore that is liable
to such a multitude of miseries could in no way be called happy, if
the men who say it is were as ready in their quest for the blessed
life to yield to the truth being convinced by the certainty of reason,
as they are to avoid unhappiness by killing themselves, and so to
discern that the perfection of beatitude is not resident in this mortal
life, when in man's greatest gifts, the greater help they afford him
against anguish, dangers, and griefs, the surer testimonies are they
of human miseries.   For if true virtues can be in none in whom
there is no true piety, then do they not promise any people, in
whom they are, any assurance against suffering of temporal sorrows.   For true virtue may not dissemble, in professing what it
cannot perform: but it aims at this only, that man's life which
being in this world is perturbed with all these extremes of sorrows,
should in the life to come be made partaker both of safety and
felicity.   For how can that man have felicity that lacks safety?
It is not therefore of the unwise, intemperate, impatient, or unjust
that St. Paul speaks, saying, 'We are saved by hope,' but of the
son of true piety, and of the observers of the real virtues: 'Hope
that is seen is not hope, for how can a man hope for that which he
seeth?   But if we hope for that we see not, we do with patience
wait for it.' [1]   Wherefore as we are saved, so are we blessed by
hope; and as we have no hold on our safety, no more have we of
our felicity, but by hope, patiently awaiting it; and being as yet
in a desert of thorny dangers, all these we must constantly endure
until we come to the paradise of all ineffable delights, having then
passed all the perils of encumbrance.   This security in the life to
come is the beatitude we speak of, which the philosophers not
beholding will not believe, but forge themselves an imaginary bliss
here, wherein the more their virtue assumes to itself, the falser it
proves to the judgment of all others.

[1] Rom. viii. 24, 25.

CHAPTER V

*Of living sociably with our neighbour : how fit it is, and yet how
subject to crosses*

WE do worthily approve their enjoining a wise man to live in mutual society; for how should our celestial city (the nineteenth book whereof we now have in hand) have ever come to its origin, development, or perfection, unless the saints live all in sociable union? But yet who is he that can recount all the miseries incident unto the societies of mortals? Hear what the comedian says, with general applause: 'I married a wife. Oh, what misery lacked I then! I begat children: so there's one care more.'[1] And those inconveniences that Terence pins on the back of love, as injuries, enmities, war, and peace again, do not all these wait upon our mortality continually? Do not these invade sometimes the friendliest affections? And does not all the world regard as certain evils injuries, enmities, and wars? And our peace is as uncertain, as we are ignorant of their hearts on whom it depends; and though we know to-day what they would do, to-morrow we may not. Who should be greater friends than those of one family? Yet how many secret plots of malice lie even amongst such, to expel security; their firmer peace becoming fouler malice; and being reputed most loyal, whereas it was only most craftily feigned? The far-spread contagion of this made Tully utter this saying which provokes our tears : 'Treason is never so dangerous, as when it lurks under the name of duty or affinity. An open foe is easily watched; but this your secret serpent both breeds and strikes ere ever you can discover it.'[2] Wherefore that which the holy scripture says, 'A man's foes are those of his own household,'[3] this we hear with great grief: for though a man have fortitude to endure it, or prevention to avoid it, yet if he be a good man, he must needs feel great grief at the badness of those so near him; be it that they have been accustomed unto this viperous dissimulation of old, or have learnt it but of late. So, then, if a man's own private house afford him no shelter from these incursions, what shall the city do, which, as it is larger, so is it fuller of squabbles, and suits, and quarrels, and accusations, even if we grant the absence of seditions and civil contentions, which are too often present, and whereof the cities are in continual danger, when they are in their safest estate?

---

[1] Terence, *Adelph.* v. v. ii. 13, 14.   [2] 2 *Verr.* i. 1, 15, 39.
[3] Mic. vii. 6; Matt. x. 36.

CHAPTER VI

The error of human judgments in cases where truth is not known

AND how lamentable and miserable are those men's judgments whom the cities must perforce use as magistrates, even in their most settled peace, concerning other men! They judge them whose consciences they cannot see, and therefore are often driven to wring forth the truth by tormenting of innocent witnesses. And what say you when a man is tortured in his own case, and tormented, even when it is a question whether he be guilty or no? And though he be innocent, yet suffers he assured pains when they are not assured he is faulty. In most of these cases the judge's ignorance turns to the prisoner's misery. Nay (which is more lamentable, and deserves a sea of tears to wash it away), the judge in torturing the accused, lest he should put him to death being innocent, oftentimes through his wretched ignorance kills that party though innocent with torture, whom he had tortured to avoid the killing of an innocent. For if (according unto their doctrine) he had rather leave this life than endure those miseries, then he says that he did the thing whereof he is clear indeed. And being thereupon condemned and executed, still the judge cannot tell whether he were guilty or no. He tortured him lest he should execute him guiltless, and by that means killed him ere he knew that he was guilty. Now, in these mists of mortal society, ought the judge to sit or no? Yes, he must sit. He is bound to it by his place, which he holds it wickedness not to discharge, and by the State's command, which he must obey. But he never holds it wickedness to torture guiltless witnesses in other men's causes; and when the tortures have overcome the patience of the innocent, and made them their own accusers, to put them to death as guilty, (whom they tortured but to try), being guiltless: nor to let many of them die even upon the very rack itself, or by that means, if they do escape the hangman. Again, what do you say to this, that some bringing a just accusation against this man or that for the good of the State, the accused endures all the tortures without confession, and so the innocent plaintiffs, not being able to prove their plea, are by the judge's ignorance cast and condemned? These now, and many more than these, the judge holds no sins, because his will is not assenting unto them, but his service to the State compels him, and his ignorance of hurt it is that makes him do it, not any will to hurt. This, now, is misery in a man, if it be not malice in a wise man. Is it the troubles of his place and of ignorance that cause those effects, and does he think that it is not enough for him to be held free from accusation, but he must needs sit in beatitude? How much more wisdom and discretion would he show in acknowledging his mortality in those troubles, and in detesting this misery in himself, crying out unto God (if he be wise) with the psalmist: 'Lord, take me out of all my troubles.' [1]

CHAPTER VII

Difference of language an impediment to human society.   The miseries of the justest wars

AFTER the city follows the whole world, wherein the third kind of human society is resident, the first being in the house, and the second in the city.   Now the world is as a flood of waters, the greater, the more dangerous: and first of all, difference of language divides man from man.   For if two meet, who perchance are compelled by some accident to abide together and confer, if neither of them can understand the other, you may sooner make two brute beasts of two different kinds sociable to one another than these two men.   For when they would commune together, their tongues do not agree; which being so, all the other helps of nature are nothing; so that a man had rather be with his own dog than with another man of a strange language.   But the great western Babylon endeavours to communicate her language to all the lands she has subdued, to procure a fuller society, and a greater abundance of interpreters on both sides.   It is true, but how many lives has this vanity cost!   And suppose that done, the worst is not past: for although she never wanted stranger nations against whom to lead her forces, yet this large extension of her empire procured greater wars than those named civil and confederate wars; and these were they that troubled the souls of mankind both while they were being waged, with desire to see them extinct, and when they had died down, with fear to see them renewed.   If I should stop to recite the massacres, and the extreme effects hereof, as I might (though I cannot do it as I should), the discourse would be infinite.   Yea, but a wise man, say they, will wage none but just war.   He will not!   As if the very remembrance that himself is man ought not to procure his greater sorrow in that he has cause of just wars, and must needs wage them, which if they were not just, it were not for him to deal in, so that a wise man should never have war.   For it is the other men's wickedness that makes his cause just that he ought to deplore, whether it produce wars or not. Wherefore he that does but consider with compassion all those extremes of sorrow and bloodshed, must needs say that this is a mystery; but he that endures them without a sorrowful emotion or thought thereof, is far more wretched to imagine he has the bliss of a god, when he has lost the natural feeling of a man.

[1] Ps. xxv. 17.

CHAPTER VIII

That true friendship cannot be secure amongst the incessant perils of this present life

BUT admit that a man be not so grossly deceived (as many in this wretched life are) as to take his foe for his friend, nor contrariwise, his friend for his foe; what comfort have we then remaining in this vale of mortal miseries, but the unfeigned faith and affection of sure friends? Yet the more they are, or the further off us, the more we fear, lest they be endamaged by some of these infinite casualties attending on all men's fortunes. We stand not only in fear to see them afflicted by famine, war, sickness, imprisonment, or slavery; but our far greater fear is, lest they should fall away through treachery, malice, or deprivation. And when this comes to pass, and we hear of it (as the more friends we have, and the farther off withal, the likelier is such news to be brought us), then who can decipher our sorrows but he that has felt the like? We had rather hear of their death, though we could not hear of either except with grief. For seeing we enjoyed the comfort of their friendships in their life, how can we but be touched with sorrowful emotions at their death? He that forbids us that may as well forbid all conference of friend and friend, all social courtesy, nay, even all human passion, and thrust them all out of man's conversation; or else prescribe their uses no pleasurable ends. But as that is impossible, so is it likewise impossible for us not to bewail him dead whom we loved being alive. For the sorrow thereof is as a wound or ulcer in our heart, unto which bewailments do serve in the stead of fomentations and plasters. For though the sounder one's understanding be, the sooner this cure is effected, yet it only proves that there is a malady that requires one application or other. Therefore in all our bewailing more or less for the deaths of our dearest friends or companions, we do yet reserve this love to them, that we had rather have them dead in body than in soul, and had rather have them fall in essence than in manners; for the last is the most dangerous infection upon earth, and therefore it was written: 'Is not man's life a temptation upon earth?'[1] Whereupon our Saviour said: 'Woe be to the world because of offences';[2] and again: 'Because iniquity shall be increased, the love of many shall wax cold.'[3] This makes us give thanks for the death of our good friends; and though it make us sad a while, yet it gives us more assurance of comfort ever after, because they have now escaped all those mischiefs which oftentimes seize upon the best, either oppressing or perverting them, endangering them in either case.

[1] Job vii. 1.   [2] Matt. xviii. 7.   [3] Matt. xxiv. 12.

CHAPTER IX

The friendship of holy angels with men: undiscernible in this life, by reason of the devils, whom all the heathen took to be good powers, and gave them divine honours

Now the society of angels with men (those whom the philosophers called the god's guardians, *lares*, and many other names), they set in the fourth place, advancing as it were from earth to the whole universe, and here including heaven. Now with regard to those friends (the angels), we need not fear to be affected with sorrow for any death or depravation of theirs, for they are impassible. But this friendship between them and us is not visibly apparent as that of man's is; which adds unto our terrestrial misery. And again, the devil, as we read, often transforms himself into an angel of light to tempt men, some for their instruction, and some for their ruin. And here is need of the great mercy of God, lest when we think we have the love and fellowship of good angels, they prove at length pernicious devils, feigned friends, and subtle foes, as great in power as in deceit. And where is this great mercy of God so needed except in this worldly misery, which is so enveloped in ignorance, and subject to be deluded? As for the philosophers of the reprobate city, who said they had gods to their friends, most sure it was they had devils indeed whom they took for deities. All the whole state wherein they lived is the devil's monarchy, and shall have the like reward with his, unto all eternity. For their sacrifices, or rather sacrileges, wherewith they were honoured, and the obscene plays which they themselves exacted, were manifest testimonies of their diabolical nature.

CHAPTER X

The reward that the saints are to receive after the overcoming of this world's afflictions

YEA, the holy and faithful servants of the true God are in danger of the devil's manifold ambushes. For as long as they live in this frail and evil-ridden world, they must be so; and it is for their good, making them more attentive in the quest of that security where their peace is without end and assured. There shall the Creator bestow all the gifts of nature upon them, and give them not only as good things but as eternal benefits, not only to the soul, by reforming it with wisdom, but also to the body, by restoring it in the resurrection. There the virtues shall not have any more conflicts with the vices, but shall rest with the victory of eternal peace, which none shall ever disturb. For it is the final beatitude,

having now attained a consummation to all eternity. We are said
to be happy here on earth when we have that little peace that
goodness can afford us. But compare this happiness with that
other, and this shall be held but plain misery. Therefore if we
live well upon earth, our virtue uses the benefits of the transitory
peace unto good ends, if we have it: if not, yet still our virtue uses
the evils, that the lack thereof produces, unto a good end also.
But then is our virtue in full power and perfection when it refers
itself, and all the good effects it can give being unto, either upon
good or evil causes, unto that end alone, wherein our peace shall
have no end, nor anything superior unto it in goodness or perfection.

CHAPTER XI

*The beatitude of eternal peace, and that true perfection wherein
the saints are installed*

WE may therefore say that peace is our final good, as we said of
life eternal; because the psalm says unto that city whereof we
write this laborious work: 'Praise thy Lord, O Jerusalem, praise
thy Lord, O Sion: for He hath made fast the bars of thy gates,
and blessed thy children within thee; He hath made peace thy
borders.' [1]   When the bars of the gates are fast, as none can come
in, so none can go out.   And therefore this peace, which we call
final, is the borders and bounds of this city: for the mystical name
hereof, Jerusalem, signifies 'a vision of peace.'   But because the
name of peace is common in this world where eternity is not resident, therefore we choose rather to call the bound wherein the
chief good of this city lies 'life eternal,' rather than 'peace.'   Of
which end the apostle says: 'Now being freed from sin, and made
servants to God, ye have your fruit in holiness, and the end, everlasting life.' [2]   But on the other hand, because such as are ignorant
in the scriptures may take this 'everlasting life' in an ill sense for
the life of the wicked which is eternally evil (either, as some philosophers held, because the soul cannot die, or as our faith teaches,
because torments cannot cease, and the wicked would not feel them
eternally, unless they have also their eternal life), therefore the main
end of this city's aim is either to be called Eternity in peace, or
Peace in eternity, and thus it is plain to all.   For the good of peace
is generally the greatest wish of the world, and the most welcome
when it comes.   Whereof I think we may ask our reader's leave
to have a word or two more, both because of the city's end, whereof
we now speak, and of the sweetness of peace, which all men do love.

[1] Ps. cxlvii. 12–14.   [2] Rom. vi. 22.

CHAPTER XII

That the bloodiest war's chief aim is peace; the desire of which is natural in man

WHO will not confess this with me, who marks man's affairs and the general form of nature? For joy and peace are desired alike of all men. The warrior would but conquer, and war's aim is nothing but glorious peace. For what is victory but a suppression of resistants, which being done, peace follows? And so peace is war's purpose, the scope of all military discipline, and the limit at which all just contentions aim. All men seek peace by war, but none seek war by peace. For they that perturb the peace they live in, do it not for hate of it, but to show their power in alteration of it. They would not disannul it, but they would have it as they like; and though they break into seditions against the rest, yet must they hold a peaceful show with their fellows that are engaged with them, or else they shall never effect what they intend. Even the thieves themselves that molest all the world besides them, are at peace amongst themselves. Admit one be so strong or subtle that he will have no fellow, but plays all his parts of roguery alone, yet with such as he can neither kill, and to whom he does not care to make known his deeds, he must needs maintain a kind of peace. And at home, with his wife and family, must he needs observe quietness; and without question he delights in their obedience unto him, which if they fail in, he chases and chides and strikes, setting all in order by force if need be, or by cruelty: which he sees he cannot do, unless all the rest be subjected under one head, which is himself. And might he have the sway of a city or province in such sort as he has that of his house, he would put off his thievish nature, and put on a king's, albeit his covetousness and malice would remain unchanged. Thus then you see that all men desire to have peace with such as they would have live according to their liking. For those against whom they wage war, they would make their own if they could; and if they conquer them they give them such laws as they like.

But let us imagine some such unsociable fellow as the poet's fable records, calling him 'half-man,' for his inhuman barbarism.

Now although his kingdom lay in a lightless cave, and his villainies were so singular that they gave him that name of Cacus, which is, evil; though his wife never had good word for him, and he never played with his children, nor ruled them in their manlier age, and though he never spoke with friend, not so much as with his father Vulcan (than whom he was far more happy in that he begat no such monster as Vulcan had in begetting him); though he never gave to any, but robbed and spoiled all that he could grip from all manner of persons, yea and the persons themselves, yet in that horrid dungeon of his, whose floor and walls were always dank with the blood of new slaughters, he desired nothing but to rest in peace therein, without molestation. He desired also to be at peace with himself; and what he had, he enjoyed; he ruled over his own body, and to satisfy his own hungry nature that menaced the separation of soul and body, he fell to his robberies with celerity; and though he were barbarous and bloody, yet in all that, he had a care to provide for his life and safety. And therefore if he would have had that peace with others, which he had in the cave with himself alone, he would neither have been called half-man nor monster. But if it were his horrible shape and breathing of fire that made men avoid him, then was it not will, but necessity that made him live in that cave and play the thief for his living. But there was no such man, or if there were, he was not such as the poets feign him. For unless they had mightily belied Cacus, they could not sufficiently have commended Hercules. But, as I said, it is likely that there was no such man, any more than there is truth in many other of their fictions. For the very wild beasts (part of whose brutishness they place in him) do preserve a peace each with other in their kind, begetting, breeding, and living together amongst themselves, being in other respects the unsociable births of the deserts. I speak not here of sheep, deer, pigeons, starlings, or bees, but of lions, foxes, eagles, and owls. For what tiger is there that does not purr over her young ones, and fawn upon them in their tenderness? What kite is there, though he fly solitarily about for his prey, but will seek his female, build his nest, sit his eggs, feed his young, and assist his mate in her motherly duty, all that in him lies? Far stronger are the bands that bind man unto society and peace with all that are peaceable. The worst men of all do fight for their fellows' quietness, and would (if it lay in their power) reduce all into a distinct form of state, drawn by themselves, whereof they would be the heads, which could never be, but by a coherence either through fear or love. For herein is perverse pride an imitator of the goodness of God, hating equality of others with itself under Him, and laying a yoke of obedience upon its fellows, under itself instead of Him. Thus hates it the just peace of God, and builds an unjust one for itself. Yet can it not but love peace, for no vice, however unnatural, can pull nature up by the roots.

But he that can discern between good and bad, and between order and confusion, may soon distinguish the godly peace from the wicked. Yet even that perverse confusion must of necessity be in, or in dependence upon, or in connection with some part of the order of things, for otherwise it would not exist at all. Let us take an example. Hang a man up with his head downwards, and all his posture is confounded; that which should be lowest having the highest place, and vice versa. This confusion disturbs the flesh, and is troublesome to it.   But it is the soul's peace with the body that causes the feeling of that disturbance.   Now if the soul leave the body by the means of those troubles, yet as long as the body's form remains it has a certain peace with itself; and the very fact that it remains suspended shows that it desires to be placed in the peace of nature, the very weight seeming to demand a place for rest; and though life be gone, yet very nature sways it unto that order wherein she placed it.   For if the dead body be preserved from putrefaction by unguents and embalmings, yet the peace of nature is kept, for the body's weight is applied thereby to a suitable earthly site, and convenient place for it to rest in.   But if it be not embalmed, but left to nature's dissolving, it is so long altered by ill-tasting vapours, until each part be wholly reduced to the particular natures of the elements, yet is not a tittle of the Creator's all-disposing law withdrawn.   For if there grow out of this carcass many more living creatures, each body of these serves the quantity of life that is in it, according to the same law of creation.   And if that be devoured up by other ravenous beasts or birds, it shall follow the ordinance of the same law, disposing all things congruently, into what form of nature soever it be changed.

CHAPTER XIII

Of that universal peace which no perturbances can seclude from the law of nature, God's just judgments disposing of every one according to his proper desert

THE body's peace therefore is an orderly disposal of the parts thereof; the unreasonable soul's, an ordered control of the appetites thereof; the reasonable soul's, a true harmony between knowledge and performance; that of body and soul alike, a temperate and undiseased habit of nature in the whole creature.   The peace of mortal man with immortal God is an orderly obedience unto His eternal law performed in faith.   Peace of man and man is a mutual concord; peace of a family an orderly rule and subjection amongst the parts thereof; peace of a city an orderly command and obedience amongst the citizens: peace of God's city a most orderly coherence in God and fruition of God; peace of all things is a well disposed order.   For order is a good disposition of discrepant parts, each in the fittest place; and therefore the miserable (as they are miserable) are out of order, lacking that peaceable and unperturbed state which order exacts.   But because their own merits have incurred this misery, therefore even herein they are imposed in a certain set order nevertheless.   Being not conjoined with the blessed, but severed from them by the law of order, and being exposed to miseries, yet these are adapted unto the places wherein they are resident, and so are digested into some kind of methodical form, and consequently into some peaceful order. But this is their misery, that although some little security wherein they live may exempt them from present sorrows, yet are they not in that state which secludes sorrow for ever, and affords eternal security. And their misery is far greater if they lack the peace of nature: and when they are offended, the part that grieves is the first disturber of their peace; for that which is neither offended nor dissolved preserves the peace of nature still. So then as one may possibly live without grief, but cannot possibly grieve unless he live; so may there be peace without any war or contention, but contention cannot be without some peace, not in so far as it is contention, but because the contenders do suffer and perform divers things herein according to nature's prescript, which things could not consist, had they not some peaceful order amongst them. And so there may be a nature (you see) where no evil may have inherence; but to find a nature utterly void of goodness is utterly impossible. For the very nature of the devils (considered as nature) is most excellent, but their own voluntary perverseness depraved it. The devil abode not in the truth, yet escaped he not the sentence of the truth; for he transgressed the peaceful law of order, yet could not avoid the powerful hand of the Orderer.

The good which God had bestowed on his nature cleared him not from God's heavy judgment by which order was maintained in punishment. Yet does not God herein punish the good which Himself created, but the evil which the devil committed. Nor did He take away his whole nature from him, but left him part, whereby to bewail the loss of the rest; which lamentation testifies both what he had and what he has; for had he not some good left, he could not lament for what he had lost. For his guilt is the greater who having lost all his uprightness should rejoice at the loss thereof. And he that is sick, even if it benefit him nothing, yet grieves at the loss of his health. For uprightness and health being both good in themselves, it behoves the losers of them to mourn, and not to rejoice (unless this loss be repaired with better recompense, seeing that uprightness of mind is better than health of body): and far more reason has the sinner to lament in his suffering than to rejoice in his transgression. Therefore even as to rejoice at the loss of goodness in sinning argues a depraved will; so likewise lament for the same loss, in suffering, proves a good nature. For he that bewails the loss of his natural peace, has his light from the remainders of that peace which are left in him, keeping his nature and him in concord.

And in the last judgment it is but reasonable that the wicked should deplore the loss of their natural goods, and feel God's hand justly heavy in depriving them of them, whom they scornfully respected not in bestowing them upon them. Wherefore the high

God, nature's wisest Creator, and most just Disposer, the Parent of the world's fairest wonder (mankind), bestowed divers good things upon him, which serve for this life only, namely the worldly and temporal peace kept by honest coherence and society; together with all the adjuncts of this peace, as the visible light, the breathable air, the potable water, and all the other necessaries of meat, drink, and clothing; but with this condition, that he that shall use them in their due manner, and with reference unto human peace, shall be rewarded with gifts of far greater moment, namely with the peace of immortality, and with unshaded glory, and full fruition of God, and of his brother in the same God: but he that uses them amiss, shall neither partake of the former nor the latter.

CHAPTER XIV

Of the law of heaven and earth which sways human society by counsel and unto which counsel human society is obedient

ALL temporal things are referred by the members thereof unto the benefit of the peace which is resident in the terrestrial city; and unto the enjoyment of the eternal peace by the citizens of the heavenly society. Wherefore if we lacked reason, we should desire only an orderly state of body, and an ordered control of desires; nothing but fleshly ease, and fullness of pleasure. For the peace of the body augments the quiet of the soul; and if it be wanting, it procures a disturbance even in brute beasts, because the emotions have not their true gratification.

Now both these combined add unto the peace of soul and body together, that is, they increase the healthful order of life. For as all creatures show how they desire their bodies' peace, in avoiding the causes of their hurt, and their souls', in following their appetites when need requires: so in flying from death they make it as apparent how much store they set by their peace of soul and body. But man, having a reasonable soul, subjects all his actions common to animals unto the peace of that soul, so to work both in his contemplation and action, that there may be a true consonance between them both; and this we call the peace of the reasonable soul. To this end he is to avoid molestation by grief, disturbance by desire, and dissolution by death, and to aim at profitable knowledge, whereunto his actions may be conformable. But lest his own infirmity in his great desire to know should draw him into any pestilent inconvenience of error, he must have a divine instruction, to whose directions and assistance he is to assent with firm and free obedience. And because during this life he is absent from the Lord, and walketh by faith, and not by sight,[1] therefore he refers all his

_____
[1] 2 Cor. v. 6, 7.

peace of body, of soul, and of both, unto that peace which mortal
man has with immortal God, to live in an orderly obedience under
His eternal law by faith.

Now God, our good Master, teaching us in the two great commandments (the love of Him, and the love of our neighbour), to
love three things, God, our neighbour, and ourselves, and seeing
that he that loves God offends not in loving himself, it follows that
he ought to counsel his neighbour to love God, and to provide for
him in the love of God, so surely as he is commanded to love him
as his own self. So must he do for his wife, children, family, and
all men besides, and wish likewise that his neighbour would do as
much for him, in his need. Thus shall he be settled in peace and
orderly concord with all the world. The order whereof is, first,
to do no man hurt, and secondly, to help all that he can. And so
his own have the first place in his care, because his place and order
in human society affords him more conveniency to benefit them.
Whereupon St. Paul says: 'He that provideth not for his own,
namely, for them that be of his household, denieth the faith, and
is worse than an infidel.'[1] For this is the foundation of domestic
peace, which is an orderly rule and subjection in the parts of the
family, wherein the providers are the commanders, as the husband
over his wife, parents over their children, and masters over their
servants: and they that are provided for, obey, as the wives do their
husbands, children their parents, and servants their masters. But
in the family of the faithful man, the heavenly pilgrim, there the
commanders are indeed the servants of those they seem to command; ruling not in ambition, but being bound by careful duty;
not in proud sovereignty, but in nourishing pity.

CHAPTER XV

*Nature's freedom; and bondage caused by sin, in which man is a slave
to his own passions, though he be not bondman to any one besides*

THUS has nature's order prescribed, and man by God was thus
created. 'Let them rule,' saith He, 'over the fishes of the sea, and
the fowls of the air, and over every thing that creepeth upon the
earth.'[2] He made him reasonable, and lord only over the unreasonable, not over man but over beasts. Whereupon the first
holy men were rather shepherds than kings, God showing herein
both what the order of the creation desired, and what the merit of
sin exacted. For justly was the burden of servitude laid upon the
back of transgression. And therefore in all the scriptures we
never read the word servant, until such time as that just man Noah
laid it as a curse upon his offending son. So that it was guilt, and

[1] 1 Tim. v. 8.   [2] Gen. i. 26.

not nature that gave origin unto that name. The Latin word *servus* had the first derivation from hence. Those that were taken in the wars, being in the hands of the conquerors to massacre or to preserve, if they saved them, then were they called *servi*, of *servo*, to save. Nor was this effected except as the desert of sin. For in the justest war, the sin upon one side causes it; and if the victory fall to the wicked (as sometimes it may) it is God's decree to humble the conquered, either reforming their sins herein, or punishing them. Witness that holy man of God, Daniel, who, being in captivity, confessed unto his Creator that his sins and the sins of the people were the real causes of that captivity.

Sin therefore is the mother of servitude, and first cause of man's subjection to man; which notwithstanding comes not to pass but by the direction of the Highest, in whom is no injustice, and who alone knows best how to proportionate His punishment unto man's offences. He Himself says: 'Whosoever committeth sin is the servant of sin';[1] and therefore many religious Christians are servants unto wicked masters; yet those masters are not freemen, for that which a man is addicted unto, the same is he slave unto. And it is a happier servitude to serve man than lust: for lust (to omit all the other passions) practises extreme tyranny upon the hearts of those that serve it, be it lust after sovereignty or fleshly lust. But in the peaceful orders of states, wherein one man is under another, as humility does benefit the servant, so does pride endamage the superior. But take a man as God created him at first, and so he is neither slave to man nor to sin. But penal servitude had its institution from that law which commands the conservation and forbids the disturbance of nature's order; for if that law had not first been transgressed, penal servitude had never been enjoined.

Therefore the apostle warns servants to obey their masters and to serve them with cheerfulness and good will: to the end that if they cannot be made free by their masters, they make their servitude a freedom to themselves, by serving them, not in deceitful fear, but in faithful love, until iniquity be overpassed, and all man's power and principality disannulled, and God only be all in all.

CHAPTER XVI

Of the just law of sovereignty

WHEREFORE although our righteous forefathers had servants in their families, and according to their temporal estates made a distinction between their servants and their children, yet in matters of religion (the fountain whence all eternal good flows), they provided

[1] John viii. 34.

for all their household with an equal respect unto each member thereof. This, nature's order prescribed, and hence came the name of 'the father of the family,' a name which even the worst masters love to be called by. But such as merit that name truly do care that all their families should continue in the service of God, as if they were all their own children, desiring that they should all be placed in the household of heaven, where command is wholly unnecessary, because then they are past their charge, having attained immortality, which until they be installed in, the masters are to endure more labour in their government than the servants in their service. If any be disobedient, and offend this just peace, he is forthwith to be corrected with strokes, or some other convenient punishment, whereby he may be readjusted into the peaceful stock from whence his disobedience has torn him. For as it is no good turn to help a man unto a smaller good by the loss of a greater, no more is it the part of innocence by pardoning a small offence to let it grow unto a fouler. It is the duty of an innocent to hurt no man, but, withal, to curb sin in all he can, and to correct sin in whom he can, that the sinner's correction may be profitable to himself, and his example a terror unto others. Every family then being part of the city, every beginning having relation unto some end, and every part tending to the integrity of the whole, it follows evidently that the family's peace adheres unto the city's, that is, the orderly command and obedience in the family have real reference to the orderly rule and subjection in the city. So that the father of the family should fetch his instructions from the city's government, whereby he may regulate the peace of his private estate by that of the common.

CHAPTER XVII

The grounds of the concord and discord between the cities of heaven and earth

BUT they that live not according to faith angle for all their peace in the sea of temporal profits; whereas the righteous live in full expectation of the glories to come, using the occurrences of this world but as pilgrims, so as not to abandon their course towards God for mortal respects, but thereby to assist the infirmity of the corruptible flesh, and make it more able to encounter toil and trouble. Wherefore the necessaries of this life are common, both to the faithful and the infidel, and to both their families; but the ends of their two usages thereof are far different.

The faithless, worldly city aims at earthly peace, and makes it its aim to have a uniformity of the citizens' wills in matters pertaining solely to mortality. And the heavenly city, or rather that part thereof which is as yet a pilgrim on earth and lives by faith, uses this peace also, as it should, until it leaves this mortal life wherein such a peace is requisite. And therefore it lives (while it is here on earth) as if it were in captivity, and having received the promise of redemption, and divers spiritual gifts as seals thereof, it willingly obeys such laws of the temporal city as order the things pertaining to the sustenance of this mortal life, to the end that both the cities might observe a peace in such things as are pertinent hereunto. But because the earthly city has some members whom the holy scriptures utterly disallow, and who either owing to their own imaginations, or being deluded by the devils, believed that each thing had a peculiar deity over it, and belonged to the charge of a separate god; as the body to one, the soul to another; and in the body itself the head to one, the neck to another, and so of every member; as likewise of the soul, one had the wit, another the learning, a third the wrath, a fourth the desire; as also in other necessaries or accidents belonging to man's life, the cattle, the corn, the wine, the oil, the woods, the coinage, the navigation, the wars, the marriages, the generations, each being a separate charge unto a particular power, whereas the citizens of the heavenly state acknowledged but one only God, to whom that worship which is called λατρεία was peculiarly and solely due; hence came it that the two hierarchies could not be combined in one religion, but must needs dissent herein, so that the good part was fain to bear the pride and persecution of the bad, had not their own multitude sometimes and the providence of God continually stood for their protection.

This celestial society while it is here on earth, increases itself out of all languages, being unconcerned by the different temporal laws that are made; yet not breaking, but observing their diversity in divers nations, so long as they tend unto the preservation of earthly peace, and do not oppose the adoration of one God alone. And so you see, the heavenly city observes and respects this temporal peace here on earth, and the coherence of men's wills in honest morality, as far as it may with a safe conscience; yea, and so far desires it, making use of it for the attainment of the peace celestial; which is so truly worthy of that name, that the orderly and uniform combination of men in the fruition of God, and of one another in God, is to be accounted the reasonable creature's only peace; which being once attained, mortality is banished, and life then is the true life indeed, nor is the carnal body any more an encumbrance to the soul, by corruptibility, but is now become spiritual, perfected, and entirely subject unto the sovereignty of the will.

This peace is that unto which the pilgrim in faith refers the other peace, which he has here in his pilgrimage; and then lives he according to faith, when all that he does for the obtaining hereof is by himself referred unto God, and his neighbour withal, because, being a citizen, he must not be all for himself, but sociable in his life and actions.

CHAPTER XVIII

That the doubtful doctrine of the new Academy opposes the constancy of Christianity

As for the new Academicians, whom Varro avouches to hold no certainty but this, that all things are uncertain, the Church of God detests these doubts as madness, having a most certain knowledge of the things it apprehends, although but in small quantity, because of the corruptible body which is a burden to the soul, and because, as the apostle says, 'We know but in part.' Besides, it believes the evidence of the senses in objects, of which the mind judges by the sensitive organs, though he would be in a gross error that trusts entirely in them. It believes also the holy canonical scriptures, both old and new, from which the just man has his faith, by which he lives, and wherein we all walk without doubt, as long as we are in our pilgrimage and personally absent from God. And this faith being kept firm, we may lawfully doubt all such other things as are not manifested unto us either by sense, reason, scripture, or testimony of grounded authority.

CHAPTER XIX

Of the dress and habits belonging to a Christian

IT is nothing to the city of God what attire the citizens wear, or what rules they observe, as long as they contradict not God's holy precepts, but each one keep the faith, the true path to salvation. And therefore when a philosopher becomes a Christian, they never make him alter his habit or his manners, which are no hindrance to his religion, but his false opinions. They respect not Varro's distinction of the Cynics, as long as they forbear unclean and intemperate actions. But as concerning the three kinds of life, active, contemplative, and the mean between both, although one may keep the faith in any of those courses, yet there is a difference between the love of the truth and the duties of charity. One may not be so given to contemplation that he neglect the good of his neighbour, nor so far in love with action that he forget divine speculation. In contemplation one may not seek for idleness, but for truth; to benefit himself by the knowledge thereof, and not to grudge to impart it unto others. In action one may not aim at power or honour, because 'all under the sun is mere vanity':[1] but to perform the work of a superior unto the true end, that is, unto

[1] Eccles. i. 23.

the benefit and salvation of the subject, as we said before. And this made the apostle say: 'If any man desire the office of a bishop, he desireth a good work.'[1] What this office was, he explains. It is an office of labour, and not of honour. The Greek word signifies that he that is herein installed is to watch over his people that are under him. *Episcopus*, a bishop, comes of ἐπί, which is 'over,' and σκοπός, which is 'a watching,' or 'an attendance': so that we may very well translate ἐπίσκοπος, 'a superintendent,' to show that he is no true bishop, who desires rather to be lordly himself than profitable unto others. No man therefore is forbidden to proceed in a laudable form of contemplation. But to desire sovereignty, though the people must be governed, and though the office be well discharged, is notwithstanding liable to be deemed unfitting. Wherefore the love of truth requires a holy retiredness; and the necessity of charity a just employment, which, if it be not imposed upon us, we ought not to seek, but betake ourselves wholly to the holy search after truth: but if we be called forth unto a position, the law and need of charity binds us to undertake it. Yet may we not for all this give over our first resolve of contemplation, lest we lose its sweetness, and be surcharged with the weight of the other.

CHAPTER XX

Hope, the bliss of the heavenly citizens during this life

THEN therefore is the good of the holy society perfect, when their peace is established in eternity, not running any more in succession as mortal men do in life and death, one to another; but confirmed unto them together with their immortality for ever, without touch of the least imperfection. What man is he that would not account such an estate most happy, or comparing it with that which man has here upon earth, would not avouch this latter to be most miserable, were it never so well fraught with temporal conveniences? Yet he that has the latter in possession, and applies it all with reference to his hope's firm and faithful object, may not unfitly be called happy already, but that is rather in his expectation of his future state than in his fruition of the present. For this present possession without the other hope is a false beautitude and a most true misery. For herein is no use of the mind's truest good, because there is lacking the true wisdom, which in the prudent discretion, resolute performance, temperate restraint, and just distribution of these things, should refer his intent in all these unto that end, where God shall be all in all, where eternity shall be firm, and peace most perfect and absolute.

[1] 1 Tim. iii. 1.

CHAPTER XXI

Whether the city of Rome had ever a true commonwealth, according to Scipio's definition of a commonwealth, in Tully

Now it is time to perform a promise which I made in the second book of this work; and that was, to show that Rome never had a true commonwealth, as Scipio defines one in Tully's book *De Re Publica*. His definition was: A commonwealth is the estate of the people, *Res publica est res populi*. If this be true, Rome never had any, for it never had an estate of the people, which he defines the commonwealth by. For he defines the people to be a multitude, united in one consent of law and profit. What he means by a consent of law, he shows himself; and shows thereby that a commonwealth cannot stand without justice; so that where true justice is wanting, there can be no law. For what law does, justice does, and what is done unjustly, is done unlawfully. For we may not imagine men's unjust decrees to be laws, for all men regard law as the fountain of justice; and that unjust assertion of some is utterly false: 'That is law which is profitable unto the greatest.' So then, where justice is not, there can be no society united in one consent of law, therefore no people, according to Scipio's definition in Tully. If no people, then no estate of the people, but rather of a confused multitude, unworthy of a people's name. If then the commonwealth be an estate of the people, and if they be no people that are not united in one consent of law, nor that a law, which is not grounded upon justice; then it must needs follow, that where no justice is, there no commonwealth is. Now then *ad propositum*. Justice is a virtue distributing unto every one his due. What justice is that then, that takes man from the true God, and gives him unto the condemned fiends? Is this distribution according to due? Is not he that takes away thy possessions, and gives them to one that has no claim to them, guilty of injustice, and is not he so likewise, that takes himself away from his Lord God, and gives himself to the service of the devil? There are wise and powerful disputations in those books, *De Re Publica*, for justice against injustice. In this work it is first argued for injustice against justice, and averred that a commonwealth could not stand without injustice. And this is brought as a principal confirmation hereof, that it is injustice for man to rule over man, and yet if the city, whose dominion is so large, should not observe this form of injustice, she could never keep the provinces under. Unto this it is answered on the behalf of justice, that this was a just course, it being profitable for such to serve, and for their good; to wit, when the power to do hurt is taken from the wicked, they will carry themselves better being curbed, because they carried themselves so badly before they were curbed. To confirm this answer this notable example is alleged, as being fetched from nature itself: 'If it were unjust to rule, why does God rule over man, the soul over the body, reason over lust and all the mind's other vicious affections?' This example teaches plainly that it is good for some to serve in particular, and it is good for all to serve God in general. And the mind, serving God, is lawful lord over the body: so is reason, being subject unto God, over the lusts and other vices. Wherefore if man serve not God, what justice can be thought to be in him, seeing that if he serve not Him the soul has neither lawful sovereignty over the body, nor the reason over the affections? Now if this justice cannot be found in one man, no more can it then in a whole multitude of suchlike men. Therefore amongst such there is not that consent of law which makes a multitude a people, whose estate makes a commonwealth. Why need I speak of the profit that is named in the definition of a people? For although none live profitably that live wickedly, that serve not God but the devils (who are so much the more wicked in that they, being most filthy creatures, dare exact sacrifices as if they were gods): yet I think that what I have said of the consent of law may serve to show that they were no people whose estate might make a commonwealth, as they had no justice amongst them. If they say they did not serve devils, but holy gods, why need we rehearse that here which we said so often before? Who is he that has read over this work unto this chapter, and yet doubts whether they were devils that the Romans worshipped or no, unless he be either senselessly thick-headed, or shamelessly contentious? But to leave the powers that they offered unto, take this place of holy writ for all: 'He that sacrificeth unto gods save unto the one God alone shall be rooted out.'[1] He that taught this in such threatening manner will have no gods sacrificed unto, be they good or be they bad.

CHAPTER XXII

Whether Christ, the Christians' God, be He unto whom alone sacrifice is to be offered

BUT they may reply: Who is that God? Or how prove you Him to be worthy of all the Romans' sacrifices, and none besides Him to have any part? Oh, it is a sign of great blindness to have yet to learn what that God is! It is He whose prophets foretold what our own eyes saw effected. It is He that told Abraham, 'In thy seed shall all the nations be blessed,'[2] which the remainders of the haters of Christianity do know, whether they will or no, to have been fulfilled in Christ, descended from Abraham in the flesh. It is that God whose spirit spake in them whose prophecies the

---

[1] Exod. xxii. 20.   [2] Gen. xxii. 18.

whole Church beholds fulfilled. The whole Church spread over
the face of the whole earth beholds them; and in that were they
fulfilled, which I related in my former books. It is that God
whom Varro called the Romans' Jove, though he know not what
he says; yet this I add because so great a scholar thought him to be
neither no God at all, nor one of the meanest, for he thought that
this was the great God of all. Briefly, it is even that God whom
that learned philosopher Porphyry (albeit he was a deadly foe to
Christianity) acknowledged to be the highest God, even according
to the oracles of those whom he called the inferior gods.

CHAPTER XXIII

Porphyry's relation of the oracles touching Christ

FOR he in his books which he entitles Θεολογία Φιλοσοφίας, 'The
Divinity of Philosophy,' wherein he sets down the oracles' answers
in things belonging to philosophy, has something to this purpose,
and thus it is from the Greek. 'One went,' says he, 'unto the
oracle, and asked unto what god he should sacrifice to obtain his
wife's conversion from Christianity. Apollo answered him thus:
"Thou mayest sooner write legible letters upon the water, or get
thee wings to fly through air like a bird, than recall thy wife from
her polluted opinion. Let her run after her mad opinions, as long
as she will: let her honour that dead God with her false lamentations, whom the wise and well-advised judges condemned, and
whom a shameful death upon the cross dispatched."' Thus far the
oracle. The Greek is in verse but our translation is not in metre.
After these verses, Porphyry adds this: 'Behold how remediless
their erroneous belief is; because as Apollo said (quoth he) the
Jews do have a better understanding of God than the Christians.'
Hear you this? He disgraces and obscures Christ, and yet says,
'The Jews receive God,' for so he interprets the oracle's verses,
where they say that Christ was condemned by well-advised judges,
as though He had been lawfully condemned and justly executed.
This lying priest's oracle let him look unto, and believe if he like:
but it may very well be that the oracle gave no such answer, but
that this is a mere fiction of his. How he reconciles the oracle,
and squares it with his own views, we shall see by and by. But,
by the way, here he says that the Jews, as the receivers of God,
judged aright in putting Christ to so ignominious and cruel a death.
So then to the Jews God said well in saying: 'He that sacrificeth
unto many gods shall be rooted out, save unto one God only.'
But to proceed, let us go to more manifest matter, and hear what
he makes of the Jews' God. He asked Apollo which was better,
the word, or the law. 'And he answered thus' (says he), and

then he adds the answer. I will relate as much of it as is necessary: 'God the Creator, and the King prior to all things, who maketh heaven and earth, the sea, and hell, yea and all the gods to tremble, on the law is their father, whom the holy Hebrews do adore.' This glory does Porphyry give the Hebrew God, according to his god Apollo, and the very deities do tremble before Him. So then this God having said, 'He that sacrifices unto many gods shall be rooted out,' I wonder that Porphyry was not afraid to be rooted out for offering to so many gods. Nay, this fellow speaks well of Christ afterwards, as forgetting the reproach he offered Him before: as if in their dreams, his gods had scorned Christ, and being awake, commended Him, and acknowledged His goodness. Finally, as if he meant to speak some marvellous matter: 'It may exceed all belief,' says he, 'which I am now to deliver. The gods affirmed Christ to be a man most godly, and immortalized for His goodness, giving Him great commendations: but as for the Christians, they avouch them to be persons stained with all corruption and error, and give them all the foul words that may be.' Then he relates the oracles which blaspheme the Christian religion, and afterwards, 'Hecate,' says he, 'being asked if Christ were God, replied thus: "His soul, being severed from His body, became immortal; but it wanders about void of all wisdom: it was the soul of a most worthy man, whom now those that forsake the truth do worship."' And then he adds his own sayings upon this oracle, in this manner: 'The goddess therefore called Him a most godly man, and said that the deluded Christians do worship His soul, being made immortal after death, as other godly souls are. Now, being asked why He was condemned then, she answered: "His body was condemned to torments, but His soul sits above in heaven, and gives all those souls unto error by destiny, who cannot attain the gifts of the gods, or come to the knowledge of immortal love. And therefore are they hated of the gods, because they neither acknowledge them nor receive their gifts, but are destined unto error by Him. Now He Himself was godly, and went up to heaven as godly men do. Therefore blaspheme not Him, but pity the poor fools whom He has bound in error."'

What man is there so foolish that he cannot observe that these oracles are either directly feigned by this crafty foe of Christianity, or else are the devil's own tricks to this end, that in praising Christ they might seem truly to reprehend the Christian profession, and so, if they could, to stop man's entrance into Christianity, the sole way unto salvation? For they think it no prejudice to their manifold deceit, to be believed in praising Christ as long as they be believed also in dispraising the Christian, so that he that believes them must be a commender of Christ, and yet a contemner of His religion. And thus although he honour Christ, yet shall not Christ free him from the clutches of the devil, because they give Christ such a kind of praise, as whoso believes it to be true shall be far from true Christianity, and rather than otherwise, a follower of Photinus' heresy, who held Christ to be man only, and no God at all; so that such a believer should never be saved by Christ, nor cleared of the devil's fowling nets.

But we will neither believe Apollo in his vituperation, nor Hecate in her commendation of Christ. He will have Christ a wicked man, and justly condemned; she will have Him a most godly man, and yet but man only. But both agree in this, that they would have no Christians, because all but Christians are in their clutches. But let this philosopher, or those that give credence to those oracles against Christianity, if they can, reconcile Apollo and Hecate, and make them both tell one tale, either in Christ's praise or dispraise. Which even if they could do, yet would we avoid them, as deceitful devils, both in their good words and in their bad. But seeing this god and this goddess cannot agree about Christ, truly men have no reason to believe or obey them in forbidding Christianity. Truly either Porphyry or Hecate in these commendations of Christ, affirming that He destined the Christians to error, yet goes about to show the causes of this error; which before I relate, I will ask this one question: If Christ did predestinate all Christians unto error, did He do this wittingly or against His will? If He did it wittingly, how then can He be just? If it were against His will, how can He then be blessed? But now to the causes of this error. There are some spirits of the earth, says he, which are under the rule of the evil demons. These, the Hebrew wise men (whereof Jesus was one, as the divine oracle, declared before, does testify) forbade the religious persons to meddle with, advising them to worship the celestial powers, and especially God the Father, with all the reverence they possibly could. And this, says he, the gods also do command us; and we have already shown how they admonish us to reverence God in all places. But the ignorant and wicked having no divine gift, nor any knowledge of that great and immortal Jove, nor following the precepts of the gods or good men have cast all the deities behind them, choosing not only to respect but even to reverence those depraved demons. And whereas they profess the service of God, they do nothing belonging to His service. For God is the Father of all things, and stands not in need of anything: and it is well for us to show Him our worship in chastity, justice, and the other virtues, making our whole life a continual prayer unto Him, by our search and imitation of Him 'For our search of Him,' quoth he, 'purifies us, and our imitation of Him deifies us by creating an affection for Himself.' Thus well has he taught God or the Father, and how to offer our service unto Him. The Hebrew prophets are full of such holy precepts, concerning both the commendation and reformation of the saints, lives. But as concerning Christianity, there he errs, and slanders, as far as his devils' pleasure is, whom he holds deities; as though it were so hard a matter, out of the obscenities practised and published in their temples and the true worship and doctrine presented before God in our churches, to discern where manners were reformed and where they were ruined. Who but the devil himself could inspire him with so shameless a falsification, as to say that the Christians do rather honour than detest the devils whose adoration was forbidden by the Hebrews? No, that God whom the Hebrews adored will not allow any sacrifice unto His holiest angels (whom we, that are pilgrims on earth, do notwithstanding love and reverence as the most sanctified members of the city of heaven) but forbids it directly in this thundering menace: 'He that sacrificeth unto gods shall be rooted out.' And lest it should be thought He meant only the earthly spirits, whom this fellow calls the lesser powers, and whom the scripture also calls gods (not of the Hebrews, but the heathens), as is evident in that one place, Psalm xcvi. 5: 'For all the gods of the heathen are devils'—lest any should imagine that the foresaid prohibition extended no further than these devils, or that it concerned not the offering to the celestial spirits, he adds: 'save only the Lord alone, but unto one God only.' Some may take the words, *nisi Domino soli*, to be 'unto the Lord, the Sun': and so understand the passage to be meant of Apollo, but the original and the Greek translations do subvert all such misunderstanding. So then the Hebrew God, so highly commended by this philosopher, gave the Hebrews a law in their own language, not obscure or uncertain, but already scattered throughout all the world, wherein this clause was literally contained: 'He that sacrificeth unto gods shall be rooted out, save only unto the Lord.' Why need we make any further search into the law and the prophets concerning this? Nay, why need we search at all? They are so plain and so manifold, that why need I elaborate my disputation with numerous quotations of those passages that exclude all powers of heaven and earth from participating in the honours due unto God alone? Behold this one passage, spoken in brief but in powerful manner by the mouth of that God whom the wisest of them do so highly extol—let us mark it, fear it, and observe it, lest we also be rooted out: 'He that sacrificeth unto more gods than that true and only Lord, shall be rooted out.' Yet God Himself is far from needing any of our services, but all that we do herein is for the good of our own souls. Hereupon the Hebrews say in their holy psalms: 'I have said unto the Lord, Thou art my God, my well-doing is nothing unto Thee.' [1] No, we ourselves are the best and most excellent sacrifice that He can have offered Him. It is His city whose mystery we celebrate in such oblations as the faithful do full well understand, as I said once

---

[1] Ps. xvi. 2.

already. For the ceasing of all the typical offerings that were
exhibited by the Jews, and the ordaining of one sacrifice, to be
offered through the whole world from east to west (as now we see
it is) was prophesied long before, from God, by the mouths of
holy Hebrews; whom we have cited, as much as needed, in convenient places of this our work.

Therefore, to conclude, where there is not this justice that God
alone rules over the society that obeys Him by grace, and yields to
His prohibition of sacrifice unto all but Himself, and where in
every member belonging to this heavenly society the soul is lord
over the body and all the bad effects thereof in obedience to God
and in rightful order, so that all the just (as well as one) live
according to faith which works by love, in which a man loves God
as he should, and his neighbour as himself—where this justice is
not, there is no society of men combined in one uniformity of law
and profit, and consequently no *populus* (if that definition hold
true), and finally no *res publica* or commonwealth; for there cannot
be a *res populi* where there is no *populus*.

CHAPTER XXIV

*A definition of a people by which both the Romans and other kingdoms
may claim to be commonwealths*

BUT omit the former definition of a people, and take this: 'A people
is a multitude of reasonable creatures conjoined in a general agreement of those things it respects': then, to discern the state of
the people, you must first consider what those things are. But
whatever they be, where there is a multitude of men, conjoined
in a common fruition of what they properly desire, there may fitly
be said to be a people: the better that their higher interests are,
the better are they themselves; and otherwise, the worse. By this
definition, Rome had a people, and consequently a commonwealth. What they embraced at the first, and what afterwards,
what goodness they changed into bloodiness, what concord they
forsook for seditions, confederacies, and civil wars, history can
testify, and we (in part) have already related. Yet this does not
bar them the name of a people, nor their state from the style of a
commonwealth, as long as they bear this our last definition un-
impaired. And what I have said of them, I may say of the Athenians, the Greeks in general, the Egyptians, and the Assyrian
Babylonians, were their dominions great or little; and so of all
nations in the world. For in the city of the wicked, where God
does not govern and men do not obey by sacrificing unto Him
alone, and consequently where the soul does not rule the body,

nor reason the passions, there is generally found wanting the virtue of true justice.

CHAPTER XXV

That there can be no true virtue where there is no true religion

FOR though there be a seeming of these things, yet if the soul and the reason serve not God, as He has taught them how to serve Him, they can never have true dominion over the body, nor over the passions: for how can that soul have any true measure of this decorum, that knows not God, nor serves His greatness, but is prostituted to the influence of the unclean and filthy devils? No, those things which she seems to account virtues, and thereby to sway her affections, if they be not all referred unto God, are indeed rather vices than virtues. For although some hold them to be real virtues, when they are desired only for their own account, and nothing else; yet even so they incur vainglory, and so lose their true goodness. For as that is not of the flesh, but above the flesh, that animates the body; so that is not of man, but above man, which beatifies the mind of man, yea, and of all the powers of the heavens.

CHAPTER XXVI

The peace of God's enemies, useful to the piety of His friends as long as their earthly pilgrimage lasts

WHEREFORE, as the soul is the flesh's life, so is God the beatitude of man, as the Hebrews' holy writ affirms: 'Blessed is the people whose God is the Lord.'[1] Wretched then are they that are strangers to that God, and yet have those a kind of allowable peace, but that they shall not have for ever, because they used it not well when they had it. But that they should have it in this life is for our good also; because during our commixture with Babylon, we ourselves make use of her peace, and though faith does free the people of God at length out of her, yet in the meantime we live as pilgrims in her. And therefore the apostle admonished the Church to pray for the kings and potentates of that earthly city, adding this reason, 'that we may lead a quiet life in all godliness and charity.'[2] And the prophet Jeremiah, foretelling the captivity of God's ancient people, commanding them (from the Lord) to go peaceably and patiently to Babylon, advised them also to pray, saying, 'For in her peace shall be your peace,'[3] meaning that temporal peace which is common both to good and bad.

[1] Ps. cxliv. 15.   [2] 1 Tim. ii. 2.   [3] Jer. xxix. 7.

CHAPTER XXVII

The peace of God's servants, the fullness whereof it is impossible in this life to comprehend

BUT as for our proper peace, we have it double with God: here below by faith, and hereafter above by sight. But all the peace we have here, be it public or peculiar to ourselves, is rather a solace to our misery than any assurance of our felicity. And for our righteousness, although it be truly such, because the end is the true good whereunto it is referred; yet as long as we live here, it consists rather of sin's remission, than of virtue's perfection—witness that prayer which all God's pilgrims use, and every member of His holy city, crying daily unto Him: 'Forgive us our trespasses, as we forgive them that trespass against us.'[1] Nor does this prayer benefit them whose faith, lacking works, is dead, but them whose faith works by love: for, because our reason, though it be subject unto God, yet as long as it is in the corruptible body, which burdens the soul, cannot have the affections under perfect obedience, therefore the justest man stands in need of this prayer. For though reason have the conquest, it is not without combat. And still one touch of infirmity or other creeps upon the best conqueror, even when he hopes that he holds all viciousness under, making him fall either by some vain word, or some inordinate thought, if it bring him not unto actual error. And therefore as long as we have to reign over sin, our peace is imperfect: because both the affections not yet conquered are subdued by dangerous conflict, and they that are under already do deny us all security, and keep us in continual anxiety. So then, in all these temptations (whereof God spake in the words, 'Is not the life of man a temptation upon earth?'[2]) who dare say he lives so, that he need not say to God: 'Forgive us our trespasses'? None but a proud fool. Nor is he mighty, but madly vainglorious, that in his own righteousness will resist Him, who gives grace to the humble, whereupon it is written: 'God resisteth the proud, and giveth grace to the humble.'[3] Man's righteousness therefore is this: to have God his Lord, and himself His subject; his soul master over his body; and his reason over sin, either by subduing it or resisting it: and to entreat God both for His grace for merit, and His pardon for sin, and lastly to be grateful for all His bestowed graces. But in that final peace, unto which all man's peace and righteousness on earth has reference, immortality and incorruption do so refine nature from viciousness, that there we shall have no need of reason to rule over sin, for there shall be no sin at all there, but God shall rule man, and the soul the body; and obedience shall there be as pleasant and easy, as the state of them that live shall be glorious and happy. And this

[1] Matt. vi. 12.   [2] Job vii. 1.   [3] Jas. iv. 6; 1 Pet. v. 5.

shall all have unto all eternity, and shall be sure to have it so; and therefore the blessedness of this peace, or the peace of this blessedness, shall be the fullness and perfection of all goodness.

CHAPTER XXVIII

The end of the wicked

BUT on the other hand, they that are not of this society are destined to eternal misery, called the second death; because there, even the soul, being deprived of God, seems not to live, much less the body, being bound in everlasting torments. And therefore, this second death shall be so much the more cruel, in that it shall never have end. But seeing war is the contrary of peace, as misery is unto bliss, and death to life, it is a question what kind of war shall reign then amongst the wicked, to answer and oppose the peace of the godly. But mark only what is the hurt of war, and it is plainly apparent to be nothing but the adverse disposal and contentious conflict of things between themselves. What then can be worse than that, where the will is such a foe to the passion, and the passion to the will, that they are for ever insuppressible and irreconcilable; and where nature and pain shall hold an eternal conflict, and yet the one never master the other? In our conflicts here on earth, either the pain is victor, and so death expels sense of it, or nature conquers, and expels the pain. But there, pain shall afflict eternally, and nature shall suffer eternally, both enduring to the continuance of the inflicted punishment. But seeing that the good and the bad are in that great judgment to pass unto those ends, the one to be sought for, and the other to be fled from, by God's permission and assistance, I will in the next book following have a little discourse of that last day, and that terrible judgment.

THE TWENTIETH BOOK OF
THE CITY OF GOD

CHAPTER I

God's judgments continually effected: His last judgment the proper subject of this book following

INTENDING now to discourse (against the faithless and the wicked) of the day of God's last judgment, we must lay down holy scriptures first as the foundation of our following structure: which some believe not, but oppose with fond and frivolous arguments, either wresting them unto quite another purpose, or utterly denying them to contain anything divine. For I do not think that man lives, who, understanding them as they are spoken, and believing that God inspired them into sanctified men, will not give his full assent unto what they aver, and must needs profess as much, whether he be ashamed or afraid to avouch it, or so obstinate that he would conceal it and study to defend what he knows to be falsehood against it. Wherefore, the whole Church believes and professes that Christ is to come from heaven 'to judge both the quick and the dead,' and this we call the day of God's judgment, the last time of all: for how many days this judgment will take we know not, but the scripture uses 'day' for 'time' very often, as none that is wont to read it can fail to discern. And we, when we speak of this day, do add 'last,' 'the last day,' because God does judge at this present and has done ever since He sent man forth of paradise and chased our first parents from the tree of life for their offences; nay, from the time that He cast out the transgressing angels, whose envious prince does all that he can now to ruin the souls of men. It is His judgment that both men and devils do live in such miseries and perturbations in air and earth, fraught with nothing but evils and errors. And if no man had offended, it had been His good judgment that man and all reasonable creatures had lived in perfect beatitude and eternal coherence with the Lord their God. And so He condemns not only men and devils in general unto misery, but He judges every particular soul for the works it has performed out of freedom of will. For the devils pray that they may not be tormented; neither does God unjustly either in sparing them or punishing them. And man, sometimes in public, but continually in secret, feels the hand of Almighty God punishing him for his trespasses and misdeeds, either in this life or in the next; though no

268

man can do well without the help of God, nor any devil can do hurt without His just permission. For, as the apostle says: 'Is there unrighteousness in God? God forbid': [1] and in another place: 'Unsearchable are His judgments, and His ways past finding out.' [2] I intend not, therefore, in this book to meddle with God's ordinary daily judgments, or with those His first, but with that great and last judgment of His (by His gracious permission) when Christ shall come from heaven, 'to judge both the quick and the dead': for that is properly called the judgment day, because there shall be no place for ignorant complaint about the happiness of the bad and the misery of the good. The true and perfect felicity on that day shall be assured only to the good, and eternal torment shall then show itself as an everlasting inheritance only for the evil.

CHAPTER II

The change of human estates ordered by God's unsearchable judgments

BUT here on earth the evils endured by the good men instruct us to endure them with patience, and the goods enjoyed by the wicked advise us not to covet them too eagerly. Thus in the things where God's judgments are not to be discovered, His counsel is not to be neglected. We know not why God makes this bad man rich, and that good man poor; why he should have joy, whose deserts we hold worthier of pains, and he pains, whose good life we imagine to merit content; why the judge's corruption or the false-ness of the witnesses should send the innocent away condemned, and the injurious foe should depart revenged, as well as unpunished; why the wicked man should live sound, and the godly lie bedrid; why lusty youths should turn thieves, and those that never did hurt in word be plagued with extremity of sickness; why infants, of good use in the world, should be cut off by untimely death, while they that seem unworthy ever to have been born attain long and happy life; or why the guilty should be honoured, and the godly oppressed; and such contrasts as these—which who could collect or recount?

And even if these absurd contrasts were constant, so that in this whole life (wherein as the prophet says in the psalm, 'Man is like to vanity, and his days like a shadow that vanisheth' [3]) the wicked alone should possess those temporal good things, and the good alone suffer evils, yet might this be referred to God's just judg-ments, yea, even to His mercies: so that such as sought not for eternal felicity might either for their malice be justly deluded by this transitory happiness, or by God's mercy be consoled by them, and that they who were not to lose the eternal bliss might for a while be exercised by temporal crosses, either for the correction of sins or the augmentation of their virtues.

But now, seeing that not only the good are afflicted, and the bad exalted (which seems injustice), but the good also often enjoy good, and the wicked, evil; this proves God's judgments more inscrutable, and His ways more unsearchable. Although, then, we see no cause why God should do thus or thus, He in whom is all wisdom, and justice, and no weakness, nor rashness, nor injustice: yet here we learn that we should not esteem too highly those goods, or misfortunes, which we see the bad share with the righteous; but should seek the good peculiar to the one, and avoid the evil reserved for the other.

And when we come to that great judgment, properly called 'the day of doom,' or 'the consummation of time': there we shall not only see all things clearly, but acknowledge all the judgments of God, from the first to the last, to be firmly grounded upon justice. And there we shall learn, and know also, why God's judgments are generally incomprehensible unto us, and how just His judgments are in that point also; although already indeed it is manifest unto the faithful, that we are justly, as yet, ignorant in them all, or at least in most of them.

CHAPTER III

Solomon's disputation in Ecclesiastes concerning those good things which both the just and the unjust do share in

SOLOMON, the wisest king that ever reigned over Israel, begins his book called Ecclesiastes (which the Jews themselves hold for canonical) in this manner: 'Vanity of vanities, all is vanity. What remains unto man of all his travails which he suffers under the sun?' [1] Unto these, he annexes the torments and tribulations of this declining world, and the short and swift courses of time, wherein nothing is firm, nothing constant. In this vanity of all things under the sun, he bewails this also for one, that though 'there is more profit in wisdom than in folly, as the light is more excellent than darkness,' and seeing 'the wise man's eyes are in his head, when the fool walketh in darkness,' [2] yet, one condition, one estate, befalls them both as touching this vain and transitory life: meaning hereby, that they were both alike exposed to those evils that good men and bad do sometimes both alike endure. He says further, that the good shall suffer as the bad do, and the bad shall enjoy good things as the good do, in these words: 'There is a vanity which is done upon the earth, that there be righteous men

---

[1] Eccles. i. 2, 3.   [2] Eccles. ii. 13, 14.

to whom it happeneth according to the work of the wicked, and there be wicked men to whom it happeneth according to the work of the just: I thought also that this is vanity.'[1] In exposition of this vanity the wise man wrote all this whole work, for no other cause but that we might discern that life, which is not vanity under the sun, but truth under Him that made the sun. But as touching this worldly vanity, is it not God's just judgment that man being made like it should vanish also like it? Yet in these his days of vanity, there is much difference between the obeying and the opposing of truth, and between partaking and neglecting of godliness and goodness. But this is not in respect of attaining or avoiding any terrestrial good or evil, but of the great future judgment, which shall distribute good things to the good, and evil to the evil, to remain with them for ever. Finally, the said wise king concludes his book thus: 'Fear God and keep His commandments, for this is the whole duty of man; for God will bring every work unto judgment of every despised man, be it good or be it evil,'[2] How can we have an instruction more brief, more true, or more wholesome? 'Fear God,' says he, 'and keep His commandments, for this is the whole duty of man,' for he that does this, is full man; and he that does it not, is in account nothing, because he is not reformed according to the image of truth, but remains still in the shape of vanity. 'For God will bring every work,' that is every act of man in this life, 'unto judgment, be it good or evil, yea the works of every despised man,' of every contemptible person, that seems not to be noted at all, yet God sees him, and despises him not, neither passes him over in His judgment.

CHAPTER IV

The author's resolution in this discourse of the judgment, to produce the testimonies of the New Testament first, and then of the Old

THE testimonies of holy scriptures, by which I mean to prove this last judgment of God, must be first of all taken out of the New Testament, and then out of the Old. For though the latter be the more ancient, yet the former are more worthy, as being the true contents of the latter. The former then shall proceed first, and they shall be backed by the latter. These, that is, the old ones, the law and the prophets afford us; the former (the new ones) are given us in the gospels and the writings of the apostles. Now the apostle says: 'By the law cometh the knowledge of sin. But now is the righteousness of God made manifest without the law, having witness of the law and the prophets, to wit, the righteousness of

---

[1] Eccles. viii. 14.   [2] Eccles. xii. 13, 14.

God, by the faith of Jesus Christ unto all and upon all that believe.' [1] This righteousness of God belongs unto the New Testament, and has confirmation from the Old, namely the law and the prophets. We must therefore first of all propound the case and then produce the confirmations, for Christ Himself so ordered it, saying: 'Every scribe which is taught unto the kingdom of heaven is like unto an householder which bringeth out of his treasury things both new and old.' [2] He says not, 'both old and new'; but if He had not respected the order of dignity more than of antiquity, He would have done so, and not as He did.

CHAPTER V

Places of scripture proving that there shall be a day of judgment at the world's end

Our Saviour therefore, condemning the cities, in whom His great miracles did not induce faith, and preferring aliens before them, tells them this: 'I say unto you, it shall be easier for Tyre and Sidon at the day of judgment than for you.' And afterwards, unto another city: 'I say unto you, that it shall be easier for them of the land of Sodom in the day of judgment than for thee.' [3] Here is a plain prediction of such a day. Again: 'The men of Nineveh,' says He, 'shall arise in judgment with this generation, and condemn it,' etc. 'The queen of the south shall rise in judgment with this generation, and shall condemn it,' etc.[4] Here we learn two things, first, that there shall be a judgment: secondly, that it shall be when the dead do arise again. For our Saviour, speaking of the Ninevites, and of the queen of the south, speaks of them that were dead long before. Now He said not, 'shall condemn,' as if they were to be the judges, but that their comparison with the aforesaid generation shall justly procure the judge's condemning sentence. Again, speaking of the present commixture of the good and bad, and their future separation in the day of judgment, He uses a simile of the sown wheat, and the tares sown afterwards amongst it, which He expounds unto His disciples: 'He that soweth the good seed is the Son of Man: the field is the world: the good seed, they are the children of the kingdom: the tares are the children of the wicked: the enemy that soweth, that is the devil: the harvest is the end of the world: and the reapers be the angels. As then the tares are gathered and burned in the fire, so shall it be in the end of this world: the Son of Man shall send forth His angels and they shall gather out of His kingdom all things that offend, and they which do iniquity, and shall cast them into a furnace of fire: there shall be weeping and gnashing of teeth. Then

---

[1] Rom. iii. 20–2.   [2] Matt. xiii. 52.   [3] Matt. xi. 22, 24.   [4] Matt. xii. 41, 42.

shall the just men shine as the sun in the kingdom of their Father. He that hath ears to hear, let him hear.' [1]

He names not the judgment day here: but He expresses it far more plainly by the effects, and promises it to befall at the end of the world. Furthermore, He says to His disciples: 'Verily I say unto you, that when the Son of Man shall sit in the throne of His majesty, then ye which followed Me in the regeneration shall sit also upon twelve thrones and judge the twelve tribes of Israel.' [2] Here we see that Christ shall be Judge, together with His apostles. Whereupon He said unto the Jews in another place: 'If I through Beelzebub cast out devils, by whom do your children cast them out? Therefore they shall be your judges.' [3] But now, in that He speaks of twelve thrones, we may not imagine that He, and only twelve more with Him, shall be the world's judges. The number of twelve includes the whole number of the judges, by reason of the two parts of seven, which number signifies totality: which two parts, four and three multiplied one by the other, make up twelve, three times four, or four times three, being twelve (besides other reasons why twelve is used in these words of our Saviour). Otherwise Matthias having Judas' place, St. Paul should have no place left him to sit as judge in, though he took more pains than them all. But that he belongs unto the number of the judges, his own words do prove: 'Know ye not that we shall judge the angels?' [4] The reason of their judgments also is included in the number of twelve. For Christ in saying, 'To judge the twelve tribes of Israel,' [5] excludes neither the tribe of Levi, which was the thirteenth, nor all the other nations besides Israel, from undergoing this judgment.

Now whereas He says, 'In the regeneration,' hereby assuredly He means the resurrection of the dead. For our flesh shall be regenerate by incorruption, as our soul is by faith. I omit many passages that might concern this great day, because inquiry may rather make them seem ambiguous, or referring to something other than this; as either unto Christ's daily coming unto His Church in His members (unto each in particular), or unto the destruction of the earthly Jerusalem, because our Saviour, speaking of that, uses the same phrase that He uses concerning the end of the world and the last judgment, so that we can scarcely distinguish them except by comparing the three evangelists, Matthew, Mark, and Luke, together, in their passages touching this point. For one has it somewhat obscure, and another more apparent, the one explaining the intent of the other. And those passages have I compared together in one of my epistles unto Hesychius (of blessed memory), Bishop of Salona. The epistle is entitled *De Fine Saeculi*, 'of the world's end.' And so I will in this place relate

---

[1] Matt. xiii. 37–43.   [2] Matt. xix. 28.   [3] Matt. xii. 27.
[4] 1 Cor. vi. 3   [5] Matt. xix. 28; Luke xxii. 30.

only that passage of St. Matthew, where Christ (the last judge, being then present) shall separate the good from the bad. It is thus:

'When the Son of Man cometh in His glory, and all the holy angels with Him, then shall He sit upon the throne of His glory, and before Him shall be gathered all nations, and He shall separate them one from another as a shepherd separateth the sheep from the goats, and He shall set the sheep on His right hand, and the goats on His left. Then shall the King say to them on His right hand, Come, ye blessed of My Father, inherit ye the kingdom prepared for you from the foundations of the world. For I was an hungered, and ye gave Me meat; I thirsted, and ye gave Me drink; I was a stranger, and ye lodged Me; I was naked, and ye clothed Me; I was sick, and ye visited Me; I was in prison, and ye came unto Me. Then shall the righteous answer Him saying, Lord, when saw we Thee an hungered and fed Thee, or athirst, and gave Thee drink? etc. And the King shall answer, and say unto them, Verily I say unto you, inasmuch as ye have done it unto one of the least of these My brethren, ye have done it unto Me. Then shall He say unto them on the left hand, Depart from Me, ye cursed, into everlasting fire which is prepared for the devil and his angels: for I was an hungered, and ye gave Me no meat: I thirsted, and ye gave Me no drink, etc. Then shall they also answer Him, saying, Lord, when saw we Thee hungry, or athirst, or a stranger, or naked, or in prison, or sick, and did not minister unto Thee? Then shall He answer them, and say, Verily I say unto you, inasmuch as ye did it not unto one of the least of these, ye did it not unto Me. And these shall go into everlasting fire, and the righteous into life eternal.' [1]

Now John the Evangelist shows plainly that Christ foretold this judgment to be at the resurrection. For having said: 'The Father judgeth no man, but hath committed all judgment unto the Son: because all men should honour the Son as they honour the Father: he that honoureth not the Son, the same honoureth not the Father that sent Him,' He adds forthwith: 'Verily, verily, I say unto you, he that heareth My word and believeth in Him that sent Me, hath everlasting life, and shall not come into judgment, but shall pass from death to life.' [2] Behold, here He avouches directly that the faithful shall not be judged. How then shall they by His judgment be severed from the faithless, unless judgment be used here for condemnation? For that is the judgment into which they that hear His word and believe in Him that sent Him shall never enter.

[1] Matt. xxv. 31-46.   [2] John v. 22-4.

CHAPTER VI

What the first resurrection is, and what the second

THEN He proceeds, in these words: 'Verily, verily, I say unto you, The hour shall come, and now is, when the dead shall hear the voice of the Son of God, and they that hear it shall live. For as the Father hath life in Himself, so likewise hath He given unto the Son to have life in Himself.' [1]

He does not speak as yet of the second resurrection, of that of the body, which is to come, but of the first resurrection, which is now. For to distinguish these two He says, 'The hour shall come, and now is.' Now this is the soul's resurrection, not the body's; for the souls have their deaths in sin, as the bodies have in nature; and therein were they dead, of whom our Saviour said, 'Let the dead bury their dead,' [2] to wit, let the dead in soul bury the dead in body. Such then is the reference in these words: 'The hour shall come, and now is, when the dead shall hear the voice of the Son of God, and they that hear it shall live.' 'They that hear it,' means they that obey it, believe it, and remain in it. He makes no distinction here between good and evil, none at all. For it is good for all to hear His voice, and thereby to pass out of the death of sin and impiety unto life and eternity. Of this death in sin the apostle speaks, in these words: 'If one died for all, then were all dead; and He died for all, that they which live should not henceforth live unto themselves, but unto Him which died for them and rose again.' [3]

Thus, then, all were dead in sin, none excepted, either in original sin, or in actual, either by being ignorant of good, or by knowing good and not performing it; and for all these dead souls, one living Son came, and died; 'living,' that is, One without all sin, that such as get life by having their sins remitted should no more live unto themselves, but unto Him that suffered for all our sins, and rose again for the justification of us all; that we, which believe upon the Justifier of the wicked, being justified out of wickedness, and raised (as it were) from death to life, may be assured to belong unto the first resurrection, that now is. For none but such are heirs of eternal bliss have any part in this first resurrection: but the second is common both to the blessed and the wretched. The first is mercy's resurrection; the second, judgment's. And therefore the psalm says: 'I will sing of mercy and judgment unto Thee, O Lord.' [4] With this judgment the evangelist proceeds, thus: 'And hath given Him power also to execute judgment, in that He is the Son of Man.' [5] Lo, here now, in that flesh, wherein He was judged, shall He come to be the whole world's Judge. For these words, 'In that He is the Son of Man,' have a direct aim at this.

[1] John v. 25–6.   [2] Matt. viii. 22.   [3] 2 Cor. v. 14, 15.
[4] Ps. ci. 1.   [5] John v. 27

And then he adds this: 'Marvel not at this, for the hour shall come, in the which all that are in the graves shall hear His voice; and they shall come forth, which have done good, unto the resurrection of life; but they that have done evil unto the resurrection of judgment.' [1]

This is the same judgment which He spoke of before, when He said: 'He that heareth My word,' etc., 'shall not come into judgment, but shall pass from death to life,' that is, because he belongs to the first resurrection, and that belongs to life, so shall he not come into 'condemnation,' which is the meaning of the word 'judgment' in this last passage, 'unto the resurrection of judgment.' Oh, rise then in the first resurrection all you that will not perish in the second! 'For the hour will come, and now is, when the dead shall hear the voice of the Son of God, and they that hear it shall live': that is, they shall not come into condemnation, which is called the second death, into which they shall all be cast headlong after the second resurrection, that arise not in the first. 'For the hour will come' (He says not here that the hour is now, because it shall be in the world's end) 'in the which all that are in the graves shall hear His voice, and shall come forth': but He says not here as He said before, 'and they that hear it shall live,' for they shall not live all in bliss, which is alone to be called life, because it is the true life: yet must they have some life, otherwise they could neither hear nor arise in their quickened flesh.

And why shall not all they live? He gives this subsequent reason:

'They that have done good shall come forth unto the resurrection of life': and these only are they that shall live: 'they that have done evil, unto the resurrection of condemnation,' and these (God wot) shall not live, for they shall die the second death. In living badly they have done badly, and in refusing to rise in the first resurrection they have lived badly, or at least in not continuing their resurrection unto the consummation. So then, as there are two regenerations, one in faith by baptism, and another in the flesh, by incorruption; so are there two resurrections, the first (that is now) of the soul, preventing the second death; the latter (future) of the body, sending some into the second death, and others into the life that despises and excludes all death whatsoever.

CHAPTER VII

Of the two resurrections: what may be thought of the thousand years mentioned in St. John's Revelation

ST. JOHN THE EVANGELIST in his Revelation speaks of these two resurrections in such a dark manner, that some of our divines, exceeding their own ignorance about the first, do wrest it unto divers

[1] John v. 28, 29.

ridiculous interpretations. His words are these: 'And I saw an angel come down from heaven having the key of the bottomless pit, and a great chain in his hand; and he took the dragon, that old serpent which is the devil and Satan, and bound him a thousand years, and he cast him into the bottomless pit, and shut him up, and sealed the doors upon him, that he should deceive the people no more, till the thousand years were fulfilled. For after he must be loosed for a little season. And I saw thrones, and they sat upon them, and judgment was given unto them; and I saw the souls of them which were slain for the testimony of Jesus, and for the word of God, and worshipped not the beast, nor his image, neither had taken his mark upon their foreheads, or on their hands: and they lived and reigned with Christ a thousand years. But the rest of the dead men did not live until the thousand years be finished: this is the first resurrection. Blessed and holy is he that hath his part in the first resurrection, for on such the second death hath no power, but they shall be the priests of God and of Christ, and reign with Him a thousand years.' [1]

The chiefest reason that moved many to think that this passage refers to a corporal resurrection, was drawn from the thousand years, as if the saints should have a continual sabbath enduring so long, to wit, a thousand years' leisure after the six thousand of trouble, beginning at man's creation and expulsion out of paradise into the sorrows of mortality; that since it is written, 'One day is with the Lord as a thousand years, and a thousand years as one day'; [2] therefore six thousand years being finished (as the six days), the seventh should follow, for the time of sabbath, and last a thousand years also, all the saints rising corporally from the dead to celebrate it.

This opinion might be allowed, if it proposed only spiritual delights unto the saints during this space (and we were once of the same opinion ourselves); but seeing the avouchers hereof affirm that the saints after this resurrection shall do nothing but revel in fleshly banquets, where the cheer shall exceed both modesty and measure, this is gross, and fit for none but carnal men to believe. But they that are really and truly spiritual do call those of this opinion Chiliasts. The word is Greek, and may be interpreted, Millenarians, or Thousand-year-ists.

This is not the place to confute them. Let us rather take the text's true sense along with us. Our Lord Jesus Christ says: 'No man can enter into a strong man's house, and take away his goods, unless he first bind the strong man, and then spoil his house': [3] meaning by this 'strong man,' the devil, because he alone was able to hold mankind in captivity; and meaning by 'the goods he would take away,' his future faithful, whom the devil held as his own in divers sins and impieties. That this strong man

[1] Rev. xx. 1–6.   [2] 2 Pet. iii. 8.   [3] Matt. xii. 29.

therefore might be bound, the apostle saw the angel coming down from heaven, having the key of the bottomless pit, and a great chain in his hand. 'And he took,' says he, 'the dragon, that old serpent, which is the devil and Satan, and bound him a thousand years,' that is, restrained him from seducing or withholding them that were to be set free. The thousand years, I think, may be taken two ways; either because this shall take place in the last thousand, that is, on the sixth day of work's continuance, and then the sabbath of the saints should follow, which shall have no night, and bring them blessedness which has no end; so that thus the apostle may call the last part of the current thousand (which make the sixth day) a thousand years, using the part for the whole: or else a thousand years is put for all the years of this age, noting the plenitude of time by a number most perfect. For a thousand is the cube of ten: ten times ten is one hundred, and this is a square, but it is but a plane one; but to produce the cube multiply ten by a hundred, and there arises one thousand.

Now if a hundred be sometimes used for perfection, as we see it is in Christ's words concerning him that should leave all and follow Him, saying: 'He shall receive an hundredfold more' [1] (which the apostle seems to expound saying, 'As having nothing, and yet possessing all things,' [2] for it had been said before: 'Unto a faithful man the whole world is his riches' [3]): why then may not one thousand be put for consummation, all the more because it is the only cube that can be drawn from ten? And therefore we interpret that text of the psalm, 'He hath alway remembered His covenant and promise that He made to a thousand generations,' [4] by taking a thousand for all in general. Let us proceed. 'And he cast him into the bottomless pit.' He cast the devils into that pit, that is, the multitude of the wicked, whose malice unto God's Church is bottomless, and their hearts a depth of envy against it. He cast him into this pit, not that he was not there before, but because the devil, being shut from amongst the godly, holds faster possession of the wicked: for he is most surely in the grip of the devils, that is not only cast out from God's servants, but pursues them also with a causeless hate. To continue: 'And shut him up, and sealed the door upon him, that he should deceive the people no more till the thousand years were expired.' 'He sealed,' that is, his will was to keep it unknown, who belonged to the devil, and who did not. For this is unknown unto this world, for we know not whether he that stands shall fall, or he that has fallen shall rise again. But nevertheless this bond restrains him from tempting the nations that are God's elected, as he did before. For God chose them before the foundations of the world, meaning to take them out of the power of darkness, and set them in the kingdom of His Son's glory, as

---

[1] Matt. xix. 29.   [2] 2 Cor. vi. 10.   [3] Prov. xvii. 6 (LXX).   [4] Ps. cv. 8.

the apostle says. For who knows not the devil's daily seducing and drawing of others unto eternal torment, though these be none of the predestinate? Nor is it wonder if the devil subvert some of those who are even regenerate in Christ, and have begun to walk in His ways. For God knows those that be His, and the devil cannot draw a soul of them unto damnation. For this God knows, as knowing all things to come, not as one man sees another in the present only, and cannot tell what shall become either of him he sees, or of himself hereafter. The devil was therefore bound and locked up, that he should no more seduce the nations (the Church's members) whom he had held in error and impiety, before they were united unto the Church. It is not said, 'that he should deceive no man any more,' but 'that he should deceive the people no more,' whereby questionless he means the Church. To proceed: 'Until the thousand years be fulfilled,' that is, either the remainder of the sixth day (the last thousand) or the whole time that the world was to continue. Nor may we understand the devil so to be barred from seducing, that when this time expired, he should seduce those nations again, whereof the Church consists, and from which he was forbidden before. But this text is like unto that of the psalm: 'Our eyes wait upon the Lord until He have mercy upon us' [1] (for the servants of God take not their eyes from beholding as soon as He has mercy upon them). Or else the order of the words is this: 'He shut him up, and sealed the doors upon him until a thousand years were fulfilled,' all that comes between, namely, 'that he should not deceive the people,' having no necessary connection hereunto, but being understood separately as if it were added afterwards; and so the sense run thus: 'And He shut him up, and sealed the door upon him until a thousand years were fulfilled, that he should not seduce the people,' that is, therefore He shut him up so long, that he should seduce them no more.

CHAPTER VIII

Of the binding and loosing of the devil

'AFTER that,' says St. John, 'he must be loosed for a season.' [2] Well, seeing that the devil is bound and locked up that he should not seduce the Church, shall he therefore be loosed to seduce it? God forbid. That Church which God predestinated, and settled before the world's foundation, whereof it is written, 'God knoweth those that be His,' [3] that Church the devil shall never seduce. And yet it shall be on earth even at the time of his loosing, as it has continued in successive estate ever since it was erected; for by and by He says that 'the devil shall bring his seduced nations in arms

---

[1] Ps. cxxiii. 2.   [2] Rev. xx. 3.   [3] 2 Tim. ii. 19.

against it, whose number shall be as the sea sands. And they went up,' says he, 'unto the plain of the earth, and compassed the tents of the saints about, and the beloved city, but fire came down from God out of heaven, and devoured them. And the devil that deceived them was cast into a lake of fire and brimstone, where the beast and the false prophets shall be tormented day and night for evermore.' [1]

But this belongs to the last judgment; which I thought good to recite, lest some should suppose that the devil being let loose again for a season should either find no Church at all, or by his violence and inducements should subvert all he finds. Wherefore the devil's imprisonment during the whole time included in this book (that is, from Christ's first coming to His last) is not any particular restraint from seducing the Church, because he could not injure the Church, were he ever so free. Otherwise, if his bondage were a set prohibition from seduction, what were his freedom but a full permission to seduce? Which God forbid should ever be! No, his binding is an inhibition of his full power of temptation, which is the means of man's being seduced, either by his violence or his fraudulence. Which if he were suffered to practise in that long time of infirmity, he would pervert and destroy the faith of many such souls as God's goodness will not suffer to be cast down. To avoid this inconvenience, bound he is. And in the last and smallest remainder of time shall he be loosed: for we read that he shall rage in his greatest malice only three years and six months, and he shall hold wars with such foes as all his enmity shall never be able either to conquer or injure. But if he were not let loose at all, his malevolence would be the less conspicuous, and the patience of the faithless the less glorious. Briefly, it would be the less apparent unto how blessed an end God had made use of his cursedness, in not debarring him absolutely from tempting the saints (though he be utterly cast out from their inward man) that they might reap a benefit from his badness; and in binding him firmly from the hearts of such as vow themselves his followers, lest if his wicked envy had the full scope, he should enter in amongst the weaker members of the Church, and by violence and subtlety together, deter and dissuade them from their faith, their only means of salvation. Now in the end, he shall be loosed, that the city of God may see what a potent adversary she has conquered by the grace of her Saviour and Redeemer, unto His eternal glory.

Oh, what are we, compared unto the saints that shall live to see this—when such an enemy shall be let loose unto them as we can scarcely resist although he be bound! (although, no doubt, Christ has had some soldiers in these our times, who if they had lived in the times to come, would have avoided all the devil's traps by their true discreet prudence, or have withstood them with undaunted

[1] Rev. xx. 7–10.

patience). This binding of the devil began when the Church began to spread from Judaea into other regions, and lasts yet, and shall do until his time be expired; for men even in these times do refuse the chain wherein he held them, infidelity, and turn unto God, and shall do, no doubt, unto the world's end. And then is he bound in respect of every private man, when the soul that was his vassal clears herself of him; nor ceases his shutting up, when they die in whom this shutting up took place: for the world shall have a continual succession of the haters of Christianity, whilst the earth endures, and in their hearts the devil shall ever be shut up. But it may be a doubt whether any one shall turn unto God during the space of his three and a half years' reign, for how can this stand good? How can a man 'enter into a strong man's house and spoil his goods, except he first bind the strong man, and then spoil his house,' [1] if he may do it when the strong man is loose? This seems to prove directly that during that space none shall be converted, but that the devil shall have a continual fight with those that are in the faith already, of whom he may perhaps conquer some certain number, but none of God's predestinated, not one. For it is not in vain that John, the author of this Revelation, says in one of his epistles, concerning some apostates: 'They went out from us, but they were not of us: for if they had been of us they would have continued with us.' [2] But what then shall become of the children? For it is incredible, that the Christians should have no children during this space; or that if they had them, they would not see them baptized by one means or other. How then shall these be taken from the devil, the spoil of whose house no man can attain before he bind him? And so it is more credible to avouch, that the Church in that time shall neither lack decrease nor augmentation; and that the parents in standing stiffly for their children's baptism (together with others that shall but even then become believers) shall beat the devil back in his greatest liberty —that is, they shall both wisely observe and warily avoid his newest stratagems, and most secret underminings, and by that means keep themselves clear of his merciless clutches. Notwithstanding, that text of scripture, 'How can a man enter into a strong man's house,' etc., is true, for all that. And according thereunto, the order was, that the strong should first be bound, and his goods taken from him, and so the Church be multiplied by weak and strong from all nations far and near, that by their true and faithful understanding of the prophecies that were to be fulfilled, they might take away his goods from him when he was in his greatest freedom. For as we must confess, 'that because iniquity increaseth, the love of many shall be cold,' [3] and that many of them that are not written in the book of life shall fall before the force of the raging newly loosed devil: so must we consider what faithful shall then be found on the earth, and how divers shall even then fly to the bosom of the Church, by God's grace, and the scripture's plainness; wherein amongst other things, that very end which they see approaching is foretold: and that they shall be both more firm in belief of what they rejected before, and also more strong to withstand the greatest assault and sorest batteries. If this be so, his former binding left his goods to all future spoil, be he bound or loose; unto which end, these words, 'How can a man enter into a strong man's house,' etc., do principally tend.

CHAPTER IX

What is meant by Christ's reigning a thousand years with the saints, and the difference between that and His eternal reign

Now doubtless whilst the devil is thus bound, Christ reigns with His saints the same thousand years, both being understood after one manner, that is, of all the time from His first coming. For that kingdom being excluded whereof He says, 'Come, ye blessed of My Father, inherit you the kingdom prepared for you,'[1] if there were not another reigning of Christ with the saints in another manner, whereof Himself says: 'I am with you alway unto the end of the world,'[2] the Church now upon earth should not be called His kingdom, or the kingdom of heaven. For the scribe that was taught unto the kingdom of God, lived in this thousand years. And the reapers shall take the tares out of the Church, which grew (until harvest) together with the good corn. This parable He expounds, saying: 'The harvest is at the end of the world, and the reapers are the angels. As then the tares are gathered and burned in the fire; so shall it be in the end of the world. The Son of Man shall send forth His angels, and they shall gather out of His kingdom all things that offend.'[3] Does He speak here of that kingdom where there is no offence? No, but of the Church that is here below. He says further: 'Whosoever shall break one of these least commandments and teach men so, he shall be called the least in the kingdom of heaven: but whosoever shall observe and teach them, the same shall be called great in the kingdom of heaven.'[4] Thus both these are done in the kingdom of heaven, both the breach of the commandments, and the keeping of them.

Then He proceeds: 'Except your righteousness exceed the righteousness of the scribes and Pharisees' (that is, of such as break what they teach, even as Christ says elsewhere of them, 'They say but do not'[5])—'unless you exceed these,' that is, both

[1] Matt. xxv. 34.   [2] Matt. xxviii. 20.   [3] Matt. xiii. 39–41.
[4] Matt. v. 19.   [5] Matt. xxiii. 3.

teach and observe, 'ye shall not enter into the kingdom of heaven.'[1]
Now the kingdom where the keeper of the commandments, and
the contemner, were both said to be, is one, and the kingdom into
which 'he that saith and doth not' shall not enter, is another.   So
then where both sorts are, the Church is as it now is: but where
the better sort is only, the Church is as it shall be hereafter, utterly
exempt from evil.   And so the Church now on earth is both the
kingdom of Christ, and the kingdom of heaven.   The saints reign
with Him now, but not as they shall do hereafter: yet the tares
reign not with them though they grow in the Church amongst the
good seed.   They reign with Him who do as the apostle says:
'If ye then be risen with Christ, seek the things which are above,
where Christ sitteth at the right hand of God: set your affections
on things which are above, and not on things which are on earth';[2]
of whom also he says, that their conversation is in heaven.[3]
Lastly, they reign with Christ who are withal His kingdom where
He reigns.   But how do they reign with Him at all, who continuing below, until the world's end, until His kingdom be purged
of all the tares, do nevertheless seek their own pleasures, and not
their Redeemer's?   This book therefore of St. John speaks of this
kingdom of warfare, wherein there are daily conflicts with the
enemy, sometimes with victory, and sometimes with loss, until the
time of that most peaceful kingdom approach, where no enemy
shall ever show his face.   This and the first resurrection are the
subject of the apostle's Revelation.   For having said that the devil
was bound for a thousand years, and then was to be loosed for a
while, he recapitulates the gifts of the Church during the said
thousand years.

'And I saw thrones,' says he, 'and they sat upon them, and
judgment was given unto them.'[4]   This may not be understood
of the last judgment: but by the thrones are meant the rulers'
places of the Church, and the persons themselves by whom it is
governed: and as for the judgment given them, it cannot be
better explained than in these words: 'Whatsoever ye bind on earth
shall be bound in heaven, and whatsoever ye loose on earth shall be
loosed in heaven.'[5]   Therefore says St. Paul: 'What have I to do
to judge them also that be without?   Do not ye judge them that
are within?'[6]   To proceed: 'And I saw the souls of them which
were slain for the witness of Jesus and for the world of God'
(understand that which follows, 'and they reigned with Christ a
thousand years'[7])—these were the martyrs' souls, not having
their bodies as yet; for the souls of the godly are not excluded from
the Church, which, as it is now, is the kingdom of God.   Otherwise
she would not mention them, nor celebrate their memories at our
communion 'of the body and blood of Christ': nor were it necessary

[1] Matt. v. 20.   [2] Col. iii. 1, 2.   [3] Phil. i'i. 20.   [4] Rev. xx. 4.
        [5] Matt. xviii. 18.   [6] 1 Cor. v. 12.   [7] Rev. xx. 4.

for us in our perils to run unto His baptism, or to be afraid to die
without it, nor to seek reconciliation to His Church, if a man have
incurred anything that exacts repentance, or burdens his conscience. Why do we those things, but that the faithful, even though
dead, are members of God's Church? Yet are they not with
their bodies, and yet, nevertheless, their souls reign with Christ,
the whole space of this thousand years. And therefore we read
elsewhere in the same book: 'Blessed are the dead which die in
the Lord. Even so, says the Spirit, for they rest from their labours,
and their works do follow them.' [1]   Thus then the Church reigns
with Christ, first 'in the quick and the dead': for 'Christ died' (as
the apostle says) 'that He might henceforth rule both over the
quick and the dead.' [2]   But the apostle here names the souls of the
martyrs only, because their kingdom is most glorious after death,
as having fought for the truth until death. But this is but a
taking of the part for the whole, for we take this passage to include
all the dead that belong to Christ's kingdom, which is, the Church.
But the sequel, 'And which did not worship the beast, neither his
image, neither had taken his mark upon their foreheads, or on
their hands': [3] this is meant both of the quick and dead. Now
although we must make a more exact inquiry what this beast was,
yet is it not against Christianity to interpret it, 'the society of the
wicked, opposed against the company of God's servants, and
against His holy city.' Now 'his image' is his dissimulation, in
such as profess religion, and practise unbelief. They feign to be
what they are not, and their pretence (not their truth) procures
them the name of Christians. For this beast consists not only
of the professed enemies of Christ and His glorious hierarchy, but of
the tares also, that in the world's end are to be gathered out of the
very fields of His own Church. And who are they that adore not
the beast, but those on whom St. Paul's advice takes effect, 'Be
not unequally yoked with unbelievers'? [4] These give him no
adoration, no consent, no obedience, nor take 'his mark,' that is,
the brand of their own sin, upon their foreheads, by professing it,
or on their hands, by working according to it. They that are
clear of this, be they living, or be they dead, reign with Christ all
this whole time, from their union unto Him to the end of the time
implied in the thousand years. 'The rest,' says St. John, 'did
not live, for now is the hour when the dead shall hear the voice of
the Son of God, and they that hear it shall live, the rest shall not
live.' [5] But the addition, 'until the thousand years be finished,'
implies that they were without life all the time that they should
have had it, attaining it by passing through faith from death to
life. And therefore on the day of the general resurrection, they
shall rise also, not unto life, but unto judgment, that is, unto con-

---

[1] Rev. xiv. 13.   [2] Rom. xiv. 9.   [3] Rev. xx. 4.
          [4] 2 Cor. vi. 14.   [5] John v. 25.

demnation, which is truly called the second death; for he that lives
not before the thousand years be expired, that is, he that hears not
the Saviour's voice, and passes not from death to life, during the
time of the first resurrection, assuredly shall be thrown both body
and soul into the second death, at the day of the second resurrection. For St. John proceeds plainly: 'This,' says he, 'is the
first resurrection. Blessed and holy is he that hath part in the first
resurrection,' [1] and part of it is his, who does not only arise from
death in sin, but continues firm in his resurrection. 'On such,'
says he, 'the second death hath no power.' But it has power over
the rest of whom he said before, 'The rest did not live until the
thousand years be finished': because in all that whole time meant
by the thousand years, although each of them had a bodily life (at
one time or other), yet they spent it, and ended it without arising
out of the death of iniquity, wherein the devil held them: which
resurrection would have been their only means to have purchased
them a part in the first resurrection, over which the second death
has no power.

CHAPTER X

*An answer to the objection of some, affirming that resurrection is proper
to the body only, and not to the soul*

SOME object this, that resurrection pertains only to the body, and
therefore the first resurrection is a bodily one; for that which falls
(say they) may rise again; but the body falls by death (for so is the
word *cadaver*, a carcass, derived of *cado*, to fall), therefore, rising
again belongs solely to the body, and not unto the soul. Well,
but what will you answer the apostle, when in as plain terms as may
be he calls the soul's bettering a resurrection? They were not
revived in the outward man, but in the inward, unto whom he
said: 'If ye then be risen with Christ, seek the things which are
above,' [2] which he explains elsewhere, saying, 'Like as Christ was
raised up from the dead by the glory of the Father, so we also
should walk in newness of life.' [3] Hence also is that text: 'Awake
thou that sleepest, and arise from the dead, and Christ shall give
thee light.' [4] Now whereas they say, none can rise but those
that fall, therefore, the body only can arise, why can they not hear
that shrill sound of the spirit: 'Depart not from Him lest ye fall'? [5]
And again, 'He standeth or falleth to his own Master'; [6] and
further, 'Let him that thinketh he standeth, take heed lest he fall.' [7]
I think these texts refer not to bodily falls but to the soul's. If
then resurrection concern them that fall, and the soul may also fall,
it must needs follow that the soul may rise again. Now St. John

[1] Rev. xx. 5, 6.   [2] Col. iii. 1.   [3] Rom. vi. 4.   [4] Eph. v. 14.
[5] Ecclus. ii. 7.   [6] Rom. xiv. 4.   [7] 1 Cor. x. 12.

having said, 'On such the second death shall have no power,'
proceeds thus: 'But they shall be the priests of God and of Christ,
and shall reign with Him a thousand years.'[1]   Now this is not
meant only of those whom the Church specifically calls bishops and
priests, but as we are all called Christians because of our mystical
chrism, our unction, so are we all priests in being the members
of one Priest.   Whereupon St. Peter calls us, 'a royal priesthood,
an holy nation.'[2]   And mark how briefly St. John insinuates the
deity of Christ in these words, 'Of God, and of Christ,' that is, of
the Father and of the Son; yet as He was made the Son of Man,
because of His servant's shape, so in the same respect was He made
a priest for ever according to the order of Melchizedek, whereof
we have spoken divers times in this work.

CHAPTER XI

*Of Gog and Magog, whom the devil (at the world's end) shall stir up
against the Church of God*

'AND when the thousand years,' says he, 'are expired, Satan shall
be loosed out of his prison and shall go out to deceive the people
which are in the four quarters of the earth, even Gog and Magog,
to gather them together into battle whose number is as the sand
of the sea.'[3]   So then the aim of his deceit shall be this war, for he
used divers ways to seduce before, and all tended to evil.   He shall
leave the dens of his hate, and burst out into open persecution.
This shall be the last persecution, hard before the last judgment,
and the Church shall suffer it, all the earth over.   The whole city
of the devil shall afflict the city of God at these times in all places.
This Gog and this Magog are not to be taken for any particular
barbarous nations, nor for the Getes and Massagetes, because of
their literal affinity, nor for any country beyond the Roman
jurisdiction.   He means all the earth when he says, 'The people
which are in the four quarters of the earth,' and then adds that
they are Gog and Magog.   'Gog' is 'a house,' and 'Magog' 'of
a house'; as if he said, 'the house and he that cometh out of the
house.'   So that they are the nations wherein the devil was bound
before; and now he is loosened, he comes from thence, they being
as the house, and he as coming out of the house.   But we refer
both these names unto the nations, and neither unto him.   They
are both the house, because the old enemy is hid and housed in
them; and they are of the house, when out of secret hate they burst
into open violence.   Now where he says, 'They went up into the
plain of the earth, and compassed the tents of the saints about, and
the beloved city,'[4] we must not think they came to any one set

---

[1] Rev. xx. 6.   [2] 1 Pet. ii. 9.   [3] Rev. xx. 7, 8.   [4] Rev. xx. 9.

place, as if the saints' tents were in any one certain nation, or the beloved city either. No, this city is nothing but God's Church, dispersed throughout the whole earth, and being resident in all places, and amongst all nations, as these words, 'the plain of the earth,' do insinuate. There shall the tents of the saints stand, there shall the beloved city stand. There shall the fury of the persecuting enemy girt them in with multitudes of all nations united in one rage of persecution. There shall the Church be hedged in with tribulations, and shut up on every side; yet shall she not forsake her warfare, which is signified by the word 'tents.'

CHAPTER XII

Whether the fire falling from heaven and devouring them implies the last torments of the wicked

BUT his following words, 'Fire came down from God out of heaven, and devoured them,'[1] are not to be understood of that punishment which these words imply: 'Depart from Me, ye cursed, into everlasting fire':[2] for then shall they be cast into the fire, and not fire be cast down upon them. But the first fire insinuates the firmness of the saints that will not yield unto the wills of the wicked: for heaven is the firmament, whose firmness shall burn them up for very zeal and vexation that they cannot draw the servants of God unto the side of Antichrist. This is the fire from God that shall burn them up, in that God has so confirmed His saints that they become plagues unto their enemies. Now whereas I said 'zeal,' know that zeal is taken in good sense or in evil; in good, as here: 'The zeal of Thine house has eaten me up';[3] in evil, as here: 'Zeal hath possessed the ignorant people.'[4] And now the fire shall eat up these opposers, but not that fire of the last judgment. Besides, if the apostle by this fire from heaven do imply the plague that shall fall upon such of Antichrist's supporters as Christ at His coming shall find left on earth, yet notwithstanding this shall not be the wicked's last plague, for that shall come upon them afterwards, when they are risen again in their bodies.

CHAPTER XIII

Whether it be a thousand years until the persecution under Antichrist

THIS last persecution under Antichrist (as we said before, and the prophet Daniel proves), shall last three years and a half. A little space! But whether it belong to the thousand years of the devil's

[1] Rev. xx. 9.   [2] Matt. xxv. 41.   [3] Ps. lxix. 9.   [4] Isa. xxvi. 11 (LXX).

bondage, and the saints' reign with Christ; or be a space of time more than the other fully accounted, is a great question. If we hold the first opinion, then we must say that the saints with Christ reigned longer than the devil was bound. Indeed, the saints shall reign with Him in the very heat of this persecution, and stand out against the devil, when he is in greatest power to molest them. But why then does the scripture confine both their reign and the devil's bondage to the exact sum of a thousand years, seeing the devil's captivity is out three years and six months sooner than their kingdom with Christ? Well, if we hold the latter opinion, that these three years and a half are beyond the exact thousand, to understand St. John that the reign of the saints with Christ and the devil's imprisonment ended both at once (according to the thousand years which he gives alike unto both), so that the said time of persecution belongs neither to the time of the one nor the other: then we must confess that during this persecution the saints reign not with Christ. But how can we dare affirm that His members do not reign with Him, when they do most firmly of all keep their coherence with him, and when at a time when the wars do rage, the more apparent is their constancy, and the more frequent is their ascent from martyrdom to glory? If we say they reign not because of the affliction that they endure, we may then infer that in the times already past, if the saints were once afflicted, their kingdom with their Saviour ceased: and so they, whose souls this evangelist beheld, namely the souls of those who were slain for the testimony of Jesus, and for the word of God, reigned not with Christ in their persecutions, nor were they the kingdom of Christ, who were Christ's most excellent possessions. Oh, this is absurd and abominable! No, the victorious souls of the glorious martyrs, subduing all earthly toils and tortures, have reigned and do reign with Christ until the expiration of the thousand years, and then shall take their bodies again, and so reign body and soul with Him for evermore. And therefore, in this sore persecution of three years and a half, both the souls of those that suffered for Christ before, and those that are then to suffer, shall reign with Him until the world's date be out, and the kingdom begin that shall never have an end. Wherefore assuredly the saints' reign with Christ shall continue longer than Satan's bondage, for they shall reign with God the Son, their King, three years and a half after Satan be loosed. It remains then, that when we hear that 'The priests of God and of Christ shall reign with Him a thousand years, and that after a thousand years the devil shall be loosed,'[1] we must understand that either the thousand years are meant of the devil's bondage only, and not of the saints' kingdom: or that the years of the saints' kingdom are longer, and they of the devil's bondage shorter; or that seeing three years and a half is but a little

[1] Rev. xx. 6, 7.

space, therefore it was not counted, either because the saints' reign
had more than it conceived, or the devil's bondage less; as we said
of the four hundred years in the sixteenth book. The time was
more, yet that sum only was set down, and this (if one observe it)
is very frequent in the scriptures.

CHAPTER XIV

*Satan and his followers condemned : a recapitulation of the resurrection
and the last judgment*

AFTER this rehearsal of the last persecution, he proceeds with the
fate of the devil and his city at the last judgment. 'And the devil,'
says he, 'that deceived them was cast into a lake of fire and brimstone, where the beast and the false prophet shall be tormented
even day and night for evermore.'[1] The beast, as I said before,
is the city of the wicked: his false prophet is either Antichrist,
or his image, the figment that I spoke of before. After all this
comes the last judgment, in the second resurrection, to wit, the
body's; and this he relates by way of recapitulation, as it was
revealed unto him. 'I saw,' says he, 'a great white throne, and One
that sat on it, from whose face flew away both the earth and
heaven, and their place was no more found.'[2] He says not, 'and
heaven and earth flew away from His face' (as though it happened
then); for that befell not until after the judgment, but, 'from
whose face flew away both heaven and earth,' meaning that afterwards, when the judgment shall be finished, then this heaven and
this earth shall cease, and a new world shall begin. But the old
one shall not be utterly consumed; it shall only pass through a
universal change; and therefore the apostle says: 'The fashion of
this world passeth away, and I would have you without care.'[3]
The fashion goes away, not the nature. Well, let us follow St.
John, who, after the sight of this throne, etc., proceeds thus: 'And
I saw the dead both great and small stand before God, and the
books were opened, and another book was opened which is the
book of life, and the dead were judged of those things which were
written in the books, according to their works.'[4]

Behold, the opening of books, and of one book! What this one
book was, he shows. It is the book of life. The others are the
holy ones of the Old and New Testament, that therein might be
shown what God had commanded: but in the book of life were
the commissions and omissions of every man on earth particularly
recorded. If we should imagine this to be an earthly book, such
as ours are, who is he that could imagine how huge a volume it
were, or how long it would take to read the contents? Shall

[1] Rev. xx. 10.   [2] Rev. xx. 11.   [3] 1 Cor. vii. 31, 32.   [4] Rev. xx. 12.

there be as many angels as men, and each one recite the deeds of
him that was committed to his charge? Then shall there not be
one book for all, but each one shall have one. Aye, but the scripture
here mentions but one in this kind. It is therefore some divine
power infused into the consciences of each individual, calling all
their works (wonderfully and strangely) unto memory, and so
making each man's knowledge accuse or excuse his own conscience.
Thus are all and each judged together. This divine power is
called a book, and fitly, for therein are read all the deeds that the
doer has committed; by the working of this he remembers all.
But the apostle, to explain the judgment of the dead more fully,
and to show how it comprises great and small, makes as it were a
return to what he had omitted (or rather deferred), saying: 'And
the sea gave up its dead which were within it, and death and hell
delivered up the dead which were in them.'[1] This was before
they were judged, and yet was the judgment mentioned before, so
that as I said, he returns to his omission; and having said thus
much, 'The sea give up its dead,' etc., he now proceeds in the
true order, saying: 'And they were judged, every man according
to his works.' This he repeats again here, to show the order of
events in the judgment whereof he had spoken before in these
words: 'And the dead were judged according to those things
which were written in the books, according to their works.'

CHAPTER XV

*Of the dead, whom the sea, and death, and hell shall give up to
judgment*

BUT what dead are they that the sea shall give up? For all that
die in the sea are not kept from hell, neither are their bodies kept
in the sea. Shall we say that the sea keeps the dead that were
good, and hell those that were evil? Horrible absurdity! Who is
so stupid as to believe this? No, the sea here is fitly understood
to imply the whole world. Christ therefore intending to show
that those whom He found on earth at the time appointed should
be judged with those that were to rise again, calls them dead men,
and yet good men, unto whom it was said: 'Ye are dead, and your
life is hidden with Christ in God.'[2] But them He calls evil of
whom He said: 'Let the dead bury their dead.'[3] Besides, they
may be called dead, in that their bodies are death's objects: wherefore the apostle says: 'The body is dead, because of sin, but the
spirit is life for righteousness' sake':[4] showing that in a mortal
man there is both a dead body and a living spirit. Yet said he
not, 'the body is mortal,' but 'dead,' although according to his

[1] Rev. xx. 13.   [2] Col. iii. 3.   [3] Matt. viii. 22.   [4] Rom. viii. 10.

manner of speech, he had called bodies mortal but a little before. Thus then the sea gave up her dead means that the world gave up all mankind that as yet had not approached the grave. 'And death and hell' (quoth he) 'gave up the dead which were in them.' [1] The sea merely presented its dead, for as they were then, so were they found; but death and hell had theirs first called to the life which they had left, and then gave them up. Perhaps it were not sufficient to say death only, or hell only, but he says both, 'death and hell,' death for such as might only die, and not enter hell, and hell for such as did both. For if it be not absurd to believe that the saints of old believing in Christ to come, were all at rest, in a place far from all torments (and yet within hell), until Christ's passion and descent thither set them at liberty; then surely the faithful that are already redeemed by that passion never know what hell means, from the time of their death until they arise and receive their rewards. After the words 'And they judged every one according to their deeds,' a brief declaration of the judgment is added. 'And death and hell,' saith he, 'were cast into the lake of fire.' [2] This is the second death. 'Death and hell' are but the devil and his angels, the only authors of death and hell's torments. This he did but recite before, when he said: 'And the devil that deceived them was cast into a lake of fire and brimstone.' [3] The obscure addition, 'Where the beast and the false prophet shall be tormented,' etc., this he explains here: 'Whosoever was not found written in the book of life, was cast into the lake of fire.' [4] Now as for the book of life, it is not meant to put God in remembrance of anything, lest He should forget, but it shows who are predestinated unto salvation, for God is not ignorant of their number, neither reads He this book to find it; His prescience is rather the book itself wherein all are written, that is, foreknown.

CHAPTER XVI

Of the new heaven and the new earth

THE judgment of the wicked being past as he foretold, the judgment of the good must follow, for he has already explained what Christ said in brief: 'They shall go into everlasting pain.' [5] Now he must express the sequel: 'And the righteous into life eternal.' 'And I saw,' says he, 'a new heaven and a new earth.' [6] The first heaven and earth were gone, and so was the sea, for such was the order described before by him when he saw the great white throne, and One sitting upon it from whose face they fled. So then they that were not in the book of life being judged, and cast into eternal fire

[1] Rev. xx. 13. [2] Rev. xx. 13, 14. [3] Rev. xx. 10.
[4] Rev. xx. 15. [5] Matt. xxv. 46. [6] Rev. xxi. 1.

(what, or where it is, I hold is unknown to all but those unto whom it please the Spirit to reveal it); then shall this world lose its form by worldly fire, as it was formerly destroyed by earthly water. Then (as I said) shall all the world's corruptible qualities be burnt away, and all those that held correspondence with our corruption shall be made fit for immortality, that the world, being so substantially renewed, may be fitly adapted unto the men whose substances are renewed also. But for that which follows, 'There was no more sea,' whether it imply that the sea should be dried up by that universal conflagration, or be transformed into a better essence, I cannot easily determine. Heaven and earth, we read, 'shall be renewed'; but as concerning the sea, I have not read of any such renewal, that I can remember; unless that other place in this book, where he says 'as it were a sea of glass, like unto crystal,' [1] import any such alteration. But in that place he speaks not of the world's end, neither does he say directly, a sea, but, as a sea. Notwithstanding, it is the prophet's custom to speak of truths in mystical manner, and to mix truths and types together, and so he might say, 'There was no more sea,' in the same sense that he said, 'The sea shall give up her dead,' intending that there should be no more turbulent times in the world, which he insinuates under the word 'sea.'

CHAPTER XVII

Of the glorification of the Church, after death, for ever

'And I, John,' said he, 'saw that holy city, New Jerusalem, coming down from God out of heaven, prepared as a bride adorned for her husband. And I heard a great voice out of heaven saying, Behold, the tabernacle of God is with men, and He will dwell with them, and they shall be His people, and He Himself shall be their God with them. And God shall wipe away all tears from their eyes, and there shall be no more death, neither tears, neither crying, neither shall there be any more pain, for the former things are passed away. And He that sat upon the throne said, Behold, I make all things new.' [2]

This city is said to come from heaven, because the grace of God that founded it is heavenly, as God says in Isaiah: 'I am the Lord that made thee.' [3] This grace of His came down from heaven even from the beginning; and ever since, the citizens of God have had their increase by the same grace, given by the Spirit, from heaven, in the fount of regeneration. But at the 'last judgment of God' by His Son Christ, this city shall appear in a state so glorious, that all the ancient shape shall be cast aside: for the bodies of each member shall cast aside their old corruption, and

[1] Rev. iv. 6. [2] Rev. xxi. 2–5. [3] Isa. xlv. 8.

put on a new form of immortality. For it were too gross impudence to think that this was meant of the thousand years aforesaid, wherein the Church is said to reign with Christ: because he adds directly: 'God shall wipe away all tears from their eyes: and there shall be no more death, neither sorrows, neither crying, neither shall there be any more pain.' Who is so obstinately absurd or so absurdly obstinate as to aver that any one saint (much less the whole society of them) shall pass this transitory life without tears or sorrows, or ever has passed it clear of them, seeing that the more holy his desires are, and the more zealous his holiness, the more tears shall bedew his supplications? Is it not the heavenly Jerusalem that says: 'My tears have been my meat day and night'?[1] And again: 'I cause my bed every night to swim, and water my couch with tears,'[2] and besides: 'My sorrow is renewed'?[3] Are not they His sons that groan being burdened because they desire not to be unclothed but clothed upon that their mortality may be reinvested with eternity; and having 'the first fruits of the Spirit do sigh in themselves, waiting for the adoption, that is, the redemption of their bodies'?[4] Was not St. Paul one of the heavenly city, nay, and that the rather, in that he had so great anxiety for the earthly Israelites? And when shall death be no more in that city, but when they may say: 'O death, where is thy sting? O grave, where is thy victory? The sting of death is sin'?[5] Sin could not be said to be there where death had no sting. But as for this world, St. John himself says: 'If we say we have no sin, we deceive ourselves, and there is no truth in us.'[6] And in this his Revelation, there are many things written for the exercising of the reader's understanding, and there are but few things whose understanding may be a key unto the rest: for he repeats the same thing so many ways that he seems to be dealing with different subjects when it is the same subject dealt with in other ways. But here where he says: 'God shall wipe away all tears from their eyes,' etc., this is directly meant of the world to come, and the immortality of the saints, for there alone shall be no sorrow, no tears, nor cause of sorrow or tears. If any one thinks this place obscure, let him look for no plainness in the scriptures.

CHAPTER XVIII

St. Peter's doctrine of the resurrection of the dead

Now let us hear what St. Peter says of this judgment. 'There shall come,' says he, 'in the last days, mockers, which will walk after their lusts, and say, Where is the promise of His coming?

---

[1] Ps. xlii. 3.   [2] Ps. vii. 6.   [3] Ps. xxxix. 2.   [4] Rom. viii. 23.
                [5] 1 Cor. xv. 55, 56.   [6] 1 John i. 8.

For, since the fathers died, all things continue alike from the beginning of the creation. For this, they (willingly) know not, that the heavens were of old, and the earth that was of the water and by the water by the Word of God, by which the world, that then was, perished, overflowed with the water. But the heavens and earth that now are are kept by the same Word in store, and reserved unto fire against the day of judgment, and of the destruction of ungodly men. Dearly beloved, be not ignorant of this, that one day with the Lord is as a thousand years, and a thousand years as one day. The Lord is not slack concerning His promise (as some men count slackness), but is patient toward us, and would have no man to perish, but would have all men to come to repentance. But the day of the Lord will come as a thief in the night, in the which the heavens shall pass away with a noise, and the elements shall melt with heat, and the earth with the works that are therein shall be burnt up. Seeing, therefore, all these must be dissolved, what manner of persons ought ye to be in holy conversation and godliness, longing for and hastening the coming of the day of God, by the which the heavens being on fire shall be dissolved, and the elements shall melt with heat? But we look for a new heaven and a new earth according to His promise, wherein dwelleth righteousness.'[1] Thus far there is not any mention of the resurrection of the dead, but enough concerning the destruction of the world, where his mention of the world's destruction already past gives us sufficient warning to believe the dissolution to come. For the world that was then perished (says he) at that time; not only the earth, but that part of the air also which the water possessed, or got above, and so consequently almost all those airy regions, which he calls the heaven, or rather in the plural the heavens, but not the spheres wherein the sun and the stars have their places; they were not touched: the rest was altered by humidity, and so the earth perished, and lost its first form by the deluge. But the heavens and earth (says he) that now are are kept by the same Word in store, and reserved unto fire against the day of judgment, and of the destruction of ungodly men. Therefore the same heaven and earth, that remained after the deluge, are they that are reserved unto the fire aforesaid, unto the day of judgment and perdition of the wicked. For because of this great change he hesitates not to say that there shall be a destruction of men also; whereas, indeed, their essences shall never be annihilated although they live in torment. Yea, but (may some say) if this old heaven and earth shall at the world's end be burned before the new ones be made, where shall the saints be in the time of this conflagration, since they have bodies, and therefore must be in some bodily place? We may answer, In the upper parts, whither the fire as then shall no more ascend than the water did in the deluge. For

[1] 2 Pet. iii. 3–13.

at this day the saints' bodies shall be movable whither their wills
do please: nor need they fear the fire, being now both immortal
and incorruptible: for the three children, though their bodies were
corruptible, were notwithstanding preserved from losing a hair
by the fire; and might not the saints' bodies be preserved by the
same power?

CHAPTER XIX

*St. Paul's words to the Thessalonians about the manifestations of
Antichrist, whose times shall immediately forerun the day of the
Lord*

I SEE I must pass over many worthy sayings of the saints concerning
this day, lest my work should grow to too great a volume: but yet
St. Paul's I may by no means omit.   Thus says he: 'Now I be-
seech you, brethren, by the coming of our Lord Jesus Christ, and
by our assembling unto Him, that you be not suddenly moved
from your mind, nor troubled neither by spirit, nor by word, nor
by letter, as if it were from us, as though the day of Christ were at
hand.   Let no man deceive you by any means; for that day shall
not come except there come a fugitive [1] first, and that man of sin
be revealed, even the son of perdition; which is an adversary, and
exalteth himself against all that is called God, or that is worshipped,
so that he sitteth as God in the temple of God, showing himself
that he is God.   Remember ye not that when I was yet with you
I told you these things?   And now ye know what withholdeth,
that he might be revealed in his due time.   For the mystery of
iniquity does already work; only he which now withholdeth shall
let, till he be taken out of the way.   And then the wicked man
shall be revealed, whom the Lord shall consume with the spirit of
His mouth, and shall abolish with the brightness of His coming;
even He whose coming is by the working of Satan, with all power,
and signs, and lying wonders, and in all deceivableness of unrighteousness amongst them that perish, because they received
not the love of the truth that they might be saved.   And therefore
God shall send them strong delusion, that they should believe a
lie, that all they might be condemned which believe not in the
truth, but had pleasure in unrighteousness.' [2]   This is doubtless
meant of Antichrist and the day of judgment.   For this day he
says shall not come until Antichrist be come before it, he that is
called here a fugitive from the face of the Lord: for if all the ungodly deserve this name, why not he most of all?   But in what
temple of God he is to sit as God, it is doubtful whether it be the
ruined temple of Solomon, or in the Church.   For it cannot be

---

[1] St. Augustine reads *refuga* instead of the Vulgate *discessio*.—ED.

[2] 2 Thess. ii. 1–12.

any heathen temple. St. Paul would never call any such the temple of God. Some, therefore, do by Antichrist understand the devil and all his domination, together with the whole multitude of his followers; and imagine that it were better to say 'He shall sit *in templum Dei*,' meaning He shall sit as the temple of God, that is, as though he were the Church: as we say *Sedet in amicum*, 'he sits as a friend,' and so forth. But whereas he says, 'And now ye know what withholdeth,' that is, what stays him from being revealed; this implies that they knew it before, and therefore he does not relate it here. Wherefore we, that know not what they knew, do strive to get the understanding of the apostle's meaning, but we cannot because his addition makes it the more mysterious. For what is this: 'The mystery of iniquity doth already work, only he that withholdeth shall let, till he be taken out of the way'? Truly, I confess that I am utterly ignorant of his meaning: but what others have conjectured about it I will relate. Some say St. Paul spoke of the State of Rome, and would not be plainer, lest he should incur a slander that he wished Rome's empire evil fortune, whereas it was hoped that it should continue for ever. By 'the mystery of iniquity' they say he meant Nero, whose deeds greatly resembled those of Antichrist, so that some think that he shall rise again and be the true Antichrist. Others think he never died, but vanished, and that he lives (in that age and vigour wherein he was supposed to be slain) until the time come that he shall be revealed and restored to his kingdom.

But this is too presumptuous an opinion. However these words, 'He that withholdeth shall let, till he be taken out of the way,' may not unfitly be understood of Rome, as if he had said, 'He that now reigneth shall reign until he be taken away.' 'And then the wicked man shall be revealed.' This is Antichrist, no man doubts it. Now some understand these words, 'Now ye know what withholdeth,' and 'The mystery of iniquity doth already work,' to be meant only of the false Christians in the Church, who shall increase unto a number which shall make Antichrist a great people. This, say they, is the mystery of iniquity, for it is yet unrevealed: and therefore does the apostle encourage the faithful to persevere, saying, 'Let him that holdeth, hold,' for thus they understand these words, 'until he be taken out of the way,' that is, until Antichrist and his troops (this unrevealed mystery of iniquity) depart out of the midst of the Church. And unto this do they hold St. John's words to belong: 'Little children, it is the last time: and as ye have heard that Antichrist shall come, even now there are many Antichrists, whereby we know that it is the last time. They went out from us but they were not of us: for if they had been of us, they would have continued with us.' [1] Thus (say they) even as before the end, in this time which St. John calls 'the last of all,' many

[1] 1 John ii. 18, 19.

heretics (whom he calls many Antichrists) went out of the Church, so likewise hereafter all those that belong not unto Christ but unto the last Antichrist shall depart out of the midst of Christ's flock, 'and then shall the man of sin be revealed.' Thus one takes the apostle's words one way, and another another way. But this he means assuredly, that Christ will not come to judge the world until Antichrist be here before Him to seduce the world (although it be God's secret judgment that he should thus seduce it), for his coming shall be (as it is said) 'by the working of Satan with all power, and signs, and lying wonders, and in all deceivableness of unrighteousness amongst them that perish.' For then shall Satan be let loose, and work by this Antichrist unto all men's admiration, and yet all in falsehood. Now here is a doubt, whether they be called lying wonders because he does but delude the eyes in these miracles, and does not what he seems to do; or because although they may be real actions, yet the end of them all is to draw ignorant mankind into this false conceit that such things could not be done but by a divine power, because they know not that the devil shall have more power given him then than ever he had before. For the fire that fell from heaven, and burnt the house and goods of holy Job, and the whirlwind that smote the building and slew his children, were neither of them false apparitions: yet were they the devil's effects, by the power that God had given him.

Therefore, in what respect these are called lying wonders, shall be then more apparent. Howsoever, they shall seduce such as deserve to be seduced, because they received not the love of the truth that they might be saved. Whereupon the apostle adds this: 'Therefore shall God send them strong delusion that they should believe a lie.' God shall send it; because His just judgment permits it, though the devil's malevolent desire performs it; that all they might be condemned which believe not in the truth, but had pleasure in unrighteousness.

Thus being condemned, they are seduced, and being seduced, condemned. But their seducement is by the secret judgment of God, justly secret, and secretly just; even His that has judged continually, ever since the world began. But their condemnation shall be by the last and manifest judgment of Jesus Christ, that judges most justly and was most unjustly judged Himself.

CHAPTER XX

St. Paul's doctrine of the resurrection of the dead

BUT the apostle says nothing of the resurrection of the dead in this place; yet in another place he says thus: 'I would not have you ignorant, brethren, concerning those which sleep, that ye sorrow not even as those which have no hope: <u>for if we believe that Jesus died, and is risen again, even so also them which sleep in Jesus will God bring with Him</u>.   For this we say unto you by the word of the Lord, that we which live and are remaining at the coming of the Lord shall not prevent those that sleep.   For the Lord Himself shall descend from heaven with a shout, with the voice of the archangel, and with the trump of God, and the dead in Christ shall arise first: then shall we which live and remain be caught up with them also in the clouds to meet the Lord in the air, and so shall we ever be with the Lord.' [1]   Here the apostle makes a plain demonstration of the future resurrection, when Christ shall come to sit in judgment over both quick and dead.   But it is a common question whether those whom Christ shall find alive at His coming (such as the apostle admits himself and those with him to be) shall ever die at all, or go immediately in a moment up with the rest to meet Christ, and so be forthwith immortalized.   It is not impossible for them both to die and live again in their very ascension through the air.   For these words: 'And so shall we ever be with the Lord,' are not to be taken as if we were to continue in the air with Him; for He shall not stay in the air, but go and come through it.   We meet Him coming, but not staying: but so shall we 'ever be with Him,' namely, in immortal bodies, wherever our stay be. And in this sense the apostle seems to urge the understanding of this question to be this, that those whom Christ shall find alive, shall nevertheless both die and revive, even as He says: 'In Christ shall all be made alive': [2] and in another place: 'That which thou sowest, is not quickened except it die.' [3]   How then shall those whom Christ shall find alive be quickened in Him by immortality, unless they do first die, if these words of the apostle be true?   If we say that the sowing is meant only of those bodies that are returned to the earth, according to the judgment laid upon our transgressing forefathers: 'Dust thou art, and unto dust shalt thou return': [4] then we must confess, that neither that text of St. Paul nor this of Genesis concerns their bodies whom Christ at His coming shall find in the body: for those are not sown, because they neither go to the earth, nor return from it, whether they have a little stay in the air, or otherwise taste not of any death at all.

But the apostle has another passage about the resurrection. 'We shall all rise again,' [5] says he, or (as it is in some copies), 'We shall all sleep.'

So then, death going alway before resurrection, and sleep in this text implying nothing but death, how shall all rise again, or sleep, if so many as Christ shall find living upon earth shall neither sleep nor rise again?   So therefore, if we do but avouch that the saints whom Christ shall find in the flesh, and who shall meet Him in the

[1] 1 Thess. iv. 13–17.   [2] 1 Cor. xv. 22.   [3] 1 Cor. xv. 36.
                    [4] Gen. iii. 19.   [5] 1 Cor. xv. 51.

air, do in this rapture leave their bodies for a while, and then take
them on again, the doubt is cleared both in the apostle's first words,
'That which thou sowest is not quickened, except it die': as also
in his latter, 'We shall all rise again,' or, 'We shall all sleep': for
they shall not be quickened unto immortality, unless they first
taste of death, and consequently have a share in the resurrection
by means of this their little sleep.   And why is it incredible that
those bodies should be sown, and revived immortally in the air,
when we believe the apostle, where he says plainly, that the resurrection shall be in the twinkling of an eye, and that the dust of the
most aged body shall in one moment unite to retain those members,
that henceforth shall never perish?   Nor let us think that that
text of Genesis, 'Dust thou art,' etc., concerns not the saints, for
all that their dead bodies return not to the earth, but are both dead
and revived whilst they are in the air.

'To dust shalt thou return,' that is, thou shalt by loss of life
become that which thou wast ere thou hadst life.   It was earth in
whose face the Lord breathed the breath of life, when man became
a living soul; so that it might be said: 'Thou art living dust, which
thou wast not, and thou shalt be lifeless dust, as thou wast.'   Such
are all dead bodies even before putrefaction, and such shall they be
(if they die) wheresoever they die, being void of life, which notwithstanding they shall immediately return unto.   So then shall
they return unto earth, by becoming earth, after being living men;
as that returns to ashes which becomes ashes, that unto putrefaction
which is putrefied, that into a pot which of earth is made a pot,
and a thousand other suchlike instances.   But how this shall be,
we do but conjecture now, nor shall know till we see it.

That there shall be a resurrection of the flesh at the coming of
Christ to judge the quick and the dead, all that are Christians must
confidently believe: nor is our faith in this point in any way frivolous, although we know not how this shall be effected.   But, as
I said before, so mean I still to proceed in setting forth such places
of the Old Testament as concern this last judgment, as far as need
shall be; which it shall not be altogether so necessary to spend
much time upon, if the reader do but aid his understanding with
that which we have mentioned before.

CHAPTER XXI

Isaiah's doctrine concerning the judgment and the resurrection

'THE dead,' says the prophet Isaiah, 'shall arise again; and they
shall arise again that were in the graves; and all they shall be glad
that are in the earth: for the dew that is from Thee is health to
them, and the land (or earth) of the wicked shall fall.' [1]   All this

[1] Isa. xxvi. 19.

belongs to the resurrection. And whereas he says, 'the land of the wicked shall fall,' that is to be understood of their bodies which shall be ruined by damnation. But now if we look well into the resurrection of the saints, these words, 'the dead shall rise again,' belong to the first resurrection, and these, 'they shall arise again that were in the graves,' unto the second. And as for those holy ones whom Christ shall meet in their flesh, this is fitly pertinent unto them: 'All they shall be glad that are in the earth: for the dew that is from Thee, is health unto them.' By health in this place is meant immortality, for that is the best health, and needs no daily refreshment to preserve it.

The same prophet also speaks of the judgment, both to the comfort of the godly, and the terror of the wicked. 'Thus saith the Lord: Behold, I will incline unto them as a flood of peace; and upon the glory of the Gentiles as a flowing stream. Then shall ye suck. Ye shall be borne upon the shoulders, and be joyful upon the knees. As one whom his mother comforteth, so will I comfort you, and ye shall be comforted in Jerusalem. And when ye see this, your hearts shall rejoice and your bones shall flourish as an herb; and the hand of the Lord shall be known unto His servants, and His indignation against His enemies. For behold, the Lord will come with fire, and His chariots like a whirlwind, that He may recompense His anger with wrath, and His indignation with a flame of fire, for the Lord will judge with fire, and with His sword, all flesh, and the slain of the Lord shall be many.' [1] Thus you hear, as touching His promises to the good. He inclines to them 'like a flood of peace': that is, in all peaceful abundance; and such shall our souls be watered with at the world's end (but of this in the last book). This He extends unto them to whom He promises such bliss, that we may conceive that this flood of beatitude does sufficiently bedew all the whole region of heaven, where we are to dwell. But because He bestows the peace of incorruption upon corruptible bodies, therefore He says, He will incline, as if He came downwards from above to make mankind equal with the angels.

By Jerusalem we understand not her that serves with her children, but our free mother (as the apostle says) which is eternal, and above; where after the shocks of all our sorrows be past, we shall be comforted, and rest like infants in her glorious arms, and on her knees. Then shall our rude ignorance be invested in that unaccustomed blessedness. Then shall we see this, and our heart shall rejoice. What we shall see is not set down. But what is it but God, that so the gospel might be fulfilled: 'Blessed are the pure in heart, for they shall see God'? [2] And all that bliss which we now believe, but as frail men, in far less measure than it is, we shall then behold and see. Here we hope, there we shall enjoy.

---

[1] Isa. lxvi. 12–16.   [2] Matt. v. 8.

But lest we should imagine that those causes of joy concerned only the spirit, He adds: 'And your bones shall flourish as an herb.' Here is a plain touch at the resurrection, relating as it were what He had omitted.

These things shall not be done even then when we do see them; but when they are already come to pass, then shall we see them. For He had spoken before of the new heaven and earth in His accounts of the promises that were in the end to be performed to the saints, saying: 'I will create new heavens and a new earth, and the former shall not be remembered nor come into mind: but be you glad and rejoice therein; for behold, I will create Jerusalem as a rejoicing, and her people as a joy, and I will rejoice in Jerusalem, and joy in My people, and the voice of weeping shall be heard no more in her, nor the voice of crying,' [1] etc. This now some apply to the proof of Chiliasm: because the prophet's manner is to mingle figurative utterances with truths, to exercise the reader in a fit inquest of their spiritual meanings. But carnal sloth contents itself with the literal sense only, and never seeks further. Thus far of the prophet's words before he wrote what we have in hand. Now let us go forward again. 'And your bones shall flourish like an herb.' That he means only the resurrection of the saints in this, his addition proves: 'And the hand of the Lord shall be known amongst His servants.' What is this but His hand distinguishing His servants from such as scorn Him? Of those it follows, 'And his indignation against His enemies': or, as another interprets it, 'against the unfaithful.' This is no threatening, but the effect of all His threatenings. 'For behold,' says he, 'the Lord will come with fire, and His chariots like a whirlwind, that He may recompense His anger with wrath, and His indignation with a flame of fire. For the Lord will judge with fire, and with His sword, all flesh, and the slain of the Lord shall be many.' [2] Whether they perish by fire or sword, or whirlwind, all refer to the pain of the judgment. For he says that God shall come as a whirlwind, that is unto such as His coming shall be penal unto. Again, His chariots, being spoken in the plural, imply His ministering angels. But when he says that all flesh shall be judged by fire and sword, we do except the saints, and apply it only to those 'which mind earthly things' (and such minding is deadly), and to such as those of whom God says: 'My Spirit shall not alway strive with man, because he is but flesh.' [3] But these words, 'The slain' (or wounded) 'of the Lord shall be many'; this implies the second death.

The fire, the sword, and the stroke, may all be understood in a good sense; for God has said He would send fire into the world. And the Holy Ghost descended in the shape of fiery tongues. Again, 'I came not,' says Christ, 'to send peace, but the sword.' [4]

[1] Isa. lxv. 17–19.   [2] Isa. lxvi. 15, 16.   [3] Gen. vi. 3.   [4] Matt .x .34.

And the scripture calls God's Word 'a two-edged sword': because
of the two Testaments. Besides, the Church, in the Canticles,
says that she is wounded with love, as though she were shot with the
force of love. But here where we read that the Lord shall come
as an avenger, etc., it is plain to whom the language refers.

Then the prophet proceeds with the destruction of the wicked,
under the types of such as in the old law refrained not from the forbidden meats, and goes on to rehearse the graciousness of the New
Testament from Christ's first coming, even unto this judgment
we have now in hand. For first, he tells how God says that He
cometh to gather the nations, and how they shall come to see His
glory.¹ 'For all have sinned,' says the apostle, 'and are come short
of the glory of God.'² He says also that He will leave signs
amongst them to induce them to believe in Him, and that He will
send His elect into many nations, and far islands that never heard
of His name, to preach His glory to the Gentiles, and to bring
their brethren, that is, the brethren of the elect Israel (of whom
He spake) into His presence; to bring them for an offering unto
God in chariots, and upon horses (that is, by the ministry of men
or angels) unto holy Jerusalem, that is now spread throughout the
earth in her faithful citizens. For these, when God assists them,
believe; and when they believe, they come unto Him. Now God
in a simile compares them to the children of Israel that offered
unto Him His sacrifices with psalms in the temple; as the Church
does now in all places: and He promises to take of them for priests
and for Levites, which now we see He does. For He has not
observed fleshly kindred in His choice now, as He did in the time
of Aaron's priesthood: but according to the New Testament, where
Christ is Priest after the order of Melchizedek, He selects each of
His priests according to the merit which God's grace has stored his
soul with, as we now behold. And these priests are not to be
respected merely for their places (for those the unworthy do often
hold), but for their sanctity, which is not common both to good
and bad.

Now the prophet having thus revealed God's mercies to the
Church, adds the several ends that shall befall the good and bad
in the last judgment, in these words: 'As the new heavens and the
new earth which I shall make shall remain before Me, saith the
Lord: even so shall your seed and your name. And from month
to month, and from sabbath to sabbath shall all flesh come to
worship before Me, saith the Lord. And they shall go forth and
look upon the members of the men that have transgressed against
Me; for their worm shall not die, neither shall their fire be quenched;
and they shall be an abhorring unto all flesh.'³ Thus ends the
prophet his book, with the end of the world. Some in this place
for 'members' read 'carcasses' hereby intimating the body's evident

¹ Isa. lxvi. 17, 18.   ² Rom. iii. 23.   ³ Isa. lxvi. 22-4.

punishment, though indeed a carcass is properly nothing but dead flesh. But those bodies shall be living. Otherwise how should they be sensible of pain, unless we say they are dead bodies, that is, their souls are fallen into the second death, and so we may fitly call them carcasses? And thus are the prophet's former words also to be taken, 'The land of the wicked shall fall.' *Cadaver*, a carcass, all know, comes from *cado*, to fall. Now the translators by saying the carcasses of the men, do not exclude women from this damnation, but they speak as by the better sex, seeing that woman was taken out of man. But note especially, that where the prophet, speaking of the blessed, says, 'all flesh shall come to worship'; he means not all men (for the greater number shall be in torments) but some shall come out of all nations, to adore Him in the heavenly Jerusalem. But as I was saying, since here is mention of the good by 'flesh,' and of the bad by 'carcasses'; verily after the resurrection of the flesh, our faith in which these words do confirm, shall be the judgment to come, which shall confine both the good and bad unto their last limits.

CHAPTER XXII

How the saints shall go forth to see the pains of the wicked

But how shall the good go forth to see the bad plagued? Shall they leave their blessed habitations, and go corporally to hell, to see them face to face? God forbid. No, they shall go in knowledge. For this implies that the damned shall be without, and for this cause the Lord calls their place outer darkness, opposite unto that ingress allowed the good servant in these words: 'Enter into thy Master's joy.' [1] And lest the wicked should be thought to go in to be seen, rather than the good should go out by knowledge to see them, being able to know that which is without (for the tormented shall never know what is done in the Lord's joy; but they that are in that joy shall know what is done in the utter darkness): therefore says the prophet, 'they shall go forth'; [2] in that they shall know what is without. For if the prophets through that small part of divine inspiration could know these things before they came to pass, how then shall not these immortals know them being passed, seeing that in them the Lord is all in all? Thus shall the saints be blessed both in seed and name. In seed, as St. John says, 'And his seed remaineth in him.' [3] In name, as Isaiah says, 'So shall your name continue; from month to month, and from sabbath to sabbath shall they have rest upon rest': [4] passing thus from old and temporal types to new and everlasting truths. But the pains of the wicked, that eternal worm, and that never dying

---

[1] Matt. xxv. 21.   [2] Isa. lxvi. 24.   [3] 1 John iii. 9.   [4] Isa. lvi. 5; lxvi. 23.

fire, are diversely expounded, either in reference to the body only, or to the soul only, or the fire to belong to the body really, and the worm to the soul figuratively; and this last is the likeliest of the three.   But here is no place to discuss particulars.   We must end this volume, as we promised, with the judgment, the separation of good from bad, and the rewards and punishments accordingly distributed.

CHAPTER XXIII

Daniel's prophecy of Antichrist, of the judgment, and of the kingdom of the saints

OF this judgment Daniel prophesied, saying, that Antichrist shall forerun it: and so he proceeds to the eternal kingdom of the saints. For having in a vision beheld the four beasts, types of the four monarchies, and the fourth overthrown by a king which all confess to be Antichrist, and then seeing the eternal empire of the Son of Man (Christ) to follow, 'I Daniel,' says he, 'was troubled in spirit, in the midst of my body, and the visions of mine head made me afraid.   Therefore I came to one of them that stood by, and asked him the truth of all this: so he told me and showed me the interpretation of these things.   These four great beasts are four kings, which shall arise out of the earth, but the saints of the Most High shall take the kingdom, and possess it for ever, even for ever and ever.   After this, I would know the truth of the fourth beast which was so unlike the other, very fearful, whose teeth were of iron, and his nails of brass, which devoured, brake in pieces, and stamped the rest under his feet.   Also would I know of the ten horns that were on his head, and of the other that came up, before whom three fell, and of the horn that had eyes, and of the mouth that spake presumptuous things, whose look was more stout than his fellows.   I beheld, and the same horn made battle against the saints, yea and prevailed against them, until the Ancient of days came, and judgment was given to the saints of the Most High: and the time approached that the saints possessed the kingdom.'[1]

All this Daniel inquired, and then he proceeds: 'Then he said, The fourth beast shall be the fourth kingdom on the earth, which shall be unlike to all the kingdoms and shall devour the whole earth, and shall tread it down and shall break it in pieces.   And the ten horns are ten kings that shall rise, and another shall rise after them, and he shall be unlike to the first, and he shall subdue three kings, and shall speak words against the Most High, and shall consume the saints of the Most High, and think that he may change times and laws; and they shall be given into his hand until a time, times, and half a time.   But the judgment shall sit and they shall take away

[1] Dan. vii. 15-22.

his dominion, to consume and destroy it unto the end: and the kingdom, and dominion, and the greatness of the kingdom under the whole heaven shall be given unto the holy people of the Most High whose kingdom is an everlasting kingdom, and all powers shall serve and obey Him. Even this is the end of the matter. I, Daniel, had many cogitations which troubled me, and my countenance changed in me but I kept the matter in mine heart.' [1] These four kingdoms, some hold to be those of the Assyrians, Persians, Macedonians, and Romans.

How fitting is this application, read Jerome's commentaries upon Daniel, and there you may have full instruction. But that Antichrist's kingdom shall be most cruel against the Church (although it last but a while) until the saints receive the sovereignty, none that reads this place can make question of. The time, times, and half a time is three years and a half; a year, two years, and half a year; and this is declared by a number of days afterwards, and by the numbers of months in other places of the scriptures. Times in this place seems indefinite; but the dual number is here used by the seventy, which the Latins have not, but which both the Greeks and Hebrews have. 'Times' then stands but for 'two times.' Now I am afraid (indeed) that we deceive ourselves in the ten kings whom Antichrist shall find as ten men by our account; but there are not so many kings in the Roman monarchy, so that Antichrist may come upon us ere we be aware. What if this number imply the fullness of royalty, which shall be expired ere he come, as the numbers of a thousand, a hundred, seven, and divers more do oftentimes signify the whole of a thing? I leave it to judgment. To go on with Daniel, 'There shall be a time of trouble,' says he, chap. xii, 'such as never was since there began to be a nation unto that same time, and at that time Thy people shall be delivered, every one that shall be found written in the book. And many that sleep in the dust of the earth shall awake: some to everlasting life, and some to shame and perpetual contempt. And they that are be wise shall shine as the brightness of the firmament, and many that turn to righteousness shall shine as the stars, for ever and ever.' [2] How like is this passage unto that of the gospel concerning the resurrection! That says: 'They that are in the graves': this, 'they that are in the dust of the earth.' That saith, 'shall come forth': this, 'shall awake,' that, 'they that have done good, unto eternal life, and they that have done evil unto everlasting damnation': [3] this, 'some to everlasting life, and some to perpetual shame and contempt.' Nor think they differ in that the gospel says, 'all that are in the graves,' and the prophet says but 'many': for the scripture sometimes uses 'many' for 'all.' So was it said unto Abraham: 'Thou shalt be a father of many nations,' [4] and yet in another place, 'In thy seed

[1] Dan. vii. 24–28. [2] Dan. xii. 1–3. [3] John v. 28, 29.
[4] Gen. xvii .5.

shall all nations be blessed.'[1] Of this resurrection, it was said thus to Daniel himself a little after: 'Go thou thy way till the end be: for thou shalt rest, and stand up in thy lot at the end of the days.'[2]

CHAPTER XXIV

David's prophecies of the world's end and the last judgment

TOUCHING this last judgment, we find much spoken of it in the psalms, but I omit the most of it, yet the plainest thereof I cannot but rehearse. 'Thou aforetime hast laid the foundation of the earth, and the heavens are the works of Thy hands. They shall perish, but Thou shalt endure: they shall all wax old as doth a garment; as a vesture shalt Thou change them, and they shall be changed: but Thou art the same, and Thy years shall not fail.'[3] What reason now has Porphyry to praise the Hebrews for their adoration of the greatest God, and yet blame the Christians for avouching that the world shall have an end, seeing that these books of the Hebrews, whose God he confesses to be terrible to all the rest, do directly aver it? 'They shall perish.' What? The heavens, the greatest, the safest, the highest part of the world shall perish; and shall not the lesser and the lower do so too? If Jove do not like this, whose oracle (as Porphyry says) has condemned the Christians' credulity, why does he not condemn the Hebrews' also, for leaving this doctrine especially recorded in their holiest writings? But if this Jewish wisdom, which he does so commend, affirms that the heavens shall perish, how vain a thing is it, to detest the Christian faith, for avouching that the world shall perish, which if it perish not, then cannot the heavens perish! Now our own scriptures, with which the Jews have nothing to do, our gospels and apostolic writings, do all affirm this. 'The fashion of this world goeth away.'[4] 'The world passeth away.'[5] 'Heaven and earth shall pass away.'[6] But I think that 'passeth away,' does not imply so much as 'perisheth.' But in St. Peter's epistle,[7] where he says, how the world perished being overflowed with water, is plainly set down both what he meant by the world, how far it perished, and what was reserved for fire, and the perdition of the wicked. And he says afterwards: 'The day of the Lord will come as a thief in the night, in the which the heavens shall pass away with a noise, the elements shall melt with heat, and the earth with the rocks that are therein shall be burnt up'; and so concludes, that 'seeing all these perish, what manner of persons ought ye to be?' Now we may understand that those heavens shall perish which he said were reserved for fire, and those elements shall melt which are

---

[1] Gen. xxii. 18.   [2] Dan. xii. 13.   [3] Ps. cii. 25–7.   [4] 1 Cor. vii. 31.
     [5] 1 John ii. 17.   [6] Matt. xxiv. 35.   [7] 2 Pet. iii. 6, 7, 10, 11.

here below in this mass of discordant natures; wherein also he says those heavens are reserved, not meaning the upper spheres that are the seats of the stars. For whereas it is written, 'that the stars shall fall from heaven,' it is a good proof that the heavens shall remain untouched. If these words be not figurative, the stars shall fall indeed, or some such wondrous apparitions shall fill this lower air, as Virgil speaks of:

> Stella facem ducens multa cum luce cucurrit,[1]
>
> A tailed star flew on, with glistering light,

and so hid itself in the woods of Ida. But this text of the psalm seems to exempt none of all the heavens from perishing. 'The heavens are the works of Thine hands. They shall perish.' Thus as He made all, so all shall be destroyed. The pagans scorn (I am sure) to call St. Peter to defend that Hebrew doctrine, which their gods do so approve, by alleging the figurative speaking hereof, *pars pro toto*. 'All shall perish,' meaning only all the lower parts; as the apostle says there, that the world perished in the deluge, when it was only the earth, and some part of the air. This shift they will not make, less they should either yield to St. Peter, or allow this meaning, that the fire at the last judgment may do as much as we say the deluge did before. Their assertion, that all mankind can never perish, will allow them neither of these evasions. Then they must needs say that when their gods commended the Hebrews' wisdom, they had not read this psalm. But there is another psalm as plain as this: 'Our God shall come, and shall not keep silence. A fire shall devour before Him, and a mighty tempest shall be moved round about Him. He shall call the heaven above, and the earth to judge His people. Gather My saints together unto Me, those that make a covenant with Me with sacrifice.'[2] This is spoken of Christ, who we believe shall come from heaven to judge 'both the quick and the dead.' He shall come openly, to judge all most justly, who when He came in secret was judged Himself most unjustly. 'He shall come and shall not be silent.' His voice now shall confound the judge before whom He was silent, when 'He was led like a sheep to the slaughter, and as a lamb before the shearer is dumb,' as the prophet says of Him, and as it was fulfilled in the gospel. Of this fire and tempest we spoke before, in our discourse of Isaiah's prophecy touching this point. But His calling the heavens above (that is the saints), this is that which St. Paul says: 'Then shall we be caught up also in the clouds, to meet the Lord in the air.'[3] For if it meant not this, how could the heavens be called above, as though they could be anywhere but above? The words following, 'and the earth,' if you add not 'above' here also, may be taken for those that are to be judged, and the heavens for those that shall judge with Christ.

[1] *Aen.* ii. 694.   [2] Ps. l. 3–5.   [3] 1 Thess. iv. 17.

And then the calling of the heavens above implies the placing of
the saints on thrones of judgments, not their being caught up into
the air. We may further understand it to be His calling of the
angels from their high places to descend with Him to judgment,
and by the earth, those that are to be judged. But if we do understand 'above' in both clauses, it intimates the saints' being caught
up directly: putting 'the heavens' for their souls, and 'the earth'
for their bodies. 'To judge (or distinguish) His people,' that is, to
separate the sheep from the goats, the good from the bad. Then
speaks He to His angels: 'Gather My saints together unto Me.'
This is done by the angels' ministry. And whom gather they?
'Those that make a covenant with Me with sacrifice.' And this is
the duty of all just men to do. For either they must offer their works
of mercy (which is above sacrifice, as the Lord says, 'I will have
mercy and not sacrifice'[1]), or else their works of mercy are the
sacrifice itself that appeases God's wrath, as I proved in the ninth
book of this present volume. In such works do the just make
covenants with God, in that they perform them for the promises
made them in the New Testament. So then Christ having gotten
His righteous on His right hand, will give them this welcome:
'Come, ye blessed of My Father, inherit ye the kingdom prepared
for you from the foundations of the world: for I was an hungered
and ye gave Me to eat': [2] and so forth of the good works, and their
eternal rewards which shall be returned for them in the last
judgment.

CHAPTER XXV

*Malachi's prophecy of the judgment, and of such as are to be purged
by fire*

THE prophet Malachiel or Malachi (otherwise called the angel, and
held by some, as Jerome says, namely by the Hebrews, to be
Esdras the priest that wrote some other parts in the canon) prophesied of the last judgment in these words: 'Behold, He shall
come, saith the Lord of Hosts: but who may abide the day of His
coming? And who shall endure when He appeareth? For He
is like a purging fire, and like fuller's soap: and He shall sit down
to test and refine the silver. He shall even refine the sons of Levi, and
purify them as gold and silver, that they may bring offerings to the
Lord in righteousness. Then shall the offerings of Judah and
Jerusalem be acceptable unto the Lord as in old time, and in the
years before. And I will come near unto you to judgment, and I
will be a swift witness against the soothsayers, and against the
adulterers, and against false swearers, and against those that wrong-
fully keep back the hireling's wages, and vex the widow and the

---

[1] Hos. vi. 6.   [2] Matt. xxv. 34, 35.

fatherless, and fear not Me, saith the Lord of Hosts: for I am the Lord, I change not.' [1]   These words do seem evidently to imply a purification of some, in the last judgment.   For what other thing can be meant by this: 'He is like a purging fire, and like fuller's soap, and He shall sit down to test and refine the silver.   He shall refine the sons of Levi, and purify them as gold or silver'?   So says Esaias: 'The Lord shall wash the filthiness of the daughters of Zion, and purge the blood of Jerusalem out of the midst thereof, by the spirit of judgment, and by the spirit of burning.' [2]   Perhaps this burning may be understood of that separation of the polluted from the pure in that penal judgment, the good living on ever after, without any commerce with the bad.   But these words: 'He shall even refine the sons of Levi, and purify them as gold and silver, that they may bring offerings to the Lord in righteousness,' do intimate a purgation even of the good, who shall now be cleansed from that unrighteousness wherein they displeased the Lord, and being cleansed, and in their perfection of righteousness, they shall be pure offerings themselves unto Him their Lord.   For what better or more acceptable oblation for Him is there than themselves?   But let us leave this theme of penal purgation unto a more fit opportunity.   By the sons of Levi, Judah, and Jerusalem, is meant the Church of God, both of Hebrews and others: but not in that state that it stands now in (for as we are now, 'if we say we have no sin, we deceive ourselves and the truth is not in us' [3]): but as it shall be then, like a threshing floor cleansed by the fan of the last judgment, all being penally purged that needed such a purification, so that now there shall be need of no more sacrifice for sin, for all that offer such are in sin, for the remission of which they offer, to be freed from it by God's gracious acceptance of their offering.

CHAPTER XXVI

Of the saints' offerings, which God shall accept as in the old time and the years before

To show that the city of God should have no more such custom, it is said that the sons of Levi shall bring offerings to the Lord in righteousness, therefore not in sin, and consequently not for sin. We may therefore gather by the words following, viz. 'Then shall the offerings of Judah and Jerusalem be acceptable unto the Lord, as in old time and in the years before'; that the Jews are deceived in believing this refers to the restorations of their old legal ceremonies: for all the sacrifices of the old instrument were offered in sin, and for sin; and the priest himself (who we must think was the holiest) was expressly commanded by the Lord to offer first for

[1] Mal. iii. 1–6.   [2] Isa. iv. 4.   [3] 1 John i. 8.

his own sins, and then for the people. We must therefore show
how these words, 'As in old time and in the years before,' are to be
taken. They may perhaps imply the time of our first parents being
in paradise, for they were then pure, and offered themselves as
unspotted oblations to the Lord. But they transgressing, and
being therefore thrust out, and all mankind being depraved and
condemned in them, since their fall no man but the Redeemer of
the world and little baptized infants were ever pure from sin—
'no, not the infant of one day's age.' [1]

If it be answered that they are worthily said to offer in righteousness that offer in faith, in that 'The just liveth by faith,' [2] though if
he say he has no sin, he deceives himself, and therefore he says
it not, because he lives by faith; I say again, Is any one so far deceived as to parallel these times of faith with those of the last
judgment, wherein those that are to offer those oblations in righteousness are to be purged and refined? Nay, seeing that after
that purgation there shall be no place for the least imperfection of
sin: assuredly the time wherein there shall be no sin is not to be
compared with any, saving with the time before our first parents'
fall in paradise, wherein they lived in spotless felicity. So that
this it is which is meant by 'the old time and the years before,'
for another such passage is there in Isaiah. After the promise of
a new heaven and a new earth, amongst the other allegorical
promises of beatitudes to the saints (which study of brevity enforced us to let pass unexpounded), this is one: 'As the days of the
tree of life, shall the days of My people be.' [3] This tree, who is it
that has read the scriptures and knows not that God planted it,
and where, and how our first parents by sin were debarred from
eating of the fruit thereof, and a terrible guard set upon it for ever
after? Some may say the prophet by that meant the days of
Christ's Church that now is, and that Christ is that tree (according
to that saying of Solomon concerning wisdom: 'She is a tree of life
to them that lay hold on her' [4]), and again, that our first parents
lived but a small while in paradise, seeing that they had no children
during that space, and therefore when we speak of the time that
they were there, we cannot speak of any years, as this text does,
'In old time and in the years before.' Well, this question is too
intricate to discuss at this time, and therefore let it pass.

There is another meaning of these words besides this, which
does also exclude the interpretation of this passage by the legal and
carnal sacrifices, as though the restoring of them were such a
benefit; for those offerings of the old law being made all of unpolluted beasts free from blemish, did signify spotless and holy
men, such as Christ Himself only was, and no other. Seeing
therefore that in the judgment all being cleansed that need clean-
sing, there shall not be any sin left in the saints, but each shall

[1] Job xiv. 4.   [2] Hab. ii. 4.   [3] Isa. lxv. 22.   [4] Prov. iii. 18.

offer himself in righteousness unto God, as an immaculate and pure oblation: thus shall it be then as in the years before, when that was represented typically which at this day shall be fulfilled truly, for then shall that purity be real in the saints, which formerly was prefigured in the sacrifices. So much for that. Now as for those that are not worthy of being cleansed, but condemned, thus says the prophet: 'I will come to you in judgment, and I will be a swift witness against the soothsayers, and against the adulterers, etc., for I am the Lord, and change not': [1] as if He said, Your fault has now made you worse, and My grace once made you better: but 'I change not.' He will be witness Himself, because He shall in that judgment need no other. Swift, because He will come on a sudden, unlooked for, and when He is thought to be farthest off; and again because He will convince the guilty conscience without making any words. 'Inquisition shall be made in the thoughts of the ungodly,' [2] says the wise man. 'Their conscience also bearing witness' (says the apostle), 'and their thoughts accusing one another or excusing, at the day when God shall judge the secrets of men by Jesus Christ according to my gospel.' [3] Thus then shall God be a swift witness in calling that suddenly unto the thoughts which shall forthwith condemn them.

CHAPTER XXVII

Of the separation of the good from the bad in the end of the last judgment

THAT also which I cited (to another purpose) in the eighteenth book out of this prophet belongs to the last judgment: 'They shall be to me, says the Lord of Hosts, in that day that I shall do this, as a flock, for I will spare them as a man spares his own son that serves him. Then shall ye return and discern between the righteous and the wicked, between him that serves God and him that serves Him not. For behold the day comes that shall burn as an oven, and all the proud, yea and all that do wickedly, shall be stubble, and the day that comes shall burn them up, says the Lord of Hosts, and shall leave them neither root nor branch. But unto you that fear My name shall the Sun of righteousness arise, and health shall be under his wings, and ye shall go forth and grow up as fat calves. And ye shall tread down the wicked, for they shall be dust under the soles of your feet in the day that I shall do this, says the Lord of Hosts.' [4] This distance of rewards and punishments severing the just from the unjust, is not seen by the transitory

---

[1] Mal. iii. 5, 6.   [2] Wisd. of Sol. i. 9.   [3] Rom. ii. 15, 16.
[4] Mal. iii. 17–iv. 3.

light of this worldly sun; but when it appears before that Sun of righteousness, in the manifestation of the life to come, then shall there be such a judgment as never was before.

CHAPTER XXVIII

Moses' law to be spiritually understood for fear of dangerous error

BUT whereas the prophet proceeds, saying: 'Remember the law of Moses My servant, which I commended unto him in Horeb for all Israel with the statutes and judgments,' [1] this is fitly added, both to follow the precedent distinction between the followers of the law and the contemners of it, as also to imply that the said law must be spiritually interpreted, that Christ, the distinguisher of the good and bad, may therein be discovered; who spoke not idly Himself, when He told the Jews, saying: 'Had ye believed Moses, ye would have believed Me, for he wrote of Me.' [2]   For these men conceiving the scriptures in a carnal sense and not apprehending those earthly promises as types of the eternal ones, fell into those wicked murmurings that they durst be bold to say: 'It is in vain to serve God, and what profit is it that we have kept His commandment, and that we walked humbly before the Lord of Hosts? Therefore we count the proud blessed; even they that work wickedness are set up,' [3] etc.   These their words seem even to compel the prophet to foretell the last judgment, where the wicked shall be so far from all shadow of happiness that they shall be visibly wretched, and the good so freed from all lasting misery, that they shall not be touched with any even the most transitory, but fully and freely be enthroned in eternal blessedness.   For their words before seem to say thus: 'All that do evil, are good in God's eye, and please Him.' [4]   These grumblings against God proceeded merely of the carnal understanding of Moses' law.   Whereupon the psalmist says that he had like to have fallen himself, and that his feet slipped, through his fretting at the foolish, seeing the prosperity of the wicked, insomuch that he says: 'How doth God know it, or is there knowledge in the Most High?'   And a little after: 'Have I cleansed mine heart in vain, and washed mine hands in innocency?'   But to clear this difficulty, how it should come to pass that the wicked should be happy, and the just miserable, he adds this: 'Then thought I to know this, but it was too hard for me, until I went into the sanctuary of God and then understood I their end.' [5]   At the day of the Lord it shall not be so, but the misery of the wicked and the happiness of the godly shall be clearly seen in far other order than the present world can discover.

[1] Mal. iv. 4.   [2] John v. 46.   [3] Mal. iii. 14, 15.
          [4] Mal. ii. 17.   [5] Ps. lxxiii. 2, 12, 13, 16, 17.

CHAPTER XXIX

Elias' coming to convert the Jews before the judgment

Now the prophet having advised them to remember the law of Moses, because he foresaw some that would hereafter misinterpret much thereof, adds: 'Behold, I will send you Elijah the prophet before the coming of the great and fearful day of the Lord: and he shall turn the hearts of the fathers to the children and of the children to the fathers, lest I come and smite the earth with cursing.'[1] That this great and mighty prophet Elijah shall convert the Jews unto Christ before the judgment, by expounding them the law, is most commonly believed and taught by us Christians, and is held as a point of infallible truth. For we may well hope for the coming of him before the judgment of Christ, whom we do truly believe to live in the body at this present hour, without having ever tasted of death. He was taken up by a fiery chariot, body and soul, from this mortal world, as the scriptures plainly avouch. Therefore when he comes to give the law a spiritual exposition, which the Jews do now understand wholly in a carnal sense, 'Then shall he turn the hearts of the fathers unto the children' (or, 'the heart of the father unto the child': for the Seventy do often use the singular number for the plural); that is, the Jews shall then understand the law as their holy forefathers had done before them, Moses, the prophets, and the rest. For the understanding of the fathers being brought to the understanding of the children, is the turning of the fathers' hearts unto the children; and the children's consent unto the understanding of the fathers, is the turning of their hearts unto the fathers. And whereas the Seventy say: 'And the heart of a man unto his kinsman'; fathers and children being the nearest of kindred are consequently meant in this place. There may be a farther and more choice interpretation of this place, namely, that Elijah should turn the heart of the Father unto the Child; not by making the Father to love the Child, but by teaching that the Father loves Him, that the Jews who had hated Him before, may henceforth love Him also. For they hold that God hates Him now, because they hold Him to be neither God nor the Son of God: but then shall His heart (in their judgments) be turned unto Him, when they are so far turned themselves as to understand how He loves Him. The sequel, 'and the heart of man unto his kinsman,' means, the heart of man unto the man Christ, for He being one God in the form of God, taking the form of a servant, and becoming man, vouchsafed to become our kinsman. This, then, shall Elias perform. 'Lest I come and smite the earth with cursing.' 'The earth,' that is, those carnal-thoughted Jews, that now are, and that now murmur at the Deity,

[1] Mal. iv. 5, 6.

saying that He delighted in the wicked, and that it is vain to serve Him.[1]

CHAPTER XXX

That it is not evident in the Old Testament in such places as say, God shall judge, that it shall be in the person of Christ, but only by some of the testimonies where the Lord God speaks

To gather the whole number of such places of scripture as prophesy His judgment, were too tedious. Suffice it that we have proved it out of both the Testaments. But the places of the Old Testament are not so evident for the coming of Christ in person as they of the New be. For whereas we read in the Old, that 'the Lord God shall come,' it is no certainty that it is meant of Christ; for the Father, the Son, and the Holy Ghost are all both Lord and God, which we may not omit to observe. We must therefore first of all make a demonstration of those places in the prophets as do expressly name the Lord God, and yet evidently refer to Jesus Christ, as also of those wherein this evidence is not so plain, and yet may be conveniently understood of Him nevertheless. There is one place in Isaiah, that has it as plain as may be. 'Hear Me, O Jacob and Israel,' says the said prophet, 'My called; I am the first, and I am the last: surely My hand has laid the foundation of the earth, and My right hand hath spanned the heavens: when I call them, they stand together. All ye, assemble yourselves, and hear. Which amongst them hath declared these things? The Lord hath loved him. He will do his will in Babel, and his arm shall be against the Chaldaeans. I, even I, have spoken it, and I have called him: I have brought him, and his ways shall prosper.

'Come near unto Me, hear ye this. I have not spoken it in secret from the beginning; from the time that the thing was, I was there, and now the Lord God and His Spirit hath sent Me.'[2] This was He that spoke here as 'the Lord God': and yet it had not been evident that He was Christ, but that He adds the last clause, 'The Lord God and His Spirit hath sent Me.' For this He spoke of that which was to come in the form of a servant, using the preterperfect tense for the future, as the prophet does elsewhere, saying, 'He was led as a sheep to the slaughter.'[3] He does not say, 'He shall be led,' but puts the time past for the time to come, according to the usual phrase of prophetical speeches.

There is also another place in Zechariah, as evident as this, which says 'The Almighty sent the Almighty': and what was that, but that the Father sent the Son? The words are these: 'Thus saith the Lord of Hosts: After this glory hath He sent Me unto the nations, which spoiled you, for he that toucheth you, toucheth the

_____
[1] Mal. ii. 17; iii. 14.   [2] Isa. xlviii. 12–16.   [3] Isa. liii. 7.

apple of His eye. Behold, I will lift My hand upon them, and they shall be a spoil to those that served them, and ye shall know that the Lord of Hosts hath sent Me.'[1] Behold here, the Lord of Hosts says that the Lord of Hosts has sent Him. Who dare say that these words proceed from any but from Christ, speaking to His lost sheep of Israel? For He says so Himself: 'I am not sent but unto the lost sheep of Israel.'[2] Those He compares here unto the apple of His eye, in His most fervent love unto them, and of those lost ones the apostles were a part themselves. But after His resurrection (before which the Holy Ghost, says John, was not yet given, because that 'Jesus was not yet glorified'[3]), He was also sent unto the Gentiles in His apostles, and so was that saying of the psalm fulfilled: 'Thou hast delivered Me from the contentions of the people: Thou hast made me the head of the heathen': [4] that those that had spoiled the Israelites and made them slaves, should spoil them no more but become their slaves. This promised He to His apostles, saying, 'I will make you fishers of men'; [5] and again, unto one of them alone, 'From henceforth thou shalt catch men.' [6] Thus shall the nations become spoils, but unto a good end, as a vessel taken from a strong man that is bound by a stronger.

The said prophet also in another place says (or rather the Lord by him says): 'In that day will I seek to destroy all the nations that come against Jerusalem, and I will pour upon the house of David and upon the inhabitants of Jerusalem the spirit of grace and of compassion; and they shall look upon Me whom they have pierced, and they shall lament for Him as one mourneth for his only son, and be sorry for Him as one is sorry for his first-born.' [7] Who is it but God that shall rid Jerusalem of the foes that come against her, that is, that oppose her faith, or (as some interpret it) that seek to make her captive? Who but He can pour the spirit of grace and compassion upon the house of David and upon the inhabitants of Jerusalem? This is properly God's own attribute, and spoken by God Himself in the prophet. And yet that this God, who shall do all the wonderful works, is Christ, the sequel shows plainly: 'They shall look upon Me whom they have pierced, and be sorry,' etc. For those Jews who shall receive the spirit of grace and compassion, in the time to come, shall repent that ever they insulted Christ in His passion, when they shall see Him coming in His majesty, and know that this is He whose baseness of parentage they had formerly flouted. And their forefathers shall see Him too, upon whom they had exercised such impiety, even Him shall they behold, but not unto their correction, but unto their confusion. These words then, 'I will pour upon the house of David, and upon the inhabitants of Jerusalem, the spirit

---

[1] Zech. ii. 8, 9.   [2] Matt. xv. 24.   [3] John vii. 39.   [4] Ps. xviii. 43.
[5] Matt. iv. 19.   [6] Luke v. 10.   [7] Zech. xii. 9, 10.

of grace and compassion,' etc., do in no way concern them, but their children only, whom the preaching of Elias shall bring to the true faith. But as we say to the Jews, 'You killed Christ,' though it was their predecessors, so shall the children of those murderers bewail the death of Christ themselves, though their predecessors (and not they) were they that did the deed. So then, though they receive the spirit of grace and compassion, and so escape the condemnation of their forefathers, yet shall they grieve, as if they had been partakers of their predecessors' villainy, yet shall it not be guilt but zeal that shall enforce this grief in them. The Seventy do read this place thus: 'They shall behold Me whom they have insulted'; but the Hebrews read it, 'whom they have pierced,' which gives a fuller intimation of the crucifying of Christ. But that 'insulting' in the Seventy was continued even through the whole passion of Christ. Their taking Him, binding Him, judging Him, apparelling Him with mock habits, crowning Him with thorns, striking Him on the head with reeds, mocking Him with feigned reverence, enforcing Him to bear His own Cross, and crucifying Him even to His very last gasp, was nothing but a continuous insulting. So that laying both the interpretations together (as we do) we express fully that the place implies Christ and none other.

Therefore, whensoever we read in the prophets that 'God shall judge the world,' though there be no other distinction, that very word 'judge' does express the Son of Man, for by His coming it is that God's judgment shall be executed. God the Father in His personal presence will judge no man, but has given all judgment unto His Son, who shall show Himself as man, to judge the world even as He showed Himself as man to be judged of the world. Who is it of whom God speaks in Isaiah under the name of Jacob and Israel, but this Son of Man that took flesh of Jacob's line? 'Jacob, My servant, I will stay upon him. Israel, Mine elect in whom My soul delighteth, I have put My spirit upon Him. He shall bring forth judgment unto the Gentiles. He shall not cry, nor lift up nor cause His voice to be heard in the streets. A bruised reed shall He not break, and the smoking flax shall He not quench. He shall bring forth judgment in truth. He shall not fail nor be discouraged until He have settled judgment in the earth, and the isles shall hope in His name.' [1]

In the Hebrew there is no mention of Jacob nor of Israel, but the Seventy being desirous to show what He meant by His servant, namely, that same form of a servant wherein the Highest was humbled, added the name of the man from whose stock He was to derive that servile form. The Spirit of God came upon Him in the form of a dove, as the gospel testifies. He brought forth judgment to the Gentiles, in foretelling them of future things

[1] Isa. xlii. 1–4.

which they never knew before. He did not cry out, yet ceased He not to preach, nor was His voice heard without (or in the street), for such as are cut off from His fold never hear His voice. He neither broke down nor extinguished those Jews His persecutors, whose lost integrity and abandoned light made them like bruised reeds and smoking flax. He spared them, for as yet He was not come to judge them, but to be judged by them. He brought forth judgment in truth, by showing them their future plagues if they perished in their malice. His face shone on the mount, His fame in the whole world. He neither failed nor fainted, in that both He and His Church stood firm against all persecutions. Therefore His foes never had nor ever shall have cause to think that fulfilled which they wished in the psalm, saying: 'When shall He die and His name perish?'[1] 'Until He have settled judgment in the earth.' Lo, here is that we seek. The last judgment is that which He shall settle upon earth, coming to effect it out of heaven. As for the last words, 'The isles shall hope in His name,' we see them fulfilled already.

Thus, then, by this which is so undeniable is that proved credible which impudence dares yet deny. For who would ever have hoped for that which the unbelievers themselves do now behold, as well as we, to their utter heart-breaking and confusion? Who did ever look that the Gentiles should embrace Christianity, that had seen the Author thereof bound, beaten, mocked, and crucified? That which one thief durst but hope for upon the cross, in that now do the nations far and wide repose their utmost confidence; and, lest they should incur eternal death, are signed with that figure whereupon He suffered His temporal death. Let none, therefore, make any doubt that Christ shall bring forth such a judgment as the scriptures do promise, except he believe not the scriptures, and stand in his own malicious blindness against that which has enlightened all the world.

And this judgment shall consist of these circumstances, partly precedent and partly adjacent. Elijah shall come, the Jews shall believe, Antichrist shall persecute, Christ shall judge, the dead shall arise, the good and bad shall sever, the world shall burn and be renewed. All this we must believe shall be, but in what order, our full experience then shall exceed our imperfect intelligence as yet. Yet verily I do think they shall fall out in order as I have rehearsed them. Now remain there two books more of this theme, to the perfect performance of our promise: the first of which shall treat of the pains due unto the wicked, and the second of the glories bestowed upon the righteous; wherein, if it please God, we will subvert the arguments which foolish mortals and miserable wretches make for themselves against God's holy and divine promises, and against the sacred nutriment given to the soul

[1] Ps .xli. 5.

by an unspotted faith, thinking themselves the only wise men in these their ungracious cavils, and deriding all religious instructions as contemptible and ridiculous. As for those that are wise in God, in all that seems most incredible unto man, if it be avouched by the holy scriptures (whose truth we have already sufficiently proved), they lay hold upon the True and Omnipotent Deity, as the strongest argument against all opposition; for He (they know) cannot possibly speak false in those scriptures, and withal, can by His divine power effect that which may seem more than most impossible to the unbelievers.

THE TWENTY-FIRST BOOK OF
THE CITY OF GOD

CHAPTER I

Why the punishment of the condemned is here disputed of before the happiness of the saints

SEEING that by the assistance of our Lord and Saviour Jesus Christ, the Judge of the quick and the dead, we have brought both the cities (the one whereof is God's and the other the devil's), unto their intended consummation, we are now to proceed (by the help of God) in this book with the declaration of the punishment due unto the devil and all his confederacy. And this I choose to do before I handle the glories of the blessed, because both these and the wicked are to undergo their sentences in body and soul, and it may seem more incredible for an earthly body to endure undissolved in eternal pains, than without all pain in everlasting happiness. So that when I have shown the possibility of the first, it may be a great motive unto the confirmation of the latter. Nor does this method want a precedent from the scriptures themselves, which sometimes relate the beatitude of the saints foremost, as here, 'They that have done good, unto the resurrection of life, but they that have done evil, unto the resurrection of condemnation,' [1] and sometimes afterward, as here, 'The Son of Man shall send forth His angels, and they shall gather out of His kingdom all things that offend, and them which do iniquity, and shall cast them into a furnace of fire; there shall be wailing and gnashing of teeth: then shall the just shine like the sun, in the kingdom of the Father,' [2] and again, 'And these shall go into everlasting pain; but the righteous into life eternal.' [3] Besides, he that will look into the prophets shall find this order often observed. It were too much for me to recite all: my reason why I observe it here, I have set down already.

CHAPTER II

Whether an earthly body may possibly be incorruptible by fire

WHAT then shall I say unto the unbelievers, to prove that a body carnal and living may endure undissolved both against death and the force of eternal fire. They will not allow us to ascribe this

[1] John v. 29.　　　[2] Matt. xiii. 41-3.　　　[3] Matt. xxv. 46.

unto the power of God, but urge us to produce it to them by some
example.   If we shall answer them that there are some creatures
that are indeed corruptible, because mortal, and yet do live untouched in the middle of the fire: and likewise, that there are a kind
of worms that live without being hurt in the fervent springs of the
hot baths, whose heat sometimes is such as none can endure, and
yet those worms do so love to live in it, that they cannot live without
it: this, either they will not believe unless they see it; or if they do
see it, or hear it affirmed by sufficient authority, then they cavil at
it as an insufficient proof for the proposed question; on the ground
that these creatures are not eternal, and living thus in this heat,
nature has made it the means of their growth and nutriment, not
of their torment: as though it were not more incredible that fire
should nourish anything rather than not consume it.   It is strange
for anything to be tormented by the fire, and yet to live: but it is
stranger to live in the fire and not to be tormented.   If then this
latter be credible, why is not the first so also?

CHAPTER III

Whether a fleshly body may possibly endure eternal pain

YEA, but (say they) there is no body that can suffer eternally but it
must perish at length.   How can we tell that?   Who can tell
whether the devils do suffer in their bodies, when, as they confess,
they are extremely tormented?   If they answer that there is no
earthly soul and visible body, or (to speak all in one) no flesh that
can suffer always and never die, what is this but to ground an
assertion upon mere sense and appearance?   For these men know
no flesh but mortal, and what they have not known and seen, that
they hold impossible.   And what an argument is this, to make pain
the proof of death, when it is rather the testimony of life!   For
though our question be, whether anything living may endure
eternal pain and yet live still, yet are we sure it cannot feel any pain
at all unless it live, pain being inseparably adherent unto life, if it
be in anything at all.   Needs then must that live that is pained,
yet is there no necessity that this or that pain should kill it: for all
pain does not kill all the bodies that perish.   Some pain indeed
must, by reason that the soul and the body are so conjoined that
they cannot part without great torment, to which the soul succumbs;
and the mortal frame of man being so weak that it cannot withstand
this violence, thereupon are they severed.   But afterwards, they
shall be so rejoined again, that neither time nor torment shall be
able to procure their separation.   Wherefore though our flesh as
now be such that it cannot suffer pain without dying; yet then
shall it become of another nature, as death also then shall be of

another nature. For the death then shall be eternal, and the soul that suffers it shall neither be able to live, having lost her God her only life, nor yet to avoid torment, having lost all means of death. The first death forces her from the body against her will, and the second holds her in the body against her will. Yet both are one in this, that they enforce the soul to suffer in the body against her will. Our opponents will allow this, that no flesh as now can suffer the greatest pain, and yet not perish: but they observe not that there is a thing above the body, called a soul, that rules and guides it; and this may suffer any torment and yet remain for ever. Behold now, here is a thing, sensible of sorrow, and yet eternal. This power then that is now in the souls of all, shall be then in the bodies of the damned. And if we weigh it well, the pains of the body are rather referred to the soul. The soul it is, and not the body, that feels the hurt inflicted upon any part of the body.

And so as we call them living and sensitive bodies, though all the life and sense is from the soul; so likewise do we say they are grieved bodies, though the grief be only in the soul. So then, when the body is hurt, the soul grieves with the body. When the mind is offended by some inward vexation, then the soul grieves alone, though it be in the body; and further, it may grieve when it is without the body, as the soul of the rich glutton did in hell, when he said: 'I am tormented in this flame.'[1] But the body lacking a soul grieves not, nor having a soul does it grieve without the soul. If therefore it were meet to draw an argument of death from the feeling of pain, as if we should say, 'He may feel pain, therefore he may die,' this should rather infer that the soul may die, because it is that which is the feeler of the pain.

But seeing that this is absurd and false, how then can it follow that those bodies, which shall be in pain, shall therefore be subject unto death? Some Platonists hold that those parts of the soul wherein fear, joy, and grief were resident, were mortal, and perished: whereupon Virgil said: 'Hinc metuunt cupiuntque, dolent gaudentque,'[2] 'Hence' (that is, by reason of those mortal parts of the soul) 'did fear, hope, joy, and grief possess them.' But touching this we proved in our fourteenth book that, after their souls were purged to the uttermost, there yet remained a desire in them to return unto their bodies: and where desire is, there grief may be. For hope being frustrate and missing the aim turns into grief and anguish. Wherefore if the soul which does principally or only suffer pain, be notwithstanding (after a sort) immortal, then it does not follow that a body should perish because it is in pain. Lastly, if the body may breed the soul's grief, and yet cannot kill it, this is a plain argument that pain does not necessarily infer death. Why then is it not as credible that the fire should grieve those bodies and yet not kill them, as that the body should

[1] Luke xvi. 24.   [2] Aen. vi. 733.

procure the soul's anguish and yet not its death? If pain exists there is therefore no sufficient argument to prove that death must needs follow it.

CHAPTER IV

Nature's testimonies, that bodies may remain undiminished in the fire

IF therefore the salamander live in the fire (as the most exact naturalists record), and if there be certain famous hills in Sicily that have been on fire continually, from beyond the memory of man, and yet remain whole and unconsumed, then are these sufficient proofs to show that all does not consume that burns, as the soul proves that all that feels pain does not perish. Why then should we have to produce any more examples to prove the perpetuity of man's soul and body, without death or dissolution, in everlasting fire and torment? That God that endowed nature with so many different and admirable qualities, shall then give the flesh a quality whereby it shall endure pain and burning for ever. Who was it but He, that has made the flesh of a dead peacock to remain always sweet, and without any putrefaction? I thought this impossible at first, and by chance being at meat in Carthage, a boiled peacock was served up, and I, to try the conclusion, took of some of the fleshy part of the breast and caused it to be laid up. After a certain space (sufficient for the putrefaction of any ordinary flesh) I called for it, and smelling it found no ill taste in it at all. I laid it up again, and thirty days after, I looked again, and it was the same as I left it. The like I did a whole year after, and found no change, save that it was somewhat more dry and solid. Who gave such cold unto chaff, that it will keep snow unmelted in it, and withal such heat, that it will ripen green apples? Who gave fire that wonderful power to make all things that it burns black, itself being so bright, and to turn a shining brand into a black coal? Neither does it always thus. For it will burn stones until they be white; and though it be red, and they whitish, yet does this their white agree with the light as well as black does with darkness. Thus the fire burning the wood, to bake the stone, works contrary effects upon objects which are not contrary. For stone and wood are different but not opposite, whereas white and black are, the one of which colours the fire produces upon the stone, and the other upon the wood, whitening the first, and darkening the latter, though it could not perfect the first except by the help of the latter.

And what strange things there are in a coal! It is so brittle that a little blow turns it to powder, and yet so durable that no moisture corrupts it, no time wastes it, so that they are wont to lay coals under boundaries and markstones for lands, to confute any one

that should come hereafter and say this is no boundary stone.
What is it that makes them endure so long in the earth, where
wood would easily rot, but that same fire that corrupts all things?
And then for lime, not only is it whitened by the fire, but it carries
fire in itself, as taken from the fire, and keeps it so secret, that it is
not discoverable in it by any of our senses, nor known to be in it
but by our experience. And therefore we call it quicklime, the
invisible fire being as the soul of that visible body. But the
wonder is that when it is killed it is quickened. For, to fetch out
the fire from it, we cast water upon it, and being cold before, that
inflames it, which cools all other things, however hot they be.
And so the lump, dying as it were, gives up the fire that was in it,
and afterwards remains cold if you water it ever so much: and then
for 'quicklime' we call it 'quenched lime.' What thing can be
more strange? Yes. If you pour oil upon it instead of water,
though oil be rather the feeder of fire, yet will it never alter, but
remain cold still. If we should have heard thus much of some
Indian stone, that we had not, and if we could not get to prove it,
we should surely imagine it either to be a stark lie, or a strange
wonder.

But things occurrent unto daily experience are debased by their
frequency, insomuch that we have left off wondering at some
things that only India (the farthest continent of the world) has
presented to our view. The diamond is common amongst us,
chiefly with our jewellers and lapidaries: and this is so hard that
neither fire, stone, nor steel can once dint it, but only the blood of
a goat. But do you think this hardness so much admired now as
it was by him that first of all descried it? Such as know it not,
may peradventure not believe it, or believing it, on seeing it, may
admire it as a rare work of nature: but daily trial ever takes off
the edge of admiration. We know that the loadstone draws iron
strangely: and surely when I observed it at first, it made me
much aghast. For I beheld the stone draw up an iron ring, and
then as if it had given its own power to the ring, the ring drew up
another and made it hang fast by it, as it hung by the stone. So
did a third by that, and a fourth by the third, and so until there was
hung, as it were, a chain of rings which merely touched one
another, without any interlinking. Who would not admire the
power in this stone, not only inherent in it, but also extending
itself through so many circles, and to such a distance? Yet
stranger was that experiment of this stone which my brother and
fellow bishop Severus, Bishop of Milevis, showed me.

He told me that he had seen Bathanarius (sometime a count of
Africa), when he feasted him once at his own house, take the said
stone and hold it under a silver plate upon which he laid a piece
of iron: and that as he moved the stone under the plate, so did the
iron move above, the plate not moving at all, and just in the same

motion that his hand moved the stone, did the stone move the iron. This I saw, and this did I hear him report, whom I will believe as well as if I had seen it myself. I have read furthermore of this stone, that if you lay but a diamond near it, it will not draw iron at all, but puts it from it as soon as ever the diamond comes to touch it. These stones are to be found in India. But if the strangeness of them be now no more admired of us, how much less do they admire them where they are as common as our lime, whose strange burning in water (which ordinarily doth quench the fire), and not in oil (which feeds it) we do now cease to wonder at because it is so frequent.

CHAPTER V

Of such things as cannot be assuredly known to be such, and yet are not to be doubted

BUT the unbelievers, hearing of miracles and such things as we cannot make apparent to their senses, fall to ask us the reason of them, which because it surpasses our human powers to give, they deride them as false and ridiculous. But let them but give us reason for all the wondrous things that we have seen, or may easily see hereafter; which if they cannot do, then let them not say that there is not, nor can be anything without a reason why it should be. Thus seeing that they are convinced by their own eyesight, I will not therefore run through all that is related by authors, but try their cunning in things which are extant for any to see, that will take the pains. The salt of Agrigentum in Sicily, being put in fire melts into water; and in water, it crackles like the fire.

The Garamantes have a fountain so cold in the day that it cannot be drunk of; so hot in the night that it cannot be touched. In Epirus is another, wherein if you quench a torch, you may light it again thereat. The Arcadian asbestos, being once inflamed, will never be quenched. There is a kind of fig-tree in Egypt whose wood sinks, and being thoroughly steeped (and the heavier, one would think), it rises again to the top of the water.

The apples of the country of Sodom are fair to the eye, but, being touched, fall to dust and ashes. The Persian pyrites, pressed hard in the hand, burns it, whereupon it has its name. The selenites is another stone wherein the waxing and waning of the moon is very visible. The mares in Cappadocia conceive with the wind, but their foals live but three years. The trees of Ceylon, an isle in India, never cast their leaves. All these, and thousands more, are no past things, but visible at this day, each in their places. It were too long for me to recite all, and my purpose is otherwise. And now let those infidels give me the reason of these things, those that will not believe the scriptures, but hold them to be fictions, in that they seem to relate incredible things, such as I have now reckoned! Reason (say they) forbids us to think that a body should burn, and yet not be consumed, that it should feel pain, and yet live everlastingly. O rare disputers! you that can give reason for all miraculous things, give me the reasons of those strange effects of nature before named, of those few only, which if you knew not to be now visible, and not future, but present to the view of those that will make trial of them, you would be more incredulous about them than in this, which we say shall come to pass hereafter. For which of you would believe us if, instead of saying that men's bodies hereafter shall burn and not consume, we were to say that there will be salt that melts in fire, and crackles in the water; or a fountain intolerably hot in the night, and intolerably cold in the day; or a stone that burns him that holds it hard, or another, that being once fired, never quenches? And so of the rest. If we had said that these things shall be in the world to come, and the infidels had bidden us give the reason why, we could freely confess we could not, the power of God in His works surpassing the weakness of human reason: and yet that we knew that God did not act without reason in these things which surpass the reason of mortal man. We know not His will in many things, yet know we that what He wills is in no way impossible, as He has told us, to whom we must neither impute falseness nor imperfection. But what say our great reasoners unto those ordinary things which are so common, and yet exceed all reason, and seem to oppose the laws of nature? If we should say they were to come, then the infidels would forthwith ask a reason for them, as they do for that which we say is to come. And therefore, seeing that in those works of God man's reason is at fault, as these things are such now, and yet why no man can tell; so shall the others be also hereafter, beyond human capacity and apprehension.

CHAPTER VI

All strange effects are not nature's. Some are man's devices; some the devil's

PERHAPS they will answer: 'Oh, these are lies. We believe them not. They are false tales. If these be credible, then believe you also if you will (for one man has related both this and those), that there was a temple of Venus wherein there burned a lamp, which no wind or water could ever quench, so that it was called the inextinguishable lamp.' This they may object, to put us in a dilemma; for if we say it is false, we detract from the truth of our former examples; and if we say it is true, we shall seem to acknowledge a pagan deity. But, as I said in the eighteenth book, we need not believe all that paganism has historically published, their histories (as Varro witnesses) seeming to conspire in voluntary contention one against another: but we may, if we will, believe such of their stories as do not contradict those books which we are bound to believe. Experience and sufficient testimony shall afford us wonders enough of nature, to convince us of the possibility of what we maintain against those infidels. As for that lamp of Venus, it rather gives our argument more scope than in any way suppresses it. For unto that, we can add a thousand strange things effected both by human invention and magical operation: which if we would deny, we should contradict those very books wherein we believe. Wherefore that lamp either burned by the artificial placing of some asbestos in it; or it was effected by art magic, to procure a religious wonder; or else some devil, having honour there under the name of Venus, continued in this apparition for the preservation of men's misbelief. For the devils are allured to inhabit certain bodies by the very creatures of God; and they are variously attracted by what is offered to them; not as other creatures are by meats, but as spirits are by characters and signs adapted to their natures, either by stones, herbs, plants, living creatures, charms, or ceremonies.

And this allurement they do subtly entice man to procure them, either by inspiring him with the secrets thereof, or teaching him the order in a false and flattering apparition, making some few scholars to them, and teachers to many more. For man could never know what they love, and what they loathe, but by their own instructions, which were the first foundations of art magic. And then do they get the fastest hold of men's hearts (which is all they seek and glory in) when they appear like angels of light. However, their works are strange, and the more marvellous, the more to be avoided, which their own natures do persuade us to do; for if these foul devils can work such wonders, what cannot the glorious angels do then? Nay, what cannot that God do, who has given such power to the most hated creatures? So then, if human art can effect such rare conclusions, that such as know them not would think them divine effects—as when an iron image was hung in a certain temple so strangely that the ignorant would have verily believed they had seen a work of God's immediate power, yet it hung so just because it was between two loadstones, whereof one was placed in the roof of the temple, and the other in the floor, without touching anything at all; and as there might be such a trick of man's art in that inextinguishable lamp of Venus; and if magicians (whom the scriptures call sorcerers and enchanters) can endow the demons with such power as Virgil, that famous poet, relates of an enchantress in these words:

> Haec se carminibus promittit solvere mentes
> Quas velit, ast aliis duras immittere curas,

Sistere aquam fluviis, et vertere sidera retro;
Nocturnosque ciet manes; mugire videbis
Sub pedibus terram et descendere montibus ornos.[1]

She said her charms could ease one's heart of pain,
Even when she list, and make him grieve again.
Stop floods, bring back the stars, and with her breath,
Rouse the black fiends, until the earth beneath
Groaned, and the trees came marching from the hills, etc.—

if all this be possible to those, how much more then can the
power of God exceed them in working such things as are incredible
to infidelity, but easy to His omnipotency, who has given virtues
unto stones, wit unto man, and such large power unto angels!
His wonderful power exceeds all wonders, His wisdom permits
and effects all and every particular of them; and cannot He make
the most wonderful use of all the parts of that world that He only
has created?

CHAPTER VII

God's omnipotency the ground of all belief in things marvelled at

WHY then cannot God make the bodies of the dead to rise again,
and the damned to suffer torment and yet not to consume, seeing
that He has filled heaven, earth, air, and water so full of innumerable
miracles, and that the world, which He made, is a greater miracle
than any it contains?   But our adversaries, believing in a God that
made the world and the other gods, by whom He governs the
world, do not deny, but avouch that there are powers that effect
wonders in the world, either voluntarily, or ceremonially and
magically; but when we give them an instance wrought neither by
man nor by spirit, they answer us: 'It is nature; nature has given
it this quality.'   So then it was nature that made the Agrigentine
salt melt in the fire, and crackle in the water.   Was it so?   This
seems rather contrary to the nature of salt, which naturally dissolves
in water, and crackles in the fire.   Aye, but nature (say they) made
this particular salt of a quality just opposite.   Good.   This, then,
is the reason also of the heat and cold of the Garamantine fountain,
and of the other that puts out the torch and lights it again, as also
of the asbestos, and those others, to rehearse all of which were too
tedious.   There is no other reason, it seems, to be given for them,
but, 'Such is their nature.'   A good brief reason verily, and a
sufficient.   But God being the Author of all nature, why then do
they exact a stronger reason of us, when we, in proving that which
they hold for an impossibility, affirm that it is thus by the will of
Almighty God, who is therefore called Almighty because He can
do all that He will, having created so many things, which, were

[1] Virg. *Aen.* iv. 487–91.

they not to be seen, and confirmed by sufficient testimony, would seem as impossible as the rest, whereas now we know them, partly all, and partly some of us. As for other things that are but reported without testimony, and concern not religion, and are not taught in scripture, they may be false, and a man may lawfully refuse to believe them. I do not believe all that I have set down so firmly that I do make no doubt of some of them; but as for those which I have tried, as the burning of lime in water and cooling in oil; the loadstone's drawing of iron and not moving a straw; the incorruptibility of the peacock's flesh, whereas Plato's flesh did putrefy; the keeping of snow and the ripening of apples in chaff; the bright fire making the stones of its own colour, and wood of the exact opposite—these I have seen and believe without any doubt at all. Such also are these—that clear oil should make black spots, and white silver draw a black line; that coals should turn white wood into black, hard wood into brittle, and make corruptible pieces incorruptible: together with many others which tediousness forbids me here to insert. For the others, excepting that fountain that quenches and kindles again, and the dusty apples of Sodom, I could not get any sufficient proofs to confirm them. Nor met I any that had beheld that fountain of Epirus, but I found divers that had seen the like near unto Grenoble in France. And as for the apples of Sodom, there are both grave authors, and eyewitnesses enough alive, that can affirm it, so that I make no doubt thereof. The rest I leave indifferent, to affirm or deny; yet I did set them down because they are recorded in our adversaries' own histories, to show them how many things they believe in their own books, without any reason, that will not give credence to us, when we say that God Almighty will do anything that exceeds their capacity to conceive. What better or stronger reason can be given for anything than to say, God Almighty will do this, which He has promised in those books wherein He promises as strange things as this, which He has performed? He will do it, because He has said He will, even He that has made the incredulous heathens believe things which they held mere impossibilities.

CHAPTER VIII

That the alteration of the known nature of any creature unto a nature unknown is not opposite unto the laws of nature

IF they reply that they will not believe that man's body can endure perpetual burning, because they know it is of no such nature, so that it cannot be said of it, that nature has given it such a quality, we may answer them out of the scriptures, that man's body before his fall was of such a nature that it could not suffer death; and yet in his fall was altered unto that mortal misery wherein now all mankind lives, to die at length; and therefore at the resurrection it may undergo such another alteration, unknown to us as yet. But they believe not the scriptures that relate man's estate in paradise. If they did, we should not need to argue long with them upon this theme of the pains of the damned: whereas now we must make demonstration out of their own authors, <u>how it is possible that there may be a full alteration of nature in any one object, from the kind of being that it had before, and yet the laws of nature be kept unviolated.</u> Thus we read in Varro's book, *Of the Race of the Roman People*, that Castor relates, that in that bright star of Venus, which Plautus [1] calls 'Hesperugo,' and Homer [2] 'the glorious Hesperus,' befell a most monstrous change both of colour, magnitude, figure, and motion; the like never was before nor since: and this, say Adrastus of Cyzicus and Dion of Naples (two famous astronomers), befell in the reign of Ogyges. A monstrous change, says Varro, and why, but that it seemed contrary to nature? Such, we say, all portents are, but we are deceived. For how can that be against nature which is effected by the will of God, the Lord and Maker of all nature? A portent, therefore, is not against nature, but against the most common order of nature. But who is he that can relate all the portents recorded by the Gentiles? Let us seek our purpose in this one. What more imperative law has God laid upon nature in any part of the creation, than He has in the motions of the heavens? What more legal and fixed order does any part of nature keep? And yet you see, that when it was the pleasure of nature's highest sovereign, the brightest star in all the firmament changed its colour, magnitude, and figure, and which is most marvellous, its very course and motion. This made a foul disturbance in the rules of the astrologers (if there were any then) when they, observing their fixed descriptions of the eternal course of the stars, durst affirm that there never was nor ever would be any such change as this of Venus was. Indeed, we read in the scriptures that the sun stood still at the prayer of Joshua, until the battle was done,[3] and went back to show Hezekiah, that the Lord had added fifteen years unto his life.[4] As for the miracles done by the virtues of the saints, these infidels know them well, and therefore aver them to be done by magic: whereupon Virgil says, as I related before of the witch, that she could

> Sistere aquam fluviis et vertere sidera retro: [5]
>
> Stop floods, bring back the stars, etc.

For the river Jordan parted, when Joshua led the people over it,[6] and when Elijah passed it,[7] as likewise when his follower Elisha divided it with Elijah's cloak: and the sun, as we said before, went

---

[1] *Amphit.* I. i, 122.   [2] *Iliad*, xxii. 318.   [3] Joshua x. 13.   [4] Isa. xxxviii. 8.
[5] *Aen.* iv. 489.   [6] Joshua iv. 18.   [7] 2 Kings ii. 8, 14.

back in the time of Hezekiah. But Varro does not say that any one desired this change of Venus. Let not the faithless therefore hoodwink themselves in the knowledge of nature, as though God's power could not alter the nature of anything from what it was before unto man's knowledge, when in truth the known nature of anything is as fully as admirable as the less known, but that men admire nothing but rarities. For what reasonable man does not see, that in that work of nature in which there is the greatest similarity and the greatest variety, the face of man, there is such an admirable quality, that were they not all of one form, they should not distinguish man from beast, and yet were they exactly all of one form, one man should not be known from another? Thus likeness and difference are both in one object. But the difference is most admirable; a common nature itself seeming to demand a uniformity; and yet because it is rarities which we admire, we do wonder far more when we see two so like that one may be easily and is oftentimes deceived in taking the one for the other.

But it may be they believe not the story of Varro, though he be one of their most learned historians, or do not respect it, because this star did not remain long in this new form, but soon resumed the former shape and course again. Let us therefore give them another example, which together with this of his I think may suffice to convince that God is not to be bound to any conditions in the allotting of a particular nature to anything, as though He could not make an absolute alteration thereof into a wholly different nature. The country of Sodom was formerly otherwise than it is now. It was once like the rest of the land, as fertile and as fair, if not more so than the rest, insomuch that the scripture compares it to paradise. But being smitten from heaven (as the heathen stories themselves record, and all travellers confirm), it now is as a field of soot and ashes; and the apples of the soil being fair without are naught but dust within. Behold, it was not such, and yet such it is at this day. Behold a terrible change of nature wrought by nature's Creator! And it remains in that sole estate now, which it was a long time ere it fell into. So then, as God can create what He will, so can He change the nature of what He has created at His good pleasure. And hence is the multitude of monsters, visions, portents, and prodigies, for the particular relation whereof here is no place. They are called monsters, from *monstro*, to show, because they betoken somewhat, and portents and prodigies from *portendo* and *porro dico*, because they portend and foretell somewhat to ensue. But whether they, or the devils, whose care it is to seduce and entangle the minds of the imperfect, and such as deserve it, do delude the world either by true predictions, or by stumbling on the truth by chance, let their observers and interpreters look to that. But we ought to gather this from all those monsters and prodigies that happen or are said to happen against nature (as the apostle implied when he spoke of 'the engrafting of the wild olive into the garden olive, whereby the wild one was made partaker of the root and fatness of the other [1]), that they all do tell us this, that God will do with the bodies of the dead according to His promise, and that no difficulty, no law of nature can or shall prohibit Him. And what He has promised, the last book declared out of both the Testaments, not in very great measure, but sufficient (I think) for the purpose of this volume.

CHAPTER IX

Of hell, and the qualities of the eternal pains therein

As God therefore by His prophet spoke of the pains of the damned, such shall they be: 'Their worm shall not die, neither shall their fire to be quenched.' [2] Our Saviour, to commend this unto us, regarding the parts that offend a man as those persons whom a man loves as his own most useful members, and bidding him cut them off, adds this: 'Better it is for thee to enter into life maimed, than having two hands to go into hell into the fire that never shall be quenched, where their worm dies not, and their fire is not quenched,' and likewise of the foot: 'Better for thee to go halting into life, than having two feet to be cast into hell,' etc. And so says he of the eye also, adding the prophet's words three several times.[3] Oh, whom would not this thunder from the mouth of God strike a chill terror into, sounding so often? Now, as for this worm and this fire, they that make them only mental pains do say that the fire implies the burning in grief and anguish of the soul, that now repents too late for being severed from the sight of God: after the manner that the apostle says: 'Who is offended and I burn not?' [4] And this anguish may be meant also by the worm, say they, as it is written: 'As the moth is to the garment, and the worm to the wood, so does sorrow eat the heart of a man.' [5] Now such as hold them both mental and real say that the fire is a bodily plague to the body, and the worm a plague of conscience to the soul. This seems more likely in that it is absurd to say that either the soul or body shall be clear of pain. Yet had I rather take part with them that say they are both bodily than with those that say that neither of them is so. And therefore by sorrow in the scriptures, though it be not expressed so, is understood a fruitless repentance conjoined with a corporal torment, for the scripture says: 'The vengeance of the flesh of the wicked is fire and the worm.' [6] He might have said more briefly, 'The vengeance of the wicked.' Why did he then add 'of the flesh,' but to show that both those plagues, the

---

[1] Rom. xi. 17, 24.   [2] Isa. lxvi. 24.   [3] Mark ix. 43–8.
[4] 2 Cor. xi. 29.   [5] Prov. xxv. 20.   [6] Ecclus. vii. 17.

fire and the worm, shall be corporal? If he added it because man shall be thus plagued for living according to the flesh (for it is therefore that he incurs the second death, which the apostle means when he says, 'If ye live after the flesh, ye die'[1]), let every man believe as he like, either giving the fire literally to the body, and the worm figuratively to the soul, or both properly to the body: for we have fully proved already that a creature may burn and yet not consume, may live in pain and yet not die: which he that denies knows not Him that is the author of all nature's wonders, that God who has made all the miracles that I formerly recounted, and thousand thousands more, and more admirable, shutting them all in the world, the most admirable work of all. Let every man therefore choose what to think of this, whether both the fire and the worm plague the body, or whether the worm have a metaphorical reference to the soul. The truth of this question shall then appear plainly, when the knowledge of the saints shall be such as shall require no trial of it, but only shall be fully satisfied and resolved by the perfection and plenitude of the divine Wisdom. For now we know but in part, until that which is perfect be come, but yet may we not believe those bodies to be such that the fire can work them no anguish or torment.

CHAPTER X

Whether the fire of hell, if it be corporal, can take effect upon the incorporeal devils

But here now is another question—whether this fire, if it plague not spiritually, but only by a bodily touch, can inflict any torment upon the devil and his angels. They are to remain in one fire with the damned, according to our Saviour's own words: 'Depart from Me, ye cursed, into everlasting fire, which is prepared for the devil and his angels.'[2] But the devils, according to what some learned men suppose, have bodies of condensed air, such as we feel in a wind; and that this air is passible, and may suffer burning, the heating of baths proves, where the air is set on fire to heat the water, and does that which first it suffers. If any will oppose, and say the devils have no bodies at all, the matter is not great, nor need there be much argument about it. For why may not unbodied spirits feel the force of bodily fire, as well as man's incorporeal soul which is now included in a carnal shape, and shall at that day be bound into a body for ever. These spiritual devils therefore, or those devilish spirits, though strangely, yet shall they be truly bound in this corporal fire, which shall torment them for all that they are incorporeal. Nor shall they be so bound in it,

---

[1] Rom. viii. 13.   [2] Matt. xxv. 41.

that they shall give it a soul as it were, and so become with it one living creature; but, as I said, by a wonderful power shall they be so bound that instead of giving it life, they shall from it receive intolerable torment; although that other coherence of spirits and bodies, whereby both become one creature, be equally as marvellous, and exceeds all human comprehension. And surely I should think the devils shall burn then, as the rich glutton did, when he cried, saying, 'I am tormented in this flame,' but that I should be answered that that fire was such as his tongue was, to cool which he, seeing Lazarus afar off, entreated him to help him with a little water on the tip of his finger. He was not then in the body but in soul only. Such likewise (that is incorporeal) was the fire he burned in, and the water he wished for, as the dreams of those that sleep and the vision of men in ecstasies are, which present the forms of bodies, and yet are not bodies indeed. And though man see these things only in spirit, yet sees he himself so like to his body, that he cannot discern whether he have it on or no. But that hell, that lake of fire and brimstone, shall be real, and the fire corporal, burning both men and devils, the one in flesh and the other in air: the one in the body adherent to the spirit, and the other in spirit only adherent to the fire, and yet not infusing life, but feeling torment. For one fire shall torment both men and devils. Christ has spoken it.

CHAPTER XI

Whether it be not justice that the time of the pains should be proportioned to the time of the sins and crimes

But some of the adversaries of God's city hold it injustice for him, that has offended but temporarily, to be bound to suffer pain eternally. This (they say) is utterly unjust. As though they knew any law that adapted the time of the punishment to the time in which the crime was committed! Eight kinds of punishment does Tully affirm the laws to inflict: damages, imprisonment, whipping, like for like, public disgrace, banishment, death, and bondage. Which of these can be performed in so little time as the offence is, excepting the fourth, which yields every man the same measure that he metes unto others, according to that of the law: 'An eye for an eye, and a tooth for a tooth'?[1] Indeed one may lose his eye by this law, in as small a time as he put out another man's by violence. But if a man kiss another man's wife, and be therefore adjudged to be whipped, is not that which he did in a moment paid for by a good deal longer sufferance? Is not his short pleasure repaid with a longer pain? And what about imprisonment? Is

[1] Exod. xxi. 24.

every one judged to lie there no longer than he was in doing his
villainy? Nay, that servant that has but violently touched his
master, is by a just law doomed unto many years' imprisonment.
And as for damages, disgraces, and banishments, are not many of
them dateless, and lasting a man's whole life, wherein they bear a
resemblance to the pains eternal? Fully eternal they cannot be,
because the life which they afflict is but temporal, and yet the sins
they punish are all committed in an instant; nor would any man
advise that the continuance of the penalty should be measured by
the time of the fact, for that, be it murder, adultery, sacrilege, or
what villainy soever, is quickly dispatched, and consequently is
not to be weighed by the length of time, but by the foulness of the
crime. And as for him that deserves death by an offence, does the
law hold the time that he is dying to be the satisfaction for his guilt,
or his being taken away from the fellowship of men? That then
which the terrestrial city can do by the first death, the celestial can
effect by the second, in clearing herself of malefactors. For as
the laws of the first cannot call a dead man back again into their
society, no more do the laws of the second call him back to salvation
that is once entered into the second death. How then are our
Saviour's words true, say they, 'With what measure ye mete, with
the same shall men mete to you again,'[1] if temporal sins be rewarded with eternal pains? Oh, but you mark not that those
words have a reference to the returning of evil for evil in our nature,
and not to an equal proportion of time—that is, he that does evil
shall suffer evil without limitation of any time; although this place
be more properly understood of the judgments and condemnations
whereof the Lord did there speak. And so he that judges unjustly,
if he be judged justly, is paid in the same measure that he meted
withal, though he does not receive what he did: for he did wrong
in judgment, and judgment he suffers; but he did it unjustly, yet
nevertheless he is repaid according to justice.

CHAPTER XII

*The greatness of Adam's sin, inflicting eternal condemnation upon all
that are out of the state of grace*

But therefore does man imagine that this infliction of eternal
torment is injustice, because his frail imperfection cannot discern
the horribleness of that offence that was the first cause of it. For
the fuller fruition man had of God, the greater impiety was it for
him to renounce Him; and therein was he worthy of everlasting
evil, in that he destroyed his own good, that otherwise had been
everlasting. Hence came condemnation upon all the stock of

[1] Luke vi. 38.

man, parent and offspring undergoing one curse, from which none can be ever freed, but by the free and gracious mercy of God, which makes a separation of mankind, to show in some the power of grace, and in others the revenge of justice. Both of which could not be expressed upon all mankind, for if all had tasted of the punishments of justice, the grace and mercy of the Redeemer had had no place in any: and again, if all had been redeemed from death, there had been no object left for the manifestation of God's justice. But now there are more so left than receivers of mercy, that so it might appear what was due unto all, without any impeachment of God's justice, who notwithstanding, having delivered so many, has herein bound us for ever to praise His gracious commiseration.

CHAPTER XIII

Against such as hold that the torments after the judgment shall be but the means whereby the souls shall be purified

SOME Platonists there are who though they assign a punishment to every sin, yet hold they that all such inflictions, be they human or divine, in this life or in the next, tend only to the purgation of the soul from enormities. Whereupon Virgil having said of the souls:

> Hinc metuunt cupiuntque, etc.,
>
> Hence fear, desire, etc.,

says immediately:

> Quin et supremo cum lumine vita reliquit,
> Non tamen omne malum miseris, nec funditus omnes
> Corporeae excedunt pestes, penitusque necesse est
> Multa diu concreta modis inolescere miris.
> Ergo exercentur poenis, veterumque malorum
> Supplicia expendunt; aliae panduntur inanes
> Suspensae ad ventos, aliis sub gurgite vasto
> Infectum eluitur scelus, aut exuritur igni.[1]

> For when the souls do leave the bodies dead,
> Their miseries are not yet finished:
> Nor all their times of torment yet complete:
> Many small crimes must needs make one that's great
> Pain therefore purgeth them, and makes them fair
> From their old stains: some hang in dusky air,
> Some in the deep do pay the debt of sin,
> And fire is chosen to cleanse others in.

They that hold this affirm that no pains at all are to be suffered after death, but only such as purge the souls; and those shall be cleared of all their earthly contagion by some of the three upper

[1] *Aen.* vi. 733–42.

elements, the air, the fire, or the water. The air, in that he says,
'suspensae ad ventos': the water, by the words, 'sub gurgite vasto':
the fire is expressly named, 'aut exuritur igni.' Now indeed we do
confess that there are certain pains of this kind during this life,
which do not properly afflict such as are not bettered but made
worse by them, but belong only to such as take them for correc-
tions. All other pains, temporal and eternal, are laid upon every
one as God pleases, by His angels good or bad, either for some sin
past, or wherein the party afflicted now lives, or else to exercise
and declare the virtue of His servants. For if one man hurt
another willingly, or by chance, it is an offence in him to do any
man harm, by will or through ignorance, but God, whose secret
judgment assigned it to be so, offends not at all. As for temporal
pain, some endure it here, and some hereafter, and some both
here and there, yet all is past before the last judgment. But all
shall not come into these eternal pains (which notwithstanding
shall be eternal after the last judgment, unto them that endure them
temporally after death). For some shall be pardoned in the world
to come that are not pardoned in this, and acquitted there and not
here from entering into pains eternal, as I said before.

CHAPTER XIV

The temporal pains of this life afflicting all mankind

BUT few there be that endure none of these pains until after death.
Some indeed I have known and heard of that never had an hour's
sickness until their dying day, and lived very long, yet nevertheless
man's whole life is a pain 'in that it is a temptation and a warfare
upon earth,' [1] as holy Job says; for ignorance is a great punishment,
and therefore you see that little children are forced to avoid it by
stripes and sorrows, that also which they learn being such a pain
to them, that sometimes they had rather endure the punishments
that enforce them to learn it, than to learn it and so avoid them.
Who would not tremble and rather choose to die than to be an
infant again, if he were put to such a choice? We begin our
life with tears, and therein predict our future miseries. Only
Zoroaster smiled (they say) when he was born: but his unnatural
mirth boded him no good; for he was, by report, the first inventor
of magic, which notwithstanding stood him not in a pin's stead in
his misfortunes, for Ninus, king of Assyria, overcame him in battle
and took his kingdom of Bactria from him. And so it is such an
impossibility that those words of the scripture, 'Great travail is
created for all men and an heavy yoke upon the sons of Adam from
the day that they go out of their mother's womb, until the day that

[1] Job vii. 1.

they return unto the mother of all things,' [1] should not be fulfilled, that the very infants ,being baptized, and therein freed from all their guilt, which then is only original, are notwithstanding much and often afflicted, yea even sometimes by the incursion of devils, which notwithstanding cannot hurt them if they die at that tenderness of age.

CHAPTER XV

That the scope of God's redeeming us is wholly pertinent to the world to come

BUT yet nevertheless in this heavy yoke that lies upon Adam's children from their birth to their burial, we have an inducement to live soberly, and to realize that our first parents' sin has made this life but a pain to us, and that all the promises of the New Testament belong only to the heritage laid up for us in the world to come. Pledges we have here, but the performance due thereto we shall not have till then. Let us now therefore walk in hope, and profiting day by day let us mortify the deeds of the flesh by the Spirit, for 'God knows all that are His,' [2] and 'as many as are led by the Spirit of God are the sons of God,' [3] but by grace, not by nature, for God's only Son by nature was made the Son of man for us, that we being the sons of men by nature might become the sons of God in Him by grace; for He remaining changeless took our nature upon Him, keeping still His own divinity, that we being changed might leave our frailty and aptness to sin through the participation of His righteousness and immortality, and might keep that which He had made good in us, by the perfection of that good which is in Him: for as we all fell into this misery by one man's sin, so shall we ascend unto that glory by one divine Man's righteousness. Nor may any imagine that he has had this change, until he be there where there is no temptation, but all are full of that peace which we seek by these conflicts of the spirit against the flesh, and the flesh against the spirit. This war had never been, had man kept his will in that right way wherein it was first placed. But refusing that, now he fights in himself; and yet this inconvenience is not so bad as the former, for happier far is he that strives against sin, than he that allows it sovereignty over him. Better is war with hope of eternal peace, than thraldom without any thought of freedom. We wish to be without this war though, and God inspires us to aim at that orderly peace wherein the inferior obeys the superior in all things: but if there were hope of it in this life (as God forbid we should imagine) by yielding to sin, yet ought we rather to stand out against it, in all our miseries, than to give over our freedoms to sin by yielding to it.

[1] Ecclus. xl. 1.   [2] 2 Tim. ii. 19.   [3] Rom. viii. 14.

CHAPTER XVI

The laws of grace, that all the regenerate are blessed in

BUT God's mercy is so great in the vessels whom He has prepared for glory, that even in the first age of man, which is his infancy, where the flesh rules without control, or in the second, his childhood, where his reason is so weak that it gives way to all enticements, and the mind is altogether incapable of religious precepts, if notwithstanding a child be washed in the fountain of regeneration, and he die at this or that age, he is translated from the powers of darkness to the glories of Christ, and freed from all pains, eternal and purificatory. His regeneration alone is sufficient to clear him after death from that which his carnal generation had contracted with death. But when he comes to years of discretion, and is capable of good counsel, then must he begin a fierce conflict with vice lest it allure him to damnation. Indeed the unseasoned soldier is the more easily put to flight, but practice will make him valorous, and enable him to pursue victory with all his endeavour, which he must evermore attempt by a weapon called 'the love of true righteousness,' and this is kept in the faith of Christ. For if the command be present, and the assisting spirit absent, the very forbidding of the crime inflames the perverse flesh to run the sooner into it, sometimes producing open enormities, and sometimes secret ones, far worse than the others, because pride, and ruinous self-conceit, persuade men that they are virtues.

Then therefore sin is quelled, when it is beaten down by the love of God, which none but He gives and He only by Jesus Christ the mediator of God and man, who made Himself mortal, that we might be made eternal. Few are so happy as to pass their youth without taint of some damnable sin or other, either in deed, opinion, or the like; but let them, above all, seek to suppress by the fullness of spirit all such evil motions as shall be incited by the looseness of the flesh. Many, having betaken themselves to the law, and becoming transgressors thereof through sin, are afterwards fain to fly unto the law of grace for help, which, making them both truer penitents and stouter opponents, subjects their spirits to God, and so they get the conquest of the flesh. He therefore that will escape hell fire, must be both baptized and justified in Christ; and this is his only way to pass from the devil unto Him. And let him assuredly believe that there are no purgatory pains except before that great and terrible judgment. Indeed, it is true that the fire of hell shall be more forcible against some than against others, according to the diversity of their deserts, whether it be adapted in nature to the quality of their merits, or remain one fire unto all, and yet be not felt alike by all.

CHAPTER XVII

Of some Christians that held that hell's pains should not be eternal

Now must I have a gentle disputation with certain tender hearts of our own religion, who think that God, who has justly doomed the condemned unto hell fire, will after a certain space, which His goodness shall think fit for the merit of each man's guilt, deliver them from that torment. And of this opinion was Origen, in far more pitiful manner, for he held that the devils themselves after a set time expired should be loosed from their torments, and become bright angels in heaven, as they were before. But this, and other of his opinions, chiefly that concerning that rotation and alternation of misery and bliss which he held that all mankind should run in, gave the Church cause to pronounce him anathema: seeing he had lost even this seeming pity of his, by assigning a true misery, after a while, and a false bliss, unto the saints in heaven, where they (if these views were true) could never be sure of remaining. But far otherwise is their tenderness of heart, which hold that this freedom out of hell shall only be extended unto the souls of the damned after a certain time appointed for every one, so that all at length shall come to be saints in heaven. But if this opinion be good and true, because it is merciful, why then the farther it extends, the better it is; so that it may as well include the freedom of the devils also, after a longer continuance of time! Why then ends it with mankind only, and excludes them? Nay, but it dares go no farther, for they dare not extend their pity unto the devil. But if any one does so, he goes beyond them in charity, and yet sins in erring more deformedly and more perversely against the express word of God, though he appears to show the more pity herein.

CHAPTER XVIII

Of those that hold that the intercession of the saints shall save all men from damnation

I HAVE talked with some that seem to reverence the scriptures, and yet are no good livers, who would make God far more merciful than these others. For as for the wicked, they confess that they deserve to be plagued, but mercy they say shall have the upper hand when it comes to judgment: for God shall give them all unto the prayers and intercession of the saints, who if they prayed for them when they insulted over them as enemies, will do it much more now when they see them prostrate at their feet like slaves. For it is incredible (say they) that the saints should forget mercy when they are most holy and perfect, who prayed for their foes,

when they were not without sin themselves.   Surely then they will
pray for them who will now become their suppliants, when they
themselves have no sin at all left in them.   And will not God hear
them, when their prayers have such perfection?   Then bring they
forth the testimony of the psalm which the others, that held the
saving of all the damned after a time, do allege also; but these
affirm that it supports them more.   The words are these: 'Hath
God forgotten to be merciful, or will He shut up His mercies in
displeasure?'[1]   His displeasure (say they) condemns all that are
unworthy of eternal life to eternal torment.   But if this condemnation continue, little or long, how can it be then that the psalm
should rightly say: 'Will He shut up His mercy in displeasure?'
It says not, 'Will He shut them up long?' but implies that He will
not shut them up at all.   Thus do they prove that the judgment of
God is not false, although He condemn none, any more than His
threatening to destroy Nineveh was false, though it was not effected
(say they) though He promised it without exception.   He said
not, 'I will destroy it unless it repent,' but plainly without addition,
'Nineveh shall be destroyed.'[2]   This threatening do they hold
true, because God foretold plainly what they had deserved, though
He spake not that which He meant to do.   For though He spared
them, yet knew He that they would repent: and yet did He absolutely promise their destruction.   This therefore (say they) was
true in the truth of His severity, which they had deserved, but not
in respect of His mercy, which He did not shut up in displeasure,
because He would show mercy unto their prayers, whose pride He
had threatened to punish.   If, therefore, He showed mercy then
(say they), when He knew He should thereby grieve His holy
prophet, how much more will He show it now when all His saints
shall entreat for it!   Now this surmise of theirs they think the
scriptures do not mention, because men should be reclaimed from
vice by fear of tedious or eternal torment, and because some should
pray for those that will not amend.   And yet the scriptures (say
they) do not utterly conceal it: for what does that saying of the
psalm intend: 'How great is Thy goodness which Thou hast laid
up for them that fear Thee!   Thou keepest them secret in Thy
tabernacle from the strife of tongues'?[3]   That means, say they, this
great sweetness of God's mercy is kept secret from us, to keep us
in the more awe, and therefore the apostle says: 'God has shut up
all in unbelief, that He might have mercy on all,'[4] to show that
He will condemn none.   Yet those who hold this opinion will not
extend this general salvation unto the devils, but make mankind
the only object of their pity, promising impunity to their own bad
lives withal, by pretending a general mercy of God unto the whole
generation of man: and in this, they that extend God's mercy unto
the devil and his angels do quite exceed these latter.

[1] Ps. lxxvii. 9.   [2] Jonah iii. 4.   [3] Ps. xxi. 19.   [4] Rom. xi. 32.

CHAPTER XIX

Of such as hold that heretics shall be saved, in that they have partaken of the body of Christ

OTHERS there are that clear not hell of all, but only of such as are baptized and partakers of 'Christ's body,' and these (they say) are saved, be their lives or doctrines whatsoever, on the ground that Christ Himself said: 'This is the bread which cometh down from heaven, that he which eateth of it should not die. I am the living bread which came down from heaven.'[1] Therefore (say these men) must all such be saved of necessity, and glorified by ever-lasting life.

CHAPTER XX

Of such as allow this deliverance only to wicked and revolted Catholics

ANOTHER sort limit the former position only to Catholics, live they never so vilely, because they have received Christ truly and been engrafted in His body: of which the apostle says: 'We that are many are one bread and one body, because we all are partakers of one Bread.'[2] And so though they fall into ever such bad heresies afterwards, yea, even into paganism, yet because they received the baptism of Christ in His Church, they shall not perish for ever, but shall receive eternal life; nor shall their guilt make their torments everlasting, but only temporal, though they may last a long time, and be extremely painful.

CHAPTER XXI

Of such as affirm that all that abide in the Catholic faith shall be saved for that faith only, be their lives never so worthy of damnation

THERE are some who, because it is written, 'He that endureth to the end, he shall be saved,'[3] do affirm that only they that continue Catholics (howsoever they live) shall be saved by the merit of that foundation, whereof the apostle says: 'Other foundation can no man lay, than that which is laid, which is Christ Jesus. And if any man build on this foundation, gold, silver, precious stones, timber, hay or stubble; every man's work shall be made manifest, for the day of the Lord shall declare it, because it shall be revealed by the fire, and the fire shall try every man's work, of what sort it is. If any man's work that he has built upon abide, he shall receive wages. If any man's work burn he shall lose, but he shall be safe himself, yet as it were by fire.'[4] And so all Christian Catholics (say they) having Christ for their foundation (which no heretics have, being cut off from His body), be their lives good or bad (as

[1] John vi. 50, 51. [2] 1 Cor. x. 17. [3] Matt. xxiv. 13. [4] 1 Cor. iii. 11–15.

those that build timber, hay, or stubble, upon this foundation), shall nevertheless be saved by fire, that is, shall be delivered after they have endured the pains of the fire which punishes the wicked in the last judgment.

CHAPTER XXII

Of such as affirm that the sins committed amongst the works of mercy shall not be called into judgment

AND some I have met that hold that none shall be damned eternally, but such as neglected to satisfy for their sins by alms-deeds, alleging that saying of James: 'There shall be judgment merciless unto him that sheweth no mercy.' [1]   Wherefore he that does show mercy (say they), though he amend not his life, but live sinfully even in these merciful works, shall nevertheless have so merciful a judgment, that he shall either not be punished at all, or, at least, shall be freed from his pain after his sufferance of them for some certain space, more or less.   And therefore the Judge of the quick and dead would mention no other thing in His words to those on both sides of Him, for the salvation of the one part and the condemnation of the other, but only the alms-deeds which they had either done or neglected.   To this also (say they) does that part of the Lord's Prayer pertain: 'Forgive us our trespasses, as we forgive them that trespass against us.' [2]   For he that forgives an offence done to him, does a work of mercy: which Christ so approved, that He said: 'If ye do forgive men their trespasses, your Heavenly Father will also forgive you, but if ye do not forgive men their trespasses, no more will your Heavenly Father forgive you your trespasses.' [3]   In the same way hereunto belongs also the aforesaid place of St. James: 'There shall be judgment merciless,' etc.   The Lord said not, 'Your small trespasses,' say they, 'nor your great,' but generally, 'your trespasses.'   And therefore they hold that those that live ever so viciously until their dying day, have nevertheless their sins absolutely pardoned by virtue of this prayer used every day, if withal they do remember freely to forgive all such as have offended them, when they entreat for pardon.   When all those errors are confuted, I will, God willing, make an end of this present book.

CHAPTER XXIII

Against those that exclude both men and devils from pains eternal

FIRST then we must show why the Church has condemned them that affirm that even the very devils after a time of torment shall be taken to mercy.   The reason is this.   Those holy men, so many

[1] Jas. ii. 13.   [2] Matt. vi. 12.   [3] Matt. vi. 14, 15.

and so learned in both the laws of God, the old and the new, did not grudge the modification of suffering and beatitude of those spirits, after their long and great extremity of torture; but they saw well, that the words of our Saviour could not be untrue, which He promised to pronounce in the last judgment, saying: 'Depart from Me, ye cursed, into everlasting fire which is prepared for the devil and his angels.'[1]   Hereby He showed that they should burn in everlasting fire.   Likewise is it stated in the Revelation: 'The devil that deceived them was cast into a lake of fire and brimstone, where the beast and the false prophet shall be tormented day and night, for evermore.'[2]   There he says, 'everlasting,' and here 'for evermore,' in both places excluding all termination and end of the time.   Wherefore there is no reason either stronger or plainer to confirm our belief that the devil and his angels shall nevermore return to the glory and righteousness of the saints, than that the scriptures, that deceive no man, tell us directly and plainly, that God hath not spared them, but cast them down into hell, and delivered them unto chains of darkness, there to be kept unto the condemnation in the just judgment, then to be cast into eternal fire and there to burn for evermore.   If this be true how can either all or any men be delivered out of this eternity of pains, if our faith whereby we believe the devil to be everlastingly tormented be not hereby infringed?   For if those (either all or some part) to whom it shall be said, 'Depart from Me, ye cursed, into everlasting fire which is prepared for the devil and his angels,' shall not continue for ever in the fire, what reason have we to think that the devil and his angels shall?   Shall the word of God, spoken alike both to men and devils, be proved true concerning the devils, and not concerning the men?   In that case would man's surmises be of more certainty than God's promises.   But seeing that cannot be, they that desire to escape this pain eternal must cease to argue against God, and take His yoke upon them while they have time.

For what foolishness were it to interpret the pains eternal as a fire only of a long continuance, but yet to believe assuredly that life eternal has no end at all, seeing that the Lord in the same place including both these parts in one sentence, said plainly: 'These shall go into everlasting pains, and the righteous into life eternal.'[3] Thus does He make them parallels.   Here are everlasting pains, and there is eternal life.   Now to say this life shall never end, but that pain shall, were grossly absurd.   Wherefore seeing that the eternal life of the saints shall be without end, so therefore is it a consequence that the everlasting pain of the damned shall be as endless as the others' beatitude.

[1] Matt. xxv. 41.   [2] Rev. xx. 10.   [3] Matt. xxv. 46.

CHAPTER XXIV

Against those that would prove all damnation frustrate by the prayers of the saints

THIS also applies to those, who under colour of more pity oppose the express word of God, and say that God's promises are true in that men are worthy of the plagues He threatens, but that they shall not be laid upon them. For He will give them (say they) unto the entreaties of his saints, who will be the readier to pray for them then, in that they are more purely holy, and their prayers will be the more powerful, in that they are utterly exempt from all touch of sin and corruption. Why then in this their pure holiness and powerfulness of prayer will they not entreat for the angels that are to be cast into everlasting fire, that it would please God to mitigate His sentence, and set them free from that intolerable fire? Some perhaps will pretend that the holy angels will join with the saints (being then their fellows) in prayer both for the angels and men also that are guilty of damnation, that God in His mercy would be pleased to pardon their wicked deserts. But there is no sound Christian that ever held this, or ever will hold it; for otherwise, there were no reason why the Church should not pray for the devil and his angels, seeing that her Lord God has willed her to pray for her enemies. But the same cause that stays the Church from praying for the damned spirits (her known enemies) at this day, the same shall hinder her from praying for the reprobate souls, at this day of judgment, notwithstanding her fullness of perfection. At present she prays for her enemies in mankind, because this is the time of wholesome repentance, and therefore her chief petition for them is, 'that God would grant them penitence and escape from the snares of the devil, who are taken by him at his will,' [1] as the apostle says. But if the Church had this light that she could know any of those who, though they live still upon the earth, yet are predestinated to go with the devil into that everlasting fire; she would offer as few prayers for them, as she does for him. But seeing that she has not this knowledge, therefore prays she for all her foes in the flesh, and yet is not heard for them all, but only for those who are predestinated to become her sons, though they be as yet her adversaries. If any shall die her impenitent foes, and not return into her bosom at all, does she still pray for them? No, because they that before death are not engrafted into Christ, are afterward reputed as associates of the devil: and therefore the same cause forbids her to pray for the reprobate souls then, as stops her from praying for the apostatical angels now; and the same reason there is why we pray for all men while living, and yet will not pray for the wicked, nor infidels, when they are dead. For the prayer

[1] 2 Tim. ii. 25, 26.

either of the Church or of some godly persons is heard for some departed this life, namely for them which, being regenerated in Christ, have not spent their life so wickedly that they may be judged unworthy of such mercy, or else so devoutly that they may be found to have no need of such mercy. So also after the resurrection there shall be some of the dead which shall obtain mercy after the punishments which the spirits of the dead do suffer, that they may not be cast into everlasting fire. For otherwise that should not be truly spoken concerning some, that 'they shall not be forgiven, either in this world, or in the world to come': unless there were some who, although they have no remission in this, yet might have it in the world to come. But when it shall be said by the Judge of the quick and the dead: 'Come, ye blessed of My Father, possess the kingdom prepared for you from the beginning of the world'; and to others on the contrary: 'Depart from Me, ye cursed, into everlasting fire which is prepared for the devil and his angels':[1] it were too much presumption to say, that any of them should escape everlasting punishment whom the Lord has condemned to eternal torments, and so be led also by the persuasion of this presumption, either to despair, or doubt of eternal life.

Let no man therefore so understand the psalmist when he says, 'Will God forget to have mercy, or will He shut up His lovingkindness in displeasure?'[2] that he suppose that the sentence of God is true concerning the good, false concerning the wicked; or that it is true concerning good men and evil angels, but that concerning evil men it is false. For that which is recorded in the psalm belongs to the vessels of mercy, and to the sons of the promise, of which the prophet himself was one, who, when he had said, 'Will God forget to have mercy: will He shut up His lovingkindness in displeasure?' straightway adds, 'And I said, It is mine own infirmity; I will remember the years of the right hand of the Highest.'[3]   Verily he has declared what he meant by these words: 'Will the Lord shut up His loving-kindness in displeasure?' For truly this mortal life is the displeasure of God, wherein 'man is made like unto vanity, and his days pass away like a shadow.' In this displeasure, nevertheless, 'God will not forget to be gracious, by causing His sun to shine upon the good and the evil, and the rain to fall upon the just and unjust.' And so He does not shut up His loving-kindness in displeasure, and especially in that which the psalm expresses here, saying, 'I will remember the years of the right hand of the Highest': because in this most miserable life, which is the displeasure of God, He changes the vessels of mercy into a better state, although as yet His displeasure remains in the misery of this corruption; because He does not shut up His mercies in His displeasure. Seeing therefore the verity of the divine song

---

[1] Matt. xxv. 34, 41.   [2] Ps. lxxvii. 9.   [3] Ps. lxxvii. 10.

may be fulfilled in this manner, it is not necessary that it should be understood of that place where they which pertain not to the city of God shall be punished with everlasting punishment. But they which please to stretch this sentence even to the torments of the damned, at least let them so understand it, that though the displeasure of God remains in them whose due is eternal punishment, yet nevertheless God does not shut up His loving-kindness in this His heavy displeasure, and causes them not to be tormented with such rigour of punishments as they have deserved (yet not so that they may escape), or at any time have an end of those punishments, but that they shall be more easy than they have deserved. For so both the wrath of God shall remain, and He shall not shut up His loving-kindness in His displeasure. But I do not confirm this thing because I do not contradict it.

But not only I, but the sacred and divine scripture does reprove and convict them most plainly and fully, which think that to be spoken rather by the way of threatening than truly, when it is said, 'Depart from Me, ye wicked, into everlasting fire'; [1] and also, 'They shall go into everlasting punishment: and their worm shall not die, and the fire shall not be extinguished,' [2] etc. For the Ninevites did sow a fruitful repentance in this life, as in the field, in which God would have that to be sown with tears, which should afterward be reaped with joy.[3] And yet who will deny that to be fulfilled in them which the Lord had spoken before, unless he cannot well perceive that the Lord does not only overthrow sinners in His anger, but likewise in His mercy? For sinners are confounded by two different ways, either as the Sodomites, in that men suffer punishments for their sins, or as the Ninevites, in that the sins of men are destroyed by repenting. For Nineveh is destroyed which was evil, and good Nineveh is built, which formerly was not; for though the walls and houses still stood, the city was overthrown in her wicked manners. And so, though the prophet was grieved because that came not to pass which those men feared would come by his prophecy, nevertheless that was brought to pass which was foretold by the foreknowledge of God; because He knew, who had forespoken it, how it was to be fulfilled in a better manner.

But that they may know, who are merciful towards an obstinate sinner, what that means which is written: 'How great, O Lord, is the multitude of Thy sweetness, which Thou hast hidden for them that fear thee,' let them also read that which follows: 'But Thou hast performed it to them which hope in Thee.' [4] For what is, 'Thou hast hidden for them that fear Thee, Thou hast performed it to them which hope in Thee,' but that the righteousness of God is not sweet because unknown unto them which establish their own righteousness for the fear of punishments, which

---

[1] Matt. xxv. 46.   [2] Isa. lxvi. 24.   [3] Jonah iii. 5–10.   [4] Ps. xxxi. 19.

righteousness is in the law? For they have not tasted of it. For they hope in themselves, not in Him, and therefore the multitude of the sweetness of God is hidden unto them; for truly they fear God, but with that servile fear which is not in love, because perfect love casteth out fear. Therefore He performs His sweetness to them which hope in Him by breathing His love into them, that when they glory with chaste fear, not in that which love casts away, but which remains for ever and ever, they may glory in the Lord. For Christ is the righteousness of God: 'Who unto us of God,' as the apostle says, 'is made wisdom, and righteousness, and sanctification, and redemption.' So it is written: 'Let him which rejoiceth, rejoice in the Lord.'[1] They which will establish their own righteousness, know not this righteousness which grace gives without merits, and therefore they are not subject to the righteousness of God which is Christ. In the righteousness there is great abundance of the sweetness of God; wherefore it is said in the psalm: 'O taste and see how sweet the Lord is.'[2] And we truly having a taste, and not our fill of it in this our pilgrimage, do rather hunger and thirst after it, that we may be satisfied with it afterward when we see Him as He is, and that shall be fulfilled which is written: 'I shall be satisfied when Thy glory shall be manifested.'[3] So Christ effects great abundance of His sweetness to those which hope in Him. But if God hide that sweetness from them which fear Him in the sense which they suppose, namely that He will not condemn the wicked, but will allow their ignorance of this and their fear of being condemned to act as an incentive to right living, and so that there may be some which may pray for the wicked, how then does He perform it to them which hope in Him, seeing that, as they dream, it is because of this sweetness that He will not condemn them which do not hope in Him? Therefore let us seek that sweetness of His, which He performs to them which hope in Him, and not that which He is thought to effect unto them which contemn and blaspheme Him. In vain therefore does man seek for that, when he is departed out of the body, which he has neglected to obtain to himself being in the body. That saying also of the apostle, 'For God has shut up all in unbelief, that He may have mercy on all,' is not spoken to that end that He will not condemn none, but it appears before in what sense it was spoken. For when the apostle spake unto the Gentiles, to whom now believing he wrote his epistles, concerning the Jews who should afterwards believe: 'As ye,' says he, 'in time past have not believed God, yet now have obtained mercy through their unbelief: even so now have they not believed by the mercy shewed unto you, that they may also obtain mercy.'[4] Then he adds these words in which these people flatter themselves in their errors, and says: 'For God hath shut up all in unbelief, that He may have mercy on

[1] 1 Cor. i. 30, 31.   [2] Ps. xxxiv. 8.   [3] Ps. xvii. 15.   [4] Rom. xi. 30, 31.

all.'[1] Who are 'they all,' but they of whom he did speak, saying, as it were 'Both ye and they'? Therefore God hath shut up both Gentiles and Jews all in unbelief, whom He foreknew, and predestinated to be made like the image of His Son: that being ashamed and cast down by repenting for the bitterness of their unbelief, and turned by believing towards the sweetness of the mercies of God, they might proclaim that saying in the psalm: 'How great is the multitude of Thy sweetness, O Lord, which Thou hast laid up for them which fear Thee: but hast performed it to them which hope, not in themselves but in Thee.'[2] Therefore He has mercy *on all* the vessels of mercy. What means 'on all'? It means, on those of the Gentiles and also on those of the Jews whom He has predestinated, called, justified, glorified (not 'on all men'), and He will condemn none of those.

~~XIX~~ ~~XX~~ ~~XXI~~   CHAPTER XXV

Whether such as being baptized by heretics and become wicked in life, or by Catholics and then fallen away into heresies and schisms, or continuing amongst Catholics and become of vicious conversation, can have any hope of escaping damnation, by the privilege of the sacraments

Now let us answer those who do both exclude the devils from salvation (as the others before do), and also all men besides, excepting such as are baptized in Christ, and made partakers of His body and blood. And these they will have saved, be their lives never so spotted by sin or heresy. But the apostle does plainly control them, saying: 'The works of the flesh are manifest, which are adultery, fornication, uncleanness, wantonness, idolatry, etc., and such like, whereof I tell you now as I told you before that they which do such things shall not inherit the kingdom of God.'[3] This were false now, if such men should become saints at any time whatsoever. But this is true scripture, and therefore that shall never come to pass. And if they be never made partakers of the joys of heaven, then shall they be evermore bound in the pains of hell, for there is no middle course, wherein he that is not in bliss might have a place free from torment.

And therefore it is fitting that we see how our Saviour's words may be understood, where He says: 'This is the bread that came down from heaven, that he that eateth of it should not die. I am the living bread which came down from heaven; if any man eat of this bread, he shall live for ever,'[4] etc. Those, whom we must answer by and by, have got an interpretation for these verses, somewhat more restrained than those whom we are to answer at

[1] Rom. xi. 32.   [2] Ps. xxxi. 19.   [3] Gal. v. 19–21.   [4] John vi. 50, 51.

this present.   For those others do not promise delivery to all that receive the sacraments, but only to the Catholics (whatever be their manner of life), for they only are those that receive the body of Christ, not only sacramentally, but truly also (say they) as being the true members of His body, whereof the apostle says: 'We that are many are one bread and one body.' [1] He therefore that is in this unity of Christ's members in one body, the sacrament whereof the faithful do daily communicate, he is truly said to receive the body and to drink the blood of Christ. And so heretics and schismatics, who are cut off from this body, may indeed receive the same sacrament, but it does them no good, but a great deal of hurt, in that great judgment, where it will both make their pains more heavy, and their continuance eternal. For they are not in that unity of peace which is expressed in this sacrament.

But now these that can observe that he that is not in Christ cannot receive His body truly, do overshoot the mark in promising absolution (at one time or other) to all the fallers away into superstition, idolatry, or heresy.   First, they ought to observe how absurd and far from all likelihood it is, that those (be they more or less) that have left the Church and become arch-heretics, should be in better estate than those whom they have seduced to be heretics with them, before they were Catholics and members of the Church; if to be baptized and to receive Christ's body in the Church be the causes of those arch-heretics' delivery. For an apostate, an opposer of the faith he has once professed, is worse than he that opposes what he did never profess. Secondly, the apostle himself contradicts them, concluding of the works of the flesh that 'They which do such things shall not inherit the kingdom of God.' [2]

Let not sinners, therefore, and wicked men, secure themselves by their continuance in the Church, in that it is written: 'He that endureth to the end, he shall be saved'; [3] nor by their iniquity renounce Christ, their justice, in committing fornication, and either all or any part of those fleshly works which the apostle recounts, or such uncleanness as he would not name: for of all such he says expressly: 'These shall not inherit the kingdom of God.' Wherefore the doers of such deeds cannot but be in eternal pains, in that they are excluded from the everlasting joys. For this kind of perseverance of theirs is no perseverance in Christ, because it is not a true perseverance in His faith, which the apostle defines to be such as worketh by love.[4] 'And love' (as he says elsewhere) 'worketh no evil.' [5] So then these are no true receivers of Christ's body, in that they are none of His true members. For (to omit other reasons) they cannot be both the members of Christ and the members of a harlot. And Christ Himself saying, 'He that eateth My flesh and drinketh My blood dwelleth in Me and I

[1] 1 Cor. x. 17.   [2] Gal. v. 21.   [3] Matt. x. 22.   [4] Gal. v. 6.
                         [5] Rom. xiii. 10.

in him,' [1] shows what it is to receive Christ not only sacramentally, but truly: for this is, 'to dwell in Christ and Christ in him.' For thus He spoke as if He had said, 'He that dwelleth not in Me, nor I in him, cannot say he eateth My flesh, or drinketh My blood.' They therefore that are not members of Christ, are not in Him. They that make themselves the members of a harlot are no members of Christ, unless they purge away their badness by repentance, and return to His goodness by a true reconciliation.

CHAPTER XXVI

What it is to have Christ for the foundation. Who they are that shall be saved (as it were) by fire

AYE, but Christian Catholics (say they) have Christ for their foundation, from whom they fell not, though they built badly upon it, in resemblance of timber, straw, and stubble. So that faith is true, which holds Christ the foundation, and though it bear some loss in that the things which are built upon it burn away, yet has it power to save him that holds it (after some time of suffering). But let St. James answer these men in a word: 'If a man say he has faith, and have no works, can the faith save him?' [2] Who then is he (say they) of whom St. Paul says: 'He shall be safe himself, yet so as by fire'? [3] Well, we will see who that is; but surely it is not those that they think it is, for otherwise the apostles contradict one another. For if one says, 'Though a man have lived wickedly, yet shall he be saved by faith, through fire': and the other, 'If he have no works, can his faith save him?' then shall we soon find who it is that shall be saved by fire, if first of all we find what it is to have Christ for the foundation. To gather this, first, from the nature of the simile, there is no work in building before the foundation. Now every one who has Christ in his heart, even though he desire temporal things (and sometimes things unlawful), still possesses Christ for the foundation thereof. But if he prefer these things before Christ, though he seem to hold his faith, yet Christ is no foundation unto him, in that he prefers those vanities before Him. And if he both contemn good instruction, and prosecute bad actions, how much the sooner shall he be convicted of setting Christ at naught, and esteeming Him of no value in vainer respects, by neglecting His command and allowance, and in contempt of both, following his own lustful extravagance. Wherefore, if any Christian love a harlot, 'and become one body with her by coupling with her,' [4] he has not Christ for his foundation. And if a man love his wife, according to Christ, who can deny that he has Christ for his foundation? Admit his love be carnal, worldly,

---

[1] John vi. 56.   [2] Jas. ii. 14.   [3] 1 Cor. iii. 15.   [4] 1 Cor. vi. 15.

concupiscential, as the Gentiles loved, that knew not Christ: all this the apostle does bear with, and therefore still may Christ be such a man's foundation. For if he prefer not these carnal affections before Christ, though he build straw and stubble upon his foundation, yet Christ is that foundation still, and therefore such a man shall be saved by fire. For the fire of tribulation shall purge away those carnal and worldly affections, which the bond of marriage acquits from being damnable: and unto this fire, all the calamities which these affections bring, as barrenness, loss of children, etc., have reference. And in this case, he that builds thus, shall lose, because his building shall not last, and these losses shall grieve him in that their fruition did delight him. Yet shall the worth of his foundation save him, in that if the persecutor should put it to his choice, whether he would have Christ, or these his delights, he would choose Christ, and leave all the rest. Now shall you hear St. Paul describe a builder upon this foundation with gold, silver, and precious stones. 'The unmarried,' says he, 'careth for the things of the Lord, how he may please the Lord.' And now for him that builds with wood, straw, and stubble. 'He that is married careth for the things of the world, how he may please his wife.' [1] 'Every man's work shall be made manifest, for the day of the Lord shall declare it,' that is, the day of tribulation, 'for it shall be revealed by the fire.' [2]

This tribulation he calls fire, as we read also in another place. 'The furnace proves the potter's vessel, and so doth the trial of affliction try man's thoughts.' [3] So then the fire shall try every man's work: and if any work abide (as his will, that careth for the things of the Lord, and how to please Him), 'he shall receive wages,' that is, he shall receive Him, of whom he thought, and for whom he cared. 'But if any man's work burn he shall lose': [4] because he shall not have his delights that he loved; yet shall he be safe, in that he held his foundation, despite all tribulation: but 'as it were by fire,' for that which he possessed in alluring love, he shall lose in the furnace of afflicting sorrow. This (think I) is the fire, that shall enrich the one and endamage the other, trying both, yet condemning neither. If we say that the fire spoken of here is that whereof Christ spoke to those on His left hand, 'Depart from Me, ye cursed, into everlasting fire'; [5] and that all such as builded timber, straw, and stubble upon their foundation, are part of the said cursed, who notwithstanding, after a time of torment, are to be delivered by the merit of their foundation; then can we not think that those on the right hand, to whom He shall say, 'Come, ye blessed,' [6] etc., are any other, saving those that built gold, silver, and precious stones upon the said foundation. But this fire of which the apostle speaks, shall be as a trial both to the

---

[1] 1 Cor. vii. 32, 33.   [2] 1 Cor. iii. 13.   [3] Ecclus. xxvii. 5.
[4] 1 Cor. iii. 15.   [5] Matt. xxv. 41.   [6] Matt. xxv. 34.

good and the bad. Both shall pass through it, for the scripture says: 'Every man's work shall be made manifest, for the day of the Lord shall declare it, because it shall be revealed by the fire, and the fire shall try every man's work of what sort it is.' If the fire try both, and he that has an abiding work be rewarded, and he whose work shall burn shall be endamaged, then cannot this be that everlasting fire. For into that shall none enter but the cursed, on the left hand, in the last judgment, whereas the blessed shall pass through this, wherein some of them shall be so tried, that their building shall abide unconsumed, and others shall have their work burned, and yet shall be saved themselves, in that their love unto Christ exceeded all their carnal imperfections. And if they be saved, then shall they stand on Christ's right hand, and shall be part of those to whom it shall be said: 'Come, ye blessed of My Father, inherit the kingdom,' etc., and not on the left hand amongst the cursed, to whom it shall be said: 'Depart from Me,' etc. For none of these shall be saved by fire, but all of them shall be bound for ever in that place where the worm never dies. There shall they burn, world without end. But as for the time between the bodily death and the last judgment, if any one say that the spirits of the dead are all that while tried in such fire as never moves those that have not built wood, straw, or stubble, afflicting only such as have wrought such works, either here, or there, or both; or that man's worldly desires (being venial) shall pass the purging fire of tribulation only in this world, and not in the other; if any hold thus, I contradict him not; perhaps he may hold the truth. To this tribulation also may belong the death of body, drawn from our first parents' sin, and inflicted upon each man sooner or later, according to his building. So may also the Church's persecutions, wherein the martyrs were crowned, and all the rest afflicted. For these calamities (like fire) tried both sorts of the buildings; consuming both works and workmen, where they found not Christ for the foundation; and consuming the works only (and saving the workmen by this loss) where they did find Him, 'and stubble,' etc., built upon Him; but where they found works remaining to eternal life, there they consumed nothing at all. Now in the last days, in the time of Antichrist shall be such a persecution as never was before: and many buildings both of gold and stubble, being all founded upon Christ, shall then be tried by this fire, which will return joy to some, and loss to others, and yet destroy none of them by reason of their firm foundation. But whosoever he be, that loves (I do not say his wife, with carnal affection) but even those relations for whom he cannot feel sensuality of this kind with such a blind desire that he prefers them before Christ, this man has not Christ for his foundation, and therefore shall neither be saved by fire, nor otherwise, because he cannot be conjoined with Christ, who says plainly of such men: 'He that loveth father or mother more than Me, is unworthy of Me. And he that loveth son or daughter more than Me, is not worthy of Me.'[1] But he that loves them carnally, and yet prefers Christ for his foundation, and had rather lose them all than Christ, if he were driven to the loss of one, such a man shall be saved, but as it were by fire, that is, his grief in the losing of them must needs be as great as his delight was in enjoying them. 'But he that loves father, mother,' etc., according to Christ, to bring them unto His kingdom, or be delighted in them because they are the members of Christ, this love shall never burn away like wood, straw, stubble, but shall stand as a building of gold, silver, and precious stones; for how can a man love that more than Christ, which he loves for Christ's sake only?

CHAPTER XXVII

Against those that think those sins shall not be laid to their charge wherewith they mixed some works of mercy

Now a word with those that hold none damned but such as neglect to do works of mercy in proportion to their sins; because St. James says, 'There shall be judgment merciless to him that sheweth no mercy.'[2] He therefore that does show mercy (say they), be his life never so burdened with sin and corruption, shall notwithstanding have a merciful judgment, which will either free him from all pains or at least deliver him after a time of suffering. And this, they say, made Christ distinguish the elect from the reprobate only by their performance, and not performance of works of mercy; the one whereof is rewarded with everlasting joy, and the other with eternal pain. And as for their daily sins, that they may be pardoned through these works of mercy, the Lord's Prayer (say they) does sufficiently prove; for as there is no day wherein a Christian says not this prayer, so likewise is there no daily sin but is pardoned when we say: 'And forgive us our trespasses as we forgive them that trespass against us,' if we perform this latter clause accordingly: for Christ (say they) did not say: 'If ye forgive men their trespasses, your heavenly Father will forgive you your small and daily ones,' but he said generally: 'He will forgive you yours.' Be they therefore never so great, never so ordinary, never so continual, yet works of mercy will wash them all away. Well, they do well in giving their advice to perform works of mercy in proportion to their sins; for if they should have said that any works of mercy may obtain pardon even for the greatest and most habitual sins, they would be guilty of much absurdity; for so might the richest man for his tenpence a day have a daily quittance for all his fornications, homicides, and other sins

---

[1] Matt. x. 37.   [2] Jas. ii. 13.

whatsoever.   But if it be an absurdity beyond comparison to affirm this, then without question if we make inquiry what those works are that are worthy of pardon for sin, and whereof St. John Baptist spoke, saying, 'Bring forth therefore fruits worthy of amendment of life,' [1] assuredly we shall find that such as stab their own souls by continual sin have no such works as are meant in this place.   First, they do take violently from others far more than they bestow charitably upon the poor; and yet in bestowing a little they think they feed Christ and purchase liberty of sinning from Him. Thus run they carelessly upon their condemnation, who if they should give away all their whole estate unto the poor members of Christ to redeem one sin alone, yet if love that does no evil did not restrain them from any more such enormities, they would thereby reap no good at all.   He therefore that will clear his sins by his works, must begin first at himself: for it is unfit to do that to our neighbour which we will not do to ourself, Christ Himself saying, 'Thou shalt love thy neighbour as thyself': [2] and again, 'Love thine own soul (if thou wilt please God).' [3]   He therefore that does not this work of mercy (that is, the pleasing of God) to his own soul, how can he be said to do works of mercy sufficient to redeem his sins?   For it is written: 'He that is wicked to himself, to whom will he be good?   For alms-deeds do lift up the prayers of men to God.' [4]   What saith the scripture?   'My son, hast thou sinned?   Do so no more, but pray for thy sins past, that they may be forgiven thee.' [5]   For this cause therefore must we do alms-deeds, that, when we pray, our prayer may be heard that we may leave our former vices, and obtain refreshment for ourselves by those works of mercy.   Now Christ says that He will impute the doing and omission of alms-deeds unto those at the judgment, in order to show how powerful they are to expiate offences past, not to protect the continuers in sin; for those that will not abjure the courses of impiety, cannot be said to perform any works of mercy.   And these words of Christ, 'Inasmuch as ye did it not unto one of these, ye did it not unto Me,' [6] imply that they did no such works as they imagined; for if they gave bread unto the hungered Christian, as if it were unto Christ Himself, the bread of righteousness, which is Christ Himself, should not be denied unto them: for God cares not to whom you give, but with what intent you give.   He therefore that loves Christ in his members, gives alms with intent to join himself to Christ, not that he may have leave to leave Him without being punished, for the more one loves what Christ reproves, the farther off does he depart from Christ. For what profiteth baptism unless justification follow it?   Does not He that said, 'Except a man be born again of water and of the Spirit, he shall not enter into the kingdom of God,' [7] say also,

---

[1] Matt. iii. 8.   [2] Matt. xxii. 39.   [3] Ecclus. xxx. 23.   [4] Ecclus. xiv. 5.
        [5] Ecclus. xxi. 1.   [6] Matt. xxv. 45.   [7] John iii. 5.

'Except your righteousness exceed the righteousness of the scribes and Pharisees, ye shall not enter into the kingdom of heaven'?[1] Why do men run to baptism for fear of the first, and do not draw near to righteousness for fear of the latter? Therefore, as he that checks his brother's sin, in charity, by telling him he is a fool, is not guilty of hell fire in spite of using the word 'fool': so, on the other side, he that loves not Christ in His members, gives no alms to a Christian (as unto a Christian) though he stretch forth his hand unto one of Christ's poor members. And he that refuses to be justified in Christ, does not love Christ in any respect.

But if one call his brother fool in reproachful contempt, rather than with intent to reform his imperfection, all the alms-deeds this man can do will never benefit him, unless he be reconciled to him whom he has injured; for it follows in the same place: 'If then thou bringest thy gift unto the altar, and there rememberest that thy brother hath aught against thee, leave there thine offering, and go thy way: first be reconciled to thy brother and then come and offer thy gift.'[2] And so it is nothing worth to do works of mercy to expiate any sin, and yet to continue in the sin still. As for the Lord's Prayer, it does indeed blot out our daily sins, it being daily said. 'And forgive us our trespasses,' if withal the following clause be not only said, but performed also: 'As we forgive them that trespass against us.' But indeed we say this prayer because we do sin, not that we might sin, for our Saviour shows us in this, that live we never so careful of shunning corruption, yet do we every day fall into some sins, for the remission of which we ought both to pray, and to pardon such as have offended us, that we may be pardoned ourselves. Wherefore Christ saith not this, 'If ye forgive men their trespasses, your heavenly Father will also forgive you yours,'[3] to give hope to any man to persevere in daily crimes (whether we put ourselves above authority, or commit them by sleight and subtlety), but to instruct us, that we are not without sin, though we may be without crime, as God advised the priests in the Old Testament, 'first to offer for their own sins, and then for the people's.' Let us mark these words of our great Lord and Master with attention and diligence. He does not say, 'Your heavenly Father will forgive you any sin whatever,' but 'He will forgive you yours,' for in this place He taught His disciples (being already justified) their daily prayer. What means He then by this same 'yours' but such sins as the righteous themselves cannot be without? Wherefore, whereas they, that would hereby take occasion to continue in sin, affirm that Christ meant the greatest sins, because He said not, 'your smaller sins,' but 'yours' in general: we on the contrary side, considering unto whom He spoke, do understand His words to concern

---

[1] Matt. v. 20.   [2] Matt. v. 23, 24.   [3] Matt. vi. 14.

small sins only, in that they to whom they were spoken were now cleared of their greater.

Nor are those great sins indeed (which every one ought to reform in himself, and avoid) ever forgiven, unless the guilty do fulfil the aforesaid clause, 'As we forgive them that trespass against us.' For if the least sins (whereunto the righteous themselves are prone) cannot be remitted but upon that condition, then much less shall the great and flagrant ones have this pardon, though they that used them do cease their further practice, if they continue inexorable in forgiving such as have offended them; for the Lord saith: 'If ye do not forgive men their trespasses, no more will your heavenly Father forgive you your trespasses.' And St. James' words are to the same purpose: 'There shall be judgment merciless to him that sheweth no mercy.' Remember but the servant whom his master pardoned of a debt of 10,000 talents, and yet made him to lie in prison for it afterwards, because he would not forgive his fellow a debt of but a hundred pence. Wherefore it is in the vessels of mercy and the sons of promise that the same apostle's words are truly effected: 'Mercy rejoiceth against (or above) judgment.'[1] For those that lived so holily that they received others into the everlasting habitations, who had made them their friends with the riches of iniquity; even they themselves were delivered by His mercy who justifies the sinner by rewarding him according to grace, not according to merit. He that professed this, 'I was received to mercy (that I might be one of the faithful),'[2] was one of this justified number. Indeed such as are received by this number into the everlasting habitations are not of that merit that they could be saved without the intercession of the Church triumphant, and therefore in them does mercy more evidently rejoice against judgment. Yet may we not think that every wicked man (being without reformation) can be admitted thither, though he have been beneficial to the saints and afforded them helps from his riches, which, whether he had gotten them by sinister means or otherwise, yet are no true riches unto him (but only reckoned as such in the thoughts of iniquity), because he knows not the true riches wherewith they abound that help such as he is into those eternal mansions. Wherefore there must be a certain mean in the lives of such doers of mercy that it be neither so bad, that the alms-deeds done unto those, who being made friends to the doers may help them to heaven, be altogether fruitless; nor yet so good, that their own sanctity without the mercies and suffrages of those whom they have made their friends, can possess for them so high a beatitude. Now I have often wondered that Virgil should have recorded this sentence of Christ: 'Make you friends of the riches of iniquity, that they may receive you into the everlasting habitations':[3] whereunto this is much like: 'He that receiveth a prophet

[1] Jas. ii. 13. [2] 1 Cor. vii. 25. [3] Luke xvi. 9.

in the name of a prophet, shall have a prophet's reward,'[1] etc.
For this poet in describing the Elysian fields, which they held the
blessed souls to inhabit, does not only place those there whose
proper merits have deserved it, but also adds this: 'Quique sui
memores alios fecere merendo,'[2] that is, such as respecting their
own future estate deserved to be remembered by those others.
Just as if he had said, as every humble Christian says commonly
in commending himself to some holy man or other, 'Remember
me,' and endeavours to procure this remembrance by desert.

But what the mean is here, and what those sins are which hinder
a man from heaven, and yet are remitted by the intercession of his
holy friends, it is both difficult to find, and dangerous to determine.
I have sought thus long myself, and yet could never find them
out. Perhaps they are concealed to stir us the rather to avoid all
sin. For if we knew for what sins we might expect the intercession
of saints, our natural idleness would draw us on carelessly in them,
and make us rely so wholly upon the help of others, that we should
never seek to avoid them by reforming ourselves, but trust only to
those our friends whom we had procured by the unrighteous mam-
mon: whereas now, although our venial sin continue with us, and
in what measure we know not, yet our study to profit by prayer is
both more fervent, and our desire to win us friends of the saints
better performed. But both these deliveries, both by ourselves
and others, tend wholly to keep us out of the fire eternal, but not to
free us after we once be in it. For such as interpret that verse of
scripture, 'Some fell in good ground, and brought forth fruit,
some thirty-fold, some sixty, some an hundred,' by the saints,
according to the diversity of their merit, that some should deliver
thirty men, some sixty, some a hundred, nevertheless do suppose
that this delivery shall be at the judgment, and not after it. By
which opinion one observing what liberty divers took to live in all
looseness and exorbitance, supposing that by this means all men
might be saved, is said to give this witty answer: 'We ought for this
cause rather to live uprightly to increase the number of the inter-
cessors, lest otherwise these should be so few, that after they had
saved each his thirty, his sixty, or his hundred, an infinite company
might still remain unsaved.' And of these why might not he be
one that comforted himself in his rash hope of help from another?
And thus much against those who, not contemning the authority
of our scriptures, do notwithstanding wrest them to evil meanings,
following their own fantasies, and not the Holy Ghost's true
intention. But since we have given them their answer, we must
now (as we promised) give an end to this present book.

---

[1] Matt. x. 41.   [2] Virg. *Aen*. vi. 664.

THE TWENTY-SECOND BOOK OF
THE CITY OF GOD

CHAPTER I

Of the estate of angels and of men

THIS present book, being the last of this whole work, shall contain a discourse of the eternal beatitude of the city of God. Which city is not called eternal, as if it should continue for the space of so many, or so many thousand ages, and then have an end, but as it is written in the gospel: 'Of His kingdom there shall be no end.'[1] Nor shall this kingdom preserve an appearance of perpetuity by one generation succeeding another, as a bay-tree seems to keep a continual verdure, though one leaf falls off and another springs up: but every citizen therein shall be immortal, and man shall attain to that which the angels have never forgone. This God the Founder of this city will effect: for so He has promised, who cannot lie, and who to confirm the rest has effected part of His promises already.

He it is that made the world, with all things sensible and intelligible therein, whose chief work the spirits were, to whom He gave an understanding, making them capable of His contemplation, and combining them in one holy and united society, which we call the city of God, holy and heavenly, wherein God is their life, their nutriment, and their beatitude. He gave a free choice also unto those intellectual natures, that if they would forsake Him, who was their bliss, they should presently be enthralled in misery. And foreknowing that certain of the angels, proudly presuming that they themselves were sufficient beatitude to themselves, would forsake Him, and all good with Him, He did not deprive them of this power, knowing it a more powerful thing to make good use of such as were evil, than to exclude evil altogether. Nor had there been any evil at all, but that those spirits (though good, yet mutable) which were formed by the omnipotent and unchangeable Deity, procured such evil unto themselves by sin; which very sin proved that their natures were good in themselves. For if they had not been so (although inferior to their Maker) their apostasy had not fallen so heavily upon them. For as blindness being a defect proves plainly that the eye was made to see, the excellency of the eye being hereby made more apparent (for otherwise blind-

[1] Luke i. 33.
358

ness were no defect), so those natures enjoying God proved themselves to be created good, in their very fall, and in that eternal misery that fell upon them for forsaking God, who has given assurance of eternal perseverance unto those that stood firm in Him, as a fit reward for their constancy. He also made man upright, endowed with free will, earthly yet worthy of heaven, if he stuck fast to his Creator; otherwise, would he partake of such misery as was appropriate to a nature of that kind. And foreknowing likewise that he would break the law that He bound him to, and forsake his Maker, He did not take away his freedom of choice, foreseeing the good use that He would make of this evil, by restoring man to His grace by means of a Man, born of the condemned seed of mankind, and by gathering so many unto this grace as should supply the places of the fallen angels, and so preserve (and perhaps augment) the number of the heavenly inhabitants. For evil men do much against the will of God, but yet His wisdom foresees that all such actions as seem to oppose His will do tend to such ends as He foreknew to be good and just. And therefore, whereas God is said 'to change His will,' that is, to turn His meekness into anger against some persons, the change in this case is in the persons, and not in Him: and they find Him changed in their sufferings, as a sore eye finds the sun sharp, and, being cured, finds it comfortable, whereas this change was in the eye and not in the sun, which keeps its office as it did at first. For God's operation in the hearts of the obedient is said to be His will; whereupon the apostle says: 'It is God that worketh in you both will and deed.' [1] For even as that righteousness wherein both God Himself is righteousness, and whereby also a man that is justified of God is such, is termed the righteousness of God; so also is that law which He gives unto man called His law, whereas it is rather pertinent unto man than unto Him. For those were men unto whom Christ said: 'It is written also in your law'; [2] though we read elsewhere: 'The law of his God is in his heart.' [3] And according unto His will, which God works in man, Himself is said to will it, because He works it in others who do will it, as He is said to know that which He makes the ignorant to know. For whereas St. Paul says, 'We now knowing God, yea rather being known of God,' [4] we may not hereby gather that God came then for the first time to the knowledge of those whom He had predestinated before the foundations of the world, but God is said to know then because He then made it known to others. Of this phrase of speech I have spoken (I remember) heretofore. And according unto this will, whereby we say that God wills that which He makes others to will, who know not what is to come, He wills many things, and yet effects them not.

---

[1] Phil. ii. 13.   [2] John viii. 17.   [3] Ps. xxxvii. 31.
[4] Gal. iv. 9.

CHAPTER II

Of the eternal and unchangeable will of God

FOR the saints do will many things that are inspired with His holy will, and yet are not done by Him; as when they pray for any one, He may not effect this their prayer, though He produces this will to pray in them by His Holy Spirit. And therefore when the saints do will and pray according to God, we may well say that God wills it and yet works it not, as we say that He wills that Himself, which He makes others to will. But according to His eternal will, joined with His foreknowledge, thereby did He create all that He pleased, in heaven and in earth, and hath wrought all things already, as well future as past or present. But when the time of the manifestation of anything, which God foreknows will come, is not yet come, we say, 'It shall be when God will': and if both the time be uncertain, and the thing itself, then we say, 'It shall be if God will.' It is not that God shall have any other will then, than He had before, but that there shall then be effected that which His eternal, unchanging will had from all eternity ordained.

CHAPTER III

The promise of the saints' eternal bliss, and the wicked's perpetual torment

WHEREFORE (to omit many words) as we see His promise to Abraham, 'In thy seed shall all nations be blessed,'[1] fulfilled in Christ, so shall that be fulfilled hereafter which was promised to the said seed by the prophet: 'The dead shall live, even with their bodies shall they rise.'[2] And where He says: 'I will create new heavens and a new earth, and the former shall not be remembered, nor come into mind; but be ye glad, and rejoice in the things I shall create. For behold I will create Jerusalem as a rejoicing, and her people as a joy,'[3] etc. And by another prophet: 'At that time shall thy people be delivered, every one that shall be found written in the book of life; and many that sleep in the dust of the earth shall awake, some to everlasting life, and some to shame and perpetual contempt.'[4] And again: 'They shall take the kingdom of the saints of the Most High, and possess it for ever, even for ever and ever.'[5] And a little after: 'His kingdom is an everlasting kingdom,'[6] etc. And further there are all such places as I either put into the twentieth book, or left untouched. All these things shall come to pass, as those have already which the infidels would never

---

[1] Gen. xxii. 18.   [2] Isa. xxvi. 19 (LXX).   [3] Isa. lxv. 17–19.
[4] Dan. xii. 1–2.   [5] Dan. vii. 18.   [6] Dan. vii. 27

believe.   For the same God promised them both, even He whom
the pagan gods do tremble before, as Porphyry, a worthy philosopher of theirs, confesses.

CHAPTER IV

*Against the wise men of the world that hold it impossible for man's body
to be transported up to the dwellings of joy in heaven*

BUT the learned of the world think that they oppose this all-con-
verting power very strongly, as touching the resurrection, when they
use that passage of Cicero in his third book *De Re Publica*.   Having
affirmed that Romulus and Hercules were both deified, he adds
that their bodies were not translated into heaven, for nature will
allow an earthly body no place except on the earth.   This is the
wise man's argument, and God knows how vain it is.   For let us
suppose that we were all mere spirits, without bodies, dwelling in
heaven, and ignorant of all earthly creatures, and that it should be
told us that one day we should be bound in corporal bodies; might
we not then use this objection and refuse to believe that nature
would ever suffer an incorporeal substance to be bound or cir-
cumscribed by a corporal one?   Yet is the earth full of vegetable
souls, strangely combined with earthly bodies.   Why then cannot
God, that made this creature, transport an earthly body into
heaven, as well as He can bring a soul (a purer essence than any
celestial body) down from heaven, and enclose it in a form of earth?
Can this little piece of earth include so excellent a nature in it, and
live by it, and yet cannot heaven entertain it, nor keep it in it,
seeing that it lives by an essence more excellent than heaven itself?
Indeed this shall not come to pass as yet, because it is not His
pleasure, who made this that we daily see and therefore respect
not in a far more marvellous manner, than that shall be which
those wise men believe not.   For why is it not more strange that
a most pure and incorporeal soul should be chained to an earthly
body, than that an earthly body should be lifted up to heaven,
which is but a body itself?   Only because the first we see daily in
ourselves, and the second we have yet never seen.   But reason
will tell one that it is a more divine work to join bodies and souls,
than to join bodies to bodies, though these be different in natures,
and the one be heavenly and the other of the earth.

CHAPTER V

Of the resurrection of the flesh, believed by the whole world excepting some few

THIS indeed was once incredible, but now we see that the whole world believes that Christ's body is taken up to heaven. The resurrection of the body and the ascension unto bliss are believed now by all the earth. Learned and unlearned embrace it, and only some few reject it. If it be credible, what fools are they not to believe it! if it be not, how incredible a thing is it, that it should be so generally believed! These two incredible things, to wit, the resurrection, and the world's belief therein, our Lord Jesus Christ promised should come to pass, before that He had effected either of them. Now one of them (the world's belief in the resurrection) we see is come to pass already. Why then should we despair of the other, that this incredible thing which the world believes, should itself come to pass; especially seeing that they are both promised in those scriptures, whereby the world believed. The manner in which belief came is even more incredible. That men, ignorant in all arts, without rhetoric, logic, or grammar, plain fishers, should be sent by Christ into the sea of this world, only with the nets of faith, and draw such an innumerable multitude of fishes of all sorts, so much the stranger, in that they took many rare philosophers! And so this may well be accounted the third incredible thing; and yet all three are come to pass. It is incredible that Christ should rise again in the flesh, and carry it up to heaven with Him. It is incredible that the world should believe this. And it is incredible that this belief should be effected by a small band of poor, simple, unlearned men. The first of these our adversaries believe not; the second they behold, and cannot tell how it is wrought, if it be not done by the third. Christ's resurrection and ascension is taught and believed all the world over. If it be incredible, why does all the world believe it? If many noble, learned, and mighty persons, or men of great sway, had said they had seen it, and should have divulged it abroad, it had been no marvel if the world had believed them, and unbelievers would have been thought hardly of. But seeing that the world believes it from the mouths of a few mean, obscure, and ignorant men, why do not our obstinate adversaries believe the whole world which believed those simple, mean, and unlearned witnesses, because the deity itself in these poor shapes did work the more effectually, and far more marvellously? For their proofs and persuasions lay not in words, but wonders: and such as had not seen Christ risen again and ascending, believed their affirmations thereof, because they confirmed them with miracles: for whereas they spoke but one language, or (at the most) but two, before, now of a sudden they spoke all the tongues of all nations. They cured a man that had been forty years lame, even from his mother's breasts, by the very name of Jesus Christ alone. Their handkerchiefs healed diseases. The sick persons got themselves laid in the way where they should pass, that they might have help from their very shadows; and amongst all these miracles done by the name of Christ, they raised some from the dead. If these things be true as they are written, then may all these be added to the three former incredibles. Thus do we bring a multitude of incredible effects to persuade our adversaries but unto the belief of one, namely, the resurrection; and yet their horrible obstinacy will not let them see the light. If they believe not that the apostles wrought any such things for confirmation of the resurrection of Christ, it is sufficient then that the whole world believed them without miracles, which is a miracle as great as any of the rest.

CHAPTER VI

That love made the Romans deify their founder Romulus, but faith made the Church love her Lord and Master Christ Jesus

LET us hear what Tully says of the fabulous deification of Romulus. 'It is more admirable in Romulus (says he) that the rest of the deified men lived in the times of ignorance, when there was more scope for fiction, and when the rude vulgar were far more credulous. But Romulus, we see, lived, within this six hundred years, since which time (and before also) learning has been more common, and the ignorance of elder times utterly abolished.' Thus says Tully; and a little after: 'Hereby it is evident that Homer was long before Romulus, so that in the later times, men grew learned, and fictions were well nigh wholly excluded, whereas antiquity has given credence to some very unlikely fables: but our modern ages being more polished deride and reject all things that seem impossible.' [1] Thus says the most learned and eloquent man, that Romulus' divinity was the more admirable, because his times were enlightened, and kept no place for fabulous assertions. But who believed this deity, but Rome, as then a little thing (God knows) and a young? Posterity indeed had to preserve the traditions of antiquity. Every one sucked this superstition from his nurse, whilst the city grew to such power, that, seeming in sovereignty to stand above the nations under it, she poured the belief of this deity of his throughout her conquered provinces, that they should affirm Romulus to be a god (howsoever they thought), lest they should scandalize the founder of their lady and mistress, in saying otherwise of him than error of love (not love of error) had

[1] *De Re Publ.* ii. 10.

induced her to believe. <u>Now in the case of Christ, though He founded the celestial city, yet does not she think Him a God for founding her, but she is rather founded for thinking Him to be a God.</u> Rome being already built and finished adored her founder in a temple: but the heavenly Jerusalem places Christ her Founder in the foundation of her faith, that hereby she may be built and perfected. Love made Rome believe that Romulus was a god: but the belief that Christ is God made His city to love Him. And so even as Rome had an object for her love, which she was ready to honour with a false belief: so the city of God has an object for her faith which she is ever ready to honour with a true and rightly grounded love. For as touching Christ, not only those many miracles but the holy prophets also did teach that He was God, long before His coming: which as the fathers believed should come to pass, so do we now see that it is come to pass. But as touching Romulus, we read that he built Rome, and reigned in it, not that this was prophesied before: but as for his deification, their books affirm that it was believed, but they show not how it was effected, for there were no miracles to prove it. The she-wolf that fed the two brethren with her milk, which is held so miraculous, what does this prove as concerning his deity? If this she-wolf were not a strumpet [1] but really a brute beast, yet as the accident concerned both the brethren alike, why was not Remus deified for company? And who is there that forbidden upon pain of death to say that Hercules, Romulus, or such are deities, had rather lose his life than profess disbelief in it? What nation would worship Romulus as a god, if it were not for fear of Rome? But on the other hand, <u>who is he that can number those that have suffered death willingly in whatever form of cruelty, rather than deny the deity of Christ?</u> A light and little fear of the Roman power compelled divers inferior cities to honour Romulus as a god: but neither fear of power, torment, nor death, could hinder an infinite multitude of martyrs, all the world through, from both believing and professing that Christ was God. Nor did His city, though she were as then a pilgrim upon earth, and had huge multitudes within her, ever go about to defend her temporal estate against her persecutors by force, but neglected that to gain her place in eternity. Her people were bound, imprisoned, beaten, racked, burned, torn, butchered, and yet multiplied. Their fight for life was the contempt of life for their Saviour. Tully, in his third *De Re Publica* [2] (or I am deceived), argues that a just city never should take arms, but either for her safety or faith. What he means by safety he shows elsewhere. From those pains (says he) which the most foolish may feel, as poverty, banishment, stripes, imprisonment, and suchlike, do private men escape, by the ready dispatch of death. But this

---

[1] *Lupa* means 'harlot' as well as 'she-wolf.'—ED.
[2] *De Re Publ.* iii. 23.

death, which seems to free private men from pains, is pain itself
unto a city. For the aim of a city's continuance should be eternity.
Death, therefore, is not so natural to a commonwealth as to a
private man. He may oftentimes be driven to wish for it: but
when a city is destroyed, the whole world seems (in a manner) to
perish with it. Thus says Tully, holding the world's eternity
with the Platonists. So then he would have a city take arms for
her safety, that is, for her continuance for ever here upon earth,
although her members perish and renew successively, as the
leaves of the olive and laurel trees and suchlike do: for death
(says he) may free private men from misery, but it is misery itself
unto a commonwealth. And therefore it is a question whether
the Saguntines did well in choosing the destruction of their city,
before the breach of faith with the commonwealth of Rome; an act
which all the world commends. But I cannot see how they could
possibly keep this rule, that a city should not take arms but either
for her faith or safety. For when these two are jointly endangered,
so that one cannot be saved without the other's loss, one cannot
determine which should be chosen. If the Saguntines had chosen
to preserve their safety, they had broken their faith: if their faith,
then would they lose their safety, as indeed they did. But the
safety of the city of God is such, that it is preserved (or rather purchased) by faith, and faith being once lost, the safety cannot possibly
but perish also. This thought, with a firm and patient resolution,
crowned so many martyrs for Christ, whereas Romulus never had
so much as one man that would die in defence of his deity.

CHAPTER VII

*That the belief of Christ's deity was wrought by God's power, not
man's persuasion*

BUT it is absurd to make any mention of the false deity of Romulus
when we speak of Christ. But if the age of Romulus, almost six
hundred years before Scipio, were so stored with men of understanding that no impossibility could enter their belief, how much
more wise were they six hundred years after, in Tully's time, in
Tiberius' time, and in the days of Christ's coming? And so His
resurrection and ascension would have been rejected as fictions and
impossibilities, if either the power of God or the multitude of
miracles had not persuaded the contrary, teaching that it was now
shown in Christ, and hereafter to be shown in all men besides, and
averring it strongly against all horrid persecutions throughout the
whole world, through which the blood of the martyrs made it
spread and flourish. They read the prophets, observed a concordance and a concurrence of all those miracles, and the truth

though new was seen to be not contrary to reason, so that at the last the world embraced and professed that which before it had hated and persecuted.

CHAPTER VIII

Of the miracles which have been and are as yet wrought to procure and confirm the world's belief in Christ

BUT how comes it, say they, that you have no such miracles nowadays, as you say were done of yore? I might answer, that they were necessary, before the world believed, to induce it to believe; and that he that seeks to be confirmed by wonders now is to be wondered at most of all himself, in refusing to believe what all the world believes besides him. But this objection of theirs implies that they believe not that there were any miracles done at all. Why then is Christ's ascension in the flesh so generally avowed? Why does the world, in such learned and circumspect times, believe such incredible things, without seeing them confirmed by miracles? Were they credible, and therefore believed? Why then do not they themselves believe them? Our conclusion is brief. Either this incredible thing which was not seen, was confirmed by other incredibles which were seen, or else this being so credible that it need no miracle to prove it, condemns their own gross incredulity, that will not believe it. This I say to silence fools: for we cannot deny that the miraculous ascension of Christ in the flesh was ratified unto us by the power of many other miracles. The scriptures do both relate them, and the end whereunto they tended. They were written to work faith in men, and the faith they wrought has made them far more famous. They are read to induce the people to believe, and yet would not be read unless they are believed. And as for miracles, there are some wrought even now in His name, partly by the sacraments, partly by the commemorations and prayers of the saints; but they are not so famous, nor so glorious as the other; for the scriptures which were to be divulged in all places have given lustre to the first, in the knowledge of all nations, whereas the latter are only known unto the cities where they are done, or some regions about them. And generally, there are few that know them even there, and many that do not, if the city be great; and when they relate them to others, they are not believed so fully and so absolutely as the others, although they be declared by one Christian to another. The miracle that was done at Milan when I was there, might well become famous, both because the city was of great largeness, and likewise for the great concourse of people that came to the shrine of Protasius and of Gervasius, where the blind man obtained his sight. The bodies of these two martyrs lay long unknown, until Ambrose, the bishop, had notice of them, by a revelation in a

dream. But that miracle at Carthage, whence Innocentius, one
that had been an advocate of a neighbour state, received his health,
was unknown unto the most; though notwithstanding I was present,
and saw it with mine eyes, for he was the man that gave entertain-
ment unto me and my brother Alypius, not being clergymen[1] as
yet, but only lay Christians; and we dwelt as then in his house.
He lay sick of many fistulas formed in the rectum. The surgeons
had lanced him, and put him to extreme and bitter pains, though
they had left one part untouched which they must perforce make
incision into ere they could possibly cure him: but though they
cured all the rest, that one part being omitted troubled them
exceedingly, and made all their applications tend to no purpose.
Innocentius marking their delays, and fearing another incision
(which a physician that dwelt in his house had told him they would
be driven to make, whom they would not suffer to see how they
cut him, whereupon Innocentius had angrily barred him his
house, and could scarcely be brought to receive him again), at last
burst forth, saying: 'Will you cut me again? Will it come to
following his sayings, whom you will not have to see your tricks?'
But they mocked at the ignorance of the physician and bade Innocentius be of good cheer, there was no such necessity. Well, the
time passed on, but no improvement of the malady could be seen.
The surgeons did still promise fair, that they would cure him by
salve and not by incision. Now they had got an old man and a
cunning surgeon called Ammonius to join with them, and he,
viewing the sore, affirmed as much as they; which assurance of his
did satisfy Innocentius that he himself did now begin to gibe and
jest at his other physician that said he must be cut again. Well, to
be brief, when they had spent some weeks more, they all left him,
showing (to their shame) that he could not possibly be cured but
by incision. This, and the excessive fear thereof, struck him
immediately beyond his senses; but recollecting himself he bade
them begone, and nevermore come to him, being enforced now by
necessity to send for a cunning surgeon of Alexandria, one that
was held a rare artist, to perform that which his anger would not
let the others do. The man coming to him, and (like a workman
observing the work of the others by the scars they had left) as an
honest man, advised him to let them finish the cure who had taken
such great pains with it, as he had with wonder observed; for
true it was that incision was the only means to cure him, but that
it was far from him to deprive those of the honour of their industry, whose pains in the cure he saw had been so exceeding
great. So the former surgeons were sent for to perform it, and
this Alexandrian was to stand by, and see them open the part which
was otherwise held to be incurable. The business was put off
until the next day. But the surgeons being all departed, the house

[1] Lat. *cleros.*—ED.

was so filled with sorrow for the grief of their master, that it showed more like a preparation for a funeral than anything else, and could scarcely be suppressed. Now he was daily visited by divers holy men, namely by Saturninus (of blessed memory), the Bishop of Uzali, and Gelosus, priest and deacon of the Church of Carthage, as also by Bishop Aurelius, who alone is yet living of all these three, a man of worthy respect, and one with whom I now and then had conferred about the wonderful works of God. I have often taken occasion to speak of this, and found that he remembered it exceeding well. These men visiting him towards the evening, he prayed them all to come again the next day to be spectators of his death, rather than his pains; for his former sufferings had so terrified him, that he made no question but that he should immediately perish under the surgeon's hands. They on the other side bade him be comforted, trust in God, and bear His will with patience. Then went we to prayers, and as we knelt down, he threw himself forcibly on his face, as if one had thrown him down, and so began to pray, with such passion of mind, such floods of tears, such groans and sobs (even almost to the stopping of his breath), that it is utterly beyond words to express. Whether the rest prayed, or marked him, I know not; for myself I could not pray a jot, only I said in my heart: 'Lord, whose prayers wilt Thou hear, if Thou hear not his?' for methought his prayer could not but procure his suit. Well we rose, and being blessed by the bishop, we departed from the room; he in the meantime entreating them to come to him in the morning, and they strengthening his spirit with as good consolations as they could give him. The feared morning was now come; the holy men came according to their promises; so did the surgeons. The terrible irons were made ready, and all things fit for such a work, whilst all the company sat silent in deep wonder. The chief and such as had more authority than the rest, comforted him as well as they could. His body was laid fit for the hand of him that was to cut him, the clothes untied, the place bared. The surgeon viewed it with his knife in his hand ready to lance it, feeling with his fingers where the ulcerous matter should lie. At length, having made a thorough examination of all the part that was before affected, he found the orifice firmly closed, and every place thereof as sound and as solid as it was first created. Then joy and praises unto God (with tears of comfort) were yielded on all sides beyond the power of my pen to describe.

In the same town, one Innocentia, a devout woman, and one of the chief in the city, had a cancer on her breast, a kind of sore, which the surgeons told her was utterly incurable: wherefore they ordinarily either cut the infected part away, or for the prolonging of the life (as Hippocrates they say does advise) omit all attempt of curing it. This a skilful physician (her familiar friend) told her, so that she now sought help of none but the Lord, who told her in a dream, that at Easter next (which then drew near) she should mark, on the women's side by the baptistry, what woman she was that (being then baptized) should first meet her, and that she should entreat her to sign the sore with the sign of the cross. She did it, and was cured. The former physician that had wished her to abstain from all attempt of cure, seeing her afterwards whole and sound whom he knew certainly to have had that incurable ulcer before, earnestly desired to know how she was cured, longing to find the medicine that had frustrated Hippocrates' aphorism. She told him. He immediately, with a voice as if he had contemned it (insomuch that she feared exceedingly that he would have spoken blasphemy), replied: 'Why, I thought you would have told me of some great discovery.' She standing all amazed replied: 'Why, is it so great a thing for Christ to heal a cancer, that could raise one to life that had been four days dead?' When I first heard of this, it grieved me that so great a miracle wrought upon so great a personage should be so concealed, whereupon I thought it good to give her a stern admonition about it, and meeting her and questioning her on the matter, she told me she had not concealed it, so that I went and inquired of her fellow matrons, who told me they never heard of it. 'Behold' (said I to her, before them), 'have you not concealed it, when your nearest familiars do not know of it?' Whereupon she fell to relate the whole order of it, unto their great wonder, and the glorification of God. There was also a physician in the same town much troubled with the gout, who having given in his name to be baptized, the night before he should receive this sacrament, in his sleep was forbidden it by a crew of curly-headed negro boys, which he knew to be devils; but he refusing to obey them, they stamped on his feet, so that they put him to most extreme pain. Yet he keeping his firm resolve, and being baptized the next day, was freed both from his pain and the cause thereof, so that he never had the gout in all his days after. But who knew this man? We did, and a few of our neighbour brethren, otherwise it had been utterly unknown.

One of Curubis was by baptism freed both from the palsy and excessive hernia, so that he went from the font as sound a man as ever was born. Where was this known but in Curubis, and unto a few besides? But when I heard of it, I got Bishop Aurelius to send him to Carthage, notwithstanding that it was first told me by men of sufficient credit. Hesperius, one that has been a captain and lives at this day by us, has a little farm called Zubedi, in the district of Fussala, which having observed (by the harm done to his servants and cattle) to be haunted with evil spirits, he entreated one of our priests (in mine absence) to go thither and expel them by prayer. One went, prayed, and administered the communion, and by God's mercy the devil was driven from the place ever after. Now he had a little of the earth whereon the sepulchre of Christ stands, bestowed upon him by a friend, which he had hung up in his chamber for the better expulsion of those wicked illusions from his own person. Now they being expelled, he knew not what to do with this earth, being not willing, for the reverence he bore it, to keep it any longer in his lodging. So as I and my colleague Maximus, Bishop of Synica, were at the next town, he prayed us to come to his house. We did. He told us all the matter, and requested that this earth might be buried somewhere, and made a place for prayer, and for the Christians to celebrate God's service in; and it was done accordingly.

Now there was a country youth that was troubled with the palsy, who hearing of this, desired his parents to bring him thither. They did so, and there he prayed, and was at once cured. Victoriana is a town some thirty miles from Hipporegium. There is a memorial there of the two martyrs of Milan, Gervasius and Protasius; and thither they carried a young man who, washing his horse in summer, at noonday, in a deep river, was possessed with a devil. Being brought hither, he lay as one dead, or very near death. Meanwhile the lady of the village (as the custom is) entered the place for evening prayers with her maids and certain votaresses, and began to sing psalms, which sound made the man start up as in a fright; and with a terrible raving he took fast hold of the altar, whence he durst not once move, but held it as if he had been bound to it. Then the devil within him began mournfully to cry for mercy, relating how and when he entered the man; and lastly saying that he would leave him he named what parts of him he would spoil at his departure, and saying these words departed. But one of the man's eyes fell down upon his cheek, and hung only by a little string, all the pupil of it (which is naturally black) becoming white, which the people (whom his cries had called) seeing, fell to help him with their prayers: and though they rejoiced at the recovery of his wits, yet sorrowed they for the loss of his eye, and advised him to get a surgeon for it. But his sister's husband, who brought him thither, replied, saying: 'The God that delivered him from the devil, hath power to restore him his eye'; which said, he put it into the place as well as he could, and bound it up with his napkin, desiring him not to loose it until certain days were past, which doing, he found it as sound as ever it was. At this place were many others cured, whom it were too long to rehearse particularly.

I knew a virgin in Hippo, who was freed from the devil, merely by being anointed with oil mixed with the tears of the priest that prayed for her. I know a bishop who by prayer dispossessed the devil present in a youth that he never saw. There was one Florentius here of Hippo, a poor and godly old man, who getting his living by mending shoes, lost his upper garment; and being not able to buy another, he came to the shrine of the Twenty Martyrs and prayed aloud unto them, to help him to raiments. A band of scoffing youths overheard him; and at his departure, followed him with mocks, asking him if he had begged fifty halfpence of the martyrs to buy him a coat with. But he, going quietly on, spied a great fish, just cast up by the sea and still panting, which fish, by their permission that were by, he took, and carried it to one Catosus a cook, a good Christian, and sold it to him for three hundred halfpence, intending to bestow this money upon wool for his wife to spin, and make into a garment for him. The cook cutting up the fish found a ring of gold in his stomach, which amazing him, his conscience made him send for the poor man, and give him the ring, saying to him: 'Behold how the Twenty Martyrs have apparelled you.'

When Bishop Projectus brought St. Stephen's relics to the town called Aquae Tibilitanae, there were many people flocked together to honour them. Amongst them there was a blind woman, who prayed them to lead her to the bishop that bore the holy relics. So the bishop gave her certain flowers which he had in his hand. She took them, put them to her eyes, and at once had her sight restored, insomuch that she passed speedily on, before all the rest, as now not needing any more to be guided. So Bishop Lucillus, bearing the relics of the said martyr, enshrined in the castle of Synice, near to Hippo, was thereby absolutely cured of a fistula wherewith he had been long vexed, and was come to that pass that he every day expected that the surgeon should lance it; but he was never troubled with it after that day. Eucharius, a Spanish priest, that dwelt at Calame, was cured of the stone by the same relics, which Bishop Posidius brought thither; and being afterwards laid out for dead from another disease, by the help of the said martyr (unto whose shrine they brought him) was restored unto his former life and soundness.

There was one Martialis, a great man of good years, but a great foe to Christ, who dwelt in this place. This man's daughter was a Christian, and married unto a Christian. The father, being very sick, was entreated by them both with prayers and tears to become a Christian, but he utterly and angrily refused. So the husband thought it good to go to St. Stephen's shrine, and there to pray the Lord to send his father-in-law into a better mind, and to embrace Christ Jesus without further delay. For this he prayed with great zeal and affection, with showers of tears, and storms of religious sighs; and then departing he took some of the flowers from off the altar, and in the night laid them at his father's head, who slept well that night, and in the morning called in all haste for the bishop, who was then at Hippo with me. So they told him. He forthwith sends for the priests, and when they came told them at once that he believed, and so was immediately baptized, to the amazement of them all. This man all the time he lived after had this saying continually in his mouth: 'Lord Jesus receive my spirit.' These were his last words, though he knew them not to be St. Stephen's, for he lived not long after. At this place also were two healed of the gout, a citizen and a stranger. The citizen knew by example what to do to be rid of his pain, but the stranger had it revealed unto him.

There is a place called Audurus, where St. Stephen has a memorial of his body remaining also. A child being in the street, certain oxen that drew a cart, growing unruly, left the way, and ran over the child with the wheel, so that it lay all crushed and past all hope of life. The mother snatched it up and ran to the shrine with it, where laying it down, it recovered both life and full strength again in an instant, being absolutely cured of all hurt whatsoever. Near this place, at Caspaliana, dwelt a votaress, who, being sick and past recovery, sent her garment to the shrine, but ere it came back she was dead, yet her parents covered her with it; which done, she presently revived and was as sound as ever. The like happened to one Bassus, a Syrian, that dwelt at Hippo. Praying for his sick daughter at St. Stephen's, and having her garment with him, word came by a boy that she was dead. But as he was at prayer, his friends met the boy (before he had been with him), and bade him not to tell him there, lest he went mourning through the street. So coming home, and finding all in tears, he laid her garment upon her, and she at once revived. So likewise when Irenaeus' son, a collector, was dead, and ready to go out for burial, one advised to anoint him with some of St. Stephen's oil. They did so, and he revived. Elusinus likewise, a captain, seeing his son dead, took him and laid him upon the shrine that is in his farm in our suburbs, where after he had prayed awhile, he found him revived. What shall I do? My promises bind me to be brief, whereas doubtless many that shall read all these things will grieve that I have omitted so many that are known both to them and me.

But I entreat their pardon that they would consider how tedious a task it is, so that my promised respect of brevity will not allow it. For if I should but relate all the miracles done on men's bodies by the memorials of St. Stephen, only at Calama and Hippo, it would be a work of many volumes, and yet not be perfect either. I could not relate all, but only such as are recorded for the knowledge of the people, for we desire, when we see our times produce wonders like to those of yore, that they should not be utterly in vain by being lost in forgetfulness and oblivion.

It is not yet two years since the shrine was built at Hippo, and although we ourselves do know many miracles done there since, that are recorded, yet are there almost seventy accounts written of those that have been done from that time to this. But at Calama the shrine is more ancient, the miracles more frequent, and the records far more in number. At Uzalis also, near Utica, have many miracles been wrought by the power of the said martyr, where Bishop Euodius erected his memorial, long before this one of ours. But there they did not use to record them, though it may be they have begun such a custom of late. For when we were there, we advised Petronia (a noblewoman who was cured of an old disease whose cure all the physicians had given up) to have the story of her miraculous cure written in a book (as the bishop of that place was willing), and that it might be read unto the people; and she did accordingly. Herein was one strange passage, which I cannot omit, though my time will hardly allow me to relate it.

A certain Jew had advised her to take a ring, with a stone set in it that is found in the reins of an ox, and sew it in a girdle of hair, which she must wear upon her skin under all her other raiments. This girdle she had on when she set forth to come to the martyr's shrine, but having left Carthage before, and come to dwell at a house of her own by the river Bagrada, as she rose to go on the rest of her journey, she spied the ring lying at her feet. Whereat wondering, she felt for her girdle, and finding it tied, as she had bound it, she imagined that the ring was broken, and so worn out. But finding it whole she took this as a good indication of her future recovery, and loosing her girdle cast both it and the ring into the river. Now they that will not believe that Jesus Christ was born without interruption of the virginal parts, nor passed into His apostles when the doors were shut, neither will they believe this. But when they examine it, and find it true, then let them believe the other. The woman is of noble birth, nobly married, and dwells at Carthage. So great a city, so great a person in the city cannot lie unknown to any that are inquisitive. And the martyr, by whose prayer she was cured, believed in Him that was born of an eternal virgin, and entered to His disciples when the doors were shut, and lastly (whereunto all this has reference), who ascended into heaven in the flesh, wherein He rose again from death. And for this faith this martyr lost his life.

And so we see there are miracles at this day wrought with what means He likes best by the same God who wrought them of yore: but they are not so famous, nor so fastened in the memory by often reading, that they might not be forgotten. For although we have gotten a good custom of late of reading the narratives of such, as these miracles are wrought upon, unto the people, yet perhaps they are read but once, which they that are present do hear, but no one else: nor do they that hear them keep them long in remembrance, nor will any of them take the pains to relate them to those that have not heard them. We had one miracle wrought amongst us, so famous and so worthy, that I think not one of Hippo but saw it or knows it, and not one that knows it that can ever forget it.

There were seven brethren and three sisters (born all of one couple in Caesarea, a city of Cappadocia). Their parents were noble. Their father being newly dead, and they giving their mother some cause of anger, she laid a heavy curse upon them all, which was so seconded by God's judgment, that they were all taken with a horrible trembling of all their whole bodies. And loathing that their countrymen should behold this ugly sight they became vagrant through most parts of the Roman Empire. Two of them, Paul and Palladia, came to us, already known by their miseries in many other places. They came some fifteen days before Easter, and every day they visited St. Stephen's shrine, humbly beseeching God at length to have mercy upon them, and to restore them their former health. Wheresoever they went they drew the eyes of all men upon them, and some that knew how they came so plagued told it unto others, that all might know it. Now was Easter Day come, and many were come to church in the morning, amongst whom this Paul was one. He had gotten him to the bars that enclosed St. Stephen's relics, and there was praying, having hold of the bars. Presently he fell flat down, and lay as if he had slept, but trembled not as he had used always to do before in his sleep.

The people were all amazed. Some feared, some pitied him. Some would have raised him, but others said: 'Nay, let us see what will happen.' Presently he started up, and rose as sound a man as ever he was born. With that all the church resounded again with loud acclamations and praises to God. And then they came flocking to me, who was about to come forth to them, every one telling me this strange and miraculous event. I rejoiced, and thanked God within myself. Presently enters the young man, and falls down at my knees. I took him up and kissed him. So forth we went unto the people, who filled the church, and did nothing but cry: 'God be thanked, God be praised!' Every mouth uttered this. I saluted them, and then the cry redoubled.

At length silence being made, the scriptures were read; and when it was sermon time I made only a brief exhortation to them, in keeping with the time and that present joy. For in so great a work of God, I did leave them to think of it themselves, rather than to give ear to others. The young man dined with us, and related the whole story of his mother and brethren's misery. The next day, after my sermon, I told the people that to-morrow they should hear the whole story of this miracle read unto them. And while doing this I made the young man and his sister stand both upon the steps that go up into the chancel (wherein I had a place aloft, to speak from thence to the people) that the congregation might see them both. So they all viewed them, the brother standing sound and firm, and the sister trembling every joint of her. And they that saw not him might know God's mercy shown to him by seeing his sister, and discern both what to give thanks for in him, and what to pray for in her. The narrative being read, I willed them to depart out of the people's sight, and began to dispute of the cause of this, when as suddenly there arose another acclamation from about the shrine. They that hearkened unto me left me, and drew thither; for the maid when she departed from the steps, went thither to pray, and as soon as she touched the gate she was wrapt in sleep as he was, and so restored to the perfect use of all her limbs. So while I was asking the reason of this noise, the people bring her unto the choir to me, being now as fully sound as her brother. And then arose such an exultation, that one would have thought it should never have end. And the maid was brought thither where she had stood before. Then the people rejoiced that she was like her brother now, who had lamented that she was unlike him before, seeing that the will of the Almighty had forestalled their intention of praying for her. This their joy was so loudly expressed, that it was able to strike the strongest ear with stupor. And what was in their hearts that rejoiced thus, but the faith of Christ, for which St. Stephen shed his blood?

CHAPTER IX

That all the miracles done by the martyrs in the name of Christ were only confirmations of that faith, whereby the martyrs believed in Christ

AND what does all this multitude of miracles do, but confirm that faith which holds that Christ rose again in the flesh, and so ascended into heaven? For the martyrs were all martyrs, that is, witnesses of this; and for this they suffered the malice of the cruel world, which they never resisted, but subdued by suffering. For this faith they died, and now are able to obtain this power from Him for whom they died. For this faith their patience made the way for the power of these so powerful miracles to follow. For if this resurrection had not taken place in Christ, or had not been to come, as Christ promised, as well as those prophets that promised Christ; how comes it that the martyrs that died for this belief should have the power to work such wonders? For whether God Himself (who being eternal can effect things temporal by such wondrous means) has wrought these things of Himself, or by His ministers, or by the souls of the martyrs as if He wrought by living men, or by His angels over whom He has an invisible, unchangeable, and incorporeal command (so that those things which the martyrs are said to do, be only wrought by their prayers, and not by their powers); be they effected by this means, or by that, they do nevertheless in every particular tend only to confirm that faith which professes the resurrection of the flesh unto all eternity.

CHAPTER X

How much greater honour the martyrs deserve in obtaining miracles
for the worship of the true God, than the devils, whose works tend
all to make men think that they are gods

BUT it may be, that at this point they will say that their gods have
also wrought wonders. Very well, they must come now to compare their deities with our dead men. Will they say, think you,
that they have gods that have been men, such as Romulus, Hercules, etc.? But we make no gods of our martyrs. The martyrs
and we have both but one God, and no more. But the miracles,
that the pagans ascribe unto their idols, are in no way comparable to
the wonders wrought by our martyrs. But as Moses overthrew
the enchanters of Pharaoh, so do our martyrs overthrow their
devils, who wrought those wonders out of their own pride, only
to gain the reputation of gods. But our martyrs (or rather God
Himself through their prayers) wrought unto another end, only to
confirm that faith which excludes multitudes of gods, and believes
but in one. The pagans built temples to those devils, ordaining
priests and sacrifices for them, as for gods. But we build our
martyrs no temples, but only erect for them monuments, as in
memory of men departed, whose spirits are at rest in God. We
erect no altars to sacrifice to them. We offer only to Him who is
both their God and ours, at which offering those conquerors of the
world as men of God have each one his peculiar commemoration,
but no invocation at all. For the sacrifice is offered unto God,
though it be in memory of them; and he that offers it is a priest of
the Lord, and not of theirs; and the offering is 'the body of the
Lord,' which is not offered unto them, because they are that body
themselves. Whose miracles shall we then believe? Theirs that
would be accounted for gods by those to whom they show them;
or theirs which tend all to confirm our belief in one God, which is
Christ? Those that would have their filthiest acts held sacred; or
those that will not have their very virtues held sacred in respect of
their own glories, but referred unto His glory, who has imparted
such goodness unto them? Let us believe them that do both
work miracles, and teach the truth: for this latter gave them power
to perform the former. A chief point of this truth is this. Christ
rose again in the flesh, and showed the immortality of the resurrection in His own body, which He promised unto us in the end
of this world, or in the beginning of the next.

CHAPTER XI

Against the Platonists that oppose the elevation of the body up to heaven, by arguments of elementary ponderosity

AGAINST this promise do many ('whose thoughts God knoweth to be vain') make opposition out of the nature of elements; Plato (their master) teaching them that the two most contrary bodies of the world are combined by other two means, that is, by air and water. Therefore (say they) earth being lowest, water next, then air, and then the heaven, earth cannot possibly be contained in heaven, every element having its peculiar gravity, and tending naturally to its proper place. See with what vain, weak, and weightless arguments man's infirmity opposes God's omnipotency! Why then are there so many earthly bodies in the air, air being the third element from earth? Cannot He that gave birds (that are earthly bodies) feathers of power to sustain them in the air, give the like power to glorified and immortal bodies, to possess the heaven? Again, if this reason of theirs were true, all that cannot fly, would live under the earth, as fishes do in the water. Why then do not the earthly creatures live in the water, which is the next element unto earth, but in the air, which is the third? And seeing they belong to the earth, why does the next element above the earth presently choke them, and drown them, and the third feed and nourish them? Are the elements out of order here, or are their arguments out of reason? I will not stay here to make a rehearsal of what I spoke in the thirteenth book, of many terrene substances of great weight, as lead, iron, etc., which notwithstanding may have such a form given them, that they will swim, and support themselves upon the water. And cannot God Almighty give the body of man such a form likewise that it may ascend, and support itself in heaven? Let them stick to their method of elements (which is all their trust), yet can they not tell what to say to my former assertion. For earth is the lowest element, and then water and air successively, and heaven the fourth and highest, but the soul is a fifth essence above them all. Aristotle calls it a fifth body, and Plato says it is utterly incorporeal. If it were the fifth in order, then were it above the rest: but being incorporeal, it is much more above all substances corporal. What does it then in a lump of earth, it being the most subtle, and this the most gross essence; it being the most active, and this the most unwieldy! Cannot the excellency of it have power to lift this up? Hath the nature of the body power to draw down a soul from heaven, and shall not the soul have power to carry the body thither whence it came itself? And now if we should examine the miracles which they parallel with those of our martyrs, we should find proofs against themselves out of their own narratives.

One of their greatest ones is that which Varro reports of a vestal votaress, who being suspected of whoredom, filled a sieve with the water of the Tiber and carried it unto her judges, without spilling a drop. Who was it that kept the water in the sieve, so that not one drop passed through those thousand holes? Some god, or some devil, they must needs say. Well, if he were a god, is he greater than He that made the world? If then an inferior god, angel, or devil had this power to dispose thus of a heavy element, that the very nature of it seemed altered; cannot then the Almighty Maker of the whole world take away the ponderosity of earth, and give the quickened body an ability to dwell in the same place that the quickening spirit shall elect? And whereas they place the air between the fire above, and the water beneath, how comes it that we oftentimes find it between water and water, or between water and earth; for what will they make of those watery clouds, between which and the sea the air has an ordinary passage? What order of the elements does appoint that those floods of rain that fall upon the earth below the air, should first hang in the clouds above the air? And why is air in the midst between the heaven and the earth, if it were (as they say) to have the place between the heavens and the waters, as water is between it and the earth? And lastly, if the elements be so disposed that the two means, air and water, do combine the two extremes, fire and earth, heaven being in the highest place, and earth in the lowest as the world's foundation, and therefore (say they) unable to be in heaven; what do we then with fire here upon earth? For if this order of theirs be kept inviolate, then, as earth cannot have any place in fire, no more should fire have any in earth. As that which is lowest cannot remain aloft, no more should that which is aloft remain below. But we see this order reversed. We have fire both on the earth, and in the earth. The mountain tops give it up in abundance. Nay, more, we see that fire is produced out of earth, namely from wood, and stones. And what are these but earthly bodies? Yea, but the elementary fire (say they) is pure, hurtless, quiet, and eternal; and this of ours, turbulent, smoky, corrupting, and corruptible. Yet does it not corrupt nor hurt the hills wherein it burns perpetually, nor the hollows within ground, where it works most powerfully. It is not like the other indeed, but adapted unto the convenient use of man. But why then may we not believe that the nature of a corruptible body may be made incorruptible, and fit for heaven, as well as we see the elemental fire made corruptible, and fit for us? And so these arguments drawn from the sight and qualities of the elements can in no way diminish the power that Almighty God has to make man's body of a quality fit and able to inhabit the heavens.

CHAPTER XII

Against the infidels' calumnies cast out in scorn of the Christian's belief of the resurrection

BUT in their scrupulous inquiries touching this point they come against us with such scoffs as these: Shall the abortive births have any part in the resurrection? And seeing the Lord says, 'There shall not one hair of your head perish,' [1] shall all men be of one stature and bigness or no? If they be, how shall abortions (if they rise again) have that at the resurrection which they lacked at the first? Or if they do not rise again because they were never born but cast out, we may make the same doubt of infants, whether they shall have that bigness of body which they lacked when they died, for they you know are capable of regeneration, and therefore must have their part in the resurrection. And then these pagans ask us: 'What height and size shall men's bodies be then?' If they be as tall as ever was any man, then both little and many great ones shall lack that which they lacked here on earth; and whence shall they have it? But if that be true which St. Paul says, 'that we shall come to the measure of the age of the fullness of Christ,' [2] and again, 'He predestinated [them] to be made like to the image of His Son,' [3] implying that all the members of Christ's kingdom shall be like Him in shape and stature, then must many men (say they) forgo part of the stature which they had upon earth. And then where is that great protection of every hair, if there be such a diminution made of the stature and body? Besides, we make a question (say they) whether man shall arise with all the hair that ever the barber cut from his head. If he does, who will not loathe such an ugly sight; for so likewise must it follow that he have on all the parings of his nails? And where is then the comeliness, which ought in that immortality to be so far exceeding that of this world, while man is in corruption? But if he does not rise with all his hair, then it is lost, and where are your scriptures then? Then they proceed unto fatness and leanness. If all be alike (say they) then one shall not be fat and another lean. And so some must lose flesh, and some must gain: some must have what they lacked and some must leave what they had. Besides, as touching the putre-faction and dissolution of men's bodies, part going into dust, part into air, part into fire, part into the entrails of beasts and birds, part being drowned and dissolved into water—these accidents trouble them much, and make them think that such bodies can never gather to flesh again. Then pass they to deformities, as monstrous births, misshapen members, scars and suchlike; in-quiring with scoffs what forms these shall have in the resurrection. For if we say they shall be all taken away, then they come upon us

[1] Luke xxi. 18.   [2] Eph. iv. 13.   [3] Rom. viii. 29.

with our doctrine that Christ arose with His wounds upon Him still. But their most difficult question of all is: Whose flesh shall that man's be in the resurrection, which is eaten by another man through compulsion of hunger; for it is turned into his flesh that eats it, and fills the parts that famine had made hollow and lean? Shall therefore he have it again that owned it at first, or he that eats it and so owned it afterwards? These doubts are raised by the scorners of our faith in the resurrection, and they themselves do either assign men's souls for ever to a state never certain, but now wretched, and now blessed (as Plato does); or else with Porphyry they affirm that after many changes through different bodies the soul finds rest at last, being utterly separated from the body for ever.

CHAPTER XIII

Whether abortions belong not to the resurrection, if they belong to the dead

To all of these objections of theirs I mean by God's help to answer. And first, as touching abortions, which die after they are alive in the mother's womb, that such shall rise again, I dare neither affirm nor deny. Yet if they be reckoned amongst the dead, I see no reason to exclude them from the resurrection. For either all the dead shall not rise again, and the souls that had no bodies, saving in the mother's womb, shall continue bodiless for ever; or else all souls shall have their bodies again, including those whose bodies perished before the time of perfection. Whichsoever of these two be received for truth, that which we will now presently affirm concerning infants is to be understood of abortions also, if they have any part in the resurrection.

CHAPTER XIV

Whether infants shall rise again in the stature that they died in

Now as touching infants, I say they shall not rise again with that littleness of body in which they died, but that the sudden and strange power of God shall give them a stature of full growth. For our Saviour's words, 'There shall not one hair of our heads perish,'[1] do only promise them all that they had before, without excluding an addition of what they had not before. The dead infant lacked the perfection of his body's size (as every perfect infant lacks), that is, it was not come to the full height and bigness, which all are born to have, and have at their birth potentially (not actually);

[1] Luke xxi. 18.

as all the members of man are potentially in the generative seed, though the child may lack of them (as for example the teeth) when it is born. In this generative seed of every substance, that which is not apparent until afterwards lies (as one might say) wrapped up from the first origin of the said substance. And in this the infant may be said to be tall or short already, because he shall prove such hereafter. This same reason may secure us from all loss of body or part of body in the resurrection: for if we should then be made all alike, ever so tall or giantlike, yet such as were reduced from a taller stature unto that should lose no part of their body: for Christ has said, 'They shall not lose an hair.' And as for the means of addition, how can that wondrous Workman of the world lack fit substance to add where He thinks good?

CHAPTER XV

Whether all of the resurrection shall be of the stature of Christ

BUT Christ Himself arose in the same stature wherein He died: nor may we say that at the resurrection He shall put on any other height or bulk than that wherein He appeared unto His disciples after He was risen again, or that He will become as tall as any man ever was. Now if we say that all shall be made equal unto His stature, then must many, that were taller, lose part of their bodies against the express words of Christ. Every one therefore shall arise in that stature which he either had at his full man's state, or should have had, if he had not died before. As for St. Paul's words of the measure of the fullness of Christ, they either imply that all His members, as being then joined with Him their head, should make up the time's consummation; or if they apply to the resurrection, the meaning is that all should arise neither younger nor older, but just of that age whereat Christ Himself suffered and rose again. For the learned authors of this world say that at about thirty years man is in his full state, and from that time he declines to an age of more gravity and decay: and so the apostle says not, 'unto the measure of the body,' nor 'unto the measure of the stature,' but, 'unto the measure of the age of the fullness of Christ.'

CHAPTER XVI

What is meant by the conformation of the saints unto the image of the Son of God

AND whereas the apostle says that the predestinate shall be made like to the image of the Son of God, this may be understood of the inward man; for he says elsewhere: 'Fashion not yourselves like

unto this world, but be ye changed by the renewing of your mind.'
So then, when we are changed from being like the world, we are
made like unto the image of the Son of God.   Besides, we may take
it thus, that as He was made like us in mortality, so we should be
made like Him in immortality, and thus it is pertinent to the resurrection.   But if it concern the form of our rising again, then it
speaks (as the other passage does) only of the age of our bodies, not
of their size.   Wherefore all men shall arise in the stature that
they either were of or would have been of in their fullness of
man's estate: although indeed it is no matter what bodies they
have, whether of old men or of infants, the soul and body being
both absolute and without any infirmity.   And so if any one say that
every man shall rise again in the same stature wherein he died, it
is not an opinion that requires much opposition.

CHAPTER XVII

Whether women will retain their proper sex in the resurrection

THERE are some, who out of these words of St. Paul, 'Till we all
meet together in the unity of faith and knowledge of the Son of
God, unto a perfect man and unto the measure of the age of the
fullness of Jesus Christ,' [2] would prove that no woman shall retain
her sex in the resurrection, but all shall become men: for God (say
they) made man only of earth, and woman of man.   But I am
rather of their mind that hold a resurrection in both sexes, for
there shall be none of that lust, which caused man's confusion:
for as our first parents before their fall were both naked, and were
not ashamed, so at the latter day, the sin shall be taken away, and
yet nature still preserved.   The sex in woman is no corruption,
but natural; and it then shall be free from childbirth; nor shall the
female parts be any more powerful to stir up the lusts of the beholders (for all lust shall then be extinguished), but praise and glory
shall be given to God for creating what was not, and for freeing
that from corruption which He had created.   For in the beginning
when a rib was taken from Adam, being asleep, to make Eve, this
was a plain prophecy of Christ and the Church.   Adam's sleep
was Christ's death, from whose side being opened with a spear as
He hung upon the cross, came blood and water, the two sacraments whereby the Church is built up.   For the word of the text
is not *formavit*, nor *finxit*, but *Aedificavit eam in mulierem*,[3] 'He
built her up into a woman.'   So the apostle calls the Church, 'the
edification of the body of Christ.' [4]   The woman therefore was
God's creature as well as the man: but was made from man for
unity's sake, and in the manner thereof was a plain figure of Christ

[1] Rom. xii. 2.   [2] Eph. iv. 13.   [3] Gen. ii. 22.   [4] Eph. iv. 12.

and His Church. He therefore that made both sexes will raise them both to life. And Jesus Himself, being questioned by the Sadducees, that deny the resurrection, which of the seven brethren should have her to wife at the resurrection whom they had all had before, answered them saying, 'Ye are deceived, not knowing the scriptures nor the power of God.' And whereas He might have said (if it had been so), 'She whom you inquire of shall be a man at that day, and not a woman,' He said no such matter, but only this: In the resurrection they neither marry wives, nor are wives bestowed in marriage, but are as the angels of God in heaven.' [1] That is, they are like them in felicity, not in flesh; nor in their resurrection, which the angels need not, because they cannot die. And so Christ does not deny that there shall be women at the resurrection, but only marriage: whereas if there had been none of the female sex, He might have answered the Sadducees more easily by saying so; but He affirmed that there should be both sexes, in these words: 'They neither marry wives,' that is, men do not marry; 'nor wives are bestowed in marriage,' that is, women are not married; so that there shall be there both such as ordinarily marry and such as are ordinarily married here in this world.

CHAPTER XVIII

Of Christ, the perfect Man, and the Church, His body and fullness

Now touching St. Paul's words, 'Till we all meet together, etc., into a perfect man,' we are to observe the circumstances of the whole speech, which is this: 'He that descended is even the same that ascended far above all heavens that He might fill all things. He therefore gave some to be apostles, and some prophets, and some evangelists, and some pastors and teachers, for the gathering together of the saints, and for the work of the ministry, and for the edification of the body of Christ, till we all meet together in the unity of faith and knowledge of the Son of God, unto a perfect man and unto the measure of the age of the fullness of Christ; that we may henceforth be no more children, wavering and carried about with every wind of doctrine, by the deceit of men, and with craftiness, whereby they lie in wait to deceive; but let us follow the truth in love, and in all things grow up into Him, which is the Head, that is, Christ, by whom all the body being coupled and knit together by every joint, for the furniture thereof, according to the effectual power which is in the measure of every part, receiveth increase of the body unto the edifying of itself in love.' [2]   Behold here the perfect man, head and body, consisting of all members, which shall be complete in due time.   But as yet the body increases

[1] Matt. xxii. 29, 30.   [2] Eph. iv. 10–16.

daily in members, as the Church enlarges, to which it is said: 'Ye are the body of Christ, and members one of another': [1] and again 'for His body's sake, which is the Church': [2] and in another place 'For we being many, are one bread and one body.' [3] Of the edification whereof you hear what St. Paul says here: 'For the gathering together of the saints, and for the work of the ministry, and for the edification of the body of Christ.' And then he adds that which all this concerns: 'Till we all meet together,' etc., 'unto the measure of the age of the fullness of Christ.' And unto what body the measure pertains, he shows, saying: 'Let us in all things grow up into Him which is the Head, that is Christ, by whom all the body,' etc.

And so both the measure of the whole body, and of each part therein, is this measure of fullness whereof the apostle speaks here, and also elsewhere, saying of Christ: 'He hath given Him to be the Head over all the Church, which is His body, the fullness of Him, who filleth all in all.' [4] But if this belong to the form of the resurrection, why may we not imagine woman to be included be man, as in that verse, 'Blessed is the man that feareth the Lord,' which giveth the same blessing also to such women as fear Him?

CHAPTER XIX

That our bodies in the resurrection shall have no imperfection at all, whatsoever they have had during this life, but shall be perfect both in quantity and quality

Now what shall I say concerning man's hair and nails? Understand that then no part of the body shall perish, yet no deformity shall abide; and this implies that such parts as do procure those deformities shall be resident only in the whole lump, not in any part where they may offend the eye. As for example, if you make a pot of clay, mar it, and make it again; it is not necessary that the clay which was in the handle before should be in the handle now again, and so on with the bottom and other parts; but only that it is the same clay as it was before.

Wherefore the cut hair and nails shall not return to deform their places, yet shall they not perish, but have their congruent place in the same flesh from whence they had their being: although our Saviour's words may rather be understood of the number of our hairs than the length, whereupon He says elsewhere: 'All the hairs of your head are numbered.' [6] In saying this I do not imply that any essential part of the body shall perish, but that that which arises out of deformity, and shows the wretched state of mortality, shall so return that the substance shall be there, and the deformity

---

[1] 1 Cor. xii. 27.   [2] Col. i. 24.   [3] 1 Cor. x. 17.   [4] Eph. i. 22, 23.
[5] Ps. cxii. 1.   [6] Luke xii. 7.

one. For if an image maker, having for some purpose made a deformed statue, can mould or cast it new and comely, with the same substance of matter, and yet without all the former mis-shapedness, neither cutting away any of the exorbitant parts that deformed the whole, nor using any other means but only the new casting of his metal or moulding of his material; what shall we think of the Almighty Moulder of the whole world? Cannot He then take away men's deformities of body, common or extraordinary (being only notes of our present misery, and far excluded from our future bliss), as well as a common statuary can re-form a mis-shapen statue of stone, wood, clay, or metal? Wherefore the fat or the lean need never fear to be such hereafter, as, if they could choose, they would not be now.

For all bodily beauty is a good congruence in the members, joined with a pleasing colour. And where there is not congruence, there is evermore dislike, either by reason of superfluity or defect. Wherefore there shall be no cause of dislike through incongruence of parts, where the deformed ones are re-formed, the defects supplied, and the excesses fitly proportioned. And for colour, how glorious will it be! 'The just shall shine as the sun in the kingdom of their Father.'[1] And this lustre was rather hidden from the apostles' eyes at Christ's resurrection, than lacking in His body; for man's weak eyes could not have endured it, and Christ's object was rather to make them to know Him than to show them His glory, as He manifested by letting them touch His wounds, by eating, and drinking with them, which He did not for any need of meat or sustenance, but because He had power to do it. And when a thing is present thus and not seen with other things that are present and seen (as this glory was unseen being with His person, which was seen), this in Greek is called ἀορασία, while the Latins translate it in Genesis, caecitas, blindness. The Sodomites were smitten with it, when they sought Lot's door, and could not find it, but if it had been direct blindness, they would rather have sought for guides to lead them home, than for this door which they could not find.

CHAPTER XX

That every man's body, however dispersed here, shall be restored him perfect at the resurrection

OUR love unto the martyrs is of that nature that we desire to behold the scars of their wounds (borne for the name of Christ) even in their glorification, and perhaps so we shall. For they will not deform, but grace them then, and give out a lustre of their virtue, not bodily, albeit in the body. But if any of them lost any member

[1] Matt. xiii. 43.

for his Saviour, surely he shall not lack that in the resurrection
for unto such was it said, 'Not an hair of your heads shall perish.'

But if Christ's pleasure be to make their scars apparent in the
world to come, then shall those members also that were cut of
have visible marks in the place whence they were cut, and when
they are re-joined; for although all their miserable hurts shall not
be there visible, yet there shall be some, which nevertheless shall
be no more called hurts, but honours. And far be it from us to
think God's power insufficient to re-collect and unite every atom
of the body, were it burnt, or torn by beasts, or fallen to dust, or
dissolved into moisture, or exhaled into air. God forbid that any
corner of nature (though it may be unknown to us) should lie hid
from the eye and power of the Almighty. Tully (their great
author) going about to define God, as well as he could, affirmed
Him to be 'mens soluta et libera, secreta ab omni concretione
mortali, omnia sentiens et movens ipsaque motu praedita sempi-
terno,' [1] 'a free and unbounded intellect, separate from all mortal
composition, moving and knowing all things and moving eternally in Himself.' This he found in the great philosophers.
So then to speak in accordance with their definition, what can lie
hid from Him that knows all? What can avoid His power that
moves all? And now may we answer the doubt that seems most
difficult, that is: Whose flesh shall that man's be at the resurrection
which another man eats? Ancient stories and late experience
have lamentably informed us, that this has often come to pass that
one man has eaten another: in which case none will say that all
the flesh went quite through the body, and that none was turned
into nutriment, for the meagre places, becoming by this mean
alone more full and fleshy, do prove the contrary. Now then my
premisses shall serve to resolve this ambiguity.

The flesh of the famished man that hunger consumed is exhaled
into air, and thence (as we said before) the Creator can fetch it
again. This flesh therefore of the man that was eaten, shall return
to the first owner, of whom the famished man does but as it were
borrow it, and so must repay it again. And his own flesh which
famine dried up into air shall be re-collected and restored into
some convenient place of his body; and even if it were so consumed
that no part thereof remained in nature, yet God could fetch it
again in an instant, and when He would Himself. But seeing
that the very hairs of our head are secured us, it were absurd to
imagine that famine should have the power to deprive us of so
much of our flesh.

These things being duly considered, this is the sum of it all, that
in the resurrection every man shall arise with the same body that
he had, or would have had in his fullest growth, in all comeliness,
and without deformity of any even the least member. To pre-

[1] *Tusc. Disp.* i. 27, 66.

serve this comeliness, if somewhat be taken from any unshapely part, and decently disposed of amongst the rest (that it be not lost, and withal, that the congruence be observed) we may without absurdity believe that there may be some addition unto the stature of the body; the inconvenience that was visible in one part being invisibly distributed amongst the rest and so annihilated. If any one avow precisely that every man shall arise in the proper stature of his growth which he had when he died, we do not oppose it, so long as he grant us an utter abolishing of all deformity, dullness, and corruptibility of the said form and stature, as things that befit not that kingdom, wherein the sons of promise shall be equal to the angels of God, if not in their bodies, nor ages, yet in absolute perfection and beatitude.

CHAPTER XXI

What new and spiritual bodies shall be given unto the saints

EVERY part therefore of the bodies, perishing either in death or after it, in the grave or wheresoever, shall be restored, renewed, and from a natural and corruptible body it shall become immortal, spiritual, and incorruptible. Be it all made into powder and dust, by chance or cruelty, or dissolved into air or water, so that no part remain undispersed, yet shall it not, yet can it not be kept hidden from the omnipotency of the Creator, who will not have one hair of the head to perish. Thus shall the spiritual flesh become subject to the spirit, yet shall it be flesh still, as the carnal spirit before was subject to the flesh, and yet a spirit still.

A proof of this we have in the deformity of our penal estate. For they were carnal in respect of the spirit indeed (not merely of the flesh) to whom St. Paul said: 'I could not speak unto you as unto spiritual men, but as unto carnal.'[1] So man in this life is called spiritual, though he be carnal still, and have a law in his members rebelling against the law of his mind. But he shall be spiritual in body, when he rises again, 'so that it is sown a natural body, but raised a spiritual body,'[2] as the said apostle says. But of the measure of this spiritual grace, what and how great it shall be in the body, I fear to determine: for it were rashness to go about it.

But seeing we may not conceal the joy of our hope, for the glorifying of God, and seeing that it was said from the very bowels of divine rapture, 'Lord, I have loved the habitation of Thine house!'[3] we may by God's help make a conjecture from the goods imparted to us in this transitory life, how great the glories shall be that we shall receive in the other, which as yet we neither have

[1] 1 Cor iii. 1.   [2] 1 Cor. xv. 44.   [3] Ps. xxvi. 8.

tried, nor can in any way truly describe. I omit man's estate before
his fall, our first parents' happiness in the fertile paradise, which
was so short, that their offspring had no taste of it. Who is he
that can express the boundless mercies of God shown unto mankind, even in this life that we all experience, and wherein we
suffer temptations, or rather a continual temptation (be we never
so vigilant) all the time that we enjoy it?

CHAPTER XXII

*Of man's miseries drawn upon him by his first parents, and taken away
from him only by Christ's merits and gracious goodness*

CONCERNING man's first origin, our present life (if such a miserable
estate can be called a life) does sufficiently prove that all his
children were condemned in him.   What else does that horrid gulf
of ignorance confirm, whence all error has birth, and wherein all the
sons of Adam are so deeply drenched, that none can be freed without toil, fear, and sorrow?   What else does our love of vanities
affirm, whence there arises such a tempest of cares, sorrows, re-
pinings, fears, mad exultations, discords, altercations, wars, trea-
sons, furies, hates, deceits, flatteries, thefts, rapines, perjuries,
pride, ambition, envy, murder, parricide, cruelty, villainy, luxury,
impudence, unchastity, fornications, adulteries, incests, several
sorts of sins against nature (filthy even to be named), sacrilege,
heresy, blasphemy, oppression, calumnies, circumventions, deceits, false witnesses, false judgments, violence, robberies, and
suchlike out of my remembrance to reckon, but not excluded from
the life of man?   All these evils are belonging to man, and arise
out of the root of that error and perverse affection which every son
of Adam brings into the world with him.   For who does not know
in what a mist of ignorance (as we see in infants) and with what a
crew of vain desires (as we see in boys) all mankind enters this
world, so that if man were left unto his own election, he would fall
into most of the aforesaid mischiefs?

But the hand of God bearing a rein upon our condemned souls,
and pouring out His mercies upon us (not shutting them up in
displeasure), law and instruction were revealed unto the capacity
of man, to awake us out of those lethargies of ignorance, and to
withstand those former incursions, which notwithstanding is not
done without great toil and trouble.   For what imply those fears
whereby we keep little children in order?   What do teachers,
rods, the strap, thongs, and suchlike, but confirm this?   And that
discipline of the scriptures that says that our sons must be beaten
on the sides while they are children, lest they wax stubborn, and
either past or very near past reformation—what is the end of all

these, but to abolish ignorance, and to bridle corruption, both of which we come wrapped into the world withal? What is our labour to remember things, our labour to learn, and our ignorance without this labour; our agility got by toil, and our dullness if we neglect it? Does it not all declare the promptness of our nature (in itself) unto all viciousness, and the care that must be had in reclaiming it? Sloth, dullness, and negligence are all vices that avoid labour, and yet labour itself is but a profitable pain.

But to omit the pains that enforce children to learn the (scarcely useful) books that please their parents, how huge a band of pains attend the firmer state of man, and are not peculiarly inflicted on the wicked, but generally impendent over us all, through our common estate in misery! Who can recount them, who can conceive them? What fears, what calamities do the loss of children, of goods or of credit, the false dealing of others, false suspicion, open violence, and all other mischiefs inflicted by others, heap upon the heart of man; being generally accompanied by poverty, imprisonment, bonds, banishments, tortures, loss of limbs or senses, prostitution to beastly lust, and other such horrid events! So are we afflicted on the other side with chances *ab externo*, with cold, heat, storms, showers, deluges, lightning, thunder, earthquakes, falls of houses, fury of beasts, poisons of airs, waters, plants, and beasts of a thousand sorts, stinging of serpents, biting of mad dogs, a strange accident, wherein a beast most sociable and familiar with man shall sometimes become more to be feared than a lion or a dragon, infecting him whom he bites with such a furious madness, that he is to be feared by his family worse than any wild beast. What misery do navigators now and then endure, or travellers by land! What man can walk anywhere free from sudden accidents? One coming home from the court (being sound enough on his feet) fell down, broke his leg, and died of it. Who would have thought this that had seen him sitting in the court? Eli the priest fell from his chair where he sat, and broke his neck. What fears are husbandmen, yea, all men subject unto, lest the fruits should be hurt by the heavens, or earth, or caterpillars, or locusts or other such pernicious things! Yet when they have gathered them and laid them up, they are secure: notwithstanding I have known granaries full of corn borne quite away with an inundation.

Who can be secure by his own innocency against the innumerable incursions of the devils, when we see that they do sometimes afflict little baptized infants (who are as innocent as can be) and (by the permission of God) even upon their harmless bodies do show us the miseries of this life, and incite us all to labour for the bliss of the life to come? Besides, how subject is man's body to diseases, more than physic can either cure or comprehend! And in most of these, we see how offensive the very medicines are that cure them, and even the very meat we eat during the time of the malady's domination. Has not extremity of heat made man to drink his own urine, and others' too? Has not hunger enforced man to eat man, and to kill one another to make meat of; and even the mother to massacre and devour her own child? Nay, is not our very sleep (which we term rest) sometimes so fraught with disquiet, that it disturbs the soul, and all her powers at once, by the appearance of such horrid terrors to the fantasy, and with such a reality that she cannot discern them from true terrors? This is ordinary in some diseases. Moreover the deceitful fiends sometimes will so delude the eye of a healthy man with such apparitions, that although they make no further impression into him, yet they persuade the sense that they are truly so as they seem; and the devil's desire is ever to deceive. From all these miserable engagements (representing a kind of hell on earth) we are freed only by the grace of Jesus Christ. For this is His name; Jesus is a Saviour, and He it is that will save us from a worse life, or rather a perpetual death, after this life: for although we have many and great comforts by the saints in this life, yet the benefits hereof are not given at every one's request, lest we should apply our faith unto those transitory respects, whereas it rather concerns the purchase of a life which shall be absolutely free from all inconvenience. And the more faithful one is in this life, the greater confirmation has he from grace, to endure those miseries without fainting, whereunto the pagan authors refer their true philosophy, which their gods, as Tully says, revealed unto some few of them. 'There was never,' says he, 'nor could there be a greater gift given unto man, than this.'[1] Thus our adversaries are fain to confess that true philosophy is a divine gift: which being (as they confess) the only help against our human miseries, and coming from above as a gift to a few, it appears that all mankind was condemned to suffer miseries. But as they confess that this help was the greatest gift that God ever gave, so do we avow and believe that it was given by no other god but Him to whom even the worshippers of many gods give the pre-eminence.

CHAPTER XXIII

Of accidents, severed from the common estate of man, and peculiar only to the just and righteous

BESIDES those calamities that lie generally upon all, the righteous have a peculiar labour to resist vice, and to be continually in combat with dangerous temptations. The flesh is sometimes furious, sometimes remiss, but always rebellious against the spirit, and the spirit has the same sorts of conflict against the flesh, so that we

[1] *Acad. Post.* i. 2, 4.

cannot do as we would, or expel all concupiscence; but we strive (by the help of God) to suppress it by not consenting, and to curb it as well as we can by a continual vigilance, lest we should be deceived by appearances or subtleties, or involved in errors; lest we should take good for evil and evil for good; lest fear should hold us from what we should do, and desire entice us to do what we should not; lest the sun should set upon our anger; lest enmity should make us return mischief for mischief; lest ingratitude should make us forget our benefactors; lest evil reports should molest our good conscience; lest our rash suspicion of others should deceive us, or others' false suspicion of us deject us; lest sin should bring our bodies to obey it; lest our members should be given up as weapons to sin; lest our eye should follow our appetite; lest desire of revenge should draw us to impropriety; lest our sight or our thought should stay too long upon a sinful delight; lest we should give willing ear to evil and indecent talk; lest our lust should become our law; and lest we ourselves in this dangerous conflict should either hope to win the victory by our own strength, or having gotten it should give the glory to ourselves, and not to His grace of whom St. Paul says: 'Thanks be unto God, who hath given us the victory through our Lord Jesus Christ': [1] and elsewhere: 'In all these things we are more than conquerors through Him that loved us.' [2]

But yet we are to know this, that stand we never so strong against sin, or subdue it never so much, yet, as long as we are mortal, we have cause every day to say: 'Forgive us our trespasses.' But when we ascend into that kingdom where immortality dwells, we shall neither have wars wherein to fight, nor trespasses to pray for; nor should we have had any here below, if our natures had kept the gifts of their first creation. And therefore these conflicts, wherein we are endangered, and whence we desire (by a final victory) freedom, are part of those miseries wherewith the life of man is continually molested.

CHAPTER XXIV

Of the good things that God has bestowed upon this miserable life of ours

Now let us see what good things the great Creator has bestowed in His mercy upon this life of ours made miserable by His justice. The first was that blessing before our parents' fall: 'Increase and multiply, fill the earth,' [3] etc. And this He revoked not, for all that they sinned, but left the gift of fruitfulness to their condemned offspring: nor could their crime abolish that power of the seed-producing seed inherent, and, as it were, woven up in the bodies

[1] 1 Cor. xv. 57.   [2] Rom. viii. 37.   [3] Gen. i. 28.

of man and woman; unto which nevertheless death was annexed, so that in one and the same current (as it were) of mankind ran both the evil merited by the parent, and the good bestowed by the Creator. In this original evil lies sin, and punishment; and in this original good lies propagation, and conformation or identity of species. But of those evils, the one whereof (sin) came from our own audaciousness, and the other (punishment) from the judgment of God, we have said sufficient already.

This book is for the goods which God has given and still gives to the condemned state of man. In this condemnation of his, God took not all from him that He had given him (for so he would have ceased to have had any being), nor did He resign His power over him, when He gave him thrall to the devil, for the devil himself is His thrall. He is cause of his subsistence. He, that is solely and absolutely essential and gives all things essence under Him, gave the devil his being also.

Of these two good things therefore, which we said that His almighty goodness had allowed our nature (however depraved and cursed), He gave the first (propagation) as a blessing in the beginning of His works from which He rested the seventh day. The second (conformation) He gives as yet unto every work which He as yet effects. For if He should but withhold His efficient power from the creatures of the earth, they could neither increase to any further perfection, nor continue in the state wherein He should leave them. So then God creating man gave him a power to propagate others, and to allow them a power of propagation also; and though God can deprive those individuals of it, whom He pleases, yet is He under necessity, for it was His gift unto the first parents of mankind, and He, having once given it, has not taken it any more away from all mankind.

But although sin did not abolish this propagation, yet it made it far less than it had been if sin had not been. For man being in honour, understood not, and so was compared unto beasts, begetting suchlike as himself:[1] yet has he a little spark left him of that reason whereby he was like the image of God. Now if this propagation should lack conformation, nature could keep no form nor similitude in her several productions. For if man and woman had not had copulation, and God had nevertheless willed to have filled the earth with men, as He made Adam without generation of man or woman, so could He have made all the rest. But man and women by coupling cannot beget unless He create. For as St. Paul says in a spiritual sense, touching man's conformation in righteousness: 'Neither is he that planteth anything, nor he that watereth, but God that giveth the increase':[2] so may we say here: Neither is he that sows anything, nor she that conceives, but God that gives the form.

---

[1] Ps. xlix. 12.   [2] 1 Cor. iii. 7.

It is His daily work that the seed unfolds itself out of a secret fold as it were, and brings the potential forms into such actual comeliness. It is He that makes that strange combination of a nature incorporeal (the ruler) and a nature corporal (the subject) by which the whole becomes a living creature. It is a work so admirable, that it is able to amaze the mind, and force praise to the Creator from it, being observed not only in man, whose reason gives him excellence above all other creatures; but even in the least fly that is one may behold this wondrous and stupendous combination! It is He that has given man's spirit an apprehension (which seems, together with reason, to lie dead in an infant, until years bring it to use) whereby he has a power to conceive knowledge, discipline, and all habits of truth and good quality, and by which he may extract the understanding of all the virtues, of prudence, justice, fortitude, and temperance, to be thereby the better armed against viciousness, and incited to subdue them by the contemplation of that high and unchangeable goodness: which height although it do not attain unto, yet who can sufficiently declare how great a good it is, and how wonderful a work of the Highest, being considered in other respects? For besides the disciplines of good behaviour, and the ways to eternal happiness (which are called virtues), and besides the grace of God which is in Jesus Christ, imparted only to the sons of the promise, man's invention has brought forth so many and such rare sciences and arts (partly necessary, and partly voluntary) that the excellency of his capacity makes the rare goodness of his creation apparent, even then when he goes about things that are either superfluous or pernicious, and shows from what an excellent gift he has those inventions and practices of his. What varieties has man found out in buildings, attires, husbandry, navigation, sculpture, and painting! What perfection has he shown in the shows of theatres, in taming, killing, and catching wild beasts! What millions of inventions has he against others, and for himself in poisons, arms, engines, stratagems, and such like! What thousands of medicines for the health, of meats for the palate, of means and figures to persuade, of eloquent phrases to delight, of verses for pleasure, of musical inventions and instruments! How excellent inventions are geography, arithmetic, astrology, and the rest! How large is the capacity of man, if we should dwell upon particulars! Lastly, how cunningly and with what exquisite wit have the philosophers and the heretics defended their very errors—it is strange to imagine! For here we speak of the nature of man's soul in general as man is mortal, without any reference to the way of truth whereby he comes to the life eternal.

Now, therefore, seeing that the true and only God, that rules all in His almighty power and justice, was the Creator of this excellent essence Himself; doubtless man had never fallen into such

misery (which many shall never be freed from, and some shall) if
the sin of those that first incurred it had not been extremely
malicious. Come now to the body. Though it be mortal as the
beasts are, and more weak than many of theirs are, yet mark what
great goodness and providence is shown herein by God Almighty.
Are not all the sinews and members disposed in such fit places,
and the whole body so composed, as if one would say: 'Such a
habitation is fittest for a spirit of reason'? You see the other
creatures have a grovelling posture, and look towards earth,
whereas man's upright form bids him continually look to the
things in heaven. The nimbleness of his tongue and hand in
speaking and writing, and working in trades, what does it but
declare the excellency of that, for whose use they were made so?
Yet (excluding its adaptation for work) the very congruence and
symmetry of the parts do so concur, that one cannot discern
whether man's body were made more for use, or for comeliness.
For there is no part of use in man, that has not the proper decorum,
as we should better discern, if we knew the numbers of the pro-
portions wherein each part is combined to the others, which we may
perhaps come to learn by those that are apparent. As for the rest
that are not seen, as the courses of the veins, sinews, and arteries,
and the secrets of the vital parts, we cannot come to know their
numbers: for, though some butcherly surgeons (anatomists they
call them) have often cut up dead men (and live men sometimes)
to learn the secret of man's inward parts, and which way to make
incisions, and to effect their cures: yet those members whereof I
speak, and whereof the harmony and proportion of man's whole
body consists, no man could ever find, or durst ever undertake
to inquire; which if they could be known we should find more
reason and pleasing contemplation in the forming of the interior
parts, than we can observe or collect from those that lie open to
the eye. There are some parts of the body that concern decorum
only, and are of no use. Such are the paps on the breasts of men,
and the beard, which is no strengthening, but an ornament to the
face, as the naked chins of women (which being weaker, should
otherwise have had this strengthening also) do plainly declare.
Now if there be no exterior part of man that is useful which is not
also comely, and if there be also parts in man that are comely and
not useful, then God in the framing of man's body had a greater
respect of dignity than of necessity. For necessity shall cease;
the time shall come when we shall do nothing but enjoy one
another's beauty without lust, for which we must especially glorify
Him, to whom the psalm says: 'Thou hast put on praise and comeliness.' [1] And then for the beauty and use of other creatures,
which God has set before the eyes of man (though as yet miserable
and amongst miseries)—what man is able to recount them? The

[1] Ps. civ. 1.

universal gracefulness of the heavens, the earth, and the sea, the brightness of the light in the sun, moon, and stars, the shades of the woods, the colours and smells of flowers, the numbers of birds, and their varied hues and songs, the many forms of beasts and fishes, whereof the least are the rarest (for the fabric of the bee or ant is more to be wondered at than the whales); and the strange alterations in the colour of the sea (as though in several garments), now one green, then another, now blue, then purple—how pleasing a sight sometimes it is to see it rough, and how much more pleasing when it is calm! And oh, what a hand is that, that gives so many meats to assuage hunger, so many tastes to those meats (without help of cook), and so many medicinal powers to those tastes! How delightful is the interchange of day and night, the temperateness of the air, and the works of nature in the barks of trees and skins of beasts! Oh, who can enumerate the particulars? How tedious should I be in every particular of these few, that I have here as it were heaped together, if I should dwell upon them one by one! Yet are all these but solaces of man's miseries, in no way pertinent to his glories.

What are they then that his bliss shall give him, if his misery has such blessings as these? What will God give them whom He has predestinated unto life, having given such great things even to them whom He has predestinated unto death? What will He give them in His kingdom, for whom He sent His only Son to suffer all injuries, even to death, upon earth? Whereupon St. Paul says unto them: 'He who spared not His own Son, but gave Him for us all unto death, how shall He not with Him give us all things also?' [1] When this promise is fulfilled, oh, what shall we be then? How glorious shall the soul of man be, without any stain and sin that can either subdue or oppose it, or against which it need to contend; perfect in all virtue, and enthroned in all perfection of peace!

How great, how delightful, how true, shall our knowledge of all things be there, without any error, without any labour, where we shall drink at the spring-head of God's wisdom, without any difficulty, and in all felicity! How perfect shall our bodies be, being wholly subject unto their spirits, and thereby sufficiently quickened and nourished without any other sustenance; for they shall now be no more natural, but spiritual, and shall have the substance of flesh quite exempt from all fleshly corruption!

CHAPTER XXV

Of the obstinacy of some few in denying the resurrection, which the whole world believes, as it was foretold

BUT as touching the good things of the mind, which the blessed shall enjoy after this life, the philosophers and we are both of one

[1] Rom. viii. 32.

mind.   Our difference is concerning the resurrection, which they
deny with all the power they have : but the increase of the believers
has left us but a few oppressors; Christ (that disproved the
obstinate even in His own body) gathering all unto His faith,
learned and unlearned, wise and simple.   The world believed
God's promise in this, who promised also that it should believe
this.   It was not Peter's magic that wrought it, but it was that
God, of whom (as I have said often, and as Porphyry confesses
from their own oracles) all their gods do stand in awe and dread.
Porphyry calls Him 'God the Father, and King of Gods': but
God forbid that we should believe His promises as they do, that
will not believe what He had promised that the world should
believe.   For why should we not rather believe as the world does,
and as it was prophesied it should, and leave them to their own idle
talk that will not believe this, that the world was promised to
believe?   For if they say we must take it in another sense, because
they will not do that God, whom they have commended, so much
injury as to say His scriptures are idle things; yet surely they injure
Him as much, or more, in saying they must be understood otherwise than the world understands them, namely, as God both
promised and performed.   Why cannot God raise the flesh unto
eternal life?   Is it a work unworthy of God?   Touching His
omnipotence, whereby He works so many wonders, I have said
enough already.   If they wish to know a thing which He cannot
do, I will tell them He cannot lie.   Let us therefore believe only
what He can do, and not believe what He cannot.   If they do not
then believe that He can lie, let them believe that He will do what
He promises.   And let them believe as the world believes, which
He promised should believe, and whose belief He both produced
and praised.   And how prove they the work of the resurrection to be
in any way unworthy of God?   There shall be no corruption therein, and that is all the evil that can befall the body.   Of the order
of the elements we have spoken already, as also of the possibility
of the swift motion of the incorruptible body.   Of man's bodily
health in this world, and the weakness of it in comparison with
immortality, I think our thirteenth book contains what will satisfy.
Let such as have not read this book or do not remember what they
have read read the passages of this present volume already recorded.

CHAPTER XXVI

*That Porphyry's opinion that the blessed souls should have no bodies,
is confuted by Plato himself, who says that the Creator promised the
inferior deities that they should never lose their bodies*

YEA, but (says Porphyry) a blessed soul must have no body; so
that the body's incorruptibility is nothing worth, if the soul cannot
be blessed unless it is without a body.   But hereof we have

sufficiently argued in the thirteenth book; and here I will rehearse
but one thing only.   If this were true, then Plato their great master
must reform his books, and say that the gods must go and leave
their bodies; for he says they all have celestial bodies, that is, they
must die, ere they can be blessed; but He that has made them,
promised them immortality and an eternal dwelling in their bodies,
to assure them of their bliss; and this should come from His
powerful will, not from their natures.   The same Plato in the same
place overthrows their reason that say there shall be no resurrection,
because it is impossible; for God, the uncreated Maker of the other
gods, promising them eternity, says plainly that He will do a
thing which is impossible.   For thus (says Plato) He said unto
them: 'Because you are created, you cannot but be mortal and
dissoluble, yet shall you never die, nor be dissolved; nor shall fate
control my will, which is a greater bond for your perpetuity than
all those whereby you are composed.'   No man that heareth this
(be he never so doltish, so he be not deaf) will make any question
that this was an impossibility which Plato's Creator promised the
deities which he had made.   For saying, 'You cannot be eternal,
yet by my will you shall be eternal,' what is it but to say, 'My will
shall make you a thing impossible'?   He therefore, that (as Plato
says) did promise to effect this impossibility, will also raise the
flesh in an incorruptible, spiritual, and immortal quality.   Why do
they now cry out that that is impossible which God has promised,
which the world has believed, and which it was promised it should
believe, seeing that Plato himself is of our mind, and says that God
can work impossibilities?   Therefore it must not be the lack of a
body, but the possession of one utterly incorruptible, that the soul
shall be blessed in.   And what body shall be so fit for their joy,
as that wherein (while it was corruptible) they endured such woe?
They shall not then be plagued with that desire that Virgil relates
out of Plato, saying:

> Rursus et incipiant in corpora velle reverti.[1]
>
> Now 'gan they wish to live on earth again.

I mean, when they have their bodies that they desired, they shall
no more desire any bodies; but shall possess those for ever, without
being ever severed from them so much as one moment.

CHAPTER XXVII

*Contradictions between Plato and Porphyry, wherein, if either should
yield unto other, both should find out the truth*

PLATO and Porphyry held diverse opinions, which if they could have
come to reconcile, they might perhaps have proved Christians.
Plato said that the soul could not be always without a body, but

[1] *Aen.* vi. 751.

that the souls of the wisest at length should return into bodies
again. Porphyry said that when the purged soul ascendeth to
the Father, it returns no more to the infection of this world. Now
if Plato had communicated unto Porphyry, that the soul's return
should be only into a human body: and Porphyry unto Plato, that
the soul should never return unto the miseries of a corruptible
body—if both of them jointly had held both these positions, I
think it would have followed, both that the souls should return
into bodies, and also into such bodies as were befitting them for
eternal felicity. For Plato says: 'The holy souls shall return to
human bodies'; and Porphyry says: 'The holy souls shall not return
to the evils of this world.' Let Porphyry therefore say with Plato:
'They shall return unto bodies,' and Plato with Porphyry: 'They
shall not return unto evils'; and then they shall both say: 'They
shall return unto such bodies as shall not molest them with any
evils, namely those wherein God has promised that the blessed
souls should have their eternal dwellings.' For this I think they
would both grant us; that if they confessed a return of the souls
of the just into immortal bodies, it should be into those wherein
they suffered the miseries of this world, and wherein they served
God so faithfully, that they obtained an everlasting delivery from
all future calamities.

CHAPTER XXVIII

*What either Plato, Labeo, or Varro might have contributed to the true
faith of the resurrection, if there had been harmony in their
opinions*

SOME of us liking and loving Plato for a certain eloquent and excellent kind of speaking, and because his opinion has been true in
some things, say that he thought something like unto that which
we do, concerning the resurrection of the dead. Tully, however,
in referring to this in his *De Re Publica*,[1] affirms that Plato rather
spake in sport, than that he had any intent to relate it as a matter
of truth. For he speaks of a man who revived, and related some
things agreeable to Plato's disputations. Labeo also says, that
there were two which died both in one day, and that they met
together in a crossway, and that afterwards they were commanded to
return again to their bodies; and then that they decreed to live in
perpetual love together, and that it was so until they died again.
Now these authors have declared that there has been such a
resurrection of body as they have had, whom truly we have known
to have risen again and to have been restored to this life; but they
do not declare it in the sense that they should not die again. Yet
Marcus Varro records a more strange, admirable, and wonderful

---

[1] *De Re Publ.* x, p. 614.

matter, in his books which he wrote *Of the Race of the Roman People.* I have thought good to set down his own words. 'Certain *genethliaci* (wizards) have written,' says he, 'that there is a regeneration, or second birth in men to be born again, which the Greeks call παλιγγενεσία. They have written that it is brought to pass and effected in the space of four hundred and forty years; so that the same body and soul which had been aforetime knit together, should return again into the same conjunction and union they had before.' Truly this Varro or those *genethliaci* (I know not who they are; for he has related their opinion concealing their names) have said something, which although it be false, because the souls returning into the bodies, which they have before managed, will never after forsake them; yet it serves to stop the mouth of those babblers, and to overthrow the stronghold of many arguments about the impossibility of resurrection. For they do not think it an impossible thing, who have thought about these things, that dead bodies resolved into air, dust, ashes, fluids, bodies of devouring beasts, or of men themselves, should return again to that which they have been. Wherefore let Plato and Porphyry, or such rather as do follow them and are now living, if they agree with us, that holy souls shall return to their bodies as Plato says, but not return to any evils as Porphyry says, and that that sequel may follow, which our Christian faith does declare, to wit, that they shall receive such bodies, as they shall live happily in eternally without any evil—let them (I say) assume and take this also from Varro, that they will return to the same bodies in which they had been aforetime. And then there shall be a sweet harmony between them concerning the resurrection of the flesh eternally.

CHAPTER XXIX

Of the quality of the vision, with which the saints shall see God in the world to come

Now let us see so far forth as the Lord shall vouchsafe to enable us, what the saints shall do in their immortal and spiritual bodies, their flesh living now no more carnally but spiritually. And truly what manner of action or rather rest and quietness it shall be, if I say the truth, I know not, for I have never seen it by the senses of the body. But if I shall say I have seen it by the mind, that is by the understanding, alas, what is our understanding in comparison of that exceeding excellency? For there is 'the peace of God which passeth all understanding,'[1] as the apostle says. What understanding, but ours, or peradventure of all the holy angels? For it does not pass the understanding of God. If therefore the saints shall live in the peace of God, without doubt they shall live in that

[1] Phil. iv. 7.

peace, 'which passeth all understanding.'   Now there is no doubt
that it passes our understanding.   But if it also pass the understanding of angels, for He seems not to except them when He says,
'all understanding'; then according to this saying we ought to
understand that we are not able, nor any angels, to know that peace
wherewith God Himself is pacified, in such sort as God knows it.
But we being made partakers of His peace, according to the measure
of our capacity, shall obtain a most excellent peace in us, and
amongst us, and with Him, according to the quantity of our excellency.   In this manner the holy angels according to their measure
do know the same; but men now do know it in a far lower degree,
although they excel in acuteness of understanding.

We must consider what a great man did say: 'We know in part,
and we prophesy in part, until that come which is perfect.   And
we see now in a glass darkly, but then we shall see Him face to
face.' [1]   So do the holy angels now see which are called also our
angels, because we being delivered from the power of darkness, and
translated to the kingdom of God, having received the pledge of the
Spirit, have already begun to pertain to them, with whom we shall
enjoy that most holy and pleasant city of God, of which we have
already written so many books.   So therefore the angels are ours,
which are the angels of God, even as the Christ of God is our Christ.
They are the angels of God, because they have not forsaken God:
they are ours, because they have begun to account us their citizens.
For the Lord Jesus has said: 'Take heed ye do not despise one of
these little ones; for I say unto you, that their angels do always
behold the face of My Father, which is in heaven.' [2]   As therefore
they do see, so also we shall see, but as yet we do not see so.   Wherefore the apostle says that which I have spoken a little before: 'We
see now in a glass darkly, but then we shall see Him face to face.'
Therefore that vision is kept for us, being the reward of faith, of
which also the apostle John says: 'When He shall appear, we shall
be like unto Him, for we shall see Him as He is.' [3]

But we must understand by 'the face of God,' His manifestation,
and not any such member as we have in the body and do call by
that name.   Wherefore when it is demanded of us what the saints
shall do in that spiritual body, I do not say that I see now, but I
say that I believe: according to that which I read in the psalm:
'I believed, and therefore I spake.' [4]   I say, therefore, that they
shall see God in the body, but whether in the same manner as we
now see by the body the sun, moon, stars, sea, and earth, is no
small question.

It is a hard thing to say, that then the saints shall have such
bodies that they cannot shut and open their eyes when they will.
But it is more hard to say, that whosoever shall shut their eyes
there shall not see God.   For if the prophet Elisha, absent in body,

[1] 1 Cor. xiii. 9, 12.   [2] Matt. xviii. 10.   [3] 1 John. iii. 2.   [4] Ps. cxvi. 10.

saw his servant Gehazi receiving the gifts which Naaman gave unto him, whom the aforesaid prophet had cleansed from the deformity of his leprosy, which the wicked servant thought he had done secretly, his master not seeing him: how much more shall the saints in that spiritual body see all things, not only if they shut their eyes, but also where they are absent from it in body? For then shall that be perfect of which the apostle speaking, says: 'We know in part, and prophesy in part: but when that shall come which is perfect, that which is in part shall be done away.' [1]

Afterwards that he might declare by some similitude how much this life differs from that which shall be, not only the life of all sorts of men, but also of them which are endowed here with an especial holiness, he says: 'When I was a child, I understood as a child, I spake as a child, I thought as a child; but when I became a man, I put away childish things. We see now in a glass darkly, but then we shall see face to face. Now I know in part, but then shall I know even as I am known.' [2] If therefore even in this life, where the prophecy of admirable men is to be compared to that life, as children to a young man, Elisha nevertheless saw his servant receiving gifts where he himself was not; shall therefore the saints stand in need of corporal eyes to see those things which are to be seen, which Elisha being absent needed not to see his servant? For when that which is perfect is come, neither shall the corruptible body any more exasperate the soul; nor shall any incorruptible thing hinder it.

For according to the Septuagint, these are the words of the prophet to Gehazi: 'Did not my heart go with thee, and I knew that the man turned back from his chariot to meet thee, and thou has received money,' [3] etc. But as Jerome has interpreted it out of the Hebrew: 'Was not my heart,' says he, 'in presence, when the man returned from his chariot to meet thee?' Therefore the prophet said that he saw this thing with his heart, wonderfully aided by the divine power, as no man doubts. But how much more shall all abound with that gift, when God shall be all things in all? Nevertheless those corporal eyes also shall have their office, and shall be in their place, and the spirit shall use them by the spiritual body. For the prophet did use them to see things present, though he needed not them to see his absent servant, which present things he was able to see by the spirit, though he did shut his eyes, even as he saw things absent, where he was not with them. God forbid therefore that we should say that the saints shall not see God in that life, their eyes being shut, since they shall always see Him by the spirit. But whether they shall also see by the eyes of the body, when they shall have them open, here there arises a question. For if they shall be able to do no more in the spiritual body by that means, as they are spiritual eyes,

[1] 1 Cor. xiii. 9, 10.   [2] 1 Cor. 11, 12.   [3] 2 Kings v. 26.

than those eyes are able to do which we have now, without all
doubt they shall not be able to see God. Therefore they shall be
of a far other power, if that incorporeal nature shall be seen by
them, which is contained in no place but is wholly everywhere.
For we do not say, because we say that God is both in heaven and
also in earth (for He says by the prophet, 'I fill heaven and earth' [1]),
that He has one part in heaven, and another in earth; but He is
wholly in heaven, and wholly in earth, not at several times, but He
is both together, which no corporal nature can be. Therefore there
shall be a more excellent and potent force of those eyes, not that
they may see more sharply than some serpents and eagles are
reported to see (for those living creatures by their greatest sharpness of seeing can see nothing but bodies) but that they may also
see incorporeal things. And it may be that great power of seeing
was granted for a time to the eyes of holy Job, even in that mortal
body, when he says to God: 'By the hearing of the ear I did hear
Thee before, but now my eye doth see Thee: therefore I despised
myself, was consumed, and esteemed myself to be earth and
ashes'; [2] although there is nothing to the contrary why the eye
of the heart may not here be understood, concerning which eyes
the apostle says: 'To have the eyes of your heart enlightened.' [3]
But no Christian man doubts that God shall be seen with them
when He shall be seen, who faithfully receives that which God the
Master says: 'Blessed are the pure in heart, because they shall
see God.' [4]

But it now is in question, whether He may be seen there also
with corporal eyes. For that which is written: 'And all flesh
shall see the salvation of God,' [5] without any knot or scruple of
difficulty may so be understood, as if it had been said: 'And every
man shall see the Christ of God,' who, as He has been seen in
body on earth, shall likewise be seen in body, when He shall judge
the quick and the dead. But that He is the salvation of God, there
are also many other testimonies of the scriptures. But the words
of that worthy and reverend old man Simeon declare it more evidently; who, after he had received the infant Christ into his hands,
'Now,' says he, 'lettest Thou Thy servant depart in peace according to Thy word: because mine eyes have seen Thy salvation.' [6]
So does that which the above recited Job says, as it is found in
many copies taken from the Hebrew: 'And I shall see God in my
flesh.' Verily he prophesied the resurrection of the flesh without
any doubt. Yet he said not, 'by my flesh.' For even if he had said
so, by God Christ might have been understood, who shall be seen
in the flesh by the flesh. But the words 'In my flesh I shall see
God' [7] may also be taken as if he had said: 'I shall be in my flesh
when I shall see God.' And that which the apostle says, 'face

[1] Jer. xxiii. 24.   [2] Job xlii. 5, 6.   [3] Eph. i. 18.   [4] Matt. v. 8.
[5] Luke iii. 6.   [6] Luke ii. 29, 30.   [7] Job xix. 26.

to face,' [1] does not compel us to believe that we shall see God by this corporal face, where there are corporal eyes, whom we shall see by the spirit without intermission. For unless there were a face also of the inward man, the same apostle would not say: 'But we, beholding the glory of the Lord with the face unveiled, are transformed into the same image from glory unto glory, as it were to the Spirit of the Lord.' [2]   Neither do we otherwise understand that which is sung in the psalm: 'Come unto Him and be enlightened, and your faces shall not be ashamed.' [3]   For by faith we come unto God, which, as it is evident, belongeth to the heart and not to the whole body.   But because we know not now how near perfection the spiritual body shall approach, for we speak of a thing of which we have no experience, and where no unmistakable and authoritative utterance of the divine scriptures comes to our aid, it must needs be that that happen in us which is read in the book of Wisdom: 'The thoughts of men are fearful, and our foresights are uncertain.' [4]   For if that manner of arguing of the philosophers, by which they dispute that intelligible things are so to be seen by the aspect of the understanding, and sensible, that is to say, corporal things, so to be seen by the sense of the body, that the understanding neither is able to behold intelligible things through the body, nor corporal things by itself without the body— if this reasoning were most certain unto us; truly it should likewise be certain, that God could not be seen by the eyes of a spiritual body.   But both true reason and prophetical authority will deride this manner of disputing.   For who is such an obstinate enemy to the truth, that he dare say, that God knows not these corporal things?   Has He therefore a body by the eyes of which He may learn those things?   Furthermore does not that which we spake a little before of the prophet Elisha declare sufficiently also, that corporal things may be seen by the spirit, and not by the body? For when his servant received rewards, though it was corporally done, yet the prophet saw it, not by the body but by the spirit. As therefore it is manifest that bodies are seen by the spirit, what if there shall be such a great power of the spiritual body, that the spirit may also be seen by the body?   For God is a Spirit.   Moreover, every man knows his own life (by which he lives now in the body, and which causes these earthly members grow and increase, and makes them living) by the inward sense, and not by the eyes of the body.   But he sees the lives of other men by the body, though they are invisible.   For how do we discern living bodies from unliving, unless we see the bodies and lives together? But we do not see with corporal eyes the lives without bodies.

Wherefore it may be (and it is very credible) that then we shall so see the material forms of the new heaven and new earth, as to see God present everywhere and also governing all corporal

[1] 1 Cor. xiii. 12.   [2] 2 Cor. iii. 18.   [3] Ps. xxxiv. 5.   [4] Wisd. of Sol. ix. 14.

things, by the bodies we shall carry, and which we shall see where-soever we shall turn our eyes, all clouds of obscurity being most evidently removed. We shall not see as the invisible things of God are seen now, being understood by those things which are made, in a glass darkly and in part, where faith prevails more in us by which we believe, than the appearances which we see by corporal eyes. But even as, so soon as we behold men, amongst whom we live, alive and performing vital motions, we do not believe that they live, but we see that they live, and though we cannot see their life without bodies, yet do we clearly behold it by the bodies, all ambiguity being removed: so wheresoever we shall turn about these spiritual eyes of our future bodies, we shall likewise by our bodies see the incorporeal God governing all things.

God therefore shall either so be seen by those eyes, because they have something of that excellency like unto the understanding, whereby the incorporeal nature may be seen (which is either hard or impossible to declare by any examples or testimonies of divine scriptures): or, what is more easily understood, God shall be so known and conspicuous unto us, that He may be seen by the spirit of every one of us, in every one of us, may be seen in one another, may be seen in Himself, may be seen in the new heaven and in the new earth, and in every creature, which shall then be: and may be seen also by the bodies in every body, whithersoever the eyes of the spiritual body shall be directed. Also our thoughts shall be open to and discovered by one another. For then shall that be fulfilled which the apostle intimated when he said: 'Judge not any-thing before the time, until the Lord come, who will lighten things that are hid in darkness, and make the counsels of the heart mani-fest, and then shall every man have praise of God.'[1]

CHAPTER XXX

Of the eternal felicity of the city of God, and the perpetual sabbath

How great shall that felicity be, where there shall be no evil thing, where no good thing shall lie hidden, where we shall have leisure to utter forth the praises of God, which shall be all things in all! For what other thing is done, where we shall not rest with any slothfulness, nor labour for any want, I know not. I am ad-monished also by the holy song, where I read, or hear: 'Blessed are they, O Lord, which dwell in Thy house; they shall praise Thee for ever and ever.'[2] All the members and bowels of the incorruptible body, which we now see distributed to divers uses of necessity, because then there shall not be that necessity, but a full, sure, secure, everlasting felicity, shall be advanced and ge

[1] 1 Cor. iv. 5.   [2] Ps. lxxxiv. 4 .

forward in the praises of God. For then all the numbers (of which I have already spoken) of the corporal harmony shall not lie hid, as they now lie hid being disposed inwardly and outwardly through all the members of the body; and with other things, which shall be seen there, both great and wonderful, shall kindle the reasonable souls with delight of such a reasonable beauty to sound forth the praises of such a great and excellent Workman. What the motions of those bodies shall be there, I dare not rashly define, when I am not able to dive into the depth of that mystery. Nevertheless both the motion and state, as the form of them, shall be comely and decent, whatsoever it shall be, where there shall be nothing which shall not be comely. Truly where the spirit will, there forthwith shall the body be; neither will the spirit will anything, which may not beseem the body nor the spirit. There shall be true glory, where no man shall be praised for error or flattery. True honour, which shall be denied unto none which is worthy, shall be given unto none unworthy. But neither shall any unworthy person covet after it, where none is permitted to be but he who is worthy. There is true peace, where no man suffers anything which may molest him, either from himself or from any other. He Himself shall be the reward of virtue, who has given virtue, and has promised Himself unto him, than whom nothing can be better and greater. For what other thing is that which He has said by the prophet: 'I will be their God, and they shall be My people,' [1] but 'I will be whereby they shall be satisfied: I will be whatsoever is lawfully desired of men, life, health, food, abundance, glory, honour, peace, and all good things'? For so also is that rightly understood, which the apostle says: 'That God may be all in all.' [2] He shall be the end of our desires, who shall be seen without end, who shall be loved without any disgust, and praised without any tediousness. This function, this affection, this action verily shall be unto all, as the eternal life shall be common to all. But who is sufficient to think, much less to utter, what degrees there shall also be of the rewards for merits, of the honours and glories? But we must not doubt but that there shall be degrees. And also that blessed city shall see this in itself—that no inferior shall envy his superior, even as now the other angels do not envy the archangels; as every one will not wish to be what he has not received, although he be bound in a most peaceable bond of concord with him who has received, even as the finger does not wish to be the eye in the body, since a peaceable conjunction and knitting together of the whole flesh contains both members. Therefore one shall so have a gift less than another has, that he also has this further gift that he does not wish to have any more. Nor shall they not have free will, because sins shall not delight them. For it shall be more free being freed from the delight of sinning to an indeclinable and steadfast delight of not sinning. For the first free will, which was given to man, when he was created righteous, had power not to sin, but it had also power to sin: but this last free will shall be more powerful than that, because it shall not be able to sin. But this also shall be by the gift of God, not by the possibility of his own nature. For it is one thing to be God, and another thing to be partaker of God. God cannot sin by nature, but he which is partaker of God receiveth from Him that he cannot sin. But there were degrees to be observed of the divine gift, that the first free will might be given, whereby man might be able not to sin, and the last whereby he might not be able to sin: and the first did pertain to the obtaining a merit, the latter to the receiving of a reward. But because that nature sinned, when it might sin, it is freed by a more bountiful grace, that it may be brought to that liberty in which it cannot sin. For as the first immortality, which Adam lost by sinning, was to be able not to die, while the last shall be not to be able to die; so the first free will was to be able not to sin, and the last not to be able to sin. For so the will to piety and equity shall be free from being lost, as the will to felicity is free from being lost. For as by sinning we neither kept piety nor felicity: neither truly have we lost the will to felicity, felicity being lost.

Is God himself in truth to be denied to have free will, because He cannot sin? Therefore the free will of that city shall both be one in all, and also inseparable in each, freed from all evil, and filled with all good, enjoying an everlasting pleasure of eternal joys, forgetful of faults, forgetful of punishments, but not therefore so forgetful of her deliverance, that she be ungrateful to her deliverer. For so much as concerns reasonable knowledge she is mindful also of her evils, which are past; but so much as concerns the experience of the senses, altogether unmindful.

For a most skilful physician also knows almost all diseases of the body, as they are known by art: but as they are felt in the body, he knows not many which he has not suffered. As therefore there are two knowledges of evils, one, by which they are not hidden from the power of the understanding, the other, by which they are fixed in the senses of him that feels them (for all vices are known in one way by the doctrine of wisdom, and in another way by the most wicked life of a foolish man); so there are two forgetfulnesses of evils. For a skilful and learned man does forget them one way, and he that has had experience and suffered them forgets them another way: the former, if he neglects his knowledge, the latter, if he lacks his misery. According to this forgetfulness which I have set down in the latter place, the saints shall not be mindful of evils past. For they shall lack all evils, so that they shall be abolished utterly from their senses. Nevertheless that power of knowledge, which shall be great in them, shall not only know their own evils past, but also the everlasting misery of the damned. Otherwise, if they shall not know that they have been miserable, how, as the psalm says, shall they sing the mercies of the Lord for ever?[1] Than which song nothing verily shall be more delightful to that city, a song sung to the glory of the grace of Christ, by whose blood we are delivered. There shall be perfected the saying, 'Be at rest and see that I am God';[2] because there shall be the most great sabbath having no evening, which the Lord commended unto us in the first works of the world, where it is read: 'And God rested the seventh day from all His works He made, and sanctified it, because in it He rested from all His works, which God began to make.'[3] For we ourselves also shall be the seventh day, when we shall be replenished and repaired with His benediction and sanctification. There being freed from toil we shall see that He is God, which we ourselves wanted to be when we fell from Him, hearing from the seducer: 'Ye shall be as gods,'[4] and departing from the true God, by whose means we should be gods by participation of Him, not by forsaking Him. For what have we done without Him, but that we have fallen from Him and gone back by His anger? But by Him being restored and perfected with a greater grace we shall rest for ever, seeing that He is God, with whom we shall be replenished, when He shall be all in all. For our good works also, when they are rather understood to be His than ours, are then imputed unto us to obtain this sabbath. But if we shall attribute them unto ourselves, they shall be servile, as it is said of the sabbath: 'Ye shall not do any servile work in it.'[5] For which cause it is said also by the prophet Ezekiel: 'And I have given my sabbaths unto them for a sign between Me and them, that they might know that I am the Lord, which sanctify them.'[6] Then shall we know this thing perfectly, and we shall perfectly rest and shall perfectly see that He is God. If therefore that number of ages be accounted as of days according to the distinctions of times, which seem to be expressed in the sacred scriptures, that sabbath day shall appear more evidently, because it is found to be the seventh. The first age, as it were the first day, is from Adam unto the flood, and the second from thence unto Abraham, not by equality of times, but by number of generations. For they are found to have the number ten. From hence now, as Matthew the evangelist doth conclude, three ages do follow even unto the coming of Christ, every one of which is expressed by fourteen generations. From Abraham unto David is one, from thence even unto the transmigration into Babylon is another, the third from thence unto the incarnate nativity of Christ. So all of them are made five. Now this age is the sixth, to be measured by no number, because of that which is spoken. 'It is not for you to

---

[1] Ps. lxxxix. 1.   [2] Ps. xlvi. 10.   [3] Gen. ii. 2, 3.   [4] Gen. iii. 5.
[5] Deut. v. 14.   [6] Ezek. xx. 12.

know the seasons, which the Father has placed in His own power.'[1] After this age God shall rest as on the seventh day, when God shall make that same seventh day which we shall be, to rest in Himself. Furthermore it would take up a long time to discourse now exactly of every one of those several ages.   But this seventh shall be our sabbath, whose end shall not be the evening, but the Lord's day, as the eighth eternal day, which is sanctified and made holy by the resurrection of Christ, prefiguring not only the eternal rest of the spirit, but also of the body.   There we shall rest and see, we shall see and love, we shall love and we shall praise.   Behold what shall be in the end without end!   For what other thing is our end, but to come to that kingdom of which there is no end?   I think I have discharged the debt of this great work by the help of God. Let those which think I have done too little, and those which think I have done too much, grant me a favourable pardon.   But let those which think I have performed enough, accepting it with a kind congratulation, give no thanks unto me, but unto the Lord with me.   Amen.

[1] Acts i. 7.

A SELECTION FROM THE COMMENTARIES OF
JOANNES LODOVICUS VIVES ON
SAINT AUGUSTINE'S 'DE CIVITATE DEI'

I. 1. *The Romans the proudest nation*

The proudest of nations, the Romans rejoiced to have this reckoned up as part of their glories, 'that they kept down the proud.' That the Romans were proud themselves, and by reason of their own pride hated it in all others, the words of Cato Censorius do prove in his oration to the senate for the Rhodians. 'They say' (quoth he) 'the Rhodians are proud. . . . They are indeed proud. What is that to us? Are you grieved that any should be prouder than ourselves?' Unto which words Gellius adds this: 'There is nothing that can be spoken either sharper or gentler than this reproof unto those most proud high-minded men, that love pride in themselves, and reprove it in others.'

I. 4. *The unconstant Greeks*

This was the Greeks' character at Rome; and therefore they called them *Graeculi*; and some copies of Augustine's books have *Graeculorum* here. Cicero in his oration for Flaccus saith: 'We earnestly desire you to remember the rashness of the multitude, and the truly Greekish levity.'

I. 9. *Paulinus of Nola*

The Goths having sacked Rome, and overrunning all Latium, their fury like a general deluge extended as far as Consentia in Calabria; and forty years after that, Genseric with the Moors and Vandals broke out again, took Rome, filled all Campania with ruin, and razed the city of Nola. Of this city at that time Paulinus was bishop, a most holy and eloquent man, exceedingly read in humane learning, and not altogether void of the spirit of prophecy, who having spent all he had in redeeming Christian captives, and seeing a widow bewailing her captive son, and pouring forth her pious lamentations mixed with tears, his pity so urged him that he could not rest until he had crossed over into Africa with the widow, where her son was prisoner; and there by exchange of himself for her redeemed her son, and gave him free unto his mother. Now his sanctity growing admirable in the eyes of the barbarians, he had the freedom of all his citizens given him, and so was sent back to his country.

I. 11. *The Romans' care, and the heathen philosophers' contempt, for sepulchres*

The Romans had great care over their burials; whence arose many observances concerning the religious performance thereof: and it was indeed a penalty of the law: 'He that doth this or that, let him be cast forth unburied.' . . . Diogenes the Cynic bade that his dead body should be cast unto the dogs and fowls of the air; and, being answered by his friends that they would rend and tear it, said: 'Set a staff by me then, and I will beat them away with it.' 'Tush, you yourself shall be senseless,' quoth they. 'Nay then,' quoth he, 'what need I fear their tearing of me?'

I. 12. *The body part of the man*

The Platonists held the soul only to be man, and the body to be but a case or cover unto it, or rather a prison. But Augustine holdeth the surer opinion that the body is a part of the man.

I. 21. *Plato's condemnation of suicide*

In the beginning of his *Phaedo*, he saith it is wickedness for a man to kill himself, and that God is angered at such an act, like the master of a family, when any of his slaves have killed themselves. And in many other places he saith that without God's command no man ought to leave this life. For here we are all as in a set battle front, every one placed as God our Emperor and General pleaseth to appoint us; and greater is his punishment that forsaketh his life than his that forsaketh his colours.

I. 26. *The old manner of baptizing*

Lest any man should mistake this place, understand that in times of old no man was brought unto baptism but he was of sufficient years to know what that mystical water meant, and to require his baptism, yea and that sundry times. Which we see resembled in our baptizing of infants unto this day. For the infant is asked (be it born on that day, or a day before) whether it will be baptized. Thrice is this question propounded unto it, unto which the godparents answer 'It will.' I hear that in some cities of Italy they do for the most part observe the ancient custom as yet.

(Omitted in the Paris edition.)

I. 27. *The meaning of 'immanent'*

Not as the grammarians take it, namely for 'uncontinuing' or 'transient'; but *immanens, quasi intus manens*, inherent, ingrafted, or staying within.

I. 29. *Labour better unto Rome than quiet*

Appius Claudius used often to say that 'Employment did far more extol the people of Rome than quiet; that excess of leisure and rest melted them into slothfulness, but the rough name of business kept the manners of the city in their pristine state, undeformed; whereas the sweet sound of quiet ever let in a great store of corruption.'

I. 30. *The Roman theatre, when first erected*

Livy in his forty-eighth book and Valerius Maximus *de Instit. Antiq.* write that Valerius Messalla and Cassius being censors had given order for a theatre to be built, wherein the people of Rome might sit and see plays. But Nasica laboured so with the senate, that it was held a thing unfit, as prejudicial to the manners of the people. So by a decree of the senate all that preparation for a theatre was laid aside; and it was decreed that no man should place any seats or sit to behold any plays within the city or within a mile of its walls. And so from a little while after the third African war until the sack of Corinth the people beheld all their plays standing; but then Lucius Memmius set up a theatre for the plays at his triumph, but it stood but for the time that the triumph lasted. The first standing theatre Pompey the Great built at Rome of square stone, the model whereof he had seen at Mytilene in the Mithridatic war. *Cavea* here in the text signifies the middle front of the theatre, which afterwards was divided into seats for the gentlemen, severed into ranks and galleries. Sometimes it is taken for the whole audience. The Grecians had theatres many ages before the Romans, and the very Greek name proves that they came first from Greece.

i. 31. *The Circensian plays*

Circenses they were called (saith Servius) because they were encompassed with swords, of *circa* and *enses*; for the (not as yet nice) antiquity, having not as yet built any places for such exercises, practised them between a river side and a rank of swords, that the idle might see danger on both sides. Afterwards Tarquinius Priscus built a ring for them. . . . They were instituted at Rome by Romulus in the fourth month after he had built the city (as Fabius Pictor recordeth) the same day that he forced away the Sabine virgins.

i. 33. *The meaning of 'asylum'*

It is a sacred place, whence it is not lawful to draw any man; for thence is the name derived coming from συράω, *rapio*, to draw or pull, and *alpha* the privative letter. And so by a figure of speech called *lambdacismus* is made *asylum* for *asyrum*. After Hercules was dead, his nephews and posterity, fearing the oppression of such as their grandfather had injured, built the first sanctuary at Athens. . . . Romulus and Remus built one between the tower and the Capitol, calling the place where it stood Intermontium, intending hereby that the multitude of offenders flocking there for hope of pardon would be a means to augment the number of inhabitants in this new city.

ii. 4. *The priests and plays of Cybele*

Her priests were called *galli*, of the river Gallus in Phrygia, the water whereof being drunk, maketh men mad. And these *galli* themselves do whirl their heads about in their madness, slashing their faces and bodies with knives, and tearing themselves with their teeth, when they are either mad in show or mad indeed. This goddess (which was nothing but a great stone upon mount Ida) the Romans transported into Italy, the day before the Ides of April, which day they dedicated unto her honours, and the plays called Megalesia on that day were acted. . . . In these the players spoke most filthy and abominable lascivious words upon Cybele and Atys; and at that time divers of the most civil Romans, disguising themselves from being known, went wandering about the streets in all licentiousness.

ii. 7. *The power of example; and the greatness of Sir Thomas More*

The examples of those whom we reverence do move us much, for we endeavour to imitate them in all things, be they gods or men. The people affect the fashion of the prince, the scholars of the master they honour, and all mortal men their conditions whom they hold immortal. . . . Plato amongst divers reasons why he will not tolerate poets in his commonwealth brings this for one, because their fictions of the gods give examples very prejudicial to the honesty of the readers, as their wars, thefts, seditions, adulteries and suchlike. Out of which Lucian hath the words he gave to Menippus in his *Necromantia*. 'I,' saith he, 'being a boy and hearing Hesiod and Homer singing of seditions, and wars, not only those of heroes and demi-gods, but even of the gods themselves, their adulteries, rapines, tyrannies, chasing out of parents, and marriages of brethren and sisters, truly I thought all these things both lawful and laudable, and affected them very zealously. For I thought the gods would never have been lechers, nor have gone together by the ears amongst themselves, unless they had allowed all these for good and decent.'

Thus far Lucian. We have rehearsed it in the words of Thomas More, whom to praise negligently, or as if we were otherwise employed, were grossness. His due commendations are sufficient to exceed great volumes. For what is he that can worthily limn forth his sharpness of wit, his depth of judgment, his excellence and variety of learning, his eloquence of phrase, his plausibility and integrity of manners, his judicious foresight, his exact execution, his gentle modesty and uprightness, and his unmoved loyalty, unless he will call them (as they are indeed) the patterns and lustres, each of his kind? I speak much, and many that have not known More will wonder at me; but such as have will know I speak the truth. So will such as shall either read his works, or but hear or look upon his actions. But another time shall be more fit to spread our sails in this man's praises, as in a spacious ocean, wherein we will take this full and prosperous wind, and write much in substance and much in value of his worthy honours; and that unto favourable readers.

II. 8. *The origin of tragedy and comedy*

Because in this book and in the other following Saint Augustine doth often makes mention of stage-plays, it seemeth a fit place here to speak somewhat thereof; and what should have been scattered abroad upon many chapters I will here lay all into one for the better understanding of the rest. And first of their origin amongst the Greeks first and the Romans afterwards; for imitation brought them from Greece to Rome.

The old husbandmen of Greece, using to sacrifice every year to Liber Pater for their fruits, first used to sing something at the putting of the fire on the altars instead of prayers; and then, to please him the better, they sung over all his victories, conquests, triumphs, and his captivation of kings. For reward of which pains of theirs a goat was first appointed, or the skin of an offered goat full of wine. So partly these rewards, and partly ostentation, set many good wits awork amongst these plain countrymen to make verses of this theme, mean and few at first; but, as in all things else, in process of time they grew more elegant and conceited; and because the kings that Liber had conquered afforded not matter enough for their yearly songs, they fell in hand with the calamities of other kings like to the former and sung of them. And this song was called a tragedy either of τράγος a goat, the reward of the conqueror in this contention, or of the wine-lees, wherewith they anointed their faces, called by the Greeks τρύγος.

Now some will have the comedy to have its origin from these sacrifices also; others from the solemnities of Apollo Nomius, that is, the guardian of shepherds and villages. Some say that both these sacrifices were celebrated at once. I will set down the most common opinion. When the Athenians lived as yet in dispersed cottages (Theseus not having yet reduced them to a city) the husbandmen used after their sacri-fices to break jests, both upon such as were at the sacrifices and such as travelled by chance that way; and by these mirthful scoffs delighted all the company. Now after the city was built, the husbandmen at the times appointed for the solemnities came into the town in carts, and jested one while at their fellows, and another while at the citizens, chiefly such as had offended them. And this was called a comedy, either of κώμη a village, because they lived in such; or of ὁδός a way and κωμάζειν to be saucy or to revel; because they were profuse and spared no man in the way with their petulant quips. And this is rather the true derivation, because the Athenians as then did not call the villages κώμας but δήμους.

This custom pleased the citizens, and made them animate those of the promptest wits to write more exactly in this kind of verse. And so little by little the country fellows were thrust out, whose quips were simple and, however envious, yet not bloody. Now the city poets, taxing at first the vices of the citizens with bitterness, did some good in reclaiming particulars from folly through fear of being impersonated; but after-wards, when they began to follow their own affects and their friends', exercising their grudges with sharpness and using their pens for their weapons, they would sometimes traduce princes that had never deserved any such matter and even name them. Which trick when Eupolis had played with Alcibiades in his comedy called *Baptis*, he caused him to be taken and thrown into the sea. When he was thrown in, it was said Alcibiades rehearsed these words oftentimes over: 'Thou hast often drowned me upon the stage, Eupolis; I will once drown thee in the sea.'

By this example the rest of the poets were so terrified that Alcibiades got a law passed that no man should dare to name any man upon the stage. So that kind of comedy called ἀρχαία, that is 'the Old Comedy' was abolished. Then came in the second, wherein many were girded at, privily suppressing names under colours; and this the nobility fell in dislike withal, lest their facts should be glanced at underhand. So that was taken quite away, and a new kind invented, which treated of persons under change of names, the argument of which was ever so different from the facts of the nobility, as each man might perceive that they were farthest from the drift of these taxations. And besides, there was such moderation used in all the effects, that no man could justly complain of them, though they had spoken of him by name. Of this kind Menander was the chief poet, who lived with Alexander the Great, being somewhat younger than he was. The old kind flourished in the wars of the Peloponnesus, and in that kind Aristophanes was most excellent. By report some say that he was very good at the second; but doubtless Antiphanes of Larissa was the best in this kind that ever wrote.

And these kinds were all in Greece. But in the four hundredth year after Rome was builded, when the city was grievously infected with the plague, by an oracle out of the books of the sibyls were stage plays called thither, a new accustomed thing to such a warlike nation. Their players they had out of Etruria, and they named them *histriones* in the language of that country. And these did dance unto the flute without speaking anything, but not without such conceited gestures as were then in use elsewhere. And then the country people of Italy after the fashion of the Greeks, having sacrificed after their harvests, used to jest one upon

another for sport sake, sparing not now and then to cast forth a sluttish
phrase and sometimes a bitter quip. And this they did interchangeably
in verses called *Fescenini*, of such a city in Etruria. These the Roman
players began to imitate but never named, for that was expressly forbidden before by a law in the Twelve Tables. So it being not allowable
to traduce any man by his name upon the stage there sprung up divers
sorts of these playing fables in Italy, after the manner of the Greeks, as
a New Comedy and the Satire, not that which taxeth vices, and is bound
to that one kind of verse, which Horace, Persius and Juvenal wrote in,
but that wherein satyrs were brought in in a sluttish and opprobrious
manner, as in hairy coats, heavy-paced, and altogether unhandsome
and slovenly. Their stage was strewed with flowers, leaves, and grass
to resemble the mountains, woods, and caves; even like as the tragic stage
resembled the state of kingly palaces, and the comical the fashion of
meaner men's houses.

II. 9. *Cicero's 'De Re Publica'*

If of all the ancient monuments of learning, which are either wholly
perished or yet unpublished, I should desire any one extant, it should be
Cicero's six books *de Re Publica*. For I doubt not but the work is
admirable, and guess but by the fragments which are extant. I do hear
that there are some that have these books, but they keep them as charily
as golden apples; but until they come forth to light, let us make use of
the conjectures recorded in other places of Cicero's works.

The greatness of Pericles

This man by his eloquence and other civil institutions did so win the
hearts of the Athenians to him, that he was made governor of that
commonwealth for many years together, being ever both wise and for-
tunate in wars abroad, and in peace at home. Eupolis, an old comedian,
saith that 'on his lips sat πειθώ,' that is the goddess of persuasion, whom
Tully calleth Lepor, and Horace Suadela. Aristophanes also, the
ancient comedian, said that Pericles cast lightning and thunder from
his lips, and confounded all Greece.

The Romans and capital punishment

There were very few crimes, which the old Romans punished with
death, and far fewer in the times which followed; for the Porcian law
forbad the death of any condemned citizen, allowing only his banishment
and so it being held death-worthy to deprave any man by writing proves
that the Romans were extremely afraid of infamy. But here let the
reader observe the meaning of this law, out of Festus, who speaking of
this *capitis diminutio*, this capital punishment, writeth thus: 'He is said
to be *capite diminutus*, capitally punished, that is banished, that of a
free man is made a bondslave to another, that is forbidden fire and water.
And this the lawyers call *maxima capitis diminutio*, the most capital
punishment of all. For there are three kinds of it: the greatest, the
mean, and the smallest.'

II. 15. *The deification of Romulus*

Romulus being dead, the people began to suspect that the senate had
butchered him secretly amongst themselves. So Julius Proculus
appeased the rage of the multitude by affirming that he saw Romulus
ascending up into heaven.

II. 16. *The strength of a town*

Here I cannot but add a very conceited saying out of Plautus' comedy *Persa*. Sagaristios the servant asks a virgin, How strong dost thou think this town is? If the townsmen (quoth she again) be well-mannered, I think it is very strong. If treachery, covetousness, and extortion be chased out, and then envy, then ambition, then detraction, then perjury, then flattery, then injury, then and lastly (which is hardest of all to get out) villainy—if these be not all thrust forth, an hundred walls are all too weak to keep out the ruin.

II. 17. *Vives sings the praises of Budaeus*

But the most copious and exact reading hereof is in Budaeus' notes upon the Pandects, explaining that place, which the lawyers did not so well understand: *jus est ars aequi et boni*. This man's sharpness of wit, quickness of judgment, fullness of diligence, and greatness of learning, no Frenchman ever paralleled, nor in these times any Italian. There is nothing extant in Greek or Latin but he hath read it, and read it over, and discussed it thoroughly. In both these tongues he is alike, and that excellently perfect. He speaks them both as familiarly as he doth French his natural tongue; nay I make doubt whether he speak them no better. He will read out a Greek book in Latin extempore, and out of a Latin book in Greek. And yet this, which we see so exactly and excellently written by him, is nothing but his extemporal birth. He writes with less pains both Greek and Latin than very good scholars in both these tongues can understand them. There is no crank, no secret in all these tongues but he hath searched it out, looked into it, and brought it forth like Cerberus from darkness into light. Infinite are the significations of words, and the proprieties of phrase, which only Budaeus hath fetched out of deep oblivion, and exposed them to men's understanding. And yet all these singular and admirable gifts hath he attained to by his own industry alone, without help of any master. O fertile wit, that found in itself alone both master and scholar and method of instruction! That whole tenth part others can hardly learn of great and cunning masters he alone without help of others drew wholly from himself. I have not yet said anything of his knowledge in the law, which he alone hath begun to restore from ruin; nor of his philosophy, whereof in his book *de Asse* he hath given such proof, as no man possibly could, but such an one as had daily conversation with such reading of all the philosophers, and deep instruction in those studies. To all this may be added that which indeed excels all things else, an honesty congruent to all this learning, so rare, and so admirable, that being but considered without the other graces of wit and learning it might seem the world's miracle. His honesty no more than his learning acknowledgeth any his superior. A man that in all the divers actions of his life gives religion always the first place: a man that having wife and many children was never drawn from his true square with any profit, or study to augment his state; but evermore swayed both himself and his fortunes, and directed both. Fortune could never lead him away, though she promised never so fair. He always had her in his power. A man continually in court, in embassages, yet never followed princes' favours, nor nuzzled them with flatteries. He never augmented his patrimony, because he would never depart an hair's breadth from

honesty. He was always a severer censurer of his own conditions than
of any others; and having offices, which were the objects of the greatest
envy, he never found calumny from any tongue, nor incurred suspicion
of any error, though he had to do with a free nation, and a people as
ready to accuse as froward to suspect. I see I have forgotten brevity's
bounds, being whirled beyond them with the love I have to relate the
virtues of mine honoured friend!

II. 19. *Augustissima or angustissima*

Augustissima it must needs be (in the closing sentence) and not *angus-
tissima*, most strait or narrow. But withal take a certain friar's note
with you, I had almost told his name, who affirmed that heaven's court
is called *angusta* here, because the way is strait (as Christ our Saviour
said) that leadeth unto life; and few there are that enter in thereat.
And that his auditors might bear it the better away, he shut it up in this
fine verse:

Arcta est via vere, quae ducit ad gaudia vitae.

The way is strait and quickly missed, that leads us to up glory's bliss.

He showed plainly that he cared not greatly for true position or quantity
of syllables, so that he made it go roundly off, and sound well.
(This note is omitted in the Paris edition.)

II. 21. *A commonwealth not governed without injustice*

It is an old saying, 'Without justice Jupiter himself cannot play the
king.' And seeing that the weal public for the general good of itself
and liberty is often compelled to use extremity against citizens private,
and also oftentimes in augmenting its power breaketh the laws of equity
in encroaching upon others, (both which notwithstanding fell still very
well out) the Romans altered the old saying and made it: 'A weal public
cannot be governed without injustice.' This Carneades touched, as
Lactantius affirmeth, and told the Romans who possessed the world,
that if they would be just, that is, restore every man his own, they must
even return to their cottages and lead their lives in all poverty and
necessity.

The meaning of the word 'tyrant'

In ancient times they called all kings tyrants, as well the best as the
worst, as Virgil and Horace do in their poems; for the name in Greek
signifieth only dominion. Plato, who was the only man that laid down
the right form of government for a city, is called τύραννος καὶ βασιλεύς,
a tyrant and a king. Festus thinketh that the word was derived from the
notorious cruelty of the Tyrrhenes; but I think rather that when the
Athenians brought in the democratical government, and other cities
through emulation followed their example, that was the cause that first
brought the word *tyrannus* into hatred and contempt; and so they
called their kings tyrants, because they governed their own wealth, but
not the commonwealth; besides that the Romans used it in that manner
also, because they hated the name of a king deadly; and in Greece also,
whosoever bore rule in a city that had before been free, was called a
tyrant, but not a king.

III. 5. *The punishment of the offending vestal*

If a virgin vestal offended but lightly, the high priest did beat her. But being convicted of neglect of chastity or whoredom she was carried in a coffin to the gate Collina, as if she went to burial, all her friends and kinsfolk bewailing her, the priests and other religious following the hearse with a sad silence. Near to the gate was a cave, to which they went down by a ladder, and shut the cave close up: and lest she should starve to death, they set by her bread, milk, and oil, of each a quantity, together with a lighted lamp. All this finished the priests departed. And on that day was no cause heard in law; but it was as a vacation, mixed with great sorrow and fear; all men thinking that some great mischief was presaged to befall the weal public by the punishment of the vestal.

III. 10. *The five ages of men*

Hesiod in his *Opera et Dies* feigneth five ages of mortality. This did Virgil, Ovid, and others imitate. The first age is the 'golden' one, and they say was under Saturn, without wars or will to wars. Humanity was locked in unity, neither were men contentious or clamorous. These were called Saturnian days. The next age was 'silver,' under Jove. Then war began to bustle; so did her daughters, care, hate, and deceit. The third 'brazen,' when war hurls all upon heaps, and quaffeth lives and blood. The fourth of the 'half-gods, heroes,' who thought they loved justice, yet their bosoms harboured an eager thirst of wars. The fifth 'iron,' where mischief goeth beyond bound and limit, and all miseries breaking their prisons assault men's fortunes. Open deceit, open hate, open wars, slaughters, vastations, burnings, rapes, and rapines are all open, violent, and common.

III. 12. *The smoke of Rome 'like a beacon'*

Either the smoke of the sacrifices; or meaning their vanity, as an allusion unto smoke; for smoke is often taken for a vain and frivolous thing, as 'to sell smoke.' In time of war or suspicion, the watchmen placed bundles of dry small sticks upon their high watch-stands, that when the enemy approached on a sudden they might fire the sticks, and so give notice unto their own soldiers and the neighbouring towns. The Greeks called those bundles φρυκτούς, and by these fires notice might be given unto the country an hundred miles about, to come betimes to the preventing of their danger.

III. 17. *Bed-spreadings*

It was an old fashion to banquet upon beds. But in their appeasing and sacrificial banquets, in the temples, and in the night orgies, they made beds in the place for the gods to lie and revel upon, and this was called *lectisternium*, 'bed-spreading' to last eight days. Three beds were fitted, one for Apollo and Latona, one for Diana and Hercules, and one for Mercury and Neptune.

The broodmen

Servius Tullius, the sixth king of Rome, divided the people into six companies or forms. In the first were those that were censured worth CM asses or more; but under that king the greatest censure was but

CXM. The second contained all of an estate between C and LXXV asses, the third them under L; the fourth them under XXXV; the fift them under XI; the last was a century of men freed from warfare *proletarii* or broodmen, and *capite censi*. A broodman was he tha was rated ML asses in the censor's book, more or less; and such wer ever forborne from all offices and uses in the city, being reserved onl to beget children, and therefore were styled *proletarii*, of *proles*, brood o offspring. The *capite censi* were poorer, and valued but at CCCLXXV asses; who, because they were not censured by their estates, were counte by the poll, as augmenting the number of the citizens. These last tw sorts did Servius Tullius exempt from all service in war, not that the were unfit themselves, or had not pledges to leave for their fealty, bu because they could not bear the charges of war, for the soldiers in thos days maintained themselves. It may be this old custom remaine after the institution of tribute, and the people of Rome thought it not fi that such men should go to war, because they accounted all by the purse

III. 18. *Plays to the hell-gods*

The infernal orgies and the secular plays seem to differ in thei origin. For Festus saith thus: The *tauri* were games made in honou of the infernal gods, upon this occasion. In the reign of Tarquin th Proud, there falling a great death amongst the child-bearing women arising out of too great plenty of bull's-flesh that was sold to the people hereupon they ordained games in honour of the infernals, calling them *tauri*.

III. 21. *The Romans' use of chickens in war*

The Romans used in their wars to carry chickens about with them in cages; and he that kept them was called *pullarius*, the chicken-keeper. If they fed greedily it was a good sign; if so greedily that part of their victuals fell to the earth it was best of all. For that was called *tripudium solistimum*, and once it was called *terripavium*, from *paviendo* of striking the earth in the fall of it, and *solistimum*, from *solum* the ground. . . . But an unlucky sign was if they fed not; but a worse if they flew out o their cages.

III. 27. *The death of Catulus*

Catulus was joint consul with Marius in his fourth consulship in the Cimbrian war, and triumphed with him over them. The whole senate entreating Marius for him, he answered he must die; which Catulus hearing of stifled himself with coals, whether swallowing them as Portia did, or enclosing the smoke close in his chamber, having newly limed it. is not certain (for this latter is a present way to death, unless remedie be forthwith gotten). Some think he died of poison, as Augustine saith here.

III. 30. *The greatness of Cicero*

He was slain being sixty-three. The divers opinions of his death are to be read in Seneca (*Suasor.*, Book I). Augustine calls him an excellen commonwealth's man, because his tongue (like a stern) did turn the ship of state which way he would; which knowing he used this verse to the great vexation of his enemies:

> Cedant arma togae, concedat laurea linguae.
> That arms should yield to arts, 'tis fit:
> Stoop then the wreath unto the wit.

Pliny the elder meeting him said: 'Hail thou that first deserved a triumph by the gown, and a garland by thy tongue.'

Cicero's short-sightedness concerning Octavius

Brutus had given Tully sufficient warning of Octavius, not to make him too powerful, nor trust him too much; that his wit was childish, though good, and better fortunes might make him insolent. And there are yet two most grave epistles of Brutus on this theme, one to Tully and the other to Atticus, wherein Brutus' manliness and judgment are clearly apparent. I think not Tully so foolish that he could not foresee this as well as he did many other events not so apparent; which he showed in his frequent use of these words: 'Octavius Caesar is to be commended, adorned, and extolled.'

Preface to Book IV. Varro's 'Antiquities'

Now must we pass from the historical acts of the Romans unto their religion, sacrifices, and ceremonies. In the first books we asked no pardon, because for the Roman acts, though they could not be fully gathered out of one author (a great part of them being lost with the writings of eloquent Livy), yet out of many they might. But in the four books following we must needs entreat pardon, if the reader find us weak either in diligence or ability. For there is no author now extant that wrote of this theme. Varro's *Antiquities* are lost, with many more. If we had but them, we might have satisfied Saint Augustine that had his assertions thence. But now we must pick them up from several places, which we here produce, lest coming without anything we should seem to want ornaments, and bare necessities. If it have not that grace that is expected, we are content in that our want is not wholly to be shamed at; and our endeavours are to be pardoned in this respect, that many learned and great scholars (to omit the vulgar sort) have become willingly ignorant in a matter of such intricate study, and so little benefit; which makes our diligence less faulty.

IV. 4. *The bestiality of war*

The world (saith Cyprian very elegantly to Donatus) is bathed in floods of mutual blood. When one alone kills a man, it is called a crime; but when many together do it, it is called a virtue. Thus not respect of innocence, but the greatness of the fact sets it free from penalty. And truly fighting belongs neither to good men nor thieves, nor to any that are men at all, but is a right bestial fury; and therefore was it named *bellum* of *bellua* a beast.

IV. 6. *The Greeks liars*

The Greeks either through desire to flourish in their styles, or for their country's admiration, or for delighting their readers, or by some natural gift, have not failed to lie wonderfully in all their histories. And the Latins that meddled with their affairs, being forced to follow them fell into the same defect.

IV. 9. *The meaning of the name Jupiter*

The Greeks call Jove ζῆνα and δια both of 'living,' because he was held to give all things life. Plato derives them both of δι᾽ αὐτὸν ζῆν 'to live by himself' (*in Cratylo*). The Romans called him Jove from *juvando* of 'helping.' The old philosophers called that same *mens*, that intellect that created all things, Jove. And therefore the wise men worshipped this, who otherwise held no mortal creature for any god, but only that immortal, almighty Prince of nature having divers names, one amongst the Greeks, another with the Persians, a third with the Phoenicians, a fourth in Egypt, etc.

IV. 11. *The origin of the Delphic oracle*

There was a deep and obscure cave there where the shrine in Delphos was first; whereunto a goat coming by chance to feed was inspired with an extraordinary spirit, and began to leap and dance beyond measure. Which the shepherd wondering at and coming to the mouth of the cave he grew rapt himself, and began to prophesy. And others upon trial did so. Whereupon it grew to pass that such as would know things to come would but bring one to lean his head into the cave, and he should answer them the truth to all that they would ask. Which afterwards they finding to be dangerous (for it had been the death of divers) they built a temple there unto Apollo, and ordained a virgin to receive the inspiration upon a frame a good height from the cave, and so give answers to the inquirers, which frame they named a tripos, of three feet, having the same shape that the brazen tripodes had afterwards. The virgin priest was called the Pythia, at first a virgin, like Diana's priest. Afterwards Echecratus lying with the Pythia they ordained that the priest should not be under fifty years of age, meddling no more with virgins at any hand: only she went virgin-like, to keep some memory of the ancient custom.

Mercury

Accounted the god of eloquence, of bargains and contracts, because words do all these. The merchants' feast was in the Ides of May, that day that Mercury's temple was dedicated. The Greeks called him ἀγοραῖος, that is market-man, and he had a statue in the market-place.

IV. 19. *Fortuna Muliebris*

After Rome's freedom from the kings eighteen years, Coriolanus warring inexorably against his country, neither departing for threats nor tears, the women's lamentations turned him away. Hereupon they erected a temple to Fortuna Muliebris in the Latin road, four miles from Rome. In which dedication the image spake twice. First this: 'Matrons, well have you seen me and dedicated me.' Liv., Val., Plut., Lactantius saith that she foretold a danger to ensue, which were questionless the words that she spake the second time.

IV. 21. *Rubigo*

Rubigo is the putrefied dew, eating and cankering the young plants. In the morning, saith Pliny, and in quiet weather doth this fall upon the corn, and on clear nights in valleys and places where the air is not moved, nor is it perceived until it be done. High hills and windy places are never troubled with this inconvenience. This feast Numa ordained to be kept on the 7th of May's Cal., for then doth this canker the most mischief.

v. 2. *Twins—a unity in diversity*

Nature never bound any one thing to another in such propriety, but she set some differences between them. What skilleth it whether those two had origin from one seed? Every man is framed and born to his own fortunes, and be they two or three born at once, their destinies promise no fraternity, but each one must undergo his particular fate.

v. 6. *Creatures that are superfoetant, that is, breeding upon breed*

Of all creatures only the hare and the coney do conceive double, upon the first conception; and having young in their bellies will conceive afresh. A woman, says Aristotle, seldom conceiveth upon her first young, but sometimes she may, if there pass but a little space between the conceptions, as Hercules and Iphicles (by report) were conceived. There was an adulteress also that bore two children at a birth, one like her husband, and another like her lemman. But these are rare examples; and if a man would oppose them he could not be brought by reason to confess that those children were conceived one after another; though I know that Erasistratus a worthy physician holdeth that all twins are conceived one after another, and so do divers Stoical philosophers also hold of many twins, but not of all. But Hippon and Empedocles held that of one act of generation by reason of the abundance of seed were all twins conceived. Asclepiades ascribeth it to the virtue, not the abundance of the seed.

v. 9. *Free will*

God created our wills free; and that because it was His will. So they make choice of contraries, yet cannot go against God's predestination. Nor questionless ever would they although they could. For sure it is that much might be done which never shall; so that the events of things to come proceed not from God's knowledge, but this from them; which notwithstanding in Him are not to come, but already present (wherein a great many are deceived). Wherefore He is not rightly said to foreknow, but only in respect of our actions, and already to know, see, and discern them. But if it seem unfit that this eternal knowledge should be derived from so transitory an object, then we may say that God's knowledge ariseth from His providence and will; that His will decreeth what shall be, and His knowledge conceiveth what His will hath appointed. That which is to come (saith Origen upon Genesis), is the cause that God knoweth it shall come. So it cometh not to pass because God knoweth it shall come so to pass; but God foreknoweth it, because it shall come so to pass.

v. 13. *Philosophy to be well read*

The philosophers' books of manners are to be read purely, diligently, nor against the will, but desirously, that we may reap profit thereby, for so doing we shall. Porphyry saith we must come with clean hands as unto a sacrifice.

v. 17. *The meaning of 'barbarians'*

The Latins were made free denizens of old; and from them it spread further into Italy, over Po, over the Alps, and the sea. Claudius Caesar made many barbarians free of Rome; affirming that it was the ruin of

Athens and Lacedaemon that they made not such as they conquered free of their cities. Afterwards under emperors that were Spaniards, Africans, and Thracians, whole provinces at first, and afterwards the whole empire was made free of Rome. And whereas before all were called 'barbarians' but the Greeks, now the Romans being lords, exempted themselves and afterwards the Latins and all the Italians from that name; but after that, all the provinces being made free of the city, only they were called 'barbarians' which were not under the empire of Rome. And thus the later historiographers use it. So the river Rhine had two banks, the nether of them was Roman, the further barbarian. Hence Claudianus:

> O quoties doluit Rhenus qua barbarus ibat,
> Quod te non geminis frueretur judice ripis.

> O how Rhine wept on the barbarian shore,
> That both his banks were not within thy power.

v. 27. *On writers who write to harm their adversaries*

Many write against others, and watch a time for the publication to the hurt of the adversary and their own profit. Such men writing only to do mischief are to be hated as the execrable enemies of all good judgments. For who cannot do injury? and what a mind hath he that thinketh his gifts and learning must serve him to use unto others' ruin? If they seek to do good by writings, let them publish them then, when they may do others the most good, and their opponents the least harm. Let them set them forth whilst their adversary lives, is lusty, and can reply to them, and defend his own cause. Pliny writes that Asinius Pollio had orations against Plancus, which he meant to publish after his death, lest he should come upon him with a reply. Plancus hearing of it: 'Tush,' saith he, 'there is none but ghosts will contend with the dead': which answer so cut the combs of the orations, that all scholars made jests and mocks of them.

VII. 32. *Prophecy and the understanding thereof*

The prophecies are not yet at an end; and though the sum of them all were fulfilled in Christ, yet by Him divers things since are to come to pass, which have particularly been intimated in the prophecies, as that (not in one prophet only) of the gathering together of the dispersed Israel at the end of the world.

All the prophets understood not their prophecies, nor did those that understood part understand all; for they spake not themselves but by God's inspiration. Whose counsels they were not fully acquainted with: nor did God use them as men skilful in future events, but as such as He meant to speak to the people by. Yet deny we not but that the sum of all the visions, the coming of the Messiah, was revealed to them by God Almighty. The Gentiles were also of the opinion that the sibyls and the other prophets understood not all their presages, for they spake them at such times as they were rapt beyond their reason, and having put off their proper minds were filled with the deity.

VIII. 9. *Plato's opinion of the greatest good*

The venerable and holy-teaching Plato, surmounting all philosophers in almost all other matters, in defining man's greatest good outstripped even himself. In his first book *de Legib*. he divides good into divine and human. The last is quite separate from virtue, the first conjoined therewith. Socrates in Plato's *Gorgias* affirms that beatitude consisteth in learning and virtue, calling only the good happy and the evil wretched. And in *Menexenus* in six hundred places (and so all Plato through) good is only honest and beauteous. As for other goods, without virtue they are the destruction of him that possesseth them. But these are but Plato's common sayings: in them he goeth with his fellows. But when he list, he riseth in spirit, and leaves all the other schools of wisdom behind him. His *Philebus* is a dialogue of the greatest good, or as some entitle it, περὶ τῆς ἡδονῆς, 'of pleasure.' Therein he maketh six ranks of goods. In the second stand the things proportionate, fair, perfect, sufficient, and suchlike. In the third, understanding and sapience. In the fourth the goods of the soul, sciences, arts, and good opinions. But in the first he putteth measure, moderation, and opportunity. All which (as he writeth to Dionysius) import that God is the proportion, cause, measure, and moderator of all goodness. And in his second *de Repub*. he calleth God the greatest good, and the idea of good.

Spain

In Spain, before silver and gold were found, there was no war, many philosophers, and the people lived wonderfully religiously. Every society had a magistrate by the year, chosen out of the most learned and judicious rank of men. Equity was the executor of Justice then. Few or no controversies were ever moved; and those that were, did either concern virtuous emulation, the reasons of nature, of the gods, of good manners, or of some such themes, which the learned disputed of at set times, and called the women to be auditors. Afterwards certain mountains that were full of metal within brake out and burned, and the melted gold and silver left admiration of such fine stuffs in men's minds. So showing this to the Phoenicians, who were then the general merchants of the world, they bartered of their metals away to them for things of no value. The Phoenicians spying this gain acquainted divers of the Asians and Greeks therewith, and so came often thither with a multitude of men, sometimes with great navies, and otherwhiles but with two or three merchants' ships. Now many either liking the air and the soil, or else loving gold better than their gods, set up their rests in Spain, and by one truck or other found means to contract alliance with others; and then began they to send colonies into Spain out of all Asia and the isles adjacent, and these spread their villainies amongst the silly ignorant souls. Then began the Spaniards to admire their own wealth, to fight, to prey upon one another, first privately, and soon after in whole armies, afterward to flat nations' war, waged under alien leaders; the Phoenicians at first, the authors both of their present and future misfortunes. Then good manners got them gone, equity was sent packing away, and laws came up together with digging of metals, so that it was farewell to philosophy, and all arts grew almost to utter ruin; for they were not written but only passed by tradition from mouth to ear. But that which remained of them was renewed by some well-wishing wits in the time of the Roman peace; for first the Goths and afterwards the Saracens rooted them utterly from amongst the vulgar. There is an old memorial extant of the ancient times written in Greek and Latin. I hope by it to illustrate the origin of my native country.

VIII. 10. *Plato and Aristotle*

From Plato and Aristotle's time unto Aphrodiseus, that lived under Severus and his son, Aristotle was rather named amongst the learned than either read or understood. Aphrodiseus first adventured to explain him, and did set many on to search farther into the author by that light he gave. Yet did Plato keep above him still, until the erection of the public schools in France and Italy, that is, as long as the Greek and Latin tongues were in account. But when learning grew mercenary and mimical, all their aim was gain and contention and verbosity and fond subtilty with vile feigned words of art and frivolous quirks, then was Aristotle's logic and physics held fit for their purpose, and many better books thrown aside. But as for Plato, because they understood him not (nay and Aristotle much less), yet because he teaches no tricks, oh never name him! I speak not this to imply Aristotle's learning more insufficient than Plato's, but it is a shame that Plato an holy philosopher should be thrust by, and Aristotle's best part also; and the rest so read that he must speak their pleasures, being such fooleries as not Aristotle, no nor any madman of his time would have held or divulged.

(This is no good doctrine in the Louvainists' opinion, for it is left out as distasteful unto the schoolmen, though not to the direct truth.)

VIII. 12. *Plato and Aristotle compared*

Comparison between Plato and Aristotle is odious because of their diversity of studies. Doubtless they were both admirable examples for all to imitate. The Greeks call Plato θεῖος, divine, and Aristotle δαίμων, which is as much. Plato's eloquence was such that it was a common saying, if Jove would speak he would speak Plato's Greek: but Aristotle's knowledge in rhetoric (I had almost said) excelled Plato's; but in use he was far short of him. For Aristotle affected a succinct phrase, lest being tedious and drawing each thing at length the discourse might become too profuse, and the rules of art too long to bear away. So his endeavour was not to admit an idle word, which made him attain unto a great perfection in the proper use of the Greek language and figures.

VIII. 17. *A Christian should disdain honours*

Christ forbids His apostles to assume the name of masters, to sit high at table, or love salutes in the streets; and commands that the chief should be but as a minister. For honour arose with heathenism, and should fall therewith and not survive in the Church: nor is it magnanimous to affect, but to contemn it.

VIII. 26. *The crocodile*

A serpent that lays eggs, four-footed, growing to seventeen cubits' length or more. He moveth his upper chap, and so doth no living creature besides him; devoureth man and beast, and lives part on the water and part on dry land. Herodot., Arist., and Plin., Senec. say that it feareth one courageous, and insulteth over one that fears it. The crocodile city is in the heart of Egypt near to the Libyan mountain

not far from Ptolemais. . . . The Egyptians, saith Porphyry, worshipped a crocodile because he was consecrated to the sun as the ram,
the buzzard, and the black beetle.

VIII. 27. *Plays of the passion of Jesus Christ unlawful*

But now, even at the celebration of Christ's passion and our redemption, it is a custom to present plays almost as vile as the old stage-
games. Should I be silent, the very absurdity of such shows in so
reverend a matter would condemn it sufficiently. There Judas playeth
the most ridiculous mimic, even when he betrays Christ. There
the apostles run away, and the soldiers follow, and all resounds with
laughter. Then comes Peter and cuts off Malchus' ear, and then all
rings with applause, as if Christ's betraying were now avenged. And
by and by this great fighter comes and for fear of a girl denies his master,
all the people laughing at her question, and hissing at his denial. And
in all these revels and ridiculous stirs Christ only is serious and severe:
but seeking to move passion and sorrow in the audience, he is so far
from it that he is cold even in the divinest matters, to the great guilt,
shame, and sin both of the priests that present this, and the people
that behold it.

(The Louvainists omit this.)

Martyrs to be reverenced but not adored

Many Christians offend in not distinguishing between their worship
of God and the saints: nor doth their opinion of the saints want much
of that which the pagans believed of their gods, yet impious was Vigi-
lantius to bar the martyrs all honour, and fond was Eunomius to forbear
the Church's, lest he should be compelled to adore the dead. The
martyrs are to be reverenced, but not adored, as God is.

IX. 15. *Commentary on Philippians ii. 7*

These are Paul's words proving that though Christ were most like to
His Father, yet never professed Himself His equal here upon earth unto
us that respected but His manhood, though He might lawfully have done
it. But the Lord of all put on Him the form of a servant, and the high
God debased Himself into one degree with us, that by His likeness to
ours, He might bring us to the knowledge of His power and essence, and
so estate us in eternity before His Father; and that His humanity might
so invite us, that His divinity did not terrify us, but take hold of our
acceptance of this invitation, and so translate us to joy perpetual. But
we could neither have been invited nor allured to this but only by one
like ourselves: nor could we be made happy but only by God the fountain
of happiness. So then there is but one way, Christ's humanity, by
which all access lieth to His deity, that is, life eternal and beatitude.

IX. 16. *God only partly known in His creation*

In the world there are some marks whereby the world's Maker may
be known; but that afar off, as a light in the most thick and spacious
dark, and not by all, but only by the sharpest wits that give themselves
wholly to speculation thereof.

IX. 21. *Christ's miracles*

Christ's miracles were more admired of the angels and devils than of men, because they knowing the cause of things saw nature's power conquered and transcended. Now men though they saw them strange, yet wanted there not some to say He cast out devils by Beelzebub their prince, not so much believing this indeed, as desiring that the simple multitude should believe it. And others of late time have charged Him with magic, against whom (by God's help) I will deal at large in my books *de Sapientia Christiana*.

X. 4. *The meaning of 'religion'*

Tully derives religion of *relegendo*, reading again, and calls it the knowledge of God, as Trismegistus doth. Lactantius had rather derive it of *religando*, binding, because the religious are bound to God in bonds of piety. Augustine of *religendo*, re-electing; I think because it was fittest for his present allusion.

The sum of all religion

O, what few laws might serve man's life! How small a thing might serve to rule not a true Christian, but a true man! Indeed he is no true man that knoweth not and worshippeth not Christ. What needeth all these digests, codes, glosses, counsels, and cautels? In how few words doth our great Master show every man his due course! Love thou Him which is above as well as thou canst, and that which is next thee as well as thyself; which doing thou keepest all the laws, and hast them perfect, which others attain with such toil and scarcely keep with so many invitations and terrors. Thou shalt then be greater than Plato or Pythagoras with all their travails and numbers; than Aristotle with all his quirks and syllogisms. What can be sweeter than love? Thou art taught neither to fear, fly, nor shrink.

Love God 'with all thy heart,' that is, refer all thy thoughts: 'with all thy soul,' that is, refer all thy life: 'with all thy mind,' that is, refer all thine understanding unto Him, of whom thou hadst them all. He leaves no part of us to be given to another, but will have the fruition of all Himself. Origen explains 'the heart,' viz. the thought, work, and memory: 'the soul,' to be ready to lose it for God's sake: 'the mind,' to profess or speak nothing but godly things.

Our friend our second self

Augustine (*de Doct. Christ.*) saith that all men are neighbours one to another. And so saith Christ in His first precept; for, as Chrysostom saith, 'Man is God's image': so that he that loves man seems to love God. This precept is so congruent to man's nature that the philosophers approved it. For nature, say they, hath joined all men in league and likeness together. And it is the first in the laws of friendship, to love our friend as ourself; for we hold him our second self.

X. 16. *Jugglers*

Men's thoughts often make them think they see that which they see not indeed; and this is often done by a phantasm, or apparition. And hence are most of our reports of spirits walking, arisen. Yea, the spirits themselves do deceive our senses; which is no wonder seeing our jugglers can do the like by legerdemain, which if another should do, you should have some make a miracle of. And their doings truly are admirable, and their manner very hard to conceive. Some think they are not done but by the devils' means. Not so. They are but the quick conveyances of art and exercise, their swift motion preventing our eyesights. So doth he that cheweth bread, and bloweth forth meal; and he that drinks and lets it out at his throat. O, how people will marvel to see them eat daggers, spew heaps of needles, laces, and counters! I omit to speak of the tricks of natural magic, making men look headless, and headed like asses, and spreading a vine all over a room. Many know the reasons hereof. They are written of, and easily done by men, much more by the devils, that are such cunning naturalists.

x. 20. *Christ's sacrifice foretold in many ways to avoid tediousness*

For variety easeth; and in discourse he that repeateth one thing twice of one fashion procureth loathing; but vary it a thousand ways and it will still pass pleasing. This is taught in rhetoric. And it is like that which Q. Flamininus saith in Livy of the divers sauces. Therefore the types of the old law that signified one thing were divers, that men might apprehend the future salvation with less surfeit; and the rude persons amongst so many might find one, whereby to conceive what was to come.

x. 23. *Whether the philosophers knew the Trinity*

It is a question that hath troubled many—whether the philosophers had any notion of the Trinity. First we ourselves, to whom the mystery of redemption is revealed, have but a small glance (God knows) of that radiant light. But what the philosophers of old wrote hereof is easily apparent that they spake it, rather than knew what they spake; it is so obscure. These secrets belonged not to their discovery. It suffered them to attain the unity of God. And if (by God's inspiration) they spake aught concerning the Trinity, it was rather to serve as a testimony of the future truth against their masters' opinions than to express any understanding they had thereof themselves.

x. 24. *Commentary on John viii. 25*

Augustine will have the Son to be a Beginning, but no otherwise than the Father as no otherwise God. And this he takes τὴν ἀρχήν for. Valla and Erasmus say that τὴν ἀρχήν can be no noun here, but an adverb, as 'in the beginning.' I will speak my mind hereof briefly, though the phrase be obscure, and perhaps an Hebraism, as many in the New Testament are. Christ seems not to say He is the Beginning; but being asked who He was, He having no one word to express His full nature to all their capacities, left it to each one's mind to think in his mind what He was, not by His sight but by His words, and to ponder how one in that bodily habit could speak such things. It was the Deity that spake in the flesh, whence all those admirable acts proceeded. Therefore He said: 'I am He in the beginning, and I spake to you as using a mortal body as an instrument giving you no more precepts by angels, but by myself.' This answer was not unlike that given to Moses: 'I am that I am'; but that concerned God's simple essence and majesty; this was more later, and declared God in the form of man.

x. 29. *The insolence of boasting of wisdom*

What an insolent thing is it to boast of wisdom! As if Plato were ashamed of his master Socrates that said he knew nothing, and did not glory in all his life that he was scholar to that stone-cutter's son, and that all his wisdom whatsoever was his master's! And as if Socrates himself (in Plato and Xenophon chief founders of that discipline) did not refer much of his knowledge to Aspasia and Diotima his two women instructors!

xi. 7. *Knowledge of the creature 'twilight'*

In *de Genes. ad lit.*, lib. 4 Augustine calleth it 'morning' when the angels by contemplating of the creation in themselves (where is deep darkness) lift themselves to the knowledge of God; and if in Him they learn all things (which is more certain than all habitual knowledge) then it is 'day.' It grows towards 'evening' when the angels turn from God to contemplate the creatures in themselves; but this 'evening' never becomes 'night,' for the angels never prefer the work before the workman. That were 'most deep dark night.' Thus much out of Augustine, the first mentioner of morning's and evening's knowledges.

xi. 10. *Religious phrases*

Words I think add little to religion, yet must we have a care to keep the old path and received doctrine of the Church; for divinity being so far above our reach, how can we give it the proper explanation? All words are man's inventions for human uses, and no man may refuse the old approved words to bring in new ones of his own invention; for whereas proprieties are not to be found out by man's wit, those are the fittest to declare things by, that ancient use hath left us, and they that have recorded most part of our religion. This I say for that a sort of smattering rash fellows impiously presume to cast the old forms of speech at their heels, and to set up their own masterships, being grossly ignorant both in the matters and their bare forms, and will have it lawful for them at their fond likings to frame or fashion the phrases of the Fathers in matter of religion into what form they list like a nose of wax.

xi. 23. *Origen's doctrine of the pre-existence of souls*

Origen in his first book *peri Archon* holds that God first created all things incorporeal, and that they were called by the names of heaven and earth, which afterwards were given unto bodies. Amongst which spirituals, our souls (*mentes*) were created, who declining (to use Rufinus' translation) from their state and dignity became souls, as their name ψυχή declareth, by waxing cold in their higher state of being *mentes*. The mind failing of the divine heat takes the name and state of a soul, which if it arise and ascend unto again, it gains the former state of a mind. Which were it true I should think that the minds of men were unequally from God, some more and some less, some should be rather souls than other some; some retaining much of their mental vigour, and some little or none. But these souls (saith he) being for their souls' falls to be put into grosser bodies, the world was made, as a place large enough to exercise them all in, as was appointed. And from the diversity and inequality of their fall from Him did God collect the diversity of things here created.

XI. 32. *Christ 'a beginning'*

I reprove not the divines in calling Christ 'a beginning.' For He is the means of the world's creation, and chief of all that the Father begot. But I hold it no fit collection from His answer to the Jews. It were better to say so because it was true than because John wrote so, who thought not so. The heretics make us such arguments to scorn us with at all occasion offered. But what that wisely and freely religious Father Hierome held of the first verse of Genesis I will now relate. Many hold (as Jason *in Papisc.*, Tertull. *contra Praxeam*, and Hilar. *in Psalm.*) that the Hebrew text hath 'In the Son God made heaven and earth,' which is directly false. For the LXX, Symmachus, and Theodotion translate it 'In the beginning.' The Hebrew is *Bereshith*, which Aquila translates *in capitulo*, not *Ba-ben*, 'in the Son.' So then the sense rather than the translation giveth it unto Christ, who is called the 'Creator of heaven and earth' as well in the front of Genesis (the head of all books) as in S. John's gospel. So the psalmist saith in his person: 'In the head of the book it is written of me,' viz. of Genesis, and John: 'All things were made by it, and without it was made nothing, etc.' But we must know that this book is called *Bereshith*, the Hebrews using to put their books' names in their beginnings. Thus much word for word out of Hierome.

XII. 22. *Discord amongst men worse than amongst beasts*

Any place will hold brute beasts without contention sooner than men. For man is wolf to man, as the Greek proverb saith; and all other creatures agree among themselves and oppose strangers. The stern lion fights not with the lion; nor doth the serpent sting the serpent. The beasts and fishes of the sea agree still with their own kind. But man doth man the most mischief. Dicaearchus (saith Tully) wrote a book of the death of men (he is a free and copious Peripatetic) and herein having reckoned up inundations, plagues, burnings, exceeding abundance of beasts and other external causes, he compares them with the wars and seditions wherewith man hath destroyed man; and he finds the latter far exceeding the former. This war amongst men did Christ desire to have abolished, and for the fury of wrath to have grafted the heat of zeal and charity. This should be preached and taught that Christians ought not to be at wars, but at love one with another, and to bear one with another. Men's minds are already too forward to shed blood, and do wickedly; they need not be set on.

XII. 25. *Women's longing that are with child*

Child-bearing women do often long for many evil things, as coals and ashes. I saw one long for a bite of a young man's neck, and had lost her birth but that she bit off his neck until he was almost dead, she took such hold. The physicians write much hereof, and the philosophers somewhat. They all ascribe it to the vicious humours in the stomach, which if they happen in men, procure the like distemper.

The influence of experiences and thoughts at conception

Pliny, lib. 7, saith that the mind hath a recollection of similitudes in it, wherein a chance of sight, hearing or remembrance is of much effect, the images taken into the conceit at the time of conception are held to be powerful in framing the thing conceived: and so is the cogitation of either party, how swift soever it be. Whereupon is more difference in man than in any other creature, the thoughts of other creatures being immovable and like themselves in all kinds. Thus much Pliny. The philosophers stand wholly upon imagination in conception. At Hertogenbosch in Brabant on a certain day of the year (whereon they say their chief church was dedicated) they have public plays unto the honour of the saints, as they have in other places also of that country. Some act saints and some devils. One of these devils spying a pretty wench grew hot, and in all haste danceth home, and casting his wife upon a bed told her he would beget a young devil upon her, and so lay with her. The woman conceived, and the child was no sooner born but it began to dance, and was just of the shape that we paint our devils in.

XII. 26. *Marriage commended in the Creation*

The woman was not made of any external parts, but of man's self as his daughter, that there might be a fatherly love of his wife in him, and a filial duty towards him in the wife. She was taken out of his side as his fellow, not out of his head as his lady, nor out of his feet as his servant.

XIII. 5. *How we follow things forbidden*

It is natural unto exorbitant minds, the more a thing is forbidden the more to desire it; as women (whose minds are most unstayed) desire that only they are prohibited. So that whereas men knew not what it was to go to the brothels, and thought not upon it, in comes the law and saith, 'Thou shalt not go,' and so taught them all what it was to go, setting their depraved natures upon pursuit of those unlawful acts. 'I knew not,' saith Paul, 'what concupiscence was, until the law told me, 'Thou shalt not covet.'' Tully saith that Solon set down no law against parricide; which being unknown, he was more afraid to declare than punish.

XIII. 15. *If man had not sinned he had not died*

Augustine often averreth directly that man had not died, had he not sinned; nor had had a body subject to death or disease. The tree of life should have made him immortal. And St. Thomas Aquinas the best school divine holds so also. But Scotus either for faction or will denies it all, making man in his first state subject to diseases, yet that he should be taken up to heaven ere he died; but if he were left on earth he should die at length, for that the tree of life could not eternize him, but only prolong his life.

XIII. 16. *Palliati*

The Romans' *toga* or gown was the Greeks' *pallium*; and they that would seem absolute Grecians went in these *pallia* or cloaks; and such were observed much for their Graecism in life and learning. For as we teach all our arts in Latin now, so did they in Greek then. They were but few, and therefore the more admired.

XIII. 18. *How man seeth*

Plato in his *Timaeus* speaking of man's fabric saith that the eyes were endowed with part of that light that shines and burns not, meaning the sun's. For the gods commanded this pure fire (brother to that of heaven) to flow forth from the apple of the eye; and therefore, when that and the day's light do meet, the conjunction of those two so well-acquainted natures produceth sight. And lest that the sight should seem effected by any other thing than fire in the same work he defineth colours to be nothing but *fulgores e corporibus manantes* 'fulgors flowing out of the bodies wherein they are.' The question whether one seeth by omission or reception, that is, whether the eye send any beam to the object, or receive any from it, is not here to be argued. Plato holds the first. Aristotle confuteth him in his book *de Sensoriis*, and yet seems to approve him in his *Problems*. The Stoics held the first also, whom Augustine (*de Trinitate*) and many of the Peripatetics follow.

XIII. 22. *How the angels and the risen Christ ate*

They did not eat as we do, passing the meat from the mouth to the stomach through the throat, and so decoct it, and disperse the juice through the veins for nutriment; nor did they delude men's eyes by seeming to move that which they had for their chaps, and yet moving them not, or seeming to chew bread or flesh and yet leaving it whole. They did not eat really but were nourished by eating. The earth, saith Bede, drinketh up water one way, and the sun another, the earth for need and the sun by his power. And so did our Saviour eat, but not as we eat. That glorious body of His took the meat, but turned it not into nutriment as ours do.

XIV. 3. *The mind's four passions*

There are four chief passions of the mind, two delightful and two sorrowful. Of the first the one belongs to things present, joy, and is an opinion of a present good: the other, desire, unto future, and is an opinion of a future good. Of the two sad ones, sorrow is an opinion of a present evil, and fear of a future. And of these passions come all the rest, envy, emulation, detraction, pity, vexation, mourning, sadness, lamentation, care, doubt, troublesomeness, affliction, desperation, all come of sorrow. Sloth, shame, error, timorousness, amazement, disturbance, and anxiety come from fear; and exultation, delight, and boasting of joy; and wrath, fury, hatred, enmity, discord, need, and affectation of desire.

XIV. 5. *The Manichees*

They held all flesh the work of the devil, not of God; and therefore forbad their hearers to kill any creatures, lest they should offend the princes of darkness from whom they said all flesh had origin. And if they used their wives, yet must they avoid generation, lest the divine substance which goeth into them by their nourishment should be bound in the fleshly bonds of the child begotten.

XIV. 11. *Envy the successor of pride*

Envy immediately succeedeth pride by nature, for a proud man so loveth himself that he grieves that any one should excel him, nay, equalize him. Which when he cannot avoid then he envies them; whence it comes that envy sits chiefly amongst the highest honours, whereas the people's favour doth not always grace the prince alone. Suetonius saith that Caligula envied even the meanest, some for that the people favoured them, others for their form or birth. So did the devil envy man's holding of so high a place; and this envy brought death into the world.

XIV. 12. *Obedience the mother of all virtue*

God lays nothing upon His creatures, men or angels, as if He needeth their help in anything, but only desireth to have them in obedience to Him. Thence is the rule: 'Obedience is better than sacrifice.'

XIV. 13. *Comment on ' You shall be as gods,' Gen. iii. 5*

Fulfil thy mind, proud woman; advance thyself to the height. What is the uttermost scope of all ambitious desire? To be a god. Why, eat and thou shalt become one! O thou fondest of thy sex, hopest thou to be deified by an apple?

XIV. 16. *Carnal copulation*

Hippocrates said that carnal copulation was a little epilepsy, or falling sickness. Architas the Tarentine, to show the plague of pleasure, bade one to imagine some man in the greatest height of pleasure that might be; and averred that none would doubt him to be void of all the functions of soul and reason, as long as delight lasted.

XIV. 20. *The Cynics and their cloaks*

Of κυνός a dog. Antisthenes Socrates' scholar was their author. Their fashions were to revile and bark at all men, to be obscene in public without blushing, and to beget all the children they could. Finally whatever we are ashamed to do even in secret that would they do openly: yet were they great scorners of pleasure, and of worldly matters, yea even of life. The Cynics wore old tattered cloaks and carried staves in their hands, called by Augustine clubs. Herein they boasted they were like Hercules, their tattered robe like his lion's skin, their staff like his club, and their enemies pleasures, as were his monsters.

XIV. 22. *The sense of scripture*

There is nothing in scripture but may be spiritually applied; yet must we keep the true and real sense. Otherwise we should make a great confusion in religion; for the heretics as they please wrest all unto their positions. But if God in saying 'Increase,' etc., had no corporal meaning, but only spiritual, what remains but that we allow this spiritual increase unto beasts, upon whom also this blessing was laid?

XIV. 24. *On sweating*

And when I was sick of a tertian at Bruges, as often as the physician told me that it was good to sweat I would but hold my breath a little and cover myself over-head in the bed, and I sweat presently. They that saw it wondered at my strange constitution, but they would have wondered more had they seen Augustine's sweater, that sweat as easily as I can spit.

xv. 7. *The text of Gen. iv. 7*

Our common translation is 'If thou do well shalt thou not be accepted? And if thou do not well, sin lieth at the door.' Hierome rehearseth the translation of the LXX and saith thus: 'The Hebrew and the Septuagint do differ much in this place.' But the Hebrew reads it as our vulgar translations have it; and the LXX has it as Augustine readeth it.

'Unto thee shall, etc.' *Apistrophe*, says the LXX. Aquila hath *societas*, and Symmachus *appetitus* or *impetus*. The meaning may be either that sin shall be our fellow, or that sin's violence shall be in our power to suppress, as the sequel declareth, and this latter is likelier to be the true meaning.

xv. 10. '*Our books*'

He means the Latin translations that the Church used then out of the LXX, ere Hierome was either published or received. And by the Hebrew books he means the original scriptures, and the Hebrew authors thereto agreeing.

xv. 13. '*Believe the original rather than the translation*'

This Hierome admireth, and reason inviteth us too. No man of wit will gainsay it. But in vain do good judgments defend this, for blockishness lies against it like a rock. Not that they only are ignorant in those tongues, for Augustine had no Hebrew, and very little Greek; but they lack his modesty. He would ever learn, and they would never learn, but would teach that wherein they are as skilful as a sort of Cumane asses.

xv. 16. *Three words for cousin german*

The sons of two brethren are called *patrueles*; of a brother and a sister *amitini*; of two sisters *consobrini*. . . . There was a law against marrying of kindred (saith Plutarch) until at length it was permitted that father or uncle might marry his brother's or sister's daughter; which arose hereupon. A good poor man, whom the people loved very well, married his brother's daughter; and being accused and brought before the judge he pleaded for himself so well that he was absolved, and this law decreed by an universal consent.

xv. 23. *The bodies of angels*

That Augustine held that the angels and devils had bodies, he that readeth his work shall see plainly. He held it himself and spake it not as another man's opinion, as Peter Lombard saith some do think. It was his own, nor followed he any mean authors herein, having the Platonists, and then Origen, Lactantius, Basil, and almost all the writers of that time on his side. It is need, saith Michael Psellus, that the spirits that are made messengers should have bodies too (as Saint Paul saith) whereby to move, to stay and appear visibly. And whereas the scripture may in some places call them incorporeal, I answer that is in respect of our grosser and more solid bodies, in comparison of which the transparent insensible bodies are ordinarily called incorporeal. Augustine gives the angels most subtle bodies, invisible, active and not passive and such as the devils had ere they fell; but then their bodies were condensate and passive, as Psellus holds also.

xv. 26. *The arrangement of the ark*

The ark was thus built, saith Origen. It was divided into two lower rooms, and over these were three other rooms, each one immediately above other. The lowest was the sink or common jakes; and the next it was the graner, or place where meat was kept for all the creatures. Then in the first of the other three were the wild beasts kept, in the second the tamer, and in the third were the men themselves. Josephus writes but of four rooms, whereas all else make five; but he perchance might omit the jakes.

xvi. 4. *Nimrod*

Josephus writeth that Nimrod first taught mankind to injure God, and to grow proud against Him; for being wondrous valiant he persuaded them that they might thank themselves and not God for any good that befell them. And so ordained he himself a sovereignty; and to provide that God should not subvert it, fell a building of this tower to resist a second deluge if God should be offended. And the multitude held it a less matter to serve man than God; and so obeying Nimrod willingly began to build this huge tower, which might stand all waters uncovered. Of this tower the sibyl writeth, saying: 'When all men were of one language, some fell to build an high tower as though they would pass through it unto heaven. But God sent a wind and overthrew it, and confounded their languages with divers, so that each one had a several tongue'; and therefore that city was called Babylon.

xvi. 11. *The original language*

Some think that Heber's house consented not unto the building of the tower, and therefore had the first language left only unto them. Herodotus writeth that Psammetichus an Egyptian king caused two children to be brought up in the woods, without hearing of any man's mouth, thinking that the language which they would speak of themselves only would be that which man spake at first. After three years they were brought unto him, and they said nothing but 'bec' divers times. Now 'bec' is 'bread' in Phrygian, whereupon he thought the Phrygian tongue to be the first: but it was no marvel if they cried 'bec,' being continually brought up amongst the goats, that could cry nothing else!

xvi. 22. *The Epistle to the Hebrews*

Jerome, Origen, and Augustine do doubt of this epistle, and so do others. The Latin Church before Jerome held it not canonical. Erasmus disputeth largely and learnedly in the end of his notes upon it.

(This note the Louvainists have left out as erroneous.)

xvi. 28. *Causes of barrenness*

The physicians hold women's barrenness to proceed of the defects of the matrix, as if it be too hard, or brawny, or too loose and spongeous, or too fat or fleshy. I omit the simples that being inwardly taken procure barrenness as the berries of black ivy, ceterach, or hart's-tongue, as Pliny saith, etc. The Stoics say that it is often effected by the contrariety of qualities in the agent and patient at copulation; which being coupled with others of more concordance, do easily become fruitful, which we may not unfitly imagine in Abraham and Sarah, because afterwards he begot children upon Keturah, unless you wind up all these matters with a more divine interpretation. For Paul calleth Abraham νενεκρωμενόν, a dead body, exhaust, and fruitless.

XVII. 1. *The patriarchs as well as the prophets were seers*

The Hebrews called the prophets seers, because they saw the Lord in their predictions or prefigurations of anything with the eyes of the spirit, though not of the full flesh. Hence it is that scriptures call a prophecy a vision, and Nathan is called the seer. The Greeks sometimes use the name of prophet for their priests, poets, or teachers. Adam was the first man and the first prophet, who saw the mystery of Christ and His Church in his sleep. Then followeth Enoch, Noah, Abraham, Isaac, Jacob and his children, Moses, etc. Yet are these not reckoned amongst the prophets, for none of them left any books of the visions but Moses, whose books concerned ceremonies, sacrifices, and civil orders also. But these were all figures of future things. Nor were those the prophetical times, as those from Samuel were, wherein there never were prophets wanting; whereas before God spake but seldom, and His visions were not so manifest as they were from the first king unto the captivity; wherein were four great books of prophecies written, and twelve of the small.

XVII. 14. *The authorship of the psalms*

James Perez, my countryman, who wrote the last (not so eloquent as learned) large commentaries upon the psalms, in the beginning of them disputeth awhile about the authors of the psalms, and affirmeth that the Jews never made question of it before Origen's time; but all both wrote and believed that David wrote them all. But when Origen began with rare learning and delicate wit to draw all the prophetical sayings of the Old Testament unto Christ already born, he made the Jews run into opinions far contrarying the positions of their old masters, and fall to depraving of the scriptures in all they could. Yet were there some Hebrews afterwards that held as the ancients did that David was the only author of all the psalms. Some again held that he made but nine, and that other prophets wrote the rest. Those that have no titles, they do not know whose they are, only that they are the works of holy men, they say. . . . Origen, Ambrose, Hilary, Augustine, and Cassiodorus make David the author of them all; unto whom James Perez agreeth, confirming it for the truth by many arguments. Read them in himself, for the books are common.

XVII. 15. *Centones*

Centones are pieces of cloth of diverse colours used any way on the back or on the bed. Metaphorically it is a poem patched out of other poems by ends of verses, as Homero-cento and Virgilio-cento, made by Probus and Ausonius.

Retrogade poems

These are Sotadical verses; that is, verses backwards and forwards, as

> Musa mihi causas memora, quo numine laesa:

and

> Laeso numine quo memora causas mihi Musa.

Sotadical verses may be turned backwards into others also, as this iambic:

Pio precare thure coelestum numina.

Turn it:

Numina coelestum thure precare pio:

it is a pentameter.

They are a kind of wanton verse (as Quintilian saith) invented, saith Strabo, or rather used (saith Diomedes) by Sotades. . . . Some of Augustine's copies read it 'a great poem,' and it is the fitter; as if one should pick verses out of some greater works concerning another purpose, and apply them unto his own, as some centonists did, turning Virgil's and Homer's words of the Greek and Trojan wars unto Christ and divine matters.

Introduction to Book XVIII

In this eighteenth book we were to pass many dark ways, and often times to feel for our passage, daring not fix one foot until we first groped where to place it, as one must do in dark and dangerous places. Here we cannot tarry all day at Rome, but must abroad into the world's farthest corners, into lineages long since lost, and countries worn quite out of memory. Pedigrees long ago laid in the depth of oblivion must we fetch out into the light (like Cerberus) and spread them openly. We must into Assyria that old monarchy, scarcely once named by the Greeks; and Sicyonia, which the very princes thereof sought to suppress from memory themselves, debarring their very fathers from having their names set on their tombs, as Pausanias relateth; and thence to Argos, which being held the most antique state of Greece is all enfolded in fables; then to Athens, whose nimble wits aiming all at their country's honour have left truth sick at the heart, they have so cloyed it with eloquence and wrapped it up in clouds. Nor is Augustine content with this, but here and there casteth in hard walnuts and almonds for us to crack, which puts us to shrewd trouble ere we can get out the kernel of truth, their shells are so thick. And then cometh the Latin gests, all hacked in pieces by the discord of authors. And thence to the Romans; nor are the Greek wisemen omitted. It is fruitless to complain, lest some should think I do it causelessly. And here and there the Hebrew runneth, like veins in the body, to show the full course of the two cities, the heavenly and the earthly. If any one travelling through those countries, and learning his way of the cunningest, should for all that miss his way sometimes, is not he pardonable I pray you though, and will any one think him the less diligent in his travel? None, I think. What then if chance or ignorance lead me astray out of the sight of divers mean villages that I should have gone by, my way lying through deserts and untracked woods, and seldom or never finding any to ask the right way of? Am I not to be borne with? I hope yes.

Varro's *Antiquities* are all lost; and the life of Rome. None but Eusebius helped me in Assyria, but Diodorus Siculus and some others set me in once or twice. I had a book by me called Berosus by the booksellers, and somewhat I had of Johannes Annius, goodly matters truly, able to fright away the reader at first sight! But I let them lie still. I love not to suck the dregs or fetch fables out of frivolous pamphlets, the very rackets wherewith Greece bandieth ignorant heads about. Had this work been a child of Berosus I had used it willingly;

but it looketh like the bastard of a Greek sire, as Xenophon's *Aequivoca* are, and many others that bear their names that never were their authors. If any man like such stuff, much good do it him. I will be none of his rival. Through Sicyonia Pausanias and Eusebius went with me, contenting themselves only with the bare names, and some other little matters. The reader shall partake of them freely. For Judaea I see no guides but the scriptures: sometimes we are put in the minds of the Gentiles hereof, only in those things that the prophets touched, not in the rest. Where the scriptures concur we need go no further. That maketh me not to trouble Cornelius Alexander Milesius Polyhistor for allegations concerning the Jews; for he goes all by the LXX interpreters in his computations both in the Hebrew stories and others. Concerning Athens, Rome, Argos, Latium, and the other fabulous subjects, the reader hath heard whatever my diversity of reading affordeth, and much from the most curious students therein that I could be acquainted withal. He that liketh not this thing may find another by and by that will please his palate better, unless he be so proudly testy that he would have these my pains for the public good of power to satisfy him only. The rest the commentaries themselves will tell you.

XVIII. 23. *An English translation in acrostic form out of the Greek of the prophecy of the Erythraean Sibyl*

I n sign of doomsday the whole earth shall sweat.
E ver to reign a King in heavenly seat
S hall come to judge all flesh. The faithful and
U nfaithful too before this God shall stand,
S eeing him high with saints in time's last end.

C orporeal shall He sit; and thence extend
H is doom on souls. The earth shall quite lie waste,
R uined, o'ergrown with thorns; and men shall cast
I dols away, and treasure. Searching fire
S hall burn the ground; and thence it shall inquire
T hrough seas and sky, and break hell's blackest gates.

S o shall free light salute the blessed states
O f saints: the guilty, lasting flames shall burn.
N o act so hid but then to light shall turn:
N or breast so close but God shall open wide.
E achwhere shall cries be heard, and noise beside

O f gnashing teeth. The sun shall from the sky
F ly forth; and stars no more move orderly.

G reat heaven shall be dissolved, the moon deprived
O f all her light; places at height arrived,
D epressed, and valleys raised to their seat.

T here shall be naught to mortals high or great.
H ills shall lie level with the plains; the sea
E ndure no burden; and the earth, as they,

S hall perish cleft with lightning; every spring
A nd river burn.   The fatal trump shall ring
U nto the world, from heaven a dismal blast,
I ncluding plagues to come for ill deeds past.
O ld chaos through the cleft mass shall be seen.
U nto this bar shall all earth's kings convene:
R ivers of fire and brimstone flowing from heaven.

Notes on the Latin text

Judicii signo. Acts i. 11. 'This Jesus who is taken up to heaven, shall
so come as you have seen him go up into heaven.'

Scilicet. This verse is not in the Greek, nor is it added here, for there
must be twenty-seven.

Sic animae. The Greek is 'Then shall all flesh come into free heaven,
and the fire shall take away the holy and the wicked for ever.' But
because the sense is harsh, I had rather read it, τῶν ἁγίων, and so make
it agree with the Latin interpretation.

Exuret. The books of consciences shall be opened, as it is in the
Revelation.

Sanctorum. Isaiah xl. 4. 'Every valley shall be exalted, and every
mountain and hill shall be laid low; the crooked shall be straight, and
the rough places plain.'

Occultos. High and low shall then be all one, and neither of them
offensive.   Pomp, height, and glory shall no more domineer in particular;
but, as the apostle saith, Then shall all principalities and powers be
annihilated, that God may be all in all.   For there is no greater plague
than to be under him that is blown big with false conceit of greatness.
He groweth rich, and consequently proud.   He thinks he may domineer.
His father was, aye marry was he: his pedigree is always in his mouth,
and (very likely) a thief, a butcher, or a swine-herd in the front of this
his noble descent.   Another tar-lubber brags that he is a soldier, an
aid unto the State in affairs military; therefore will he rear and tear down
whole cities before him (if any leave their own seats and come into his
way, or to take the wall of him; not else).

The Latins have no word beginning with u that could fit the same. For
the Greek υ beginning a word is always aspirate.   Now if we bring it
into Latin aspirate, we must put *h* before it, and this deceives the ignorant.

XVIII. 25. *The mottos of the Seven Sages*

Thales' motto was, *Nosce te: Know thyself.*   Pittacus', *Nosce occa-
sionem:* Take time while time is.   Solon's, *Nihil nimis:* The mean is
the best.   Chilon's, *Sponsioni non deest jactura:* Bargains and losses
are inseparable, or, He that will adventure must lose.   Periander's,
Stipandus imperator non est armis sed benevolentia: Love and not arms
guard him that would rule.   Cleobulus', *Cave inimicorum insidias,
amicorum invidias:* Beware of your foes' enmity, and your friends' envy.
Bias', *Plures mali:* the worse are the more.   So agree Augustine and
Eusebius, who saith their inventions were nothing but short sentences,
tending to the institution of honest disciplines into men's hearts.

XVIII. 30. *The text of Micah v. 2, 'And thou, Bethlehem,' etc.*

Augustine and the LXX do differ here from the Hebrew. St. Matthew readeth it thus: 'And thou, Bethlehem in the land of Judah, art not the least among the princes of Judah, for out of thee shall come the governor that shall feed my people Israel.' Sr. Hierome saith that this quotation of Matthew accordeth neither with the Hebrew nor the LXX. This question putting the holy father to his plunges, he is fain to say that either the apostle cited it, not having the book before him, but out of his memory, which sometimes doth err; or else he cited it as the priests had given it in answer to Herod, herein showing their negligence. The first he affirmeth as the opinion of others. It is an hard thing to make the apostle speak just contrary to the prophet. Neither Porphyry nor Celsus would believe this in a matter that concerned not themselves. But the scope of both being one maketh this conjecture indeed the more tolerable. For it is a weak hold to say that the priests spake it thus. It were extremely absurd in their practice of the scriptures to alter a prophecy, intending especially to show the full aim of it. But before the apostle (nay, the Spirit of God) shall be taxed with such an error, let the latter conjecture stand good, or a weaker than it, as long as we can find no stronger. But if we may lawfully put in a guess after Hierome in the extrication of those holy labyrinths, to grant that the Hebrew and the LXX read this place affirmatively and the evangelist negatively, read this place with an interrogation, and they are both reconciled; I mean, with an interrogation in the prophet, as is common in their works and befitting the order of their affections, but in the evangelist the bare sense is only fit to be laid down without figure or affection.

XVIII. 35. *Translators ought to change no names*

Malachi's name interpreted is 'His angel,' and so the LXX called him; whereupon Origen upon this prophet saith that he thinketh it was an angel that prophesied this prophecy, if we may believe Hierome's testimony herein. Others call him Malachi; for indeed names are not to be altered in any translation. No man calleth Plato 'broad'; or Aristotle 'good perfection,' or Joshua 'the saviour,' or Athene 'Minerva.' Names are to be set down in the proper idiom. Otherwise the names of famous men, being translated into several tongues, should obscure their persons' fame by being the more dispersed; which makes me wonder at those, which will wring the Greek names, etc., unto their several idioms, wherein their own conceit doth them gross wrong. Caesar was wise to deal plainly in giving the French and German each his country's names, only making them declinable by the Latin.

The meaning of Matt. xxi. 25

The evangelist St. Matthew readeth it: 'upon a colt, and the foal of an ass used to the yoke.' The Jews that were yoked under so many ceremonies were prefigured herein. But the free and young colt (as the LXX do translate it) was the type of the Gentiles. Take which you will. God sitteth upon both, to cure both from corruption and to bring both salvation.

XVIII. 39. *The wisdom of the ancient Egyptians*

Geometry, arithmetic, and astronomy were the ancient Egyptians' only studies. Necessity made them geometers, for Nilus' inundations every year took away the bounds of their lands, so that each was fain to know his own quantity, and how it lay and in what form; and thus they drew the principles of that art. Now aptness made them astronomers, for their nights were clear, and never cloud came on their land, so that they might easily discern all the motions, stations, rising and fall of every star; a study both wondrous delectable and exceeding profitable, and beseeming the excellence of man. Now these two arts could not consist without number, and so arithmetic got up for the third.

XVIII. 41. *The vainglory of ancient authors*

Vainglory led almost all the ancient authors wrong, stuffing arts with infamous errors, gross and pernicious; each one seeking to be the proclaimer of his own opinion rather than the preferrer of another's. Blind men! They say not how laudable it is to obey good counsel, and to agree unto truth. I knew a man once (not so learned as arrogant) who professed that he would write much, and yet avoid what others had said before him, as he would fly a serpent or a basilisk; for that he would rather affirm a lie than assent unto others' opinions.

XVIII. 47. *Israelites not 'of Israel,' and Christians who know not Christ*

Nature being unpolluted with vicious opinion might possibly guide one to God as well as the law of Moses; for what these got by the law, those might get without it, and come to the same perfection that the Jews came, seeking the same end; nor was their difference other than if one traveller should carry an itinerary of his way with him, and the other trust only his memory. So may he also nowadays that liveth in the faithless isles of the ocean, and never heard of Christ, attain the glory of a Christian by keeping the two abstracts of all the law and the prophets, perfect love of God and his neighbour. Such a conscience is a law unto a man, and according to the psalmist: 'He remembereth the name of the Lord in the night, and keepeth His law.' This hath he that seeth the Lord's righteousness: so great a blessing is it to be good, although you have not one to teach you goodness. And what wanteth here but water? For here is the Holy Spirit as well as in the apostles; as Peter witnesseth of some who received that, before ever the water touched them. So the nations that have no law but nature's are a law unto themselves. The light of their living well is the gift of God coming from His Son, of whom it is said: 'He is the light that lighteth every one that cometh into the world.'

(The Louvain copy is defective in all this.)

XVIII. 52. *Suetonius and Tacitus against the Christians*

Suetonius calls the Christians 'men of new and pernicious superstitions.' And Tacitus calleth them 'hated for their wickedness, guilty, and worthy of utmost punishment.' O senseless men, Tacitus and Suetonius! Can your bestial and luxurious Jove seem a god unto you, and Christ seem none? Call you an union in innocency 'execrable superstition,' and hold you them worthy of punishment, whose chief law is to do no man hurt and all men good? If you have not read our laws, why condemn you us? If you have, why reprove you us, seeing we embrace those virtues, which your best writers so highly admire?

Diocletian and Maximian

Diocletian was subtle and cruel, and could easily lay his butcheries on another's neck. Maximian was barbarous, and brutish even in aspect, and served for Diocletian's hangman, who grew to such price that he commanded himself to be adored as a god, and that his foot should be kissed, whereas but before they used but to kiss their hands. He persecuted the Church, and on Easter week the nineteenth year of his reign, commanded all the churches to be pulled down, and the Christians to be killed. Decius' persecution was the greatest, but this was the bloodiest.

XVIII. 53. *Against calculators*

Christ forbiddeth all curiosity, referring the knowledge of things to come only to Himself. Now let my figure-flingers, and mine old wives, that hold ladies and scarlet potentates by the ears with tales of 'thus and thus it shall be'—let them all go pack. Nay, sir, he doth it by Christ's command. Why, very good, you see what Christ's command is. Yet have we no such delight as in lies of this nature; and that maketh them the bolder in their fictions, thinking that we hold their mere desire to tell true a great matter in so strange a case.

XVIII. 54. *The time of Christ's death*

First sure it is Christ suffered under Tiberius the Emperor. Luke the evangelist maketh His baptism to fall in the fifteenth year of Tiberius' reign. So then His passion must be in the eighteenth or nineteenth, for three years He preached salvation. So saith Eusebius, alleging heathen testimonies of that memorable eclipse of the sun, as namely out of Phlegon a writer of the Olympiads, who saith that in the fourth year of the two hundred and second Olympiad (the eighteenth of Tiberius' reign) the greatest eclipse befell that ever was. It was midnight at midday, the stars were all visible, and an earthquake shook down many houses in Nicaea a city of Bithynia.

XIX. 1. *On virtue natural and acquired*

The old philosophers have a great ado about virtue in man, whether it be by laborious acquisition or natural infusion. Some hold the latter, and some the first. Plato is variable. Assuredly virtue is not perfected in any one without both nature and exercise. Three things, φύσις, λόγος, καὶ ἄσκησις, nature, reason, and practice, are as necessary in the attaining of arts and all good habits, as a fat soil, a good seed, and a painful husbandman are unto the obtaining of a fruitful harvest.

XIX. 13. *The perverse nature of those who love dissensions*

S. Augustine in this chapter proveth all things to consist by peace and concord; so that consequently discord must needs be the fuel to all ruin and confusion. Wherefore I wonder at the perverse nature of men that love dissensions and quarrels as their own very soul, hating peace as it were a most pernicious evil. Surely they had but their due, if their bosoms within and their states without were wholly fraught with this their so dearly affected darling, war. Men do turn all goods nowadays into contentious uses, as if they were ordained for no other end, never thinking that there is a place of eternal discord prepared for them to dwell in hereafter, where they may enjoy their damned desires for ever. The whole goodness of peace, and of that especially, which Christ left us as His full inheritance, is gone, all but for the name and imaginary shade thereof. All the rest we have lost. Nay, we have made a willing extrusion of it, and expelled it wittingly and of set purpose, imagining our whole felicity to consist in the tumults of wars and slaughters. And O, so we brave it, that we have slain thus many men, burned thus many towns, sacked thus many cities, founding our principal glories upon the destruction of our fellows! But I may begin a plaint of this here, but I shall never end it.

xix. 19. On bishops

Ἐπίσκοπος comes either of ἐπισκόπτω, to consider, or of ἐπισκέπτομαι, to visit. The scriptures, where the LXX translated ἐπίσκοπος, do read it 'a watchman,' as in Ezekiel and Hosea chap. v, where the Lord complaineth that they have been a snare in their watching, and a net upon mount Tabor. As if He had spoken of the bishops of these times, who set snares for benefices, and spread large nets for money, but not too wide wasted, lest the coin should scatter forth. . . . O, but some fine brains have now brought it about that bishoprics may not only be sued for, but even bought and sold without any prejudice at all unto this law. . . . Augustine showeth that a bishop should converse with the holy scriptures often, and draw himself home unto God now and then from all his businesses, living (if he did well) as a pilgrim of God in this life, and one that had a charge of God, and His own souls in hand, not any temporal trash; and yet ought he not to forsake his ministry, to which he should be preferred by an heavenly calling and not by an heavy purse.

xx. 3. The authorship of Ecclesiastes

Many of the Hebrews say that Solomon wrote this in the time of his repentance for the wicked course that he had run. Others say that he foresaw the division of his kingdom under his son Rehoboam, and therefore wrote it in contempt of the world's unstable vanity.

xx. 23. The four kingdoms of Daniel's prophecy

The first beast was like a lioness, bloody and lustful; and like an eagle, proud and long-lived, and such was the Assyrian Empire. The second was like a bear, rough and fiery. Such was Cyrus founder of the Persian monarchy. The third was like a winged leopard, headlong, bloody, and rushing upon death. Such was the Macedon who seemed rather to fly to sovereignty than go on foot; for how soon did he bring all Asia under! The fourth, the strangest, strongest, bloodiest of all, and such was the Roman Empire, that exceeded barbarism in cruelty, filling all the world with the rust of her own breeding, with bones of her massacring, with ruins of her causing.

xx. 26. The sinlessness of the Virgin Mary

The question of the Virgin Mary was not yet on foot, but grew afterward between the two orders of friars, both fiery, and led with undaunted generals, the Dominicans by Thomas Aquinas, and the Franciscans by John Duns Scotus. Now the Council of Basle decreed that she was wholly pure from all touch of sin; but the Dominicans objected that this was no lawful council, and the minorities of the other side avowed that it was true and holy, and called the Dominicans heretics for slandering the power of the Church; so that the matter had come to a shrewd pass, but that Pope Sixtus forbade this theme to be any more disputed of. Thus do these men esteem councils or canons, be they against their pleasures, just as an old wives' tale in a flax-shop, or at an ale-house gossiping.

(Omitted in the Louvain copy.)

xx. 30. *Smoking flax*

It was a custom of old (saith Plutarch *in Quaestionibus*) never to put out the snuff of the lamp, but to let it die of itself, and that for divers reasons. First, because this fire was somewhat like in nature to that inextinguishable immortal fire of heaven. Secondly, they held this fire to be a living creature, and therefore not to be killed but when it did mischief. (That the fire was a living creature, the want that it hath of nutriment, and the proper motion, besides the groan it seemeth to give when it is quenched, induced them to affirm.) Thirdly, because it is unfit to destroy anything that belongeth to man's continual use, as fire or water, etc. But we ought to leave them to others when our own turns are served. Thus far Plutarch. The first reason tendeth to religion, the second to mansuetude, the third to humanity.

xxi. 24. *Prayers for the departed*

In the ancient books printed at Bruges and Cologne, the ten or twelve lines beginning 'For the prayer either of the Church' are not to be found; for it is written in this manner: 'For the prayer either of the Church or of some godly persons is heard for some departed this life, but for them whose life hath not been spent so wickedly being regenerate in Christ, etc.' Those things which follow are not extant in them, neither in the copies printed at Freiburg. Nevertheless the style is not dissonant from Augustine's phrase. Peradventure they are either wanting in some books, or else are added here out of some other work of Augustine, as the first scholion, afterwards adjoined to the context of the speech.

xxi. 27. *Almsgiving*

Behold here Saint Augustine reckoneth tenpence a day for a small alms. But how many have we now that give so much? How many potentates see you give fourpence a day to the poor? Nay they think much with a penny or twopence. But after the dice let ducats go by thousands. Their fools and jesters shall have showers of their beneficence poured upon them. It is a great man's part, an emblem of nobleness. But ask them a penny for Christ's sake, and they are either as mute as stones, or grieve at the sight of the gift they part from. Respect of virtue now is laid low. So you shall have divers take up freely they care not where, not of whom, nor in what fashion; and then break, turn counterfeit bankrupts, and satisfy their creditors with ten at the hundred, and think they have made a good hand of it, and shall redeem all with a little alms. O fools that think that God is taken with pence! No it is the mind He respecteth, such as is resident only in honest breasts. Thieves and villains have now and then money in good store, and disperse it bountifully. But let no man trust in his wealth, or to purchase heaven with a piece of silver.

XXII. 30. *Eternal felicity*

Innumerable things might be said, but Augustine is to be imitated in this, and we must neither speak nor write anything rashly upon so sacred or holy a matter; neither is it lawful for us to search out that by philosophy and disputations of men, which the Lord hath commanded to be most secret, neither hath unveiled to the eyes, nor uttered to the ears, nor hath infused into the thoughts and understandings of mortal men. It is His will that we should believe them to be great and admirable, and only to hope after them, and then at last to understand them, when we being made partakers of our desire, shall behold openly all things being present even with our eyes, and so conjoined and affixed unto ourselves, that we may so know as we are known. Neither ought we to inquire whether that blessedness be an action of the understanding or rather of the will; whether our understanding shall behold all things in God, or whether it shall be restrained from some things; lest if we inquire these things over contentiously there be neither blessedness of our understanding nor of our will, nor we see anything in God. All things shall be full of joys and beatitudes, not only the will and understanding, but the eyes, hands, ears, the whole body, the whole mind, the whole soul. We shall see all things in God, which we will, and every one shall be content with the degree of his own felicity, nor will envy another, whom he shall behold to be nearer to God, because every man shall be so blessed as he shall desire.

Vives on the completion of his work

And I likewise think that I have finished no less work, and disburdened myself of no less labour than Augustine thinketh he hath done. For the burden of these mean and light commentaries hath been as heavy to our imbecility and unskilfulness, as the admirable burden of those volumes was to the vigour and strength of his wit, learning, and sanctity. If I have said anything which may please, let the reader give thanks unto God for me; if anything which may displease, let him pardon me for God's sake; and let things well-spoken obtain favour for things ill-spoken. But if he shall kindly amend and take away the errors, he shall deserve a good turn of me and the readers, which peradventure relying upon me might be deceived.

EVERYMAN'S LIBRARY
A CLASSIFIED LIST OF THE 977 VOLUMES

In each of the thirteen classifications in this list (except BIOGRAPHY) the volumes are arranged alphabetically under the *authors' names*, but Anthologies and works by various hands are listed under titles. Where authors appear in more than one section, a cross-reference is given, viz.: (*See also* FICTION). The number at the end of each item is the number of the volume in the series.

BIOGRAPHY

The Publishers regret that, owing to wartime difficulties and shortages, some of the volumes may be found to be temporarily out of print.

BIOGRAPHY—*continued*

CLASSICAL

ESSAYS AND BELLES-LETTRES

ESSAYS AND BELLES-LETTRES—*continued*

FICTION

FICTION—*continued*

FICTION—*continued*

FICTION—*continued*

Mickiewicz's (Adam) Pan Tadeusz. 842

Modern Humour. Edited by Guy Pocock and M. M. Bozman. 957

Modern Short Stories. Edited by John Hadfield. 954

Moore's (George) Esther Waters. 933

Mulock's John Halifax, Gentleman. Introduction by J. Shaylor. 123

Neale's (J. M.) The Fall of Constantinople. 655

Paltock's (Robert) Peter Wilkins; or, The Flying Indians. Intro. by A. H. Bullen. 676

Pater's Marius the Epicurean. Introduction by Osbert Burdett. 903

Peacock's Headlong Hall and Nightmare Abbey. 327

Poe's Tales of Mystery and Imagination. Intro. by Padraic Colum. 336
    (*See also* POETRY)

Prévost's Manon Lescaut, with Mérimée's Carmen. Introduction by Philip Henderson. 834

Priestley's Angel Pavement. 938

Pushkin's (Alexander) The Captain's Daughter and Other Tales. Trans. by Natalie Duddington. 898

Quiller-Couch's (Sir Arthur) Hetty Wesley. 864

Radcliffe's (Ann) Mysteries of Udolpho. Intro. by R. Austin Freeman. 2 vols. 865–6

Reade's (C.) The Cloister and the Hearth. Intro. by A. C. Swinburne. 29
    ,,   Peg Woffington and Christie Johnstone. 299

Richardson's (Samuel) Pamela. Intro. by G. Saintsbury. 2 vols. 683–4
    ,,   ,,   Clarissa. Intro. by Prof. W. L. Phelps. 4 vols. 882–5

Russian Authors, Short Stories from. Trans. by R. S. Townsend. 758

Sand's (George) The Devil's Pool and François the Waif. 534

Scheffel's Ekkehard: a Tale of the Tenth Century. 529

Scott's (Michael) Tom Cringle's Log. 710

SIR WALTER SCOTT'S WORKS:

Abbot, The. 124	Ivanhoe. Intro. Ernest Rhys. 16
Anne of Geierstein. 125	Kenilworth. 135
Antiquary, The. 126	Monastery, The. 136
Black Dwarf and Legend of Montrose. 128	Old Mortality. 137
	Peveril of the Peak. 138
Bride of Lammermoor. 129	Pirate, The. 139
Castle Dangerous and the Surgeon's Daughter. 130	Quentin Durward. 140
	Redgauntlet. 141
Count Robert of Paris. 131	Rob Roy. 142
Fair Maid of Perth. 132	St. Ronan's Well. 143
Fortunes of Nigel. 71	Talisman, The. 144
Guy Mannering. 133	Waverley. 75
Heart of Midlothian, The. 134	Woodstock. Intro. by Edward
Highland Widow and Betrothed. 127	Garnett. 72

    (*See also* BIOGRAPHY *and* POETRY)

Shchedrin's The Golovlyov Family. Translated by Natalie Duddington. Introduction by Edward Garnett. 908

Shelley's (Mary Wollstonecraft) Frankenstein. 616

Sheppard's Charles Auchester. Intro. by Jessie M. Middleton. 505

Shorter Novels, Vol. I. Elizabethan and Jacobean. Edited by Philip Henderson. 824
    ,,   ,,   Vol. II. Jacobean and Restoration. Edited by Philip Henderson. 841
    ,,   ,,   Vol. III. Eighteenth Century (Beckford's Vathek, Walpole's Castle of Otranto, and Dr. Johnson's Rasselas). 856

Sienkiewicz (Henryk). Tales from. Edited by Monica M. Gardner. 871
    ,,   ,,   Quo Vadis? Translated by C. J. Hogarth. 970

Smollett's Humphry Clinker. Intro. by Howard Mumford Jones; Notes by Charles Lee. 975
    ,,   Peregrine Pickle. 2 vols. 838–9
    ,,   Roderick Random. Introduction by H. W. Hodges. 790

Stendhal's Scarlet and Black. Translated by C. K. Scott Moncrieff. 2 vols. 945–6

Sterne's Tristram Shandy. Introduction by George Saintsbury. 617
    (*See also* ESSAYS)

FICTION—*continued*

HISTORY

HISTORY—*continued*

Gibbon's Decline and Fall of the Roman Empire. Edited, with Introduction and Notes, by Oliphant Smeaton, M.A. 6 vols. 434-6, 474-6
(*See also* BIOGRAPHY)

Green's Short History of the English People. Edited and Revised by L. Cecil Jane, with an Appendix by R. P. Farley, B.A. 2 vols. 727-8

Grote's History of Greece. Intro. by A. D. Lindsay. 12 vols. 186-97

Hallam's (Henry) Constitutional History of England. 3 vols. 621-3

Holinshed's Chronicle as used in Shakespeare's Plays. Introduction by Professor Allardyce Nicoll. 800

Irving's (Washington) Conquest of Granada. 478
(*See also* ESSAYS *and* BIOGRAPHY)

Josephus' Wars of the Jews. Introduction by Dr. Jacob Hart. 712

Lutzow's Bohemia: An Historical Sketch. Introduction by President T. G. Masaryk. Revised edition. 432

Macaulay's History of England. 3 vols. 34-6
(*See also* ESSAYS *and* ORATORY)

Maine's (Sir Henry) Ancient Law. 734

Merivale's History of Rome. (An Introductory vol. to Gibbon.) 433

Mignet's (F. A. M.) The French Revolution. 713

Milman's History of the Jews. 2 vols. 377-8

Mommsen's History of Rome. Translated by W. P. Dickson, LL.D. With a review of the work by E. A. Freeman. 4 vols. 542-5

Motley's Dutch Republic. 3 vols. 86-8

Parkman's Conspiracy of Pontiac. 2 vols. 302-3

Paston Letters, The. Based on edition of Knight. Introduction by Mrs. Archer-Hind, M.A. 2 vols. 752-3

Pilgrim Fathers, The. Introduction by John Masefield. 480

Pinnow's History of Germany. Translated by M. R. Brailsford. 929

Political Liberty, The Growth of. A Source-Book of English History. Arranged by Ernest Rhys. 745 [2 vols. 397-8

Prescott's Conquest of Mexico. With Intro. by Thomas Seccombe, M.A.
,, Conquest of Peru. Intro. by Thomas Seccombe, M.A. 301

Sismondi's Italian Republics. 250

Stanley's Lectures on the Eastern Church. Intro. by A. J. Grieve. 251

Tacitus. Vol. I. Annals. Introduction by E. H. Blakeney. 273
,, Vol. II. Agricola and Germania. Intro. E. H. Blakeney. 274

Thierry's Norman Conquest. Intro. by J. A. Price, B.A. 2 vols. 198-9

Villehardouin and De Joinville's Chronicles of the Crusades. Translated, with Introduction, by Sir F. Marzials, C.B. 333

Voltaire's Age of Louis XIV. Translated by Martyn P. Pollack. 780

ORATORY

Anthology of British Historical Speeches and Orations. Compiled by Ernest Rhys. 714

Bright's (John) Speeches. Selected, with Intro., by Joseph Sturge. 252

Burke's American Speeches and Letters. 340 (*See also* ESSAYS)

Demosthenes: Select Orations. 546

Fox (Charles James): Speeches (French Revolutionary War Period). Edited, with Introduction, by Irene Cooper Willis, M.A. 759

Lincoln's Speeches, etc. Intro. by the Rt. Hon. James Bryce. 206
(*See also* BIOGRAPHY)

Macaulay's Speeches on Politics and Literature. 399
(*See also* ESSAYS *and* HISTORY)

Pitt's Orations on the War with France. 145

PHILOSOPHY AND THEOLOGY

A Kempis' Imitation of Christ. 484

Ancient Hebrew Literature. Being the Old Testament and Apocrypha. Arranged by the Rev. R. B. Taylor. 3 vols. 253-6

Aquinas, Thomas: Selected Writings. Edited by Rev. Fr. D'Arcy. 953

Aristotle, The Nicomachean Ethics of. Translated by D. P. Chase. Introduction by Professor J. A. Smith. 547 (*See also* CLASSICAL)

Bacon's The Advancement of Learning. 719 (*See also* ESSAYS)

PHILOSOPHY AND THEOLOGY—*continued*

Berkeley's (Bishop) Principles of Human Knowledge, New Theory of Vision. With Introduction by A. D. Lindsay. 483

Boehme's (Jacob) The Signature of All Things, with Other Writings. Introduction by Clifford Bax. 569

Browne's Religio Medici, etc. Intro. by Professor C. H. Herford. 92

Bunyan's Grace Abounding and Mr. Badman. Introduction by G. B. Harrison. 815 (*See also* ROMANCE) [3 vols. 886–8

Burton's (Robert) Anatomy of Melancholy. Intro. by Holbrook Jackson.

Butler's Analogy of Religion. Introduction by Rev. Ronald Bayne. 90

Chinese Philosophy in Classical Times. Translated and edited by E. R. Hughes. 973

Descartes' (René) A Discourse on Method. Translated by Professor John Veitch. Introduction by A. D. Lindsay. 570

Ellis' (Havelock) Selected Essays. Introduction by J. S. Collis. 930

Gore's (Charles) The Philosophy of the Good Life. 924

Hindu Scriptures. Edited by Dr. Nicol Macnicol. Introduction by Rabindranath Tagore. 944

Hobbes's Leviathan. Edited, with Intro., by A. D. Lindsay, M.A. 691

Hooker's Ecclesiastical Polity. Intro. by Rev. H. Bayne. 2 vols. 201–2

Hume's Treatise of Human Nature, and other Philosophical Works. Introduction by A. D. Lindsay, M.A. 2 vols. 548–9

James (William): Selected Papers on Philosophy. 739

Kant's Critique of Pure Reason. Translated by J. M. D. Meiklejohn. Introduction by A. D. Lindsay, M.A. 909

Keble's The Christian Year. Introduction by J. C. Shairp. 690

King Edward VI. First and Second Prayer Books. Introduction by the Right Rev. E. G. S. Gibson. 448

Koran, The. Rodwell's Translation. 380

Latimer's Sermons. Introduction by Canon Beeching. 40

Law's Serious Call to a Devout and Holy Life. 91

Leibniz's Philosophical Writings. Selected and trans. by Mary Morris. Introduction by C. R. Morris, M.A. 905

Locke's Two Treatises of Civil Government. Introduction by Professor William S. Carpenter. 751

Malthus on the Principles of Population. 2 vols. 692–3

Mill's (John Stuart) Utilitarianism, Liberty, Representative Government. With Introduction by A. D. Lindsay, M.A. 482

  ,,   Subjection of Women. (*See* Wollstonecraft, Mary, *under* SCIENCE)

More's Utopia. Introduction by Judge O'Hagan. 461

New Testament. Arranged in the order in which the books came to the Christians of the First Century. 93

Newman's Apologia pro Vita Sua. Intro. by Dr. Charles Sarolea. 636 (*See also* ESSAYS)

Nietzsche's Thus Spake Zarathustra. Trans. by A. Tille and M. M. Bozman. [892

Paine's Rights of Man. Introduction by G. J. Holyoake. 718

Pascal's Pensées. Translated by W. F. Trotter. Introduction by T. S. Eliot. 874 [403

Ramayana and the Mahabharata, The. Translated by Romesh Dutt, C.I.E.

Renan's Life of Jesus. Introduction by Right Rev. Chas. Gore, D.D. 805

Robertson's (F. W.) Sermons on Christian Doctrine, and Bible Subjects. Each Volume with Introduction by Canon Burnett. 3 vols. 37–9

Robinson's (Wade) The Philosophy of Atonement and Other Sermons. Introduction by Rev. F. B. Meyer. 637

Rousseau's (J. J.) The Social Contract, etc. 660 (*See also* ESSAYS)

St. Augustine's Confessions. Dr. Pusey's Translation. 200

St. Francis: The Little Flowers, and The Life of St. Francis. 485

Seeley's Ecce Homo. Introduction by Sir Oliver Lodge. 305

Selection from St. Thomas Aquinas. Edited by The Rev. Father M. C. D'Arcy. 953

Spinoza's Ethics, etc. Translated by Andrew J. Boyle. With Introduction by Professor Santayana. 481

Swedenborg's (Emmanuel) Heaven and Hell. 379

    ,,   ,,   The Divine Love and Wisdom. 635

    ,,   ,,   The Divine Providence. 658

    ,,   ,,   The True Christian Religion. 893

POETRY AND DRAMA

POETRY AND DRAMA—*continued*

Minor Elizabethan Drama. Vol. I. Tragedy, Selected, with Introduction, by Professor Thorndike. Vol. II. Comedy. 491–2
Minor Poets of the 18th Century. Edited by H. I'Anson Fausset. 844
Minor Poets of the 17th Century. Edited by R. G. Howarth. 873
Modern Plays. By Somerset Maugham, R. C. Sherriff, A. A. Milne, Noel Coward, and Arnold Bennett and E. Knoblock. 942
Molière's Comedies. Introduction by Prof. F. C. Green. 2 vols. 830–1
New Golden Treasury, The. An Anthology of Songs and Lyrics. 695
Old Yellow Book, The. Introduction by Charles E. Hodell. 503
Omar Kháyyám (The Rubáiyát of). Trans. by Edward FitzGerald. 819
Palgrave's Golden Treasury. Introduction by Edward Hutton. 96
Percy's Reliques of Ancient English Poetry. 2 vols. 148–9
Poe's (Edgar Allan) Poems and Essays. Intro. by Andrew Lang. 791
   (*See also* FICTION)
Pope (Alexander): Collected Poems. Introduction by Ernest Rhys. 760
Proctor's (Adelaide A.) Legends and Lyrics. 150
Restoration Plays. A Volume of. Introduction by Edmund Gosse. 604
Rossetti's Poems and Translations. Introduction by E. G. Gardner. 627
Scott's Poems and Plays. Intro. by Andrew Lang. 2 vols. 550–1
   (*See also* BIOGRAPHY *and* FICTION)
Shakespeare's Comedies. 153
   „   Historical Plays, Poems, and Sonnets. 154
   „   Tragedies. 155
Shelley's Poetical Works. Introduction by A. H. Koszul. 2 vols. 257–8
Sheridan's Plays. 95
Spenser's Faerie Queene. Intro. by Prof. J. W. Hales. 2 vols. 443–4
   „   Shepherd's Calendar and Other Poems. Edited by Philip Henderson. 879
Stevenson's Poems, A Child's Garden of Verses, Underwoods, Songs of Travel, Ballads. 768   (*See also* ESSAYS, FICTION, *and* TRAVEL)
Swinburne's Poems and Prose. Selected and Edited by Richard Church.
Synge's (J. M.) Plays, Poems, and Prose. 968   [961
Tchekhov. Plays and Stories. 941
Tennyson's Poems. Vol. I. 1830–56. Introduction by Ernest Rhys. 44
   „   „   Vol. II. 1857–70. 626
Twenty One-Act Plays. Selected by John Hampden. 947
Webster and Ford. Plays. Selected, with Introduction, by Dr. G. B. Harrison. 899
Whitman's (Walt) Leaves of Grass (I), Democratic Vistas, etc. 573
Wilde (Oscar): Plays, Prose Writings, and Poems. 858
Wordsworth's Shorter Poems. Introduction by Ernest Rhys. 203
   „   Longer Poems. Note by Editor. 311

REFERENCE

Atlas of Ancient and Classical Geography. Many coloured and line Maps; Historical Gazetteer, Index, etc. 451
Biographical Dictionary of English Literature. 449
Biographical Dictionary of Foreign Literature. 900
Dates, Dictionary of. 554
Dictionary of Quotations and Proverbs. 2 vols. 809–10
Everyman's English Dictionary. 776
Literary and Historical Atlas. I. Europe, Many coloured and line Maps; full Index and Gazetteer. 496
   „   „   „   II. America. Do. 553
   „   „   „   III. Asia. Do. 633
   „   „   „   IV. Africa and Australia. Do. 662
Non-Classical Mythology, Dictionary of. 632
Reader's Guide to Everyman's Library. Revised edition, covering the first 950 vols. 889
Roget's Thesaurus of English Words and Phrases. 2 vols. 630–1
Smith's Smaller Classical Dictionary. Revised and Edited by E. H. Blakeney, M.A. 495
Wright's An Encyclopaedia of Gardening. 555

ROMANCE

Aucassin and Nicolette, with other Medieval Romances. 497
Boccaccio's Decameron. (Unabridged.) Translated by J. M. Rigg. Introduction by Edward Hutton. 2 vols. 845–6
Bunyan's Pilgrim's Progress. Introduction by Rev. H. E. Lewis. 204
Burnt Njal, The Story of. Translated by Sir George Dasent. 558
Cervantes' Don Quixote. Motteaux's Translation. Lockhart's Introduction. 2 vols. 385–6
Chrétien de Troyes: Eric and Enid. Translated, with Introduction and Notes, by William Wistar Comfort. 698
French Medieval Romances. Translated by Eugene Mason. 557
Geoffrey of Monmouth's Histories of the Kings of Britain. 577
Grettir Saga, The. Newly Translated by G. Ainslie Hight. 699
Gudrun. Done into English by Margaret Armour. 880
Guest's (Lady) Mabinogion. Introduction by Rev. R. Williams. 97
Heimskringla: The Olaf Sagas. Translated by Samuel Laing. Introduction and Notes by John Beveridge. 717
    „   Sagas of the Norse Kings. Translated by Samuel Laing. Introduction and Notes by John Beveridge. 847
Holy Graal, The High History of the, 445
Kalevala. Introduction by W. F. Kirby, F.L.S., F.E.S. 2 vols. 259–60
Le Sage's The Adventures of Gil Blas. Intro. by Anatole Le Bras. 2 vols. 437–8
MacDonald's (George) Phantastes: A Faerie Romance. 732
    (See also FICTION)
Malory's Le Morte d'Arthur. Intro. by Professor Rhys. 2 vols. 45–6
Morris (William): Early Romances. Introduction by Alfred Noyes. 261
    „   „   The Life and Death of Jason. 575
Morte d'Arthur Romances, Two. Introduction by Lucy A. Paton. 634
Nibelungs, The Fall of the. Translated by Margaret Armour. 312
Rabelais' The Heroic Deeds of Gargantua and Pantagruel. Introduction by D. B. Wyndham Lewis. 2 vols. 826–7
Wace's Arthurian Romance. Translated by Eugene Mason. Layamon's Brut. Introduction by Lucy A. Paton. 578

SCIENCE

Boyle's The Sceptical Chymist. 559
Darwin's The Origin of Species. Introduction by Sir Arthur Keith. 811
    (See also TRAVEL)
Eddington's (Sir Arthur) The Nature of the Physical World. Introduction by E. F. Bozman. 922
Euclid: the Elements of. Todhunter's Edition. Introduction by Sir Thomas Heath, K.C.B. 891
Faraday's (Michael) Experimental Researches in Electricity. 576
Galton's Inquiries into Human Faculty. Revised by Author. 263
George's (Henry) Progress and Poverty. 560
Hahnemann's (Samuel) The Organon of the Rational Art of Healing. Introduction by C. E. Wheeler. 663
Harvey's Circulation of the Blood. Introduction by Ernest Parkyn. 262
Howard's State of the Prisons. Introduction by Kenneth Ruck. 835
Huxley's Essays. Introduction by Sir Oliver Lodge. 47
    „   Select Lectures and Lay Sermons. Intro. Sir Oliver Lodge. 498
Lyell's Antiquity of Man. With an Introduction by R. H. Rastall. 700
Marx's (Karl) Capital. Translated by Eden and Cedar Paul. Introduction by G. D. H. Cole. 2 vols. 848–9
Miller's Old Red Sandstone. 103
Owen's (Robert) A New View of Society, etc. Intro. by G. D. H. Cole. 799
Pearson's (Karl) The Grammar of Science. 939
Ricardo's Principles of Political Economy and Taxation. 590
Smith's (Adam) The Wealth of Nations. 2 vols. 412–13
Tyndall's Glaciers of the Alps and Mountaineering in 1861. 98
White's Selborne. Introduction by Principal Windle. 48
Wollstonecraft (Mary), The Rights of Woman, with John Stuart Mill's The Subjection of Women. 825

TRAVEL AND TOPOGRAPHY

A Book of the 'Bounty.' Edited by George Mackaness. 950
Anson's Voyages. Introduction by John Masefield. 510
Bates's Naturalist on the Amazon. With Illustrations. 446
Belt's The Naturalist in Nicaragua. Intro. by Anthony Belt, F.L.S. 561
Borrow's (George) The Gypsies in Spain. Intro. by Edward Thomas. 697
 ,, ,, The Bible in Spain. Intro. by Edward Thomas. 151
 ,, ,, Wild Wales. Intro. by Theodore Watts-Dunton. 49
  (See also BIOGRAPHY)
Boswell's Tour in the Hebrides with Dr. Johnson. 387
  (See also BIOGRAPHY)
Burton's (Sir Richard) First Footsteps in East Africa. 500
Cobbett's Rural Rides. Introduction by Edward Thomas. 2 vols. 638-9
Cook's Voyages of Discovery. 99
Crèvecœur's (H. St. John) Letters from an American Farmer. 640
Darwin's Voyage of the Beagle. 104
  (See also SCIENCE)
Defoe's Tour through England and Wales. Introduction by G. D. H.
 Cole. 820-1 (See also FICTION)
Dennis' Cities and Cemeteries of Etruria. 2 vols. 183-4
Dufferin's (Lord) Letters from High Latitudes. 499
Ford's Gatherings from Spain. Introduction by Thomas Okey. 152
Franklin's Journey to the Polar Sea. Intro. by Capt. R. F. Scott. 447
Giraldus Cambrensis: Itinerary and Description of Wales. 272
Halkuyt's Voyages. 8 vols. 264, 265, 313, 314, 338, 339, 388, 389
Kinglake's Eothen. Introduction by Harold Spender, M.A. 337
Lane's Modern Egyptians. With many Illustrations. 315
Mandeville's (Sir John) Travels. Introduction by Jules Bramont. 812
Park (Mungo): Travels. Introduction by Ernest Rhys. 205
Peaks, Passes, and Glaciers. Selected by E. H. Blakeney, M.A. 778
Polo's (Marco) Travels. Introduction by John Masefield. 306
Roberts' The Western Avernus. Intro. by Cunninghame Grahame. 762
Speke's Discovery of the Source of the Nile. 50
Stevenson's An Inland Voyage, Travels with a Donkey, and Silverado
 Squatters. 766
  (See also ESSAYS, FICTION, and POETRY)
Stow's Survey of London. Introduction by H. B. Wheatley. 589
Wakefield's Letter from Sydney and Other Writings on Colonization. 828
Waterton's Wanderings in South America. Intro. by E. Selous. 772
Young's Travels in France and Italy. Intro. by Thomas Okey. 720

FOR YOUNG PEOPLE

Aesop's and Other Fables: An Anthology from all sources. 657
Alcott's Little Men. Introduction by Grace Rhys. 512
 ,, Little Women and Good Wives. Intro. by Grace Rhys. 248
Andersen's Fairy Tales. Illustrated by the Brothers Robinson. 4
 ,, More Fairy Tales. Illustrated by Mary Shillabeer. 822
Annals of Fairyland. The Reign of King Oberon. 365
 ,, ,, The Reign of King Cole. 366
Asgard and the Norse Heroes. Translated by Mrs. Boult. 689
Baker's Cast up by the Sea. 539
Ballantyne's Coral Island. 245
 ,, Martin Rattler. 246
 ,, Ungava. Introduction by Ernest Rhys. 276
Browne's (Frances) Granny's Wonderful Chair. Intro. by Dollie Radford. 112
Bulfinch's (Thomas) The Age of Fable. 472   [112
 ,, ,, Legends of Charlemagne. Introduction by Ernest
  Rhys. 556
Canton's A Child's Book of Saints. Illustrated by T. H. Robinson. 61
  (See also ESSAYS)
Carroll's Alice in Wonderland, Through the Looking-Glass, etc. Illus-
 trated by the Author. Introduction by Ernest Rhys. 836
Clarke's Tales from Chaucer. 537

FOR YOUNG PEOPLE—*continued*

Collodi's Pinocchio: the Story of a Puppet. 538
Converse's (Florence) The House of Prayer. 923
  (*See also* FICTION)
Cox's (Sir G. W.) Tales of Ancient Greece. 721
Defoe's Robinson Crusoe. Illustrated by J. A. Symington. 59
  (*See also* FICTION)
Dodge's (Mary Mapes) Hans Brinker; or, The Silver Skates. 620
Edgar's Heroes of England. 471
  (*See also* FICTION)
Ewing's (Mrs.) Jackanapes, Daddy Darwin's Dovecot, illustrated by
    R. Caldecott, and The Story of a Short Life. 731
  ,,   ,,   Mrs. Overtheway's Remembrances. 730
Fairy Gold. Illustrated by Herbert Cole. 157
Fairy Tales from the Arabian Nights. Illustrated. 249
Froissart's Chronicles. 57
Gatty's Parables from Nature. Introduction by Grace Rhys. 158
Grimm's Fairy Tales. Illustrated by R. Anning Bell. 56
Hawthorne's Wonder Book and Tanglewood Tales. 5
  (*See also* FICTION)
Howard's Rattlin the Reefer. Introduction by Guy Pocock. 857
Hughes's Tom Brown's School Days. Illustrated by T. Robinson. 58
Ingelow's (Jean) Mopsa the Fairy. Illustrated by Dora Curtis. 619
Jefferies' (Richard) Bevis, the Story of a Boy. Intro. by Guy Pocock. 850
Kingsley's Heroes. Introduction by Grace Rhys. 113
  ,,   Madam How and Lady Why. Introduction by C. I. Gardiner,
            M.A. 777
  ,,   Water Babies and Glaucus. 277
  (*See also* POETRY *and* FICTION)
Kingston's Peter the Whaler. 6
  ,,   Three Midshipmen. 7
Lamb's Tales from Shakespeare. Illustrated by A. Rackham. 8
  (*See also* BIOGRAPHY *and* ESSAYS)
Lear (and Others): A Book of Nonsense. 806
Marryat's Children of the New Forest. 247
  ,,   Little Savage. Introduction by R. Brimley Johnson. 159
  ,,   Masterman Ready. Introduction by R. Brimley Johnson. 160
  ,,   Settlers in Canada. Introduction by R. Brimley Johnson. 370
  ,,   (Edited by) Rattlin the Reefer. 857
  (*See also* FICTION)
Martineau's Feats on the Fjords, etc. Illustrated by A. Rackham. 429
Mother Goose's Nursery Rhymes. Illustrated. 473
Plays for Boys and Girls. Edited by John Hampden. 966
Poetry Book for Boys and Girls. Edited by Guy Pocock. 894
Reid's (Mayne) The Boy Hunters of the Mississippi. 582
  ,,   The Boy Slaves. Introduction by Guy Pocock. 797
Ruskin's The Two Boyhoods and Other Passages. 688
  (*See also* ESSAYS)
Sewell's (Anna) Black Beauty. Illustrated by Lucy Kemp-Welch. 748
Spyri's (Johanna) Heidi. Illustrations by Lizzie Lawson. 431
Story Book for Boys and Girls. Edited by Guy Pocock. 934
Stowe's Uncle Tom's Cabin. 371
Swiss Family Robinson. Illustrations by Chas. Folkard. 430
Verne's (Jules) Abandoned. 50 Illustrations. 368
  ,,   ,,   Dropped from the Clouds. 50 Illustrations. 367
  ,,   ,,   Five Weeks in a Balloon and Around the World in Eighty
                Days. Translated by Arthur Chambers and P. Desages.
  ,,   ,,   Twenty Thousand Leagues Under the Sea. 319   [779
  ,,   ,,   The Secret of the Island. 50 Illustrations. 369
Yonge's (Charlotte M.) The Book of Golden Deeds. 330
  ,,   ,,   The Lances of Lynwood. Illustrated by Dora
                Curtis. 579
  ,,   ,,   The Little Duke. Illustrated by Dora Curtis. 470
  (*See also* FICTION)